Selected Readings on Electronic Commerce Technologies:
Contemporary Applications

Wen-Chen Hu
University of North Dakota, USA

INFORMATION SCIENCE REFERENCE

Hershey · New York

Director of Editorial Content:	Kristin Klinger
Director of Production:	Jennifer Neidig
Managing Editor:	Jamie Snavely
Assistant Managing Editor:	Carole Coulson
Typesetter:	Lindsay Bergman
Cover Design:	Lisa Tosheff
Printed at:	Yurchak Printing Inc.

Published in the United States of America by
Information Science Reference (an imprint of IGI Global)
701 E. Chocolate Avenue, Suite 200
Hershey PA 17033
Tel: 717-533-8845
Fax: 717-533-8661
E-mail: cust@igi-global.com
Web site: http://www.igi-global.com

and in the United Kingdom by
Information Science Reference (an imprint of IGI Global)
3 Henrietta Street
Covent Garden
London WC2E 8LU
Tel: 44 20 7240 0856
Fax: 44 20 7379 0609
Web site: http://www.eurospanbookstore.com

Library of Congress Cataloging-in-Publication Data

Selected readings on electronic commerce technologies : contemporary applications / Wen-Chen Hu, editor.

    p. cm.

  Summary: "This book offers research articles focused on key issues concerning the technologies and applications of electronic commerce"--Provided by publisher.

  Includes bibliographical references and index.

  ISBN 978-1-60566-096-7 (hbk.) -- ISBN 978-1-60566-097-4 (ebook)

  1. Electronic commerce. I. Hu, Wen Chen, 1960-

  HF5548.32.S453 2009

  658.8'72--dc22

                            2008020495

British Cataloguing in Publication Data
A Cataloguing in Publication record for this book is available from the British Library.

All work contributed to this book set is original material. The views expressed in this book are those of the authors, but not necessarily of the publisher.

Table of Contents

Section III
Tools and Technologies

Section IV
Utilization and Application

Section V
Criticial Issues

Section VI
Emerging Trends

Detailed Table of Contents

Section I
Fundamental Concepts and Theories

This chapter introduces XML-based e-commerce standards that have emerged within the past decade. The history of e-commerce standards is first described, and then representative horizontal and vertical e-commerce standards are presented by detailing their functionality, and how their development has been shaped by various stakeholders. These standards have the potential to transform B2B practice, which is shown using three industry examples. Due to the central role these standards are likely to play in future e-commerce activity, most firms will at some point need to become aware of their capabilities, their application, and potential impact. This chapter is intended to provide an overview of the situation as it is understood today, and presents likely scenarios for how these standards may progress.

Chapter II

This chapter examines the relationship between electronic commerce and the U.S. state sales and use tax system. A framework of a high-quality tax system is used in this study, and it is applied to taxing electronic commerce sales. The first part of this article analyzes nine principles of an effective tax system. In the second part of this article, these principles are tested to determine what impact electronic commerce taxation has on an effective revenue system. The results of these initial tests suggest that taxation of electronic commerce was associated with fairness in the tax system. In particular, the results suggested that states that had fairer tax systems were more likely to rely less on a sales tax and more on taxing Internet access. These results reinforce the existing public finance and legal theories that argue that the sales tax is not a fair revenue stream and that it should be reevaluated.

Chapter III

Craig Standing, Edith Cowan University, Western Australia
Patricia McManus, Edith Cowan University, Western Australia
Susan Standing, Edith Cowan University, Western Australia
Heikki Karjaluoto, University of Oulu, Finland

Mobile services (m-services) have become an important part of the e-commerce landscape. This chapter addresses the question of why and how individuals adopt and appropriate m-services with a particular focus on m-communication. The authors of this chapter propose the use of means-end chains and laddering techniques to determine the basic primitive values that are fulfilled for the individual by using various m-services. The examples presented show that mobile services often fulfill such basic needs as self esteem, achievement, individuality, belonging, and well-being. Exploring the realization of values as a theoretical framework offers researchers a way forward in environments characterized by individual technology decisions.

Chapter IV

Luiz Antonio Joia, Getulio Vargas Foundation, Brazil
Paulo Sergio Sanz, Getulio Vargas Foundation, Brazil

This chapter explores the transaction profitability of frequent and sporadic buyers in the e-commerce arena. Evidence in relationship marketing literature stressing the impact of purchase frequency on customer transaction profitability as well as recent academic research challenging this approach and pointing out the importance of sporadic clients is analyzed and presented. In order to gather relevant input to carry out this research, one of the largest retailing groups in Brazil was investigated. Conclusions are drawn showing that greater frequency of purchases does not necessarily translate into increased customer transaction profitability. Implications are presented, enabling practitioners and academics to grasp fully the real value of customers — both frequent and sporadic buyers — in order to develop coherent approaches for dealing with them adequately.

Section II
Development and Design Methodologies

Chapter V

P. Benou, University of Peloponnese, Greece
V. Bitos, TIM HELLAS, Greece

Recent advances in wireless and mobile communication technologies enable users to conduct commercial activities anywhere and at any time. In this new environment, designing appropriate applications is necessary in order to effectively support mobile users' needs. This chapter investigates the environment in which these applications operate, identifies possible categories for these applications, and proposes guidelines outlining their development.

The growth of the Internet is increasing the deployment of e-commerce B2C services within such areas as e-retailing, e-learning, and e-health. However, a major impediment to the growth of e-commerce on the Internet is the lack of consumer trust in the provider of the e-service. This chapter presents a literature survey of recent contributions to building trust in e-commerce, followed by a description of seven ways for the B2C Internet service provider to build trust in the use of its services among consumers.

Chapter VII

This chapter examines the importance of trust in business-to-consumer e-commerce. The author explores the issue of trust in the development and implementation of e-commerce and focuses on the context and role of users and consumers in transactions. The author contends that trust is more than a technical consideration and emphasizes the non-technical components such as community, identity, and experiences and their relevance to e-commerce. Despite the growing ubiquity of e-commerce, analysts and commentators continue to draw our attention to the issue of trust in e-commerce transactions. In particular, stories of "hacking," "phishing," and illegitimate online transactions have been an on-going public and private concern. These breaches are seen as cyber crimes and detrimental to the development of an efficient and effective business practice. Resolving these breaches are costly; businesses have to outlay financial resources not only to fix the breaches but, in the eyes of their clients, such breaches call into question the efficacy, integrity, and security of these businesses, creating both disquiet and a potential shift to alternative providers.

Chapter VIII

Electronic commerce or e-commerce has the potential to streamline existing functions and services in the public sector by reducing transaction costs or the cost of doing business. This chapter provides an overview of some of the critical e-commerce issues for the public sector focusing on its impact on reducing transaction costs.

Chapter IX

Today, a high volume of goods and services are being traded using online auction systems. The growth in size and complexity of architectures to support online auctions requires the use of distributed and cooperative software techniques. In this context, the agent software development paradigm seems appropriate both for their modeling, development, and implementation. This chapter proposes an agent-oriented patterns analysis of best practices for online auction. The patterns are intended to help both IT managers and software engineers during the requirement specification of an online auction system while integrating benefits of agent software engineering.

Section III
Tools and Technologies

Chapter X

Nir Kshetri, University of North Carolina at Greensboro, USA
Nicholas Williamson, University of North Carolina at Greensboro, USA
David L. Bourgoin, University of Hawaii at Manoa, USA

China is emerging as a global capital of m-commerce applications. China is the world's biggest mobile market in terms of subscriber base and the fastest growing in the history of telecommunications. Although China currently lacks advanced mobile applications compared to Europe, North America, Japan and Korea, a number of mobile players are rapidly launching sophisticated mobile applications. Unique institutions and the nature of mobile market conditions in China, however, superimpose in a complex interaction that harbors a paradoxical nature. The Chinese m-commerce market is thus drastically different from that of the Western world. This chapter examines and analyzes China's m-commerce landscape.

Chapter XI

Pierre Vialle, STORM Research Group, GET-INT, France
Olivier Epinette, STORM Research Group, GET-INT, France

This chapter introduces the emerging m-commerce market in France. Despite the current low level of use, this market is characterized by the implementation of an increasingly efficient m-commerce value chain by network operators, content providers and content enablers. As a result, innovative and attractive services are being introduced for both consumers and businesses, which are analyzed here with the help of the CLIP framework. Furthermore, the authors argue that an m-commerce strategy should be designed in synergy with a fixed network-based e-commerce strategy while carefully following and anticipating the progressive implementation of significant technological advances.

Chapter XII

David Wright, University of Ottawa, Canada

This article identifies the capabilities needed for mobile computing and commerce and assesses their technology and business implications. It identifies developments in the wireless networks that can be used for mobile computing and commerce, together with the services that can be provided over such networks. It provides a business analysis indicating which network operators can profitably deploy new networks, and which network operators need to establish business and technology links with each other so as to better serve their customers. The resulting range of next generation service, technologies and network operators available for mobile computing and commerce is identified.

Chapter XIII
    Haroun Alrayalat, Brunel University, UK
    Yogesh Kumar Dwivedi, Brunel University, UK
    Jasna Kuljis, Brunel University, UK
    Ray J. Paul, Brunel University, UK

Internet connectivity has a profound impact on almost all aspects of human lives, including social interaction and individual behavior. This chapter focuses on evaluating the impact of broadband Internet on the growth and development of business-to-consumer (B2C) electronic commerce. Results indicate that broadband use has a significant impact on consumer behavior towards adoption of B2C electronic commerce. This chapter illustrates how broadband use has an influence on off-line purchase behavior, online B2C electronic commerce, and overall online experience.

Chapter XIV
    Valli Kumari Vatsavayi, Andhra University, India
    Ravi Mukkamala, Old Dominion University, USA

With mobile operators having a large customer base and e-payments getting popular, there is a shift of focus on the huge potential that the mobile commerce (m-commerce) market offers. Mobile payment (m-payment) service is the core for the success of m-commerce. M-payments allow customers to buy digital goods from anywhere and anytime using Internet and mobile environments. Ubiquity, reachability, localization, personalization, and dissemination of information are the characteristics that favor m-payments and encourage the consumers and merchants to use them. This chapter examines various aspects of m-payments like architectures, limitations, security, and trust issues. It also discusses and compares the existing payment procedures of several different companies providing m-payment services. While exploring the advantages of shifting to m-payments, the problems that have to be dealt with when adopting new solutions are discussed. Finally, the chapter concludes by identifying a common set of requirements criteria for successful global m-payments.

Chapter XV
    Eusebio Scornavacca, Victoria University of Wellington, New Zealand
    Stuart J. Barnes, University of East Anglia, UK

One pertinent area of recent m-commerce development is in methods for personal transaction and information transfer. Several companies around the world have begun to use barcodes for the provision of m-commerce services. This chapter provides background on the enabling technological platform for providing such services. It then continues with three cases where mobile barcodes have been used—in

Japan, New Zealand, and the UK. Subsequently, these are used as the basis for a discussion and analysis of key business models and strategic implications for particular markets. The chapter concludes with predictions for the market and directions for future research.

Section IV
Utilization and Application

Chapter XVI

Ayman Abuhamdieh, Indiana State University, USA
Julie E. Kendall, Rutgers University, USA
Kenneth E. Kendall, Rutgers University, USA

This chapter presents the experience of the New York Theatre Group (NYTG), a nonprofit performing arts organization, in integrating e-commerce in its business practices. The case study of this organization begins with a very broad overview of the nonprofit sector, the performing arts industry, its delivery channels, and the theatrical production process in general. Then, attention turns to NYTG itself in terms of its history, organizational structure, its market segmentation, market trends, and forecasted growth. The strategic planning at NYTG, and the programs put in place to help it achieve its objectives and mission, are detailed. A survey that maps the demographic attributes of NYTG's patrons and subscribers is discussed. The case concludes with the current e-commerce challenges facing NYTG in particular and the nonprofit performing arts organizations in general.

Chapter XVII

Sylvie Feindt, SFC, Germany
Judith Jeffcoate, University of Buckingham, UK
Caroline Chappell, The Trefoyle Partnership, UK

The objective of this chapter is to evaluate the use of e-commerce across the value chains of several companies. In order to fulfill this objective, two different types of supply chain are analyzed: the first type consists of buyer groups in the consumer goods sector; the second is dynamic networks in the manufacturing sector. Having identified what value activities are automated, the chapter examines the level of ICT and how value activity interactions between organizations are supported with e-commerce. Building on the analysis of e-commerce technology usage, the development of virtual structures is examined and the roles that SMEs can play in these. The chapter seeks to demonstrate that, with the introduction of e-commerce technologies in value activities across companies, the role of the current players is changing.

Chapter XVIII

Fahim Akhter, Zayed University, UAE
Zakaria Maamar, Zayed University, UAE
Dave Hobbs, University of Bradford, UK

This chapter presents an application of fuzzy logic to human reasoning about e-commerce transactions. This research uncovers some of the hidden relationships between critical factors such as security, familiarity, design, and competitiveness. The authors analyze the effect of these factors on human decision process and how they affect the Business-to-Consumer (B2C) outcome when they are used collectively. A toolset for B2C vendors to access and evaluate a user's transaction decision process is provided along with an assisted reasoning tool for the online user.

Chapter XIX

Trust is widely recognized as an essential factor for the continual development of business-to-customer electronic commerce. Many trust models have been developed, however, and most are subjective and do not take into account the vagueness and ambiguity of EC trust and the customer's intuitions and experience when conducting online transactions. In this chapter, the authors develop a fuzzy trust model using fuzzy reasoning to evaluate EC trust. This trust model is based on the information customers expect to find on an EC Web site and is shown to increase customers trust towards online merchants. Fuzzy logic, the authors argue is suitable for trust evaluation as it takes into account the uncertainties within e-commerce data and like human relationships; it is often expressed by linguistics terms rather than numerical values.

Chapter XX

This chapter introduces a new transaction protocol using mobile agents in electronic commerce. The authors first propose a new model for transactions in electronic commerce—mutual authenticated transactions using mobile agents. They then design a new protocol by this model. Furthermore, the authors analyze the new protocol in terms of authentication, construction, and privacy. The aim of the protocol is to guarantee that the customer is committed to the server, and the server is committed to the customer. At the same time, the privacy of the customer is protected.

Section V
Criticial Issues

Chapter XXI

This chapter briefly examines existing literature regarding important factors that affect online shopping, forming the basis for speculation on factors that may be important for consumers shopping via their mobile phones. One such factor is the kind of online shopping, which should resemble, to some degree, other forms of shopping on the Internet. Hypotheses are formulated and a methodology is developed. After presenting the results, the authors discuss the implications and conclusions of this study.

Chapter XXII

This chapter presents a value exchange model of privacy and security for electronic customer relationship management within an electronic commerce environment. Enterprises and customers must carefully manage these new virtual relationships in order to ensure that they both derive value from them and minimize unintended consequences that result from the concomitant exchange of personal information that occurs in e-commerce. Based upon a customer's requirements of privacy and an enterprise requirement to establish markets and sell goods and services, there is a value exchange relationship. The model is an integration of the customer sphere of privacy, sphere of security, and privacy/security sphere of implementation.

The authors of this selection develop a new model of Web IS success that takes into account both intrinsic and extrinsic motivating factors. The proposed model begins with the Garrity and Sanders (1998) model of technologic acceptance and develops an extended nomological network of success factors that draws on motivation and flow theory. The authors conclude, through their current research, that future studies should both enhance and understand IS success measurement and prediction.

Chapter XXIV

Along with the exponential increase in online business transactions, the online payment system has gained in popularity because vendors and creditors realize its growing importance as a foundation to improve their information infrastructure and to achieve "paperless" operating efficiency. However, due to per se different characteristics among customers and Web-systems, both sides' perspectives and technology factors could cause a significant level of variation in customers' acceptance of online payment methods.

Our research involving 148 subjects who participated in a field survey examined the impact of a series of possible decision factors including perceived risk, perceived benefits, vendor's system features, and customers' characteristics on the intention to use an online payment system by customers.

Chapter XXV

David Gefen, Drexel University, USA
Tsipi Heart, Ben-Gurion University of the Negev, Israel

Trust and trust beliefs (trustworthiness) are key to e-commerce success but depend, to a large extent, on culture. With e-commerce being an international phenomenon, understanding the cross-cultural aspects of trust creation is arguably required although mostly ignored by current. This exploratory study examines whether definitions of trust beliefs as conceptualized and verified in the U.S. apply in Israel which differs markedly in individualism, uncertainty avoidance, and power distance. The data, cross-validating the scale of trust and its antecedents in both cultures, generally support the proposition that trust beliefs apply across cultures, and may be a relatively unvarying aspect of e-commerce. However, as expected, the effects of predictability and familiarity on trust beliefs may differ across national cultures. Implications about the need to include national culture in the research on trust, in general, and in e-commerce in particular, are discussed.

Chapter XXVI

Jeff Baker, Texas Tech University, USA
Jaeki Song, Texas Tech University, USA

The recent growth of business-to-consumer (B2C) Internet auctions challenges researchers to develop empirically-sound explanations of critical factors that allow merchants to earn price premiums in these auctions. The absence of a comprehensive model of Internet auctions leads the authors to conduct an exploratory study to elucidate and rank critical factors that lead to price premiums in Internet auctions. Classification and Regression Trees (CART), a decision-tree induction technique, is employed to analyze data collected in a field study of eBay auctions. The current research finds that shipping cost, reputation, initial bid price, and auction ending time as the factors most predictive of price premiums in B2C Internet auctions.

Section VI
Emerging Trends

Chapter XXVII

Robert C. MacGregor, University of Wollongong, Australia
Lejla Vrazalic, University of Wollongong, Australia

Over the last decade, the Internet and Internet technologies such as electronic commerce have experienced phenomenal growth. However, research shows that small businesses have been slow to adopt and to implement e-commerce due to a variety of barriers or impediments. This chapter presents an exploratory study of regional small businesses in Sweden that aims to improve our knowledge about e-commerce adoption barriers and to determine if there are any differences in the level of importance assigned to different barriers by males and females. The results of the study suggest that e-commerce adoption barriers fall into one of two distinct groupings: too difficult to implement or unsuitable to the business. The results of the study have significant implications for government organizations engaged in promoting e-commerce adoption, particularly among small businesses in regional areas.

Chapter XXVIII

This chapter discusses the growing significance of m-commerce with special focus on Bluetooth and WiMax. There is a detailed investigation of the components involved with, and the marketplace for, m-commerce transactions. The chapter concludes with the future opportunities and obstacles for m-commerce. The authors hope that readers will gain a better understanding of not only m-commerce, but also the impact of Bluetooth and WiMax.

Chapter XXIX

Consumer-to-consumer (C2C) e-commerce is a growing area of e-commerce. This study adapts constructs from a business-to-consumer (B2C) e-commerce study of satisfaction (Devaraj, Fan, & Kohli, 2002) to determine what, if any, the differences are in the C2C e-commerce arena. The constructs include elements of the technology acceptance model (TAM), which includes perceived ease of use and usefulness; transaction cost analysis (TCA), which includes uncertainty, asset specificity, and time; and service quality (SERVQUAL), which includes reliability, responsiveness, assurance, and empathy. Findings indicate that TAM, TCA, and SERVQUAL all impact satisfaction in C2C e-commerce. Reliability and responsiveness (areas of service quality) were found to influence C2C e-commerce satisfaction, whereas as they were not found to be an influence in the B2C study. These findings warrant further research in the C2C e-commerce arena.

Advances in wireless communications and information technology have made the Mobile Web a reality. The Mobile Web is the response to the need for anytime, anywhere access to information and services. As communications and other IT usage becomes an integral part of many people's lives and the available products and services become more varied and capable, users expect to be able to personalize a service to meet their individual needs and preferences. The involved sectors have to meet these challenges by reengineering their front-end and back-end office. This chapter examines the interaction requirements for a friendlier, personalized and more effective multi-channel services environment. It will present the mobility challenges and constraints implemented into the business sector, investigating the current m-commerce situation and the extended user characteristics and presenting a high level user-centric m-commerce architecture.

Prologue

INTRODUCTION

Electronic commerce or *e-commerce* can be briefly defined as the buying and selling of goods, information and services and the transfer of funds using digital communications. The term "electronic commerce" is now very familiar and most people are used to performing many of their everyday transactions through electronic commerce. The future of electronic commerce looks even brighter according to the following market research:

- Online Publishers Association (2007) found that about 15% of Internet activities were related to electronic commerce in the first five months of 2007 and the increase in content's share of time was fairly steady from 2003 to 2007 based on a monthly gauge of the time being spent on e-commerce, communications, content, and search functions.
- More than 85% of the world's online population, 875 million consumers, have shopped on the World Wide Web, up 40% in the two years since 2005 (Nielsen Company, 2008).
- Electronic commerce sites are the most frequent users of paid search engine marketing. The top ten paid search advertisers, generating 16% of all sponsored links, were all retail or comparison shopping sites. eBay, the number one spot, achieved 802 million sponsored link exposures. (comScore, Inc., 2007).

Companies and research organizations provide a host of software and methodologies for electronic commerce implementations. However, given the wide variety of technologies and methodologies available, IT workers often have difficulty selecting the most suitable technology for a specific electronic commerce application. This book presents a set of first-class articles on contemporary electronic commerce technologies written by renowned scholars, scientists, and industrialists from all over the world. Its aim is to help readers better understand the electronic commerce technologies that are available and how best to apply the technologies to electronic commerce implementations.

Compared to electronic commerce, the term "electronic commerce technologies" is vague and rarely used because it covers so many different disciplines. This prologue discusses electronic commerce technologies, dividing them into two categories for convenience:

A. *Technologies for electronic commerce implementations*: This refers to technologies such as the languages and software, for example ASP.NET and Adobe Flash, that are used to facilitate the construction of electronic commerce systems and applications.
B. *Technologies used by electronic commerce*: Here, the technologies include the methods and algorithms such as Web mining and information retrieval that are used by electronic commerce.

The relationships between these two kinds of technologies are shown in Figure 1.

Figure 1. Two kinds of technologies for electronic commerce

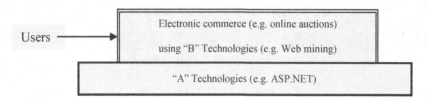

The rest of this prologue is organized as follows. Section 2 introduces a generic structure of electronic commerce systems and explains the four system components: (i) applications, (ii) client computers, (iii) wired networks, and (iv) host computers. A list of electronic commerce applications is given in Section 3. Section 4 discussed two kinds of electronic commerce programming: (i) client-side programming using languages and software like CSS and Adobe Dreamweaver and (ii) server-side programming using software and tools such as the LAMP stack and ASP.NET. Electronic commerce security and payment methods are also discussed in this section. Technologies used by electronic commerce are introduced in Section 5, with two of the technologies, Web mining and Web searching, examined in more detail. The final section gives a summary of this prologue.

ELECTRONIC COMMERCE SYSTEMS

An electronic commerce system is inherently interdisciplinary and there are many different ways to implement it. Figure 2 shows a generic structure of a traditional electronic commerce system and a typical example of such a system. The system structure includes four components (Hu, Yang, Yeh, & Hu, 2008):

- *Electronic commerce applications*: Typical applications include business transactions and electronic markets. Several popular applications will be discussed in the next section.
- *Client computers*: Client computers, specifically their browsers, are used to interactively communicate with electronic commerce applications.
- *Wired networks*: Wired networks are used to transmit data for electronic commerce. There are three major types of wired networks:

  - *Local Area Networks (LAN)* span a relatively small space of only a few square kilometers or less, such as an office building. They generally offer a throughput of 10 Mbps or 100 Mbps and are usually based on Ethernet technology, which is a network protocol using a bus topology and defining a specific implementation of the Physical and Data Link Layers in the OSI model (IEEE 802.3).
  - *Metropolitan Area Networks (MAN)* span a geographical area greater than a LAN but less than a WAN, such as few city blocks or a whole city. MANs typically use wireless infrastructure or optical fiber connections to link sites and may connect multiple LANs. Their maximum throughput is no less than 44 Mbps and they use the Distributed Queue Dual Bus technology based on the IEEE 802.6 standard.

Figure 2. An electronic commerce system structure

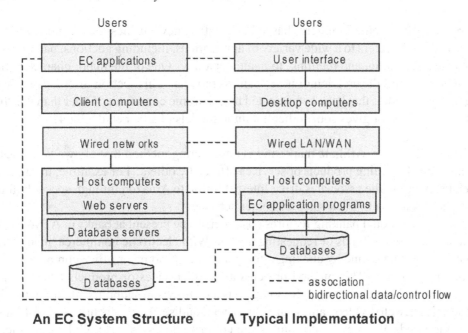

An EC System Structure   **A Typical Implementation**

- *Wide Area Networks (WAN)* span a wide geographic area, such as state or country, and use specialized computers to connect smaller networks, such as LANs. They generally offer a throughput of 1.5 Mbps or more. WANs typically use wide area network services from tele-communications carriers, whose technologies include standard phone lines, ISDN (Integrated Services Digital Network), or other high-speed services.
- *Host computers*: Most electronic commerce application programs reside in this component, except for client-side programs such as cookies or user interfaces using markup languages. User requests such as checking out or adding items to the shopping cart are actually processed at a host computer, which contains three major kinds of software specifically written for e-commerce transactions:

  - *Web servers*: These are server-side application programs that manage the Web pages stored in the Web site's databases or files. Three popular Web servers are (i) Apache HTTP Servers, (ii) Microsoft's Internet Information Services (IIS), and (iii) Sun Java System Web Servers.
  - *Databases and database servers*: Databases store electronic commerce data such as user and product information; database servers manage databases and provide database access functions, such as locating the actual records being requested or updating the data in databases. Some popular databases include: (i) IBM DB2, (ii) Microsoft's Office Access and SQL Servers, and (iii) Oracle databases.
  - *Application programs and support software*: These are responsible for handling server-side processing such as user interface creation and user input processing. The software used to build the application programs will be discussed later.

ELECTRONIC COMMERCE APPLICATIONS

The emergence of electronic commerce has led to countless new business opportunities and applications. Electronic commerce refers to a wide variety of applications, including auctions, banking, marketplaces and exchanges, recruiting, and retailing, to name but a few. One of the major characteristics of e-commerce is that it enables the creation of new business models. This section discusses some of the newly possible business models that have been created by electronic commerce. Other than the "buy-and-sell" model, the following list gives some other common models (Turban et al., 2004):

- *Affiliate marketing*: Affiliate marketing is a marketing method that allows Web sites to receive a commission by selling products or services offered by others. For example, in Amazon.com's Associates Program the associates drive Internet traffic to Amazon through specially formatted links that allow Amazon to track sales and other activities.
- *Banking*: Traditional banking requires customers to be present at banks or ATMs to perform tasks such as transferring funds or requesting a loan. With electronic commerce, many banking operations can be done online by clicking a few buttons on a home or office computer.
- *Comparing prices*: This method presents a list of services or products based on a consumer's specifications. For example, mySimon.com is a comparison shopping site for apparel, computers, electronics, jewelry, video games, and other merchandise. It gathers prices on millions of products from thousands of stores, so customers can compare products and find the best price before they purchase an item.
- *Customization and personalization*: Customization or personalization allows the design and creation of content that meets a customer's specific needs. For example, Dell Inc. sells computer systems directly to the public, with each unit tailor-made to the customer's specifications. This direct business model eliminates the time and costs involved in purchasing through traditional bricks-and-mortar retailers.
- *Electronic marketplaces and exchanges*: Electronic marketplaces are Internet Web sites that act as a meeting point between supply and demand; electronic exchanges serve as central marketplaces with established rules and regulations where buyers and sellers meet to trade futures and options contracts or securities. Electronic marketplaces and exchanges provide benefits to both buyers and sellers because they are more efficient than their traditional counterparts.
- *Electronic tendering systems*: For large purchases of services or goods potential suppliers bid competitively for a contract, quoting a price to the buyer who then selects the most advantageous. Large buyers usually make their purchases through a tendering (bidding) system, which becomes more effective and efficient with the help of electronic commerce.
- *Group purchasing*: Items purchased in bulk benefit from quantity discounts; electronic commerce allows a group of customers or organizations to place their orders together and negotiate a better deal. For example, Amerinet members saved more than $300 million in 2003 through group purchasing health care equipment and products.
- *Name your price*: With this model, the product/service prices are set by customers instead of sellers. Priceline.com was the first company to apply this method. The following example shows how this works. With Priceline.com's "Name Your Own Price" hotel reservation service, customers choose the star level of hotel they want, along with the desired neighborhood, dates and price they want to pay. Priceline.com then searches for a hotel room at the customer's desired price. Priceline.com is able to offer this sale as a result of

- certain hotel suppliers agreeing to make lower rates available for particular properties through Priceline.com's hotel service and/or
- the application by Priceline.com of a variable subsidy to certain offers.

- *Online auctions*: Traditional auctions usually require bidders to attend the auctions in person, and the items offered are limited. Online auctions allow bidders from everywhere to bid products or services provided by various sellers without needing to show up. eBay.com is the world's largest online auction site, offering an online platform where millions of items are traded each day. Several hundred other companies, including Amazon.com and Yahoo.com, also conduct online auctions.
- *Recruiting*: Electronic commerce makes recruiting easy, fast, and effective. Jobs posted by recruiters can be searched by job seekers from all over the world, while job seekers can post their resumes and requests on the Internet for potential interested recruiters.
- *Retailing*: In the past, customers had to drive to stores to purchase groceries or appliances and carry them home. Now all kinds of online retail stores are available. Customers can purchase clothes, toys, and even fresh foods from the Internet and have them delivered directly to their homes.
- *Virtual communities*: A virtual community is a collection of people sharing common interests, ideas, and feelings over the Internet or other collaborative networks. People in a virtual community tend to be more comfortable performing transactions with other members of their community.

TECHNOLOGIES FOR ELECTRONIC COMMERCE IMPLEMENTATIONS

Figure 3 shows another structure of an electronic commerce system or a database-driven web site, which is often implemented using a `three-tiered client-server architecture` consisting, as the name suggests, of three layers:

1. *User interface*: This runs on a desktop PC or workstation (the client) and uses a standard graphical user interface. The main function of this tier is to translate tasks and results to something the user can understand.
2. *Function modules*: This tier coordinates the application, processes commands, makes logical decisions and evaluations, and performs calculations. It also relays data between the other two tiers.
3. *Database management system (DBMS)*: A DBMS on a host computer stores and manages the data required by the middle tier for further processing. The middle tier then sends the processed data back to the user.

The three-tier design has many advantages over traditional two-tier or single-tier designs, the chief one being: *The added modularity makes it easier to modify or replace one tier without affecting the other tiers*.

Electronic Commerce Programming

Electronic commerce is popular and widely used. A variety of languages and software are available for building electronic commerce systems and applications. Each of the languages or software belongs to one of two kinds of electronic commerce programming:

Figure 3. Three-tiered client-server web system structure

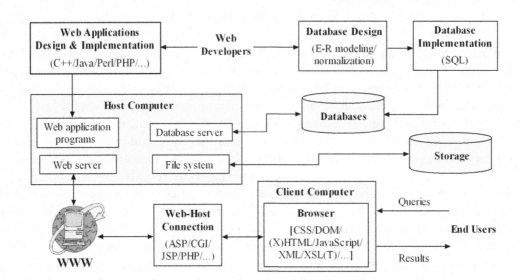

Table 1. A list of client-side languages and software for electronic commerce implementations

Markup/Programming Languages	Multimedia Editors	HTML Editors
AJAX, CSS, DOM, DTD, (X)HTML, JavaScript, XML, XSL(T)	Adobe Flash, Adobe Photoshop	Adobe Dreamweaver, Microsoft Expression Web, Microsoft SharePoint Designer

- *Client-side programming* uses the software that runs on client computers/devices, in particular the Web interface. Popular languages for Web interfaces include CSS, DOM, (X)HTML, JavaScript, XML, and XSL(T). In addition to the Web interface, this can include client-side applications such as address and schedule books. The tools and languages used for client-side application development depend on the client-side operating systems being used, for example Visual Studio is used for Windows or C/C++ for Linux. Table 1 lists some popular client-side languages and software for electronic commerce implementations.

- *Server-side programming* involves the software that runs on servers. This normally deals with requests from browsers and sends the results from databases/files/programs back to the browsers for display. Popular server-side languages include C/C++, Java, Perl, and PHP. Server-side programming also implements numerous applications such as instant messaging and e-mails, but as these types of applications are related to standard network programming tasks such as TCP/IP programming they will not be covered in this book.

- Table 2 lists some popular server-side software and tools, including integrated development environments (IDEs) and the LAMP stack (Lawton, 2005), that are used for electronic commerce implementations.

Table 2. A list of server-side software and tools for electronic commerce implementations

IDEs	
	IBM DB2,
	Microsoft Access,
	Microsoft SQL Server,
Adobe CodeFusion,	MySQL,
Microsoft ASP.NET,	Oracle 11gAJAX,
Microsoft Visual Studio,	SOAP,
NetBeans,	Web services,
Ruby On Rails (ROR),	XQueryLinux,
Sun Java Studio,	Apache HTTP Server,
Zend Core	MySQL,
	PHP,
	Perl,
	Python

Electronic Commerce Security and Payment Methods

Another important issue of electronic commerce technologies is related to security and payment methods. Secure commercial information exchange and safe electronic financial transactions are essential for both content providers and potential customers. A secure electronic commerce system must have the following properties: (i) confidentiality, (ii) authentication, (iii) integrity, (iv) authorization, (v) availability, and (vi) non-repudiation. To achieve these security goals, digital data are encrypted and decrypted based on cryptographic algorithms, which can be divided into two categories (Lee, Kou, & Hu, 2005):

- *Symmetric key systems*: In this category, the sender and receiver participating in a secure session both own the same digital key. The sender encrypts messages using this key and then sends it to the receiver through the public network. The receiver then decrypts the messages received using the same key.
- *Asymmetric key systems*: These are also called "public key systems." Unlike in symmetric key systems, a participating entity in an asymmetric key system uses two keys—a public key that is accessible to everyone in the world and a private key known only to itself. Applying one or both of these two keys in different orders to data messages provides security services such as authentication and digital signature.

Among the many issues that arise with electronic commerce security, payment methods are probably the most crucial. A typical payment scenario is as follows:

1.   A user registers for the services via a PC or notebook computer.
2.   The user submits his/her payment for the services he/she has received.
3.   The service/content provider deals with the request by authenticating and authorizing the user and then contacting a financial institution.
4.   A confirmation of the completed transaction is delivered to the user.

The Secure Sockets Layer (SSL) is one of the most popular techniques used by electronic commerce payment methods. It works as follows (VeriSign, Inc., n.d.). An SSL Certificate, issued by the Certificate Authority (CA), is created for a particular server in a specific domain for a verified business entity. Each SSL Certificate contains unique, authenticated information about the certificate owner. When a Web browser points to a secured domain, an SSL handshake authenticates the server (Web site) and the client (Web browser) and an encryption method is established with a unique session key. The server and client can start a secure session with message privacy and integrity guaranteed. VeriSign at http://www.verisign.com/ is one of the companies providing SSL payment services for electronic commerce.

TECHNOLOGIES USED BY ELECTRONIC COMMERCE

Unlike the technologies used for building electronic commerce systems and applications, the technologies discussed in this section are usually not related to any specific languages or software but are instead methodologies or algorithms. Almost all kinds of information technologies have been used by electronic commerce, but the three most widely used are:

- *Artificial intelligence (AI)*: Artificial intelligence uses computer programs to mimic human intelligence, such as reasoning, learning, problem solving, and decision making. Many AI methods such as data mining and data warehousing have been applied to electronic commerce.
- *Information retrieval (IR)*: Information retrieval is the study of indexing, searching, and managing data. IR has been widely used by computer systems such as digital libraries for a long time. Recently, IR methods such as relevance feedback have been adapted for use with electronic commerce.
- *Business management*: Business management methods such as supply chain management and enterprise resource planning (ERP) have been widely used by traditional commerce. Many of these methods are also used by electronic commerce.

It is not possible to cover all of these technologies in detail in the limited space available here, which instead focuses on providing an extensive list of methods and means. The next two sections discuss two major technologies used by electronic commerce: Web usage mining of artificial intelligence and Web searching of information retrieval.

World Wide Web Usage Mining

World Wide Web Data Mining includes content mining, hyperlink structure mining, and usage mining. All three approaches attempt to extract knowledge from the Web, produce useful results from the

Figure 4. A Web usage mining system structure

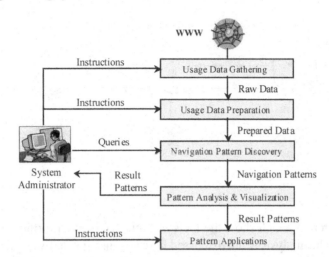

knowledge extracted, and apply the results to specific real-world problems. The first two apply data mining techniques to Web page contents and hyperlink structures, respectively. The third approach, Web usage mining, is the application of data mining techniques to the usage logs of large Web data repositories in order to produce results that can be applied to many practical subjects, such as improving Web sites/pages, making additional topic or product recommendations, user/customer behavior studies, and so on. A Web usage mining system such as the one shown in Figure 4 performs five major tasks, discussed in turn below (Hu, Zuo, Wiggen, & Krishna, 2008).

Usage Data Gathering

Web usage data are usually supplied by two sources: trial runs by human operators and Web logs. The first approach is impractical and rarely used because of its intrinsically high time and expense costs and its bias. Most usage mining systems therefore use log data as their data source. A Web log file records activity information when a Web user submits a request to a Web server. A log file can be located in three different places: (i) web servers, (ii) web proxy servers, and (iii) client browsers, as shown in Figure 5.

Usage Data Preparation

The information contained in a raw Web server log does not reliably represent a user session file. The Web usage data preparation phase is thus used to restore users' activities in the Web server log in a reliable and consistent way. This phase should at a minimum achieve the following four major tasks: (i) removing undesirable entries, (ii) distinguishing among users, (iii) building sessions, and (iv) restoring the contents of a session (Cooley, Mobasher, & Srivastava, 1999).

Navigation Pattern Discovery, Analysis, and Visualization

Many data mining algorithms are dedicated to finding navigation patterns. Among these, most algorithms use the method of sequential pattern generation, while the remaining methods tend to be rather ad

Figure 5. Three Web log file locations

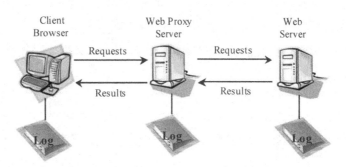

hoc. Navigation patterns, which show the facts of Web usage, need further analysis and interpretation before application. The analysis is not discussed here because it usually requires human intervention or is distributed to the two other tasks: navigation pattern discovery and pattern applications. Navigation patterns are normally two-dimensional paths that are difficult to perceive if a proper visualization tool is not supported.

Usage Pattern Applications

The results of navigation pattern discovery can be applied to the following major areas, among others: (i) improving site/page design, (ii) making additional topic or product recommendations, and (iii) Web personalization. Learning user/customer behavior (Adomavicius & Tuzhilin, 2001) and Web caching (Lan, Bressan, & Ooi, 1999), as well as other less important applications for navigation patterns, are also worth studying.

- *Web site/page improvements*: The most important application of discovered navigation patterns is to improve Web sites/pages by (re)organizing them. In addition to manually (re)organizing the Web sites/pages, it is possible to use automatic methods to achieve this. Adaptive Web sites (Chibing & Nordahl, 2005) automatically improve their organization and presentation by learning from visitor access patterns. They mine the data buried in Web server logs to produce easily navigable Web sites.
- *Additional topic or product recommendations*: Electronic commerce sites use recommender systems or collaborative filtering (Zhou, Hui, & Chang, 2004) to suggest products to their customers or to provide consumers with information to help them decide which products to purchase. For example, each account owner at Amazon.com is presented with a section of *Your Recommendations*, which suggests additional products based on the owner's previous purchases and browsing behavior.
- *Web personalization*: Web personalization (re)organizes Web sites/pages based on the Web experience to fit individual users' needs (Suryavanshi, Shin, & Mudur, 2005). This is a broad area that includes adaptive Web sites and recommender systems as special cases. The WebPersonalizer system (Mobasher et al., 2002) uses a subset of Web log and session clustering techniques to derive usage profiles, which are then used to generate recommendations.

World Wide Web Searches

One of the most commonly performed tasks on the Web is to search Web pages, and it is also one of the most frustrating and problematic. The situation is getting worse because of the Web's fast growing size and lack of structural style, as well as the inadequacy of existing Web search engine technologies (Lawrence & Giles, 1999). Traditional search techniques are based on users typing in search keywords that the search services can then use to locate the desired Web pages. However, this approach normally retrieves too many documents, of which only a small fraction are relevant to the users' needs. Furthermore, the most relevant documents do not necessarily appear at the top of the query output list.

Search Engine Structure

Two different approaches are applied to Web search services: genuine search engines and directories. The difference lies in how their listings are compiled:

- Search engines, such as Google, create their listings automatically.
- A directory, such as Yahoo!, depends on human operators for its listings.

Figure 6 shows the system structure of a typical search engine (Hu, et al., 2007). Some search engines, known as hybrid search engines, maintain an associated directory. Search engines traditionally consist of three components: the crawler, the indexing software, and the search and ranking software:

- *Crawlers*: A crawler is a program that automatically scans a sequence of Web sites and collects Web documents from them. Crawlers follow the links on a site to find other relevant pages. Two

Figure 6. System structure of a Web search engine

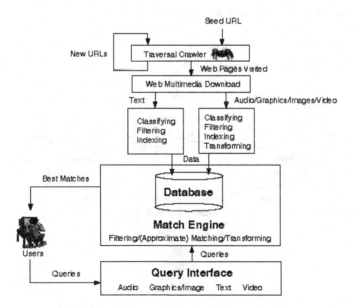

search algorithms, breadth-first searches and depth-first searches, are widely used by crawlers to traverse the Web.

- *Indexing software*: Automatic indexing is the process of algorithmically examining information items to build a data structure that can be quickly searched. Filtering is one of the most important pre-processes for indexing and is a typical transformation in information retrieval that is often used to reduce the size of a document and/or standardize it to simplify searching.
- *Search and ranking software*: Query processing is the activity of analyzing a query and comparing it to indexes to find relevant items. A user enters a keyword or keywords, along with Boolean modifiers such as "and," "or," or "not," into a search engine, which then scans indexed Web pages for the keywords. To determine in which order to display pages to the user, the engine uses an algorithm to rank pages that contain the keywords. For example, the engine may count the number of times the keyword appears on a page.

Price Comparison Using Metasearch Engines

One popular electronic commerce application is price comparison, which can be implemented by using a metasearch engine. Metasearch engines (Goldberg, Taksa, & Spink, 2008) conduct a search using several other search engines simultaneously and then present the results in some sort of integrated format. Figure 7 shows the system structure of a metasearch engine, which consists of three major components:

- *Dispatch*: Determines to which search engines a specific query is sent. The selection is usually based on network and local computational resources, as well as the long-term performance of search engines on specific query terms.
- *Interface*: Adapts the user's query format to match the format of a particular search engine, which varies from engine to engine.
- *Display*: Here, raw results from the selected search engines are integrated for display to the user. Each search engine will produce different raw results, with different formats, from other search engines and these must be combined to give a uniform format for ease-of-use.

Figure 7. System structure of a metasearch engine

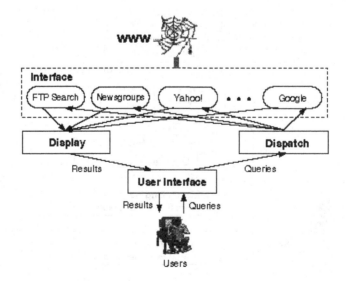

SUMMARY

The introduction of electronic commerce in the 1990s has had an enormous impact on our daily life, particularly for activities such as shopping, banking, and traveling. This prologue has introduced important issues connected with electronic commerce technologies and applications, including the following themes:

- *Electronic commerce systems*: An e-commerce system consists of four components: (i) applications, (ii) client computers, (iii) wired networks, and (iv) host computers.
- *Electronic commerce applications*: The applications cover almost all transactions.
- *Technologies for electronic commerce implementations*: Electronic commerce programming involves a wide variety of technologies and languages. It consists of two kinds of programming:

  - *Client-side programming*, which develops the software that runs on client computers or devices. This is mostly related to web interface construction, and popular languages for web interface construction include CSS, DOM, (X)HTML, JavaScript, XML, and XSL(T).
  - *Server-side programming*, which develops the software that runs on servers. The software normally receives requests from browsers and sends the results from databases/files/programs back to the browsers for display. Popular server-side languages include C/C++, Java, Perl, and PHP.

Cryptography used by electronic commerce security including symmetric and asymmetric key systems and a payment method using Secure Sockets Layer (SSL) are discussed.

- *Technologies used by electronic commerce*: Three major technologies used by electronic commerce are (i) artificial intelligence, (ii) information retrieval, and (iii) business management. Web mining of artificial intelligence and Web searching of information retrieval have also been discussed in this prologue.

The Selected Readings on Electronic Commerce Technologies: Contemporary Applications presents a set of first-class articles on contemporary electronic commerce technologies written by renowned scholars, scientists, and industrialists from all over the world. Its aim is to provide assorted, seamless, up-to-date high-quality research publications of electronic commerce technologies and applications for class use. Students will smoothly gain valuable knowledge from this book and lecturers will be greatly benefited by its convenience and effectiveness.

REFERENCES

Adomavicius, G. & Tuzhilin, A. (2001). Using data mining methods to build customer profiles. *IEEE Computer*, 34(2), 74-82.

Chibing, G. & Nordahl, M. (2005). Building an adaptive Website based on user access patterns. In *Proceedings of International Conference on Cyberworlds (CW'05)*, 5 pages, Singapore.

comScore, Inc. (2007). *E-Commerce Sites Dominate Search Engine Marketing*. Retrieved April 2, 2008, from http://www.researchrecap.com/index.php/2007/06/07/e-commerce-sites-dominate-search-engine-marketing/

Cooley, R., Mobasher, B., & Srivastava, J. (1999). Data preparation for mining World Wide Web browsing patterns. *Knowledge and Information Systems*, 1(1), 5-32.

Goldberg, R., Taksa, I., & Spink, A. (2008). Metasearch engines and information retrieval: computational complexity of ranking multiple search results. In *Proceedings of 5th International Conference on Information Technology: New Generations*, pages 315-320, Las Vegas, Nevada.

Hu, W.-C., Bemgal, S., Fu, L., & Yang, H.-J. (2007). A focused mobile web search engine using a topic-specific knowledge base. In *Proceedings of the 40th Annual Midwest Instruction and Computing Symposium (MICS 2007)*, Grand Forks, North Dakota.

Hu, W.-C., Yang, C.-H., Yeh, J.-h., & Hu, W. (2008). Mobile and electronic commerce systems and technologies. *Journal of Electronic Commerce in Organizations*.

Hu, W.-C., Zuo, Y., Wiggen, T., & Krishna, V. (2008). Handheld data protection using handheld usage pattern identification. In *Proceedings of IEEE International Conference on Electro/Information Technology*, Ames, Iowa.

Lan, B., Bressan, S., & Ooi, B. O. (1999). Making Web servers pushier. In *Proceedings of the Workshop on Web Usage Analysis and User Profiling*, pages 112-125, San Diego, California.

Lawrence, S. & Giles, C. L. (1999). Accessibility of information on the Web. *Nature*, 400, 107-109.

Lawton, G. (2005). LAMP lights enterprise development efforts. *IEEE Computers*, 38(9), 18-20.

Lee, C.-w., Kou, W., & Hu, W.-C. (2005). Mobile commerce security and payment methods. In Hu, W.-C., Lee, C.-w., & Kou, W., editors, *Advances in Security and Payment Methods for Mobile Commerce*, pages 1-18, Idea Group, Inc.

Mobasher, B., Dai, H., Luo, T., & Nakagawa, M. (2002). Discovery and evaluation of aggregate usage profiles for Web personalization. *Data Mining and Knowledge Discovery*, Kluwer Publishing, 6(1), 61-82.

Nielsen Company. (2008). *Over 875 Million Consumers Have Shopped Online—The Number of Internet Shoppers up 40% in Two Years*. Retrieved April 12, 2008, from http://www.nielsen.com/media/2008/pr_080128b_download.pdf

Online Publishers Association. (2007). *Content, Not Communications, the Primary Use of Today's Internet*. Retrieved April 10, 2008, from http://www.researchrecap.com/index.php/2007/08/14/content-not-communications-the-primary-use-of-todays-internet/

Suryavanshi, B. S., Shin, N., & Mudur, S. P. (2005). Improving the effectiveness of model based recommender systems for highly sparse and noisy Web usage data. In *Proceedings of IEEE/WIC/ACM International Conference on Web Intelligence*, pages 618-621, Compiegne University of Technology, France.

Turban, E., King, D., Lee, J., & Viehland, D. (2004). *Electronic Commerce 2004: A Managerial Perspective*. Prentice Hall.

VeriSign, Inc. (n.d.). *Secure Sockets Layer (SSL): How It Works*. Retrieved April 23, 2008, from http://www.verisign.com/ssl/ssl-information-center/how-ssl-security-works/index.html

Zhou, B., Hui, S. C. & Chang, K. (2004). An intelligent recommender system using sequential Web access patterns. In *Proceedings of IEEE Conference on Cybernetics and Intelligent Systems*, pages 393-398, Singapore.

About the Editor

Wen-Chen Hu received a BE, an ME, an MS, and a PhD, all in computer science, from Tamkang University, Taiwan, the National Central University, Taiwan, the University of Iowa, Iowa City, and the University of Florida, Gainesville (1984, 1986, 1993, and 1998, respectively). Currently, he is an associate professor in the Department of Computer Science of the University of North Dakota, Grand Forks. Dr. Hu has taught more than 10 different computer courses and advised over 50 graduate students, has published more than 70 articles in refereed journals, conference proceedings, books, and encyclopedias and edited two books, and is solely authoring one book. His current research interests include handheld computing, electronic and mobile commerce systems, Web technologies, and databases.

Section I
Fundamental Concepts and Theories

Chapter I
E-Commerce Standards:
Transforming Industry Practice

Stephen Hawk
University of Wisconsin-Parkside, USA

Weijun Zheng
University of Wisconsin-Parkside, USA

ABSTRACT

This chapter introduces XML-based e-commerce standards that have emerged within the past decade. The chapter describes the history of e-commerce standards, and then presents representative horizontal and vertical e-commerce standards by detailing their functionality, and how their development has been shaped by various stakeholders. The chapter also describes the potential for these standards to transform B2B practice by providing three industry examples. The chapter finishes by suggesting directions for future research by describing factors that could influence the future of these standards. Due to the central role these standards are likely to play in future e-commerce activity, most firms will at some point need to become aware of their capabilities, their application, and potential impact. This chapter is intended to provide an overview of the situation as it is understood today, and presents likely scenarios for how these standards may progress.

INTRODUCTION

E-commerce (electronic-commerce) refers to business over the Internet. The two major forms of e-commerce are business-to-consumer (B2C) and business-to-business (B2B). While B2C caters mostly to consumers, B2B e-commerce refers to one business selling to another business via the Web. According to the Gartner Group, B2B e-commerce is expected to grow from $145 billion in 1999 to more than $7 trillion by 2004, which will represent more than 7% of all sales transactions worldwide.[1] Traditional electronic data interchange (EDI) standards are well developed and are what have been used for decades as the basis for pre-Internet B2B e-commerce. However, it has been widely recognized that traditional EDI will eventually be supplanted by newer Internet-based B2B standards. These standards have only begun to be significantly adopted in select industries the past few years so their impact can be discussed mostly in terms of potential. As a great majority of e-commerce revenue comes from B2B transactions, and most of that comes from transactions carried out via traditional EDI (Knorr, 2002), the newer standards have the potential for becoming a foundation technology for generating a majority of e-commerce revenue in the not-too-distant future.

The mission of this chapter is to introduce these newer e-commerce standards. We begin by describing some basic background and history of e-commerce standards. The chapter then presents representative horizontal and vertical e-commerce standards by detailing their functionality, and how their development has been shaped by various stakeholders (e.g., formal standards bodies, vendors, etc.). The chapter also describes the potential for these standards to transform B2B practice in industries where they are adopted by providing three industry examples. The chapter finishes by suggesting directions for future research by describing factors that could influence the future of these standards. Although we have tried to reduce the technique jargon, there are still a number of basic terms that are necessary in order to discuss these standards, how they have developed, and are beginning to be used.

BACKGROUND

E-commerce is fundamentally changing both companies' business processes and the value chains in which they operate. Greater automation speeds up business processes and makes them more efficient, promising productivity gains—and greater prosperity—both now and in the future. In order to enable e-commerce, common format conventions, or standards, are fundamental to the success of e-commerce.

A standard is a framework of specifications that has been approved by a recognized standards organization (de jure standard), is accepted as a de facto standard by the industry or is one of the open standards (Hawkins, Mansell, & Skea, 1995). Standards provide a blueprint for the future of industries, offering both stability and neutrality to a set of specifications. By providing a target for development, standards reduce the time and cost needed to develop systems and services, increase market access and acceptance, and reduce administrative and materials overhead. In today's e-commerce, standards have become a strategic tool for delivering innovation, reducing costs, improving the quality of goods and services produced, and opening new business opportunities (Kotok, 2002a, 2002b).

To better understand why standards are crucial to business, consider a relatively simple process: requesting a quote. Typically, the customer requests a product quote by sending its supplier a message with different kinds of specifications. After receiving the message, a supplier could respond by performing three different activities: checking availability of the product in its inventory; sending back the quote to the customer if its inventory matches the specification; and if not, referring the customer to another supplier. These activities are normally carried out by the supplier's own internal systems that are not visible to the customer. Without a clearly defined dialog between trading partners, the electronic exchange of messages for this transaction would be very difficult to accomplish. Similar to this case, many other transactions and information relevant to e-commerce must also be depicted (or "mapped") electronically in ways so that they can be exchanged between companies. There could be multiple companies in collaboration with one another along a supply chain. These companies normally have very different internal systems, but need to share some aspects of their business processes and exchange many different types of business documents as part of their interactions, which makes the electronic exchange of messages even more complex.

Implemented through various technologies, e-commerce standards provide a common language and format that make it possible for all trading partners to develop the processes and systems needed to exchange business information with each other. The development of e-commerce standards, according to CEN/ISSS eBusiness Standards Focus Group, will alleviate concerns about data protection and security, ensure interoperability, lower the cost of entry through free reference implementations, give good guidance, establish a more mainstream e-commerce software market; provide practical guidance by example, and aim for maximal ease of use (Li, 2003). All of these will help to remove some of the major barriers for e-commerce development and transform industry practice.

History of E-Commerce Standards

Today's B2B electronic commerce actually started with traditional electronic data interchange (EDI), the computer-to-computer exchange of business data in a standardized format. Starting from the late 1960s, as businesses began to computerize their internal operations, EDI was developed in an effort to reduce the burden of paperwork, and also as an attempt at implementing the fictional "paperless" office.

Traditional EDI users used leased or dedicated telephone lines or a value-added network (VAN)[2], such as those run by IBM, GE, or AT&T, to carry data exchanges. These lines would then be used to connect participating trading partners who in turn would need to install the VAN's proprietary software to translate and transmit their business documents in EDI formats. Although traditional EDI could result in faster transfer of documents at a lower cost and with fewer errors, it unfortunately was complex and expensive to implement. This, and its use of proprietary communication protocols,[3] effectively blocked most small-to-medium

sized enterprises (SMEs) from its advantages (Scala & McGrath, 1993).

In the 1970s, several industries sponsored a shared EDI system that they usually turned over to a third-party network. In some cases, the shared system was developed by the third party for the group of common companies or an industry trade group. In 1975, the Transportation Data Coordinating Committee (TDCC) developed the first set of interindustry EDI standard covering air, motor, ocean, rail, and some banking applications (Berge, 1991).

The milestone of EDI development came in 1985, when X12 was released by the American National Standards Institute (ANSI). X12 was the primary North American standard for defining EDI transactions. Along with ANSI X12, EDIFACT (EDI for administration, commerce, & transport) started out as an international standard through the auspices of the United Nations. Following the implementation of ASC X12 and EDIFACT, EDI became crucial to nearly every industry. In 1997, X12 merged with EDIFACT, the global standard for EDI transactions.[4]

As the Internet became widely used in the 1990s, companies began to realize that EDI could reach well beyond those who could afford the traditional VAN approach. While traditional EDI is still widely used, companies needed a common language through which to exchange structured information between their computer systems over the Internet. HTML, the first-generation language of the Internet, is not suited for this task as it defines only the formatting of information, not its meaning. The introduction of the Extensible Markup Language (XML) in 1997 launched a new series of efforts towards redefining languages for diverse industry sectors and business communities.

XML is a data-description standard designed by the World Wide Web Consortium (W3C) to simplify Web-based e-commerce transactions among supply-chain partners. XML itself is neither a language nor syntax, but a formal grammar, meant to build languages and syntaxes that exist in a neutral format (operating system and language independent). This explains its flexibility and strength, but also the proliferation of XML-based specialized languages and applications. XML is well suited to represent both data and documents, and allows specifying a model of documents and a means of validation of those documents against a given model. XML has rapidly become a key technology in two domains: (1) document and content management; (2) data interchange. In the document and content management domain, all EDI communities are working hard to develop new sector-specific languages. In the data interchange area, most tools being developed for messaging, enterprise application integration (EAI), and e-commerce (e.g., RosettaNet, ebXML, SOAP and Web services) are based on XML-encoded data (IDA, 2003). Major IT suppliers and user groups have enthusiastically embraced XML as the way to go in the future. It is expected that XML will soon become the dominant world standard for B2B e-commerce transactions over the Internet.

However, in any business application, XML itself is not the answer. It is only a standard foundation on which answers can be built. There is not just one XML-based standard emerging, but many. Some standards address particular industry sectors, and others that are intended as a basic platform for e-commerce in any industry. In the next section, we will describe several significant initiatives to develop contemporary e-commerce standards. These initiatives are first described by their functionalities. Then, the supporting standard bodies behind each are introduced.

REPRESENTATIVE CONTEMPORARY E-COMMERCE STANDARDS

There are a number of e-commerce standards that have been developed the past few years. They cover a broad range of functionality and represent dif-

ferent approaches for handling interactions. These standards rarely work alone to support Web-based B2B e-commerce transactions. Instead, they exist in a hierarchy of standards from the foundational Internet standard, communication protocols, interaction standards, to data exchange formats (Zhao, Xia, & Shaw, 2005). It is beyond this book chapter's scope and objective to systematically introduce and describe each of these standards. However, it is noted that e-commerce standards generally fit into one of two categories: *vertical* or industry-specific standards that address the unique needs of firms within the industry, and *horizontal* standards that provide more general capabilities that would be useful in a wide variety of industries (Markus, Steinfield, & Wigand, 2003). Examples of vertical standards include RosettaNet, MISMO®, and STAR. Prominent examples of horizontal standards are SOAP, ebXML, and Web services using UDDI and WSDL. This chapter presents several of the well-developed and influential standards with the goal of giving readers an idea of what these standards are attempting to accomplish. The following presents vertical standards, followed by a discussion of horizontal standards.

Vertical Standards

A vertical standard is one that is specific to some kind of activity and/or some industrial sector (Aklouf, Piera, Ameur, & Drias, 2005). As a data-description standard, XML is not enough to handle interapplication communication between a wide range of companies and services. Nothing in XML ensures that the XML documents exchanged by two firms are mutually intelligible; it only provides the rules for how to create a properly structured document.

Since XML itself does not address the semantics of document content, it can be used to describe anything the creator of the document wishes. The problem is how to ensure that others understand what the document's creator intended.

One potential solution might be for two trading partners to agree on the same set of XML tags. This, however, would still not be sufficient to address the meaning of data in a document, as the same tag could be interpreted differently by different parties. For example, one firm may use a *"Price"* element to mean *"RetailPrice"* while another firm could use the same element to mean *"WholesalePrice."* Without standardization of semantics, perhaps the best that could be hoped for would be for a business offering Web services to unambiguously explain the meanings of the tags contained its XML documents.

For documents to be understood by the two parties, they must agree on the meaning and organization of the data elements contained in them. While a pair of business partners might agree on the XML documents that are the inputs and outputs of their respective services, and create the mappings between the data used by their internal systems and the XML documents, this approach does not scale well when the number of trading partners increases. New mappings would have to be created for each additional partner.

Vertical standards attempt to address the preceding problem. A vertical standard represents the business knowledge of a specific industry, product, or process, and could:

- Provide a standard dictionary of data elements, their names, meanings, technical representations, and coding standards
- Define the structure of XML documents that will be exchanged
- Define business processes; for instance, what sequence of steps would occur in particular kinds of interactions between parties?

Standardizing industry-specific vocabulary would be a significant step toward semantic interoperability. This would also provide the foundation that would allow the creation of standard business documents for the industry. By addressing these two issues, firms that implement the standard would be able to understand the documents exchanged with each other. This does not mean, however, that both firms would have agreed on when to use any of the documents. For a given business process, for instance, how are these interactions "choreographed"? Defining the choreography for a given process specifies a series of ordered message exchanges and the conditions under which these messages are exchanged. In some cases, the context for using a document may be well understood or simple enough so that it need not be addressed by a vertical standard, while in others the choreography defined in the standard

Table 1. Representative vertical standards

		Issues Addressed by the Standard		
Standard	**Industry**	**Data Dictionary & XML docs**	**Business Process**	**Other**
AgXML	Oilseed and grain	Yes	Yes	-
CIDX	Chemical	Yes	Yes	Security
MISMO	Mortgage	Yes	No	-
OTA	Travel	Yes	Yes	-
RosettaNet	Semiconductor, IT, and Electronic components	Yes	Yes	Messaging & infrastructure
STAR	Automotive retail	Yes	No	Dealer infrastructure and messaging

could clarify how two parties would interact with each other via the XML documents.

There are a large number of vertical standards, and it is therefore beyond the scope of this chapter to enumerate them. The following are some representative, well-established vertical standards. Table 1 shows the standards, the industries where they are used, and a basic summary of the issues addressed by each. All of the following standards provide a data dictionary of industry-specific terms and define the structure of documents, but not all define the processes where the documents are used.

Among all the vertical standards, RosettaNet is one of the most extensive and detailed. The core of the RosettaNet standard is the partner interface process (PIP) that defines the sequence of steps required to execute a specific, predefined business process between supply-chain partners as well as the documents that are exchanged during each of the steps. As an example, the "Request Quote" PIP starts with a buyer sending a "product quote request" to a vendor, with two possible responses from the vendor; a quote or a referral to another vendor. For two firms to conduct business using RosettaNet, they both must have implemented one or more PIPs in common. The more PIPs two trading partners have both implemented in common, the more their B2B interactions can be conducted using RosettaNet.

In addition to PIPs, RosettaNet also defines data dictionaries and data guidelines for terms used in PIP documents. The RosettaNet Business Dictionary defines the properties used in basic business activities between trading partners. The RosettaNet Technical Dictionary defines properties for products, components, devices, and services relevant for the supply chains in the IT/electronics industry. Together, these define both business properties and terms found in technical product descriptions that are used across PIP documents.

Finally, the RosettaNet implementation framework (RNIF) provides messaging standards that are common to all of the PIPs. RNIF lays out the basic message structure that is common to all PIP exchanges by defining the envelope that contains RosettaNet messages. This envelope includes the headers required in any PIP document exchange, whereas the XML document defined in a PIP would be the "payload" contained within this envelope. RNIF also sets general standards for how the interactions found in PIPs are carried out. RNIF, for example, specifies a mechanism for reliable messaging based on acknowledgements and supplies choreography models that all PIPs must follow. It also specifies schemas[5] for acknowledgment and exception (error) messages. RNIF makes RosettaNet different from the other vertical standards in that it deals much more extensively with issues that are typically the domain of horizontal standards. After the discussion of horizontal standards in the next section, the discussion will return to a recap of how RosettaNet compares to them.

Finally, one useful feature of RosettaNet is not part of the standard itself, but is included in the RosettaNet Web site. Firms that have implemented a PIP can register themselves with RosettaNet's "Trading Partner Directory," a registry of firms that have implemented each PIP. Their Web site can be searched to locate firms that have implemented a given PIP with the ability to use additional search criteria such as industry and location.

Horizontal Standards

A horizontal standard "is a general set of standards that defines exchange protocols and information formats without referencing any product or service." (Aklouf et al., 2005, p. 71). Horizontal standards have broad applicability and are not tied to the requirements of any particular industry or application. Figure 1 describes a Web-service architecture that is based on a particular horizontal standard: Web services using UDDI and WSDL.[6] It is general enough, however, to describe much of the functionality found in other horizontal

Figure 1. Web service oriented architecture[7]

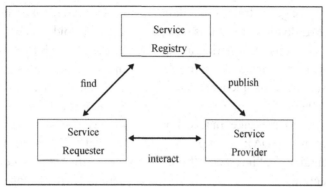

standards to provide a useful overview of many issues addressed by these standards.

The two parties shown at the bottom of Figure 1 are the ones that interact with each other to carry out some business process: The service requester interacts with the service provider by sending an XML document requesting the service and providing the data needed by the provider. The provider maps this request into the format used by its internal systems, and generates a response in the form of an XML document that is returned to the service requester. But, how does the requester know how to structure the XML document expected by the service provider and what data to provide?

The service registry addresses the problem of knowing how to request a service by enabling prospective requesters to locate and understand requirements for invoking services offered by a provider. A service registry may be hosted by the service provider or a third party. In either case, a horizontal standard can provide a way to describe services and how to invoke them. The service provider creates the service description and the requester uses the description to understand what is needed to invoke the service. Finally, horizontal standards specify how service providers publish their descriptions to a registry, and how service requesters find descriptions therein. This general

framework is broadly relevant for interactions related to different industries, and for different products, services, and business processes.

The following provides an overview of the three main horizontal standards included in this chapter: SOAP, ebXML, and Web services.

SOAP

Simple object access protocol (SOAP) provides methods for a program running under one operating system to communicate with a program in the same or another operating system using XML to structure the information exchange (Alexander & Zhang, 2005). SOAP (http://www.w3.org/TR/soap/) was originally developed as a means of invoking remote procedures over the Internet. If used by itself, remote procedure invocation is the function normally performed by a SOAP message. SOAP, however, does not require a SOAP message to contain a remote procedure call. A common use of SOAP is its inclusion in other standards, where its purpose is to provide an envelope for some other type of message instead of invoking a procedure. The envelope in this case would serve as a container for the "payload," where the payload is the real content of the SOAP message, and surrounding SOAP fields contain information used to help the recipient process the payload.

The content of a SOAP message may be a UDDI, WSDL, or ebXML message, or transaction data in the form of an XML document. In this case, the SOAP envelope contains information about the message's payload. For instance, it could contain information about the recipient or sender, encoding style, and other information about how to process and interpret the message. In terms of what is shown in Figure 1, SOAP could provide the envelope that contains the "interact," "find," and "publish" interactions.

ebXML

ebXML (http://www.ebxml.org) strengths lie in the area of representing the business process semantics that allow trading partners to understand each other's capabilities and requirements for engaging in e-commerce. It provides a framework and processes for e-commerce collaborations without defining the specific terms and processes to be used in any particular collaboration between trading partners. It allows for these to be defined, but leaves it to others to do so.

"Core components" are ebXML's means for providing a standard data dictionary. They are intended to be industry-neutral, and contain definitions (individual data elements and aggregations of elements) that are relevant across industries. These serve as low-level building blocks that are used throughout ebXML, for instance, when defining ebXML documents. How industry-specific terms are decided upon and standardized are not part of the ebXML standard.

Messaging services in ebXML use another standard, SOAP (simple object access protocol), as an envelope for ebXML messages. As noted earlier, a SOAP message can hold a payload that could be any XML document, such as one that represents a business document. SOAP, therefore, provides an envelope for ebXML messages. ebXML does not simply use SOAP as-is for messaging. SOAP is extensible, and allows for higher-level protocols to add entries to serve their unique purposes. For instance, the MessageHeader element is a required ebXML element added to SOAP message when used to hold an ebXML messages. One of the things it does is to identify the version of ebXML in the current message.

Security of ebXML interactions is provided through a combination of *XML Signature* and *XML Encryption*. XML Signature provides message integrity and authentication information about the originator of a message. The XML signature defines XML elements that would be embedded in an XML document that would allow the receiver to verify that the message has not been modified from what the sender originally sent. With XML encryption, either part or all of an XML message can be secured through encryption, so that the encrypted portion of the message would not be visible to other parties besides the originator and ultimate recipient.[8]

A strong point of ebXML is its ability to represent semantic information that can be used to assess the compatibility of the processes of prospective trading partners, and for coming to a mutual agreement on how business is to be conducted electronically. Collaboration protocol profile (CPP) and collaboration profile agreements (CPA) are the two main components that support this.

A CPP allows a firm to express its business processes and business service interface requirements in a way that can be understood by others. A CPP can be used by prospective trading partners to assess the requirements of and options for conducting business via ebXML. If prospective trading partners determine that their CPPs are compatible, they could develop a collaboration profile agreement to specify exactly how business will be conducted between them. The CPA defines terms and conditions for document exchange as well as all the valid, visible, and enforceable interactions, and how to execute them. A CPA is formed from CPPs of the parties involved, and contains only those elements that are in common. The two parties then negotiate the parameters to produce a final CPA. CPAs serve as the basis for configuring the technical details of conducting e-commerce in ebXML.

ebXML also provides mechanisms for firms to locate each other: the ebXML registry and ebXML repository. Repositories are where data about firms and their processes are stored. In it are stored descriptions of products, services offered, basic firm information, CPP, CPA, core components, predefined messages, and other objects to enable parties to exchange data electronically. Registries store information about items in a repository; it is where relevant repository items and metadata about them can be registered. Registries can be queried to find the location of repository information. The registry information model (ebRIM) provides a high-level blueprint for metadata in the ebXML registry, and any ebXML registry must follow ebRIM.

The general model for how ebXML works is for prospective trading partners to discover each other, and the services and products they offer, using ebXML registries/repositories. Then, based on their CPPs, the firms determine which shared business processes and associated document exchanges need to be used for interacting with each other. Once they decide to collaborate, the firms would agree on contractual terms relating to the processes used, and documents exchanged by creating a CPA. The firms would then exchange information and services in accordance with these agreements.

Web Services Using WSDL, UDDI, and SOAP

Two standards that work together in enabling Web services are Web services Description Language (WSDL) and universal description, discovery, and integration (UDDI). These, in turn, rely on an existing standard, SOAP, as the primary means of sending messages that invoke Web services, and as an envelope for UDDI and

WSDL messages (http://www.uddi.org/: http://www.w2.org/TR/wsdl).

WSDL is used to describe services offered by businesses. WSDL uses XML to describe a Web service in a generic way that can be mapped to the capabilities provided by the actual internal systems. WSDL allows for the definition of how to invoke a service, its input requirements, and what, if any, response is provided as a result.

WSDL provides two modes of using Web services; a remote procedure (RPC) style and a document style. With the RPC style, the service corresponds to a remote procedure call. The input requirements define data elements that correspond to the method's input parameters and the response corresponds to the method's output. The RPC style provides a synchronous response that would be appropriate when real-time requirements exist for invoking the service. The document style follows the asynchronous approach found in traditional EDI, ebXML, and RosettaNet. The input and output "documents" normally correspond to business documents that would be exchanged during the business transaction, for example, a purchase order. Processing is asynchronous so this could be used when the initiating firm is not expecting an immediate response.

UDDI provides a registry for businesses to list themselves on the Internet. Its goal is to help companies find each other and assess the interoperability of their systems (Newcomer, 2002). UDDI can be viewed as an online version of a telephone book's white, yellow, and green pages as follows:

- **White pages:** Provide name and contact for the business
- **Yellow pages:** Describes type of business, its location, and products offered
- **Green pages:** Details about the business' processes and how to invoke them; a pointer to the business' WSDL file could be placed here

UDDI registries are hosted by members of the UDDI consortium. Once a potential business partner is found using a UDDI query, details about invoking the desired services would be retrieved. The details of how to invoke the service in a UDDI entry are somewhat general, and can optionally point to a WSDL description of the service. UDDI, however, allows for entries to refer to other types of services such as ebXML or RosettaNet. A firm could offer its Web services and make WSDL descriptions available on its own without using UDDI. UDDI, however, provides a way to make it easier for other firms to locate the firm and understand the services offered.

The typical scenario for service discovery and invocation is as follows. A business would locate potential trading partners using UDDI queries. Based on whatever factors are relevant for making this choice (e.g., location, products offered, Web services offered, etc.), the business would select trading partners and the services to invoke using SOAP. Its systems would then use the WSDL description of the service to configure the translation between its internal processes and the needed messages that are sent and received via SOAP. Finally, the interactions with other businesses would be carried via SOAP message exchanges according to the WSDL description of the service.

WS-Security defines enhancements to SOAP to provide three capabilities: credential exchange, message integrity, and confidentiality. WS-Security delivers a foundation for implementing security functions such as integrity and confidentiality in messages implementing higher-level Web services applications. The WS-Security specifications describe a mechanism for securing Web services message exchanges using a variety of existing security technologies and methodologies.[9]

Table 2. Overview of horizontal e-commerce standards

Standard	ebXML	Web services using WSDL & UDDI
Data dictionary	Core components – defines basic terms in that cross industries	
Use of SOAP for requesting services	SOAP – containing ebXML documents	2 modes of using SOAP: • document-style (asynchronous), or • remote procedure call style (synchronous)
Business process descriptions	CPP – collaboration protocol profile • Provide details of how to invoke a service, where services are defined in the context of a series of process steps. CPA – collaboration protocol agreement • Uses CPPs to develop a mutually feasible agreement	WDSL – Provide details on how to invoke a service and what data to provide
Registries – publish, store, and find business partners and their processes	ebRIM	UDDI

Summary of Standards

SOAP is a relatively simple standard when compared to Web services and ebXML, as well as being a component in those two standards. Web services and ebXML both provide a number of similar features, but still differ considerably in some of the capabilities included.

Table 2 summaries ebXML and Web services to highlight the similarities and differences between the two standards. Both standards provide a registry with similar capabilities ebXML is the only one to provide some support for defining business terms using its core components. Both protocols use SOAP as envelope for messaging. When it comes to requesting a service, however, Web services provides two options. A request for service under ebXML is similar to Web service's document-style use of SOAP and both are similar to traditional EDI. Web service's RPC style could be useful in situations that require a quick response to a service request.

Another significant difference between ebXML and Web services is how they define and use business process descriptions. WSDL/UDDI and SOAP were originally intended for straightforward transactions found in B2B marketplaces (Havenstein, 2005). WSDL describes how to invoke Web services, but does little to help firms to understand the semantics involved. ebXML, on the other hand, has much greater capability for describing how interactions are choreographed. ebXML can be used to develop mutual understanding, negotiating differences, and agreeing on a mutual process to follow. Web services' view of business processes is restricted to a technical view of what is required to invoke a single process, while ebXML attempts to deal with the semantics of processes requiring a sequence of interactions between parties.

Although Web services' simpler view of process definition might be a deficiency, it could be strength in some cases. SOAP, WSDL, and UDDI address an important problem in a rela-

tively simple, easy-to-implement manner, and this may often be a sufficient solution. Although Web services could be used to handle a series of interactions between parties, it does not address how to represent or set up such agreements. If this is needed, one solution would be if the firms are in an industry where a vertical standard defined the relevant processes. In this case, the horizontal standard's capability to represent business processes and allow for negotiating a trading agreement would be less important. Such capability has the potential to provide value if there is in fact a lot of variation in the services exposed by firms over the Internet. It should be noted, however, that a forthcoming enhancement to WSDL called "Web Services Choreography Description Language" (WS-CDL) will allow Web services to approach ebXML's ability to represent processes as a series of interactions.[10]

The core of vertical standards is the creation of a data dictionary and the definition of standard documents used in particular industries. This feature enables standard documents to be exchanged and interpreted by all firms that have implemented interfaces to the standard. Many vertical standards go beyond this to define processes carried out using the standard documents. In some cases, processes are provided as examples of business interactions; in others an extensive set of processes are defined.

RosettaNet is the most comprehensive of the vertical standards presented herein. RosettaNet also overlaps what ebXML and Web services do in that it defines message structure and generic interaction patterns that apply to any transaction. The fact that RosettaNet was developed prior to the horizontal standards may help explain this; without existing horizontal standards to address these general problems RosettaNet developers chose to incorporate this capability. However, RosettaNet is not in competition with the horizontal e-business standards like ebXML or Web services. It actually benefits from the horizontal standards, as they enable RosettaNet to concentrate its efforts on standardizing e-business processes, by no longer having to develop and maintain infrastructure pieces that can be adopted from horizontal standards like ebXML.

As other e-business standards emerged, RosettaNet has remained flexible and seek convergence where possible. Currently, RosettaNet is in the process of adopting the ebXML Registry and Repository specifications, the ebXML BPSS (business process specification schema), the ebMS (messaging services), and the CPPs (the partner profiles). While ebXML and Web services are relatively new and have few implementations to boast of, RosettaNet's maturity comes from billion of dollars worth of real e-business being conducted by business partners using RosettaNet specifications. This has lead to further RosettaNet adoption in Europe and Asia.

DEVELOPING B2B E-COMMERCE STANDARDS

The development of B2B e-commerce standards has involved many stakeholders' efforts, including companies, industry associations, government agencies, academic institutions, and international organizations, and so forth. Among them, standards developing organizations (SDOs) have played a fundamental role for initiation, facilitation, and implementation of B2B e-commerce standards. These SDOs can produce either horizontal or vertical standards. A brief discussion of both would give the readers a better idea of the landscape of e-commerce SDOs.

Horizontal SDOs

Among the different horizontal SDOs or groups, there are several that are worthy of particular attention in the process of B2B e-commerce standardization. Their ongoing works have or will have tremendous impacts on the development of B2B e-commerce standards. The next table, fol-

lowed by a brief explanation of each SDO, gives a short list of several representative horizontal B2B e-commerce SDOs and their standard developing work.

UN/CEFACT was established in 1996 by the Economic Commission for Europe (UN/ECE) within the United Nations.[12] Open to participation from member states, intergovernmental organizations, and industry associations, UN/CEFACT also has participation from many private-sector associations work at the policy level and hundreds of private-sector technical experts in UN/CEFACT working groups.

UN/CEFACT's activities, in general, focus on developing and expanding global EDI standards with a network of supporting private and public sector institutions. It publishes the UN/EDIFACT standards that are used internationally. One of UN/CEFACT's milestones is the launch of ebXML by UN/CEFACT and the Organization for the Advancement of Structured Information Standards (OASIS) in September 1999. After the completion of the first phase of ebXML framework in May 2001, the UN ECE and OASIS split the remaining tasks, with UN/CEFACT responsible for process-related work including business processes and core components and OASIS responsible for infrastructure work including transport, routing and packaging, registry and repository, collaboration-protocol profile and agreement, security, and conformance.

The ANSI Accredited Standards Committee X12

The ANSI Accredited Standards Committee (ASC) X12 (http://www.x12.org) is a membership based not-for-profit standard body chartered in 1979 by the American National Standards Institute (ANSI). ANSI represents the U.S. in the International Organization for Standardization (ISO). ASC X12 memberships are open to "any individual, company, or organization that may be directly and materially affected by ASC X12 ac-

Table 3. Representative horizontal standards bodies and their work

Standard bodies	Standards Developed		
	Framework Standards	Document & Data Standards	Infrastructure Standards
Government Authority Type			
ISO[11]	ebXML		
UN/CEFACT	ebXML	Core components	
X12		Core components	
Consortia Type			
W3C			WSDL: Web-service description language WS-CDL: Web-service choreography description language SOAP: Simple object access protocol
OASIS	ebXML	UBL: Universal business language	UDDI: Universal description, discovery, and integration XACML: Extensible access control markup language
OAG		OAGIS & OAMAS	

tivities."[13] Since 1987, Data Interchange Standards Association (DISA) has served as the secretariat for the X12 standards development process.

ANSI itself does not write standards. Instead, ANSI develops the procedures that other standards bodies, such as IEEE, use to develop standards. It also reviews the procedures and processes that these standards-developing bodies use, and in the end approves the standards they develop as ANSI standards. ASC X12 has developed its standard system through different years releases (a complete set of X12 standards), subreleases (republished releases), technical reports and guidelines, as well as workbooks and alphabetic code lists. While it continues to develop and enhance business message standards based on the X12 EDI syntax, ASC X12 now intends to clarify its message design architecture, XML schema syntax, and XML design rules and guidelines with the collaboration of the UN/CEFACT. Both

of ANSI X12 and UN/CEFACT recently have agreed to focus all XML subcommittee efforts into the ebXML framework specification development initiative.[14] In addition, ASC X12 and UN/CEFACT jointly developed object oriented EDI (OO-EDI) to meet a mutual goal to provide one global EDI standard.

Organization for the Advancement of Structured Information

OASIS (http://www.oasis-open.org/) is a not-for-profit international consortium founded in 1993. More than 3,000 members of OASIS are venders, users, and specialists of standards-based technologies that represent over 600 organizations and individual members in 100 countries. OASIS has its members themselves (excluding individual members) set the OASIS technical agendas, form technical committees, and vote on the completed works. The National Institute of Standards and Technology (NIST) plays an active role within OASIS.

OASIS produces "worldwide standards for security, Web services, conformance, business transactions, supply chain, public sector, and interoperability within and between marketplaces"[15] through an open, democratic, vendor-neutral process. It is especially active on Web services standards in comparison to the other standard organizations. However, OASIS is more like a standardizer rather than inventors of technology like W3C. The work of OASIS helps to make structured information standards easy to adopt and the products practical to use in the real world, thereby complementing those of the other standard organizations rather than create more. One of the most important works OASIS has done in the e-commerce area is the joint ebXML project with the UN/CEFACT in November 1999. In addition, OASIS now hosts two of the most widely respected information portals on XML and Web services standards: XML.org and Cover Pages.[16] Many organizations, technologists, and business people rely on XML cover pages for daily updates on XML resources and industry initiatives.

World Wide Web Consortium

Created on October 1994, W3C is the main technology standards body for the World-Wide Web (http://www.w3.org/)and the most influential standard body by far in XML related standards. W3C is now hosted by the Laboratory for Computer Science (LCS) at MIT, the French National Institute for Research in Computer Science and Control (INRIA), and Keio University. Membership at W3C is only open to organizations and is not free, but W3C Web site serves as a central location to disseminate the technical specifications written by the consortium, as well as other related information, which is free to all. Today, over 450

members and nearly 70 full-time staff around the world are contributing to the development of W3C specifications and software.[17]

W3C's activities and other work are primarily in four domains: architecture domain, interaction domain, technology and society domain, Web Accessibility Initiative (WAI). Through these activities, W3C provides technical reports, open source software, and services (e.g., validation services). The network protocols that the W3C established with the collaboration of global community include the XML specification and its complementary specifications (often referred to as the "XML Family of Standards"). In addition, XML schemas and resource description format (RDF) have received great attention from the W3C.

Open Applications Group

Open Applications Group (OAG) (http://www.openapplications.org/) is a nonprofit consortium founded in February 1995 by leading enterprise application software developers. To date, the OAG is comprised of nearly 50 members including customer organizations, systems integrators, middleware vendors, as well as application software vendors. Prominent stakeholders, such as AT&T, Microsoft, Compaq, Lucent Technologies, Ford Motors, and so forth, are in OAG's membership.

OAG is the largest publisher of XML-based content for business software interoperability in the world.[18] The OAG builds and publishes the detailed specifications necessary to use the XML content and a common middleware application programming interfaces (APIs) specification.[19] From its first year of existence, OAG continues to release specifications with richer functions, and has done extensive prototyping with XML to successfully validate its applicability for business software, primarily, the open applications group integration specification (OAGIS), and the open applications group common middleware API specification (OAMAS).

Vertical SDOs

Due to their focused and in-depth coverage of standards that are of direct interest to firms within an industry, vertical SDOs are more attractive to firms than industry neutral SDOs. For example, Electronics Industry Data Exchange Group (EIDX) is a vertical e-commerce SDO in the electronics industry, and only 5 out of 46 EIDX members also join ASC X12, the US-based cross-industry e-commerce SDO. Many horizontal SDOs also have industry-focused groups within them in order to motivate firms to participate in the consortium. For instance, ASC X12 has subcommittees working in the insurance, transportation, and health-care industries. The content of standards from horizontal and vertical SDOs may overlap or complement one another. Therefore, collaborations between them are common, especially for firms engaging across

Table 4. Industry and their vertical SDOs[20]

Industry	SDOs
Agriculture	AgXML (http://www.agxml.org)
Accounting	XBRL (http://www.xbrl.org)
Automobile	AIAG (http://www.aiag.org)
Automobile retail	STAR(http://www.starstandard.org)
Chemical	CIDX (http://www.cidx.org)
Electronics	EIDX (http://eidx.comptia.org)
Energy	PIDX, PPDM, POSC
Financial–banking	BITS
Financial–insurance	ACORD (http://www.acord.org)
Financial–mortgage	MISMO (http://www.mismo.org)
Financial–real estate	RETS, MITS
Financial	FISD, FIX Protocol (http://www.fixprotocol.org), FPML (http://www.fpml.org), IFX (http://www.ifxforum.org)
Geography	OpenGIS (http://www.opengeospatial.org/ogc)
Healthcare	CDISC (http://www.cdisc.org), HL7 (http://www.hl7.org)
Human Resources	HR-XML (http://www.hr-xml.org)
Legal	Legal XML (http://www.legalxml.org
Marine	EMSA, Maritime
Paper	PapiNet (http://www.papinet.org)
Retail	ARTS (http://www.nrf-arts.org)
Semiconductor, IT, & electronic components	RosettaNet (www.rosettanet.org)
Transportation	LandXML (http://www.landxml.org)
Travel	OTA (http://www.opentravel.org)

industries transactions. For instance, ebXML proposed by OASIS has gained support from some vertical SDOs such as OTA and RosettaNet. It is also possible that standards from the two camps have significant overlap and therefore compete with each other (Zhao et al., 2005). Table 4 lists several major vertical SDOs.

The standards-developing approaches used by the SDOs are either *de jure* or *de facto*. Traditional standards development organizations (ISO, IEEE, etc.), scientific or professional societies, trade associations, or industrial standard organizations that can have a liaison with formal official bodies, establish *de jure* standards by their legal authority, and as such, face no challenges in the marketplace. They usually serve coordinating and distributing functions that the paying-members of the organization manage. They facilitate the development of standards, but volunteers do the bulk of the work, and no royalties are paid. In contrast, vertical industry groups or consortia, usually formed in response to intense competition among the largest companies, primarily rely on participants' voluntary consensus that later on emerge as industry *de facto* standards (Toth, 1996). These SDOs can charge fees to members to fund their standard development activities. In order to permit smaller companies to participate, the rates usually vary according to companies' revenue level. During the past few years, many industries have recognized the importance of developing common B2B e-commerce standards to facilitate information sharing in the value chain. A great number of industry-led SDOs or "forums," therefore, have emerged for industry participants to collaboratively develop e-commerce standards (Mähönen, 1999).

Unfortunately, the B2B e-commerce standard landscape has become much more complex and confusing today due to that many standards groups or bodies are involved in the process of B2B e-commerce standardization. The need for common B2B e-commerce standards had long been recognized by many industries and governments. However, the current situation has a long way to go before convergence on common standards occurs.

TRANSFORMING THE INDUSTRY WITH E-COMMERCE STANDARDS

The changes that new e-commerce standards have brought about in the practices of industries are broad and deep. Although starting slowly, the new e-commerce standards are emerging in and across various industries. Both horizontal B2B standards such as ebXML, and vertical standards such as RosettaNet are finding their ways into the practices in a number of industries.

Case 1: Automotive Industry

The automotive industry is one of the industries that ebXML has attracted significant attention from. Beginning in April of 2004, General Motors began to replace its traditional EDI with a messaging services based on ebXML.[21] GM will support traditional EDI, but plans to migrate to ebXML through EDI services provide by Covisint (Industrial Distribution, 2002). The approach towards providing both EDI and ebXML called "Covisint Connect" was developed by an industry consortium that included General Motors, DaimlerChrysler, Delphi, Ford Motor Company, and Johnson Controls.[22] Covisint Connect was designed with automotive specific functionality to simplify and improve communications between companies in the industry. It provides a direct replacement for current EDI methods and a foundation for the exchange of XML documents utilizing ebXML. Covisint Connect includes features specifically designed to enable smaller companies, even those not currently using EDI, to connect to their customers and suppliers.[23]

The migration from their current EDI provider to Covisint Connect will involve more than 6,000 GM suppliers. During the transition to Internet-based ebXML, Covisint will continue to route EDI messages to and from the prior value-added network of those suppliers who have yet to migrate to Covisint Connect. In addition to being based on ebXML, Covisint Connect will use Open Application Group's (OAG) standards for document content. Not only will this reduce the cost of supporting and operating its EDI systems, it will allow GM to enable a larger number of (mostly smaller) suppliers to use it who currently do not use EDI. Other automakers in the consortium and their suppliers will follow suit and migrate towards ebXML for supplier interactions (Meehan, 2001).

Automakers also have begun using ebXML to interact with its dealerships. One estimate suggests that EDI costs will be cut in half as a result of replacing traditional EDI with ebXML (Sullivan & Babcock, 2004). Cost savings will accrue both to dealerships and automakers.

Although these efforts are still underway, the automotive industry is among the more advanced industries in its migration from traditional EDI to newer e-commerce standards. The benefits are twofold. First, the estimated cost of using ebXML is substantially less than traditional EDI in dealing with suppliers who currently use EDI (Sullivan & Babcock, 2004). Second, due to reduced cost and the ease of set up and operation, the industry is able to switch a number of smaller suppliers to using ebXML that heretofore were not EDI-capable. Thus, ebXML allows the auto industry to extend the benefits from EDI to a larger number of suppliers (e.g., greater responsiveness and reduced cost of transacting business).

Case 2: Electronics Industry

As a vertical standard, RosettaNet has certainly established a reputation in the global high-technology industry for bringing businesses closer together. The global consortium now involves more than 500 of the world's leading electronics components, information technology, logistics, semiconductor manufacturing, and telecommunications companies.[24] Some giant players, such as Intel, Nokia, Sony, and Cisco Systems, have been particularly bullish on RosettaNet's developments and advocate the implementation of RosettaNet for the electronic industry. Not only have these companies lent highly placed executives to the consortium, they have also shown enough confidence in RosettaNet to actually rip out much of its EDI connections in deference to RosettaNet PIPs. Intel, for instance, conducts more than 30,000 RosettaNet-based transactions per month, with more than 90 customers and suppliers who are based in 17 countries.[25]

In the electronic industry, those who have started using RosettaNet standard primarily for supply-chain processes, such as price changes, catalog updates, and product introductions, have reported efficiencies, even if they are using it only on a limited basis. Implementing XML-based RosettaNet standards allows the use of the Internet as a low-cost transmission medium while supporting much higher transaction volumes and performance scalability than traditional Web-based tools. For instance:

- 3Com has begun using a catalog-update PIP with reseller CompUSA to speed up the introduction of new products. Typically, if 3Com has a new product it wants its distributors and resellers to put into their catalogs, it communicates this by phone, fax, or e-mail. With the PIP for product catalogs, it can send single product introductions automatically, cutting down the rate of inaccuracy and the process time from several weeks to hours (Medina, 2000).

- Arrow Electronics has also started using a PIP from RosettaNet. The PIP significantly reduces the time it takes to change product orders. Traditionally, Arrow would accumulate change orders throughout the day in its inventory-management system and then submit them overnight through an EDI transmission. The next day, the customer would check its sales order-entry system to see if the product was available and then respond that evening. The process could take anywhere from 36 to 48 hours. With a PIP, the purchase-order change happens immediately (Medina, 2000).

• Shinko's collaboration with Intel previously required a multilevel, mostly manual procurement process involving spreadsheets, e-mail, manual paperwork, and costly faxes between the U.S. and Japan. This process required a lot of exception management, and information regarding work-in-process, procurement, and settlement was exchanged through various manual and semi-manual methods that required a great deal of effort. Figure 2 illustrates the old process and the new process under RosettaNet. The most obvious benefit for Shinko in making this change was the elimination of substantial faxing costs between the U.S. and Japan. Shinko was able to achieve a 50% reduction in manual workload, and at the same time establish a 100% error-free process environment. In addition, order management throughput time was reduced from 24 hours to less than 1 hour.

However, the benefits of RosettaNet implementation go beyond the stated numbers. In the collaboration of Intel and Shinko, for instance, Intel has not included the value of additional tasks that employees can now perform with the time available as a result of implementing RosettaNet. Also, the benefits of extending supply-chain visibility into the entire business environment are just beginning to be understood. "The promise of increased supply chain visibility is extremely compelling," explains Brown. VP at Intel Manufacturing Group, "Making business decisions with good, hard data from the entire business environment instead of just local ERP systems allows a business to anticipate changes in the business climate much sooner and to respond to those changes with greater agility."[27]

RosettaNet has taken a leadership role in driving global e-business process standards for

Figure 2. Process changes in Shinko's order management[26]

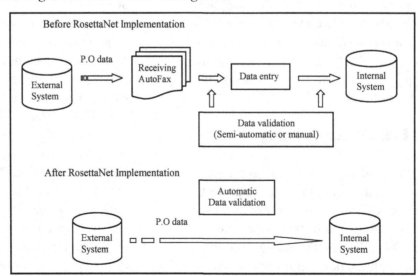

its partners. From 2000, when the first set of RosettaNet PIPs was released, the number of companies adopting RosettaNet grew rapidly. In 2002, the total number of distinct trading partners using RosettaNet to trade with board members grew by 207%. In Asia, millions of dollars from government funds are used to promote RosettaNet implementations and projects because it is believed that the use of the RosettaNet could simplify the coordination of the fragmented high-tech outsourcing process in Asia and reduce high-inventory expense and production stoppages (McFarlan & Belokhvostova, 2004). The success of RosettaNet has also caused several industry organizations to adopt the RosettaNet messaging specification as an industry standard. The Chemical Industry Data Exchange has defined the CIDX protocol, which is based on RNIF1.1, and the American Petroleum Industry has defined the Petroleum Industry Data Exchange (PIDX),which is based on RNIF2.0 specifications. "Looking ahead, RosettaNet will continue to focus on the creation and adoption of standards and services driven by its members as well as expand into adjacent industries, such as logistics, consumer electronics and aerospace."[28]

Case 3: Mortgage Industry

The home mortgage industry is highly fragmented, with most processes requiring the efforts of more than one organization. Example processes are loan origination and underwriting, loan closing, mortgage recording, loan servicing, and sales of mortgages to secondary investors. An X12 standard developed for this industry did not achieve much success for a number of reasons; chief among them was that the bureaucracy involved in the X12 effort produced a standard that was not specific enough to their industry (Cooley, 2005). The Mortgage Industry Standards Maintenance Organization (MISMO® Inc.) was formed in 1999 to develop, promote, and maintain XML-based e-commerce standards for the mortgage industry. More than 100 companies and 600 individuals are involved in the MISMO standards setting process, with membership in MISMO being voluntary and open to all. MISMO uses workgroups to concentrate on the various aspects of the mortgage industry's value chain.

An important motivation for developing e-commerce standards for this industry is the high cost of many processes wherein a good proportion

Figure 3. SMART Doc™ structure [29]

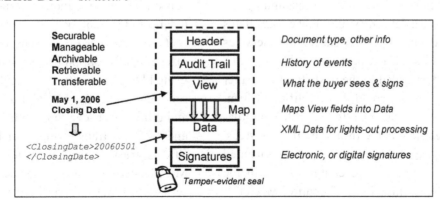

of those costs come from data collection and data entry. The costs of underwriting and closing a loan, for example, run between $800 and $1,000. Estimates indicate that more than one third of the loan origination effort involves collecting and entering data and correcting errors. Every time the paperwork for a loan application moves between parties, much of the data needs to be reentered into different systems with additional effort to detect and correct errors (Story, 2003). MISMO developed standard XML documents for the mortgage industry with the intent of solving this problem by allowing a given XML document to move from step to step and between organizations without the need for reentry.

MISMO standards include a data dictionary that identifies the names, meaning, representation, and coding information for elements. MISMO standards also define a number of documents that use these elements such as the mortgage application, underwriting, credit report, and mortgage insurance application. These two components are standard content of any vertical standard. A feature unique to MISMO is embedding these business-oriented XML documents within what is termed a "SMART™ Document" as shown in Figure 3.

Besides the data they contain, SMART™ documents use XHTML to embed formatting information so that the document itself can be displayed within a Web browser. A SMART document can be "what the buyer sees and signs," and serves as a data entry form that encapsulates the XML document. This data can then serve as input to software that processes it "lights out," or can be forwarded to the next step for further processing, which could be in a different firm. The document contains a record of the cumulative changes that come from the different steps. The sequence of these changes and any needed electronic signatures are contained within the SMART™ document itself. The entire SMART™ document is embedded in an envelope with a tamper-evident seal. This reduces the need to reenter the data when documents go from step to step or between organizations. Besides greatly lowering the costs of processing and reducing errors that come from duplicate data entry, the use of SMART™ document can speed up the entire process since documents can move quickly from one step to the next.

MISMO standards have become well enough established that software for this industry has begun to be certified as to whether it meets MISMO standards. Additionally, there may be competitive pressure for software firms to integrate MISMO standards into their products so that not only could their systems support the internal processes of a customer, they would allow a firm to easily exchange documents electronically with others. Use of MISMO has considerably reduced costs for firms that adopt it, and provide improved service to customers in the form of faster response time. If use of MISMO becomes widespread enough, the whole home mortgage industry could be radically transformed. Not too long ago, this industry made very little use of electronic communications between firms. The long-term vision is for the whole value chain to be totally carried out electronically using the MISMO standard. The impacts on the industry are as yet difficult to predict, as it could both have the result of leveling the playing field, which would be helpful to smaller firms, while also allowing for a concentration of data in the hands of larger firms, which would facilitate consolidation in the industry among those firms (Markus et al., 2003)

One of the future directions for MISMO are to offer users the option to interface with MISMO using PDF documents and to integrate with Web services. Currently, MISMO uses SMART doc and other lower level protocols such as HTTPS and FTP for transferring data between firms. Efforts are underway to provide interfaces to MISMO-based systems via Web services, described in WSDL whereby a firm could invoke a Web service, and receive a SMART™ document in response.

CLOSING COMMENTS

The synergy or interoperability of applications from different vendors enabled by e-commerce standards allows the industries to create more customizable, advanced, and powerful systems. However, partly due to the diverse and broad scope that e-commerce standards have, little is known about the process of e-commerce standardization. Given the literature addressed in the chapter, we will offer suggestions for further investigation on the emergence of new e-commerce standards.

For instance, which standards are finally finding their way into widespread use vs. those that are still in limited use, and why? Given the large number of overlapping and competing standards and the expense of building systems based on them, understanding the likelihood of a standard becoming widely accepted could help in making a wise choice when identifying the best standard for an application. Many businesses that engage in traditional forms of EDI, such as X12, have yet to be convinced of the benefit of switching to the newer e-commerce standards. An interesting research question would be why have they not yet made the switch to these newer standards? Conversely, for those firms that have made the switch to using newer standards, why did they choose to make this transition, what factors influenced their choice of standard(s), and what lessons can be learned from their experiences?

A different area of examination would be the organizational and industry transformations that have resulted or could result from e-commerce standards adoption. What are the impacts of standards adoption on the operations and effectiveness of businesses? What organizational changes were necessary in order to achieve these impacts? Since e-commerce standards would cost less to use than traditional EDI, they should increase the participation in B2B e-commerce by SMEs. The broader functionality included in these standards over traditional EDI provides additional opportunities for altering how businesses interact. The examples reported earlier provide some evidence about this in selected industries. However, a more systematic cross-industry investigation would be useful in this regard.

Finally, examining the standards-setting environment could be useful. Developing an understanding of the dynamics of how standards groups, vendors, and other players interact to shape standards and influence their adoption could help in devising strategies that companies could apply to coping with standard bodies, as well as the potential development direction of e-commerce standards themselves.

Can an ultimate standard for e-commerce be reached in the same way that X12 and EDIFACT have dominated traditional EDI? Achieving a single dominant standard seems unlikely since these newer standards collectively cover much more ground, with no one standard being comprehensive. In certain areas of functionality, however, emergence of stable winners should do much to convince firms that are sitting on the standards sideline to finally get into the game. This in turn would provide incentive for other firms to do the same.

One factor that would facilitate a standard's adoption would be the availability of software that supports it. This could take the form of either a software vendor enhancing an existing application package, such as ERP, to provide a Web service interface according to the standard, or by creating middleware that translates between existing internal systems to a Web interface according to the standard. The availability of software of this kind should reduce the cost and effort of adopting a standard and thus should accelerate its adoption. However, software vendors may be unlikely to invest in creating this kind of software unless there already is a good market for it. Given this, it may take a while for a critical mass of firms to adopt a standard before it begins to be well supported by the offerings of software vendors. Once a standard achieves both a critical mass of users and software products that support it, a likely scenario would be for the standard to experience a surge of firms adopting it. This, of course, begs the question of how a standard gets to this point. Except for SOAP perhaps, none of the standards are yet there. Some possible scenarios for the future of the standards are as follows:

- SOAP already is widely used and is used in conjunction with a number of other standards. No matter which standards gain acceptance, SOAP will likely play a role.

- ebXML is being promoted by standards bodies that brought us traditional EDI. It is the chosen successor to X12 and EDIFACT. However, it is more complicated than other standards. While the capability for setting up trading agreements using CPPs and CPAs is appealing and potentially powerful, it may prove too difficult for many firms to implement. The ebXML standard has been developed in a top-down manner by standards-bodies, while the actual demand for the whole set of standards is not clear. If industry-specific document standards and standardized CPPs emerge (similar to what has happened in the automotive industry) this would simplify the use of CPPs and CPAs by providing some degree of uniformity across businesses within the industry. This could make these components become similar to RosettaNet's PIPs in the electronics industry.

- The combination of UDDI, WSDL, and SOAP is likely to continue gaining acceptance. It is relatively simple and straight-forward when compared to ebXML. SOAP already enjoys relatively wide adoption. UDDI may become widely used beyond WSDL and SOAP-based Web services. It is flexible enough to serve as a registry for other types of Web services, and is therefore in a good position to become the most widely used registry standard. WSDL and SOAP are oriented towards simpler marketplace

transactions and may not receive much direct competition here from ebXML.

- RosettaNet is driven by a consortium of firms that are its potential adopters, so it therefore is tailored to their needs. RosettaNet is on the way to becoming widely adopted. Although many of the vertical standards address some of the issues encompassed in horizontal standards, RosettaNet has gone much further than others in this regard. When RosettaNet was developed, there was an absence of horizontal standards that resulted in horizontal components becoming part of this standard. Since its formation, a number of viable horizontal XML standards have appeared and are gaining some acceptance. In the long run, it is likely that the traditional components of vertical standards will remain at the core of RosettaNet. The horizontal components, however, will likely be supplemented by, and perhaps replaced by, other horizontal standards. Aside from the costs transitioning to different horizontal standards, there would not be much reason to incur the costs of maintaining RosettaNet's separate horizontal components unless they address important needs of this industry much better than the other horizontal standards. At this point, it is not clear that this is the case.

- A wide variety of vertical standards have emerged that address the unique needs of their respective industries. Some of these, such as MISMO, are also beginning to see significant implementation and use. It appears, however, that these standards have been developed without much attempt to rely on other horizontal standards to provide a framework for their use. Perhaps the emphasis was to develop the highest value vertical components (data dictionary and standard documents) while providing some horizontal capabilities sufficient for creating functional solutions. As firms gain experience with the vertical standards and as horizontal standards mature, will there be a greater convergence of the two types of standards? In many cases, Web services and ebXML should provide added-value functionality not present in the vertical standards. Over time, therefore, one would expect vertical standards to be extended to specify how their vertical components could be implemented using the capabilities of other horizontal standards. One example of this that was mentioned earlier is efforts to extend MISMO so that interfaces to it could be exposed via Web services.

In conclusion, few businesses have much real experience applying the new e-commerce standards. Others are either in the investigation or experimental phases of standards adoptions. Many others, of course, have yet to seriously consider them or perhaps are only vaguely aware of them. The ultimate usefulness and applicability of these standards, therefore, is hard to predict, and the standards themselves will continue to evolve as businesses gain more experience with them. Due to the central role these standards are likely to play in future e-commerce activity, most firms, especially those already engaged in e-commerce, will at some point need to become aware of their capabilities, their application, and potential impact. This chapter provides an overview of the situation as it is understood today, with some attempt to suggest likely scenarios for how things may progress.

REFERENCES

Aklouf, Y., Pierra, G., Ameur, Y., & Drias, H. (2005). PLIB ontology: A mature solution for products characterization in B2B electronic commerce. *Journal of IT Standards & Standardization Research, 3*(2), 66-81.

Alexander, D., & Zhang, D. (2005). A comparative study of SOAP and DCOM. *Journal of Systems and Software, 76*(2), 157-169.

Berge, J. (1991). *The EDIFACT standards.* Manchester, UK: NCC Blackwell.

Champion, M., Ferris, C., Newcomer, E., & Orchard, D. (2002, November 14). *Web services architecture* (W3C working draft). World Wide Web Consortium. Retrieved February 28, 2006, from http://www.w3.org/TR/2002/WD-ws-arch-20021114/.

Cooley, S. (2005). The jury is in: MISMO is a win. *Mortgage Banking, 66*(3), 109-110.

Havenstein, H. (2005). Registry demand grows. *Computerworld, 39*(13), 10.

Hawkins, R., Mansell, R., & Skea, J. (1995). *Standards, innovation and competitiveness: The politics and economics of standards in natural and technical environment.* Brookfield, VT: Edward Elgar,.

IDA (Interchange of Data between Administrations). (2003). *Evaluation of XML frameworks.* XML based business frameworks serials. Retrieved March 6, 2006, from http://europa.eu.int/idabc/en/document/1564/5587

Industrial Distribution (no author). (2002). Covisint adopts XML standards. *Industrial Distribution, 91*(3), 28-29.

Knorr, E. (2002). ebXML: A B2B standard on hold. *ZDNet,* March 15, 2002. Retrieved March 6, 2006, from http://techupdate.zdnet.com/techupdate/stories/main/0,14179,2865508,00.html

Kotok, A. (2002a, February). Standards-based methodology for U.S. e-government initiatives. *Data Interchange Standards Association (DISA) white paper.* Retrieved March 5, 2006, from http://www.disa.org/pdfs/white_paper02.pdf

Kotok, A. (2002b, June). Utility deregulation requires effective e-business atandards. *Data*

Interchange Standards Association (DISA) white paper. Retrieved March 6, 2006, from http://www.disa.org/pdfs/white_paper03.pdf

Li, M. (2003, July 3). CEN/ISSS report and recommendations on key eBusiness standards issues 2003-2005. *CEN/ISSS eBusiness Standards Focus Group*. Retrieved March 6, 2006, from http://www.eeurope-standards.org/Docs/Roadmap.pdf

Mähönen, P. (1999). Chapter III: The standardization process in IT—too slow or too fast? In K. Jakobs (Ed.), *Information technology atandards and atandardization: A global perspective*. Hershey, PA: Idea Group Publishing.

Markus, M., Steinfield, C., & Wigand, R. (2003). The evolution of vertical IS standards: Electronic interchange standards in the US home mortgage industry. In *Proceedings of the Workshop on Standard Making: A Critical Research Frontier for Information Systems MISQ Special Issue Workshop*. Retrieved March 6, 2006, from http://www.si.umich.edu/misq-stds/proceedings/130_80-91.pdf

McFarlan, F., & Belokhvostova, V. (2004, October). RosettaNet and ebXML: Betting on the right e-commerce standard. *Harvard Business School Case, 9-305-006*.

McFarlan, F., & Mähönen, P. (1999). Chapter III: The standardization process in IT—too slow or too fast? In K. Jakobs (Ed.), *Information technology standards and standardization: A global perspective*. Hershey, PA: Idea Group Publishing.

Medina, H. (2000). The paradox of Rosettanet. *Line 56: The E-business Executive Daily*, September, 2000. Retrieved September 14, 2005, from http://www.line56.com/articles/default.asp?NewsID=1257

Meehan, M. (2001). Covisint exchange vows it will support ebXML Automakers' marketplace deems standard to be critical to open, global e-commerce. *Computerworld, 35*(23), 16.

Newcomer, E. (2002). *Understanding Web services: XML, WSDL, SOAP, and UDDI*. Boston: Addison-Wesley Professional.

Scala, S., & McGrath, R. (1999). Advantages and disadvantages of electronic data interchange: An industry perspective. *Information and Management, 25*(2), 85-91.

Story, C. (2003). A smart alternative. *Mortgage Banking, 63*(6), 71-79.

Sullivan, L, & Babcock, C. (2004, March 1). Driving standards. *Information Week*, (978), 22-23.

Toth, B. (1996). Putting the U.S. standardization system into perspective. *StandardView, 4*(4), 160-178.

Zhao, K, Xia, M., & Shaw, M. (2005). Vertical e-commerce standards and standards developing organizations: A conceptual framework. *Electronic Markets, 15*(4), 289-300.

ENDNOTES

[1] Cited from http://computing-dictionary.thefreedictionary.com/B2B+e-commerce (accessible through March 3, 2006)

[2] A VAN was a system whereby a third party (the VAN provider) leased lines from local telecommunications providers, often enhancing them with elements such as error detection.

[3] A protocol is the special set of rules that end points in a telecommunication connection use when they communicate.

[4] AXC X12 Web site: http://www.x12.org/x12org/about/faqs.cfm#a1 http://www.x12.org/x12org/about/faqs.cfm#a1

[5] XML schemas express shared vocabularies and allow machines to carry out rules made by people

[6] "Web services" can be used generically to refer to any service exposed via some inter-

face over the Web. "Web services," however, normally refers to a specific standard based on SOAP, WSDL and UDDI.

7   Adapted from Champion et al. (2002)

8   http://www.w3.org/Signature/

9   http://xml.coverpages.org/ws-security.html

10   Source: World Wide Web Consortium (http://xml.coverpages.org/ni2004-12-29-a.html)

11   International Standards Organization (http://www.iso.org/iso/en/ISOOnline.frontpage)

12   Source: UN/CEFACT site (http://www.unece.org/cefact/)

13   Source: ANSI Web site (http://www.ansi.org/)

14   As of today, four ebXML specifications have been approved by ISO as the ISO 15000 (1~4): 2004 serial standards.

15   Source: OASIS Web site (http://www.oasis-open.org/home/index.php)

16   Web sites: http://www.xml.org and http://xml.coverpages.org

17   Source: W3C Web site (http://www.w3.org/)

18   Source: OAG Web site (http://www.openapplications.org/)

19   Middleware is a class of software technologies designed to help manage the complexity and heterogeneity inherent in distributed systems. It is defined as a layer of software above the operating system but below the application program that provides a common programming abstraction across a distributed system.

20   Cited from Zhao et al. (2005)

21   Cited from http://www.covisint.com/migration/gm/ (accessed through 03/03/2006)

22   Cited from http://www.informationweek.com/showArticle.jhtml?articleID=16700279 (accessed through 03/03/2006)

23   Cited from www.covisint.com (accessed through 03/03/2006)

24   Source: www.rosettanet.org

25   Intel News Release, "Intel Uses RosettaNet e-Business Technology Standards," from http://www.intel.com/pressroom/archive/releases/20021210comp.htm (accessible through March 6, 2006)

26   Same as endnote 27

27   "Intel and Shinko use RosettaNet standards to build forecast-to-cash procurement process," cited from: http://www.rosettanet.org/RosettaNet/Doc/0/FSG4VFMC6RA4B47H0FJB0NNPED/IntelShinkoROICaseStudy.pdf (accessible through March 6, 2006)

28   RosettaNet Annual Summary Report 2002-2003. (2003). Cited from http://www.rosettanet.org/rosettanet/Doc/0/6CA862VN341KH1QV5ASQEEBM31/RosettaNet+Annual+Sumary6-2-03.pdf (accessible through March 6, 2006)

29   Adapted from http://www.efscouncil.org/EFSCconference/documents/Gardner-eMortgageOverview.pdf

Chapter II
Electronic Commerce and the State Sales Tax System:
An Issue of Tax Fairness

Christopher G. Reddick
University of Texas at San Antonio, USA

EXECUTIVE SUMMARY

This article examines the relationship between electronic commerce and the U.S. state sales and use tax system. A framework of a high-quality tax system is used in this study, and it is applied to taxing electronic commerce sales. The first part of this article analyzes nine principles of an effective tax system and divides these principles into the categories of adequacy of revenue, fairness of revenue, and management of revenue. In the second part of this article, these principles are tested to determine what impact electronic commerce taxation has on an effective revenue system. The results of these initial tests suggest that taxation of electronic commerce was associated with fairness in the tax system. In particular, the results suggested that states that had fairer tax systems were more likely to rely less on a sales tax and more on taxing Internet access. Management and adequacy of the revenue systems of states were not found to have a significant bearing on taxing electronic commerce. These results reinforce the existing public finance and legal theories that argue that the sales tax is not a fair revenue stream and that it should be reevaluated, especially in light of the contentious issue of taxing electronic commerce.

INTRODUCTION

Taxing of electronic commerce is one of the most pressing tax policy issues that U.S. state governments face in the 21st century. This article examines how electronic commerce affects the sales tax system and its adherence to the standards of a high-quality tax system. This study uses several principles to devise measures of revenue capacity, or the ability of state governments to have a high degree of adequacy, fairness, and management in their revenue systems. Revenue capacity is different from tax capacity; the latter represents the ability of a government entity to finance its public services (Berry & Fording, 1997). Revenue capacity is broader, encompassing not just state revenue raising ability but also the management of the revenue system and equity issues.

This study attempts to discern how states deal with taxing electronic commerce, particularly if they have a high-quality revenue system. Specifically, areas such as taxing Internet access, having a state sales tax, taxing digital downloads, and participation in the Streamlined Sales Tax Project (SSTP) (an effort created by state governments to simplify and modernize sales and use tax collection and administration) are examined.

The study is notably different from existing empirical work, in that it examines how the taxing of electronic commerce affects revenue capacity. This article qualitatively applies nine principles of an effective tax system, dividing them into the categories of adequacy of revenues, fairness of revenues, and management of revenues to the taxation of electronic commerce. These three categories then are tested quantitatively to determine the impact that taxing electronic commerce has on revenue capacity. The key question is: *For states that are less reliant on taxing electronic commerce sales, will they have higher levels of revenue capacity?*

Taxing Electronic Commerce and Information Systems (IS) Research

A common argument for not taxing Internet sales is that the Internet is viewed by some as an infant industry that requires protection. In information systems (IS) research, we would like to know whether taxing Internet sales would lead to less use of this communication media because of the higher price. There are potentially positive spillover effects arising from the size of the Internet. The idea is that aiding the Internet early will yield large benefits to future generations (Goolsbee & Zittrain, 1999). Furthermore, as the number of

Internet transactions rises, the value of Internet commerce rises, as well. There is some empirical evidence that supports a ban on taxing Internet sales in the short run (Goolsbee & Zittrain, 1999) and other evidence suggesting that it makes no difference to sales if Internet access is taxed (Bruce, Deskins, & Fox, 2004).

Another common argument in favor of banning taxes on the Internet relates to a "digital divide" in Internet access in America. The Internet and other information technologies are more prevalent among wealthier people than among lower income individuals (Bruce et al., 2004). Therefore, taxing Internet sales will affect the poor more than the rich in the United States. Lower income individuals will not have as much Internet access in order to take advantage of purchasing online and potentially avoiding paying sales tax. These two arguments are especially pertinent to IS research and are explored in more detail later in this article.

This article is divided into three parts. The first part of the study looks at how the existing system of sales taxation adheres to the standards of a high-quality revenue system and how electronic commerce affects this relationship. The second part of the study uses the information presented in the first part to build hypotheses and to test relationships of how the presence of electronic commerce and taxation affects the revenue capacity of states. The third part presents recommendations, limitations, and avenues for future research on taxing electronic commerce sales.

PRINCIPLES OF HIGH-QUALITY STATE TAX SYSTEM APPLIED TO SALES TAXES ON ELECTRONIC COMMERCE

There are nine principles of a high-quality state tax system that can be applied to the taxing of electronic commerce. The comparison is based upon criteria outlined in the 1992 document titled

Table 1. Comparing principles of high-quality tax system and taxing of electronic commerce

Category	Principle	Is principle found in taxing electronic commerce sales? (Yes or No)	Comments	Key Literature
Adequacy	1. Elements that are complementary in state and local finances	No	Different rate structures in state and local sales taxes, which makes electronic commerce compliance extremely difficult for vendors	Brunori (2001)
	2. Revenue-reliable manner (i.e., stability, certainty, and sufficiency)	No	**Stability.** Not stable since sales tax is diminishing because of increase in remote purchases. **Certainty.** Remote sales make this source less certain for the future. **Sufficiency.** Because of exemptions to the base, partly because of electronic commerce, states are turning to income taxes and user fees or higher sales tax rates in order to make up for lost revenues.	Bruce and Fox (2001a, 2001b); Cline and Neubig (1999); Goolsbee and Zittrain (1999)
	3. Relies on a balanced variety of revenue sources	No	Electronic commerce sales decrease sales tax revenue, making it difficult for states that have a heavy reliance on sales taxes (e.g., Texas).	Mikesell (2001); Bruce and Fox (2001a)
Fairness	4. Treats taxpayers equitably	No	The sales tax is regressive and even more so because of electronic commerce sales. The wealthy have more access to the Internet.	McLure (2002a, 2002b)
	5. Responsive to international and interstate competition	No	Interstate advantages to those firms that do not have a presence in a purchaser's state. International competition is distorted, since consumers can purchase electronic commerce goods overseas and not pay sales tax.	Hellerstein (1998); Bruce, et al. (2003)
	6. Accountable to taxpayers	No	Not accountable, since most taxpayers are not aware that they are supposed to pay the use tax on remote sales, if it is not collected from the vendor.	Due and Mikesell (1994); Mikesell (2004); Cornia, et al. (2004)
Management	7. Facilitates taxpayer compliance	No	Taxing electronic commerce sales is not transparent. Most consumers do not know that they owe tax on remote purchases.	McLure (2002a, 2002b); Due and Mikesell (1994)
	8. Simple to administer	No	Electronic commerce sales and collection are difficult to administer because of nexus rules. Issue of taxpayer fairness comes into play.	McLure (2000, 2002b)
	9. Minimize its involvement in spending decisions	No	Firms and individuals will change their spending decisions in order to reduce their sales tax liability, electronic commerce is one factor.	Fox and Murray (1997); Goolsbee (2000); Cornia, et al. (2004)

"Principles of a High-Quality State Revenue System" prepared by the Foundation for State Legislatures and the National Conference of State Legislators (NCSL, 1992). The nine principles have been placed into three groups, representing key issues that state governments face in revenue capacity. These groups are adequacy, fairness, and management of revenues. The principles and their impact on taxing electronic commerce sales are summarized in Table 1. Each of the principles as well as applications to taxing electronic commerce sales are discussed.

Adequacy of Revenue

The principles under this group include 1, 2, and 3. Principle 1 of a high-quality tax system is that the state revenue system should be complementary. For example, different rates and filing requirements across jurisdictions increase the costs of taxpayer compliance. State and local governments should cooperate in order to avoid a patchwork of rate structures across the state, since a revenue system that minimizes complexity eases compliance costs and improves efficiency of revenue collection. Many state sales taxes have separate local rates piggy backed on top of state rates, adding complexity to an already complicated system.

How does Principle 1 apply to electronic commerce and sales tax? When calculating potential tax liability, it is not just the 45 different sales taxes that must be taken into account; there are other numerous local rates that must be applied. Local government's use of sales taxes indicates there are about 7,600 jurisdictions that have a general sales tax program authorized by 34 states. This wide variation makes it extremely complicated when collecting the sales and use taxes, especially on electronic commerce purchases (Brunori, 2001). Principle 1 clearly is violated, if there is an effort to tax electronic commerce without simplification of all the tax rates.

Principle 2 deals with the revenue system producing revenue in a reliable manner. This involves stability, certainty, and sufficiency of the tax system. There should be stability in that the amount of revenue collected should be relatively constant over time and not subjected to unpredictable fluctuations. A diversified revenue structure with a broad tax base tends to be more stable than an undiversified structure with a narrow tax base. Certainty implies that the number and types of tax changes will be kept to a minimum. Individuals should not be subjected to frequent changes in tax rates and bases, because frequent changes interfere with their economic choices and the ability to make long-term financial plans and decisions. In this principle, sufficiency means that a high-quality revenue system produces enough revenue to finance the level of services that the state chooses to provide.

In taxing electronic commerce, revenue collected in a reliable manner is being eroded due to remote sales. This makes the necessity of taxing electronic commerce especially important in order to produce additional tax revenue in tight economic times (GAO, 2000). As Bruce and Fox (2001a, 2001b) note, the economic losses from not taxing electronic commerce will be substantial in the near future. They estimate that by 2011, states will lose anywhere from 2.6% to 9.9% of their total state tax collections to electronic commerce. Other research indicates that revenue losses will be lower. For instance, Cline and Neubig (1999) found revenue losses for 1998 to be only one-tenth of 1% of total sales tax revenue. Goolsbee and Zittrain (1999) estimated that revenue losses in 1998 were less than one-fourth of 1% of sales tax revenue, and that by 2003, losses would be less than 2% of total sales tax revenue. Some argue that once the issues of trust and risk of using the Internet have been resolved, electronic commerce will begin to have real tax implications for states (Clay & Strauss, 2000).

Principle 3 is that a high-quality revenue system should rely upon a diverse and balanced range of sources. One goal of a revenue system is economic neutrality to prevent the distortion of individual and business behavior. If reliance is divided among numerous sources and if their bases are broad, rates can be kept low in order to minimize their impact on behavior. A broad-based tax system helps to meet the goal of diversification, since it spreads the burden of the tax among more payers. States should attempt to avoid excessive reliance on any single revenue source.

The taxing of electronic commerce partly violates Principle 3, because many states rely heavily on the sales tax. However, the important question for this study is whether the taxation of electronic commerce is causing a narrowing of the tax base. For example, the sales tax base equaled 51.4% of the state's personal income in 1979 but has fallen to 42% in 2000 (Mikesell, 2000, 2001). The narrowing of the sales tax base is attributed to three major factors (Yang & Poon, 2001). The first is remote sales, including electronic commerce, catalogue and telephone sales, and cross-state shopping, all of which have been expanding greatly in recent years. The second factor is the shift in consumption patterns toward greater consumption of services (exempt from taxes in most states) and less consumption of goods. Third, continued legislative exemptions have narrowed the base in essentially every state. As a result, states have responded to the narrowing tax base by raising rates (Bruce & Fox, 2001a). For instance, the median sales tax rate increased across states from 3.25% in 1970 to 5.3% in 2003. The existing evidence shows that there is an increased reliance on the sales tax and the narrowing of its base. Both of these factors can be attributed partly to the loss of tax revenue from electronic commerce sales.

Fairness of Revenue

The principles under this group include 4, 5, and 6. Principle 4 refers to the fairness of revenue cat-

egory. A high-quality tax system treats taxpayers equitably. This is measured by horizontal equity and vertical equity. Horizontal equity requires that individuals in similar circumstances have similar tax burdens. Vertical equity refers to the distribution of tax burdens among people in different circumstances. Reliance on sales taxes tends to make state and local revenue systems regressive, and a high-quality tax system should minimize regressivity.

Not taxing electronic commerce sales makes the sales tax even more regressive for low-income groups, since the effective rate is higher for them. Therefore, Principle 4 is violated due to electronic commerce, and the sales tax lacks horizontal equity. Higher income groups have greater Internet access and will be able to avoid paying sales taxes more easily than lower income groups, which makes their effective rate lower (McLure 2002b). McLure (2002a) believes that it is unfair to exempt electronic commerce purchases that are disproportionately made by the relatively affluent while taxing purchases from local vendors are made disproportionately by the less affluent, increasing the regressivity of the sales tax.

Principle 5 is that a high-quality tax system should be responsive to interstate and international economic competition. If there are different sales tax rates between states, economic distortions are created, because businesses will locate in jurisdictions where they have the least tax burden. Therefore, states are under increasing pressure to make revenue systems a tool for economic development. The problem is that tax breaks can erode tax bases. A state that imposes a tax burden far different from that of its neighboring states runs a risk of hurting its local economy. Therefore, taxes should provide similar treatment for all industries and all firms within a given industry and state.

The taxing of electronic commerce violates Principle 5, since the current sales tax system provides some economic incentives for businesses to locate in jurisdictions where their customers have the least tax burden. Taxing electronic commerce has not provided an additional problem, since it has existed before the Internet because of mail order and phone retailers. However, the rise of the Internet has exasperated this problem in terms of competition and the economic distortions that it creates. This tax wedge affects location decisions of businesses that face paying use taxes (Bruce, Fox, & Murray, 2003). The tax wedge between local and remote purchases occurs when citizens either can buy locally and pay sales tax or buy remotely and, more often than not, avoid paying sales or use tax on the purchase. The tax differential can amount to a discount of up to 10%. Sales taxes encourage firms to locate their production facilities in the lowest tax rate states in order to evade use taxes (Cornia, Sjoquist, & Walters, 2004).

For example, Amazon.com has admitted that one of the reasons for its location in the state of Washington is to limit the percentage of sales on which it must collect taxes. In addition, Walmart. com claimed that it was a separate online entity from its brick-and-mortar Wal-Mart stores. Therefore, Walmart.com asserted that it did not have to collect sales taxes on online transactions with customers within states where Wal-Mart maintains retail stores, which is every state in the United States (Cockfield, 2002). Firms are required to collect sales tax in states where operations exist because of nexus, or having a physical presence. Therefore, Wal-Mart, being in 50 states, should be obligated to collect sales taxes in all applicable states for its Internet operations. In addition, Barnes & Noble avoided this issue by organizing BN.com as a separate entity, so only its warehouses and management (initially in the states of New York and New Jersey) were counted as taxable locales. Traditional nexus rules are based upon concepts of territory and the physical presence of the taxpayer in the state. However, such an approach makes little sense, since the Internet has no geographic borders (Hellerstein, 1998).

Principle 6 is that a high-quality tax system should be accountable to taxpayers. Tax laws should be explicit and not hidden, and proposed changes should be well publicized in advance to stimulate debate. Lawmakers have a responsibility to ensure that policy produces the intended effect and does so at a reasonable cost.

The sales tax system violates Principle 6 in the taxation of electronic commerce. In the existing system, most taxpayers are not aware that they must pay taxes on remote sales, which does not make it accountable to taxpayers. This is probably why taxpayer compliance is only around 1% for use taxes (Due & Mikesell, 1994). The greatest problem is that taxpayers do not understand what the use tax is and how it fits into the overall tax system (Cornia et al., 2004). In addition, the existing literature argues that direct collection of the use tax from consumers is not feasible (Mikesell, 2001).

Management of Revenue

The principles under this group include 7, 8, and 9. Principle 7 fits into the management of revenue category, arguing that a high-quality tax system facilitates taxpayer compliance. It does this by avoiding a maze of taxes, forms, and filing requirements. The reduction in complexity helps taxpayers to understand the tax system and reduces the costs of compliance. It is important for the taxpayer to feel that the system is fair, because taxpayer compliance is largely voluntary.

The sales tax system and electronic commerce violate the transparency requirement, because they are dependent upon the business having a physical presence, or nexus, in the purchaser's state (McLure, 2002a). If this is not the case, it is incumbent upon the consumer to remit what is called a use tax to the taxing authority. However, most people are not aware that if they do not pay a sales tax on a remote purchase, they are responsible for remitting the corresponding use tax to their taxing authority (Cornia et al., 2004; Due & Mikesell, 1994). In addition, the exemptions for food and services also make the sales tax system more complicated, and higher statutory rates are required to cover these exemptions (Mikesell, 2001, 2004). The vendor has the complicated task of trying to figure out what is taxable and what is not taxable, all of which increases compliance costs. Differing state exemptions for digital downloads and taxing Internet access are other problems that violate the transparency requirement (McLure, 2002b).

Principle 8 is that a high-quality tax system that is easy to administer reduces the likelihood of errors and facilitates fairness. Poor tax administration will mean that tax burdens are distributed among taxpayers in ways that the law did not intend. If the tax system is administered fairly, individuals and businesses are more likely to pay their respective shares of the tax burden. Therefore, a fair tax system should increase taxpayer compliance.

Electronic commerce diminishes fairness, since individuals can choose to purchase items online to avoid paying sales taxes. This significantly diminishes tax fairness and equity in administration (McLure, 2002b). For instance, determining who should remit the tax for tangible goods is a manageable problem. The goods must be shipped to a location, which is a reasonable approximation of where it will be used, and the opportunities for businesses and consumers to behave in ways that minimize their taxes are not that burdensome. Digital goods, by contrast, are not subject to similar constraints. Even if the sellers of such goods decided to collect sales tax, buyers conceivably could have the digital product shipped to an Internet location and pay for the product with a credit card, whose billing address lists a state without a sales tax. The anonymity of Internet transactions seriously complicates both tax administration and tax compliance, if taxes are based on the destination of sales or the source of income (McLure, 2000).

Principle 9 is that a high-quality tax system minimizes its involvement in spending decisions and makes involvement explicit. For example, tax deductions, credits, and exemptions shift tax burdens from a favored set of taxpayers to less favored taxpayers. For this reason, the costs should be explicit or transparent and should be reviewed annually.

The taxing of electronic commerce favors online purchases over main-street vendors (Fox & Murray, 1997). Research shows that differences in sales tax rates along state borders cause consumers to switch their purchases from the higher to lower tax jurisdictions (CBO, 2003). Goolsbee (2000) found that the probability of buying something online decreases, as the local sales tax rate rises. Specifically, this author found that controlling for demographic characteristics while applying existing tax rates to the Internet reduces the number of buyers online by 20-25% and reduces sales by 25-30%. There appears to be tax sensitivity of consumers that could have a negative impact on electronic commerce. However, taxing electronic commerce would have a positive impact on taxpayer equity (McLure, 2002a).

The application of taxing electronic commerce and the nine principles of high-quality taxation reveal that this system fails on all counts. It is the existence of the sales tax that creates the problem, but it is exacerbated by taxing electronic commerce. These nine principles are used to test the impact that taxing electronic commerce has on revenue capacity. A model is created in the next part of this article that tests the relationship among the nine principles. Principles 1 to 3 examine adequacy of revenue, Principles 4 to 6 examine fairness of the revenue system, and Principles 7 to 9 examine the impact of management on the revenue system. However, before this article specifies the hypothesis and models, there is a brief examination of the existing empirical studies on the taxation of electronic commerce in order to see how this study fits into the literature.

Table 2. Existing empirical studies on taxing electronic commerce

Consumers and Taxing Electronic Commerce	Existing Empirical Studies	State Governments and Taxing Electronic Commerce	Existing Empirical Studies
a. Taxing Internet access	Bruce, et al. (2004) a	. Participation in SSTP	Cornia, et al. (2004); Cameron (2004)
b. Taxing Internet sales G	oolsbee and Zittrain (1999); Goolsebee (2000); Vijayasarathy (2002); Alm and Melnik (2005)	b. Taxing Internet access, downloads, Internet sales	Nesbary (2000); Best and Teske (2002)

TAXING ELECTRONIC COMMERCE SALES AND STATE GOVERNMENT REVENUE CAPACITY

There are several empirical studies that examine the impact of electronic commerce taxation on Internet sales, Internet access, and digital downloads (see Table 2). These studies can be divided either into consumers and taxing electronic commerce sales or state governments and taxing Internet sales. Both will be reviewed.

Consumers and Taxing Electronic Commerce

Taxing Internet Access. Bruce, et al. (2004) examine the effect that Internet access taxation has on Internet access rates. Their empirical results show that taxing Internet access does not have a statistically significant effect on Internet access rates. The strongest impact was from income, with Internet access rising as the individual's income rose.

Taxing Internet Sales. Using public opinion data from Forrester, a market research firm, Goolsebee and Zittrain (1999) did an analysis of consumer behavior and taxing Internet sales. First, they found that aggressive enforcement of taxes on Internet commerce raised only a small amount of revenue in the short term. Second, enforcing taxes on Internet sales disproportionately benefited higher-income and highly educated people, but this effect lessened substantially because of the proliferation of the Internet. Third, the costs of complying with taxes on Internet commerce were unlikely to be very large for most online transactions. Finally, there are positive externalities or spillover effects of the Internet that should be considered before aggressively applying taxes.

In the literature on consumers' reactions to taxing Internet sales, Goolsbee (2000) conducted an empirical analysis on how local taxation affects the decision of consumers to buy goods over the Internet. Controlling for individual characteristics, consumers living in places with higher tax rates are significantly more likely to buy online. The magnitude of the tax effect suggests that applying existing sales taxes to the Internet might reduce the number of online buyers by as much as 24%.

Vijayasarathy (2002) examined whether the shopping orientations of consumers would change their behavior as a result of sales taxes being charged for online purchases. The survey results indicated that charging sales tax would not have a negative impact on online shopping.

Finally, Alm, and Melnik's (2005) study attempted to determine the impact of sales taxes on the probability of online shopping. Their results indicated that sales taxes typically have a positive and statistically significant impact on the probability of consumers buying online. For instance, a

1% change in the tax price reduces the probability of buying online by roughly 0.5%, which is one-fourth the size of Goolsbee's (2000) estimates. In addition, the probability of online purchases tends to be greater for higher income groups and lower for most minorities, which is similar to Goolsbee and Zittrain's (1999) finding.

State Governments and Taxing Electronic Commerce

Participation in the SSTP. Cornia, et al. (2004) explored the hypothesis that if the sales and use tax structures are simplified, then remote vendors voluntarily would collect and remit the sales tax, if it was in their commercial interests. These authors conducted a simulation, and their results revealed that large firms without nexus would prefer a voluntary system to a mandatory collection system, but participation would hinge on the compensation level for compliance set by the state.

In another study on this issue, Cameron (2004) attempted to identify state characteristics that increased the likelihood of participation in the SSTP. This author found three factors that were supported: the more business vitality, the less likely to participate in the SSTP; the higher the technological innovation of the state, the less likely to participate in the SSTP; and the greater the reliance on the sales tax, the more likely to participate in the SSTP.

Taxing Internet Access, Downloads, and Internet Sales. Nesbary (2000) tested a model that examined the impact of taxation of goods and services sold over the Internet, taxation of Internet access fees, and taxation of digital downloads from the Internet. This author tested these as dependent variables against fiscal, organizational, and demographic factors as predictor variables. Overall, the results did not show significant relationships among these common factors that were perceived to be associated with taxing Internet sales.

In a similar line of inquiry, Best and Teske (2002) examine the impact of interest groups and political and economic factors and found that they were correlated with adoptions of taxing Internet access and digital downloads. Their study was similar to the Nesbary (2000) study; however, Best and Teske (2002) found some significant relationships. The results of their models indicate that interest groups are extremely influential in states' decisions to tax Internet sales.

This study is different from the existing empirical work, since it focuses on testing whether electronic commerce taxation is associated with being a high-revenue-capacity state. This has not been modeled previously in the literature. It fits into the existing empirical studies outlined in Table 2 on state governments and electronic commerce taxation. The following section formally outlines the hypotheses tested in this study that are derived from some of these empirical studies.

Hypotheses

In order to examine the impact that revenue capacity has on the taxation of electronic commerce, four groups of hypotheses are tested. These hypotheses will be mentioned briefly, followed by a detailed discussion of how each is specified. It should be noted that this study does not outline all 32 tests conducted here as hypotheses but mentions the most important ones, showing their impact on electronic commerce and revenue capacity.

Adequacy of Revenue

Hypothesis 1a. State governments that tax Internet access will have more adequate revenue capacity.

Hypothesis 1b. State governments that do not have a sales tax will have more adequate revenue capacity.

Hypothesis 1c. State governments that tax Internet downloads will have more adequate revenue capacity.

Hypothesis 1d. State governments that do not participate in the SSTP will have more adequate revenue capacity.

Fairness of Revenue

Hypothesis 2a. State governments that tax Internet access will have a fairer tax system.

Hypothesis 2b. State governments that do not have a sales tax will have a fairer tax system.

Hypothesis 2c. State governments that tax digital downloads will have a fairer tax system.

Hypothesis 2d. State governments that do not participate in the SSTP will have a fairer tax system.

Management of Revenue

Hypothesis 3a. State governments that tax Internet access will have a greater ability to manage their revenue system.

Hypothesis 3b. State governments that do not have a sales tax will have a greater ability to manage their revenue system.

Hypothesis 3c. State governments that tax digital downloads will have a greater ability to manage their revenue system.

Hypothesis 3d. State governments that do not participate in the SSTP will have a greater ability to manage their revenue system.

Revenue Capacity

Hypothesis 4a. State governments that tax Internet access will increase their overall revenue

capacity (or adequate revenue capacity, fair tax system, and better management of revenues).

Hypothesis 4b. State governments that do not have a sales tax will increase overall revenue capacity.

Hypothesis 4c. State governments that tax digital downloads will increase overall revenue capacity.

Hypothesis 4d. State governments that do not participate in the SSTP will increase overall revenue capacity.

Hypotheses 1 through 4 examine the impact of electronic commerce variables on the adequacy of revenue, fairness of revenue, management of revenue, and overall revenue capacity. For instance, in Hypotheses 1a, the existing empirical research has investigated the relationship between taxing Internet access and electronic commerce (Best & Teske, 2002; Bruce et al., 2004; Nesbary, 2000). For Hypothesis 1b, the reaction of government to having a sales tax on electronic commerce has been investigated by Nesbary (2000) and Best and Teske (2002). For Hypothesis 1c, taxing digital downloads also has been examined by these authors. Finally, for Hypothesis 1d, there is existing research on the relationship of the SSTP and electronic commerce (Cameron, 2004; Cornia et al., 2004). These hypotheses can be operationalized with data that measure state revenue capacity.

Revenue-Capacity-Dependent Variables

The following section discusses the dependent variables used in this study to test the impact of revenue capacity on electronic commerce taxation. In order to measure the impact that the electronic commerce variables have on revenue capacity, data were compiled from *Governing Magazine*

(Barrett, Greene, Mariani, & Sostek, 2003). They collected data in 2003 on the nine previously mentioned principles of high-quality tax systems and narrowed them down to the following four measures of state revenue capacity:

1. **Adequacy of Revenue:** Several issues are measured here. Does the state have adequate revenues currently and for the foreseeable future in order to provide reasonable support for the programs that the legislature historically has seen fit to fund? Is there a balanced, multi-tax approach that does not rely excessively on any one tax? Is the state experiencing budget shortfalls that can be attributed to a weakness in tax revenues? Are there long-term trends that call into question the ability of the current tax system to deliver sufficient revenue down the road? Are there structural issues that make it particularly difficult to deal with obvious tax problems?

2. **Fairness of Revenue:** This measures the following issues. Are similar taxpayers taxed similarly, and as a result, is the broadest possible base being taxed at the lowest possible rates? Is the system overly regressive? How thoroughly does the state tax services? Do the sales taxes on goods have a broad base with minimum unnecessary exemptions? Do the state's taxes avoid excessive exemptions and deductions that are not mean-tested? Is there anything extremely unfair about the state's approach to corporate taxes?

3. **Management of Revenue:** This measures the following issues. Does the state have adequate resources and management capacity in order to optimize voluntary compliance, to find and get taxes from those who do not voluntarily comply, and to do this with optimal efficiency for both the state and its taxpayers? How accurate have been its revenue estimates and assessments of the impact of tax changes over time? Does the

state engage in studies of its tax system and use them to create better policies? Does it have good information and data to facilitate understanding of the tax system? What is the quality of human resources? Is there high turnover, lack of training, lack of workforce planning, or many line budget cuts? To what extent has the state engaged in taxpayer education efforts and taken steps to improve customer relations?

4. **Revenue Capacity:** This measures the adequacy, fairness, and management of the state revenue system. This variable is compiled by adding up the values for each of the three previously mentioned categories for each of the states and by dividing them by three to get an overall revenue capacity score (to be discussed more thoroughly later in this article).

The *Governing Magazine* rating methodology consisted of a general outline of the elements that contribute to adequacy, fairness, and management through interviews and document reviews in order to determine how successful states had been establishing them. For example, *Governing Magazine* staff conducted interviews with heads of the revenue departments or designated officials in most states. Interviews were conducted with tax experts, and documents that shed further light on the state revenue systems were evaluated. The following four-star rating system was devised:

- **Four Stars:** The state has done very well in the area under consideration and generally has at least one or two elements that make it stand out from other states in a positive way.

- **Three Stars:** Although, in general, there is room for improvement, the state essentially is performing well. This means that the structure of the state is such that in the near future, the revenue streams will be adequate.

Table 3. State revenue capacity and taxing electronic commerce issues (Sources: (a) Barrett et al., 2003; (b) CCH, 2004)

State	Adequacy of Revenue[a] (Max 4 Stars)	Fairness of Revenue[a] (Max 4 Stars)	Management of Revenue[a] (Max 4 Stars)	Revenue Capacity (Max 4 Stars)	Tax Internet Access[b] (1=Tax Internet Access)	Sales Tax[b] (1=Sales Tax)	Tax Down-loads[b] (1=Tax Downloads)	SSTP[b] (1=SSTP)
Alabama	1	1	2	1.3	0	1	1	0
Alaska	1	3	2	2.0	0	0	0	0
Arizona	2	2	2	2.0	0	1	1	0
Arkansas	2	2	2	2.0	0	1	0	1
California	1	2	2	1.7	0	1	0	0
Colorado	1	2	2	1.7	0	1	1	0
Connecticut	2	2	2	2.0	1	1	1	0
Delaware	4	3	4	3.7	0	0	0	0
Florida	1	1	4	2.0	0	1	0	0
Georgia	3	2	2	2.3	0	1	0	0
Hawaii	3	4	2	3.0	0	1	1	0
Idaho	3	2	3	2.7	0	1	1	0
Illinois	2	1	2	1.7	0	1	1	0
Indiana	3	2	3	2.7	0	1	1	1
Iowa	3	2	2	2.3	0	1	0	1
Kansas	2	2	3	2.3	0	1	1	1
Kentucky	2	2	2	2.0	0	1	0	1
Louisiana	2	2	2	2.0	0	1	1	0
Maine	2	2	3	2.3	0	1	1	0
Maryland	2	2	3	2.3	0	1	0	0
Massachusetts	2	2	3	2.3	0	1	0	0
Michigan	2	2	4	2.7	0	1	1	0
Minnesota	2	2	4	2.7	0	1	1	1
Mississippi	2	2	1	1.7	0	1	1	0
Missouri	2	2	4	2.7	0	1	0	0
Montana	1	3	2	2.0	0	0	0	0
Nebraska	2	2	3	2.3	0	1	1	1
Nevada	1	1	1	1.0	0	1	0	1
New Hampshire	2	2	3	2.3	0	0	0	0
New Jersey	2	2	3	2.3	0	1	0	0
New Mexico	4	3	1	2.7	1	1	1	0
New York	2	2	3	2.3	0	1	1	0
North Carolina	2	2	3	2.3	0	1	0	1
North Dakota	4	3	2	3.0	1	1	1	1
Ohio	2	2	3	2.3	1	1	1	1
Oklahoma	2	2	2	2.0	0	1	0	1
Oregon	1	3	3	2.3	0	0	0	0

(continued on following page)

Table 3. cont.

State	Adequacy of Revenue[a] (Max 4 Stars)	Fairness of Revenue[a] (Max 4 Stars)	Management of Revenue[a] (Max 4 Stars)	Revenue Capacity (Max 4 Stars)	Tax Internet Access[b] (1=Tax Internet Access)	Sales Tax[b] (1=Sales Tax)	Tax Downloads[b] (1=Tax Downloads)	SSTP[b] (1=SSTP)
Pennsylvania	3	2	2	2.3	0	1	0	0
Rhode Island	2	2	2	2.0	0	1	0	0
South Carolina	2	2	2	2.0	0	1	0	0
South Dakota	3	3	3	3.0	1	1	1	1
Tennessee	1	1	2	1.3	0	1	1	1
Texas	1	1	3	1.7	1	1	1	1
Utah	3	2	3	2.7	0	1	1	1
Vermont	3	3	2	2.7	0	1	0	1
Virginia	2	2	2	2.0	0	1	0	0
Washington	1	2	4	2.3	0	1	1	1
West Virginia	2	2	2	2.0	0	1	1	1
Wisconsin	2	3	3	2.7	1	1	1	0
Wyoming	4	2	2	2.7	0	1	1	1

- **Two Stars:** The state could continue to function as it currently does into the near future. However, there are clear elements to the tax system that would benefit from change.
- **One Star:** The area under review needs some kind of dramatic reform. Alteration at the margins will not be enough to fix the state's tax problems.

Some of the states that had four stars for adequacy of their revenue system included Delaware, New Mexico, North Dakota, and Wyoming (Table 3). Hawaii was the only state that had four stars for fairness of the revenue system. For management capacity of the revenue system, four stars were reported for Delaware, Florida, Michigan, Minnesota, Missouri, and Washington. In the revenue capacity variable, which is the average of the three scores for each state, the highest score was 3.7, reported for the state of Delaware, out of a maximum attainable score of four.

The lowest scores for revenue adequacy also can be found in Table 3. Some of the states with low revenue adequacies included Alabama and Nevada. In total, there were 11 states with only one star for adequacy of the revenue system. For fairness of the revenue system, there were six states with only one star: Alabama, Florida, Illinois, Nevada, Tennessee, and Texas. For the management capacity variable, there were three states with only one star: Mississippi, Nevada, and New Mexico.

In order to measure the impact of electronic commerce and taxation on revenue capacity, an index was composed using the scores obtained from *Governing Magazine*. One star is worth one point, two stars two points, and so forth. The average score for the 50 states was just over two points for adequacy and fairness and just over two and one-half points for management capacity (Table 4). Two points indicates that the state could continue to function at its current level, but there are structural changes that could be beneficial to the current tax system.

Total revenue capacity also is measured, which is compiled by adding the adequacy, fairness, and management scores and dividing this score by three in order to get an overall value out of four. This study used the score for each of the adequacy, fairness, and management-of-revenues variables for each state government in order to create an overall revenue capacity score (Table 4). Therefore, if a state did well on each of these scores, this would be reflected in the overall revenue capacity score. A limitation of using this four-star rating system is that there are only four choices, which reduces the precision of the dependent variables and should be kept in mind when interpreting the results. Variability of the ratings could come from a number of factors that may not be captured in the models presented here. The following section discusses the independent

variables that are used to explain state government revenue capacity.

Predictor Variables

The electronic commerce independent variables are reported in Table 4. Internet access is used as a predictor of revenue capacity, which has been modeled in prior research on taxing Internet sales (Best & Teske, 2002). The results in Table 4 indicate that 14%, or seven states, taxes Internet access. In accordance with the Internet Tax Freedom Act (ITFA) of 1998, these states represent only those that were able to tax Internet access before it was banned by Congress. There are 90%, or 45 states, that has a sales tax; this variable also has been studied in the literature on taxing electronic commerce (Bruce et al., 2004; Nesbary, 2000). In addition, 54% of the states taxes digital downloads. Best and Teske (2002) incorporated digital downloads in their models of taxation of Internet sales. Finally, there were 20 states in 2003 that had adopted the provisions of

Table 4. Descriptive statistics of variables (Sources: (a) Barrett, et al. [2003]; (b) CCH [2004]; (c) Bruce and Fox [2001a]; (d) Governing Magazine [2003]; and NA=Not Applicable

	N	Minimum	Maximum	Mean	Predicted Impact
Adequacy of Revenue[a]	50	1.00	4.00	2.12	NA
Fairness of Revenue[a]	50	1.00	4.00	2.10	NA
Management of Revenue[a]	50	1.00	4.00	2.52	NA
Revenue Capacity Index	50	1.00	3.67	2.25	NA
Tax Internet Access[b]	50	0.00	1.00	0.14	+
Sales Tax[b]	50	0.00	1.00	0.90	-
Tax Downloads[b]	50	0.00	1.00	0.54	+
Streamlined Sales Tax Project[b]	50	0.00	1.00	0.40	-
Sales Tax % State Revenue[c]	50	0.00	62.60	32.08	-
Sales Tax Base % Personal Income[c]	50	0.00	109.20	44.42	+
% Households with Internet Access[d]	50	36.10	64.10	50.23	+
State Retail Sales % of U.S.[d]	50	0.18	10.69	2.00	-

the SSTP. Cameron (2004) examined the impact on state participation in the SSTP from business and economic conditions of the state and found an empirical connection; therefore, it should be included in the models.

In addition to the electronic commerce variables, this research has controlled for the amount of sales taxes collected as a percent of total state revenue. This variable can be used to demonstrate how dependent a state is on sales taxes. Existing literature indicates that the sales tax base is narrowing (Mikesell, 2001). States that have a smaller base would benefit greatly from taxing electronic commerce. Therefore, a measure of this is the state tax base as a percentage of personal income. In addition, this research uses the amount of household Internet access as a predictor variable. States that have higher Internet access are more likely to be concerned about collecting taxes on Internet sales. The state's retail sales as a percentage of total retail sales are used to measure the dependence of the state on the retail industry. Higher state dependence on retail sales indicates a greater need to collect sales taxes. The following section presents the models that were tested to determine the impact of taxing electronic commerce on revenue capacity.

Models

The models used in this study test four types of revenue capacity issues. The results initially are suggestive of some correlations. The first dependent variable measures how adequate revenues are for the state. The second dependent variable examines fairness of the state revenue system. The third dependent variable tests state management of the revenue system. The final dependent variable is a revenue capacity index, a combination of the three measures.

It is anticipated that taxing Internet access will have a positive impact on the revenue capacity dependent variables, because states will be able to collect more tax revenue from these fees (the direction of predicted causality for all of the independent variables is shown in Table 4). Existing work has indicated a relationship between taxing Internet access and sales tax reliance (Best & Teske, 2002). However, other empirical studies have found no relationship between Internet access and taxing electronic commerce (Bruce et al., 2004; Nesbary, 2000).

If the state has a sales tax, negative coefficients are anticipated for the capacity variables, since the state may be more dependent upon this tax compared to other forms of taxation such as income taxes. As discussed in the first part of this article, there has been a tendency for state governments to raise their sales tax rates, and electronic commerce is one cause of a decreased sales tax base. In terms of the principles mentioned in the first part of this article, the sales tax and electronic commerce fails in terms of providing adequate revenues (exemptions to the base and loss of sales tax revenues from electronic commerce), fairness (it is a regressive tax, more so with electronic commerce), and management (nexus rules make it difficult for vendor compliance).

If a state taxes digital downloads, it is an indication that the state will have a higher capacity score due to a more balanced revenue system. This is associated with the fairness principle, in that digital downloads should be taxed similarly to purchases made off-the-shelf. Fairness would decrease, since consumers would choose to purchase more digital downloads. Management capacity would be applicable, because it would make compliance more difficult, sorting between what is taxable and not taxable.

In addition, states that have implemented the SSTP initiative should experience a negative impact on revenue capacity, since they are trying to override the physical presence rules of the *Quill* decision. This implies that they are more dependent on sales taxes. This is related to the adequacy principle, in that these states are not getting enough revenue from the sales tax because of the loss in tax revenues from electronic commerce sales. Second, fairness is not achieved, since consumers that purchase online can escape the sales tax. Finally, management capacity is impaired, since there are compliance costs associated with vendors and consumers trying to discern what is taxable.

Some of the other predictor variables also should be mentioned briefly. One of them is the state sales tax as a percentage of state revenue. This is anticipated to have a negative impact on capacity. A higher sales tax base as a percentage of personal income is anticipated to increase revenue capacity. Household Internet access should increase revenue capacity, because it represents a greater threat to taxing remote sales and an increased need to diversify revenue sources. A high level of dependence by the state on retail sales should decrease revenue capacity.

Results

The results of the models of adequacy of revenue, fairness of revenue, management of revenue, and revenue capacity are illustrated in Table 5.

Ordinary Least Squares (OLS) regression is the appropriate statistical procedure to use when working with a continuous dependent variable. The results from the OLS regressions of the revenue adequacy variable suggest no statistically significant coefficients for the taxing of electronic commerce variables. Other results show that as state sales tax as a percent of revenue increases, there will be a decrease in adequacy of revenue by about half of a point. Second, as the tax base increases, there will be a rise in adequacy of state revenue by half of a point. Third, as state retail sales tax rises, there will be a decrease in adequacy by one-third of a point. The adjusted R^2 for the adequacy model was 0.41, and the F-statistic suggested that the model as a whole was statistically significant.

The second capacity variable tested was the fairness of the state revenue system, which suggests more robust results than the adequacy variable (Table 5). The results of the regression suggest that states that tax Internet access will increase fairness of their tax system by around one-third of a point. Second, for states that have a

Table 5. Regressions of adequacy, fairness, management, and revenue capacity tested against taxing electronic commerce issues

	Dependent Variables											
	Adequacy of Revenue			Fairness of Revenue			Management of Revenue			Revenue Capacity Index		
Independent Variables	Beta	t-statistic	Significant	Beta	t-statistic	Significant	Beta	t-statistic	Significant	Beta	t-statistic	Significant
Constant	1.72	(1.52)	0.14	1.55	(2.39)**	0.02	0.21	(0.18)	0.85	1.16	(1.75)	0.09
Tax Internet Access	0.22	(1.58)	0.12	0.30	(2.76)***	0.01	-0.10	(-0.68)	0.50	0.20	(1.43)	0.16
State Sales Tax	0.16	(0.71)	0.48	-0.39	(-2.23)**	0.03	-0.04	(-0.16)	0.87	-0.09	(-0.41)	0.68
Tax Downloads	-0.03	(-0.19)	0.85	-0.04	(-0.31)	0.76	0.22	(1.36)	0.18	0.09	(0.56)	0.58
Streamlined Sales Tax Project	0.00	(0.01)	0.99	-0.11	(-1.04)	0.31	0.19	(1.26)	0.22	0.05	(0.37)	0.71
State Sales Tax % State Revenue	-0.45	(-2.16)**	0.04	-0.52	(-3.16)***	0.00	0.06	(0.26)	0.79	-0.45	(-2.12)**	0.04
Sales Tax Base % Personal Income	0.49	(2.23)**	0.03	0.72	(4.19)***	0.00	-0.23	(-1.00)	0.32	0.47	(2.08)**	0.04
% Households with Internet Access	0.02	(0.14)	0.89	0.23	(2.09)**	0.04	0.36	(2.39)**	0.02	0.31	(2.10)**	0.04
State Retail Sales % of U.S.	-0.31	(-2.09)**	0.04	-0.25	(-2.19)**	0.03	0.22	(1.43)	0.16	-0.17	(-1.10)	0.28
Model Diagnostics												
F-statistic		(2.59)**	0.02		(7.31)***	0.00		(1.78)*	0.10		(2.15)**	0.05
Adjusted-R^2		0.41			0.71			0.30			0.36	
N		50			50			50			50	

Notes: ** significant at 0.05 level; *** significant at 0.01 level; electronic commerce variables are shaded.

sales tax, which implies the ability to tax Internet sales, fairness decreases by more than one-third of a point. Third, as sales tax revenue increases as a percentage of revenue, the fairness of the revenue system will decrease by around half of a point. Fourth, as the sales tax base of the state rises, fairness increases by more than two-thirds of a point. An increase in household Internet access means that fairness will increase by about one-fifth of a point. Finally, an increase in retail sales tax will decrease fairness by a quarter of a point. The adjusted R^2 for this model was significantly higher than the previously mentioned adequacy model, suggesting that two-thirds of the variance is explained by fairness.

The third capacity variable examined was management capacity (Table 5). The only predictor of management capacity was household Internet access, which increased by one-third of a point. This would suggest that wealthier states have a greater ability to access the Internet, having more resources devoted to management of their revenue systems.

The last OLS regression model is a combination of the previously mentioned capacity variables (Table 5). First, an increase in sales tax revenue as a percentage of state revenue will decrease revenue capacity by almost half of a point. Second, as the tax base rises, the revenue capacity will increase by half of a point. Third, Internet access increases capacity by one-third of a point. The results for the revenue capacity variable, however, do not show any significant impact from taxing electronic commerce.

The overriding message from the empirical results suggests some initial support only for Hypotheses 2 of the impact of electronic commerce tax variables on revenue fairness. If a state has a sales tax, there will be a decrease in revenue fairness. In addition, those states that tax Internet access will increase the fairness of the revenue system.

The following section concludes by providing an assessment of why fairness is the most important predictor of taxing electronic commerce and discusses some policy recommendations and limitations of this research.

CONCLUSION

This article has demonstrated how the existing sales tax system compares to the principles of a high-quality revenue system. The key contribution of this study is looking at the impact of electronic commerce on revenue capacity in contrast to the existing empirical work, which has focused on consumers' reactions to electronic commerce taxation or the socioeconomic and political factors that influence electronic commerce taxation.

The first part of this article showed that, when it comes to taxing Internet sales, the existing sales tax system violates all nine principles in areas broadly defined as adequacy, fairness, and management of the state revenue system. In adequacy of revenues, some states have incurred significant revenue losses because of remote sales. These losses are estimated to be in the range of 1-10%. In addition, losses are compounded by the sales tax base shrinking, partly because electronic commerce is no longer the dominant revenue source for states. In the fairness of revenue system category, the sales tax is already a regressive tax. The taxing of Internet sales makes it even more so, because those that are more affluent have greater Internet access. Finally, management of revenues is difficult, since vendors are not required to collect sales taxes on remote purchases (but they can volunteer to do so), unless they have a physical presence or nexus within the purchaser's state. On the one hand, businesses want to avoid charging sales taxes to customers, because it represents a discount for customers and an increase in the vendors' profits. On the other hand, the public is generally not aware that they are required to pay the use tax, if it is not collected by vendors. This explains the low consumer compliance rate.

The second part of this article tested several models that examined the impact of electronic commerce on state revenue capacity; it essentially tested the nine principles of a high-quality tax system outlined in the first part of this article. The results suggested that the most important determinant of taxing electronic commerce was the fairness of the state revenue system. Referring back to the first part of this article, only Principles 4 through 6 (fairness of the revenue system) of a high quality revenue system were supported in the empirical results. There was some initial evidence that fairness decreases when states have a sales tax and that it increases when states tax Internet access. These quantitative results are similar to those reported by existing public finance and legal scholars (McLure, 2002a, 2002b; Mikesell, 2001). Indeed, with the narrowing of the sales tax base, there has been a shift away from the sales tax as the dominant revenue source for state governments (Mikesell, 2004).

Long-Term and Short-Term Policy Recommendations

Some long-term and short-term policy recommendations for taxing electronic commerce sales are outlined in this section. One long-term solution is for state and local governments that now depend on sales tax revenues to substitute other taxes, such as income taxes (Litan & Rivlin, 2001). If the decline in the sales tax base accelerates because of a rapid increase in electronic commerce sales, some or many jurisdictions may be tempted to act on their own, replacing the revenue with other sources. Another long-term solution is for the federal government to reduce its dependence on income taxes in favor of a national sales tax or value-added tax. Since the federal government can tax sales wherever they occur, a federal sales or value-added tax automatically would solve the

problem of treating electronic commerce and other remote sales equally. However, with the general anti-tax sentiment in the United States, this may be a difficult sell for politicians in the short term (Mikesell, 2001).

Since it is not very likely that there will be a major overhaul of the tax systems of state or federal governments in the near future, then what can be done in the short-term? One possible solution is for states to be more aggressive in the enforcement of collecting use taxes owed by consumers. What often gets confused is that the sales tax is not owed, if the firm does not have nexus, or a physical presence, in the state where the Internet purchaser resides. When this is the case, the consumer is required to remit the use tax to his or her state taxing authority. Two approaches are used for collecting use taxes from consumers. The first approach is the individual income tax reporting booklet that is mailed to taxpayers with filing instructions. The second approach is a use tax reporting line on the state income tax return itself, with instructions on how the owed amount would be computed. In 2003, 19 of 38 states provided information for taxpayers to report use tax obligations on their individual state income tax returns, and another eight provide information about the use tax in the individual income tax booklets (Manzi, 2003). The consumer participation rates for use tax compliance are extremely low at around 1.5%. However, states such as Maine, Michigan, and North Carolina have been more successful and have achieved compliance rates moderately above that level.

Limitations of this Study

There are some limitations to this study that should be mentioned. First, the four-star rating system cannot capture many factors that possibly could influence revenue capacity, because it is limited to a small number of categories. Second, this study has conducted 32 tests (four dependent variables times eight independent variables) with a sample size of 50. As a result, the chances of including errors are greater with such a small sample size. Therefore, the findings should be viewed as suggestive and not definitive. Third, there is also the limitation of using secondary data in the analysis of the impact of electronic commerce on revenue capacity, since the four-star rating system is a subjective measure. However, this study is different from existing work, in that it combines both qualitative research (how taxing electronic commerce compares against nine principle of an effective revenue system) and quantitative research (testing these principles with a model of how electronic commerce affects revenue capacity).

Future research could examine citizens' perceptions concerning the taxing of electronic commerce. There is much written on state governments' reaction to taxing electronic commerce; however, more needs to be known about citizens' perceptions of taxing Internet sales. The existing literature indicates that politically it is very difficult to find enough common ground among 45 states and 36 local governments on streamlining their sales tax systems through the SSTP (Cornia et al., 2004). Discerning what public support exists for taxing electronic commerce should provide some indication of the extent of reform that politicians could achieve by addressing this important tax issue.

ACKNOWLEDGMENT

The author would like to thank the associate editor and anonymous reviewers of this article for their helpful comments.

REFERENCES

Alm, J., & Melnik, M.I. (2005). Sales taxes and the decision to purchase online. *Public Finance Review, 33*(2), 184-212.

Barrett, K., Greene, R., Michele Mariani, M., & Sostek, A. (2003). The way we tax: A 50 state report. *Governing Magazine, 16*(5), 20-97.

Berry, W. D., Richard, C., & Fording, R. C. (1997). Measuring state tax capacity and effort. *Social Science Quarterly, 78*(1), 158-166.

Best, S., & Teske, P. (2002). Explaining state Internet sales taxation: New economy, old-fashion interest group politics. *State Politics and Policy Quarterly, 2*(1), 37-51.

Bruce, D., Deskins, J., & Fox, W. F. (2004). Has Internet access taxation affected Internet use? *Public Finance Review, 32*(2), 131-147.

Bruce, D., Fox, W., & Murray, M. (2003). To Tax or not to tax? The case of electronic commerce. *Contemporary Economic Policy, 21*(1), 25-40.

Bruce, D., & Fox, W. F. (2001a). *State and local sales tax revenue losses from e-commerce: Updated estimates*. Knoxville, TN: Center for Business and Economic Research.

Bruce, D., & Fox, W. F. (2001b). E-commerce and local finance: Estimates of direct and indirect sales tax losses. *Municipal Finance Journal, 22*(3), 24-47.

Brunori, D. (2001). *State tax policy: A political perspective*. Washington, DC: The Urban Institute Press.

Cameron, A. C. (2004). Factors leading to state participation in the streamlined sales tax project. *Journal of Public Budgeting, Accounting, & Financial Management, 16*(4), 80-108.

CCH. (2004). *CCH tax research network*. Riverwoods, IL: CCH Incorporated.

Clay, K., & Strauss, R. P. (2000). Trust, risk, and electronic commerce: 19th century lessons for the 21st century. *State Tax Notes, 19*, 1701-1710.

Cline, R. J., & Neubig, T. S. (1999). *Masters of complexity and bearers of great burden: The sales tax system and compliance costs for multistate retailers* [technical report]. Ernst and Young.

Cockfield, A. J. (2002). Walmart.com: A case study of entity isolation. *State Tax Notes, 25*, 633-701.

Congressional Budget Office (CBO). (2003). *Economic issues in taxing Internet and mail-order sales.* Washington, DC: Congress of the United States Congressional Budget Office.

Cornia, G. C., Sjoquist, D. L., & Walters, L. C. (2004). Sales and use tax simplification and voluntary compliance. *Public Budgeting & Finance, 24*(1), 1-31.

Due, J. F., & Mikesell, J. L. (1994). *Sales taxation: State and local structure and administration* (2nd ed.). Washington, DC: Urban Institute Press.

Fox, W. F., & Murray, M. (1997). The sales tax and electronic commerce: So what's new? *National Tax Journal, 50*(3), 573-592.

General Accounting Office (GAO). (2000). *Sales taxes: Electronic commerce growth presents challenges; revenue losses are uncertain.* Washington, DC: United States General Accounting Office.

Goolsbee, A. (2000). In a world without borders: The impact of taxes on Internet commerce. *Quarterly Journal of Economics, 115*(2), 561-576.

Goolsbee, A., & Zittrain, J. (1999). Evaluating the costs and benefits of taxing Internet commerce. *National Tax Journal, 52*(3), 413-428.

Governing Magazine. (2003). *State and local source book 2003.* Washington, DC: Congressional Quarterly Press.

Hellerstein, W. (1998). Electronic commerce and the future of state taxation. In D. Brunori (Ed.), *The future of state taxation* (pp. 207-222). Washington, DC: The Urban Institute Press.

Litan, R. E., & Rivlin, A. M. (2001). *beyond the dot.coms: The economic promise of the Internet.* Washington, DC: Brookings Institution Press.

Manzi, N. (2003). *Use tax collection on income tax returns in other states* [policy brief]. Minneapolis: Minnesota House of Representatives Research Department.

McLure, C. E. (2000). The taxation of electronic commerce: Background and proposal. In N. Imparato (Ed.), *Public policy and the Internet: Privacy, taxes, and contract* (pp. 49-113). Stanford, CA: Hoover Institution Press.

McLure, C. E. (2002a). Thinking straight about the taxation of electronic commerce: Tax principles, compliance problems, and nexus. *NBER/Tax Policy & the Economy, 16*(1), 115-140.

McLure, C. E. (2002b). Sales and use taxes on electronic commerce: Legal, economic, administrative, and political issues. *The Urban Lawyer, 34*(2), 487-520.

Mikesell, J. L. (2000). Remote vendors and American sales and use taxation: The balance between fixing the problem and fixing the tax. *National Tax Journal, 53*(4), 1273-1285.

Mikesell, J. L. (2001). The threat to state sales taxes from e-commerce: A review of the principal issues. *Municipal Finance Journal, 22*(3), 48-60.

Mikesell, J. L. (2004). The prospects for general sales taxation in American state and local government finance: Challenges for a fiscal workhorse unready for the new millennium. *Journal of Public Budgeting, Accounting, & Financial Management, 16*(1), 63-79.

National Conference of State Legislatures (NCSL). (1992). *Principles of a high-quality state revenue system.* Washington, DC: National Conference of State Legislatures. Retrieved June 1, 2005, from www.ncsl.org.

Nesbary, D. (2000). The taxation of Internet commerce. *Social Science Computer Review, 18*(1), 17-39.

Vijayasarathy, L. R. (2002). Internet taxation, privacy and security: Opinions of the taxed and legislated. *Quarterly Journal of Electronic Commerce, 3*(1), 53-71.

Yang, J., & Poon, W. (2001). Taxable base of Internet commerce. *Municipal Finance Journal, 22*(3), 70-80.

This work was previously published in Journal of Electronic Commerce in Organizations, Vol. 4, Issue 2, edited by M. Khosrow-Pour, pp. 40-61, copyright 2006 by IGI Publishing, formerly known as Idea Group Publishing (an imprint of IGI Global).

Chapter III
Searching for Value in Researching the Adoption and Use of M-Services

Craig Standing
Edith Cowan University, Western Australia

Patricia McManus
Edith Cowan University, Western Australia

Susan Standing
Edith Cowan University, Western Australia

Heikki Karjaluoto
University of Oulu, Finland

ABSTRACT

Mobile services (m-services) have become an important part of the e-commerce landscape. Although research has been conducted on which services people use and the benefits they attach to those services, the values associated with the adoption and use of m-services at the individual level is still unclear. This article addresses the question of why and how individuals adopt and appropriate m-services with a particular focus on m-communication? In the information systems field, various technology adoption models have been proposed and validated in relation to technology adoption within an organisational setting, but personal adoption and use of technology is less researched. We propose the use of means-end chains and laddering techniques to determine the basic primitive values that are fulfilled for the individual by using various m-services. The examples presented show that mobile services often fulfill such basic needs as self-esteem, achievement, individuality, belonging, and well-being. Exploring the realization of values as a theoretical framework offers researchers a way forward in environments characterised by individual technology decisions.

INTRODUCTION

Various theories are used in information systems to determine the patterns of adoption of technologies at an organisational level. However, the reasons for adoption of technologies and services at the individual level are less understood. The aim of this article is to determine the reasons for m-services adoption and usage at the individual level. Means-end chains and laddering are explained and examples are used to show the reasons underpinning different consumer value choice perceptions. Finally, the significance of value based theories, as an explanatory theory at the individual level, is assessed.

Industry analysts have high expectations of the consumers' willingness to adopt mobile services. However, there is still uncertainty in relation to understanding why an individual adopts electronic channels, and the intrinsic influential factors, such as consumers' attitudes and values in relation to electronic channels (Venkatesh & Brown, 2001; Anckar, 2002). Anckar (2002, p. 3) pointed out that "The main reason for value-adding elements in m-commerce, the consumers' actual reasons—the primary drivers for adopting m-commerce remain unclear." The importance of understanding what motivates adoption becomes even more critical for m-services as adoption rates are expected to rapidly increase (Anckar, 2002). Some of the reasons behind this optimistic forecast are the low cost associated with m-commerce hardware (e.g., mobile telephones) and consumers' familiarity with mobile telephones (Ropers, 2001; Anckar, 2002).

DEFINITIONS OF MOBILE COMMERCE

Mobile services embrace terms such as mobile communication, mobile collaboration, and mobile commerce (Sarker & Wells, 2003). Whilst there is some overlap between these terms, it can be argued that mobile communication includes voice, Short Messaging Service (SMS), and Multimedia Messaging Service (MMS), whilst the same services can be used to collaborate on projects and can additionally draw upon information and news from Web sites. Mobile commerce involves information, news, and the purchase of physical goods and services. In this article, the term m-services is used to describe the ability to send and receive communication and purchase goods/services through a wireless public (e.g., Internet) or private network enabled device, like a mobile telephone or a personal digital assistant (Balasubramanian, Peterson, & Jarvenpaa., 2002; Clark, 2001, Han, Harkke, Landor, & Mio, 2002; Junglas, 2002).

It is argued that the main difference between e-commerce and m-commerce is that m-commerce is associated with wireless technologies (Clark, 2001; Anckar & D'Incau, 2002; Han et al., 2002; Turban, McLean, & Wetherbe, 2002). For example, Turban et al. (2002, p. 28) have defined m-commerce as the "Conduct of e-commerce via wireless devices." The basic definition of wireless is: "The absence of a physical link between the sending and receiving devices," (Balasubramanian et al., 2002). It is important to clarify the terminology, since it is easy for the concept of m-commerce to be mistaken for its underlying technologies (applications and devices) (Balasubramanian et al., 2002; Han et al., 2002).

Three key characteristics of m-commerce are portability, ubiquity, and addressability.

Portability

Portability refers to the mobility aspects of communication devices. The portability construct implies that there is no fixed physical location at the device or application level, that is, an individual can take the device anywhere (Muller, 1999; Balasubramanian et al., 2002; Turban et al., 2002; Junglas, 2002; Microsoft, 2003).

Ubiquity

The ubiquity construct comprises the two characteristics of reach and accessibility. The combination of these two characteristics mean that an individual can be contacted or make a contact at any time from anywhere, in other words, time and space are made irrelevant (Muller, 1999; Balasubramanian et al., 2002; Turban et al., 2002; Junglas, 2002; Lyytinen & Yoo, 2002).

Addressability

Blattberg and Deighton (1991, p. 6) have defined an address as "Anything that locates the customer uniquely in time and space." In most m-commerce definitions, authors have used the word localization (see Muller, 1999; Junglas, 2002; Turban et al., 2002) to describe the characteristics of positioning services like Global Positioning System (GPS) that enable consumers and marketers to push (send) or receive information in the context of where the consumer is located at that moment.

These three concepts help us to define the conceptual significance of mobile commerce independent of the hardware.

THEORETICAL PERSPECTIVES ON M-SERVICES ADOPTION AND USE

This section of the article examines the factors that drive consumers' adoption and willingness to adopt and use m-services.

There has been a number of m-commerce consumer adoption studies conducted. Barnes and Huff (2003) use Rogers' (1995) innovation and diffusion theory to examine the diffusion of Internet access via mobile telephones (iMode). Rogers developed a number of characteristics that explain innovation diffusion: (1) Relative advantage: the degree to which the technology provides an advantage over other methods, (2) Compatibility: the degree to which the technology is compatible with how people work or behave, (3) Complexity: whether people perceive the technology as easy to understand and use, (4) Trialability: the degree to which a technology can be trialled before being adopted, and (5) Observability: the level of visibility of the product to the other members of the adopter's social group.

Barnes and Huff (2003) conclude that iMode's success in Japan is unlikely to be replicated to the same extent in other countries, since the conditions that prevailed in Japan do not exist elsewhere to the same extent. The low level of PC adoption, high market saturation of mobile telephones, and fierce competition between trusted brands, who are putting together cost-effective mobile Internet packages, enable consumers in Japan to readily access mobile services.

Studies related to advertising and marketing are closely associated with consumer attitudes and built around the Theory of Reasoned Action (TRA) (Ajzen & Fishbein, 1980; Fishbein & Ajzen, 1975) and its applications to IT settings. The theory provides a framework to understand why people behave as they do when making decisions. TRA proposes that the use of technology can be predicted by a person's behavioural intention and that this is determined by a person's attitude towards using the technology. A person's attitude is shaped by their positive or negative feelings towards performing a specific behaviour (or using a technology) and whether people who are personally important, typically in the workplace, think that they should or should not perform the behaviour.

Using a form of TRA, Tsang, Ho, and Liang (2004) examine the link between attitude, intention, and behaviour in relation to m-marketing. In their model entertainment, information content, irritation, and credibility are seen to shape attitudes with permission having a major impact. The availability of incentives, such as free calls, impacts on the intention to receive m-marketing for certain attitudes. Intention is directly related to behaviour in relation to m-marketing. Their study findings indicate that consumers have a negative attitude towards mobile advertising, unless they have consented to it. All four attributes of mobile advertising impact significantly on attitude towards mobile advertising. Attitude was significantly correlated to intention, with incentives also positively impacting on intention. There was a strong correlation between intention and behaviour. This study was conducted in Taiwan with a large percentage of respondents regularly using SMS, although it is unclear from the results presented the extent to which respondents had received mobile advertising.

The Technology Acceptance Model (TAM) (Davies, 1989; Davis, Bagozzi, & Warshaw, 1989; Davis & Venkatesh, 1996; Mathieson, 1991) is tailored to information systems contexts and is designed to predict IT acceptance and usage in the workplace. It focuses on perceived usefulness of the technology and perceived ease of use. In m-commerce adoption research, Wu and Wang (2004) perceived ease of use was not found to be significant. TAM has been extended to include a third belief called perceived enjoyment (Davis, Bagozzi, & Warshaw, 1992), where using the computer is perceived to be enjoyable in its own right (hedonic) and quite separate from performance issues (Van der Heijden, 2004). The consumer behaviour literature shows that utilitarian, in the sense of instrumental value, or hedonic benefits, determine the intention to consume. In some m-commerce studies, hedonistic factors, including entertainment value, have been considered as

significant (Bauer, Barnes, Reichardt, & Neumann, 2005).

As there are a number of adoption models available to researchers, Venkatesh, Morris, Davis, and Davis (2003) synthesized the main models in order to provide a unified view of user acceptance. The unified model identifies determinants and moderators related to intention and it suggests intention is a predictor of user behaviour. Four factors impact on intention and usage: performance expectancy, effort expectancy, social influence, and facilitating conditions. The key moderators are gender, age, experience, and voluntary use. Interestingly, attitude was considered to overlap with performance and effort expectancies. The non-significance of attitude in the presence of these two other constructs has been supported in a number of other studies (Taylor & Todd, 1995). In empirical studies, the unified model was found to be a substantial improvement on any of the other earlier models. Standing, Benson, and Karjaluoto (2005) used a version of the unified theory to determine significant factors in the decision to participate in m-marketing schemes and found that granting permission, financial savings, and highly relevant information were significant factors in the decision to participate, but that the time and effort involved in processing m-marketing messages were not considered important. Work on technology acceptance is still evolving with, for example, studies that integrate user satisfaction constructs with technology acceptance constructs (Wixom & Todd, 2005).

Consumer adoption related factors can be summarized as including the consumer's general attitude toward the technology, level of involvement, innovation, response to stimuli, trust, and perceptions of utility, choice, control, and risk. Demographic factors (age, gender, income, education) have also been found to be important control variables to consider when looking at consumer acceptance of m-services (Barnes & Scornavacca, 2004; Tsang et al., 2004).

Although it is widely recognized that younger consumers have embraced mobile technology, it is being increasingly recognized that factors beyond age or gender may be important. It can be argued that segmenting people on the basis of their acceptance and use of technology as well as their lifestyle motivations is more representative of their actual behaviour (Sultan & Rohm, 2005). Consumers' adoption of new technologies/services depends on a number of factors, for example, the type of service to be offered, how comfortable people feel using the technology, how user friendly the service interface is, socio-economic factors, motivations (benefits), culture, demographics and psychographics, amount of time that the customer expects to use the service, and past experience (Daghfous, Petrof, & Pons, 1999; Sultan & Henrichs, 2000). Sarker and Wells (2003) provide a framework for understanding the adoption and use of mobile devices that includes most of these factors. Their model considers not only the decision made in the initial adoption, but also how users appropriate the technology and services through exploration and experimentation. They argue that users assess their experiences on three dimensions: functional (e.g., time savings), psychosocial (e.g., safety, elevated self-worth, sense of freedom), and relational (building relationships).

THE CONCEPTUALISATION OF VALUE AND VALUES

The concept of values is a theme of research in a range of social science disciplines including: anthropology, economics, education, history, marketing, political science, psychology, and sociology (Rokeach, 1973). Generally, the concept of value has two different connotations: Values as an individual core belief, and as a perceived direct or indirect benefit of a product/service (Rokeach, 1973). The meaning of "perceived value" (or value) is drawn from definitions related to the "value-for-money" concept. Valerie Zeithaml's (1988) definition is one of the most widely accepted (see Woodruff, 1997, Sweeney, Soutar, & Johnson, 1999; Anckar & D'Incau, 2002). She depicts value as: "The consumers' overall assessment of the utility of a product based on their perception of what is received and what is given," (Zeithaml, 1988, p. 14). The concept of perceived value can be called product value as it refers to what consumers' value in terms of product characteristics/benefits. This concept has been considered an important source of competitive advantage for manufactures and retailers (Sheth, Newman, & Gross, 1991a; Woodruff, 1999; Forester, 1999; Sweeney & Soutar, 2001).

Sheth, Newman, and Gross (1991a, 1991b) conceptualized a model to help explain how consumers make decisions in the marketplace. They based their model on the principle that the choices consumers make are based on their perceived values in relation to what the authors called "market choice." Sheth et al., (1991a) classify five categories of perceived value. Functional values are associated with the utility level of the product (or service) compared to its alternatives. Social values could be compared with the subjective norm dimension in the Theory of Planned Behaviour, as it is associated with willingness to please and social acceptance. Emotional values are those choices made based upon feelings and aesthetics. Epistemic values can be used to describe the early adopters in the sense that it relates to novelty or knowledge searching behaviour. Finally, the conditional value refers to a set of circumstances that depend upon the situation (e.g., Christmas, wedding, and so forth). Socio-economic and physical aspects are included in this value. These five values were conceptualised based on a diversity of disciplines including: social psychology, clinical psychology, sociology, economics, and experimental psychology (Sheth et al., 1991a).

Means-End Chains

The concept of values is also addressed through means-end chains. The means-end chain concept concentrates on the systematic relationship between three level of values: product/service attributes, consequences, and personal values (Gutman, 1982; Reynolds & Gutman, 1988). This model represents how the consumption of a product enables the consumer's realization of his/hers desired ends. The central aspect of this theory is that "…consumers choose actions that produce desired consequences and minimize undesirable consequences," (Gutman, 1982, p. 61).

In Gutman's (1982) model, product attributes are understood as all tangible and intangible product characteristics such as size, weight, colour, and so forth. Consequences are defined as the physiological or psychological results acquired directly or indirectly by the consumer from his/her behaviour (product or service use). Sheth's et al. (1991a) theory of Consumption Values does not represent end states of existence, but expected benefits (consequences) from consuming that particular product or service.

The personal value construct in this model is drawn from the concept used in psychology and sociology and relates to Rokeach's construct of human/personal values. Rokeach (1973) identified two types of values: instrumental and terminal. Instrumental values relate to those values that act like tools in achieving end-state behaviours (values like courage, honesty, ethics, and so forth). Terminal values, also used by Gutman (1982), refer to "Preferred end-states of existence" (Gutman, 1982, p. 63), for example: accomplishment, happiness, and satisfaction. Gutman's model (1982) has two basic underlying assumptions: (1) Values are connected to consequences as long as the consequences have positive or negative connotations, and (2) Consequences have a direct relationship with product attributes as long as

Figure 1. Means-end chain

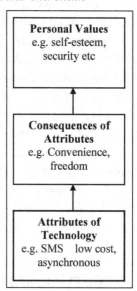

Table 1. Personal values (Gutman, 1982; Rokeach, 1973)

Self esteem	Achievement/fulfilment
Security	Nurturer
Belonging	Well Being
Independence	Honesty/responsibility
Acceptance	Grounded
Individuality	Moral
Happiness	

consumers obtain the products which may cause the desired benefits.

The three levels of product attributes, consequences, and personal values are hierarchically interconnected (Figure 1). The lower level values are an instrument for consumers to reach their desirable end values (higher levels) (Gutman, 1982; Reynolds & Gutman, 1988). The central aspect of this model assumes that consumers will behave in a way to obtain the desired or positive consequences and minimize the undesirable or negative consequences (Leao & Mello, 2001, 2002). The end values as explained previously are ideal end-states or goals.

Laddering Technique

The laddering technique is a method used to reveal the means-end hierarchy (Gutman, 1982; Reynolds & Gutman, 1988; Leao & Mello, 2002). This ladder refers to the relationship between the three levels of values or abstractions (attribute, consequence, and value). It represents the connection between the actual product and the user's cognitive process that leads to a direct and useful understanding of his/hers perceptual orientation in relation to the service. The laddering technique is an in-depth individual interview used to understand consumers' decisions. It translates product attributes into associations relevant to the users "self," based on the means-end chain model. This is done through sequentially asking the respondent the reason why that attribute/consequence was important to him or her (Reynolds & Gutman, 1988). The goal of this strategy of enquiry is to allow the researcher to get to users' actual root reasons for using that particular mobile service (Reynolds & Gutman, 1988). Because this technique can be perceived by the respondent as obvious and intrusive, it is paramount that the researcher pays particular attention to the interview environment. The environment needs to be friendly and conducive to introspection in order to seek the underlying drivers behind a given mobile service (Reynolds

& Gutman, 1988). It is fundamental that the interviewee perceives the interviewer as very interested and, at the same time, as neutral; his only job is to record the information provided (Reynolds & Gutman, 1982).

The result of the laddering process is a series of cognitive maps or hierarchical value maps (HMV) that show the aggregate consumer means-end chains that link the product or service characteristics with consumer's values.

We applied the mean-end chain and laddering approach to the investigation of the adoption of m-services. For each person, an interview lasting between forty minutes to an hour involving closed and open-ended questions was carried out. The questions asked addressed issues related to the respondents' background, personal and family life (significant life events), and personality traits. Then, questions were asked about the mobile services they use, usage intensity, and reasons for using those particular services/features. An assessment of motives for using particular services was analysed following a laddering approach. This involved why they used the service and what benefits they obtained and this line of enquiry was pursued to obtain the personal values behind the consequences. The following conceptual maps are the result of analysing 28 interviews with mobile service users. The interviewees represent a convenience sample of m-service users and covered late teenagers through to retirees.

When the data are synthesised and analysed from the 28 interviews, three broad patterns emerge. These patterns can be classified under relational, achievement, and individual/well-being. The relational map (Figure 2) centres around the use of communication to keep in contact and stay connected in order to achieve a sense of belonging and/or acceptance by a group (typically work group). Both of these values can have a positive impact on self-esteem.

Mobile services, including games, streaming video, and ring tones, provide fun and entertainment, which create a sense of well-being and

Figure 2. Relational map

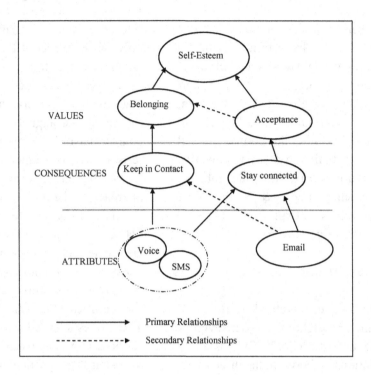

Figure 3. Individuality/well being map

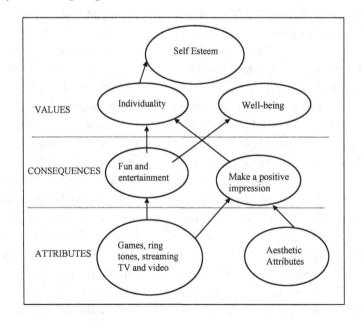

individuality that also link to self-esteem. The aesthetic appeal of mobile phones (colour, style) can make a positive impression on people and can support the value of individuality (Figure 3). Figure 4 revolves around the use of communication to provide convenience and organisation to improve efficiency. The key value here is sense of achievement, which also links to self-esteem.

CONCLUSION

In this article, we have proposed that adoption of m-services at the individual level can be better understood through the use of means-end theory and a laddering methodology. We argue that the emphasis given to values through means-end theory takes research on the adoption of technology and services to another level. Much of the research to date on technology adoption has examined technology adoption in organisational settings. Adoption of mobile services typically requires decisions to be made at the individual level, yet few researchers are investigating the primitive value drivers. Our study with a small sample of mobile-service users illustrates how means-end chain theory and a laddering style of enquiry can uncover the real value of m-services.

The three cognitive association maps may not be a definitive group for the m-services area. Rather, we propose them as a starting point for further research. Nor are the maps mutually exclusive. Mobile services have a functional value as they are convenient, but the decision to adopt may often be combined with the desire to feel part of a group or community of use. Indeed, the erosion of boundaries between work, home, leisure, learning, and education, partly brought about by mobile technology, means that people may have multiple reasons for adopting or using services. Mobile technology can serve multiple needs including, family, friends, work, and curiosity, or learning.

The ideas proposed in this article are currently being tested through a large scale study that involves interviewing over a hundred users of m-services. When this is completed we should be nearer developing a predictive model of m-service adoption. These findings may also be applicable to the adoption of other technologies at the individual level.

REFERENCES

Anckar, B. (2002). Adoption drivers and intents in the mobile electronic marketplace: Survey findings. *Journal of Systems and Information Technology, 6*(2), 1-17.

Anckar, B., & D'Incau, D. (2002). Value creation in mobile commerce: Findings from a consumer survey. *The Journal of Information Technology Theory and Application (JITTA), 4*(1), 43-64.

Ajzen, I., & Fishbein, M. (1980). *Understanding attitudes and predicting social behavior.* Englewood Cliffs, NJ: Prentice-Hall.

Balasubramanian, S., Peterson, R. A., & Jarvenpaa, S. L. (2002). Exploring the implications of m-commerce for markets and marketing. *Journal of the Academy of Marketing Science, 30*(4), 348-36.

Barnes, S., & Huff, S. (2003). Rising sun: iMode and the wireless Internet. *Communications of the ACM, 46*(11), 79-84.

Barnes, S., & Scornavacca, E. (2004). Mobile marketing: The role of permission and acceptance. *International Journal of Mobile Communications, 2*(2), 128-139.

Bauer, H. H., Barnes, S. J., Reichardt, T., & Neumann, M. M. (2005). Driving consumer acceptance of mobile marketing: A theoretical framework and empirical study. *Journal of Electronic Commerce Research, 6*(3), 181-192.

Blattberg, R. C., & Deighton, J. (1991). Interactive marketing: Exploiting the age of addressability. *Sloan Management Review, Fall*, 5-14.

Carroll, A., Barnes, S. J., & Scornavacca, E. (2005, July 11-13). Consumers' perceptions and attitudes towards SMS mobile marketing in New Zealand. In *Proceedings of the Fourth International Conference on Mobile Business (ICMB)* (pp. 434-440). Sydney, Australia.

Clark III, I. (2001). Emerging value propositions for m-commerce. *Journal of Business Strategies, 18*(2), 133-148.

Daghfous, N., Petrof, J. V., & Pons, F. (1999). Values and adoption of innovations: A cross cultural study. *Journal of Consumer Marketing, 16*(14), 314-331.

Davies, F. (1989). Perceived usefulness, perceived easy of use and user acceptance of information technology. *MIS Quarterly, 13*(3), 319-340.

Davis, F. D., Bagozzi, R. P., & Warshaw, P. R. (1989). User acceptance of computer technology: A comparison of two theoretical models. *Management Science, 35*(8), 982-1003.

Davis, F. D., Bagozzi, R. P., & Warshaw, P. R. (1992). Extrinsic and intrinsic motivation to use computers in the workplace. *Journal of Applied Social Psychology, 22*(14), 1111-1132.

Davis, F.D., & Venkatesh, V. (1996). A critical assessment of potential measurement biases in the technology acceptance model: Three experiments. *International Journal of Human-Computer Studies, 45*(1), 19-45.

Dickinger, A., & Haghirian, P. (2004, January, 5-8). An investigation and conceptual model of SMS marketing. In *Proceedings of the 37th Hawaii International Conference on System Sciences (HICSS-37)*, Hawaii, USA, CD-ROM.

Fishbein, M., & Ajzen, I. (1975). *Belief, attitude, intention, and behavior: An introduction to theory and research*. Reading, MA: Addison-Wesley.

Forester, M. (1999). Deja vu discussion delivers message emphasizing value. *Chain Store Age, 75(April)*, 12.

Gutman, J. (1982). A means-end chain model based on consumer categorization processes. *Journal of Marketing, 46(Spring)*, 60-72.

Haghirian, P., & Madlberger, M. (2005). Consumer attitude toward advertising via mobile devices - an empirical investigation among Austrian users. In *Proceedings of the 13th European Conference on Information Systems, Regensburg, Germany, May 26-28*. Retrieved February 21, 2006, from http://is2.lse.ac.uk/asp/aspecis/20050038.pdf.

Han, J., & Han, D. (2001). A framework for analysing customer value of internet business. *Journal of Information Technology Theory and Application (JITTA), 3*(5), 25-38.

Han, S., Harkke, V., Landor, P., & Mio, R. R. D. (2002). A foresight framework for understanding the future of mobile commerce. *Journal of Systems & Information Technology, 6*(2), 19-39.

Junglas, I. A. (2002). *U-commerce an experimental investigation of ubiquity and uniqueness*. Unpublished Dissertation, University of Georgia, Athens.

Leao, A. L. M. d. S., & Mello, S. C. B. d. (2002). *Conhecendo o valor do cliente virtual: Uma analize utilizando a teoria de cadeias de meios-fim*. Paper presented at the XXVI ENAMPAD, Salvador, Bahia, Brazil.

Lyytinen, K., & Yoo, Y. (2002). Issues and challenges in ubiquitous computing. *Communications of the ACM, 45(12)*, 63-65.

Mathieson, K. (1991). Predicting user intentions: Comparing the technology acceptance model with the theory of planned behavior. *Information Systems Research, 2*(3), 173-191.

Microsoft (2003). *Internet & networking dictionary*. Redmond: Microsoft Press.

Muller, F. (1999). *Mobile commerce report* [Internet]. Retrieved June 11, 2003, from http://www.durlacher.com/bbus/resreports.asp

Rettie, R., & Brum, M. (2001). M-commerce: The role of SMS text messages. In *Proceedings of the Fourth Biennial International Conference on Telecommunications and Information Markets (COTIM 2001)*, Karlsruhe, Germany. Retrieved from http://www.ebusinessforum.gr/content/downloads/047_brum_mcommerce.pdf

Reynolds, T., & Gutman, J. (1988). Laddering theory, theory, method, analysis, and interpretation. *Journal of Advertising Research, 28*(1), 11-31.

Rogers, E. M. (2003). *Diffusion of innovations (5th ed.)*. New York: Free Press.

Rokeach, M. (1973). *The nature of human values*. New York: The Free Press.

Ropers, S. (2001). New business models for the mobile revolution. *EAI, (February)*, 53-57.

Sarker, S., & Wells, J. D. (2003). Understanding mobile handheld device use and adoption. *Communications of the ACM, 46(12)*, 35-40.

Sheth, J. N., Newman, B. I., & Gross, B. L. (1991a). *Consumption values and market choice: Theory and applications* (1991 ed.). South-Western Publishing Co.

Sheth, J. N., Newman, B. I., & Gross, B. L. (1991b). Why we buy what we buy: A theory of consumption values. *Journal of Business Research, 22*, 150-170.

Standing, C., Benson, S., & Karjaluoto, H. (2005, December 5-7). Consumer perspectives on mobile advertising and marketing. In *Proceedings of the Australia and New Zealand Marketing Academy Conference* (pp. 135-141). Perth, Australia [CD-ROM].

Sultan, F., & Rohm, A. (2005). The coming of the era of "brand in the hand" marketing. *MIT Sloan Management Review, 47*(1), 83-90.

Sultan, F., & Henrichs, R. B. (2000). Consumer preferences for Internet services over time: Initial explorations. *Journal of Consumer Marketing, 17*(5),386-402.

Sweeney, J. C., Soutar, G. N., & Johnson, L. W. (1999). The role of perceived risk in the quality-value relationship: A study in a retail environment. *Journal of Retailing, 77*(1), 75-105.

Sweeney, J. C., & Soutar, G. N. (2001). Consumer perceived value: The development pf a multiple item scale. *Journal of Retailing, 77*(2001), 203-220.

Taylor, S., & Todd, P. A. (1995). Assessing IT usage: The role of prior experience. *MIS Quarterly, 19*(2), 561-570.

Tsang, M. M., Ho, S., & Liang, (2004). T. Consumer attitudes toward mobile advertising: An empirical study. *International Journal of Electronic Commerce, 8*(3), 65-78.

Turban, E., McLean, E., & Wetherbe, J. (2002). *Information Technology for management: Transforming business in the digital economy* (3rd ed.). Milton, Queensland: John Wiley & Sons.

Van der Heijden, H. (2004). User acceptance of hedonic information systems. *MIS Quarterly, 28*(4), 695-703.

Venkatesh, V., & Brown, S. A. (2001). A longitudinal investigation of personal computers in homes: Adoption determinants and emerging challenges. *MIS Quarterly, 25*(1), 71-102.

Venkatesh, V., Morris, M. G., Davis, G. B., & Davis, F. D. (2003). User acceptance of information technology: Toward a unified view. *MIS Quarterly, 27*(3), 425-479.

Wixom, B., & Todd, P. A. (2005). A theoretical integration of user satisfaction and technology acceptance. *Information Systems Research, 16*(1), 85-102.

Wu, J.-H., & Wang, S.-C. (2004). What drives mobile commerce? An empirical evaluation of the revised technology acceptance model. *Information & Management, 42*(5), 719-729.

Woodruff, R. B. (1997). Customer value: The next source of competitive advantage. *Journal of the Academy of Marketing Science, 25*(2), 139-153.

Zeithaml, V. A. (1988). Consumer perception of price, quality, and value: A means-end model and synthesis of evidence. *Journal of Marketing, 52*(July), 2-22.

Chapter IV
The Financial Potential of Sporadic Customers in E–Retailing:
Evidence from the Brazilian Home Appliance Sector

Luiz Antonio Joia
Getulio Vargas Foundation, Brazil

Paulo Sergio Sanz
Getulio Vargas Foundation, Brazil

EXECUTIVE SUMMARY

The scope of this article is to explore the transaction profitability of frequent and sporadic buyers in the e-commerce arena. Evidence in relationship marketing literature stressing the impact of purchase frequency on customer transaction profitability as well as recent academic research challenging this approach and pointing out the importance of sporadic clients is analyzed and presented. A single case study research methodology was chosen for this article due to the exploratory facets associated with the subject and the industry under investigation. In order to gather relevant input to carry out this research, one of the largest retailing groups in Brazil was investigated. Conclusions are drawn showing that greater frequency of purchases does not necessarily translate into increased customer transaction profitability. Implications are presented, enabling practitioners and academics to grasp fully the real value of customers — both frequent and sporadic buyers — in order to develop coherent approaches for dealing with them adequately.

INTRODUCTION

Traditional marketing literature suggests that the benefits accrued from long-term relationships between firms and customers are greater than the returns reaped from short-term relationships. Conceptual evidence on this theory was collated from several researchers who have addressed the importance of retaining customers for corporate profitability (Kenny & Marshall, 2000; Kotler, 1999; McKenna, 1993; Peppers & Rogers, 1997; Reichheld & Sasser, 1990; Reichheld & Teal, 1996; Seybold, 1998).

Notwithstanding the perceived importance of frequent buyers, recent research has challenged this conventional approach, highlighting the fact that companies either fail to comprehend or assess correctly the true value associated with their customers, be they frequent or sporadic purchasers. This behavior may lead firms to make strategic mistakes as well as perpetuate managerial errors, such as high spending for retention of unprofitable customers or failing to perceive the importance of a high-value sporadic consumer (Dowling & Uncles, 1997; Reinartz & Kumar, 2000, 2002, 2003; Schultz & Hayman, 1999).

The correct understanding of how to manage both frequent and sporadic buyers has assumed a truly important dimension, mainly in the e-commerce realm, due to the very high churn rate of customers in this arena. Reichheld and Shefter (2000) point out that up to 50% of consumers abandon an e-retailing company before the third year of their commercial relationship.

The impact of other issues related to the Internet regarding customer defection and transaction profitability is also relevant. The low information asymmetry generated by this technology makes customers far more aware of products and services, readily enabling them to search and locate where the best price can be found, thereby reducing switching costs (Smith et al., 1999). According to Bakos (1997), if the search cost is low enough, buyers will tend to look for prices and products among all available and potential sellers.

The scope of this research is to explore in an empirical manner the transaction profitability derived from sporadic and frequent customers in the home appliance e-commerce sector. The company analyzed is one of the largest retailing groups on the Brazilian market, serving the major and minor appliance industry both through conventional channels and via its Web site. Due to confidentiality issues, the name of the group is omitted from this article.

This study is divided into five sections. The first section identifies literature dealing with the relationship between customer retention and transaction profitability, The second section addresses the Brazilian environment with respect to Internet users and the e-commerce industry, comparing the latter to that of the U.S. The third section presents the research methodology used to gather and analyze data and the propositions to be tested, and discusses the criteria applied for categorizing clients according to their value to the company as well as the inherent limitations of such criteria. In the fourth section, the evidence obtained is analyzed, and the propositions about customer transaction profitability are tested statistically. Finally, the last section summarizes and discusses the academic and managerial implications derived from the article's findings and also recommends further research tracks.

CUSTOMER RETENTION AND TRANSACTION PROFITABILITY

In relationship marketing literature, several authors have pointed out the beneficial impact of customer retention on corporate profitability. Kotler (1999) claims that the longer a client remains with a supplier, the more profitable this customer becomes. According to the aforementioned author, frequent buyers are more profitable for four main reasons: (1) they purchase more over the course of time; (2) the cost of serving a frequent client decreases with the passing of time; (3) satisfied consumers usually recommend the supplier favorably to others; and (4) frequent customers are less sensitive to price.

Day (1999) suggests that companies achieve higher profitability by building long-term relationships with their clients. Peppers and Rogers (1993) claim that there is only one way a business can guarantee its financial sustainability; namely, by cultivating loyal and satisfied customers. These authors allege that the more purchases a consumer makes, the higher the markup obtained by the company. McKenna (1993) stresses this concept, stating that the development of strong ties with the customer is an effective way to leverage the firm's competitive advantage.

Seybold (1998) ratifies these ideas, stating that when a company loses a client, it loses not only the potential profit that would be derived from this customer but also the profits from the chain of consumers who hear the disgruntled customer's negative commentaries. Reichheld and Sasser (1990) declare that the loss of clients can have a greater impact on profitability than on other traditional factors associated with a company's competitive advantage, such as market share and unit cost. According to these authors, the efficient management of customer retention is relevant in order to ensure that cumulative profits accrued from purchases made by clients supersede the investments made to acquire and retain them. In a later study, Reichheld and Teal (1996) state that businesses with a high rate of customer loss will face a difficult future with reduced profits; slow growth, if any; and shorter life expectancy.

In view of this, it is essential to assess the financial potential of all customers in order to quantify their importance vis-à-vis corporate profitability. Kotler (1999) recommends the use of LTV (Lifetime Value) methodology, which depicts the total spending of customers within a specific product or service category during their lives, irrespective of the company with which the business is transacted. According to Peppers and Rogers (1997), LTV represents the profit generated by clients minus the costs associated with their acquisition and retention throughout the course

of their relationship with a specific firm. Rust et al. (2000) point out that LTV is influenced by several factors, such as cost of capital, cross sales, and word of mouth.

Stone (1984) suggests the use of RFM (Recency, Frequency, Monetary Value) metrics for classifying customers according to recency (time of most recent purchase), frequency (frequency/number of past purchases), and monetary value (ticket value per transaction). For the aforementioned author, the best customers (i.e., those who have the highest likelihood of buying again) are those who have purchased more recently, those who have purchased more frequently within a given time frame, and those who have spent a sizable sum of money.

These metrics seek to predict the financial potential of each consumer according to the share-of-wallet concept, as the firm tries to increase its share in customer spending rather than its share in the mass market (Sheth et al., 2000).

A relevant issue in customer retention is the acquisition cost. Relationship marketing theory often suggests that the cost of acquiring a new customer is five times greater than the cost involved in keeping an existing client satisfied. According to Goodman (1999), this metric originated from a study developed in 1984 by TARP (Technical Assistance Research Program) that sought to examine acquisition vs. retention costs in an automobile company in the U.S. Recent numbers from TARP suggest that the relationship between these two former variables can vary from 2:1 to 20:1, depending on the state of the economy and the industry analyzed (Goodman, 1999).

In the industry under scrutiny in this article, the acquisition costs are mainly concentrated in advertising, which belongs to the promotion dimension of the traditional marketing mix (McCarthy, 1960). A report from CrossRoads (2001) indicates that the growth of advertising spending worldwide has been 30% greater than economic growth. According to this report, this pattern results from the belief that companies have that continuous investment in advertising allows them to sustain their market share.

In marked contrast with the authors quoted, recent research has challenged the traditional methods adopted by most executives for retaining customers as well as the resulting managerial implications involved. Schultz and Hayman (1999) warn that if all the benefits accrued from customer retention claimed by firms were true, loyalty would not be so good for their clients, as they would be paying higher prices and advertising the company for free in addition to receiving worse attention from the company.

Dowling and Uncles (1997) suggest that customer loyalty is probably a consequence of the industry within which the firm operates as well as the power of brand name. According to them, investments in customer retention do not reap the desired benefits for the strategic positioning and brand equity of the company. Moreover, it is quite possible that these investments generate neither a significant rise in the number of frequent clients nor an increase in corporate profitability.

Some of the ideas of Dowling and Uncles (1997) tally with an empirical study conducted by Reinartz and Kumar (2000) in a catalog-based retailing company in the U.S. In this research, evidence was found, which ran counter to some traditional concepts of relationship marketing, such as the following:

1. The relationship between customer lifetime and the corresponding firm's cumulative profitability was only verified in a moderate way with frequent higher-income clients (i.e., merely a small percentage of all customers). Sporadic clients with higher incomes have higher LTV than those of frequent customers with lower incomes. The authors suggest that companies should focus not only on retaining clients but also on developing effective tools to attract sporadic consumers.

2. The commercial transaction value diminishes during the course of the relationship between a company and its customers. Based on this statement, the notion that profits generated by frequent buyers always increase over the course of time is duly challenged.

3. As commercial transactions were analyzed individually, frequent customers were considered less profitable both in terms of higher- and lower-income clients. In contrast with traditional relationship marketing literature, Reinartz and Kumar (2000) suggest that frequent buyers are more price-sensitive than sporadic purchasers.

4. The concept that servicing costs are lower for frequent customers was rejected. In order to back their theory, the authors used the ratio between mailing costs and customer revenues. The differences observed in the ratio between frequent and sporadic consumers were not statistically significant.

In a recent study, Reinartz and Kumar (2002) concluded that firms should not focus exclusively on their frequent clients. The previously mentioned authors warn that mismanagement of customer retention can lead a company to make excessive investments in an attempt to retain unprofitable consumers as well as undervalue the financial potential of sporadic buyers.

This issue is even more relevant when applied to e-commerce, in which industry-specific characteristics influence customer defection and profitability. According to Smith et al. (1999), the reduced information asymmetry provided by electronic markets makes the customers more aware of their options, which leads to lower search costs for products and services. Bakos (1997) shows that if the search cost is low enough, buyers examine all products offered and purchase the one that best suits their needs, resulting in decreased price premiums and customer profitability. Consequently, for customers, the decrease in search costs leads to lower switching costs, allowing them to change their allegiance to suppliers very easily.

SOCIAL AND ECONOMIC CONTEXT OF INTERNET USERS AND THE E-RETAILING INDUSTRY

Brazil is a federation with the three following levels of government:

- **Central:** Federal Government
- **Intermediary:** 27 states plus the Federal District (Brasília — the capital of Brazil)
- **Local:** More than 5,500 municipalities with the constitutional status of autonomous members

The Federation was not created on a base-upward premise. Instead, it was based on consciousness about the perceived need to divide the unitary state.

Furthermore, Brazil is a country with no significant cultural friction generated by differences of language, religion, or race.

Most of the bibliography about Internet users addresses the OECD countries (OECD, 2002). Some developing countries, such as India, Brazil, Mexico, and so forth, use Information Technology in a very intensive way. This fact in itself may constitute a highly optimistic opportunity related to e-retailing initiatives.

However, since these countries have large populations, absolute figures can lead the reader to misconceptions. If, for instance, one compares Canada and Brazil, it can be seen that while Brazil has almost the same number of Internet users as Canada, nearly 50% of the population of the latter is digitally included, whereas little more than 5% of the population of the former has access to the Internet (Joia, 2004).

The number of Internet users in Brazil is estimated at around 10 million. Thus, as stated

earlier, it represents a very small percentage of the 170 million total population of a country whose GDP was close to US$588 billion in 2000 (Afonso, 2001; Neri, 2003).

According to Afonso (2001), fixed-line telephones are the predominant option for the Internet (62.5 million lines, of which 38.8 million are hard-wire and 23.7 are mobile cell phones). Individual services still only reach 39% of the population. Hence, reduced line access remains a limiting factor for Internet expansion, both for individual users and service providers. The high price for conventional telephone services represents another barrier in a country where the income per capita is around US$3,500 per year.

Connections between the local and international backbones are still very expensive. Furthermore, ISPs do not offer local-line Internet connections in many small towns.

As may be imagined, the price of hardware is another obstacle to providing nationwide Internet access, since per-capita income in Brazil remains very low. Besides, the predominance of English-based content on Web sites limits accessibility to a very small percentage of the Brazilian population; namely, that with the highest educational level.

The lack of training, not just to deal with the Internet but also to provide support to infrastructure and to develop new services and software, is another obstacle in Brazil.

Furthermore, all of these issues constitute an environment that fosters digital inequalities. Most of these inequalities are merely the consequence of longstanding social and economic disparities in Brazil (Joia, 2004).

Nonetheless, monthly e-retailing sales grew by 40.6% in Brazil between September 2003 and September 2004, totaling nearly US$222 million, according to figures released by the Brazilian Chamber of Electronic Commerce (Camara-e, 2004), whereas the retailing industry as a whole in Brazil grew by only 11.8% during the same period, according to the Brazilian Institute of Geography and Statistics (IBGE, 2004). E-commerce sales in September 2004 accounted for 3.4% of the total sales (Camara-e, 2004).

According to E-bit (2004), only 1.5% of the entire Brazilian population has made at least one online purchase to date. The average monthly income per household of these customers is US$1,392, and the average age is 35. More than 60% of these B2C consumers are male, and 57% of them have an undergraduate degree.

Interestingly, when compared with the U.S. (in percentage), Brazil is in a slightly better position with regard to the e-commerce realm; according to data from the U.S. Census Bureau (2004), e-retailing sales in the U.S. grew by 23.1% between the second quarter of 2003 and the second quarter of 2004, while the total retailing industry grew by 7.8% over the same period. In addition, e-commerce sales in the second quarter of 2004 in the U.S. accounted for 1.7% of total sales.

As we have seen, the main problem in Brazil is not related to percentage figures (which are better than those in the U.S.). It has more to do with the absolute number of consumers on the Web due to the heavy digital gap prevailing in that country (Joia, 2004).

RESEARCH METHODOLOGY

In order to gather relevant input to carry out this research, one of the largest retailing groups in Brazil was investigated. The firm's database was analyzed quantitatively to assess the transaction profitability derived from sporadic and frequent customers purchasing via the company's digital channel; namely, its Web site.

A single-case research methodology was chosen for this article, due to the exploratory facets associated with the subject and the industry investigated, in order to reveal relevant and updated information for practitioners, executives, and academics.

This is an instrumental case study, where a particular object is examined in order to offer enhanced understanding about some question or theory (Eisenhardt, 1989; Stake, 1994). According to Yin (1994), a single-case design is appropriate when it serves an innovative purpose, where an observer may gain access to a phenomenon that was previously inaccessible. In particular, this work presents two aspects that were previously inaccessible to scientific investigation; namely, the real transaction profit margins of sporadic and frequent buyers (previous research merely estimated the profitability of transactions) and the transposition of the customer transaction profitability discussion to the Brazilian B2C arena.

From the theoretical background presented earlier, the article aims to test the following quantitative propositions in order to examine the transaction profitability of frequent and sporadic buyers:

P1: The transaction profit derived from frequent customers increases as they purchase more frequently.

P2: The ticket value of frequent clients increases as they buy more frequently.

P3: Frequent customers purchase more profitable products than sporadic consumers.

P4: Frequent clients purchase more expensive products than sporadic buyers.

Due to the characteristics of the products commercialized (i.e., major and minor home appliances) (see Santos and Costa [1997] for more information about this segment), this research is based on the premise that customers may only be considered frequent buyers if they make at least one purchase during every 12-month period. These are the same criteria adopted by the firm under analysis to categorize its frequent customers.

The company was selected because it sells a broad range of products throughout the year without seasonal variations in supply and demand. The analysis includes all customers who made purchases between the day the firm's Web site was inaugurated (July 1, 1999) and the day on which the data were extracted from the database (December 31, 2002).

The statistical tests that supported the conclusions drawn in this research were based on variance analysis — ANOVA (Schau & Mattern, 1997) and regressions of the data collected, which were developed with a significance level of 5% (a = 0.05), performed by SPSS. From a total of 149,062 customers, a sample of 14,906 buyers was selected at random (10% of the total), of which 10,421 were sporadic consumers, and 4,482 were frequent purchasers.

The real value of all the monetary amounts involved in this research was calculated using the inflation rate during the 42 months under analysis (Rossi, 1997). The investigation conducted does not take into account customer acquisition costs, as the amounts for each specific client are not considered by the company under scrutiny.

The quantitative analysis dealt with the following selected attributes:

1. **Customer Purchasing Frequency.** Number of purchases made by customers.
2. **Transaction Profit.** Profit accrued from purchases made by clients.

3. **Ticket Value.** Value of purchases made by customers.

Finally, as stated earlier, the customers were divided into two main groups: sporadic buyers and frequent buyers. They were classified according to their average ticket and segmented according to a Pareto level, as suggested by Roos (cited in Chatzkel, 2002) and Reinartz and Kumar (2000), as presented in Table 1.

Methodology Limitations

It is important to stress some limitations associated with the methodology adopted in this study. The first limitation refers to the premise that frequent customers of home appliances are clients who make at least one purchase during every 12-month period. The lack of literature clearly addressing the concept of how to define a frequent client within different industries led the authors to use the same criteria as those adopted by the firm under analysis.

The second limitation is the fact that the Web site has been deployed only recently (i.e., the data refer to the period between July 1999 and December 2002 [42 months], which might be considered a relatively short period of observation).

Furthermore, customer segmentations other than the Pareto Analysis might have been taken into consideration. In fact, the customer's ticket value was the major element considered for

Table 1. Customer segmentation

Category	Description
Sporadic 20%	Sporadic consumers with the highest 20% average ticket
Sporadic 80%	Other sporadic consumers
Frequent 20%	Frequent customers with the highest 20% average ticket
Frequent 80%	Other frequent customers

analyzing customer behavior in this virtual organization.

Another issue involves the research methodology chosen. A single case study presents considerable limitations in terms of generalization (external validity), especially in instrumental cases, where the analysis is restricted to the elements being tested (in this case, anomalies in the transaction profitability of frequent customers). However, the firm under scrutiny revealed its profit margins for analysis, and this facet proved to be highly relevant and revealing, as explained in the next section.

The last important limitation is the impossibility of calculating total client profitability, since the costs of customer acquisition and retention are not computed by the firm under scrutiny. Consequently, this research deals exclusively with customer transaction profitability.

DATA ANALYSIS AND FINDINGS

As stated earlier, the researchers in this study were granted access to individualized transaction profit margins, discounting taxes and the cost of capital (financing taxes, credit card commissions, etc.), allowing them to calculate customer transaction profitability in a more reliable way than had been possible in previous research that sought to estimate the profitability of commercial transactions (Reinartz & Kumar, 2000).

In line with the theoretical background and research methodology herein exposed, this work set out to test quantitatively four propositions concerning the profitability derived from sporadic and frequent customers in the e-retailing realm.

Proposition 1. The transaction profit derived from frequent customers increases as they purchase more frequently.

Regressions were used to analyze the commercial transaction markup as dependent on the purchase frequency of each frequent customer in order to test this hypothesis. The regressions took the two segments of frequent customers into account (Pareto 20% and 80%). Table 2 summarizes this analysis, where the sign of the coefficient indicates the type of relationship between transaction profitability and purchase frequency (positive or negative).

From the regressions, it can be seen that the coefficient is negative (-6.18) for the segment of frequent customers with the highest average ticket (Pareto 20%), indicating an inverse relationship between transaction profit and customer purchasing frequency. In the other segment of frequent buyers (Pareto 80%), the coefficient is 0.34, indicating that transaction profitability increases slightly as more purchases are made by customers. In other words, this proposition cannot be supported for the frequent buyers with the highest average ticket (Pareto 20%).

Proposition 2. The ticket value of frequent customers increases as they buy more frequently.

Regressions were used to analyze the ticket value as dependent on the purchase frequency of

Table 2. Regressions of transaction profitability as a function of purchase frequency

	R^2	Coefficients	Std Error	t Stat	P-value
Frequent 20%	0.74	-6.18	1.38	-4.46	< 0.01
Frequent 80%	0.56	0.34	0.12	2.76	< 0.05

Table 3. Regressions of average ticket as a function of purchase frequency

	R^2	Coefficients	Std Error	t Stat	P-value
Frequent 20%	0.63	-17.86	5.12	-3.48	< 0.05
Frequent 80%	0.51	-0.02	0.01	-2.49	< 0.05

Table 4. ANOVA: Average markup of frequent and sporadic customers

	Markup of Frequent Customers	Markup of Sporadic Customers	F Calc	P-value	F Crit
Pareto 20%	R$ 80.34	R$ 86.07	0.62	0.43	3.84
Pareto 80%	R$ 16.40	R$ 14.92	31.61	< 0.01	3.84

Table 5. ANOVA: Average tickets of frequent and sporadic customers

	Ticket of Frequent Customers	Ticket of Sporadic Customers	F Calc	P-value	F Crit
Pareto 20%	R$ 375.54	R$ 455.43	34.05	< 0.01	3.84
Pareto 80%	R$ 126.62	R$ 103.71	449.61	< 0.01	3.84

each frequent client in order to test this hypothesis. The regressions took the two segments of frequent customers into account (Pareto 20% and 80%). Table 3 summarizes this analysis, where the sign of the coefficient indicates the type of relationship between ticket value and purchase frequency (positive or negative).

The coefficient is negative (-17.86) for the segment of frequent customers with the highest average ticket (Pareto 20%), indicating an inverse relationship between ticket value and customer purchasing frequency. In the other segment of frequent buyers (Pareto 80%), the coefficient is -0.02, indicating that the average ticket decreases only slightly as more purchases are made by clients. In other words, this proposition cannot be supported for all frequent customers using the digital sales channel of the firm investigated.

Proposition 3. Frequent customers purchase more profitable products than sporadic consumers.

For this test, the average markups of frequent and sporadic consumers within each segment (Pareto 20% and 80%) are compared. The variance analysis is presented in Table 4.

The low value of *F Calc* for the segment of buyers with the highest average ticket (Pareto 20%) indicates that the difference between averages is not significant. In the other segment of consumers (Pareto 80%), frequent clients present a higher transaction profit (R$16.40; approximately US$5.86) than the respective value associated with sporadic buyers (R$14.92; approximately US$5.33). Such evidence seems not to support Proposition 3, as the statement that frequent customers buy more profitable products than sporadic purchasers could not be verified for those consumers with the highest ticket value (Pareto 20%).

Proposition 4. Frequent customers purchase more expensive products than sporadic buyers.

For this test, the average tickets of frequent and sporadic consumers within each segment (Pareto 20% and 80%) are compared. The variance analysis is presented in Table 5.

The high value of *F Calc* for all segments indicates that the difference between averages is significant. In the segment of buyers with the highest ticket (Pareto 20%), sporadic consumers present a higher average transaction value (R$455.43; approximately US$162.65) than the respective value associated with frequent customers with the highest ticket (R$375.54; approximately US$134.12). This evidence led the researchers not to support Proposition 4, as the statement that frequent customers buy more expensive products than sporadic purchasers could not be verified for those consumers with the highest ticket value (Pareto 20% segment).

DISCUSSION, MANAGERIAL IMPLICATIONS, AND FUTURE RESEARCH

The empirical evidence revealed by this study ratifies some of the findings presented by Reinartz and Kumar (2000), which was the main research stream used in the theoretical framework of this article. According to Campbell and Stanley (1963), the generalization of evidence transposed to different scenarios, populations, and moments is an important factor for improving the external validity of the research.

The following findings are presented in this article:

- The analysis of Proposition 1 showed that the profit associated with transactions made by frequent customers with the highest average ticket (Pareto 20%) decreases progressively over the course of their purchasing history. This finding allows the researchers to challenge the contention that customer retention always enables firms to obtain a premium price, as suggested by relationship marketing theories (Brondmo, 2000; Day, 1999; Kotler, 1999; Peppers & Rogers, 1993; Reichheld & Teal, 1996).

- The test of Proposition 2 showed that the average ticket of frequent customers decreases as they purchase more frequently. This finding is directly opposed to some conceptual evidence from relationship marketing theories (Brondmo, 2000; Day, 1999; Kotler, 1999; Peppers & Rogers, 1993; Reichheld & Teal, 1996).

- The test of Proposition 3 showed that it is not true to say that frequent customers always purchase more profitable products than sporadic consumers, as stated in relationship marketing literature (Brondmo, 2000; Kotler, 1999; McKenna, 1993; Reichheld & Teal, 1996). This evidence cannot be supported for those consumers who purchase products with the highest average ticket (Pareto 20%).

- The test of Proposition 4 challenges traditional marketing literature, which contends that frequent customers always purchase more expensive products than sporadic consumers (Brondmo, 2000; Kotler, 1999; McKenna, 1993; Reichheld & Teal, 1996). This proposition cannot be supported for frequent buyers with the highest ticket value (Pareto 20%).

This evidence does not invalidate the importance of frequent customers for firms. The key question seems to be why and when transaction profitability associated with sporadic purchasers can be higher than that derived from frequent buyers. For traditional sales channels, this phenomenon might be explained by the increase in customer bargaining power (Porter, 1980). However, there is no possibility of price negotiation via the e-retailing channel of the company under analysis. In this case, the reduction of information asymmetry and increased access to market information afforded by the Internet could make it easier for frequent customers to reduce transaction costs and to become aware of promotions (Bakos, 1997; Smith et al., 1999). Hence, it is important to investigate the anomalies revealed here in other sectors of e-retailing in order to better understand the kind of factors that influence the transaction profitability of frequent and sporadic consumers on the Web. In other words, it would seem to be of paramount importance to analyze the influence of managerial practices on the transaction profitability of frequent and sporadic customers. Marketing and e-commerce literature abounds with innumerable managerial approaches associated with profitable relationships between firms and clients (Bakos, 1997; Brown et al., 2002; Homburg et al., 2000; Kotha et al., 2004; Mitra & Lynch, 1996). Future research could replicate the quantitative methodology adopted here and also include qualitative elements that convey to different marketing praxis. Following this line of reasoning, it is suggested that five practices accrued from relationship marketing literature should be tracked in further studies, presented as follows:

1. **Supply of Homogenous or Differentiated Products.** Alba et al. (1997) contend that price plays a highly relevant role when products are easily comparable. Consequently, utilization of differentiated products assures greater profitability for the retailer. Concomitantly, Lynch and Ariely (2000) point to empirical evidence showing that price sensitivity is reduced by offering differentiated products and increased by the supply of homogenous goods.

2. **Product Dissemination Strategy.** According to Mitra and Lynch (1996), dissemination of information not related to price favors a decision based on quality, thereby helping consumers to select products that best suit their specific desires and needs. Bakos (1997) adds that greater qualitative information

transparency may mitigate the importance of price, thereby ensuring higher profitability for electronic retailers.

3. **Customizing Communications with Clients.** Conceptual evidence suggests that e-mail customization results in higher profitability for e-retailers (Chen & Sudhir, 2002). This tactic allows the implementation of differentiated offers, exploiting the individual potential of each consumer, respecting areas of interest, periods, and frequency of communication.

4. **Marketing Orientation Adopted.** To Day and Montgomery (1999), the more firms change the focus of their marketing approach from products to clients, the more they begin to gain a full insight into the habits and needs of their consumers. Homburg et al. (2000) contend that a strategy geared to clients enables companies to exploit their financial potential in an efficient way.

5. **Customer Retention Mechanisms.** According to Schouten and McAlexander (1995), one of the most important tactics for developing relationship marketing is based on the creation of communities of customers, gathering clients that share the same values and behavior patterns. Brown et al. (2002) show empirically how the construction of a solid structure of virtual communities represents an important source of profit in electronic retailing. For their part, Bolton et al. (2000) point out that clients involved in loyalty programs pay little heed to negative evaluations of a given company vis-à-vis its competitors. Kotha et al. (2004) show a positive association between the market value of firms and the existence of relationship services, such as virtual communities and the personalization of Web sites.

Therefore, if it can be proved that the company under analysis does not take these critical success factors into consideration, it might be possible to understand why frequent customers are not performing better than sporadic buyers, thereby validating the marketing relationship theory via the Web.

In other words, qualitative analysis is needed in order to investigate whether the firm under analysis is complying with the best managerial praxis accrued from the marketing relationship theory developed for virtual organizations. It can be speculated that these anomalies might be the effects of managerial practices that are at odds with those that one would expect to find in a world-class digital store.

These are, undoubtedly, the next research tracks to be pursued.

REFERENCES

Afonso, J. R. (2001). E-government in Brazil: Experiences and perspectives. *Proceedings of the Forum of Federations*, Montreal, Canada.

Alba, J., et al. (1997). Interactive home shopping: Consumer, retailer, and manufacturers incentives to participate in electronic marketplaces. *Journal of Marketing, 61*, 38-53.

Bakos, J. Y. (1997). Reducing buyer search costs: Implications for electronic marketplaces. *Management Science, 43*(12), 1676-1692.

Bolton, R., Kannan, P., & Bramlet, M. (2000). Implications of loyalty program membership and service experiences for customer retention and value. *Journal of the Academy of Marketing Science, 28*(1), 95-108.

Brondmo, H. P. (2000). *The engaged customer. The new rules of Internet direct marketing.* New York: Harper Business.

Brown, S., Tilton, A., & Woodside, D. (2002). The case for on-line communities. *The McKinsey Quarterly, 1*. Retrieved from http://www.mckinsey quarterly.com

Camara-e. (2004). Index of electronic retail. *Brazilian Chamber of Electronic Commerce.* Retrieved November 4, 2004, from http://www. e-consulting corp.com.br/vol/

Campbell, D. T., & Stanley, J. C. (1963). *Experimental and quasi-experimental designs for research.* Chicago: Rand McNally.

Chatzkel, J. (2002). A conversation with Göran Roos. *Journal of Intellectual Capital, 3*(2), 96-117.

Chen, Y., & Sudhir, K. (2002). When shopbots meet emails: Implications for price competition on the Internet. *Review of Marketing Science, 1*(3). Working paper No. 20021139.

Crossroads. (2001). *A sector report: Consumer products.* Irvine, CA: Crossroads.

Day, G. (1999). *The market driven organization.* New York: Free Press.

Day, G., & Montgomery, D. (1999). Charting new directions for marketing. *Journal of Marketing, 63*, 3-13.

Dowling, G., & Uncles, M. (1997). Do customers loyalty programs really work? *Sloan Management Review, 38*(4), 71-82.

E-bit. (2004). Web shoppers. Retrieved November 4, 2004, from http://www.camara-e.net/_upload/ WebShoppers10.pdf

Eisenhardt, K. M. (1989). Building theories from case study research. *Academy of Management Review, 14*, 532-550.

Goodman, J. (1999). *Basic facts on customer complaint behavior and the impact of service on the bottom line.* TARP.

Homburg, C., Workman Jr., J., & Jensen, O. (2000). Fundamental changes in marketing organization: The movement toward a customer-focused organizational structure. *Journal of the Academy of Marketing Science, 28*(4), 459-478.

IBGE. (2004). Monthly survey of commerce. *Brazilian Institute of Geography and Statistics.* Retrieved November 4, 2004, from http://www.ibge.gov. br/home/estatistica/indicadores/comercio/pmc

Joia, L.A. (2004). Bridging the digital divide: Some initiatives in Brazil. *Electronic Government, 1*(3), 300-315.

Kenny, D., & Marshall, J. (2000). Contextual marketing: The real business of the Internet. *Harvard Business Review, 78*(6), 119-125.

Kotha, S., Rajgopal, S., & Venkatachalam, M. (2004). The role of online buying experience as a competitive advantage: Evidence from third-party ratings for e-commerce firms. *Journal of Business, 77*(2), 100-134.

Kotler, P. (1999). *How to create, win, and dominate markets.* New York: Free Press.

Lynch, J., & Ariely, D. (2000). Wine online: Search costs affect competition on price, quality, and distribution. *Marketing Science, 19*(1), 83-103.

McCarthy, E. J. (1960). *Basic marketing: A managerial approach.* Homewood, IL: R.D. Irwin.

McKenna, R. (1993). *Relationship marketing: Successful strategies for the age of the customer.* Cambridge, MA: Perseus Publishing.

Mitra, A., & Lynch, J. (1996). Advertising effects on consumer welfare: Prices paid and liking for brands selected. *Marketing Letters, 7*(1), 19-29.

Neri, M. (2003). *Mapa da exclusão digital.* Retrieved October 9, 2003, from http://epge.fgv.br/portal/pesquisa/livros/2003.html

OECD. (2002). *Measuring the information economy 2002.* Retrieved October 9, 2003, from http://www.oecd.org/document/5/0,2340,en_2649_37409_2765701_1_1_1_37409,00.html

Peppers, D., & Rogers, M. (1993*). The one to one future: Building relationships one customer at a time.* New York: Doubleday.

Peppers, D., & Rogers, M. (1997). *Enterprise one to one: Tools for competing in the interactive age.* New York: Doubleday.

Porter, M. E. (1980). *Competitive strategy: Techniques for analyzing industries and competitors.* New York: Free Press.

Reichheld, F., & Sasser Jr., W. E. (1990). Zero defections: Quality comes to services. *Harvard Business Review, 68*(5), 105-111.

Reichheld, F., & Schefter, P. (2000). E-loyalty: Your secret weapon on the Web. *Harvard Business Review, 78*(4), 105-113.

Reichheld, F., & Teal, T. (1996). *The loyalty effect: The hidden force behind growth, profits, and lasting value.* Boston: Harvard Business School Press.

Reinartz, W., & Kumar, V. (2000). On the profitability of long-life customers in a noncontractual setting: An empirical investigation and implications for marketing. *Journal of Marketing, 64,* 17-35.

Reinartz, W., & Kumar, V. (2002). The mismanagement of customer loyalty. *Harvard Business Review, 80*(7), 86-94.

Reinartz, W., & Kumar, V. (2003). The impact of customer relationship characteristics on profitable lifetime duration. *Journal of Marketing, 67,* 77-99.

Rossi, J. W. (1997). A guide for present value models. *Institute of Applied Economic Research,* Text n° 482.

Rust, R. T., Zeithmal, V. A., & Lemon, K. N. (2000). *Driving customer equity: How customer lifetime value is reshaping corporate strategy.* New York: Free Press.

Santos, A. M., & Costa, C. S. (1997). General characteristics of retail in Brazil. *National Bank for Social and Economic Development*, Setorial nº 5.

Schau, C., & Mattern, N. (1997). *Use of map techniques in teaching applied statistics courses. The American Statistician, 51*(2), 171-175.

Schouten, J., & McAlexander, J. (1995). Subcultures of consumption: An ethnography of the new bikers. *Journal of Consumer Research, 22*(1), 43-61.

Schultz, D., & Hayman, D. (1999). The two sides of loyalty. *Interactive Marketing, 1*(1), 31-43.

Seybold, P. B. (1998). *Customers.com: How to create a profitable business strategy for the Internet and beyond.* Auckland: Random House Publishing.

Sheth, J. N., Sisodia, R. S., & Sharma, A. (2000). The antecedents and consequences of customer-centric marketing. *Journal of the Academy of Marketing Science, 28*(1), 55-66.

Smith, M. D., Bailey, J., & Brynjolfsson, E. (1999). *Understanding digital markets: Review and assessment.* Retrieved August 4, 2000, from http://ecommerce.mit.edu/papers/ude/ude.pdf

Stake, R. E. (1994). Case Studies. In N. K. Denzin & Y. S. Lincoln (Eds.), *Handbook of qualitative research.* Thousand Oaks, CA: Sage.

Stone, B. (1984). *Successful direct marketing methods* (3rd ed.). Lincolnwood, IL: NTC Publishing.

U.S. Census Bureau. (2004). *Retail e-commerce sales in second quarter* 2004. *Retrieved* August 28, 2004, from http://www.census.gov/mrts/www/ecom.pdf

Yin, R. (1994). *Case study research: Design and methods.* Beverly Hills, CA: Sage.

This work was previously published in Journal of Electronic Commerce in Organizations, Vol. 4, Issue 1, edited by M. Khosrow-Pour, pp. 18-32, copyright 2006 by IGI Publishing, formerly known as Idea Group Publishing (an imprint of IGI Global).

Section II
Development and Design Methodologies

Chapter V
Developing Mobile Commerce Applications

P. Benou
University of Peloponnese, Greece

V. Bitos
TIM HELLAS, Greece

ABSTRACT

The recent advances in wireless and mobile communication technologies enable users to conduct commercial activities anywhere and at any time. In this new environment, the designing of appropriate applications constitutes both a necessity and a challenge at the same time in order to support effectively the movable user. This article investigates the environment in which these applications operate, identifies possible categories of them and proposes guidelines for their development process.

INTRODUCTION

The exponential growth in wireless and mobile communication technologies, coupled with the impressive mass adoption of mobile phone and the increasing number of users that possess other handheld devices, such as personal digital assistants (PDAs) and smartphones, pave the way to the extension and evolution of e-commerce to m-commerce.

Mobile commerce or *m-commerce* is defined as any activity that is related with a commercial transaction (or a potential one)—an exchange of services or goods for money—and is conducted via wireless and mobile communication networks and uses wireless and mobile devices as user interface. A few of the existing e-commerce services can be successfully expanded to the new mobile environment and brand new services can be built by reason of the distinct attributes of the mobile setting (Durlacher, 2000; Turban, King, Lee, & Viehland, 2004). These special attributes include:

- **Ubiquity:** It refers to the advantage of a mobile device to be available at any time and anywhere, fulfilling the need of both real-time information and communication independent of the user's location.

- **Reachability:** Holding a mobile terminal, the user can be instantly reached at any time.
- **Convenience:** It has to do with the easiness that the user interacts in the mobile environment, just using a smartphone or a PDA, without booting up a PC or placing a call via a modem.
- **Instant Connectivity:** It relates to the ability of the mobile device to connect easily and quickly to the Internet, intranets, other devices and wireless networks.
- **Context-Sensitiveness:** It refers to the ability of the mobile applications to sense and exploit the context—the information that surrounds the human-computer interaction—in order to offer personalized, localized and generally purpose-suitable services.

In this article we discuss issues related to the development of mobile commerce applications. We describe the framework in which the m-commerce operates and the possible categories of m-commerce applications. We also address the important issues of context and context-awareness and propose guidelines for the development process.

More precisely, in the section entitled *"The Framework of Mobile Commerce"* we present the most important participating entities in m-commerce operations. Regarding the section *"Mobile Commerce Application's Categories,"* we describe some of the possible m-commerce application categories. In the section *"The Special Issue of Context and Context-Awareness,"* we discuss the concept of context and highlight an important dimension of it, the location. In this section we also define the context-aware applications and the requirements that these applications should meet. In the section *"Guidelines for M-Commerce Applications Development"* we propose some guidelines for the m-commerce application development process organized in the following categories: (i) management-related propositions, (ii) development process-related propositions, (iii) user-related propositions and (iv) context-related propositions. The section *"Conclusion"* concludes the article.

THE FRAMEWORK OF MOBILE COMMERCE

Mobile commerce is a complex process and involves a number of participating entities that constitute the m-commerce value chain (Giaglis, 2004). Although an analysis of the strategic goals, the key advantages and the values which these entities share is beyond the scope of this paper; we address them briefly in order to have a comprehensive view of the framework in which the m-commerce operates.

The value chain of m-commerce consists of the following:

- **Mobile network operators (MNOs):** The main role of MNOs is to implement and operate the countrywide mobile networks. They also act as mobile service providers by owning a portal, exploiting the already known billing relationship with the customer.
- **Network equipment providers:** They consist of companies that manufacture the infrastructure and equipment needed to operate a mobile or wireless network.
- **Device manufactures:** The manufactures of all kinds of mobile devices are found under this category.
- **Technology platform vendors:** They deliver the operating systems and microbrowsers for portable devices.
- **Wireless internet service providers (WISPs):** They either provide access to Internet through mobile networks or they

operate public access wireless local area networks (WLANs) providing access to the Internet through WLAN hotspots.

- **Wireless application service providers (WASPs):** Their role is to develop and host wireless applications for companies that wish to conduct m-commerce activities but do not have the necessary resources.

- **Application developers:** They build applications that are used off-line, run over the wireless networks or operate as mobile Internet services.

- **Content providers:** They originate and provide content that is delivered to the end-user. The content provider who collects content from various content providers and delivers the aggregated content in a most appropriate package is called content aggregator. For example, a provider of this kind acquires real-time stock price content from a stock exchange, financial news content from a news agency and financial analysis content from a consulting firm and bundles them into a new package.

- **Mobile portal providers:** The mobile portals act as entry points to a wide spectrum of content and services. They can be characterized as *horizontals* if they contain content and services regarding to a wide spectrum of markets or *vertical* if they target to a particular market. When their primary concern is the information distribution they are called *information* or *content-oriented*; *communication-oriented* when they provide communication mechanisms such as e-mail, instant messaging and calendars, and *commerce-oriented* when they provide transaction services such as banking, shopping, auctions, and so forth.

- **Trading companies:** They are firms that conduct the m-commerce activities.

- **Consumers:** The target audience of the m-commerce is the consumers, which are individuals, companies or business customers.

The above mentioned m-commerce participating entities utilize the available technology that underpins the mobile commerce and leads it to growth and spreading. These technologies include standards such as WiFi, and Bluetooth for communication through the wireless networks. It also includes global system for mobile communications (GSM), general packet radio services (GPRS) and universal mobile telecommunications system (UMTS) for communication through the mobile networks. A multitude of diverse mobile devices is available including both cellular phones, smartphones, PDAs and hybrid handheld devices that combine voice, data processing and communication capabilities. Operating systems like Windows CE, Palm OS, EPOC, Linux and proprietary systems as well, such as RTOS and GEOS, enable the various mobile devices to operate. Java 2 Micro Edition (J2ME), a light version of Java, has been introduced to meet the limitations and peculiarities of mobile devices. The wireless application protocol (WAP), based on existing Internet and network technologies, optimizes the wireless Internet access. The connectivity gateways lie between the Web application servers and mobile devices in order to adapt the various device specific network protocols, such as WAP, to the common TCP/IP-based communication protocols applied on the server side. Standards like XML, WML and various kinds of HTML are used for content delivery; furthermore voice XML technologies offer convenient user interfaces (Hansmann, Merk, Nicklous, & Stober, 2003).

In the relatively new mobile environment, the application's designers and developers are invited to design and implement innovative mobile commerce solutions, taking into account the constraints that this new environment imposes, but also exploiting the distinct benefits, which this offers.

MOBILE COMMERCE APPLICATION CATEGORIES

Just like e-business is a wide concept that contains the e-commerce, m-business includes m-commerce; moreover it has a common section with e-business, as shown in *Figure 1*. M-business, excluding the m-commerce, includes other activities as well, such as mobile office, mobile medicine and mobile learning; but in this work we focus on the m-commerce applications.

Although there is an unlimited number of potential m-commerce applications, under both business to business (B2B) and business to consumer (B2C) models, here we are going to discuss only some important classes of them, including mobile financial applications, mobile advertising, mobile shopping and some others in more details.

Mobile Financial Applications

Mobile financial applications are one of the most important components of m-commerce and constitute a new service distribution channel for financial institutions. This new channel enables them to offer more value-added services and at the same time to further cut the operational costs. These applications include mobile banking, mobile brokerage services and mobile payments.

- **Mobile banking:** The simplest of the mobile banking solutions enable users to receive information about their account balance via an SMS request or via a voice call to an IVR (interactive voice response) system. More complex banking services can be offered through the wireless Internet (Mallat, Rossi, & Tuunainen, 2004). Customers can track their account and credit card transactions, transfer funds between accounts and pay bills using a menu-based interface (Herzberg, 2003). Additionally they can be informed about check exchange and interest rates and learn about new investment solutions. Furthermore they have access to information regarding housing, consumer and professional loans, and they can find out the location of automatic teller machines (ATMs) and branches of banks.

- **Mobile broking:** More and more brokerage firms are moving towards mobile broking as they realize the opportunity for service differentiation in order to attract and retain customers (Loney, Jessup, & Valacich, 2004). Investors—private or professional ones—are no longer constrained by wires and can complete their investment activities while out of the office or away from home. Mobile broking offers functionalities such

Figure 1.

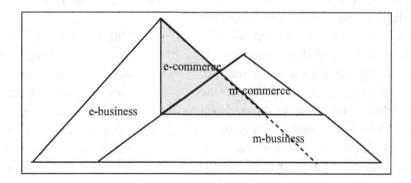

as: receive alerts about price movements, buy and sell stocks, options, mutual funds and other investment products, browse and delete existing orders, receive a message when an order is executed and manage portfolio (Muntermann, Rossnagel, & Rannenberg, 2004).

- **Mobile payments:** One of the interesting applications of m-commerce is mobile payments. They are commonly categorized into small payments—for small purchase less than 10 euros—and large payments. They are further subdivided into proximity and remote payments, depending on whether the purchase takes place at the point of sale (POS) or at a distance via a mobile network (Herzberg, 2003). POS small payments include small purchases in shops and kiosks, such as of soft drinks, cigarettes, fast food and instant photos. An example of remote small payments is the purchase of mobile content such as ring tones, logos, games and information. Paradigms of POS large payments are car washing, parking services, taxi payments, retail shopping and paying at restaurants. Examples of remote large payments constitute receiving services and purchasing goods such as books, roses and gifts. A common way to charge mobile payments is to add them to the monthly mobile phone bill, providing the user with the advantage of no additional service enrollment. There is also the credit card billing scheme, where the mobile payments are included in the consumer's credit card bill (Durlacher, 2000). Another billing solution is the direct debit of the customer's bank account or a special account used only for mobile payments for security reasons. Additionally there is the possibility, for the POS purchases, the payment to be made via Bluetooth technology (McKitterick & Dowling, 2003). Electronic cash can be loaded on the mobile handheld and transferred in the

vending machine through a personal area network.

Mobile Advertising

Mobile advertising applications deliver promotional information to consumers using mobile phones and PDAs. Advertisements can be sent via SMS or MMS for various on-going specials (shops, malls, restaurants) in the surrounding area of the user, using the mobile network (Bulander, Decker, & Schiefer, 2005). When WiFi or Bluetooth communication has been established, advertisements can be sent as notification messages (Aalto, Gothlin, Korhonen, & Ojala, 2004). The advertisements can be sent to all users in a specific area or to users with specific needs and interests regardless of their current location (Kurkovsky & Harihar, 2006). This is known as the "push" method of advertising. In addition to the "push" method for advertising, the "pull" method is available as well, enabling the user to request a page where information about the product or service concerned is embedded. MNOs lie in a very advantageous position as far as exploiting the mobile advertising is concerned, because they have the demographic information of the user, knowing his current location and his purchasing habits—if they own a portal—so that a more targeted advertising can be achieved.

Mobile Shopping

Mobile shopping includes retailing, ticketing, reservations and auctions.

- **Mobile retailing:** Many vendors allow customers to shop from wireless devices enabling them to perform quick searches, compare prices, order and view the status of their order using cell phones or PDAs (Turban et al., 2004). Books, CDs and groceries (Kourouthanassis, Spinellis, Roussos, & Giaglis, 2002) are everyday items, which the user knows very well and he just needs a tool to make the purchase. He can buy them in his spare time, regardless of the shop's opening hours and his current location (Newcomb, Pashley, & Stasko, 2003).

- **Mobile ticketing:** One of the most compelling mobile services is ticket purchasing. The user makes a phone call to a service number and the tickets are delivered as an SMS or MMS message (Mobile Electronic Transaction, 2003). The ticket can contain comprehensive information about the transaction—customer's name, number of persons travelling, means of payment used, time of departure, time of arrival and so on. Potential applications of mobile ticketing include: transportation (flights, trains, boats, ferries, buses, trams), events (concerts, theatres, fairs, museums, sports events) and facilities (gyms, solariums, spas).

- **Mobile reservations:** Mobile reservations are one of the most featured applications in mobile commerce. The customers are able, using their mobile devices, to access hotel and restaurant reservation systems to check prices or availability and to make or change a reservation.

- **Mobile auctions:** Mobile devices provide the ideal environment for auctions and many firms, such as eBay, which conduct online auctions, have moved towards the wireless environment. The main reason for this extension is that bidders want to continue to participate even when they are not in front of a PC. Additional capabilities, except the mobile biting that can be offered by the mobile auctions, are searching for the items, looking at pictures depicting the items and checking the auction lists.

Mobile Information Provisioning

As in the Web, the information that can be provided using the mobile devices is unlimited. It can take the shape of an MMS message or can be offered through the mobile information portals. It can contain general news, sports news, program information of cinemas/theatre, TV and radio, and travel information such as train, bus and flight schedules.

Mobile Entertainment

The available entertainment services and the increased communication bandwidth enable the consumers to buy games, music and video.

Mobile Inventory Management

This category of applications includes the tracking of goods, trucks, or even people. Tracking goods help the providers to determine the time of delivery to the customer, thus improving the customer service. Tracking trucks and people can be exploited for efficient fleet management. Another example is the just-in-time delivery of components in an assembly plant based on the rate of consumption of existing components.

Mobile Supply Chain Integration

The integration of business processes along the supply chain is of significant importance for efficient trading. Additionally accurate and on time information, for the on the move business person, is critical to business success. With the wireless technology there is the possibility—for a pharmaceutical sales representative on the road, for example—to check availability of a particular item in the warehouse, order particular products, or have security access to obtain financial data from the backend enterprise resource planning (ERP) systems.

Mobile CRM

Mobile access expands the reach of customer relationship management (CRM) systems outside the company to employees and partners. One of the attractive functions of the mobile CRM is the sales force automation. Key data that can be retrieved by the sales force on the road could include contact management information, order entry and product availability.

THE SPECIAL ISSUE OF CONTEXT AND CONTEXT-AWARENESS

The Notion of Context

Unlike desktop computing, where the applications are designed to operate in the relatively stable environment of office or home, mobile applications are intended to operate in the dynamic environment of everyday life. The users change their location and social roles during the day: they are professionals at work, consumers while shopping, tourists when traveling and investors when they conduct stock trading activities. Additionally the computing environment varies, as the users have the ability to choose between their cellular phones, PDAs or other handheld devices. All this information surrounding the human-computer interaction, which can be exploited by applications, constitute the *context*.

First Schilit & Theimer (1994) refer to context as location, identities of nearby people and objects, and changes to those objects. Brown, Bovey, & Chen (1997) define context as location, identities of the people around the user, the time of day, season, temperature, and so forth. Pascoe (1998) defines context as the subset of physical and conceptual state of interest to a particular entity. Schmidt & Laerhoven (2001) identify context as the knowledge about the user's and the device's state, including surroundings, situation and location.

Dey & Abowd (1999) propose a more generic definition that states that context is any information that can be used to characterize the situation of an entity. An entity is a person or object that is considered relevant to the interaction between a user and an application, including the user and the application themselves. For example, when a user wants to book a room in a hotel, the preferences of the user constitute valuable "context," which can be exploited to propose alternative solutions to him.

The contextual information can be classified, according to which entity it concerns, into the following categories (Schilit, Adams, & Want, 1994; Chen, & Kotz, 2000):

- **User context:** user identity, collection of nearby people, user's profile, and so forth.
- **Computing context:** hardware characteristics, software characteristics, network connectivity, communication bandwidth, nearby resources such as printers, displays and other devices and so forth.
- **Physical Context:** lighting, noise level, temperature, humidity, and so forth.
- **Spatio-temporal context:** location, place, time of the day, week, month, season of year, time zone, and so forth.
- **Task context:** the goals, tasks and actions of the user.

The types of the context according to the manner of its acquisition can be divided in three categories:

- **Sensed context:** this context is acquired from the environment by means of physical or software sensors (identity, location, temperature, time)
- **Derived context:** this kind of contextual information is computed (for example the name of the city from GPS coordinates through a relation mechanism).
- **Context explicitly provided:** the context that the user provides explicitly (for example the entries in the user profile).

During the last ten years of the context's exploration, many techniques have been proposed for its modeling and representation, including key-value pairs, object-oriented, markup schemes and ontology-based models (Strang & Linnhoff-Popien, 2004).

Positioning Techniques

The accurate knowledge of the position of mobile devices and portable objects can be beneficial for a lot of mobile applications, such as mobile advertising, fleet management, object tracking and location-based information services, for example, find the nearest facilities—restaurants, theaters, parking, and so forth. The significance of the location context element prompts us to discuss in detail the various positioning techniques that currently exist. These techniques include satellite-based, cellular network-based, WLANs-based and RFID-based systems, as they are described in the following paragraphs.

GPS and Assisted GPS (A-GPS): This is a handset-based mobile positioning technique, called so because the handset itself is the primary means for positioning the user and relies on the global positioning satellite system (GPS). The GPS consists of 24 satellites put into orbit, 20,000 kilometers above the surface of the earth, which transmit encoded signals. The GPS receiver, which is integrated in the mobile device, uses these signals to determine its position in 3D—in latitude, longitude and altitude—with accuracy of 10 meters or less. The GPS device needs to have a clear line-of-sight with at least four satellites before it can calculate its position. In the assisted GPS technique, the mobile network provider can, through an assistant server, aid the handset by directing it to look at specific satellites and by collecting data from the handset to perform location identification calculations that the handset is unable to perform due to its limited power.

Indoor GPS: The indoor global positioning system has been developed due to the fact that satellite GPS can not be applicable indoors, because the signal strength is too low to penetrate buildings. The signal of an indoors GPS is emitted by a number of pseudo-satellites and is similar to satellite GPS signal (Zeimpekis, Giaglis, & Lekakos, 2003).

Cell Identification or Cell of Origin (COO): This is referred to as a network-based method, because the mobile network is used to position the mobile device. This method relies on the fact that the mobile network operator is able to identify approximately the position of a mobile device by knowing the cell that the mobile device uses at a given time. Higher location precision can be achieved through the *angle of arrival (AOA)* and *time of arrival (TOA)* methods.

Wireless Local Area Networks (WLANs): In WLAN's environment, the position of the mobile device is determined by the location of the access point of the connection (Varshney, 2003).

Radio Frequency Identification (RFID): According to this method the location of a device, an object or a user, which carries an RFID card, can be determined from the location of the stationary reader that captures the signals emitted by the RFID card.

Context-Aware Applications

The context, which has been discussed in the previous paragraphs, could be exploited in order to provide more valuable services to the end-user. The ability of an application to have knowledge about the context that surrounds it, and to adapt its interface, content and behavior accordingly, is called *context-awareness*

Context-aware computing was first introduced by Schilit & Theimer (1994) to be software that adapts according to the location of use and the collection of nearby people and objects, as well as to changes to such things over time. Pascoe (1998) defines context-awareness as the ability of a device or program to sense, react or adapt to its environment of use. Brown, Bovey, & Chen (1997) define context-aware applications as applications that automatically provide information and/or take actions according to the user's present context as detected by the sensors. Fickas, Korteum, & Segall (1997) define context-aware applications (called environment-directed) to be applications that monitor changes in the environment and adapt the operation according to predefined or user-defined guidelines. Dey & Abowd (1999) characterizes a system as context-aware if it uses context to provide relevant information and/or services to the user, where relevancy depends on the user's task.

The functions that a context-aware application should implement (Schilit, Adams, & Want, 1994) are:

- **Proximate selection:** a user interface-level technique where the nearby-located objects are emphasized or otherwise made easier to choose.
- **Automatic contextual reconfiguration:** a process of adding new components, removing existing components, or altering the connections between components due to context changes.
- **Contextual information and command:** queries on contextual information can produce different results according to the context in which they are issued. Similarly, context can parameterize "contextual commands."
- **Context-triggered actions:** "If-then" rules used to specify how context-aware systems should be adapted.

Dey & Abowd (1999) propose that the features that context-aware applications may support are:

- **Presentation:** of information and services to the user or use context to propose appropriate selections

- **Automatic execution:** of a service according to context changes
- **Tagging of context:** to information for later retrieval.

GUIDELINES FOR M-COMMERCE APPLICATIONS DEVELOPMENT

Mobile commerce applications have a number of unique properties that differentiate them from traditional e-commerce applications and demand new development approaches. Although no comprehensive suggestions have yet been presented, many researchers have pointed out the necessity for new design methodologies and have put forward recommendations for each development phase. Kohler & Gruhn (2004) and Valiente & Heijden (2004) attempt to put forward methods for the identification of the business processes, which could be automated in the mobile environment. Stanoevska-Slabeva (2003), Gebauer, Gribbins & Shaw (2006) and Andreou et al. (2002) propose alternations of existing development approaches in brief. Holtzblatt (2005) has focused on a customer-center design while Rupnik & Krisper (2003) and Tarasewich (2003) point out the importance of context exploitation. Van de Kar (2005) reveals the importance of the interests of the participating entities; Krogstie et al. (2003) and Banavar et al. (2000) highlight the character of mobility, while Kemper & Wolf (2002) relies their proposal on the axis of *innovation*, *risk* and *speed of development*.

Moving to the direction of shaping a comprehensive m-commerce applications' development methodology, we present the unique properties of mobile applications and propose the following guidelines:

Management-Related Propositions

Property 1: *The usage of m-commerce applications is extended over time and space.*

Due to this characteristic, new innovative services can be devised, enabling the companies to remain in a competitive position in the future.

Guideline 1: *Managers should encourage the generation of novel ideas regarding the m-commerce solutions.*

This can be done through the examination of the e-commerce counterpart applications for opportunities to expand in the mobile environment, the observation of advances in technology, the investigation of international practices and the encouragement of brainstorming discussions.

Property 2: *Sometimes the return of investment—in terms of absolute numbers—doesn't justify the cost of the mobile undertaking.*

Guideline 2: *The undertaking of innovative m-commerce solutions does not only aim at generating revenues but also diffusing the reputation, acquiring knowledge and gaining competitive advantage.*

Property 3: *The development of m-commerce applications is a complex process and involves enough participating entities.*

The involving entities could be the trading company, the service provider, the mobile network operator, the content provider, the payment institution and so on.

Guideline 3: *The roles and the interests of the participating entities should be carefully determined, as well as the values that they will share in "a win to win situation."*

Property 4: *There is a relative lack of experience regarding the development of mobile information systems.*

The wireless and mobile technology is relatively new as well as the m-commerce undertakings.

Guideline 4: *Companies should form inter-organizational ties during the development of m-commerce solutions to complement their cognitions and competitive advantages.*

Development Process-Related Propositions

Property 1: *There is a plethora of available technologies that support the moving user.*

Guideline 1: *The alternative technologies, in each mobile case, should be carefully compared with each other and the suitable tools, platforms, protocols, devices and networks should be selected.*

Property 2: *There is a lack of long-time experience regarding the development of mobile information systems among the designers and developers.*

In the mobile environment, it is even harder than in the traditional case to identify non-anticipated difficulties arising from the new technology and new usage situations.

Guideline 2: *In the development of m-commerce information systems, prototyping development approaches should be adopted (Krogstie et al., 2003).*

Property 3: *Time to market for a mobile application is short (Kolos-Mazuryk, Poulisse, & Eck, 2005).*

The speed of development is crucial in the mobile environment since the technology is quickly bypassed and often strong competition factors press for quick solutions.

Guideline 3: *For the development of m-commerce information systems, rapid development approaches should be selected.*

Property 4: *The gathering and exploitation of the context in the m-commerce applications make the code more complicated.*

The mixing of context management and adaptivity code with the applications' core code renders the application code more complex, difficult to maintain and impossible to reuse.

Guideline 4: *During the m-commerce application's design, techniques of separation of context and adaptivity concerns from the core functionalities should be searched out.*

Property 5: *The mobile applications are intended to be used in many different devices with different interfaces, for example, voice interface.*

The main concern of m-commerce applications—in an interface independent design—is the tasks and subtasks that they implement (Banavaar et al., 2000).

Guideline 5a: *The structure of a mobile program should be described in terms of tasks and subtasks and their navigation order.*
Guideline 5b: *The logic of an application should be materialized through distinct services that can be bound into a presentation unit.*

Property 6: *The users don't have great experience of m-commerce applications; therefore it is difficult to identify their requirements.*

Guideline 6: *For the user requirements gathering, repetitive and scenario-driven approaches should be adopted.*

Property 7: *The spatio-temporal environment in which mobile applications operate make the evaluation of mobile services hard, since it is often not possible to create a realistic usage situation (Holmquist, Hook, Juhlin, & Persson, 2002).*

Guideline 7a: *Field test and evaluation planning should be carefully designed and executed.*
Guideline 7b: *The mobile applications should be refined and adapted to the working environment through an iterative process and repeated feedback loops.*

User-Related Propositions

Property 1: *The target audience of mobile applications is broader than desktop applications, with lack of homogeneity.*

Guideline 1 a: *During the mobile application design it is crucial to identify the potential target user groups, their age, cultural background, cognitive capabilities, as well as their information and communication needs.*
Guideline 1 b: The widespread adoption of mobile applications is highly dependent on their usability in terms of ease to learn and ease to use.

Property 2: *The user can only pay intermittent and limited attention to the mobile application over a long period of time.*

When the user interacts with a mobile application he is usually busy, as he simultaneously conducts other activities such as walking, meeting somebody or shopping.

Guideline 2 a: *The mobile application should offer clearly value-added services, such as saving time and increasing efficiency.*

Guideline 2 b: *Simple solutions will work better than complicated solutions.*

Guideline 2c: *Only the information that is absolutely critical should be displayed.*

Guideline 2 d: *During the mobile applications design the minimization of clicks should be sought.*

Guideline 2 e: *Convenient user interfaces, such as voice or sound interfaces, should be investigated.*

Property 3: *User activity occurs in spurts (Kolos-Mazuryk et al., 2005).*

Guideline 3: *There should be a matching between the mobile applications services and the tasks that the mobile user tries to complete.*

This can be done through the identification of the core tasks and subtasks that the user performs in order to achieve a certain goal.

Property 4: *In the mobile environment, the devices are usually personal.*

Although there is a need for generalization, the fact that the mobile devices are personal dictates the need for specialization.

Guideline 4: *Personalized services, tailored to users' preferences, could be provided.*

Context-Related Propositions

Property 1: *The mobile environment is dynamic and the context is rapidly changing.*

Guideline 1: *The context can be captured and exploited in order to provide adaptive mobile applications. These applications recommend content and services to the user or provide suitable information and services in each situation.*

Property 2: *Compared to desktop computers, mobile devices have small screens, limited interaction facilities, low processing power, limited memory and restricted network capabilities.*

Guideline 2: *During the mobile applications' design performance issues, regarding the computing devices and the network should be considered.*

Property 3: *The cellular networks have broadcasting capabilities.*

Guideline 3: *Mass information dissemination can be achieved through mobile networks to users with same interests or in the same location, for example, stock prices or advertising messages.*

Property 4: *The same application could operate on different devices.*

Guideline 4: *The mobile applications should provide consistent functionality and user interfaces through the different devices in which they run.*

CONCLUSION

In this article we discuss issues regarding the development of mobile commerce applications. We explore possible categories of them and address context-related topics. We strongly believe that the successful development of the m-commerce applications is highly dependent on the exact specification and efficient exploitation of the context. The collection and implementation of the context information should be done in a way so that it is reusable and easily extended to cover not yet predictable aspects of it. Moreover, new methods should be investigated in order to separate the core applications logic from the adaptive functionality.

Additionally, we realize that the distinct characteristics of the mobile setting reveal the necessity for new development methodologies. Although some researchers have pointed out the necessity for new development approaches—especially due to the device's characteristics and the changing context—there has not been suggested a complete proposition yet. While working on the shaping of a comprehensive methodology as such, we propose some guidelines for the development process.

Finally, although in this paper we do not address these matters, we believe that security and privacy factors will intensely influence the widespread adoption of m-commerce. The user's personal data, his potentially depicted behaviour and his preferences should be utilized in a clear way and with his consent. In addition, although current communication technologies incorporate strong authentication systems and cryptographic techniques, security issues should be taken into account in the nodes in which decryption and re-encryption occur.

REFERENCES

Aalto, L., Gothlin, N., Korhonen, J., & Ojala, T. (2004). Bluetooth and WAP push based location-aware mobile advertising system. In *Proceedings of the 2nd International Conference on Mobile Systems, Applications, and Services* (pp. 49-58). ACM.

Andreou, A., Chrysostomou, C., Leonidou, C., Mavromoustakos, S., Pitsillides, A., Samaras, G. (2002). *Mobile commerce applications and services: A design development approach.* The First International Conference on Mobile Business M-Business2002, July 8-9, Athens, Greece, 2002.

Banavar, G., Beck, J., Gluzberg, E., Munson, J., Sussman, J., & Zukowski, D. (2000). Challenges: An application model for pervasive computing. In *Proceedings of the 6th Annual International Conference on Mobile Computing and Networking* (pp. 266-274).

Brown, J., Bovey, D., & Chen, X. (1997). Context-aware applications: From the laboratory to the marketplace. *IEEE Personal Communications, 4*(5), 58-64.

Bulander, R., Decker, M., & Schiefer, G. (2005). Comparison of different approaches for mobile advertising. In *Proceedings of the Second IEEE International Workshop on Mobile Commerce and Services* (pp. 174-182).

Chen, G., & Kotz, D. (2000). *A survey of context-aware mobile computing research.* Technical Report TR2000-381. Department of Computer Science, Dartmouth College.

Dey, A., & Abowd, G. (1999). *Towards a better understanding of context and context-awareness.* Technical Report 99-22. Georgia Institute of Technology.

Durlacher Research Ltd. (2000). *Mobile commerce report.* Retrieved from http://www.durlacher.com/fr-research-reps.htm.

Fickas, S., Korteum, G., & Segall, Z., (1997). Software organization for dynamic and adaptable wearable systems. In *Proceedings of the 1st IEEE International Symposium on Wearable Computers* (pp. 56-63).

Gebauer, J., Gribbins, J., & Shaw, J. (2006). *Task-technology fit for mobile information systems.* Working Paper, 06-0107. University of Illinois at Urbana-Champaign, College of Business.

Giaglis, G. (2004). Κινητό και Ασύρματο Επιχειρείν. Εκδόσεις Ι. ΣΙΔΕΡΗΣ. ISBN 960-08-0331-5.

Hansmann, U., Merk, L., Nicklous, M., & Stober T. (2003). *Pervasive computing.* Berlin, Heidelberg, New York: Springer-Verlag.

Herzberg, A. (2003). Payments and banking with mobile personal devices. *Communications of the ACM, 46*(5), 53-58.

Holmquist, L., Hook, K., Juhlin, O., & Persson P. (2002). Challenges and opportunities for the design and evaluation of mobile applications. In *Proceedings of the Workshop on Main Issues in Designing Interactive Mobile Services.*

Holtzblatt, K. (2005). Customer-centered design for mobile applications. *Personal and Ubiquitous Computing, 9*(4), 227-237.

Kemper, H.G., & Wolf, E. (2002). Iterative process models for mobile application systems: A framework. In *Proceedings of the Twenty-Third International Conference on Information Systems* (pp. 401-413).

Kohler, A., & Gruhn, V. (2004). Analysis of mobile business processes for the design of mobile information systems. In *Proceedings of the 5th International Conference on Electronic Commerce and Web Technologies* (3182) (pp. 238–247).

Kolos-Mazuryk, L., Poulisse, G., & van Eck, P. (2005). Requirements engineering for pervasive services. In *Proceedings of the Second Workshop on Building Software for Pervasive Services* (pp. 18-22).

Kourouthanassis, P., Spinellis, D., Roussos, G., & Giaglis, G. (2002). Intelligent Cokes and diapers: MyGROCER ubiquitous computing environment. In *Proceedings of the 1st International Mobile Business Conference* (pp. 150-172).

Krogstie, J., Lyytinen, K., Ophahl, A., Pernici, B., Siau, K., & Smolander K. (2003). *Mobile information systems—Research challenges on the conceptual and logical level.* Lecture Notes in Computer Science—Advanced Conceptual Modeling Techniques (Vol. 2784) (pp. 124-135). Berlin, Heidelberg: Springer-Verlag.

Kurkovsky, S., & Harihar, K. (2006). Using ubiquitous computing in interactive mobile marketing. *Personal and Ubiquitous Computing Journal,* 227-240.

Loney, C., Jessup, L., & Valacich, J. (2004). Emerging mobile business models for mobile brokerage services. *Communications of the ACM, 47*(6), 71-77.

Mallat, N., Rossi, M., & Tuunainen, V.K. (2004). Mobile banking services. *Communications of the ACM, 47*(5), 43-46.

McKitterick, D., & Dowling, J. (2003). *State of the art review of mobile payment technology.* Technical Report, TCD-CS-2003-24.

Mobile Electronic Transaction Ltd. (2003). MeT white paper on mobile ticketing. Retrieved from http://www.mobiletransaction.org/pdf/R200/white_papers/MeT_White_paper_on_mobile_ticketing_v1.pdf.

Muntermann, J., Rossnagel, H., & Rannenberg, K. (2004). Mobile financial information services, security and certification. In *Post-Proceedings of the CSES 2004 2nd International Workshop on Certification and Security in Inter-Organizational E- Services, IFIP 18th World Computer Congress 2004.*

Newcomb, E., Pashley, T., & Stasko, J. (2003). Mobile computing in the retail arena. In *Proceedings of the ACM Conference on Human Factors in Computing Systems* (pp. 337-244). New York: ACM Press.

Pascoe, J. (1998). Adding generic contextual capabilities to wearable computers. In Proceedings of the 2nd International Symposium on Wearable Computers (pp. 92-99).

Rupnik, R., & Krisper, M. (2003). Mobile applications: A new application model in information systems. In *Proceedings of the 2nd International Conference on Mobile Business.*

Schilit, B., & Theimer, M. (1994). Disseminating active map information to mobile hosts. *IEEE Network, 8*(5), 22-32.

Schilit, B., Adams, N., & Want, R. (1994). Context-aware computing applications. In *Proceedings of the 1ˢᵗ International Workshop on Mobile Computing Systems and Applications* (pp. 85-90).

Schmidt, A., & Laerhoven, K. (2001). How to build smart appliances. *IEEE Personal Communications, 8*(4), 66-71

Stanoevska-Slabeva, K. (2003). Towards a reference model for m-commerce applications. In Proceedings of the 11th European Conference on Information Systems.

Strang, T., & Linnhoff-Popien, C. (2004). A context modeling survey. In *Proceedings of the 1st International Workshop on Advanced Context Modelling, Reasoning And Management* (pp. 34-41).

Tarasewich, P. (2003). Designing mobile commerce applications. *Communications of the ACM, 46*(12), 57-60.

Turban, E., King, D., Lee, J., & Viehland, D. (2004). *Electronic commerce.* New Jersey: Prentice Hall.

Valiente, P., & Heijden H. (2004). A method to identify opportunities for mobile business processes. In *Proceedings of E-Commerce and Web Technologies* (EC-Web 2004). Lecture Notes in Computer Science (pp. 238-247). Berlin, Heidelberg: Springer-Verlag.

Van De Kar, E. (2005). Guidelines for designing mobile information service systems in a value network. In *Proceedings of the 5ᵗʰ ACM International Conference on Electronic Commerce* (Vol. 50) (pp. 413-421). New York: ACM Press.

Varshney, U. (2003). Location management for mobile commerce applications in wireless Internet environment. *ACM Transactions on Internet Technology, 3*(3), 236-255.

Zeimpekis, V., Giaglis, G., & Lekakos, G. (2003). A taxonomy of indoor and outdoor positioning techniques for mobile location services. *ACM SIGECOM Exchanges, 3*(4), 19-27.

This work was previously published in Journal of Electronic Commerce in Organizations, Vol. 6, Issue 1, edited by M. Khosrow-Pour, pp. 63-78, copyright 2008 by IGI Publishing, formerly known as Idea Group Publishing (an imprint of IGI Global).

Chapter VI
Building Consumer Trust for Internet E-Commerce[1]

George Yee
National Research Council Canada, Canada

ABSTRACT

The growth of the Internet is increasing the deployment of e-commerce B2C services within such areas as e-retailing, e-learning, and e-health. However, a major impediment to the growth of e-commerce on the Internet is the lack of consumer trust in the provider of the e-service (Van Slyke, Belanger, Comunale, 2004). This chapter presents a literature survey of recent contributions to building trust in e-commerce, followed by a description of seven ways for the B2C Internet service provider to build trust in the use of its services among consumers.

INTRODUCTION

Accompanying the growth of the Internet has been the availability of a diverse number of e-services. Most consumers are familiar with online banking or online retailing via the Internet. Other Internet-based services such as e-learning (online courses), e-government (online government services such as tax information), and e-health (online medical advice and others) are becoming more commonplace as well. Yet, the pace of such growth can be many times the current rate if consumers found these services trustworthy. According to Van Slyke et al. (2004), worldwide Internet commerce was expected to reach $8.5 trillion in 2005, of which online retail sales is the most evident, with U.S. consumers spending $51.3 billion online in 2001, $72.1 billion in 2002, and a projected $217.8 billion in 2007. However, Van Slyke et al. (2004) also report that not all forecasts are as rosy: while total online spending is increasing, per person online spending is quickly declining. These authors indicate that concerns over privacy and trust are among the most important factors that turn an online buyer into a nonbuyer. Kim and Prabhakar (2004) examine the role of trust in consumers' first adoption of Internet banking. They report that consumers' initial trust in the e-banking service is necessary for making use of the service and that this initial trust is based on trust for the "e-channel," the electronic channel through which service transactions are conducted (i.e., the Internet). Kim and Prabhakar (2004) state that trust of the e-banking service calls for trust in the provider of the service (the bank) and trust in the e-channel.

This chapter has two main objectives. The first objective is to present a literature survey of recent contributions to building trust for e-commerce. The second objective is to provide a description of seven methods that can be taken by the B2C Internet service provider to increase consumer trust in its services. These methods are (1) branding, (2) seal of approval (including privacy seals), (3) trustable user interface, (4) trusted subproviders, (5) reputation, (6) insurance, and (7) economic incentives. Thus, the reader will gain from this work: (a) an awareness of what research has been done in the area of building trust for e-commerce, and (b) knowledge of seven practical approaches that can be used to make B2C services trustworthy to consumers (and thereby increase sales and profits).

It is useful in a chapter on "trust" to define the meaning of trust. Gefen (2002) defines trust as "a willingness to be vulnerable to the actions of another person or people" or "the expectation that commitments undertaken by another person or organization will be fulfilled." Gefen (2002) also states that "overall trust is the product of a set of trustworthiness beliefs" that are primarily about the ability, integrity, and benevolence of the trusted party. "Integrity is the belief that the trusted party adheres to accepted rules of conduct, such as honesty and keeping promises. Ability is beliefs about the skills and competence of the trusted party. Benevolence is the belief that the trusted party, aside from wanting to make a legitimate profit, wants to do good to the customer." Of course, trust is important for many social and business relationships, setting the stage for interactions and expectations. Trust is even more important for e-commerce than ordinary commerce, since the business environment of the Web is less verifiable and less controllable. When consumers supply private information needed by a Web service, they expose themselves to possible unethical use and disclosure of their data.

The remainder of this chapter is organized as follows. The "Literature Survey" section summarizes the content and findings of recent works on building trust for e-commerce. The section "Seven Ways to Build Consumer Trust for Internet E-Commerce" describes the seven methods mentioned above for building trust. The section "Future Trends" discusses the likely evolution of trust and e-commerce in the coming years. Finally, the section "Conclusion" concludes the chapter.

LITERATURE SURVEY

Many papers describing trust and e-commerce have appeared in recent years in response to the growth of the Internet and e-commerce. We present a nonexhaustive review of some of the more recent papers here (Table 1), categorizing them according to the following focus areas: "overall trust factors," "trust models and frameworks," "aspects of trust or methods for trust," "trust in specific sectors or geographic areas," "privacy and security," and "user interface issues." It is recommended that the reader peruse this table to find entries of interest and then read the corresponding original papers, as the summaries and key findings in the table may not do the original papers justice. In addition to the review here, we will refer to these papers in the remaining sections of this work as appropriate.

The above survey indicates that much work has been done in terms of trust models and frameworks for understanding the role of trust in e-commerce. All studies point to the same conclusion, that trust plays a key role in consumers' decisions to adopt e-commerce. Some of the more interesting conclusions arrived at by these authors include (i) consumers' private information

Table 1. Survey of recent papers on trust in e-commerce

Focus Area / Paper	Summary of Content	Key Findings
Overall Trust Factors		
Araujo & Araujo (2003). Developing trust in Internet commerce.	Describes factors that can influence a consumer's trust; also presents key elements for improving such trust.	A weighted checklist or automated tool can be developed to improve the trustworthiness of Web sites.
Gefen (2002). Reflections on the dimensions of trust and trustworthiness among online consumers.	Based on the premise that trust is multi-dimensional, proposes a three dimensional scale of trustworthiness dealing with integrity, benevolence, and ability; shows the importance of examining each dimension individually.	May be better to regard online consumer trustworthiness beliefs as a set of interrelated beliefs about the vendor rather than as one overall assessment; need to realize that trust may be multi-dimensional as well as uni-dimensional.
Kim & Tadisina (2005). Factors impacting customers' initial trust in e-businesses: An empirical study.	Uses previous studies and logical reasoning to define initial trust and examines its predictors. Empirical results explaining the factors impacting customers' initial trust in e-businesses are also presented.	The results provided evidence that Web site quality has the largest effect on customers' beliefs that an e-business had competence and goodwill. Other predictors like company profile and supporting organization, had lesser effects. Authors caution that these results should be used with caution since they were based on old data gathered under limited conditions.
Van Slyke et al (2004). Factors influencing the adoption of Web-based shopping: the impact of trust.	Using the literature on trust and diffusion of information, discusses the role of trust on consumers' intention to use B2C e-commerce; presents the results of a consumer survey to determine the influence of trust on decisions to make purchases.	Perceptions of trust are related to intentions to shop on the Web. Further, perceived ideas of relative advantage, complexity, compatibility, and image are also related to such intentions. While trust is important, the influence of trust seems to be less than some other factors.
Trust Models and Frameworks		
Bhattacharya & Saha (2004). Trust dimensions in e-retailing: A strategic exploration.	Focuses on development of trust through understanding and risk analysis as perceived by the consumer; provides a conceptual model and framework for future studies on why people are apprehensive to buying on the Internet.	Tips to help providers gain the trust of their customers; building trust is a long-term proposition; propensity of customers to trust an online shopping process can only be supported, not controlled, since trust needs to be earned.
Chen & Park (2004). Trust and privacy in electronic commerce.	Proposes a research model with trust and privacy as two endogenous variables along with other exogenous variables such as independent self-construal, interdependent self-construal, technological knowledge, and Web site quality, that are expected to affect the trust level and privacy concerns of Internet consumers.	Identified several major factors that affect trust and privacy in e-commerce; proposed eight hypotheses regarding trust, privacy, and self-construals. An example of a hypothesis is (Hypothesis 3) *Internet consumers with interdependent self-construals will have lower level of privacy concerns when shopping online.*
Chen, Gillenson, & Sherrell (2004). Consumer acceptance of virtual stores: A theoretical model and critical success factors for virtual stores.	Proposes a theoretical model, the Model of Consumer Acceptance of Virtual Store, for predicting consumer acceptance of virtual stores. Results of testing this model are also presented.	The proposed model can explain and predict consumer acceptance of virtual stores substantially well. The authors give advice to modify model input and parameters for additional research studies.

(continued on following page)

Table 1. continued

Kong & Hung (2006). Modeling initial and repeat online trust in B2C e-commerce.	Proposes an integrated model of online trust, and identifies the fundamental drivers of the online trust attitude formation process by adopting the dual cognitive processing notions of the Elaboration Likelihood Model of persuasion. Attempts to identify the fundamental drivers of information processes that lead to customers' trust decisions.	Identified two fundamental drivers that aid customers in their trust decision-making processes: motivation and ability to process relevant information. Authors believe that their model provides a basis to understand the relationships between initial and repeat customer online trust.
McKnight, Kacmar, & Choudhury (2003). Whoops... did I use the wrong concept to predict e-commerce trust? Modeling the risk-related effects of trust vs. distrust concepts.	Makes the point that mistrust is better suited at addressing issues of high risk (e.g., perceptions that the Web is risky), and proposes a model making use of both trust and mistrust to better predict high risk Web constructs.	E-commerce risk needs to be addressed by both trust and distrust concepts. Disposition to trust tends to affect low- or medium-risk constructs; disposi-tion to distrust tends to affect high risk constructs (e.g., willing-ness to depend on the Web site).
Nefti, Meziane, & Kasiran (2005). A fuzzy trust model for e-commerce.	Presents a trust model based on fuzzy logic. The authors argue that fuzzy logic is suitable for trust evaluation because it takes into account the uncertainties within e-commerce data. The trust model is validated using two case studies.	The fuzzy trust model addresses many issues that other trust models do not, such as taking into account the fuzzy nature of trust and the use of a substantial number of variables. Future trust systems should allow customers to rank trust variables according to their own perception and experience.
Salam, Iyer, Palvia, & Singh (2005). Trust in e-commerce.	Provides a comprehensive framework, based on four main research themes, for understand-ing trust in the context of Internet-enabled exchange re-lationships between consumers and Web-based vendors.	Trust is complex, containing technological, behavioral, social, psychological, and organizational interaction elements. Technical approaches to establishing trust are necessary but not sufficient. A comprehensive view of how consumer trust evolves related to specific actions is needed.
Serva, Benamati, & Fuller (2005). Trustworthiness in B2C e-commerce: An examination of alternative models.	Presents a study to clarify and advance the theoretical conceptualization of trustworthi-ness within a B2C context by synthesizing previous research and testing three alternative conceptualizations.	Viewing trustworthiness as a one-dimensional construct may be limited, in that it may not fully represent the underlying data. Instead, trustworthiness is better represented as a multidimensional construct, and both first and second-order conceptualizations are useful in e-commerce trust research, depending on purpose.
Tsygankov (2004). Evaluation of Web site trustworthiness from customer perspective, a framework.	Proposes a trust evaluative framework with 20 evaluation positions for use in reviewing commercial Web site trustworthiness from the customer perspective.	It would be useful to have a set of rules and recommendations for establishing trusted e-commerce environments. The presented framework may be used for evaluation of commercial Web site trustworthiness rate.
Yang, Hu, & Chen (2005). A Web trust-inducing model for e-commerce and empirical research.	Presents a Web trust-inducing model consisting of four dimensions, namely graphic design, structure design, content design, and social-cue design, along with four hypotheses. Presents the results of an online survey carried out to test the model and hypotheses. Identifies 12 trust-inducing features that can be applied to foster optimal levels of trust in customers.	Results of this study support the majority of the original model features. Some relationships did not receive significant support from the data, but the original model seems to hold fairly well after some moderate revision. The revised model is a reasonable starting point for developing a friendly interface for inducing trust in e-commerce.

(continued on following page)

Table 1. continued

Zhang, Kang, & He (2005). Towards a trust model with uncertainty for e-commerce systems.	Presents a trust model to account for the uncertain nature of trust using the cloud model. The traditional cloud model is extended to reason and describe the uncertainty of trust relationships scientifically and effectively.	Compared the proposed trust model with three other trust models in simulation experiments; results show that the proposed model performs better than the other three models. The proposed model has been applied in real e-commerce systems.
Aspects of Trust or Methods for Trust		
Atif (2002). Building trust in e-commerce.	Proposes a trust Web model based on a distributed search algorithm and a network of trusted intermediaries that can establish a trusted channel through which end parties deal virtually directly and risk free with each other.	Future e-commerce systems must support trust services to gain loyalty from both consumers and providers. The proposal here builds trust by negotiating a customers' request to complete a transaction using a sequence of trustworthy intermediaries.
Kim & Prabhakar (2004). Initial trust and the adoption of B2C e-commerce: The case of Internet banking.	Presents a conceptual model proposing that initial trust in the electronic channel as a banking medium and trust in the bank are major determinants of consumer acceptance.	A significant relationship exists between initial trust in the electronic channel and the adoption of Internet banking. However, trust could be neces-sary but not sufficient for the adoption of Internet banking.
Kim, Steinfield, & Lai (2004). Revisiting the role of Web assurance seals in consumer trust.	Examines consumers' awareness of Web assurance seal services and consumers' perceived importance of assurance seals found on B2C Web sites.	Consumer education increases the perceived importance of the seals, but consumers still are not likely to use these seals as indicators of site trustworthiness.
Kim & Kim (2005). A study of online transaction self-efficacy, consumer trust, and uncertainty reduction in electronic commerce transaction.	Explores self-efficacy as a factor that influences trust during an online transaction. Self-efficacy is an important factor in explaining motives and motivations of individual behaviors and choices.	Self-efficacy plays an important role in online transactions by negatively influencing perceived risk and positively influencing consumer trust. Online trans-action self-efficacy is a stronger predictor of risk perception than disposition to trust.
Lee, Ahn, & Han (2006). Analysis of trust in the e-commerce adoption.	Studies the trust of virtual communities to better understand and manage e-commerce. Proposes a theoretical model to clarify the factors as they are related to a Technology Acceptance Model. In particular, the relationship between trust and intentions is hypothesized.	When the users of a virtual community consider information exchange between one another, they are more sensitive to the trust between members than the trust in service providers. However, when they are interested in online purchasing, trust in service providers has a stronger impact on intention to purchase than trust between members.
Moores (2005). Do consumers understand the role of privacy seals in e-commerce?	Describes a study aimed at answering the basic question of whether online consumers understand or care about privacy seals and whether such measures have any impact on their online shopping.	While respondents to the study understand that privacy seals have something to do with promoting trust online, they are generally unaware of what a site must do to acquire a seal, or even what a genuine seal actually looks like. Furthermore, while almost all of the respondents had bought online, less than one-third would only trust a site with a seal. Serious questions need to be asked of the role of privacy seals in developing online trust.
Moores & Dhillon (2003). Do privacy seals in e-commerce really work?	Examines whether privacy seals in e-commerce really work.	Good news: the three main seals (TRUSTe, WebTrust, BBB-Online) have sensible data privacy principles and strive to ensure compliance by recipient Web sites. Bad news: Serious abuses by recipient sites continue. Perhaps legislation is required.

(continued on following page)

Table 1. continued

Salam, Rao, & Pegels (2003). Consumer-perceived risk in e-commerce transactions.	Examines consumer-perceived risks of transactions over the Internet focusing on the financial dimension. A framework is developed to identify critical aspects that need to be present or developed to reduce perceived risk.	One way to reduce consumer-perceived risk is to develop institutional trust using financial and social institutions as guarantors of e-commerce activity. Another way is for vendors to offer economic incen-tives (e.g., competitive pricing).
Tang, Thom, Wang, Tan, Show, & Tang (2003). Using insurance to create trust on the Internet.	Examines the use of insurance as a proxy in order to create trust for e-commerce activities over the Internet.	People surveyed were enthu-siastic about using insurance to effect trust, but expressed reservations about paying for it. The insurance value proposition needs further study but arguments can be made for its viability.
Trust in Specific Sectors or Geographic Areas		
Barnard & Wesson (2004). A trust model for e-commerce in South Africa.	Proposes a trust model for e-commerce in South Africa based on guidelines identified as significant for e-commerce in South Africa.	Guidelines identified can be applied to the design and eval-uation of e-commerce sites. The guidelines and the trust model together can improve the usability and level of consumer trust in South African e-commerce.
Kim, Ferrin, & Rao (2003). A study of the effect of consumer trust on consumer expectations and satisfaction: the Korean experience.	Proposes an e-commerce framework for the relationship between consumer trust, satisfaction, and expectation. The proposed models are tested using Internet consumer behavior data from two major Korean universities.	Both consumers' trust and expectation have positive influ-ences on consumers' satisfaction. The more consumers trust the seller, the higher the expectation they have, and the more likely to be satisfied. Consumer satis-faction may also affect the future trust and expectation of the consumer.
Luo & Najdawi (2004). Trust-building measures: A review of consumer health portals.	Analyzes trust building measures used by 12 major health portals and identifies the potential effects of these measures on consumer trust.	Each trust building measure affects the trustworthiness of the portal in different ways. Such measures are widely deployed, but the number and type used vary considerably among the portals.
Siau & Shen (2003). Building customer trust in mobile commerce.	Explores various facets of gaining consumer trust for mobile commerce.	Customer trust is crucial for the success of mobile commerce. Building this trust is complex, involving technology and business practices.
Sillence, Briggs, Fishwick, & Harris (2004). Trust and mistrust of online health sites.	Examines the question of how trust develops for online health information Web sites.	There is evidence for a staged model of trust in which visual appeal determines early decisions to mistrust sites, while credibility and personalization of informa-tion content influences the decision to select or trust them.
Sillence, Briggs, Fishwick, & Harris (2005). Guidelines for developing trust in health Web sites.	Similar to Sillence et al. (2004). Explores the question of how people decide which health Web sites to trust and which to reject.	Design guidelines for health Web sites. Staged model of trust as in Sillence et al. (2004). Within a health domain, it appears that personalization, site impetus, and social identity are especially important for site acceptance.
Privacy and Security		
Korba, Yee, Xu, Song, Patrick, & El-Khatib (2005). Privacy and trust in agent-supported distributed learning.	Explores the challenges, issues, and solutions for satisfying requirements for privacy and trust in agent-supported distributed learning.	Described many aspects of building privacy into agent-supported distributed learning. Not all described technologies would be required for every e-learning environment; need to use them where required, including in other types of e-business.

(continued on following page)

Table 1. continued

Levy & Gutwin (2005). Security through the eyes of users: Improving understanding of Web site privacy policies with fine-grained policy anchors.	Tackles the problem of understanding Web site privacy policies that make it difficult for the consumer to determine the cause and origin of conformance conflicts.	Integrated Privacy View that uses fine-grained policy anchors to present visual conformance information in the context of specific input fields. Users prefer this approach and could better determine the existence and source of privacy conflicts.
Nilsson, Adams, & Herd (2005). Building security and trust in online banking.	Examines the question of what influences users' perceptions of online banking security and trust.	One challenge for online banking is to maintain the balance between perceived trust, security, and usability for users. Authentication mechanisms can have a significant impact upon perceived trust in online banking.
Roussos & Moussouri (2004). Consumer perceptions of privacy, security, and trust in ubiquitous commerce.	Discusses the market forces that make the deployment of ubiquitous commerce infra-structures a priority for grocery retailing. Report on a study on consumer perceptions of security and privacy for MyGrocer, a recently developed ubiquitous commerce system.	Rather than focusing solely on the trustworthiness of a system, design should also address the affective aspects of interaction between ubiquitous commerce services and the consumer. It is unlikely that without allowing some degree of control over the system, consumers will be persuaded to use it. Indeed, controlling the flow of personal data is core in developing a trusting relationship between consumer and retailer.
Spiekermann, Grossklags, & Berendt (2001). E-privacy in 2nd generation e-commerce: Privacy preferences vs. actual behavior.	Examines the relationship between study participants' self-reported privacy preferences and their actual private data disclosing behavior during an online shopping episode.	In the study, participants disclosed private information contrary to their stated preferences. Therefore, current approaches to protect online privacy such as EU data protection regulation or P3P may not be effective since they assume that consumers will act according to their preferences.
User Interface Issues		
Barnard & Wesson (2003). Usability issues for e-commerce in South Africa: An empirical investigation.	Discusses an empirical study conducted in South Africa to determine if there were any usability problems on three well-known South African e-commerce sites and one international site.	A comparison of the strengths and weaknesses of each site. The five best and five worst features of the sites. Example best feature: home page gives clear indication of what site sells. Example worst feature: supply enough detail to enable product comparison.
Fang & Salvendy (2003). Customer-centered rules for design of e-commerce Web sites.	Describes a study in which real customers were interviewed to obtain information on what they liked and what difficulties they had in each stage of e-commerce Web site operation.	Nineteen most important design rules addressing customer concerns on home page, navigation, categorization, product information, shopping cart, checkout, and registration, and customer service.
Hussin, Keeling, Macaulay, & McGoldrick (2005). A trust agent for e-commerce: looking for clues.	Reviews the concept of trust in e-commerce and investigates 90 e-commerce Web sites to identify the presence of "clues" in the Web sites that signal the presence of several types of trust attributes; tests the presence of "clues" and trust attributes on Web sites against consumer perceptions of trustworthiness.	The results show that the clues correspond to the consumer search strategy for trust attributes. The clues are used as a basis for developing a personal trust agent (PTA) to assist consumers in assessing the trustworthiness of e-commerce Web sites.

(continued on following page)

Table 1. continued

Korba et al. (2005). Privacy and trust in agent supported distributed learning.	For this category of User Interface Issues, contains a section discussing the building of trustworthy user interfaces for distributed learning systems.	Interface design techniques, if properly used, can increase users' feelings of trust and reduce their perceptions of risk. Giving due consideration to users' privacy needs in terms of comprehension, consciousness, control, and consent, and making sure that the service satisfies these needs will be an important step for a usable and trusted environment.
Lanford & Hübscher (2004). Trustworthiness in e-commerce.	Examines the multifaceted notions of trust and trustworthiness and how they can be applied to e-commerce stores. Argues that high usability does not imply that the store is also trustworthy; formulates design guidelines for designing for trust.	Design guidelines for making a site more trustworthy, for example, fulfill the customer's expectations, show technical competence, let the user feel in control. Many e-commerce sites need major improvements to be successful. Improved usability is definitely key, but so is trustworthiness.
Pu & Chen (2006). Trust building with explanation interfaces.	Explores the potential of building users' trust with explanation interfaces. Presents major results from a survey that identified the most promising areas for investigating design issues for trust-inducing interfaces. Describes a set of general principles for constructing explanation interfaces that mostly contribute to trust formation.	Explanation interfaces have the greatest potential for competence-inspired trust with its users. A recommender agent's competence is positively correlated with users' intention to return, but not necessarily with their intention to purchase. An organization-based explanation interface should be more effective than the simple "why" interface, since it would be easier to compare different products and make a quicker decision.
Riegelsberger (2003). Interpersonal cues and consumer trust in e-commerce.	Investigates the effect of visual interpersonal cues (e.g., photo-graphs) on consumers' trust in e-commerce. Human trust decisions are also based on affective reactions, which can be triggered by interpersonal cues.	First results: visual interpersonal cues such as photographs have an effect on consumers' decision making. However, this effect strongly depends on context variables as well as individual differences.

disclosure behavior may not follow their stated privacy preferences (Spiekermann, Grossklags, & Berendt, 2001), (ii) the type of authentication mechanism used affects the level of user trust in online banking (Nilsson et al., 2005), (iii) technical approaches (i.e., security technology) for creating trust are necessary but not sufficient (Salam et al., 2005), (iv) trust could be necessary but not sufficient for consumers to adopt Internet banking (Kim & Prabhakar, 2004), (v) consumers may not use seals of approval (aka Web assurance seals) as indicators of Web site trustworthiness (Kim et al., 2004), and (vi) privacy seals do not appear to work as expected and their roles need to be seriously questioned (Moores, 2005; Moores & Dhillon, 2003).

These authors represent excellent references for our presentation of the seven methods to build trust in e-commerce (next section).

SEVEN WAYS TO BUILD CONSUMER TRUST FOR INTERNET E-COMMERCE

The following seven methods for building trust in Internet e-commerce are known approaches in one form or another. As most of these ideas (except for trusted subproviders and reputation) are already well described by other authors, we will keep our descriptions to a minimum and refer the interested reader to these other authors. In addition, these methods are presented here for information purposes only and not to be construed as recommendations. Finally, the methods differ in effectiveness and at least one is controversial.

Branding

Branding refers to the association of an unknown product or a service to a name that is well known and trustworthy among consumers. The intention (and hope) is that the trustworthiness of the name will be transferred to the product or service in the eyes of the consumer, that is, the consumer will also believe that the product or service is trustworthy. Branding is well described in terms of a company, a product, and a third party in Araujo and Araujo (2003).

An example of branding in e-commerce can be found in Amazon.com, where the consumer can directly purchase goods (usually used goods) from third-party sellers using the Amazon.com Web site. In this way, the third-party sellers hope to enjoy the trustworthiness and reputation that consumers associate with Amazon.com.

Seal of Approval (including privacy seals)

A seal of approval is an attestation by a recognized and trusted party that the receiver of the seal has lived up to or complied with a set of standards of good conduct, reliability, or trustworthiness. This is an old idea (e.g., Good Housekeeping Seal of Approval on household products) applied to modern e-commerce where the e-commerce Web site displays one or more seal(s) of approval to show that it is trustworthy, as attested to by the recognized and trusted parties. Seals of approval can be specialized to approve different aspects of

a consumer's Web site experience (e.g., Verisign Secure Site seal, BBBOnline Privacy seal). There is some controversy as to whether consumers are aware of these seals (Kim et al., 2004) and whether they really work as expected (Moores, 2005; Moores & Dhillon, 2003). Since, the main problem in this controversy appears to be lack of consumer awareness and recognition of the seals, perhaps the answer lies in educating consumers on the seals. However, Kim et al., (2004) state that although consumer education increases the perceived importance of the seals, consumers are still not likely to use them as indicators of Web site trustworthiness. Additional research is needed.

Trustable User Interface

When consumers purchase goods on an e-commerce Web site, they must make decisions about the trustability of the vendor as well as the technology they are using. A number of factors come into play in influencing those trust decisions. One of the most important contributors to trust is a well-designed visual interface. We quote from Korba et al. (2005): "A visual appearance that is clean, uses pleasing colors and graphics, is symmetrical, and is professional looking is usually rated as more trustable. Other design factors that can build trust are the amount of information provided to the user, such as the information on how a system operates and the status of any processing….Predictable performance can also be an important factor, with systems that respond rapidly and consistently, instilling higher levels of trust." Other ideas for building trustable visual interfaces include the use of 19 design rules derived from interviews with real consumers (Fang & Salvendy, 2003), allowing consumers some degree of control over the flow of personal data (Araujo & Araujo, 2003; Lanford & Hübscher, 2004;Roussos & Moussouri, 2004;), fulfilling customer expectations and showing technical competence (Lanford & Hübscher, 2004), and the use of visual interpersonal cues such as photographs (Riegelsberger, 2003).

Trusted Subproviders

A subprovider is a secondary provider that a primary provider uses to supply one or more components of its service. Components of a service could range from a functional component such as data mining to a logistical component such as payment for the service. By using trusted subproviders, the primary provider hopes that the trustworthiness of the trusted subproviders will be transferred to itself in the eyes of the consumer, that is, the consumer will see the primary provider as trustworthy because it uses subproviders that the consumer trusts. The trust effect is similar to branding. The most famous example of a trusted subprovider is Paypal.com for payment services.

In the literature, the closest reference to trusted subproviders is the work by Atif (2002), where the author recommends the use of third-party trusted intermediaries to guarantee payment and delivery. Atif (2002) proposes a "trust Web model based on a distributed search algorithm and a network of trusted intermediaries that can establish a trusted channel through which terminal transacting parties deal virtually directly and risk-free with each other." This approach differs slightly from our use of trusted subproviders in that the intermediaries do not provide components of the service itself but instead act like brokers, forming a trust path between consumer and vendor through which to forward the payment or the goods. Another related work is Salam et al. (2003), who recommend reducing consumer-perceived risk by developing institutional trust using financial and social institutions as guarantors of e-commerce activity. This is similar to the use of trusted intermediaries as guarantors in Atif (2002).

Reputation

The reputation of an e-commerce service provider directly determines whether a consumer will trust the provider's service. The higher the reputation of the provider, the higher the level of trust the consumer will have for the service. Thus, in order to use reputation to build consumer trust in a provider's service, (1) the provider has to be reputable, and (2) there needs to be some way to easily calculate and display the provider's reputation for all consumers to see or access.

The most famous e-commerce reputation system in actual use is the buyer/seller rating system in eBay.com. In this reputation system, buyers rate sellers on how well they carried out their part of the transaction, for example, *goods delivered in a timely manner?*, *goods arrived in condition advertised?*. Sellers rate buyers on how well the buyers fulfilled their end of the bargain, for example, *accurate payment?*, *prompt payment?*. The resultant scores are administered by eBay itself and are posted for all to see. Moreover, the actual text of the buyer or seller rating (e.g., "very fast delivery") is posted as well for all to see. A buyer thinking of making a purchase can check the seller's rating and perhaps peruse the text of all the seller's ratings to make sure the seller has a good reputation before committing to the purchase. By so doing, the buyer can ascribe some trust to the seller if the seller has a good reputation.

A reputation system similar to the one at eBay. com can be set up for general e-commerce providers and consumers. Consumers can rate providers, and vice versa, using the Web site of a trusted authority that would administer the ratings and make sure that ratings are secure and fair. The authority would investigate outlandish ratings to ensure that one party is not "badmouthing" another party. Consumers or providers could then access the authority's Web site to ascertain the reputation of the transacting partner before committing to the transaction. The trusted authority could be a role played by a government agency as a public service and for the good of the economy so that there would be no charges for use of its services. Actually, in traditional commerce, the existing network of Better Business Bureau (BBB) offices, where consumers can lodge complaints against providers, is somewhat like what we are proposing. However, with BBB, consumers do not rate every transaction and consumers themselves are not rated. Nevertheless, traditional commerce consumers can, in many cases, check the BBB for the reputation of a provider.

We did not find any references in the literature to the direct use of reputation to build consumer trust in e-commerce as we describe here. However, other methods such as branding, seal of approval, and trusted subproviders are of course based on the reputation of the name brand, the giver of the seal of approval, and the trusted subprovider, respectively.

Insurance

In today's world, insurance can be found for many areas, as long as the insurance companies find it profitable. It is no surprise then that insurance be proposed as a means of building trust in e-commerce. Tang et al. (2003) is the definitive reference for this method of building trust. In their paper, trust for e-commerce is divided into three types of trust: market space trust (trust that both buyers and sellers must have in the market space where the transaction will occur), buyer's trust (the trust of the buyer that the goods will be delivered as agreed), and seller's trust (the trust of the seller that s/he will be paid for the delivered goods). Tang et al. (2003) then propose specific insurance policies to cover each of the areas in which these types of trust must arise. The different types of trust will then arise as a result of the insurance policies being in place. The authors also conducted interviews

with insurance and technology organizations to determine the feasibility of their insurance approach. They report that: "most of the people surveyed and interviewed were enthusiastic about using insurance as a proxy for effecting trust on the Internet. However, there were reservations about paying for such a product." To counter these reservations, the authors cite the example of bottled water, which is a popular purchase item now, but there may have been reservations about paying for bottled water when it was first proposed. Tang et al. (2003) conclude that building e-commerce trust with insurance would provide too many benefits to be ignored. We refer the interested reader to Tang et al. (2003) for the details.

Economic Incentives

The use of economic incentives to build trust in e-commerce refers to incentives to purchase such as reduced pricing, more product for the same price, or free delivery offered by a seller to a potential buyer. The principal behind economic incentives is the observation by researchers (Salam et al., 2003) that some consumers will make purchases if there is sufficient economic incentive, even if their trust level for the vendor is low. In this sense, it may not really be building up the consumer's trust but rather reducing the consumer's perceived risk of the service, that is, the consumer believes that s/he is getting such a good deal that it is "worth the risk." Nevertheless, if the consumer makes the purchase the end result is the same.

FUTURE TRENDS

Consumer trust for e-commerce is a key enabler of e-commerce success. We have seen how various researchers have tackled the problems of both understanding trust and how it can be built up. This research will of course continue and will involve a melding of diverse disciplines from engineering, computer science, and the social sciences such as psychology and sociology. A rapidly developing area of trust is how to build trust through trustable interfaces, that is, human-machine interfaces that inspire trust in the machine. Another growing area of research that is related to trustable interfaces is the role of usability in building consumer trust. The more usable the device, the more likely it should be trusted. However, the question is: How can usability be improved so that the result inspires trust? Trustable interfaces and usability have important applications in the new field of biometrics, where trust is needed to sooth the consumer's concerns over the use of biometric devices that can be awkward to use. Still, a further area of research will be towards expanding the number of ways of building consumer trust, as described previously.

One goal of improving consumer trust in e-commerce may be stated simply as *arriving at some future state where consumers trust e-commerce to the same extent as they trust brick and mortar commerce.* Achieving this goal will require a thorough understanding of the nature of trust and how to achieve it. It will no doubt require the application of some of the ways of building trust given previously, as well as new methods of building trust that are yet to be discovered. We are still far from achieving this goal, but we have made a reasonable start.

CONCLUSION

We began by surveying the recent literature on contributions to building consumer trust in e-commerce and found that there are many works in this area, especially on trust frameworks and models. However, all such studies conclude that trust is an important and key factor for e-commerce success. A number of authors had remarkable or counter-intuitive findings such as (1) consumers' private information disclosure behavior may not follow their stated privacy preferences (Spiekermann et al., 2001), (2) the type of authentication mecha-

nism used affects the level of user trust in online banking (Nilsson et al., 2005), and (3) technical approaches (i.e., security technology) for creating trust are necessary but not sufficient (Salam et al., 2005). We then proceeded to describe seven practical ways for e-commerce service providers to build consumer trust in their services. Most of these methods are already known and described in the literature but we contributed two, hopefully new ones or variations over existing ones, that as far as we can tell are not in the literature, namely the use of trusted subproviders and the use of reputation. We hope that this work has provided the reader with some useful insights and tools for building trust in e-commerce.

REFERENCES

Araujo, I., & Araujo, I. (2003, October). Developing trust in Internet commerce. In *Proceedings of the 2003 Conference of the Centre for Advanced Studies on Collaborative Research* (pp. 1-15).

Atif, Y. (2002). Building trust in e-commerce. *IEEE Internet Computing, 6*(1), 18-24.

Barnard, L., & Wesson, J. L. (2003, September). Usability issues for e-commerce in South Africa: An empirical investigation. In *Proceedings of the 2003 Annual Research Conference of the South African Institute of Computer Scientists and Information Technologists on Enablement Through Technology (SAICSIT '03)* (pp. 258-267).

Barnard, L., & Wesson, J. (2004, October). A trust model for e-commerce in South Africa. In *Proceedings of the 2003 Annual Research Conference of the South African Institute of Computer Scientists and Information Technologists on Enablement Through Technology (SAICSIT '04)* (pp. 23-32).

Bhattacharya, K. K., & Saha, S. (2004, October). Trust dimensions in e-retailing: A strategic exploration. In *Proceedings, 2004 IEEE International*

Engineering Management Conference (Vol. 2, pp. 825-828).

Chen, J.-C. V., & Park, Y. I. (2004, March 28-31). Trust and privacy in electronic commerce. In *Proceedings of the 2004 IEEE International Conference on E-Technology, E-Commerce, and E-Service (EEE'04)* (pp. 117-120).

Chen, L., Gillenson, M. L., & Sherrell, D. L. (2004). Consumer acceptance of virtual stores: A theoretical model and critical success factors for virtual stores. *ACM SIGMIS Database, 35*(2), 8-31.

Fang, X., & Salvendy, G. (2003). Customer-centered rules for design of e-commerce Web sites. *Communications of the ACM, 46*(12), 332-336.

Gefen, D. (2002). Reflections on the dimensions of trust and trustworthiness among online consumers. *ACM SIGMIS Database, 33*(3), 38-53.

Hussin, A. R. C., Keeling, K., Macaulay, L., & McGoldrick, P. (2005, March 29-April 1). A trust agent for e-commerce: Looking for clues. In *Proceedings of the 2005 IEEE International Conference on E-Technology, E-Commerce, and E-Service (EEE '05)* (pp. 286-289).

Kim, D. J., Ferrin, D. L., & Rao, H. R. (2003, September). A study of the effect of consumer trust on consumer expectations and satisfaction: The Korean experience. In *Proceedings of the 5th International Conference on Electronic commerce (ICEC '03)* (pp. 310-315).

Kim, D. J., Steinfield, C., & Lai, Y. (2004, March). Revisiting the role of Web assurance seals in consumer trust. In *Proceedings of the 6th International Conference on Electronic Commerce (ICEC 2004)* (pp. 280-287).

Kim, E., & Tadisina, S. (2005, January 3-6). Factors impacting customers' initial trust in e-businesses: An empirical study. In *Proceedings of the 38th Annual Hawaii International Conference on System Sciences (HICSS '05)* (pp. 170b-170b).

Kim, K. K., & Prabhakar, B. (2004). Initial trust and the adoption of B2C e-commerce: The case of Internet banking. *ACM SIGMIS Database, 35*(2), 50-64.

Kim, Y. H., & Kim, D. J. (2005, January). A study of online transaction self-efficacy, consumer trust, and uncertainty reduction in electronic commerce transaction. In *Proceedings of the 38th Annual Hawaii International Conference on System Sciences (HICSS '05)* (pp. 170c-170c).

Kong, W.-C., & Hung, Y.-T. (2006, January 4-7). Modeling initial and repeat online trust in B2C e-commerce. In *Proceedings of the 39th Annual Hawaii International Conference on System Sciences (HICSS '06)* (Vol. 6, pp. 120b-12b).

Korba, L., Yee, G., Xu, Y., Song, R., Patrick, A. S., & El-Khatib, K. (2005). Privacy and trust in agent-supported distributed learning. In F. Oscar Lin (Ed.), *Designing distributed learning environments with intelligent software agents* (pp. 67-114). Information Science Publishing.

Lanford, P., & Hübscher, R. (2004, April). Trustworthiness in e-commerce. In *Proceedings of the 42nd Annual Southeast Regional Conference* (pp. 315-319).

Lee, H., Ahn, H., & Han, I. (2006, January 4-7). Analysis of trust in the e-commerce adoption. In *Proceedings of the 39th Annual Hawaii International Conference on System Sciences (HICSS '06)* (Vol. 6, pp. 113c-113c).

Levy, S. E., & Gutwin, C. (2005, May). Security through the eyes of users: Improving understanding of Web site privacy policies with fine-grained policy anchors. In *Proceedings of the 14th International Conference on World Wide Web* (pp. 480-488).

Luo, W., & Najdawi, M. (2004). Trust-building measures: A review of consumer health portals. *Communications of the ACM, 47*(1), 108-113.

McKnight, H., Kacmar, C., & Choudhury, V. (2003, January). Whoops... did I use the wrong concept to predict e-commerce trust? Modeling the risk-related effects of trust vs. distrust concepts. In *Proceedings of the 36th Annual Hawaii International Conference on System Sciences* (10 pp.).

Moores, T. (2005). Do consumers understand the role of privacy seals in e-commerce? *Communications of the ACM, 48*(3), 86-91.

Moores, T. T., & Dhillon, G. (2003). Do privacy seals in e-commerce really work? *Communications of the ACM, 46*(12), 265-271.

Nefti, S., Meziane, F., & Kasiran, K. (2005, July 19-22). A fuzzy trust model for e-commerce. In *Proceedings, Seventh IEEE International Conference on E-Commerce Technology* (pp. 401-404).

Nilsson, M., Adams, A., & Herd, S. (2005, April). Building security and trust in online banking. In *CHI '05 extended abstracts on human factors in computing systems* (pp. 1701-1704).

Pu, P., & Chen, L. (2006, January). Trust building with explanation interfaces. In *Proceedings of the 11th International Conference on Intelligent User Interfaces (IUI '06)* (pp. 93-100).

Riegelsberger, J. (2003, April). Interpersonal cues and consumer trust in e-commerce. In *CHI '03 extended abstracts on human factors in computing systems* (pp. 674-675).

Roussos, G., & Moussouri, T. (2004). Consumer perceptions of privacy, security and trust in ubiquitous commerce. *Personal and Ubiquitous Computing, 8*(6), 416-429.

Salam, A. F., Iyer, L., Palvia, P., & Singh, R. (2005). Trust in e-commerce. *Communications of the ACM, 48*(2), 72-77.

Salam, A. F., Rao, H. R., & Pegels, C. C. (2003). Consumer-perceived risk in e-commerce transactions. *Communications of the ACM, 46*(12), 325-331.

Serva, M. A., Benamati, J., & Fuller, M. A. (2005). Trustworthiness in B2C e-commerce: An examination of alternative models. *The DATABASE for Advances in Information Systems, 36*(3), 89-108.

Siau, K., & Shen, Z. (2003). Building customer trust in mobile commerce. *Communications of the ACM, 46*(4), 91-94.

Sillence, E., Briggs, P., Fishwick, L., & Harris, P. (2004, April). Trust and mistrust of online health sites. In *Proceedings of the SIGCHI Conference on Human Factors in Computing Systems* (pp. 663-670).

Sillence, E., Briggs, P., Fishwick, L., & Harris, P. (2005, May). Guidelines for developing trust in health Web sites. *Special Interest Tracks and Posters of the 14th International Conference on World Wide Web* (pp. 1026-1027).

Spiekermann, S., Grossklags, J., & Berendt, B. (2001, October). E-privacy in 2nd generation e-commerce: Privacy preferences vs. actual behavior. In *Proceedings of the 3rd ACM conference on Electronic Commerce* (pp. 38-47).

Tang, F., Thom, M. G., Wang, L. T., Tan, J. C., Chow, W. Y., & Tang, X. (2003). Using insurance to create trust on the Internet. *Communications of the ACM, 46*(12), 337-344.

Tsygankov, V. A. (2004, March). Evaluation of Web site trustworthiness from customer perspective, a framework. In *Proceedings of the 6th International Conference on Electronic Commerce (ICEC 2004)* (pp. 265-271).

Van Slyke, C., Belanger, F., & Comunale, C. L. (2004). Factors influencing the adoption of Web-based shopping: The impact of trust. *ACM SIGMIS Database, 35*(2), 32-49.

Yang, Y., Hu, Y., & Chen, J. (2005, August). A Web trust-inducing model for e-commerce and empirical research. In *Proceedings of the 7ᵗʰ International Conference on Electronic Commerce (ICEC '05)* (pp. 188-194).

Zhang, G., Kang, J., & He, R. (2005, October 12-18). Towards a trust model with uncertainty for e-commerce systems. In *Proceedings, IEEE International Conference on E-Business Engineering (ICEBE 2005)* (pp. 200-207).

ENDNOTE

[1]   NRC Paper Number: NRC 48509

Chapter VII
Trust in E–Commerce:
Risk and Trust Building

Loong Wong
University of Canberra, Australia

ABSTRACT

This chapter examines the importance of trust in business-to-consumer e-commerce. The author explores the issue of trust in the development and implementation of e-commerce and focuses on the context and role of users and consumers in transactions. The author contends that trust is more than a technical consideration and emphasizes the non-technical components such as community, identity, and experiences and their relevance to e-commerce. Despite the growing ubiquity of e-commerce, analysts and commentators continue to draw our attention to the issue of trust in e-commerce transactions. In particular, stories of "hacking," "phishing," and illegitimate online transactions have been an on-going public and private concern. These breaches are seen as cyber crimes and detrimental to the development of an efficient and effective business practice. Resolving these breaches are costly; businesses have to outlay financial resources not only to fix the breaches but, in the eyes of their clients, such breaches call into question the efficacy, integrity,

and security of these businesses, creating both disquiet and a potential shift to alternative providers. For individuals, it boils down to an invasion of privacy and a lack of trust in the integrity of business systems and practices. This chapter examines the critical import of trust in business-to-consumer e-commerce. The chapter begins by exploring the issue of trust in the development and implementation of e-commerce; in particular, it focuses on the context and the central role of users and consumers in the transaction process. I argue that this development is an evolutionary one congruent with increasing complexities and the shift towards a risk society. The author argues that there is a growing virtualization of social life and that this virtualization plays an important role in our everyday lives. In particular, it transforms our views of agency, interactionism and community, generating both new identities and new possible spheres of autonomous action. Businesses have cashed in on these developments and sought to provide users with choices and ease of use, contributing to a pervasive and critical reception to e-commerce business practices. Via their Web sites and information conveyed, we learn to trust the information we receive. As such, we tend to equate trust with information. Trust becomes no more than a technical consideration. However, trust is and cannot simply be reducible to information. Its nontechnical components—the issues of community, identity and experiences—are critically important. As such, I seek to examine these issues in this chapter and their relationships to the building of trust and consequently, their relevance to e-commerce.

INTRODUCTION

E-commerce has become ubiquitous and according to some, will be a high trust community (Davidson & Rees-Mogg, 1997, p. 371). Yet, numerous studies point out that obstacles remain in the uptake of-commerce for many consumers. One of the reasons was identified by Hoffman, Novak, and Paralta (1999): the fundamental lack of faith between most businesses and consumers remain a key consideration for many. Frauds, on-line scams, hacking and phishing are common occurrences and the everyday consumer is increasingly concerned over breaches of privacy and security. In their study of "Consumer Reactions to Electronic Shopping," Jarvenpaa and Todd (1997) found concerns with risk, both personal and performance, were recorded by over 50% of Web shoppers. On the other hand, Cheskin Research (1999) found that only 10% of participants in their survey on e-commerce usage considered little or no risk when purchasing on the Web. Clearly, there are significant differences in views. In e-commerce, critical and vital information essential for effecting transactions is carried from site to site.

Increasingly, there are concerns over security breaches and the misuse of data. For the consumer, companies that profess to be reliable and dependable can appear and disappear in an instant, jeopardizing many of their personal and economic details. Industry sources have, however,

claimed that the rapid technological evolution of the Internet as a medium for social intercourse and commerce will in itself deliver new solutions and in the process offer new possibilities and context for trust creation and maintenance mechanisms (Bhimani, 1996). Such a technologically determinist viewpoint is indeed common and suggests that through the use of, and exposure to, these new technologies, users will adopt new forms of behavior explicitly linked to the technology itself. Further, it suggests that these forms of behavior will be novel—they neither grow out of, nor bear any relation to, users' everyday actions, experiences, or routine practices. It implies that there is a special and new category of human behavior which will come into being and is substantially different from the everyday systems of trust that we use to routinely order our behavior. However, it is posited that such a viewpoint is unsustainable and patently inaccurate. Instead, the chapter suggests that a more considered approach to the understanding of trust and the ways in which it affects people's e-commerce practices (and also their decision not to practise) is needed if we are to understand and further develop e-commerce.

First, the chapter examines how the notion of trust can be applied to consumer e-commerce, exploring the ways in which trust is relevant and applied by users engaging in shopping transactions. The chapter then draws on previous sociological research on trust, interaction, and everyday experiences, particularly in trying to show that trust is best understood as a non-technical or deterministic process. The chapter demonstrates how users approaching e-commerce bring with them previous experiences of trust and apply them to the new computer-mediated situations rather than being merely acted upon in e-commerce systems that affect their preferred actions and responses. The chapter then examines five areas at which interactions and e-commerce systems intersect and argue that these areas are critical for those building, managing and maintaining e-commerce projects and strategies.

WHAT IS TRUST?

Everyday, we place our trust in people, even strangers, and in the services these people provide. We trust that our friends, our accountants, and our lawyers will not betray our confidences, that the food we consume will not poison us, that the car we travel in will not break down, that people will listen to us when we talk to them, that our parents and children will tell us the truth and, indeed, the list goes on. If we do not place our trust so routinely in others, life would be practically unbearable, and we would be enveloped by all sorts of fearful possibilities and risks. Our life would rapidly descend into chaos or helplessness and we would rapidly be tagged as neurotic, schizophrenic, obsessive-compulsive. For most of us, this scenario is nowhere near our day to day reality—instead we learn to interact and trust people and strangers.

However, there are different levels of trust. Blanket trust is seldom applied toward another party. As Baier points out, there needs to be "an answer not just to the question, Whom do you trust? but to the question, What do you trust to them?" (Baier, 1986, p. 236). Indeed, to say I trust you seems almost always to be elliptical, as though we can assume some other phrase as "to do X" or "in matters Y" (Hardin, 1993, p. 506). It follows that trust is situational where A trusts B to do X and that X is often narrowly defined and that A distrusts B with regard to Y and that A has no conscious view of B's trustworthiness with regard to all other matters.

For the most part, much of the literature on trust written by marketing researchers implicitly embraces this view of blanket trust even though they often stress the multidimensionality of trust (Anderson & Naurus, 1990; Butler, 1991). Other disciplines have each approached the notion of trust differently. However, the majority of writers have sought to locate the discourse of trust within related discussions of security, confidence, vulnerability, uncertainty, and risk

(Abdul-Rahman & Hailes, 2000; Barber & Kim, 2000; Blois, 1999; Giddens, 1990; Lane & Bachman, 1998; Lewicki & Bunker, 1995; Lewis & Weigert, 1985b; Luhmann, 1988; Tan & Thoen, 2002; Yuan & Sung, 2004). Several factors, such as shared norms, repeated interactions, and shared experiences have been suggested to facilitate the development of trust (Baier, 1986; Bradach & Eccles, 1998; Lewis & Weigert, 1985; Mayer et Al., 1995). Another factor seen as critical in promoting trust and cooperation is the anticipation of future association (Anderson & Naurus, 1990; Powell, 1990); others see face-to-face encounters as irreplaceable for building trust and repairing shattered trust (Nohria & Eccles, 1992; O'Hara-Devereaux & Johansen, 1994).

Sociologically, the idea of trust has had a long intellectual career (Gambetta, 1988; Seligman, 1997; Silver, 1985; Sztompka, 1999) dating back to Garfinkel's works in the early sixties (Garfinkel, 1963). From his work, a number of crucial observations around trust develop:

- Trust is manifest in the actions of individuals
- We judge how to act based upon the trust we have in others
- Trust is used to the benefit of both parties involved in an action
- Where trust is offered is it generally expected in return
- Trust is offered based upon "expectancies" of other's behavior
- Trust is used to define one's relationship to others

For Garfinkel, trust is active, interactive, symbolic, and a transaction involving interactions and negotiations between individuals. There will be rules governing these interactions but they are context sensitive as can be seen from the differences in interactions between family members, friends in a social environment, business acquaintances. These rules and the routines, scripts, or "practical consciousness" that organize our everyday behavior are "tacit or taken-for-granted qualities [which] form the essential condition which allows actors to concentrate on tasks in hand" (Giddens, 1991, p. 36). Further, these organizational techniques must be mutual to all those involved in an encounter, and indeed have been incorporated into the business literature, for example, the concepts of embeddedness and networks, among others.

In the business discipline, trust is, however, often viewed from a rational-calculative and social perspective—the effecting of self-interest (Coleman, 1990; Gulati, 1995; Lane, 1998). Increases in trust decrease transaction costs and the converse applies (Barber & Kim, 2000; Casson, 1995). Trust, as such, mediates and manages risks (Sztompka, 1999, pp. 29-32). Socially, trust enables relationships and high-levels of cooperation and inter-organizational relationship (Kramer & Tyler, 1996; Zand, 1972), particularly where a contract does not or cannot fully specify the nature of a relationship between two parties. Thus, for example, business networks, close supplier relationships and economic clusters are key examples of such trust-engendered mechanisms, allowing companies to be cooperative, more effective, efficient and productive (Axelrod, 1990). They are also more predictable (Rose & Miler, 1992).

E-COMMERCE, TRUST, AND THE SOCIOLOGICAL IMAGINATION

The world of e-commerce is often seen as one in which teenagers are making their dotcom fortunes before they are old enough to have to pay taxes. Consumer computer technology has developed at such a speed that people who were using e-mail 10 years ago remember the advent of Mosaic at the end of 1993,[1] or still feel a little uncomfortable using a mouse. The industry moves so fast that it is very seductive to start thinking in the compressed perspective of "Internet time" in which things move faster, change quicker, and become outdated almost immediately, or are blurred. For most people, the only access they have to computing (if at all) is at work and using computers is still a chore. Despite recent growth in PC ownership in homes, the technology is still not seen as a domestic one. Many homes do not have it and it does not have the same place as the television does within the majority of people's daily routines (see, for example, Lull, 1990; Moores, 1993). Because of this, manufacturers and e-commerce strategists have sought to harness the television to further increase their penetration, for example, via the integrated media player and digital television. Clearly, this strategy of co-opting the television is significant for it suggests that far from technology alone, familiarity with the technologies and its place in our daily lives and routines may actually be more important and may actually act as the prime basis for trust in e-commerce.[2]

In this chapter, the Internet can be seen as a place in which the rules and knowledge that have informed our everyday experiences are not seen to apply and as such it is a place of potentially high risk for those that venture into it. There have indeed been numerous reports of consumers' concerns over security on the Internet (Hancock, 1999). Given these concerns and its seemingly lawlessness, the Internet can be best seen as an exemplar of Giddens' vision of post-traditional society in which rather than going about our everyday interactions offering trust to others without thought or reflection, the winning of trust is constantly necessary (Beck, Giddens, & Lash, 1994). This, he argues, is due to living an urban existence in which we do not know most of the people or institutions we have contact with and are forced to inhabit situations that are beyond our control. In this "risk society" both our perceptions of risk and our exposure to actual risk is higher than before. In such an environment, our approach to using e-commerce can hardly be greatly different.

This chapter puts at the centre of its proposition that trust is a human quality that is observable through interaction (Golembiewski & MConkie, 1975) and that this interaction shapes interactions among transacting members. This chapter looks at e-commerce not as a mere technical development or even a new type of online interaction but as a technology which mediates already established and long-practiced routines of human behavior. As such, while not disregarding the importance of online security and the evolving systems that support it, this chapter believes that security has little to do with general consumer trust. This is the case not only because of consumers' lack of the expertise needed to make informed choices but, more importantly, because of their general lack of interest in the technology of security. This, among other reasons, is seen as a little protection against "disreputable or careless people" who will take credit card details and use them for their own gain and the owner's loss (Fukuyama, 1999; Ratnasingham, 1998). As such, it is of little surprise that significant numbers of Internet users have never bought anything online or have taken part in e-commerce. Clearly central here is the issue of trust, and numerous researchers have suggested that trust is a key actor in e-commerce adoption (Bons, Lee, & Wagenaar, 1998; Castelfranchi & Tan, 2002; Keen, 1999; Tan & Thoen, 2000).

However, while trust is important in understanding why consumers choose to use or refrain from using e-commerce and understanding how they make choices about which B2C retailer they use, the opposite side of this coin is that for the firms' consumers, trust offers initial and repeat purchases, strong brand loyalty and encourages word-of-mouth recommendation. Trust is a valuable (if intangible) asset which, as Fukuyama (1995) has persuasively argued, is firmly linked with economic success. Indeed, although the link between commerce and culture (Casson, 1995) has long been recognized, the nature of these links still remains under-explored and under-developed in many areas.

Garfinkel's (1963) views offer us an opportunity to further examine these links to better understand trust drawn from the observation of participants' action rather than through modeling or technological systems. In accepting Garfinkel's (1963) work as a basis for approaching consumer trust in e-commerce, it becomes clear that trust has very little relationship to technical security. In fact, it is suggested that people do not mistrust technology because they are inherently Luddite and have a view of technology as wrong, bad, or evil. But, because following Garfinkel's insights, trust is a basically a transaction involving individuals, rather than people and mediating technologies. It is apparent that phrases such as "I trust my PC to help my do my home accounts" or "I trust this network with my credit card details," are somewhat strange personifications. As neither of these objects can accept my trust it is not possible for me to bestow it.[3]

Trust, indeed, as many have pointed out, is something which one individual offers to another and is prepared to be vulnerable to the actions of another party, predicated on the premise that the other party will perform an appropriate action important to the trustor (see also Hosmer, 1995; Sako, 1994; Sztompka, 1999). In this formulation, to trust somebody means that you do not believe that it is necessary to safeguard against possible harmful actions by them. Indeed our actions might be unconscious and even habitual, narrowing down the set of possible acceptable actions by the other actor (Sako, 1994, p. 4). As Luhmann suggests, trust "reduces social complexity by going beyond available information and generalizing expectations of behavior in that it replace missing information with an internally guaranteed certainty" (Luhmann, 1979, p. 93).

This mutuality of interaction is as important in business to consumer e-commerce transactions as it is elsewhere (Gefen, 2000). The parties involved in the transaction must have a shared perspective of what is going on and the routines that generally (and acceptably) govern that interaction. Now the idea that both client and merchant know what is going on and behave accordingly may not appear to be a ground-breaking observation. If we, however, unpack the process a little, its profound relevance to successful e-commerce becomes apparent. Questions arise about who is doing what, what preconceptions are they bringing to the interaction and how responsive (or alive) are they to the situation.

Take, for example, a user new to e-commerce. When approaching this new experience, what people try to do is apply rules that have governed previous similar experiences. For the new e-commerce users this will most likely be that of shopping. However, even the most sophisticated and well developed e-commerce sites remove the situated experience usually associated with shopping: gone are geographical, temporal, tactile, and social experiences of shopping. Now, in routine forms of shopping such as regular food purchases (which forms the majority of household shopping expenditure along with petrol and mortgages) this may be a good thing but for leisure and recreational purchases (which make up the majority of B2C e-commerce) it means that the e-commerce experience stops being shopping and is reduced to buying things. What happens in such e-commerce interactions is that mutuality can begin to fall apart. Site designers and merchants believe, for their part, they are entering into a selling interaction while consumers are not necessarily involved in a buying interaction and therefore can often be uncertain as to what is required of them as their previous shopping routines fail to work. As the rules that usually apply to our social relationships cease to remain valid, people become uneasy. Such an uncertainty heightens the importance of trust for the consumer and increases the need for the merchant to respond to it. The interaction that online retailers often believe themselves to be involved in is one of collecting customer data first and selling the goods, second. Customers, especially those new to the Internet and e-commerce, will be looking for a shopping interaction. The two are bound to be irreconcilable. This is not to say that either is wrong or that

the future of e-commerce will not continue to be data collection orientated. Placed in interactional situations in which the customer is uncertain as to what is going on, entering fully into the interaction becomes difficult and potentially risky In such a situation, issues of trust are paramount especially when the retailer makes demands on the consumer without offering anything either upfront or in return. Further, if trust in e-commerce is simply reduced to a matter of consumers "learning" to understand e-commerce systems or putting into place increasingly sophisticated security and validation systems, the lack of real interactions means that it is highly likely to be less successful.

Despite this, most e-commerce writers have ignored sociological aspects of users' interactions and aims to reify trust when exploring network communications. For example, Gerck (1998) defines the goal of his research on trust as producing a practical definition of trust is one which allows considerations to "be viewed non-antromorphically [sic] when dealing with the concept of trust in communication engineering and security design." Such a view claims to solve the problem of trust by removing trust from the equation; trust has somehow been technologically integrated and therefore not problematic. In such an argument, it is however unclear who is trusting or what it is that trust is being placed in. This is a vital question when addressing trust's implication for business-to business (B2B) e-commerce.

According to Gerck (1998), "trust is that which is essential to a communication channel but cannot be transferred from a source to a destination using that channel." Clearly, here, Gerck is suggesting that we trust the information we receive. This is an over technological and deterministic view as we cannot trust information per se but rather, based on our previous experiences, the provider of that information or our own informed evaluation of it. Trust is not reducible to information; it "does not reside in integrated circuits or fibre optic cables" and cannot be digitized and transmitted (Fukuyama, 1995, p. 25). If these propositions have some validity, how can e-commerce solution providers and online merchants then promote and exploit trust? It is simply not enough to demonstrate that consumer trust is not related in any significant way to technical security without offering at least some suggestions as to what it is related to. The next section of this chapter discusses a few possibilities that derive from the framework above and examines their practical attendant effects.

HOW CAN E-COMMERCE FOSTER TRUST?

Keeping up-to-date in any broad manner with developments in the e-commerce industry has become difficult as its fortunes and directions fluctuate wildly. A plethora of organizations, market research, academic, industrial and journalistic, often with irreconcilable perspectives and always in need of revision further down the line map out their gyrations and, indeed, the new economy's speed makes it very easy to ignore the relatively stable aspects of business which would make strategies, decisions, and plans firmer (Porter, 2001).

Drawing on sociological insights, I have attempted to highlight a few key areas of concern relevant to e-commerce and consumer trust. These are community, flow, brand identity, personal experience, and the idea of institutions. In developing these five areas, I am not claiming that other areas are inconsequential; indeed, the sociological interest in other areas, for example, virtuality (Carrier & Miller, 1998) and mobility (Urry, 2000), among others, are equally significant. In concentrating on the five areas I have nominated, I have sought to proximate and relate some of these sociological concepts with the broader business discipline.

Community

The idea of online communities has become an attractive concept, and despite their notorious fluidity, they offer the online retailer a valuable resource for promoting user trust. They also promote site "stickiness" and add value to the site and the products being offered by providing (at little cost to the retailer beyond initial development) reviews, overviews, hints and tips, buying advice, and so forth. Although a richly discussed term, the following covers some of the main features of community as far as sociological research stands. *Community* stands as a convenient shorthand term for the broad realm of local social arrangements beyond the private sphere of the home and family but more familiar to us than the impersonal institutions of the wider society (Crow & Allan, 1994, p. 1). In such a context we can see that what is happening in communities which pivot around online retail sites is the development of relationships.[4]

The virtual basis of these communities is largely irrelevant to the interaction involved and does not mean that the relationships involved are in any way less real as members increasingly feel part of the community and begin to align themselves with the community and, by extension, the community host (Jones, 1995; Rheingold, 1993; Smith & Kollock, 1999). Being part of the community—especially if one is seen as a core or long-term member—begins to carry with it its own kudos or cultural capital as community membership begins to carry with it its own value. Therefore, as a community evolves, members will begin to actively demonstrate membership of the community, for example, through techniques such as displaying specialist knowledge of the community history and its members and outside of it through recommendation or favourable comparison with other, similar communities. This contributes not only to the sense of community found within the group but also the development of boundaries around it that marks it as separate from other online communities. In such communities, trust is central and is the glue binding members together—it fosters, maintains and helps develop community relationships.

By developing an imagined community (Anderson, 1991), for example, eBay, retailers become seen as a trusted part of the community rather than merely an institution. Further, the development of a community and its relationship to trust is a cyclic process: members of communities demonstrate trust in other members they know and also in the other members by virtue of their membership of the community. The longer people remain a member of the community the more they are likely to offer greater amounts of trust to the community. As Fukuyama observes, "community depends on trust, and trust in turn is culturally determined" (Fukuyama 1995, p. 25). Indeed, this is discernable in numerous examples of Web practices, for example, the peer-to-peer facilitating networks (Kaaza, YouTube and Napster) where members of the community develop trust with each other through thick interactive information transactions and exchanges and in e-commerce retailing, for example, eBay.

Since its founding in 1995, eBay hosted person-to-person online auctions for the members of its community. That community was composed of anonymous and remote individuals who were unlikely to have repeat dealings. Trade was impersonal with, for example, a seller knowing only the user name of bidders until the winner of the auction provided a shipping address. Buyers did not have an opportunity to inspect the goods on which they bid, and the winning bidder paid for the item prior to shipment (Livingston, 2005). Trades were neither supported by contracts nor in most cases by public enforcement of implicit contracts but rather by relied on trust engendered within the eBay community and its institutional practices. The rules and regulations on member-

ship practices and its online reputation mechanism were based on feedback provided by the transacting parties (Dellacros & Resnick, 2003; Li & Lin, 2004). Members established informal norms, standards, provided feedback on other members' performance and policed the site. Standards were thus maintained and reputations managed. eBay's strategy, while far from perfect, illustrates the types of responses that can strengthen a reputation, reduce the cost of trust, lower transaction costs and amplify the value of community practices. In fact, there is anecdotal evidence suggesting that customers are relying more and more on online opinions when making their online purchasing decisions (Guernsey, 2000). The Web community, it appears, can enable businesses to grow and develop when properly harnessed.

Flow

Although Csikszentmihalyi's (1975, 1988) notion of *flow*,[1] the way computer users become absorbed in their activity to the exclusion of other things, is usually applied to athletes, it has also been used in understanding e-commerce (Hel, van Niekerk, Berthon, & Davies, 1999) and, more generally, to the online experience (Novak & Hoffman, 1997). According to Mihaly Csikszentmihalyi, flow is the "holistic sensation that people feel when they act with total involvement" (Csikszentmihalyi, 1975, p. 36). Csikszentmihalyi wanted to understand the experience of enjoyment which we do for the sheer joy of it (Csikszentmihalyi, 1975, p. 4). Flow is a positive, highly enjoyable state of consciousness that occurs when our perceived skills match the perceived challenges we are undertaking. When our goals are clear, our skills are up to the challenge, and feedback is immediate, we become involved in the activity. In the process, we lose our sense of self and time is distorted. The experience becomes autotelic or intrinsically rewarding (Csikszentmihalyi, 1990, p. 34).

This mode is characterized by a narrowing of the focus of awareness so that irrelevant perceptions and thoughts are filtered out by loss of self-consciousness, by a responsiveness to clear goals and unambiguous feedback, and by a sense of control over the environment. It is this common flow experience, an intense, immersive and emotional involvement, that people adduce as the main reason for performing the activity (Csikszentmihalyi, 1975). Thus, for flow to exist, there must be a level of challenge involved in the activity but that level of challenge must not be so great as to make those involved feel out-maneuvered so that they lose interest. Such challenge is often designed into computer games such as motor racing simulations. In such games when a player is performing badly and slips to the back of the race the cars at the front will start to gently slow down in order for there to be more of a possibility of the less skilled player to catch up. Conversely, the computer-driven cars will increase their speed and driving accuracy to maintain challenge and interest for the experienced gamers (Poole, 2000). Successful Web sites are not about navigating content, but rather about staging and managing experiences where participants, when in the flow state, shift into a common mode of experience as they become absorbed in their activity. Such flow, as Novak and her collaborators found, "is determined by: (1) high levels of skill and control; (2) high levels of challenge and arousal; (3) focused attention; and (4) enhanced interactivity and telepresence" (Novak, Hoffman & Yung, p. 24). They found that speed had the greatest effect on the amount of time spent online and on frequency of visits for Web applications. For repeat visits, the most important factors were skill/control, length of time on the Web, importance, and speed.

For the Web developer or e-commerce solution provider, this in itself presents a substantial challenge and in many ways runs contrary to common knowledge of site design in which everything must be simple and transparent for the users as they navigate through the site. To facilitate flow, designers have to ensure that visitors to a site are given clear information and receive feedback but it also needs to include a variable element of challenge to the interaction users have with the site. The combination of goal orientated challenge, feedback, and interaction with other users in auctions is one such strategy. When the idea of flow is applied to e-commerce, this engagement encourages users' involvement with a site, increases the amount of time they will spend on it, and makes the likelihood of their returning often greater. To enter into a flow state, many of the same conditions that are necessary for trust are required. For example, there must be an established and recognizable set of rules that govern the interaction and which people can expect others to adhere and by which to judge their actions. Given this situation, despite the challenge involved which will itself fulfil users' expectancies, the interaction will avoid situations in which the site user is faced with the unexpected or situations in which mutual interaction fails to operate. Given such a relationship, it is highly likely that trust will develop. Again, here the example of eBay is instructive. On logging onto eBay, users are directed to their interests through a process of interactive flows, learn to absorb the rules and practices of the site, and are socialized into its institutional practices. These experiences can be seen in other sites which seek to engage users and to buy more products, making the site experiences more compelling and engaging.

Brand Identity

Brands have been critical in instances of information asymmetries and where consumers rationally depend on brand names in making their purchase decisions. This has not changed that much online. KPMG (1999) found that more than 50% of Internet users claimed that they would shop online more if major financial institutions or vendors guaranteed their transactions. The emphasis here of placing trust in organizations rather than systems is clear (even if the organization stands as a metonym for the individuals who make it). Theoretically, as trust is fostered through relationships, it would appear that the trust that e-commerce users demonstrate would favour familiar brands. If this was so it is likely that there will be growing number of users visiting a select number of the largest e-commerce providers.

Branding is also linked strongly with trust services such as Verisign, TrustUK, PayPal and *Which? WebTrader*. In situations in which a retailer is a member of such a professional or regulatory organization it is easy to simply assume that trust can be produced by a regulatory agency. However, the problem arises about why we should trust e-Trust or *Which?* in the first place. These services rely on a previous trustworthy relationship between the consumer and the trust service. Trust in a firm is not about doing business with them because PayPal will refund me the $50 that my credit card company may not if the company disappears with my money and fails to deliver the new television set I ordered from them. Such safety nets (like the emphasis Fukuyama places on hierarchy) are the product of distrust and act to minimize the effects of wrongful behavior. In a trusting relationship, the display of a trust service's logo or banner on the retailer's site assures the consumer that the business done there will conform to a set of norms which are already established, available for review, and familiar to the parties involved. It restores a sense of mutuality as discussed and highlighted above. If I have trust in the behavior sanctioned by the trust service then such legal assurance become less important (Fukuyama, 1995, p. 27). It is like being introduced to a friend of a friend. We assume, because of the trust relationship we have with our friend, that our new acquaintance will demonstrate similar points of view to ourselves, that they will not be untrustworthy, offensive, abusive, and so forth. In such close relationships, the recognition of the power of this trust can make it embarrassing to point out that we do not like our friend's friends and, conversely, to have a friend we have

introduced act in an inappropriate manner. This ensures that trust is therefore not breached.

As consumers become better educated and seek greater protection and privacy online (Homburg & Furst, 2005), branding coupled with strategies to develop more efficacious privacy practices, for example, the appointment of chief privacy officers and the development of a more rigorous privacy guideline, offers protection to online consumers and, unwittingly, a distinct competitive advantage vis-à-vis their competitors (Andrews & Shen, 2000; Frombrun, 1996; Tadelis, 1999). Banks, finance companies, and credit providers have, in particular, crafted their strategies accordingly, and through their Web protection strategies, enhanced their reputation (Barr, Knowles, & Moore, 2003) and makes them more trustworthy in the eyes of their customers (Dellacros, 2005; Melnik & Alm, 2002; Windley, Tew, & Daley, 2006; Yu & Singh, 2000). Conversely, if consumer expectations (and their complaints) are not handled appropriately, this may lead to the magnification of prevailing negative perceptions and the brand is consequently affected. Custom and business invariably suffers.

Personal Experiences

All of the above three aspects of trust inform our personal experiences. That is, trust is a quality which grows out of, and informs, our local interactional experiences. This is because personal experience and narratives have profound importance in the creation of trust (see also Jones & Vijayasarathy, 1998; Lane & Bachmann, 1998). We make decisions to trust through our own (often limited or misrepresented) satisfied experiences and the anecdotes offered by those we trust more readily (and pragmatically) than by any rational evaluation of available facts. Trust, as such, may have components of rationality (especially when it is institutionally processed) but this does not mean it is a rational system.

As the Cheskin Research (1999) points out, "Trust is understood by most customers to be a dynamic process. Trust deepens or retreats based on experience." As such, there is a pattern to the development of trust through personal experience which applies as readily to e-commerce as it does to friendships. In the early stages of a relationship, the level of trust is low for both parties involved. As neither party knows much about each other, mutuality appears lows and the risk of having an offering of trust abused is potentially high. It is at this stage that trust services, consumer law, well formulated and displayed return policies play their major role in the trust process. This is when the new customer seeks reassurance that the level of damage they open themselves up to, the risks they take, and the amount of misappropriation that can be done by the company is limited through law and officially sanctioned regulation. It is only as the trust relationship builds through successive and successful interactions that more informal transactions can be comfortably entered into. As the level of satisfactory service the customer receives grows so does the level of trust they have in the retailer. Indeed, successful e-tailers often remarked on their customers' satisfaction.

Linked to this search for certainty is the growth in tolerance towards variability of service, for example, the occasional mix-up in order or slightly delayed delivery so long as recompense is made and apology is offered. Such repairs demonstrate to the consumers (as does an apology to a friend) that the relationship is valued and that there is a desire to maintain the relationship and its development. Such an observation, which effectively boils down to a commitment to provide a service or regular quality with a focus of customer recognition and satisfaction, is not new but as online retailing continues to be more about the service offered than the product sold the quality of that service becomes increasingly important. Again, here, I refer to the earlier brief discussion of eBay and its practices, where its feedback mechanism enables the development of customers' feedback, satisfac-

tion, and the refinement of its base of customers' knowledge (Morgan, Anderson, & Mittal, 2005) as it seeks to enhance its appeal.

Institutions

Research has clearly shown that individuals involved in human-computer interaction have tended to rely on social attitudes and rules in vesting trust in machines. Nass and Moon (2000), for example, found that many people mindlessly and readily concede their trust to computers. Somehow, computers are seen as part of the institution of knowledge, science, and technology; hence, they are reliable and can only but induce trust. According to Zucker (1986), there has been a shift to certification institutions derived and supported by governments because local personal-trust networks are and have been disintegrating. Through their "power" and authority, these practices, protocols, standards, and regulations induce compliance and trust in the control procedures (see also Rea, 2001; Benassi, 1999; Keen, 1999; Lane & Bachman, 1997). Indeed, without this support, understanding, and the ability to exploit this social background, neither security nor trust will be effected and/or effective.

Norbert Elias (1994) has argued that the civilizing process is synonymous with reducing the unpredictability of encounters with strangers. Long distance trade and financial exchange promoted new forms of discourse and practice—written documents, orders, promissory notes and bills of exchange—during the Middle Ages (Braudel, 1981; Kerridge, 1988), allowing "strangers with no basis for trust to work with one another" (Fukuyama, 1995, p. 150). These new practices enabled and ensured promises were rendered more stable, mobile and containable. In contemporary virtual trading environments, while risks can be amplified, sociotechnical solutions have been advanced to fix the ensuing problems of trust and distrust/control (Kyas, 1997). Stability, predictability and normalcy is restored and maintained, and clearly the new ICT solutions civilize and induct us into the process of a new sociotechnical age. For example, users of the Internet have structural assurance that legal and technological safeguards protect them from privacy infractions, identity loss or online fraud. This institution-based trust provides assurances that things will go well, normalizes our roles and expectations, and increases our dispositions to trust (Baier, 1986; Benassi, 1999; Gefen, 2000; Lewis & Weigart, 1985; McKnight & Chervany, 2002; Shapiro, 1987; Zucker, 1986). Trust, as such, is constructed for and by people to enact some form of predictability and reliability. In e-commerce transactions, trust can be seen at different levels of interactions:

- Trust in the environment and infrastructure
- Trust in the computing agent and in mediating agents
- Trust in potential partners
- Trust in the authorities to enforce compliance, for example, protocols and procedures and laws

In the Internet context, beliefs that there are legal and regulatory protections for consumers clearly influence and effect trust to be built and developed. Trust and confidence is thus based on abstract systems resting on the validity of commonly acceptable and accepted technical and social norms and standards of business behavior and practice, and the power these technologies of trust invokes and maintains, as a new social contract emerges. Perhaps, the clearest manifestation of this institutional trust is best seen in discussions of communities of practice, global networks of innovation, and supply chain relations (Bachman, 2003; Lane & Bachman, 1998). In these communities and networks, members are concerned with both practical outcomes for customers and learning, combining an agency's focus on personal development with traditional community's foundation of shared purpose.

CONCLUSION

Trust is a complex and slippery subject; it "is a cultural norm which can rarely be created intentionally because attempts to create trust in a calculative manner would destroy the affective basis of trust" (Sako, 1994, p. 6). Because of this, Baier warned, trust "is a fragile plant, which may not endure inspection of its roots, even when they were, before the inspection quite healthy" (Baier, 1986, p. 260). In the case of trust, particularly in virtual economic environments, both fragility and complexity are preset, and sensitive handling of these issues is required if e-commerce is to be properly understood and effected. By looking at Web-based business-to-consumer e-commerce this chapter has placed trust within a context of everyday routines, interactions and local experiences. It is therefore suggested that regardless of who is involved or how business is conducted, e-commerce will continue to change our routine behavior and our approaches to trust interactions. As such, there will remain a need to build upon social science research in general, and interactional sociology in particular, in order to develop the initial observations that have been offered above. The task that this chapter leaves us with is not only to refine our understanding of trust for the online consumer but to see how this understanding corresponds to research in other fields and explore how it can inform the development of e-commerce solutions.

In this chapter, I have sought to show trust as a social process through which control is affected in the sense that people, actions, and events can be rendered relatively predictable. I have also argued that a sociologically-informed view of trust will readily reveal that e-commerce solutions predicated on technological solutions are therefore flawed and unable to deliver expected outcomes as they failed to understand the different logics induced by trust. Trust is central to predictability but is not rule-bound but rather is invoked by power relationships through which relationships are created, maintained, enacted and negotiated. Via standardization and a set of *communal* values, individuals are potentially controlled and controllable, predictable, and familiar. Individuals may thus seize upon, enact, and thereby reproduce mechanisms of trust governing their conduct and behavior.

From a practical standpoint, it is clear that successful e-commerce sites and practices need to integrate these complementary notions of community, flow, branding, personalization, and systemic practices into their Web business strategies. Businesses need to be cognizant and respond to the larger desire from consumers for voices and attention to those voices. Customers not only want to be heard but also want their personal experiences to be taken seriously through feedback mechanisms. In addition, they want businesses to respond actively to their negative comments and to devise appropriate strategies to respond to their concerns. In so doing, businesses also invariably manage their customers and socialize them into acceptable institutional arrangements.

While the five areas discussed in this chapter may help to consolidate and refine Web business strategies, it is also clear that culture may affect the notion of community participation, the perception of flows and, accordingly, color personal experiences. These cultural variables are often under-emphasized in much of the e-commerce literature but they can be particularly important. For example, the response and reception of mobile commerce in East Asia has been attributed to cultural (and institutional) practices. Clearly, prevailing institutional arrangements in different countries, such as the lack of bandwidth, censorship practices, access, flow, and personal experiences, also impact e-commerce experiences and these arrangements and issues need further consideration and research.

REFERENCES

Abdul-Rahman, A.,& Hailes, S. (2000). Supporting trust in virtual communities. In *Proceedings of the Hawaii International Conference on System Sciences* (pp. 55-63).

Anderson, B. (1991). *Imagined communities: Reflections on the origin and spread of nationalism.* London: Verso.

Anderson, J.C., & Naurus, J.A. (1990). A model of distributor firm and manufacturing firm working partnerships. *Journal of Marketing, 54,* 42-58.

Andrews, S., & Shen, A. (2000). *Laws or regulations posing barriers to electronic commerce.* Washington, DC: Electronic Privacy Information Center.

Axelrod, R. (1990). *The evolution of co-operation.* Harmondsworth, UK: Penguin.

Bachman, T. (2003). Trust and Power as a Means of Coordinating the Internal Relations of the Organisation: A Conceptual Framework. In B Nooteboom & F. Six (Eds.) *The Trust Process in Organisations: Empirical Studies of the Determinants and the Process of Trust Development.* Cheltenham, UK: Edward Elgar.

Bachmann, R. (1998). Trust: Conceptual aspects of a complex phenomenon. In C. Lane & R. Bachmann (Eds.), *Trust within and between organisations: Conceptual issues and empirical applications* (pp. 298-322). Oxford: Oxford University Press.

Baier, A. (1986). Trust and antitrust. *Ethics, 96,* 231-260.

Balachander, S. (2001). Warranty signaling and reputation. *Management Science, 47*(9), 1282-1289.

Barber, K.S., & Kim, J. (2000). *Belief revision process based on trust: Agents evaluating reputa-*

tion of information sources. Retrieved March 9, 2007, from http://www.istc.cnr.it/T3/download/aamas2000/Barber-Kim.pdf

Barr, T., Knowles, A., & Moore, S. (2003). Trust in transactions: Australian Internet research. Paper presented at the Communications Research Forum 2003. Retrieved March 9, 2007, from http://www.dcita.gov.au/crf/papers03/barr3final.pdf

Beck, U., Giddens, A., & Lash. S. (1994). *Reflexive modernisation.* Cambridge, UK: Polity.

Benassi, P. (1999). TRUSTe: An online privacy seal program. *Communications of the ACM, 42*(2), 56-59.

Bhimani, A. (1996). Securing the commercial Internet. *Communications of the ACM, 39*(6), 29-35.

Blois, K.J. (1999). Trust in business to business relationships: An evaluation of its status. *Journal of Management Studies, 36*(2), 197-215.

Bons, R.W.H., Lee, R.M., & Wagenaar (1998). Obstacles for the development of open electronic commerce. *International Journal of Electronic Commerce, 2*(3), 61-83.

Bradach, J.L., & Eccles, R.G. (1989). Price, authority and trust: From ideal types to plural forms. *Annual Review of Sociology, 15*, 97-118.

Braudel, F. (1981). *Civilisation and capitalism, 15ᵗʰ-18ᵗʰ century.* London: Collins/Fontana.

Butler, J.K. (1991). Toward understanding and measuring conditions of trust. *Journal of Management, 17*, 643-663.

Carrier, J., & Miller, D. (1998) *Virtuality: A new political economy.* Oxford, UK: Berg Publishers.

Casson, M. (1995). *The organisation of international business: Studies in the economics of trust.* Aldershot, UK: Edward Elgar.

Castelfranchi, C. (2000). Why computers will (necessarily) deceive us and each other. *Ethics and Information Technology, 2*, 113-119.

Castelfranchi, C., & Falcone, R. (2001). *Social trust: A cognitive approach.* In C. Castelfranchi & Y.H. Tan (Eds.), *Deception, fraud and trust in virtual societies* (pp. 55-90). Dodrecht, The Netherlands: Kluwer.

Castelfranchi, C. & Tan, Y.H. (2002). The Role of Trust and Deception in Virtual Societies. *International Journal of Electronic Commerce 6*(3), 55-70.

Cheskin Research & Studio Archetype/Sapient (1999). *eCommerce trust study.* Retrieved March 9, 2007, from http://www.sapient.com/cheskin

Clayman, S.E. (1993). Booing: The anatomy of a disaffiliative response. *American Sociological Review, 58*, 110-130.

Coleman, J. (1990). *Foundations of social theory.* Boston: Harvard University Press.

Cranor, L.F. (1999). Internet privacy. *Communications of the ACM, 42*(2), 28-31.

Crow, G., & Allan, G. (1994). *Community life: An introduction to local social relations.* Hemel Hempstead, UK: Harvester Wheatsheaf.

Csikszentmihalyi, M. (1975). *Beyond boredom and anxiety.* San Francisco: Jossey-Bass.

Csikszentmihalyi, M. (1988) *Optimal experience.* New York: Cambridge University Press.

Csikszentmihalyi, M. (1990). *Flow: The psychology of optimal experience.* New York: Harper and Row.

Davidson, J., & Rees-Mogg, W. (1997). *The sovereign individual.* London: Pan.

Dellarocas, C. (2003). The digitization of the word of mouth: Promise and challenges of online feedback mechanisms. *Management Science, 49*(10), 1407-1424.

Dellarocas, C. (2005). Reputation mechanism design in online trading environments with pure moral hazard. *Information Systems Research, 16*(2), 209-230

Dellarocas, C., & Resnick, P. (2003). *Online reputation mechanisms: A roadmap for future research.* Summary Report of the First Interdisciplinary Symposium on Online Reputation Mechanisms. Retrieved March 9, 2007, from http://www2.sims.berkeley.edu/research/conferences/p2pecon/papers/s8-dellarocas

Elias, N. (1994). *The civilising process.* Oxford: Blackwell.

Fombrun, C.J. (1996). *Reputation: Realizing value from the corporate image.* Boston: Harvard Business School Press.

Fukuyama, F. (1995) Trust: The social virtues and the creation of prosperity. New York, NY: Free Press.

Gambetta, D.G. (Ed.). (1988). *Trust, making and breaking of cooperative relations.* New York: Basil Blackwell.

Garfinkel, H. (1963). A conception of, and experiments with, "trust" as a condition of stable concerted action. In O.J. Harvey (Ed.), *Motivation and social interaction* (pp. 187-238). New York: Ronald Press.

Gefen, D. (2000). E-commerce: The role of familiarity and trust. *Omega, 28*(6), 725-737.

Gerck, E. (1998). *Towards real-world models of trust: Reliance on received information.* Retrieved March 9, 2007, from http://www.mcg.org.br/trustdef.com

Giddens, A. (1984). *The constitution of society.* Cambridge, UK: Polity.

Giddens, A. (1990). *The consequences of modernity.* Cambridge, UK: Polity.

Giddens, A. (1991). *Modernity and self-identity.* Cambridge, UK: Polity.

Giddens, A. (1994). Living in a post-traditional society. In U. Beck, A. Giddens, & S. Lash (Eds.), *Reflexive modernisation* (pp. 56-109). Cambridge, UK: Polity.

Golembiewski, R.T., & McConkie, M. (1975). The centrality of interpersonal trust in group processes. In G.L. Cooper (Ed.), *Theories of group processes* (pp. 131-85). London: John Wiley.

Guernsey, L. (2000). Suddenly, everybody's an expert on everything. Retrieved March 9, 2007, from http://www.nytimes.com/library/tech/00/02/circuits/articles/03info.html

Gulta, R. (1995). Does Familiarity Breed Trust? The Implications of Repeated Ties for Contractual Choice in Alliances. *Academy of Management Journal 38*, 85-112.

Hancock, B. (1999). Security Views. *Computers and Security 19*(7), 553-64.

Hardin, R. (1993). The street-level epistemology of trust. *Politics and Society, 21*(4), 505-529.

Hel, D., van Niekerk, R., Berthon, J.P., & Davies, T. (1999). Going with the flow: Web sites and customer involvement. *Internet Research, 9*(2), 109-116.

Hoffman, D., Novak, T.P., & Peralta (1999). Building consumer trust online. *Communications of the ACM, 42*(4), 80-85.

Hoffman, D.L., & Novak, T.P. (1996). Marketing in hypermedia computer-mediated environments: conceptual foundations. *Journal of Marketing 60*, 50-68.

Homburg, C., & Furst, A. (2005). How organizational complaint handling drives customer loyalty: An analysis of the mechanistic and the organic approach. *Journal of Marketing, 69*(3), 95-114.

Hosmer, L.T. (1995). Trust: The connecting link between organisational theory and philosophical ethics. *Academy of Management Review, 20*(2), 379-403.

Jarvenpaa, S.L., & Todd, P. (1997). Consumer reactions to electronic shopping. *International Journal of Electronic Commerce, 1*(2), 59-88.

Jones, S.G. (1995). Understanding community in the information age. In S.G. Jones (Ed.), *Cybersociety: Computer-mediated communication and community*. Thousand Oaks; London: Sage.

Jones, J., & Vijayasarathy, L.R. (1998). Internet consumer catalog shopping: Findings from an exploratory study and directions for future research. *Internet Research, 8*(4), 322-333.

Keen, P.G.W. (Ed.). (1999). *Electronic commerce relationships: Trust by design*. Englewood Cliffs, NJ: Prentice-Hall.

Kerridge, E. (1988). *Trade and banking in early modern England*. Manchester, UK: Manchester University Press.

KPMG (1999). *The new mass medium*. USA: Ziff-Davis/Dell/Intel.

Kramer, R.M., & Tyler, T.R. (Eds.). (1996). *Trust in organisations: Frontiers of theory and research*. Thousand Oaks, CA: Sage.

Kyas, O. (1997). *Internet security: Risk analysis, strategies and firewalls*. New York: International Thomson Publishing.

Lane, C., & Bachman, R. (1996). The social constitution of trust: Supplier relations in Britain and Germany. *Organisation Studies, 17*(3), 365-395.

Lane, C., & Bachman, R. (1997). Co-operation in Inter-Firm Relations in Britain and Germany: The Role of Social Institutions. *British Journal of Sociology 48*(2), 226-54.

Lane, C., & Bachman, R. (Eds.). (1998). *Trust within and between organisations: Conceptual issues and empirical applications*. Oxford, NY: Oxford University Press.

Latane, B., Liu, J.H., Nowak, A., Bonevento, M., & Zheng, L. (1995). Distance matters: Physical space and social impact. *Personality and Social Psychology Bulletin, 21*(8), 795-805.

Lewicki, R.J., & Bunker, B. (1995). Trust in relationships: A model of trust development and decline. In B.B. Bunker & J.Z. Rubin (Eds.), *Conflict, cooperation and justice* (pp. 133-73). San Francisco: Jossey-Bass.

Lewicki, R.J., & Bunker, B. (1996). Developing and maintaining trust in work relationship. In R. Kramer & T. Tyler (Eds.), *Trust in organisations: Frontiers of theory and research* (pp. 114-139). Thousand Oaks, CA: Sage.

Lewis, J.D., & Weigert, A. (1985a). Trust as a social reality. *Social Forces, 63*(4), 967-985.

Lewis, J.D., & Weigert, A. (1985b). Social atomism, holism and trust. *Sociological Quarterly, 26*(4), 455-471.

Li, D., & Lin, Z. (2004, December 5-8). Negative reputation rate as the signal of risk in online consumer-to-consumer transactions. In *Proceedings of ICEB 2004*.

Livingston, J. (2005). How valuable is a good reputation? A sample selection model of Internet auctions. *The Review of Economics and Statistics, 87*(3), 453-465.

Luhmann, N. (1988). Familiarity, confidence, trust: Problems and alternatives. In D. Gambetta (Ed.), *Trust: Making and breaking co-operative relations*. Oxford, UK: Basil Blackwell.

Luhmann, N. (1979). *Trust and power*. New York, NY: John Wiley.

Lull, J. (1990). *Inside family viewing: Ethnographic research on television's audience*. London: Routledge.

Mayer, R.C., Davis, J.H., & Shoorman, F.D. (1995). An Integrative Model of Organizational Trust. *Academy of Management Review, 20*(3), 709-34.

McKnight, D.H., & Chervany, N.L. (2002). What trust means in e-commerce customer relationships: An interdisciplinary conceptual typology. *International Journal of Electronic Commerce, 6*(2), 35-59.

Melnik, M.I., & Alm, J. (2002). Does a seller's e-commerce reputation matter? Evidence from eBay auctions. *Journal of Industrial Economics, 50*(3), 337-349.

Moores, S. (1993). *Interpreting audiences: The ethnography of media consumption.* Thousand Oaks, CA: Sage.

Morgan, N.A., Anderson, E.W., & Mittal, V. (2005). Understanding firms' customer satisfaction information usage. *Journal of Marketing, 69*(3), 131-151.

Morgan, R.M., & Hunt, S.D. (1994). The commitment-trust theory of relationship marketing. *Journal of Marketing, 58,* 20-38.

Nass, C., & Moon, Y. (2000). Machines and mindlessness: Social responses to computers. *Journal of Social Issues, 56*(1), 81-103.

Nohria, N., & Eccles, R.G. (1992). Face-to-face: Making network organisations work. In N. Nohria & R.G. Eccles (Eds.), *Networks and organisations* (pp. 288-308). Boston: Harvard Business School Press.

Novak, T.P., & Hoffman, D.L. (1997). A new marketing paradigm for electronic commerce. *The Information Society: An International Journal 13*(1), 43-54.

Novak, T.P., & Hoffman, D.L. (1997). *Measuring the flow experience among Web users* (Working Paper). Vanderbilt University. Retrieved March 7, 2007, from http://www.2000.osgm.vanderbilt.edu/novak/flow.julv.1997/flow.htm

Novak, T.P., Hoffman, D.L., & Yung, Y.F. (2000). Measuring the customer experience in online environments: A structural modeling approach. *Marketing Science, 19*(1), 22-42.

Oakes, G. (1990). The sales process and the paradox of trust. *Journal of Business Ethics, 9,* 671-679.

O'Hara Devereaux, M., & Johansen, R. (1994). *Global work: Bridging distance, culture and time.* San Francisco: Jossey-Bass Publishers.

Poole, S. (2000). *Trigger happy: The inner life of video games.* London: Fourth Estate.

Porter, M. (2001). Strategy and the Internet. *Harvard Business Review (March),* 63-78.

Powell, W.W. (1990). Neither market nor hierarchy: Network forms of organisation. *Research in Organisational Behavior, 12,* 295-336.

Ratnasingham, P. (1998). The importance of trust in electronic commerce. *Internet Research, 8*(4), 313-321.

Rea, T. (2001). Engendering trust in electronic environments: Roles for a trusted third party. In C. Castelfranchi & Y.H. Tan (Eds.), *Deception, fraud and trust in virtual societies* (pp. 221-234). Dodrecht, The Netherlands: Kluwer.

Rheingold, H. (1993). *The virtual community: Homesteading on the electronic frontier.* New York: Addison-Wesley.

Rose, N., & Miller, P. (1992). Political power beyond the state: Problematics of government. *British Journal of Sociology, 43*(2), 173-205.

Sako, M. (1994). Price, quality and trust: Inter-firm relations in Britain and Japan. Cambridge, UK: Cambridge.

Schoorman, D.F., Mayer, R.C., & Davis, J.H. (1996). Including versus excluding ability from the definition of trust. *Academy of Management Review, 21*(2), 339-340.

Seligman, A. (1997). *The problem of trust.* Princeton, USA: Princeton University Press.

Shapiro, S.P. (1987). The Social Control of Impersonal Trust. *American Journal of Sociology, 93,* 623-658.

Silver, A. (1985). Trust in social and political theory. In G.D. Suttles & M.N. Zald (Eds.), *The challenge of social control* (pp. 52-70). Greenwich, CT, USA: Ablex.

Silver, A. (1989). Trust as a moral ideal: An historical approach. *Archives Europeenes de Sociologie, 30*(2), 69-87.

Silver, A. (1998). Two different sorts of commerce: Friendship and strangership in civil society. In

J.Weintraub & K. Kumar (Eds.), *Private and public in thought and practice* (pp. 43-74). Chicago: University of Chicago Press.

Sitkin, S.B., & Roth, N.L. (1993). Explaining the limited effectiveness of legalistic "remedies" for trust/distrust. *Organisation Science, 4*(3), 367-392.

Smith, M.A., & Kollock, P. (Ed.) (1999). *Communities in cyberspace*. London: Routledge.

Sztompka, P. (1999). *Trust: A sociological theory*. Cambridge, UK: Cambridge University Press.

Tadelis, S. (1999). What's in a name? Reputation as a tradeable asset. *American Economic Review, 89*(3), 548-563.

Tan, Y.H., & Thoen, W. (2000). A generic model of trust in electronic commerce. *International Journal of Electronic Commerce, 5*(2), 61-74.

Tan, Y.H., & Thoen, W. (2002). Formal aspects of a generic model of trust for electronic commerce. *Decision Support Systems, 33*(3), 233-246.

Urry, J. (2000). *Sociology beyond societies*. London: Routledge.

Wang, H., Lee, M.K.O., & Wang, C. (1998). Consumer privacy concerns about Internet marketing. *Communications of the ACM, 41*(3), 63-70.

Williams, R. (1974). Television, technology and cultural form. London, UK: Fontana.

Williamson, O. (1993). Calculativeness, trust and economic organisation. *Journal of Law and Economics, 30*, 131-145.

Windley, P.J., Tew, K., & Daley, D (2006). *A framework for building reputation systems*. Retrieved March 9, 2007, from http://www.windley.com/essays/2006/dim2006/framework_for_building_reputation_systems

Yamagishi, T., & Yamagishi, M. (1994). Trust and commitment in the United States and Japan. *Motivation and Emotion, 18*(2), 129-166.

Yu, B., & Singh, M.P. (2000). A social mechanism of reputation management in electronic com-
munities. In M. Klusch & L. Kerschberg (Eds.), *Proceedings of the 4ᵗʰ International Workshop on Cooperative Information Agents*.

Yuan, S.T., & Sung, H. (2004). A learning-enabled integrative trust model for e-markets. *Applied Artificial Intelligence, 18*, 69-95.

Zand, D.E. (1972). Trust and managerial problem solving. *Administrative Science Quarterly, 17*(2), 229-239.

Zucker, L.G. (1986). Production of trust: Institutional sources of economic structure 1840-1920. In B.M. Staw & L.L. Cummings (Eds.), *Research in organisational behavior* (pp. 53-111). JAI Press, CT, USA.

ENDNOTES

[1] The exact release dates of the GUI browser, Mosaic, are hard to pin down as versions for different operating systems were often released at different times. While the first official release is dated November 1993, x-mosaic dates back to December 1992. The release of Mosaic 3 in January 1997 marked the end of the browsers development by NCSA. See http://www.ncsa.uiuc.edu/SDG/Software?XMosaic.

[2] This focuses primarily on Web-based e-commerce throughout and assumes access via a desktop computer. This is not in any way a rejection of the importance of other platforms—from interactive mobile telephony to games consoles—will have in future access to e-commerce but a recognition of their current marginal ownership and use.

[3] Giddens' notion of "ontological security" (Giddens, 1984, 1990, 1991) and the work of Fukuyama (1995, 1998) demonstrates better than the brief remit of this paper can why this is not merely linguistic play.

[4] Elsewhere, Giddens (1991, p. 88) has suggested that quest for intimacy is a central

feature of contemporary social life. He has suggested that relationships are possible and develop where mutual trust exists and intimacy formed through working at the relationship.

⁵ This is not to be confused with Raymond Williams concept of flow—that is, the way items run into each other without marked separation—which is as applicable to Web sites as it is to television.

This work was previously published in Computer-Mediated Relationships and Trust: Managerial and Organizational Effects, edited by L. L. Brennan and V. E. Johnson, pp. 177-194, copyright 2008 by Information Science Reference, formerly known as Idea Group Reference (an imprint of IGI Global).

Chapter VIII
Public Sector E-Commerce

Christopher G. Reddick
The University of Texas at San Antonio, USA

INTRODUCTION

Electronic commerce or e-commerce has the potential to streamline existing functions and services in the public sector by reducing transaction costs or the cost of doing business. This article provides an overview of some of the critical e-commerce issues for the public sector focusing on its impact on reducing transaction costs.

BACKGROUND

E-commerce in the public sector has been defined as any process or transaction conducted by a government organization over a computer-mediated network that transfers ownership of or rights to use, goods, services, or information (Stowers, 2001). Public sector e-commerce has also been defined as the subset of e-government involving the exchange of money for goods and services purchased over the Internet by citizens and businesses (Reddick, 2005). The main aspect that defines e-commerce is transactions between government and citizens or businesses involving the exchange of money. Therefore, e-commerce is the use of the Internet and the Web to transact business. More formally, e-commerce is digitally enabled commercial transactions between and among organizations and individuals (Reddick, 2004b).

Generally speaking, one definition of electronic government or e-government refers to the use of technology, particularly Web-based Internet applications, to enhance the access to and delivery of government information and services to citizens, business, partners, employees, other agencies, and entities (GAO, 2001). E-commerce is a subset of e-government, is more restrictive in that it focuses on government transactions over the Internet. E-commerce is one way for government to reduce transaction costs and hence save budgetary resources, an especially critical function in fiscally restrained governments as witnessed by some of the transactional services offered online.

E-COMMERCE TRANSACTIONS

Survey data on the U.S. state government use of e-government was compiled by this author and was taken from the Center for Digital Government (2003) (Table 1). The 2002 data indicates that the top five most popular online services were job searches (done by 48 states), unclaimed property searches (46 states), college admissions (45 states), legislative tracking (45 states), and personal tax filing (43 states). Other interesting observations were that driver's license renewals were done in eight states and auto registration renewals were provided in 18 states. Therefore, many of the top services involve information searches such as online job searches and unclaimed property search.

The results in Table 1 indicate that e-government has changed the traditional way of advertising for a government job. It has also made it much

Table 1. Top 35 U.S. state government online services. Ranking of services in 2002 (0 to 50 scale) (Compiled from data from the Center for Digital Government, 2003)

Ranking of Service	Online Services	Number of States offering these Online Services	Ranking of Service	Online Services (continued)	Number of States offering these Online Services
1	Online Job Search	48	19	UI Filing and Payment	17
2	Unclaimed Property Search	46	20	Retirement Benefits	15
3	College Admissions	45	21	Contractor Look Up	14
4	Legislation Tracking	45	22	Personal Property Tax Payments	13
5	Personal Tax Filing	43	23	UCC Filings	12
6	Court Decisions Look Up	34	24	Social Service Directory	9
7	Sex Offender Look Up	33	25	Driver's License Renewal	8
8	Business License Look Up	32	26	Adoption Services	7
9	Vital Records	31	27	Corp. Biennial Reports	7
10	Business Tax Filing	30	28	Criminal History Lookup	6
11	Professional License Look UP	30	29	Motor Vehicle Citation Payments	6
12	Fishing and Hunting Licenses	28	30	Vanity Plates	6
13	List of Active Contracts	27	31	Auto Licensing	5
14	Apply as a state employee	23	32	Child Support Payments	4
15	Park Reservations	22	33	Lobbyist Registration	4
16	Renew Professional Licenses	22	34	Court Filings	2
17	Auto Registration Renewal	18	35	Online Voter Registration	2
18	Business Registration	18			

Note: UCC = Uniform Commercial Code; Top five e-commerce services in bold

easier for citizens to locate lost property. The college admissions process has been streamlined because of the Internet. In terms of e-commerce and transactions being completed online, filing personal taxes, for instance, was done in almost all of the states. This article focuses on the development of transaction-based e-commerce, since e-commerce is not possible unless there is a transaction between two parties over the Internet. A model of e-government adoption can be used to explain the evolution of e-commerce.

There are several stages of e-government growth. In the first stage, there is the cataloging of information on government Web sites (Layne & Lee, 2001). In this stage, there is no interaction with the citizen or business, just the presentation of downloadable forms or Web content for users. Most governments are in this stage of development because they have their own government Web sites disseminating information to the public. However, e-commerce is not prevalent in this stage because there are no transactions taking place between the user of the government Web site and the agency providing information or services.

The second stage is the transaction phase (Layne & Lee, 2001). There is some initial evidence in the United States suggesting that e-government has entered the transaction-based phase of e-government adoption (Edmiston, 2003; Holden, Norris, & Fletcher, 2003; Layne & Lee, 2001; Reddick, 2004a; Reddick, 2004b; Reddick, 2005; Wang & Rubin, 2004; West, 2004). This phase is where e-commerce comes to life. Governments make available working databases that support online transactions such as renewing a driver's license or filing taxes (Table 1). As a result of putting live databases online, governments can cut back on staffing offices since citizens and businesses now have the option of going online for selected services. There is, of course, still the problem of the digital divide where certain groups, such as minorities, elderly, low income, and those with disabilities do not have as much

access to the Internet or are not as Web savvy, although this gap is shrinking over time (U.S. Department of Commerce, 2002). Besides the important issue of the digital divide, this article examines transaction costs theory and its impact on e-commerce adoption.

TRANSACTION COSTS THEORY

One of the reasons for the adoption of information technology, and especially the Internet, is the reduction of transaction costs. Information technology helps government decrease in size because it can reduce transaction costs—the costs incurred when government buys on the marketplace what it cannot make for itself (Fountain, 2001; Laudon & Laudon, 2003; Thurmaier & Chen, 2005; Williamson, 1985). The principle idea of transaction cost theory in its application to e-commerce is that governments incur transaction costs when they conduct business. Simply stated transaction costs are the costs of making an economic exchange. The costs in government transactions include search and information costs, bargaining costs, and policing and enforcement costs (Thurmaier & Chen, 2005).

Information technology with the aid the Internet can also reduce internal management costs. According to the agency theory, the government can be viewed as a "nexus of contracts" among self-interested individuals rather than a unified entity (Horn, 1995). In this theory, a principal (e.g., departmental manager) employs "agents" (employees) to perform work on his or her behalf, however, agents need constant supervision from management because they will tend to pursue their own interests rather than those of their managers. Information technology permits public organizations to reduce agency costs because it becomes easier for managers to oversee a greater number of employees, when the number of middle management and clerical workers is reduced. Other issues of e-commerce that should be discussed address impacts from management, policy, and technology capacity.

STATE PUBLIC SECTOR E-COMMERCE ISSUES

The National Electronic Commerce Coordinating Council (NECCC) in conjunction with the Center for Digital Government addressed some of the issues that state governments will face in the implementation of electronic commerce (NECCC, 1999). These issues are common to e-commerce at most levels of government. There are four areas: enterprise administration, technologies, management, and policy. Each area will be briefly discussed along with its key issues (Table 2).

In terms of enterprise administration, some issues in this category are leadership and governance (Table 2). An enterprise approach to governance is recommended to maximize efficiencies and create a sense of empowerment in the implementation of new business processes. Leadership and vision at the executive level are critical elements of successful e-commerce (GAO, 2001). A second issue in the enterprise administration category is privacy. There should be informed consent at the

point of collection, limiting collection to required elements, allowing subjects to view and correct information, obtaining consent for any additional use of information. The third issue in the category is security. In implementing security solutions, governments should support open standards and choose commercially accepted technologies. The fourth issue in the enterprise administration category is electronic payments. Governments need to explore the full range of electronic payment mechanisms for both inflows and outflows including credit cards, debit cards, electronic funds transfer, micropayments, electronic wallets, and e-checks. Laws must be in place to support new and emerging technologies such as digital signatures, electronic records management, and electronic payments (NECCC, 2002).

Another important issue in state use of e-commerce is technologies (Table 2). Governments have been trying to create a "single face" by re-engineering their Web sites into service delivery mechanisms (i.e., Web site portals). The two general models prevail: a government-funded approach that uses an appropriation of the state budget and a self-funded model (Johnson, 2003). Each service offered on the Web portal may have its own financial model, advertising revenue, convenience fees, and documented cost savings

Table 2. A selection of e-commerce issues for governments

Enterprise Administration	Technologies	Management	Policy
• Leadership and governance	• Portals	• Funding	• Digital divide
• Privacy	• Applications	• Marketing	• Economic development
• Security	• Infrastructure	• Personnel and training	• Taxation
• Electronic payments	• Standards	• Economies of scale	

that all contribute to an overall financial strategy. A second issue in the technologies' category is applications developed from electronic commerce. By leveraging a standards-based infrastructure and browser-based tools, government agencies can streamline their internal processes and applications, enabling employees to use self-service tools. A third issue in the technologies' category is infrastructure. The most common challenge to almost any information technology project is funding. Governments must figure out how to pay for their e-commerce projects. The fourth issue in the category of technologies is standards. Consistent standards are important in order to ensure interoperability, compatibility, and shared usage of electronic commerce resources.

Management is the third category of successful e-commerce, and I argue that it is the most important issue (Table 2). Some of the existing literature supports the conclusion that more effective management leads to greater e-government adoption (Holden, Norris, & Fletcher, 2003; Reddick, 2004b). Funding is one of the issues in management that has its own set of challenges. There are three main funding and financing models for government Web site portals (Johnson, 2003). In the traditional model, monies are appropriated from the general fund and sometimes charge-back pricing occurs. The second model is the infrastructure finance model. The funding scheme is from debt proceed funds generated from the sale of state or local government bonds. The third funding model is the Internet based approach. The funding stream for this model is either advertising and or transaction-based revenue. Another often-overlooked issue in the category of management of public sector e-commerce is marketing. Edminston (2003) suggests that if e-commerce is to become successful, governments will be required not only to build and maintain useful Internet Web sites and portals, but also to educate their constituents about the availability of online public services and the benefits of us-

ing digital government resources. The third issue in the category of management is personnel and training. Some of the issues involved with electronic commerce and training include the short lifecycle of technology and the variety of technologies. Both of these require management to make strategic decisions regarding technology training. The fourth issue in the management category of e-commerce development is economies of scale in service provision. Since governments obviously have limited goods to sell to the public or business, one would expect to see the most e-commerce applications in the areas where funds exchange hands—taxes, licenses, permits, and procurement (Stowers, 2001).

The fourth category is electronic commerce policies and one key issue in this category is the digital divide (Table 2). There is a large group of citizens and small businesses without access or any real knowledge of the tools required to use the Web as a medium for conducting affairs (Edmiston, 2003). The second issue in the policy category is that of economic development. When private businesses can do everything online from obtaining permits to renewing licenses, the government offering these services is considered business friendly. The last issue in the policies category is taxation. If an Internet business has no physical presence in the jurisdiction, the company is not collecting sales tax, paying business license fees, property tax, real-estate tax, income tax, or employing local citizens (Nesbary, 2000).

FUTURE TRENDS

Public sector e-commerce in the future will increasingly expand as citizens and businesses grow accustomed to using online services. In addition, as some of the aforementioned issues such as management, privacy, and technology capacity receive greater attention, e-commerce should significantly expand. The potential for e-commerce to reduce transaction costs for government agencies makes it very desirable for them to accept online payments for services.

CONCLUSION

Public sector e-commerce is different from e-government in that it focuses on citizens or businesses using the Internet to conduct transactions with government such as renewing a driver's license or filing taxes. Governments often take part in e-commerce initiatives in order to reduce transaction costs. Governments in the United States are mostly cataloging information online; there is not as much development into conducting transactions online. Some of the e-commerce issues discussed in this article that should be addressed before more transactions are completed online are enterprise administration, technologies, management, and policy.

REFERENCES

Center for Digital Government. (2003). *Digital government navigator*. Retrieved January, 2005, from http://www.centerdigitalgov.com

Edmiston, K. D. (2003). State and local e-government: Prospects and challenges. *American Review of Public Administration, 33*(1), 20-45.

Fountain, J. E. (2001). *Building the virtual state: Information technology and institutional change.* Washington, DC: The Brookings Institution.

GAO. (2001). *Electronic government: Challenges must be addressed with effective leadership and management.* GAO-01-959T. (Washington, DC; General Accounting Office).

Holden, S. H., Norris, D. F., & Fletcher, P. D. (2003). Electronic government at the local level: Progress to date and future issues. *Public Performance & Management Review, 26*, 325-344.

Horn, M. J. (1995). *The political economy of public administration.* Cambridge, MA: Cambridge University Press.

Johnson, C. L. (2003). Financing and pricing e-service. In M. A. Abramson & T. L. Morin (Eds.), *E-government 2003.* Oxford, Rowan & Littlefield Publishers, Inc.

Laudon, K. C., & Laudon, J. P. (2003). *Essentials of management information systems: managing the digital firm* (5th ed.). Upper Saddle River, NJ: Prentice Hall.

Layne, K., & Lee, J. (2001). Developing fully function e-government: A four stage model. *Government Information Quarterly, 18*(1), 122-136.

NECCC. (1999). *Electronic commerce: A blueprint for states.* Lexington, KY: National Electronic Commerce Coordinating Council. Retrieved January, 2005, from www.ec3.org

NECCC. (2002). *Electronic payments primer.* Lexington, KY: National Electronic Commerce Coordinating Council. Retrieved January 2005, from www.ec3.org

Nesbary, D. (2000). The taxation of Internet commerce. *Social Science Computer Review, 18*(1), 17-39.

Reddick, C. G. (2004a). A two-stage model of e-government growth: Theories and empirical evidence for U.S. cities. *Government Information Quarterly, 21*(1), 51-64.

Reddick, C. G. (2004b). Public sector e-commerce and state financial management: Capacity versus wealth. *Social Science Computer Review, 22*(3), 293-306.

Reddick, C. G. (2005). Government e-commerce adoption: A study of Texas counties. *Journal of E-Government, 2*(2), 45-73.

Stowers, G. (2001). Commerce comes to government on the desktop: E-commerce applications in the public sector. In M. A. Abramson & G. E.

Means (Eds.), *E-government 2001* (pp. 44-84). Oxford: Rowan & Littlefield Publishers, Inc.

Thurmaier, K., & Chen, Y. (2005). *Financing eGovernment business transactions: Empirical estimates of willingness to pay.* International Association of Schools and Institutions of Administration. Retrieved November, 3, from http://das.ite.iowa.gov/governance/IAC/documents/Thurmaier-Chen-IASIA05b.pdf

U.S. Department of Commerce. (2002). *A nation online: How Americans are expanding their use of the Internet.* Washington, DC: U.S. Department of Commerce Economics and Statistics Administration and the National Telecommunications and Information Administration.

Wang, H., & Rubin, B. L. (2004). Embedding e-finance in e-government: A new e-government framework. *Electronic Government, 1*(4), 362-373.

West, D. M. (2004). E-government and the transformation of service delivery and citizen attributes. *Public Administration Review, 61*(1), 15-27.

Williamson, O. E. (1985). *The economic institutions of capitalism.* New York: Free Press.

KEY TERMS

Convenience Fees: A fee charged to the public or businesses for the privilege of using an online government service such as renewing a driver's license online.

Digital Divide: Large differences in Internet access and e-commerce access among income, ethnic, and age groups.

Digital Wallet: Authenticates the consumer through the use of digital certificates or other encryption methods, stores and transfers payment, and secures the payment process from consumer to government.

Government-Funded Portal: The government uses its own funds to start up an e-commerce Web site.

Micropayments: Part of a digital wallet function. Used for payments under $5 anywhere on the Web based on credit cards.

Privacy: Includes both the claim that certain information should not be collected from the Internet at all by governments, and the claims of individuals to control the use of whatever information that is collected about them.

Public Sector E-Commerce: Public sector e-commerce is defined as the subset of e-government involving the exchange of money for goods and services purchased over the Internet by citizens and businesses.

Security: Educates and trains users, keeps management aware of security threats and breakdowns, and maintains the tools chosen to implement security on a government Web site.

Self-Funded Portal: Private vendors pay for the start-up costs of an e-commerce Web site and recoups their costs of investment through online transaction charges and subscription fees.

Web Site Portal: Is an integrated gateway into a government Web site and provides visitors with a single point of contact for online service delivery.

This work was previously published in Encyclopedia of Digital Government, edited by A. Anttiroiko and M. Malkia, pp. 1383-1387, copyright 2007 by Information Science Reference, formerly known as Idea Group Reference (an imprint of IGI Global).

Chapter IX
Multi−Agent Patterns for Deploying Online Auctions

Ivan Jureta
University of Namur, Belgium

Manuel Kolp
University of Louvain, Belgium

Stéphane Faulkner
University of Namur, Belgium

ABSTRACT

Today, a high volume of goods and services is being traded using online auction systems. The growth in size and complexity of architectures to support online auctions requires the use of distributed and cooperative software techniques. In this context, the agent software development paradigm seems appropriate for their modeling, development, and implementation. This article proposes an agent-oriented pattern analysis of best practices for online auctions. The patterns are intended to help both IT managers and software engineers during the requirement specification of an online auction system while integrating benefits of agent software engineering.

INTRODUCTION

The emergence and growing popularity of electronic commerce in general and online auctions in particular has raised the challenge to explore scalable global electronic market information systems, involving both human and automated traders (Rachlevsky-Reich, Ben-Shaul, Tung Chau, Lo, & Poggio, 1999).

Online auctions are a particular type of Internet-based electronic markets (i.e., worldwide open markets in which participants buy and sell goods and services in exchange for money). Most online auctions rely on classical auction economics (Bikhchandani, de Vries, Schummer, & Vohra, 2001; Beam & Segev, 1998). In the economics literature, "an auction is an economic mechanism for determining the price of an item. It requires a pre-announced methodology, one or more bidders who want the item, and an item for sale" (Beam & Segev, 1998). The item usually is sold to the highest bidder. An online auction can be defined as an auction that is organized using an information system (IS) and is accessible to auction participants exclusively through a Web site on the Internet.

Recently, online auctions have become a popular way to trade goods and services. In 2002, eBay.com, the leading online marketplace, provided a trading platform for 638 million items of all kinds. The value of all goods that were traded amounted to nearly $15 billion, which represented, at the time, a third of all online sales in the U.S. This trend results from specific advantages of online auctions over traditional ones (as discussed in the section "Current State of Online Auctions") as well as the fact that people are becoming increasingly comfortable with online shopping, which is reflected in strong growth of online sales on both auction-based and other e-commerce platform types (e.g., fixed-price marketplaces such as Amazon.com).

Today, with the increasing number of online auctions being organized, there is a need for distributed, large-scale, dynamic IS architectures to support online auction marketplaces (Rachlevsky-Reich, Ben-Shaul, Tung Chau, Lo, & Poggio, 1999). From the IS development perspective, multi-agent systems (MASs) are a powerful new software engineering paradigm for designing and developing complex ISs (Yu, 1997). The use of agents as intentional, autonomous, social entities that act according to their self interests (Yu, 2001) provides advantages in both the modeling of an online auction system and its implementation using an agent-oriented IS.

In this article, we propose agent-oriented analysis patterns for deploying an online auction information system (OAIS). These patterns are intended to help both IT managers and software engineers during the analysis of OAIS. We develop the social dimension of patterns on the basis of the analysis of leading existing OAISs.

Our motivation stems from the fact that auction mechanisms for exchanging goods and services will become more and more popular with both consumers and companies (Resnick & Zeckhauser 2002). Providing agent-oriented patterns for such systems can reduce their development cost and time while integrating benefits of agent-orientation in software development. Patterns of current best practices in the online auction domain facilitate the development of new auction systems by showing clearly the functionalities that are particularly valued by auction participants. These should be included in any auction system, if it wishes to attract both consumers and corporate users.

The rest of this article is organized as follows. The second section gives an overview of the core concepts and of their relevance in the context of online auctions. The third section describes our analysis method and identifies existing online auction systems on which we base our analysis. The fourth section describes the patterns of a basic OAIS. The fifth section describes best practices in the domain of OAIS. The sixth section concludes the text and discusses the limitations of our approach.

ONLINE AUCTIONS, AGENTS, AND AGENT PATTERNS

Our work revolves around three main concepts: online auctions, agents, and patterns. In the following subsections, we present each one and discuss reasons why agent orientation is appropriate for modeling, design, and implementation of OAIS.

Current State of Online Auctions

There is currently multi-billion-dollar annual activities in the online auction market with a growing variety of sophisticated trading mechanisms (Pinker, Seidmann, & Vakrat, 2001). There are numerous reasons for the popularity of online auction marketplaces (Lucking-Reiley, 2000; Pinker, Seidmann, & Vakrat, 2001; Re, Braga, & Masiero 2001). We classify them into following categories: market efficiency, accessibility, managing complexity, and information gathering.

There have been several studies that have presented online auction business models (Beam & Segev, 1998; Lucking-Reiley, 2000). These studies propose different classification criteria for online auctions, such as the auction mechanism (English, Vickrey, Dutch, etc.), the type of participants (businesses and/or consumers), the number of participants, and so forth. We retain here the classification proposed by Pinker, Seidmann, and Vakrat (2001), which is based primarily on the number of participants. This classification is shown in Figure 1.

In bilateral negotiations, the two parties negotiate the sale of an item. Negotiation involves the price of the item but also may involve its qualitative characteristics.

Figure 1. Classification of online auction types, according to Pinker, Seidmann, and Vakrat (2001)

	ONE BUYER	MANY BUYERS
ONE SELLER	Bilateral negotiations	Web-based sales auctions
MANY SELLERS	Web-based reverse procurement auctions	Web-based exchanges

In Web-based reverse procurement auctions, many sellers compete to win a single buyer (e.g., a government accepts bids for a construction project from several companies).

In Web-based exchanges, many buyers face multiple sellers (e.g., the stock market). In Web-based sales auctions, a single seller offers an item for sale to many bidders (e.g., eBay.com).

In Web-based sales auctions on the Internet, the most common auction mechanisms are the English, Vickrey, Dutch, and first-price-sealed-bid auctions. Next we briefly describe their mechanisms.

English Auction. Each bidder sees the highest current bid and can place a bid and update it many times. The winner of the auction is the highest bidder who pays the price bid (i.e., the final auction bid that this bidder placed). An example is eBay.com. English auctions are by far the most popular auction type, and their success lies most probably in the familiarity of English auctions as well as in the entertainment they provide to participants (in the form of bidder competition).

First-Price Sealed Bid Auction. Each bidder makes a single secret bid; the winner is the highest bidder, and the price paid is the highest bid. An example is The Chicago Wine Company (tcwc.com).

Vickrey Auction. Each bidder makes a single secret bid; the winner is the highest bidder. However, the price paid is the amount of the second highest bid. Some online auction systems propose it as an option (e.g., iauction.com).

Dutch Auction. The seller steadily lowers the price of the item over time. The bidders can see the current price and must decide if they wish to purchase it at that price or wait until it drops further. The winner is the first bidder to pay the current price (e.g., klik-klok.com).

In the context of the classification proposed in Figure 1, our analysis focuses on *Web-based sales auctions*. The analysis is applicable on any type of auction as far as the participant type is concerned. Both the seller and buyers may be either customers and/or businesses. Our analysis is independent of the auction mechanism, as long as it is a mechanism involving a single seller and many buyers.

Benefits of Agent Orientation

An agent can be defined as an intentional, autonomous, social entity that acts according to its self-interest (Yu, 2001). In the IS development perspective, an agent is an autonomous software entity that is responsive to its environment, proactive (i.e., it exhibits goal-oriented behavior), and social (i.e., it can interact with other agents to complete goals) (Kauffman &Walden, 2001). Multi-agent systems involve the interaction of multiple agents, both software and human, so that they may achieve common or individual goals through cooperative or competitive behavior.

The use of agent orientation in the modeling, design, and implementation of OAIS provides at least the following benefits:

- When modeling an OAIS, we can represent (using, for example, the *i** modeling framework) (Yu, 1995) the intentional dimension of agents participating in the auction process as well as their interdependencies. Consequently, the use of agents as the core modeling concept makes it possible to understand more profoundly the environment in which IS will be used. We then can explore alternative IS structures incorporating different functionalities during the requirements engineering phase of the IS development. We can evaluate alternative IS structures in terms of their contribution to users' needs (e.g., ease of use, speed, etc.) and to the system's other non-functional requirements

(e.g., security, reusability, development cost, development time, etc.) in order to select the most adequate IS structure.

- OAISs are large-scale, complex, and distributed systems. The use of MAS as a powerful new software engineering paradigm for designing and developing complex IS has been advocated in Faulkner, Kolp, and Do (2004). Social organization-based MAS (Kolp, Giorgini, & Mylopoulos, 2003; Faulkner et al., 2004) match the system architecture with its operational environment (Do, Kolp, & Pirotte, 2003). They provide a strong basis for the development of robust and highly customizable software that is able to cope with the changing environment while being sufficiently secure to protect personal data and other belongings of system agents. Agent architectures are more flexible, modular, and robust than, for example, object-oriented ones. They tend to be open and dynamic, as their components can be added, modified, or removed at any time (Yu, 1997).

Online Auction Patterns

Patterns are reusable solutions to recurring IS design problems and provide a vocabulary for communicating these solutions to others (Weiss, 2003). They aid in the reuse of IS analysis and design experience, as each pattern describes a reusable and flexible solution for a specific problem type.

Patterns for OAIS already have been proposed by Re, Braga, and Masiero (2001). However, these patterns are specified using the UML. Consequently, they do not show agents as intentional, autonomous, and social entities. In addition, the pattern language provided by Re, Braga, and Masiero (2001) does not integrate best practices that can be identified on currently operating auction IS on the Internet. Kumar and Feldman (1998) only provide a global architecture of a basic online auction system in the context of object-oriented software development. GEM (Rachlevsky-Reich et al., 1999) provides system architecture for developing large distributed electronic markets, but it only addresses the system's basic functionalities that are required to organize trading among agents. It provides patterns without treating intentional aspects and uses agents at the implementation level.

ANALYSIS METHOD

Our analysis is based on three leading OAISs on the Internet: eBay.com, Amazon.com Auctions, and Yahoo.com Auctions. We examined the Web sites of these systems and used literature that provides either strategic analysis (Pinker et al., 2001) or economic analysis (Lucking-Reiley, 2000; Resnick & Zeckhauser, 2002) of aspects of auctions being conducted on these systems.

We do not provide a comparative analysis of the three. However, it is necessary to note that eBay is by far the leading online auction marketplace and provides the most advanced functionalities that support both the auction process and the exchange of items and valuables that follows the auction. eBay is also the only one for which online auctions constitute its core business, making it particularly sensitive to the needs of its users (Amazon is specialized in fixed-price retailing, and Yahoo is an all-purpose Web portal). We have found that both Yahoo.com Auctions and Amazon.com Auctions are late entrants to the online auction market and that they copy the eBay business model. Consequently, we focus the analysis of the IS structure and the identification of best practices on eBay, while comparing our findings with its two main competitors.

We model the social dimension of each pattern using the *i** modeling framework (Yu, 1995). *i** is an agent-oriented modeling framework that is used to support the early phase of requirements engineering (Yu, 1997), during which we wish to represent and understand the wider context

in which the IS will be used. The framework focuses on dependencies that exist among actors and provides two types of models to represent them: a strategic dependency (SD) model used for describing processes as networks of strategic dependencies among actors, and the strategic rationale (SR) model used to describe each actor's reasoning in the process as well as to explore alternative process structures.

Main modeling constructs of the *i** framework are Actors, Roles, Goals, Softgoals, Resources, and Tasks. Both the SD and SR models can represent dependencies among Actors or Roles. A dependency is a relationship in which an Actor or Role A_1 depends on some other Actor or Role A_2, for the provision of a dependum. We call A_1 the depender and A_2 the dependee in the relationship. Each dependency can be seen as a matching of a want from the depender side to an ability on the dependee side (Liu & Yu, 2004). The following dependency types exist:

- **Goal Dependency.** A Goal is a condition or state of affairs in the environment that the actors would like to achieve. In a Goal dependency, the depender depends on the dependee to achieve a Goal. The dependee has the freedom to choose the way in which the Goal will be achieved.
- **Softgoal Dependency.** A Softgoal is similar to a Goal but differs in that there are no clear-cut criteria for knowing whether the Softgoal has been achieved or not. It is then up to the stakeholders to judge whether a particular IS structure sufficiently satisfies the Softgoal. In a Softgoal dependency, the depender depends on the dependee to act in such way so as to contribute to the Softgoal.
- **Task Dependency.** A Task specifies a particular way of doing something. In a Task dependency, the depender specifies the course of action to be taken by the dependee.

- **Resource Dependency.** A Resource is a physical or informational entity that may serve some purpose. In a Resource dependency, the depender requires the dependee to provide some Resource.

In *i**, software agents are represented as Actors. Actors can play Roles. A Role is an abstract characterization of the common behaviour of an Actor in some specific context (e.g., a consumer, a salesman, a buyer, a seller, etc.).

BASIC AGENT-ORIENTED PATTERNS ANALYSIS

We focus on an online auction process that is appropriate for the cited auction types (English, Vickrey, Dutch, and First-Price Sealed Bid Auction) involving a single seller and multiple buyers. We first provide the social dimension of separate patterns that are required to run an OAIS. We then integrate these patterns in order to show how they constitute an OAIS that provides basic auction functionality.

Basic Patterns

In our analysis, we identified system actors (Figure 2). The figure shows that these actors are specializations of common generic e-business agents from the business agent typology proposed in Papazoglou (2001). This is useful, since much work has been put in to the specification, development, and testing of these generic agent types (Guttman, Moukas, & Maes, 1998; Papazoglou, 2001).

Personal Agents work directly with the human user to help support the creation and management of the user's profile. *User Agents* can play the roles of Buyers and Sellers with regard to selling and/or buying in auctions. *Negotiating and Contracting Agents* negotiate terms of business transactions in terms of transaction rules, payment methods, and so forth. *Security Agents* manage security aspects of the system, such as user registration, access authorization, and so forth. *Information Brokering Agents* manage, summarize, and manipulate information. They search for information on behalf of *User Agents*.

Figure 2. Actors and roles in the online auction information system

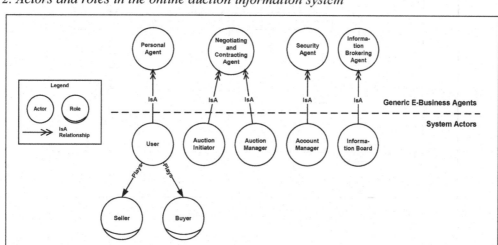

Figure 3. Social dimension of the user authentication pattern

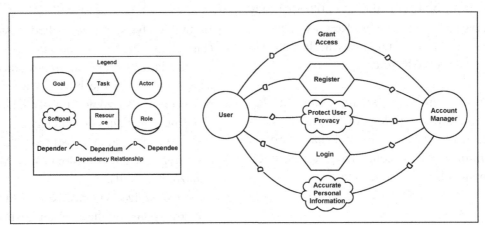

Figure 4. Dynamic dimension of the User Authentication pattern

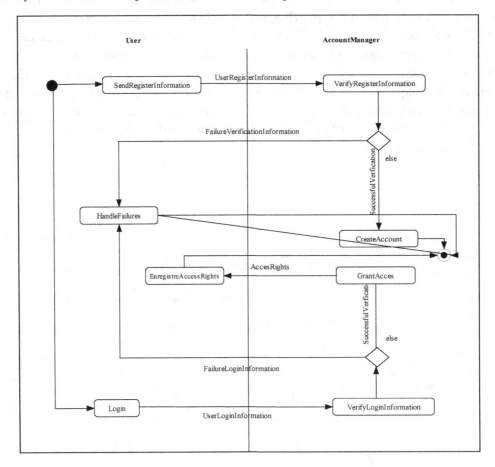

Figure 5. Social dimension of the auction setup pattern

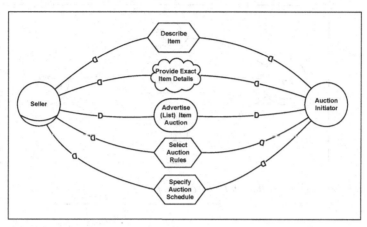

Figure 6. Dynamic dimension of the auction setup pattern

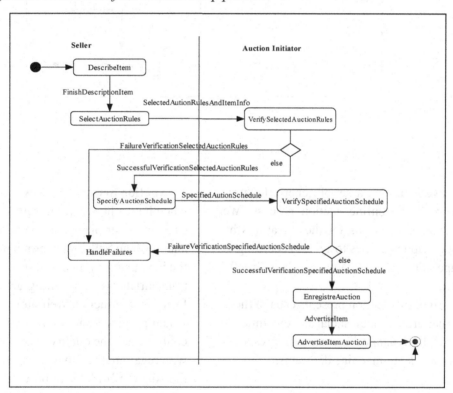

Figure 7. Social dimension of the auction search pattern

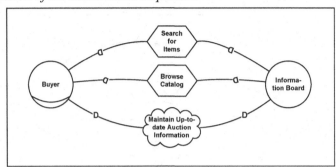

Figure 8. Dynamic dimension of the auction search pattern

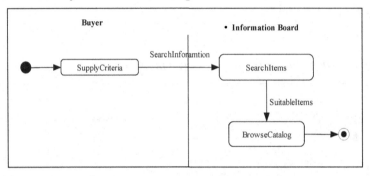

We have identified a set of generic features that compose the online auction process. We provide analysis patterns for these features by allocating responsibilities to agents according to their capabilities that already have been briefly described.

The rest of this section presents each of these analysis patterns through social and dynamic dimensions. The dynamic dimension is represented with classical state-machine diagrams.

User Authentication. In order to use the system, Users first need to register on the system by providing personal data. The data are necessary for identification when they return to participate in auctions. They can then access and use the system by logging on.

Auction Setup. A User will set up an auction when he or she wishes to sell an item. In such a case, the User plays the role of the Seller in the auction. The Seller must provide a description of the item using a procedure specified by the Auction Initiator (i.e., by filling out a series of Web forms on the auction Web site). Ideally, the Seller would provide Exact Item Details, which would contribute to the quality of service of the system with regard to the Buyers. The Seller depends on the Auction Initiator to provide a procedure for selecting among alternative auction rules (e.g., English Auction, Dutch Auction, etc.) and to specify the schedule of the auction. The Seller depends on the Auction Initiator to advertise the item that the Seller has put on auction so that potential Buyers can be informed about the auction event.

Figure 9. Social dimension of the auction bidding pattern

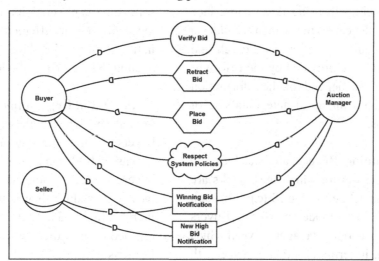

Figure 10. Dynamic dimension of the auction bidding pattern

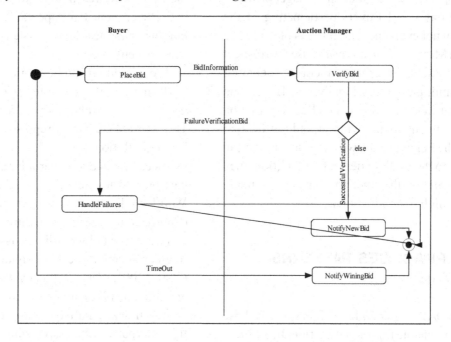

The Auction Setup pattern is independent of the auction type. However, specific constraints do apply for specific auction types. For example, if the User selects the English auction rules, he or she must specify the minimum bid increment.

The same information is irrelevant for a Dutch auction, for example. The specification of such constraints is outside the scope of this text and should be discussed with specialists of the auction domain.

Auction (Item) Search. A User looks for auctioned items either by using a search interface or by browsing the catalogue, which provides a hierarchical organization of items. Search and browsing features are provided by the Information Board. The User depends on the Information Board to maintain an up-to-date database of current auctions.

Auction Bidding. Buyers can place bids and retract bids. The way in which these tasks are accomplished is defined in the IS (e.g., through a specific Web/wap/i-mode interface). Buyers depend on the Auction Manager to verify bids that they place, in terms of bid coherence with the auction rules (e.g., is the minimum bid increment respected?). The Auction Manager provides notifications to all Buyers participating in the auction whenever a new high bid is placed. The Auction Manager depends on the users to respect system policies in terms of incorrect behavior such as multiple bidding. Finally, both Buyers and the Seller in the auction depend on the Auction Manager to supply the winning bid notification so that the Seller and the winning Buyer then can proceed to the trade settlement. In addition, they both depend on the Auction Manager to supply the new high bid notification.

BEST PRACTICES PATTERNS ANALYSIS

Today's OAISs offer additional features to those that automate the traditional auction. In addition to enhancing the user experience, these additional features are essential to the commercial success of an OAIS. We provide patterns for several additional features that we consider to be best practices in the domain of online auctions.

We will see that some of the features can be introduced in the system in several ways, requiring comparison and evaluation. To select the most adequate alternative, we represent relevant system qualities (e.g., security, privacy, usability, etc.) as softgoals and use contribution links to show how these softgoals are affected by each alternative, as in the Non-Functional Requirements framework (Chung, Nixon, Yu, & Mylopoulos, 2000).

Proxy Bidding. Online auctions can last for several days, which makes it impossible for human buyers to follow the auction in its integrity, as is the case in traditional ones. Proxy bidding allows buyers to specify their maximum willingness to pay. A procedure then is used to automatically increase their bid until the specified maximum is reached or until the auction is closed (Kurbel & Loutchko, 2001). This enables human buyers to be represented in the auction without requiring their physical presence in order to interact with their Buyer agent. It is important to note that proxy bidding is applicable only when English auction rules are enforced.

Proxy bidding can be introduced in the basic OAIS in several ways in terms of responsibility assignment. Two alternatives are shown in Figure 11. Each alternative is represented as a simple Strategic Rationale model. A series of softgoals has been selected as criteria for alternative comparison: Privacy, Security, Reliability, Speed, and Workload. These are non-functional requirements (Chung et al., 2000) for the information system and were selected according to issues often raised in e-commerce IS design (Mylopoulos, Kolp, & Castro, 2001; Weiss, 2003), OAIS design (Kumar & Feldman, 1998), and so forth.

The first alternative seems more adequate. In this alternative, the responsibility of managing proxy bidding is allocated to the Buyer agent. Several reasons support this choice:

- When the Buyer manages proxy bidding, price preferences are not communicated to outside agents. Consequently, privacy is higher than in the second alternative, which requires the transfer of price preferences to the Auction Manager.

Figure 11. Two alternative responsibility assignments expressed in two strategic rationale models of the proxy bidding feature. Positive (favorable) (+) and negative (not favorable) (-) contributions of each alternative structure are shown. They aid in alternative selection

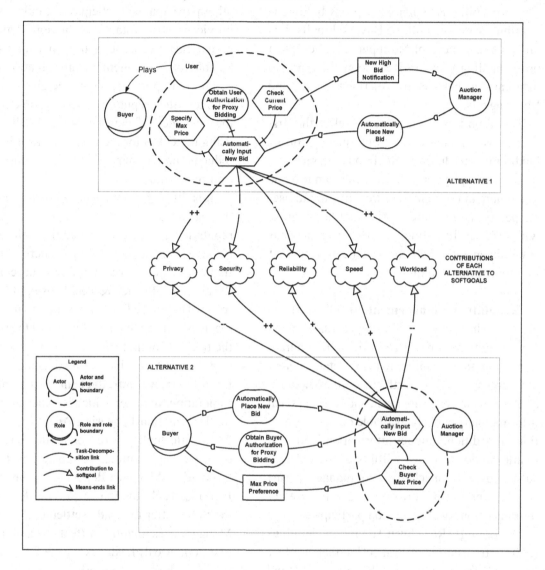

- Workload of the system is lower, since automatic bidding is distributed among multiple Buyer agents participating in the auction. We consider that system workload is much higher when all proxy bidding activity in one auction is centralized at the Auction Manager.

- We consider that security of data transfers between the Buyer and Auction Manager is not of high priority in an English online auction, since the bid made by the Buyer is made publicly available by the Auction Manager.

Reliability concerns the probability of error in terms of, for example, a new proxy bid not being taken into account by the Auction Manager. This probability is higher when proxy bidding is distributed among multiple Buyers. Finally, it is probable that speed of bid input is higher when proxy bidding is centralized, since there are no data transfers between the Auction Manager and Buyer agents.

Based on this discussion, we select the first alternative in Figure 11. Consequently, proxy bidding is introduced in the IS as a service that a User agent playing the Buyer role can provide to the human user, and requires the human user to specify the maximum price that he or she is willing to pay. In addition, the Buyer agent needs to obtain an authorization from the user in order to initiate proxy bidding.

Reputation Management. In classical exchanges where buyers and sellers actually meet, trust[1] results from repeated buyer-seller interactions, from the possibility to inspect items before the purchase, and so forth. In online auctions, sellers and buyers do not meet, and little personal information is publicly available during the auction. In addition, product information is limited to information provided wilfully by the seller. In such a context, a mechanism for managing trust should be provided in order to reduce uncertainty in transactions among auction participants.

According to Ramchurn, Huynh, and Jennings (2004), "trust is a belief an agent has that the other party will do what it says it will (being honest and reliable) or reciprocate (being reciprocate for the common good of both), given an opportunity to defect to get higher payoffs." Trust can be favored in an OAIS through a reputation mechanism, which should satisfy specific requirements (Ramchurn et al., 2004); it should be costly to change identities in the community; new entrants should not be penalized by initially having a low reputation rating; participants with low ratings should be able to rebuild reputation; it should be costly

for participants to fake reputation; participants with high reputations should have more influence on reputation ratings that they attribute to other participants; participants should be able to provide more qualitative evaluations than simply numerical ratings; and finally, participants should be able to keep a memory of reputation ratings, and more importance should be given to the latest ones. Such reputation mechanism can reduce the hesitancy of new buyers and sellers when using the OAIS for the first time, as it implicitly reduces the anonymity and uncertainty among trading partners.

It is difficult to construct a reputation system that satisfies all of these requirements. Seller reputation can be established through feedback of buyers on the behavior of sellers during the trade settlement, which follows the closure of the auction (Resnick & Zeckhauser, 2002). As a result of buyer feedback in repetitive sales, a seller receives a rating that is indicative of the trust that the trading community has in him or her.

In order to enable the management of trust in an OAIS, we introduce an additional agent: Reputation Manager, which is a specialization of the Information Brokering Agent (Papazoglou, 2001). Informally, its responsibility is to collect, organize, and summarize reputation data. The Reputation Manager depends on the winning Buyer of each auction to provide feedback on the Seller after the trade settlement. Reputation Manager uses qualitative (textual) and quantitative (numerical) feedback on the Seller in order to establish reputation ratings of users that have played the role of Sellers in auctions. As information on reputation is valuable to any user of the OAIS, any user depends on the Reputation Manager to manage feedback forum in which the feedback and rating information is contained and organized. Each Buyer depends on the Reputation Manager to provide summarized seller reputation information so that the Buyer can have an indication on the trust that he or she can put into the relationship with the Seller. The Seller can post

Figure 12. Social dimension of the reputation management pattern

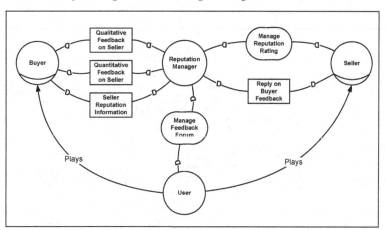

replies on feedback provided by Buyers. Finally, the Seller depends on the Reputation Manager to manage reputation rating.

This pattern satisfies all but one of the requirements previously specified: it does not make it costly for participants to change identities. For example, eBay deals with this problem by requiring each seller to provide a valid credit card number. We do not introduce such a possibility into the pattern, since it is not a standardized solution (eBay applies it only for its U.S. users and none of its competitors applies it anywhere in the world).

Dispute Resolution. The trade settlement that follows the closure of the auction may not be successful for many reasons (e.g., late deliveries, late payment, no payment at all, etc.). It then results in a dispute that can require mediation by a third party in order to be resolved. The third party (here, a Negotiation Assistant) can be either a software agent that manages an automated dispute resolution process or a human mediator.

The Negotiation Assistant collects Buyer and Seller arguments and makes them available to both parties. On the basis of these arguments and its

solution knowledge base, the agent selects solution (both the Buyer and the Seller depend on the agent to suggest a solution to their dispute).

Payment. Payment can be accomplished in numerous ways in the context of an online auction. It either can be managed (in part) through the OAIS (e.g., credit-card-based transactions) or outside the scope of the IS (e.g., cash, checks, etc.). The payment choice of auction participants is not repetitive and differs according to the payment cost, convenience, and protection. Consequently, it is important to take these criteria into account when structuring an OAIS.

In the payment pattern, the Payment Agent (specialization of the Negotiating and Contracting Agent) (Papazoglou, 2001) mediates the payment interaction between the Seller and the Buyer. This agent depends on the Account Manager for data on users, which is then used in providing payment details to the payment system. In addition to user identification, payment details also should contain transaction-related data. The Payment Agent depends on the payment system to realize payment and to provide money transfer confirmation, which is used to confirm money transfer to the

Figure 13. Strategic rationale model of the dispute resolution pattern with focus on negotiation assistant agent rationale

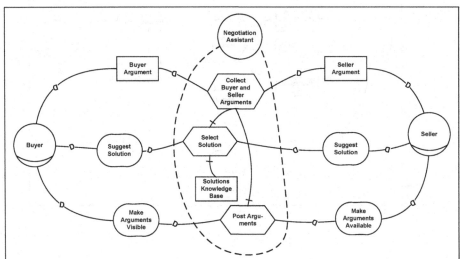

Figure 14. Social dimension of the payment pattern

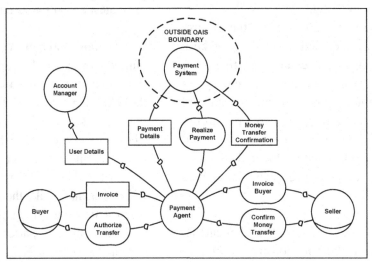

Seller. The payment system is outside the boundary of the OAIS. Upon closure of the auction, the Seller depends on the Payment Agent to invoice the Buyer. The Buyer depends on the payment system to provide an invoice, and in return, the Buyer is expected to authorize transfer.

The pattern structure in Figure 14 is adapted to all common credit-card-based payment systems. Any of these payment systems intervenes in the pattern as the payment system, which is specialized in money transfers.

CONCLUSION

Online auctions have become increasingly popular in e-business transactions. Companies require such systems to be developed on tight budgets and in a short time in order to deploy auctions in managing relationships with their suppliers and clients. Patterns of best practices of online auctions can provide significant aid in the development process of such systems.

This article explores such patterns by analyzing some advanced online auctions functionalities through the lens of the agent paradigm. Compared to the literature, our approach is innovative in several respects: we consider that multi-agent systems are adapted particularly to modeling and implementing online auction systems; we provided the *i** agent-oriented modeling perspective of each of the patterns we considered, and we focused on specifying best practices in current online auction systems.

There are limitations to our work. We have not provided dimensions other than the *i** (social and intentional) ones for the patterns. This is well beyond the scope of this article, as it requires much more time and space. As future work, the patterns will be modeled using UML-based notations as well as formally specified with the Z language.

REFERENCES

Beam, C., & Segev, A. (1998). *Auctions on the Internet: A field study* (Working Paper 98-WP-1032). Berkeley, CA: University of California.

Bikhchandani, S., de Vries, S., Schummer, S., & Vohra, R.V. (2001). *Linear programming and vickrey auctions: Mathematics of the Internet: E-auction and markets.* Springer-Verlag.

Chung, L.K., Nixon, B.A., Yu, E., & Mylopoulos J. (2000). *Non-functional requirements in software engineering.* Kluwer Publishing.

Do, T.T., Kolp, M., & Pirotte, A. (2003). Social patterns for designing multiagent systems. In *Proceedings of the 15th International Conference on Software Engineering and Knowledge Engineering, SEKE'03,* San Francisco.

Faulkner, S., Kolp, M., & Do, T.T. (2004). The SKwyRL perspective on agent-oriented design patterns. In *Proceedings of the 6th International Conference on Enterprise Information Systems, ICEIS'04,* Porto, Portugal.

Guttman, R.H., Moukas, A.G., & Maes, P. (1998). Agent-mediated electronic commerce: A survey. *Knowledge Engineering Review, 13*(3), 45-69.

Kauffman, R.J., & Walden, E.A. (2001). Economics and electronic commerce: Survey and research directions. *International Journal of Electronic Commerce, 5*(4), 5-117.

Kolp, M., Giorgini, P., & Mylopoulos, J. (2003). Organizational patterns for early requirements analysis. In *Proceedings of the 15th International Conference on Advanced Information Systems Engineering, CAiSE'03,* Velden, Austria.

Kumar, M., & Feldman, S.I. (1998). Internet auctions. In *Proceedings of the 3rd USENIX Workshop on Electronic Commerce,* Boston.

Kurbel, K., & Loutchko, I. (2001). A framework for multi-agent electronic marketplaces: Analysis and classification of existing systems. In *Proceedings of the International Congress on Information Science Innovations, ISI'01,* Dubai.

Liu, L., & Yu, E. (2004). Designing information systems in social context: A goal and scenario modelling approach. *Information Systems, 29,* 187-203.

Lucking-Reiley, D. (2000). Auctions on the Internet: What's being auctioned, and how? *Journal of Industrial Economics, 48*(3), 227-252.

Mylopoulos J., Kolp M., & Castro, J. (2001). UML for Agent-oriented software development:

The tropos proposal. In *Proceedings of the 4th International Conference on the Unified Modeling Language, UML'01,* Toronto, Canada.

Papazoglou, M.P. (2001). Agent-oriented technology in support of e-business. *Communications of the ACM, 44*(4), 71-77.

Pinker, E.J., Seidmann, A., & Vakrat, Y. (2001). *The design of online auctions: Business issues and current research* (Working Paper CIS-01-05). Rochester, Canada: University of Rochester.

Rachlevsky-Reich, B., Ben-Shaul, I., Tung Chau, N., Lo, A., & Poggio, T. (1999). GEM: A global electronic market system. *Information Systems, 24*(6), 495-518.

Ramchurn, S.D., Huynh, D., & Jennings, N.R. (2004). Trust in multi-agent systems. *The Knowledge Engineering Review, 19*(1), 1-25.

Re, R., Braga, R.T.V., & Masiero, P.C. (2001). A pattern language for online auctions management. In *Proceedings of the 8th Conference on Pattern Languages of Programs, PLoP'01,* Illinois.

Resnick, P., & Zeckhauser, R. (2002). Trust among strangers in Internet transactions: Empirical analysis of ebay's reputation system. *Advances in Applied Microeconomics, 11,* 77-106.

Weiss, M. (2003). Pattern-driven design of agent systems: Approach and case study. In *Proceedings of the 15th International Conference on Advanced Information Systems Engineering, CAISE'03,* Velden, Austria.

Yu, E. (1995). *Modelling strategic relationships for process reengineering.* Doctoral dissertation, University of Toronto, Toronto, Canada.

Yu, E. (1997). Why agent-oriented requirements engineering. *In Proceedings of 3rd International Workshop on Requirements Engineering: Foundations for Software Quality,* Barcelona, Spain.

Yu, E. (2001). Agent-oriented modelling: Software versus the world. In P*roceedings of the 2nd International Workshop on Agent-Oriented Software Engineering, AOSE'01,* Montreal, Canada.

ENDNOTE

[1]   The issue of trust between Buyers and Sellers in online auctions is an often-treated topic in economics research (Resnick & Zeckhauser, 2002; Pinker et al., 2001).

This work was previously published in International Journal of Intelligent Information Technologies, Vol. 2, Issue 3, edited by V. Sugumaran, pp. 21-39, copyright 2006 by IGI Publishing, formerly known as Idea Group Publishing (an imprint of IGI Global).

Section III
Tools and Technologies

Chapter X
China:
M–Commerce in World's Largest Mobile Market

Nir Kshetri
University of North Carolina at Greensboro, USA

Nicholas Williamson
University of North Carolina at Greensboro, USA

David L. Bourgoin
University of Hawaii at Manoa, USA

ABSTRACT

China is emerging as a global capital of m-commerce applications. China is the world's biggest mobile market in terms of subscriber base and the fastest growing in the history of telecommunications. Although China currently lacks advanced mobile applications compared to Europe, North America, Japan and Korea, a number of mobile players are rapidly launching sophisticated mobile applications. Unique institutions and the nature of mobile market conditions in China, however, superimpose in a complex interaction that harbors a paradoxical nature. The Chinese m-commerce market is thus drastically different from that of the Western world. This chapter examines the Chinese m-commerce landscape and analyzes its drivers. We also examine the Chinese market from the CLIP perspective.

INTRODUCTION

Consider the following observations on the development of mobile technology and the potential of m-commerce in China:

For the tech industry, it's China—not Europe, or Japan, or other Asian countries—that will soon be its [USA's] main rival. The implications are profound. No longer content to cheaply make other people's products, a task it has clearly mastered,

China wants to be a global standards setter. ... One place to watch the flexing of power is in mobile phones[1]. The mobile Internet has really saved China's Internet industry[2].

As the above statement indicates, China has emerged as a capital of the global mobile market. The growth rate achieved by the Chinese mobile network, the biggest in the world, is the fastest in the history of telecommunications. Rapid development in the Chinese mobile market has driven increasingly China-centric activities of major players in the global mobile market (Kshetri, 2004a, 2004b).

Unique institutions and the nature of mobile market conditions in China, however, superimpose in a complex interaction that harbors a paradoxical nature (Kshetri, 2005). This chapter provides a brief survey of the paradoxical Chinese m-commerce market and analyzes its driving force. The chapter structure is as follows: The next section provides a brief overview of the Chinese mobile market. The paper then analyzes some major forces behind China's rapid growth in this market. Next, we examine the Chinese market from the CLIP perspective. Finally, the paper presents its conclusions.

A BRIEF SURVEY OF THE CHINESE MOBILE MARKET

The Chinese mobile market became the largest in the Asia Pacific in 2000 and the world's largest in 2002 (Stout, 2001). By the end of 2004, there were over 300 million mobile subscribers in China and an additional 75 million "Little Smart"[3] users (BBC News, 2004). During 2004, mobile phone users in China grew by 27 per cent (Reuters, 2004). An estimate by the telecom analyst firm, EMC, suggests that China will have 36 million 3GSM[4] (W-CDMA) subscribers by 2009 (globalsources.com, 2004).

In 2002, 120 million handsets, or 27 percent of the world total, were produced in China. The proportion increased to 33 percent in 2003, 35.1 percent (233.5 million) in 2004 (*SinoCast, China Business Daily News*, 2005a) and is estimated to reach 50 percent by 2008 (Symbianphone.com, 2003). China's handset exports increased from 22.75 million in 2000 (*GIS News*, 2001) to 55 million in 2002. During the first half of 2003, China exported 37 million handsets.

China's Time Division—Synchronous Code Division Multiple Access (TD-SCDMA)—developed by Datang is currently accepted as a global third generation (3G) standard. Among 16 proposals submitted for IMT-2000[5] standards, TD-SCDMA was one of the three 3G mobile standards selected by the International Telecommunications Union (ITU) in May 2000. The other two standards are the U.S. based CDMA2000 system and Europe's WCDMA. The Third Generation Partnership Project (3GPP) accepted the TD-SCDMA in March 2001.

TD-SCDMA is scheduled for launch in the second half of 2005. Estimates are that following its launch, the TD-SCDMA will capture 30 percent of the Chinese market and 10 percent outside China (Einhorn, 2003). It is also interesting to note that some innovative m-commerce applications were first developed and employed in China. To take one example, the world's first electronic stock trading over a wireless network, took place on byair.com in Shanghai, China, in 1998[6] (see Box 1).

By 2008, China's wireless mobile market is estimated to exceed US$200 billion[7]. An estimate by Lehman Brothers Inc. suggests that revenues of mobile portals generated by sending news updates, games and online dating amounted to $200 million in 2001, and was estimated at $3 billion in 2004. China Mobile, the world's largest mobile operator, was the most profitable telecom operator in the Asia-Pacific region in 2002, with a profit of $3.5 billion on revenues of $12.2 billion. A 28 percent

Box 1. GWcom's mobile portal in China[13]

> GWcom is a mobile wireless ASP in China. It launched its wireless portal, byair.com[14], in 1998 to provide timely information and e-commerce capabilities such as stock trading and banking to users with mobile phone or wireless palmtop devices in the U.S. and Greater China. The company provides its networks and handheld device (netset) to individual investors. By 2002, GWcom had partnered with over 30 Internet content providers and e-commerce portals in the U.S. and Greater China and was connected with more than 20 securities trading firms.
>
> By March 2000, byair.com had over 6,000 subscribers, with the number of stocks traded as high as 3,500 daily and 250,000 page views daily. By early 2002, it delivered services to over 250,000 mobile users and more users on Information on Demand (IOD) and messaging services. GWcom users mostly use the two-way paging capability for trading stock electronically, and such transaction-type services have turned out to be its "killer application" (TDAP, 2002).
>
> The company's pricing structure made stock investment on its paging network more attractive than on the fixed network. Because of low PC penetration and relatively higher Internet access fees, the only way to trade stock for a large proportion of Chinese is to read newspapers or magazines and then pick up a phone[15]. These factors have made GWcom's Web portal more attractive (Ebusinessforum.com, 2000). GWcom describes its network product, PLANET, as a "high-capacity and low cost cellular packet data network that is optimized for serving wireless palm computers and PDAs."[16] The users pay a monthly service charge of only about US$5-10. With the increasing demand, GWcom has decided to specialize in the mobile wireless data network infrastructure and outsource the equipment manufacturing to Ericsson and Chinese vendors. This is likely to result further reduction in price.
>
> China's stock market is growing very fast[17] and the stock exchange companies are located in Shanghai and Shenzhen. GW Trade selected these two cities for its initial trial. Wireless users have been using GWcom's application platforms to conduct online trading since 1998 in Shanghai and since 1999 in Shenzhen. In March 2000, 3,000 investors in Shanghai and 100 in Shenzhen were trading stocks over the paging networks managed by GWcom. The average daily volume of 3,000 Shanghai users in early-2000 was $3.6 million, about 30 times as much as the average trading volume on stockstar.com, the largest and most popular Web-based stock trading company in China.
>
> ---
>
> In developing countries like China, non-voice technologies (such as paging) have potential to offer a cheap and reliable way to transmit data that will be a viable alternative to the mobile phone. In other parts of the world, big players are not following such paging routes (Holland, 2000). The GWcom case also provides some evidence of he leapfrogging potential of mobile technologies. For instance, the world's first electronic stock trading over the wireless network took place on the GWcom network in 1998 in Shanghai.

return on revenue is an excellent indication of where the Chinese market is developing.

China introduced Wireless Fidelity (Wi-Fi) technology in 2002 and is diffusing rapidly (Clark & Harwit, 2004). By mid 2003, 80 percent of China's five-star hotels, airports and high-grade office buildings in its four largest cities were connected to China Netcom's Wi-Fi network[8]. At the end of 2003, China Telecom, China Netcom and China Mobile had about 10,000 hotspots deployed or planned for rollout (Clark & Harwit, 2004).

One estimate suggested that the Chinese Wi-Fi market was at $24 million in 2003 (compared to the worldwide market of $600 million) (Koprowski, 2004). Another estimate suggests that China's Wi-Fi market will reach $250 million by 2005[9]. This growth from 4 percent to 30 percent of the market

is astonishing. Venture capital companies such as Intel Capital are capitalizing on the huge Wi-Fi potential in China by funding the deployment of Wi-Fi technology (Clark & Harwit, 2004).

The Chinese mobile market, however, is characterized by a high degree of bias towards urban areas. For instance, in 1999, 78 percent of the population owned mobile phones in the three wealthy cities—Beijing, Shanghai and Guangzhou (Tsuchiyama, 1999)—compared with the national average of 3.42 percent that year (UNDP, 2001). This disparity can indicate a huge potential market for future investment and development, or, conversely, show the sophistication of the Chinese wealth sector, with its high technology development and implementation that is close to the cutting edge.

CHINA'S RAPID MOBILE DIFFUSION[10]

Starting the mid-1980s, China invested heavily in the telecom sector. The heavy investment was supplemented by a series of programs designed to accelerate telecom development, including extensive re-engineering of and intense competition in the mobile sector. China Unicom, formed in 1994, competes with the former monopoly China Telecom and is licensed for mobile, paging, data, Internet and long-distance (James, 2001).

Fierce competition in the Chinese mobile sector led to low connection fees as well as lower subscription fees for mobile services. In the late 1990s, for instance, monthly subscription rates as well as connection charges for mobile services in China were lower than the average in lower-middle income countries or in general across the world (Table 1). Fixed line connection, on the other hand, was more expensive than both of these comparative averages. Competition and technological development have steeply reduced the costs of mobile phones. When mobile handsets were first introduced in China in 1994, the

price was US$850, which decreased to about US$200 in 1999 (Tsuchiyama, 1999). Similarly, the connection fee declined from US$600 in 1994 (Tsuchiyama, 1999) to US$60 in 1999 (Table 1). By mid-2001, China Mobile eliminated its mobile connection fees in many cities.

To penetrate the market, mobile subscribers have reduced subscription fees and introduced other promotional measures. Examples of such measures include China Mobile's heavy discount plans in Beijing, Shanghai and Guangzhou (*Wall Street Journal*, 2003), and China Unicom's plan allowing users to set five local phone numbers at 1.2 cents per minute (one-sixth of normal rate) and up to 60 percent discounts for heavy users of short messages. The planned rollout of Xiaolingtong (Little Smart)[11] and the ongoing heavy price competition among mobile suppliers have intensified the promotion.

The Chinese government expects that a richer and more technology-orientated economy might help increase respect for the nation. The government also has the ambition of providing every household with a telephone. To achieve these objectives, top priority was given to building

Table 1. A comparison of fixed and mobile charges in China and the world

	China	Lower-middle income countries average	World average
Mobile network (1999)			
Connection ($)	*60*	90	86
Monthly subscription ($)	*6.04*	20.99	21.40
Tariff per minute (peak) ($)	*0.05*	0.25	0.27
Tariff per minute (off-peak) ($)	*0.05*	0.18	0.18
100 minute basket ($)	*10.87*	39.69	38.15
Fixed network (1998)			
Residential connection ($)	*226*	133	109
Business connection ($)	*226*	212	155
Residential monthly subscription ($)	*1.9*	4.8	6.9
Business monthly subscription ($)	*2.9*	8.8	11.5
Cost of 3 minute local call ($)	*0.01*	0.05	0.09
Subscription as a % of GDP per capita	*3.1*	3.8	7.5

Source: ITU (1999), Adapted from Kshetri and Cheung (2002)

R&D capacity in mobile telephony in the late 1990s (Niitamo, 2000). The government is also promoting mobile phones as the "people's phone" and is actively encouraging Chinese consumers in cities and the countryside to buy mobile phones (Kshetri & Cheung, 2002).

Innovations in mobile pricing, such as the introduction of mobile prepaid cards, have been the major driving force for the rapid diffusion of mobile phones across the world. Mobile prepaid cards were introduced in China at the end of 1999 and are contributing to the high mobile growth rates.

CHINESE MOBILE MARKET FROM THE CLIP ANGLE

China differs widely from the developed world in terms of the four CLIP dimensions: communications (C), information (I) exchange, payments (P) and "locatability" (L). Compared to developed countries, voice communications account for a significantly higher proportion of the Chinese mobile market.

In data communications, technologies that are a decade old and outdated in most developed countries are among the most profitable in China. For instance, SMS, a standard feature on almost every wireless phone, which sends text messages at 80 percent less cost than voice transmission is very popular in China[12]. The popularity can be attributed to its low cost and the fact that even basic wireless handsets can perform it.

Nevertheless, more advanced m-commerce applications are rapidly emerging in China. For instance, through revenue-sharing deals with China Mobile and China Unicom, China-based Web portals such as Sina, Sohu and NetEase have launched new business models that are tailor-made for the Chinese market. These companies charge the users for news updates, games and online dating information on mobile phones. The services have thus evolved beyond simple text messages.

Sohu, for instance, sends out color greeting cards accompanied with voice messages from basketball star Yao Ming (Einhorn, 2004). By April 2003, Sohu provided 150 fee-based wireless products (such as the Japanese game "Kung-Fu Boy") to its over one million SMS services subscribers (*World IT Report*, 2003).

Virtual games played on mobile devices are also growing rapidly in popularity. By the end of 2004, there were over 10 million mobile game players in China generating about $100 million in revenue (*SinoCast China Business Daily News*, 2005c). The Chinese mobile game market is expected to grow by 80 percent in 2005 (*SinoCast China Business Daily News*, 2005b). IDC suggests that the Chinese online game market will reach $809 million by 2007. Virtual games offered on mobile devices are becoming increasingly popular. For instance, in a game offered by Mtone Wireless Corp in late 2003, 500,000 people signed up in three months (Einhorn, 2004). Chinese and foreign mobile players are planning to launch a wide array of business models for the Chinese mobile market. In mid 2005, for instance:

a. Global cellular NetVillage was at a final stage to distribute its pinball game to Java-enabled handsets in China and aimed to develop a variety of business models (Tsukioka, 2005).

b. Tom Online and Warner Bros. Online were planning to launch a Chinese-language Web site featuring cartoon characters such as Bugs Bunny and Scooby-Doo for mobile phones (*Wall Street Journal*, 2005).

Mobile payment is less attractive in China compared to Europe and North America. A major hindrance is China's cash-based economy—over 90 percent of business transactions takes place on a cash basis. Nonetheless, companies are launching a variety of innovative business models to facilitate m-payment (see Box 2). In the payment realm of business, in 2002 Sumit Mobile Systems Ltd.,

Box 2. M-payment in China

Although m-payment is in a nascent stage in China, it is growing exponentially. One estimate suggests that wireless payment will be 15 percent of e-commerce payments in 2006 (Rashtchy, 2004). Mobile companies with innovative business models are capitalizing on this rapid growth rate. Smartpay, a multi-province mobile payment system which allows subscribers to pay phone bills simply by sending an SMS message (DMAsia.com, 2004) had over 100,000 users as of December 2004 (Ortolani, 2005). The company also has partnerships with seven banks, including China Construction Bank and Agricultural Bank of China (Ortolani, 2005).

The Chinese mobile market, however, lacks more sophisticated m-payment services. M-payment in China is hindered by a number of factors, including a lack of secure network with an efficient authentication system in banks, lack of a retail network that accepts codes linking to customers' bank accounts and perceived fraud in transactions (chinanex.com, 2004). Basic services such as handset banking, in which a cell phone user can check his/her account online and transfer funds within the same bank have been available for some time (chinanex.com, 2004). China Mobile and China Unicom launched one-way payment services in 2003. China Unicom's one-way payment card launched in 2003 attracted over 20,000 new users in three days (*SinoCast China Business Daily News*, 2005d).

Nonetheless, major players such as China Mobile are aggressively expanding m-payments (Rashtchy, 2004). In May 2005, for instance, China Mobile and China UnionPay announced their cooperation with ten banks to launch m-payment services in Beijing (pacificepoch.com, 2005).

working with mobile network providers, banks and utility companies in Shanghai, designed a system that allows users to pay their bills by cell phone. When a payment is due, a message displays on the screen that shows the amount due and where the user can then authorize the payment from a bank account by typing a secret code. The service attracted 90,000 users in Shanghai in nine months (Manuel, 2003). Similarly, in mid 2005, The Music Engine (TME), a UK-based technology and online marketing solutions provider, was planning to provide m-payment services in China (Salz, 2005).

The Chinese mobile landscape is also developing rapidly on the locatability dimension. In the mid-2004, Cambridge Positioning Systems (CPS) partnered with Wisemax, a Beijing-based supplier of multimedia messaging and SMS, to provide the Chinese wireless market with location-based services supported by its Matrix software solution (Geospatial Solutions, 2004). Similarly, in November 2004, Sichuan Yingda, a China-based mobile value-added service provider, launched location-based services based on the Matrix location system of CPS to track its vehicles, security personnel as well as other assets of the company (*Wireless News*, 2004).

CONCLUDING REMARKS

The discussion in this paper makes clear that m-commerce in China is expanding quickly while unusual paradoxes coexist. For instance, the Chinese mobile market is the biggest in the world and penetration rates in some of the wealthiest Chinese cities are much higher than the averages of many developed countries. Yet mobile phones are virtually non-existent in many Chinese villages. Similarly, some of the most modern m-commerce applications are emerging from China. At the same time, decade-old mobile technologies that are outdated in the developed countries are widely used in China and are among the most profitable applications. A technology marketer's success in the Chinese m-commerce market, thus, is a function of its capability to go beyond superficial indicators and understand how the company can capitalize on the paradoxes.

QUESTIONS FOR DISCUSSION

1.   What are the most important factors that are driving the diffusion of mobile technology in China?

2. How does the Chinese mobile market differ from European and the U.S. mobile markets? What do you think are the opportunities created by the Chinese mobile market that do not exist in European and U.S. markets?

3. Basing your examination from the CLIP perspective, how does the Chinese mobile market differ from mobile markets in Western Europe and North America?

REFERENCES

BBC News (2004). Virgin plans China mobile service. Retrieved December 7, 2004 from, http://news.bbc.co.uk/1/hi/business/4074933.stm

Chinanex.com (2004). Mobile payment market. Retrieved July 15, 2004, from http://www.chinanex.com/insight/mopay0704.htm

Clark, D., & Harwit, E. (2004). *Wi-Fi in China*. Paper presented at the Pacific Telecommunications Council, Honolulu, HI.

Dholakia, N., & Kshetri, N. (2003) Mobile commerce as a solution to the global digital divide: Selected cases of e-development. In S. Krishna & S. Madon (Eds.), *The digital challenge: Information technology in the development context* (pp. 237-250). Aldershot: Ashgate Publications.

DMAsia.com (2004). Smartpay launches payment services in Anhui. Retrieved October 28, 2005 from, http://www.digitalmediaasia.com/default. asp?ArticleID=4074

Ebusinessforum.com (2000). *GW trade: Serving a high-tech niche in China*. Retrieved 2005 from, http://www.ebusinessforum.com

Einhor, B. (2003, April). Master of innovation? China aims to close its technology gap with Korea and Japan. *Business Week Online* (pp. 22-28). Retrieved July 19, 2005, from http://www. businessweek.com/magazine/content/03_15/ b3828010.htm

Einhor, B. (2004, March 15). China.Net; China will soon be No. 1 in Web users. That will unleash a world of opportunity. *Business Week*.

Geospatial Solutions. (2004, May). Location-based services. *Geospatial Soutions, 14*(5), 51.

GIS News (2001). China outstrips Korea in IT industry growth: Samsung. Retrieved September 11, 2005, from http://www.gisdevelopment. net/news/2001/oct/news111001.htm

globalsources.com (2004). Asia to lead worldwide 3GSM subscribers. Retrieved November 26, 2004, from http://www.globalsources.com/gsol/I/GSM-phone/a/9000000058313.htm

Holland, L. (2000, Feb 24). Turning a new pager. *Far Eastern Economic Review, 163*(8), 44.

ITU (1999). *World telecommunications development report*. Geneva: International Telecommunications Union.

James, D. (2001). China's sizzling circuits. *Upside, 13*(1), 60-67.

Kahn, G. (2003, Sept 22). World business; what's old is new: A Chinese Internet company has thrived by focusing on a seemingly obsolete technology. *Wall Street Journal*, R.4.

Koprowski, G. J. (2004). Wireless world: China's WiFi revolution. United Press International. Retrieved July 5, 2004, from http://chineseculture. about.com/gi/dynamic/offsite.htm?site=http:// www.upi.com/view.cfm %3FStoryID=2004050 6%2D101652%2D8297r

Kshetri, N. (2004a, March 11-12). China's emergence as an epicenter of the global mobile market. *Proceedings of the Austin Mobility Roundtable, Center for Business, Technology and Law*, Mc-Combs Business School at the University of Texas at Austin.

Kshetri, N. (2004b, July 10-13). Internationalization of the Chinese cellular industry: The inward-outward connection. *The 2004 Annual Meeting of the Academy of International Business (AIB)*, Stockholm, Sweden.

Kshetri, N. (2005). *Six paradoxes of China imperative for technology companies*. Working Paper, Department of Business Administration, University of North Carolina at Greensboro.

Kshetri, N., & Cheung, M. K. (2002). What factors are driving China's mobile diffusion? *Electronic Markets, 12*(1), 22-26.

Manuel, G. (2003, Oct 20). E-commerce; dialing for dollars: Will people use their cell phones to buy lots of stuff? Phone companies are determined they will. *Wall Street Journal*, 3.

Niitamo, V. (2000). Making information accessible and affordable for all. *Wider Angel*. Retrieved July 20, 2001, from http://www.wider. unu.edu/newsletter/angle2000-1.pdf

Ortolani, A. (2005, Feb 2). Chinese begin paying by cellphone. *Wall Street Journal*, p. 1.

Pacificepoch.com (2005). *China Mobile joins China UnionPay for mobile payment service*. Retrieved March 25, 2005, from http://www.paci-ficepoch.com/newsstories/25207_0_5_0_M/

Rashtchy, S. (2004). *The China analyst*. Retrieved September 2, 2005, from http://www.piperjaffray. com/760

Reuters. (2004). *China's mobile subscribers rise 27% in 2004*. Retrieved January 20, 2005, from http://147.208.132.198/news/181_1206466,0003. htm

Salz, P. A. (2005). Power to the people: Do it yourself content distribution. *EContent, 28*(6), 36-41.

SinoCast. (2005a, July18). Shenzhen produced 10% world's cellphones in 2004. *China Business Daily News*, p. 1.

SinoCast. (2005b, July 12). Mobile game market to grow 80% this year. *China Business Daily News*, p. 1.

SinoCast. (2005c, July 5). China mobile game market to reshuffle in 2005. *China Business Daily News*, p. 1.

SinoCast. (2005c, May 31). China unicom Chongqing branch launches one-way payment service. *China Business Daily News*, 1.

Stout, K. L. (2001). China mobile has eyes only for 2.5G. *CNN.Com*. Retrieved June 5, 2005, from http://archives.cnn.com/2001/BUSINESS/ asia/06/05/hk.chinamobile2.5g/

Symbianphone.com. (2003). Every third mobile phone made in China. Retrieved April 1, 2005, from http://www.symbianphone.com/?l=apr03. htm

TDAP. (2002). China's new regulatory environment spurs UNICOM's subscriber growth. Interview with Wang Jianzhou, Executive Vice President of China Unicom, *Telecommunications Development, Asia-Pacific*. Retrieved July 10, 2003, from http://www.tdap.co.uk/uk/archive/interviews/inter(unicom_0012).html

Tsuchiyama, R. (1999). The cellular industry in China: Politics, rewards, and risks. *Pacific Telecommunications Review*, 2nd quarter, 149-160.

Tsukioka, A. (2005, July 15). NetVillage, KA-ZeNet form alliance in mobile game business in China. *JCNN News Summaries - Japan Corporate News Network*, p. 1.

UNDP. (2001). *Human development report 2000*. New York: United Nations Development Program. Retrieved July 11, 2001 from, http://www.undp. org/hdr2001/completenew.pdf

Vogelstein, F., Boyle, M., Lewis, P., & Kirkpatrick, D. (2004, Feb 23). 10 tech trends to bet on. *Fortune*, 75-80.

Wall Street Journal. (2003). China's mobile operators bring discounts to big cities. Retrieved April 21, 2005, from http://www.bdachina.com/content/about/pressquotes/P1051109819/en

Wall Street Journal. (2005, June 21). Tom online signs deal with Warner Bros. to distribute content. p 1.

Wireless News. (2004, Nov 26). China's Sichuan Yingda turns to CPS software for location-based solution. p. 1.

World IT Report. (2003, April 9). Sohu launches interactive cellular game in China. p. 1.

ENDNOTES

[1] See Vogelstein et al. (2004).

[2] Victor Wang, CEO of Mtone Wireless Corp, quoted in *Einhorn* (2004).

[3] "Little Smart" is a low-cost, limited-roaming service provided by several fixed-line operators.

[4] The 3GSM standard builds on GSM to allow the integration of IP (Internet Protocol) technology and new features such as video calling, faster Internet, WAP access and downloadable content (http://www.wave-telecom.com/content/shared_content/mobile/downloads/Wave_FAQs.doc).

[5] International Mobile Telecommunications (IMT- 2000) is a general term for technologies planned for inclusion in ITU world standards for 3G mobile communications.

[6] See http://www.mobic.com/news/2000/01/gwcom_receives_capital_investmen.htm.

[7] See http://mobile2004.com/ (4G/B3G-OWA Will Reshape China's Future Mobile Communications Research).

[8] WiFi Makes Internet Plus Coffee Possible in Beijing and Tianjin , SinoCast, *China Business Daily News.* July 25, 2003, p. 1

[9] See http://www.itfacts.biz/index.php?id=P448

[10] This section draws from Kshetri and Cheung (2002).

[11] Xiaolingtong is provided by fixed-line phone companies and is much cheaper than mobile services provided by China Mobile and China Unicom.

[12] See Kahn (2003).

[13] This case draws from Dholakia and Kshetri (2003).

[14] GWcom restructured the corporation in April 2002, dividing the business into two companies. The short messaging service (SMS) business has been renamed to byair Corporation, which encompasses the mobile media services. The network business is GWcomPlanet Corporation.

[15] See http://www.gwcom.com.cn/gwcom_news-m17.htm

[16] See http://www.chinatelecomconference.com/china-dc/bio/bio13.html

[17] See http://www.gwcom.com.cn/gwcom_news-m17.htm

This work was previously published in M-Commerce: Global Experiences and Perspectives, edited by N. Dholakia, M. Rask, and R. R. Dholakia, pp. 34-45, copyright 2006 by IGI Publishing, formerly known as Idea Group Publishing (an imprint of IGI Global).

Chapter XI
France:
Mobile Communications and Emerging M–Commerce

Pierre Vialle
STORM Research Group, GET-INT, France

Olivier Epinette
STORM Research Group, GET-INT, France

ABSTRACT

This chapter introduces the emerging m-commerce market in France. Despite the current low level of use, this market is characterized by the implementation of an increasingly efficient m-commerce value chain by network operators, content providers and content enablers. As a consequence, innovative and attractive services are being introduced progressively for both consumers and businesses, which are analyzed here with the help of the CLIP framework. Furthermore, the authors argue that an m-commerce strategy should be designed in synergy with a fixed network-based e-commerce strategy while carefully following and anticipating the progressive implementation of significant technological advances.

INTRODUCTION

Despite the significant growth exhibited in previous years, France has the lowest wireless penetration in Europe, 73.9 percent, compared with an average penetration rate of 77 percent in Western Europe, and 80 percent in Italy, Finland or Sweden (Jupiter Research, 2004). This is consistent with several other ICT indicators (OECD Key ICT Indicators, n.d.; Vialle, 2003) where the French market scores lower than average in Western Europe.

In addition, the French mobile telecommunications market exhibits three other characteristics. First, a relative concentration of service supply, since there are only three mobile operators in France and Mobile Virtual Network Operators

(MVNOs) are quasi-absent from the market. Second, it is the only large European country where Vodafone does not directly operate a mobile telecommunications company. Third, the market for both voice and data services tends to be somehow less developed than in other European countries. However, with 44.5 million subscribers, the French market is the fourth most important market in Europe and is expected to become the second market by 2007 (Salcedo, 2004).

Multimedia Services Market

Nearly one quarter of the market, or 10.3 million subscribers, uses a diversified range of multimedia services. The bulk of the market concerns messaging services. The most popular service is SMS: 10.7 billion SMS were sent in the year 2004, corresponding to a monthly average of 23.6 messages per subscriber. The SMS+[1] traffic enjoyed a 66 percent growth in 2004, reaching 228 million messages and generating revenues amounting to 135 million euros. The MMS consumption is also increasing, but is limited by the number of compatible handsets—around 12 million in 2004 — technical complexity and high tariffs. Tariffs can vary according to the operator and the type of message (text, picture, video and postcard), from around 0.10 to around 2 euros.

The bulk of the content services market concerns ringtones, then icons, wallpapers, logos and animations, followed by mobile alerts, and finally mobile games (Salcedo, 2004). According to Bigot (2004), 58 percent of mobile handset owners regularly send SMS, 29 percent download icons, logos and games, 18 percent use vocal information services, 13 percent send SMS+, 11 percent send MMS and 8 percent consult mobile Internet sites[2]. The current usage of services involving monetary transactions is very limited, and is not expected to represent a large share of revenues in the near future.

This rather undeveloped picture of the mobile multimedia market corresponds to the "old" supply environment: that of the relatively low bandwidth of GPRS supported services with an effective bit-rate, usually not exceeding 50 Kbps. Furthermore, the market was limited by the number of multimedia-enabled handsets used, about 14.2 million in 2004 (Salcedo, 2004).

Limited deployment and security concerns seem to be the main barriers for adoption. The higher bit-rate allowed by UMTS (up to 384 Kbps) or EDGE (up to 150 Kbps) may trigger market development in France. Video telephony, which has been a mythic telecommunications service in the mind of the French for more than twenty years[3], could well be the killer application for UMTS in France. The French operators have taken care to ensure interoperability between UMTS and other technologies and to provide dual mode handsets. This should allow them to avoid the difficulties encountered by NTT DoCoMo in Japan, because of the limited coverage of UMTS combined with the impossibility to use the 2.5G network with 3G handsets. Location-based services could also trigger the use of transaction services in the future. However, price may constitute a significant barrier to adoption: Tariff plan subscriptions are still expensive, starting at 52 euros for SFR and 55 euros for Orange, and the cheapest handset is priced at 199 euros. One minute of video telephony is priced as two minutes of voice call[4], and 30 minutes of video or TV cost between 10 and 15 euros.

Structure of the Chapter

French mobile operators are presented first in order to provide some background information on the French market. A selection of m-commerce services is then introduced, followed by the assessment of the state of service provision in France with the help of the CLIP framework. Furthermore, the role of content-enabling companies is outlined in reducing complexity for both users and suppliers. Significant technological and managerial lessons are suggested in the conclusion.

BACKGROUND

There are currently three mobile operators in France offering GSM services (Table 1): Orange (France Télécom), SFR and Bouygues Télécom. All three implemented 2.5G GPRS services in 2002 and hold a 3G UMTS license. Compared to most other large European mobile markets, which have four or more operators, this situation may be detrimental to competition. On the other hand, it may facilitate the deployment of UMTS, due to the high investment involved and the uncertainty of market development.

Orange France is a 100 percent subsidiary of Orange SA (100% France Télécom), created in 2001 after the acquisition of Orange plc by France Télécom in August 2000. The wireless activities of the two companies were merged to create an international wireless group with a strong focus on Europe. France Télécom has been present on the mobile market since 1985 with analog services and launched GSM services in 1992. The former national monopoly is now a strong group with a significant international presence. With 47.2 billion euros in revenue, the group ranked fifth in the world and second in Europe in the year 2004. With 19.7 billion euros in revenue, Orange SA was the seventh largest mobile operator in the world and the third in Europe. It is present in 18 countries and has shown a strong commitment to mobile Internet with the acquisition of UMTS licenses in six countries. In Europe, Orange is the leader in the UK in number of customers, but is not present in the three other main markets: Germany, Italy and Spain. In August 2003, it formed an alliance with Telefonica Moviles, TIM (Telecom Italia Mobile) and T-Mobile, which aims to deliver a seamless customer experience across its combined geographical footprint. The creation of this alliance is obviously a response to the threat represented by Vodafone, whose extensive presence allows the provision of seamless, advanced services in Europe.

In December 2004, Orange France officially launched its UMTS services under the "Orange Intense" name. It is part of France Télécom's broader strategy to offer seamless broadband services to its customers, such as video telephony, across various network accesses such as UMTS, EDGE, Internet, Wi-Fi or Wimax. With an initial network investment of 500 million euros, the UMTS services were targeted to reach 40 percent of the French population by the end of the year 2004. Orange will also roll out EDGE technology on its network in order to provide complementary "medium bandwidth" services, which will result in coverage of 85 percent of the population. For the launch, six dual mode UMTS/GPRS handsets were available, and UMTS/EDGE handsets should be available during the year 2005.

SFR is a subsidiary of SFR Cegetel (56 percent Vivendi Universal, 44 percent Vodafone),

Table 1. French mobile market in 2004 (France and overseas departments and territories)

Operator	Number of subscribers	Market share	Contract Customers	SMS/Month Q4 2004[5]
Orange 2	1,251,500	47.7%	60.6%	21.9
SFR	15,819,800	35.5%	60.7%	26.4
Bouygues Télécom	7,468,400	16.8%	66.1%	22.3
Others [6]	12,100	NS	11.5%	NA
Total	44,551,800	100%	61.5%	23.6

Source: Le tableau de bord du marché national (2005)

and reached 6.7 billion euros in revenue in 2003. SFR launched analog NMT services in 1988 and GSM services in 1992. With 8.3 billion euros in revenue in 2004, SFR Cegetel is the second largest French telecommunications company for both fixed and mobile telephony, and thus France Télécom's main challenger. Its major stakeholder, Vivendi-Universal, is a large international entertainment and media group, with 21.4 billion euros in revenue in the year 2004. Its other stakeholder, Vodafone, is the number one mobile operator in the world, with £43,602 million in revenue in 2004. It has an extensive international presence, and operates mobile networks in nearly all the European countries, including four of the "big five" European markets: Germany, UK, Italy and Spain. France is the only major European country where it does not control a subsidiary, and Vodafone is seen as a possible candidate for a takeover of Vivendi-Universal. SFR Cegetel is focused on the French market, but is also present through other Vivendi Universal subsidiaries in five other countries. Despite its independent management, SFR benefits from the same international services as a Vodafone controlled subsidiary, such as roaming agreements, access to the Vodafone live!™ portal, business solutions or a wide range of suitable handsets.

After testing UMTS in Monaco and other cities, SFR launched its services in November 2004. The initial network investment is similar to that of Orange (500 million euros) for a coverage of 38 percent of the total population at the end of 2004. The range of services corresponds broadly to Vodafone's offering, with continuity of 3G services in 12 countries. For the launch, eight dual mode UMTS/GPRS handsets were available. SFR also claims interoperability between 3G and Wi-Fi.

Bouygues Télécom is a subsidiary of Groupe Bouygues (83 percent), a large building and media company with 23.4 billion euros in revenues in 2004. Created in 1994, it launched its DCS 1800 services in 1996, and generated sales of 3.7 billion

euros in 2004. As the latest operator on the market, Bouygues Telecom has used innovation to differentiate itself from the two market leaders: It was the first to target the mass market with offers of rate plans by the minute, and introduced high resolution sound on its network. It remained mainly focused on the mass market, and its prime target market is in the 18-38 age bracket. Interestingly enough, it signed a contract with NTT DoCoMo in April 2002 in order to launch i-Mode services in France. Taking advantage of the technical resources and the knowhow previously developed in Japan, it was able to launch i-Mode services at the end of November 2002. Bouygues Télécom claimed to have one million i-Mode subscribers in December 2004, having access to 300 services on its portal and 3,000 independent sites. i-Mode represents a major stake for Bouygues Télécom and is allocated 50 percent of its advertising budget. An average i-Mode subscriber represents an ARPU increase of 13 euros compared to a non-i-Mode subscriber for the same user range. Bouygues Télécom belongs to the i-Mode alliance with Telefonica, KPN mobile and Wind, allowing joint procurement of handsets.

Bouygues Télécom did not participate in the first UMTS license contest, but applied for one in May 2002 as the French government had decided to lower the license fees from 4.9 billion euros to 619 million (plus one percent of revenues). The license was awarded in September 2002 and the operator has been testing this technology since 2003. However, Bouygues Télécom has announced its intention to implement EDGE technology for a transitory phase from the year 2005, before rolling out UMTS. The data rate of 150 Kbps is lower than the 384 Kbps data rate of the first UMTS generation, but is estimated to provide enough comfort to users. EDGE could be implemented at a reasonable cost in order to cover 90 percent of France by the end of the year 2005, an advantage over non-continuous UMTS networks. Bouygues Télécom prefers to wait for the second UMTS generation using the HSDPA format that should be available from 2006 and would provide a data rate of 2 Mbps.

Three MVNOs operate in France with very limited market presence. Transaltel has had a contract since 2001 with Bouygues Télécom and concentrates on cross-border travelers between France and Belgium. Under pressure of the ART, the French regulator, two new agreements were signed in 2004: one between SFR and Debitel, a company formerly marketing mobile services on behalf of mobile operators, and one between Orange and Omer Telecom. Under the Breizh Mobile brand, the latter company is focused on the Brittany region. One radio station, NRJ, and one TV chain, M6, have also signed an MVNO agreement with Orange and SFR, with young people as the specific target.

The French market is somehow atypical in Europe. It is the only large European market where Orange has a leader and not a challenger position, as it is a subsidiary of the main incumbent. This position may be also explained by the fact that Vodafone does not operate directly in France.

SELECTED SERVICES IN FRANCE'S MOBILE SECTOR

In this section, we present a selection of m-commerce services because of their popularity, their usefulness or the innovative way they exploit technical capabilities in order to answer customer requirements.

Location-Based Services: The Cityneo Case

Location-based services allow mobile users to get useful information according to their geographical location. They are all the more attractive in that the intensity of needs may be very high, as mobile handsets may be the only available or most practical link to information for users. They are challenging for suppliers because information needs to be accurate and up-to-date, and these services must correspond to the temporal requirements of users. For example, indicating a restaurant or a pharmacy that is closed at the time it is requested would be useless to users. The variety of the possible needs and tastes also means offering a high level of personalization and selection. The services provided by Cityneo provide a good example of how to answer customers' needs.

Created in October 2000, Cityneo aims to provide localized information to mobile users through services that are attractive, exhaustive and easy to use. Cityneo provides information concerning the 50 main cities of France by combining maps, an updated database of information and the location information provided by mobile network operators or users. Its services can be accessed through the three French operators, with both WAP and i-Mode technology. Information is selected according to different criteria, but the most important are location, as well as the date and time of day. The services are the following (Cityneo Press Releases, n.d.):

- "Cityneo Plan" is a map and itinerary calculation service. Users indicate the departure and arrival points and get a recommended detailed itinerary, depending on whether they walk or drive, with an estimation of the travel time;
- "Cityneo Guide" provides access to addresses of bars, restaurants, clubs and various cultural events, corresponding to user location and time of day. A specific feature is the possibility of selection according to the user's mood: hype, Zen, sexy, air, culture, fun, in love or surprise;
- "Cityneo Pratik" allows localized practical information to be found, such as an open pharmacy, a cash dispenser, a tobacco shop or a gas station, provided with the relevant map; and
- Cityneo also offers related services in partnership with other companies: "Guide

Nova," providing advice on concerts and other cultural and social activities recommended by the trendy Radio Nova station; "Guide Pudlo" for gastronomic information; and "Le Petit Futé," a French tourist guide.

Cityneo relies on continuous innovation in order to improve its services. For example, in December 2004 it introduced a new service, providing the location of automated speed traps on an itinerary or a city, in response to the increasing use of such speed traps by the French police. Due to its experience with i-Mode in France, and particularly with DoJa[7], Cityneo has been able to extend its service to three other European countries where i-Mode services are also proposed: Italy (with Wind), The Netherlands (with KPN) and Spain (with Telefonica). Interestingly enough, starting from a pure mobile player position, it also began offering its city guide on the Web in March 2004.

Charity: The "One SMS for Asia" Case

One of the most impressive cases is not related to business, but to charity. Potential donors are often discouraged by unknown or uneasy access to charity organizations, or by practical matters such as writing and sending checks. SMS appears to be a good way to reduce this loss of potential donations by providing a quick and easy solution. After the devastating tsunami of December 25 and 26, 2004 in Asia, the three French mobile operators launched a charity campaign called "one SMS for Asia."[8] By typing "ASIE" on their mobile handset and sending an SMS, mobile users could send an SMS+ to one of the three charity organizations associated with this campaign. By doing so, they could donate one euro, plus the cost of the SMS that was donated by the operator. From January 2 to January 31, 2005, more than 3.4

million SMS were sent, generating more than 3.8 million euros of donations (Bilan de l'opération "Un SMS pour l'Asie," 2005). This campaign was so successful that other charity organizations, which had not been asked to be associated to it, complained about it.

Community Service: The Orange Moblogging Case

Blogs have become very popular on the Internet. The large number of mobile handsets, their increased functionalities and the possibility for users to take advantage of their spare time suggest a high potential for mobile blogging. The mobile blogging service launched in June 2004 by Orange is becoming the most successful community service of this company. Reserved for Orange France subscribers, this service enables them to create their own mobile blog, which can be accessed by either Web or WAP. Users can update their page through SMS, MMS or on the Orange Internet Portal, and can also send messages to other bloggers in the same way. Only Orange subscribers can view the Website with their mobile, but everybody can access it on the Web. Six months after its launch in June, 20,000 blogs have been created, with 90,000 submissions by bloggers every month (Guerrier, 2004). In November, three million pages were viewed on the Web and seven million via WAP.

One of the reasons for this success is that, unlike other mobile operators that have launched similar blogs, such as O2 Ireland or T-Mobile USA, Orange has chosen not to charge its subscribers for the service. Revenues for Orange come through increased data, SMS and MMS traffic. Interestingly enough, even though users can update their blog for free on the net, 65 percent of the image posts are via MMS, which is more than 10,000 MMS a month. With UMTS, this service will be upgraded in order to allow videos to be posted.

MUSIC ENTERTAINMENT SERVICES: THE MUSIWAVE CASE

Musiwave is a French company that has become the European leader for mobile music entertainment services. The added value of Musiwave's offer relies on the quality of content cleared of rights, state-of-the-art mobile technology and marketing and content management expertise. Musiwave provides turnkey mobile music entertainment services to mobile operators such as Vodafone or T-Mobile, and media companies such as AOL or MTV. In France, although working with the three mobile operators, it has c form in 2004.

The platform now integrates a wide range of advanced services, such as streaming music (Smart Radio), full track downloads, music recognition, superdistribution (DRM enabled P2P) and a large mobile music library. The services provided by Musiwave are the following (Musiwave Press Releases, n.d.):

- "Musitones" (excerpts of original music as ringtones), "Pictones" (multimedia ringtones);
- "Ringback tones" (audio files that callers will hear while the phone is ringing), and music-related images;
- "MODS" (Music on Demand Service), a full track purchasing and downloading of music, giving access to a 50,000-track catalogue that includes major record labels. Consumers start listening to songs immediately as the rest of the song downloads, and can also retrieve their purchased tracks on their PC through a secured music storage vault;
- "Superdistribution," a P2P-type legal trading of music via messaging, Bluetooth, etc., essentially making one's friends an interface for mobile music;
- "Music Wizard," a music recognition service that works with any handset;
- "Smart Radio," a streaming music service, providing unlimited listening, storage and music channels. While traditional streaming technologies use pre-programmed channels, Musiwave's Smart Radio technology allows users to seamlessly create their own personalized streaming music channels. Personalized music channels are automatically created through real-time analysis of the user's behavior with powerful profiling technologies; and
- "Cross-selling," a service that allows the buyer of a full-length, hi-fi title to be offered the opportunity to buy content type from the same artist or musical genre.

Travel: The SNCF Case

The French railway company SNCF has always been an advanced user of information and communications technology, and its on-line information and reservation system has been quite popular in France. This service was first offered on the French Teletel[9] system in the mid-eighties, and then extended to the Internet. The use of these technologies is a way to provide its customer with accurate and up-to-date information and facilitate the reservation and purchasing of train tickets. SNCF has been eager to simultaneously reduce the manpower and facility cost of its sales network and the waiting time of its customers by providing online services and installing automated ticket distributors in train stations. Providing extensive high-speed train services towards the main destinations in France and neighboring countries, SNCF holds a large share of a market —particularly the business travel market—which would be served by airlines in other countries. In this respect, quality of service and customer care may be more crucial than for other railway companies.

Due to the growing popularity of mobile data services, SNCF has launched new services based on SMS (Services SMS SNCF, n.d.). By sending an SMS+ with INFO and the train number, users receive an SMS informing them if the train is on time, late or cancelled. When customers make an on-line reservation, they can get the details of their reservation by SMS, including the reservation number in order to get the ticket. They also have the option to cancel their reservation by SMS. Customers can also personalize their service by creating a "preference account" online. For example, if they frequently travel from Paris to Lille, they can create a LILLE preference file. In this case, they can send an HORA LILLE message to get timetables for this destination or RESA LILLE to make a reservation.

Consumer Portals

There are several multimedia portals offered to French mobile users, three proposed by the incumbents (Orange World, SFR Vodafone live! and Bouygues Télécom). Four more are expected to be proposed by the MVNOs: Breizh Mobile, Debitel, NRJ and M6.

All mobile operators' portals are proposed around three main "categories": tools, fun and information. All types of data services are proposed besides voice services: video call, SMS, MMS, WAP, chat, forum and mblog. The three incumbents propose similar services on their M-portal, available whatever the service solution used by the consumers. What differentiates them is the way they organize the services and the content in the portal and how they package and price services.

Business Portals

Due to the international (and mostly European) positioning of Orange and its mother company, this new business was conceived from the start with an international focus. This international positioning is based on the cooperation between two subsidiaries of France Télécom: Orange and Equant, producing a global company aimed at international business customers. In this cooperation, the two subsidiaries put together their

resources and expertise in mobile and data services respectively. Under the name Orange MIB (Mobile Internet for Business), a taskforce was created in February 2000 and the Orange MIB portal was launched in July 2000 in France. In June 2001, the joint venture Orange MIB was created.

To the basic offer (Internet access, e-mail, diary, task planning, company directory, SMS and access to business applications), other services were added such as Lotus Notes access, geographical location and industrial applications. This is a specific feature of Orange, which offers:

- Road on line: a specific application for truck transportation to better manage logistics, for 1,000 euros plus 30 euro/month/line; and
- MIB City: aimed at local authorities to manage maintenance activities, for 1,000 euros plus 11 euro/month/line.

Orange also introduced a partnership strategy, with two types of partnerships. The first concerns information providers that are accessible through portals (services such as news, weather reports and reservations). The second concerns companies such as software houses, computing service firms, equipment manufacturers, developers, integrators or consultants, for which a partner pack has been designed. The objective is to help partners develop mobile solutions and products by providing a test and demonstration platform, privileged access to new technologies, commercial and technical support and a development forum. In fact, the objective is twofold: to increase the number and variety of products and applications around its portal, and to benefit from the prescriptive power of the partners on the market (Vialle & Epinette, 2003). The partner pack is available for 2000 euros plus 8 euro/month/user.

Under the name of PIM (Portail Intranet Mobile), SFR introduced a partial version of its portal in 1999, and the final launch occurred in September 2000. The services offered are similar to that of Orange. SFR also has a partnership strategy. To launch its portal, it proposed a trial offer "PIM découverte," that allows customers to test some functions of the portal before adopting it.

Bouygues Telecom launched its portal in September 2001. The content is similar to the others, but the presentation of services appears to be clearer and easier to understand. It has also developed a partnership program.

In February 2002, the three companies announced the launch of their GPRS services (Vialle & Epinette, 2002). Apart from the increased bandwidth (with a real expected bit-rate of 30 to 50 Kbps), this technology allows billing according to the volume of information instead of airtime for plain GSM. They applied the package approach to data, which has spurred the diffusion of voice cellular services, and launched packages tailored for different market/usage segments, including an allowance of data volume.

Two types of services are promoted:

- Portal services, or Intranet access; and
- Mobile office (Internet, e-mail and WAP/i-Mode).

With the introduction of UMTS, operators focus their promotion on PC cards, allowing GPRS/UMTS/Wi-Fi access to the mobile office or Intranet services, and launched specific call plans, ranging from 100 Mo to 2 Go.

VIEWING FRANCE'S MOBILE SERVICES IN THE CLIP FRAMEWORK

As was outlined above, there is little differentiation between the three main mobile operator's portals, as competitive imitation tends to neutralize service differentiation. This phenomenon is also reinforced by cooperative initiatives such as Gallery or SMS+ association. Moreover, homogenization also takes place at the European and international levels, with powerful groups such as Vodafone and France Télécom/Orange, or alliances such as the i-Mode alliance or FreeMove. However, the CLIP framework presented in Chapter I proves itself useful to assess the general level of development of m-commerce in France.

Concerning communications (C), the two main trends are increased bandwidth and integration. The increased bandwidth provided by networks allows services to be enriched, from the plain voice and text services to more advanced multimedia services incorporating image, music and video. Mobile communications in France must also be situated in a more general context of integration of fixed, mobile and wireless communication, such as the France Télécom's initiative to provide video telephony across all its networks. Moreover, national telecommunications companies are cooperating in order to provide seamless European services. As shown above, this is supported by an expanding and innovative content enabling layer, allowing technical and marketing integration.

Location (L) applications are scarce and not highly sophisticated. They are found at the level of specific services, such as maps and itinerary provision or city guides, and not at the level of an m-portal. The localization is determined by the operator's network, identification of the cell where the user is located or manually by the user. More advanced services are currently being tested, such as navigation services for cars, using GPS technology.

Information (I) and content services represent the most innovative and sophisticated type of services, as shown in the Musiwave and Cityneo cases. It is at this level, for example, that we find the most advanced services in terms of personalization, using large databases and profiling techniques. These services are often integrated with online Internet services, as they are either providing access to the same information in a different format or providing complementary services. For example, in the SNCF case, the mobile access is used to access or modify a file created online, or to get updated information. In the Musiwave case, online fixed access allows stable storage on a PC, whereas mobile access provides impulsive purchase and instant listening.

Concerning payment (P), different options are available: on the operator's bill, by e-wallet, by credit card or indirectly by SMS+. However, except for information services and downloads charged on the operator's bill, m-payment is still underdeveloped. Only a few services using e-wallet systems can be found, for example for car park or bus ticket payments.

From this assessment, it appears that m-commerce supply in France is still at an emergent stage. Advanced features such as location, payment and personalization are not sufficiently developed. For example, personalization is found essentially at the content provider level and not so much at the portal level. When such a feature is present, for example in the Orange World portal, it is determined manually by the user and not by profiling techniques. A certain level of integration is provided, but clearly not enough to generate the customer's enthusiasm. For example, it is possible to know the theatre programs in your neighborhood, but not to click to make a reservation or pay for a ticket.

To some extent, our observations are challenging the m-commerce concept. In particular, we question to some extent an "isolated" view of m-commerce. Our analysis identifies two concurrent trends of complementarity and homogeneity linking the fixed and mobile environments, giving rise to different service strategies (Table 2).

Service providers tend to complement their main offering in respectively the fixed or mobile environment by offering a limited set of functions, or specific functions in the other environment. The functions offered in the other environment are conditioned by technical, security or specific use. This can be the case of originally fixed service suppliers, such as the SNCF, offering a limited set of functions corresponding to urgent use situations, as well as limitations due to the current GPRS mobile handsets and networks. On the other hand, Cityneo extended its pure mobile offering to a fixed service, complementing its "instant location" services on mobile with "anticipated location" services on the fixed Internet.

Technological progress also facilitates homogenization between the fixed and mobile environments. The higher bandwidth available through 3G technologies and wireless Internet technologies (such as Wi-Fi and Wimax), as well as the availability of terminals with larger screens (Laptops, PDAs and other terminals), allow mobile users to benefit progressively from the same services as in the fixed environment. Communications services should first benefit from this trend, but information and entertainment services should follow the extended availability of mobile bandwidth and larger screen terminals.

THE ROLE OF CONTENT-ENABLING COMPANIES: REDUCING COMPLEXITY FOR USERS AND SUPPLIERS

The content-enabling layer includes a wide range of actors that allow content to be delivered to

Table 2. Fixed and mobile service strategies

Stand alone fixed or mobile service	Fixed as complement to mobile; Cityneo, Musiwave and Orange Moblogging
Mobile as complement to fixed SNCF	Homogenization; Videophony and PC Connect services

networks and terminals, taking into account the specificity of mobile Internet. They assist the content providers to adapt content to a rapidly moving context of multiple terminals and interfaces. They also contribute to simplifying the users' lives by providing easy access to services, from a technical or a marketing point of view.

Sabat (2002) identifies five types of actors contributing to the development of wireless platforms and utility applications:

- Service bureaux, developing open platforms to convert and format all forms of data information (i.e., messaging, advertising, billing, location-based services, voice-enabled services and hosting);
- Middleware and content delivery applications providers, facilitating the transmission of content with different networks, operating systems and format (i.e., application platforms, content management, corporate data access, synchronization, network monitoring, data optimization and security applications);
- Portals, aggregating, presenting, navigating and delivering a wide range of communication, commerce and content services. A distinction can be made between Internet portals such as Yahoo!, general mobile Internet portals, such as mobile operators' portals and specialized portals providing entertainment, streaming video or gaming services, as well as vertical solutions (financial, education, CRM and sales force management, IT management, transportation and logistics and field force);
- Systems integrators and consultants, specialists in the development of end-to-end wireless Internet offerings, for operators, service providers or large business users.

These content enabling activities are all the more important as a rather high level of complexity characterizes the current situation. The provision of wireless services has to cope with three mobile operators, numerous Wi-Fi hotspot operators and five access-related technologies: GSM, GPRS, EDGE, UMTS and Wi-Fi.

Moreover, the formatting of information must take into account various information access and display modes, such as:

- HTML, the current fixed Internet language for Web pages, and the new language XML;
- WAP (Wireless Application Protocol), specifically designed for mobile phones and using WML language or XML. It exists in different versions, especially for black and white or color screens;
- I-mode, developed by NTT DoCoMo, is provided on Bouygues Telecom's network, and uses the C-HTML language; and
- SMS (Short Message Services), EMS (Enhanced Message Services) and MMS (Multimedia Message Services).

For the content providers, it means that the information must be adapted to the different languages, applications and screen sizes. For example, in the current situation in France, a content provider should offer at least seven different style sheets in order to be accessed by most of the terminals on the market.

Reducing Technical and Transaction Complexity: The Netsize Case

A French company created in 1998, Netsize actually began its operations in 2000 as a wireless messaging operator. Its main activities are the development of customized mobile solutions in order to link its customers' information systems to mobile terminals, with a strong focus on SMS, and now also on EMS and MMS. Starting with revenues of 0.6 million euros in 2000, Netsize has reached 62 million euros in 2003. Netsize operates a network of gateways connected with more than 60 mobile operators (essentially in Europe), allowing the provision of pan-European messaging services and offering access to 500 million mobile users. Netsize has developed a network of 70 business partners, such as Microsoft, Oracle, Sun Microsystems and Atos Origin, and over 500 clients, mostly large businesses. It is now a small multinational with 200 employees, 17 subsidiaries in Europe and two in the NAFTA region. The company has extended its offer with innovative applications and platforms, allowing its customers to quickly implement entertainment, business or machine-to-machine services. Netsize was ranked as the second fastest growing technology in the 2004 Deloitte Technology Fast 500 EMEA. The company achieved its position on the basis of a five-year growth rate of 75.901 percent (Netsize Corporate Brochure, n.d.).

Reducing Technical Complexity of Integrating Different Formats: The Atos Origin Case

Atos Origin is a French company providing consulting, system integration, outsourcing and online services solutions. Atos Origin is the result of the merging or acquisition of significant IT services and consulting companies such as Axime, Sligos, Origin, KPMG Consulting (UK and The Netherlands) and the SEMA Group. With more than 5 billion euros of revenues, 45,000 employees and a presence in 50 countries, it is a large e-business and IT services provider in Europe (Atos, 2005). From its extensive experience in online services as an integrator and hosting provider, the company naturally extended its activities to include mobile Internet. It now has a multimedia platform offering access to all distribution channels, such as Internet, GSM, GPRS, UMTS, WAP, SMS, Videotex, satellite and voice systems for different terminals. Benefiting from an initially strong presence in the banking industry, it has developed m-banking and m-payment solutions.

Reducing Transaction Complexity: The SMS+ Association Case

SMS+ is a premium SMS service allowing a payment for the content or service provider. The SMS + association is a non-profit organization set up in May 2002 by the three French mobile operators. It allows the provision of one-stop shopping services to service editors, a common tariff structure and a single 5-digit number to mobile users, whatever the mobile operator concerned. It has four functions: to manage the available short numbers optimally for the service editors, to book a short number before editing it, to make sure that ethics are respected and to promote the use of SMS+.

Two types of SMS+ services are offered: per act or per session. The *per act* payment option is adapted to the purchase of content from a single source, such as ringtones, icons, poll, weather forecasting or traffic forecasting. The *per-session* option is aimed at services putting different participants in contact, such as games or chat. There are five tariff levels, allowing a service charge from 0.05 to 1.50 euros in addition to the standard SMS tariff. In 2004, 143 services editors reserved 500 short numbers (336 in 2003) of which 350 were open to services; the revenues amounted to 135,000 k, more than twice that of 2003. The SMS+ offer generated 228,000,000 SMS against 137,000,000 in 2003, representing a growth rate of 66 percent. The three mobile operators are soon expected to offer a premium MMS service, called MMS+. The service is forecast to be as successful as the SMS+; since May 2004, new 2G devices can receive MMS, thus enlarging the potential user market (SMS+ Info, n.d.).

Reducing Transaction Complexity: The Gallery Case

The popularity of Minitel as an electronic content delivery channel is widely acknowledged. In

1994, the installed base of terminals reached 6.5 million, the number of services offered reached 24,000 and the total revenues were 6.6 billion French Francs (about 1 billion euros plus inflation), out of which 3.1 billion were given back to service providers (Steinfield, Caby, & Vialle, 1992). One of the main reasons for its success was the provision of a simple billing system and the sharing of a large portion of revenues with content providers (Vialle, 1998). The three French mobile operators have decided to team up in order to offer a similar system to Minitel for mobile users. Content providers can advertise their services directly to end users with a single access point and under a single brand, "Gallery," adopted by the three French mobile operators. The service editor choosing Gallery is certain that any mobile user will access its service whatever the mobile operator he/she subscribed to, and does not need to advertise directly on their respective portals, such as Orange world. The mobile user will pay for the access communication (according to his tariff plan) plus a fee to Gallery, and his mobile operator will bill him according to his tariff plan (pay as you go or monthly plan). Depending on the service, five tariff formulas are proposed: free, day plan, week plan, monthly plan and per download. In the same way as SMS+, several tariffs are available to service editors. The revenues are shared between content providers and mobile operators.

TECHNOLOGICAL AND MANAGERIAL LESSONS FROM FRANCE'S MOBILE EXPERIENCE

For the time being, the French market is not the most developed market for mobile use and mobile commerce. Concerning multimedia services, the bulk of the market concerns mainly messaging services and the download of ringtones and icons. However, the three mobile operators, content providers and an expanding content-enabling

industry are paving the way for future market development. Infrastructures are being progressively upgraded with EDGE and UMTS technologies in order to provide more bandwidth, and thus more attractive and user-friendly services. A wide range of services and applications has been implemented for both consumers and businesses, and the innovation potential of the new network technologies, such as UMTS, is far from being fully exploited. What can also be observed is a general trend of integration at different levels: integration between fixed, mobile and wireless networks, provision of seamless European services, integration of Internet-based business and m-business by companies and content providers.

What lessons can be drawn from the French experience? First, that technology matters, and in the following different ways. There was a clear gap between the promises expressed in advertising and the limits and imperfections of the first systems. Only with EDGE and UMTS, and with the user-friendliness of the most recent services, could the full potential of m-commerce be revealed. Although the market is yet to achieve its full potential, one reason for current growth is the European and French approach of *ex ante* standardization and integration, ensuring compatibility between brands, services, devices and equipment at an early stage of development. Second, it is interesting to note that, while competition is heavily promoted, cooperation seems to be a key success factor for the development of m-commerce, and various players are engaged in a network of cooperative relationships. These partnerships can be vertical, such as the relations between equipment and device manufacturers, content providers and enablers and network operators. They can also be horizontal, such as the case of Gallery or SMS+. Mobile operators or alliances of operators seem to have achieved a powerful position because of their buying power and because they have the customers; payment via their phone bill for most current services puts them in a privileged situation. The respective success of these large mobile operators or alliances will also depend on their network-orchestration capability, that is to say, their capacity to influence a whole new business network (Möller, Rajala, & Svahn, 2005) However, innovative companies such as Musiwave or Netsize have also reached a key position because of their skills and their ability to reduce transaction complexity. Finally, organizations using m-commerce (or intending to do so) should carefully analyze the specificity of fixed and mobile telecommunications and design a synergistic strategy across the two media. Simultaneously, they should also anticipate the diffusion of new technologies and products that induce some form of homogenization between fixed and mobile services.

In conclusion, we note the development of a very dynamic content provision and content enabling industry backed by national operators, one of which has a significant international dimension. From a national perspective, m-business appears to be an opportunity for France and other European countries to play a leading role compared to their laggard positions in Internet-related industries. We do not observe the same dominance of United States firms in the m-business economy, as in the fixed Internet economy.

QUESTIONS FOR DISCUSSION

1. How would you describe the opportunities for 3G in France?
2. Choose a type of company (e.g., automobile or banking) and design an m-commerce strategy for the French context. How would it complement the prevailing e-commerce strategies of such a company?
3. Discuss the relative strengths, weaknesses, opportunities and threats for members of the m-commerce value chain in the French context: mobile operators, terminal equipment vendors, content-enablers and content providers.

REFERENCES

About Orange. (n.d.). Retrieved May 25, 2005, from http://www.orange.com/English/aboutorange/default.asp

ATOS Corporate Brochure. (2005). Retrieved February 28, 2005, from http://www.atosorigin.com/corporate/download/corp_brochure.pdf

Bilan de 'opération "Un SMS pour 'Asie." (2005) Retrieved February 15, 2005, from http://www.atelier.fr/article.php?artid=29103

Bigot, R. (2004). La diffusion des technologies de l'information dans la société française. *Enquête Conditions de vie et Aspirations des Français.* Paris: Credoc. Retrieved February 15, 2005, from http://www.art-telecom.fr/publications/etudes/et-credoc2004.pdf

Bouygues Chiffres clés. (2005). Retrieved June 29, 2005, from http://www.bouygues.fr/

Bouygues Telecom I-mode portal. (n.d.). Retrieved February 15, 2005, from http://www.imode.fr/home.asp

Bouygues Telecom Mobile Business Solutions. (n.d.) Retrieved February 15, 2005, from http://www.entreprises.bouyguestelecom.fr/

Bouygues Telecom Services. (n.d.). Retrieved February 15, 2005, from http://www.services.bouyguestelecom.fr/

Cegetel Chiffres Clés. (2005). Retrieved June 29, 2005, from http://www.groupecegetel.fr/

Cityneo Press Releases. (n.d.) Retrieved February 15, 2005, from http://www.cityneo.com/presse.htm

France Télécom Investor factsheet full year 2004. (n.d.). Retrieved May 15, 2005, from http://www.francetelecom.com/en/financials/investors/data/memento/an2004/

Gallery services. (n.d.) Retrieved February 15, 2005, from http://www.gallerymobile.fr/

Guerrier P. (2004). Les jeunes abonnés d'Orange séduits par le moblogging. *VNUnet*. Retrieved February 15, 2005, from http://svm.vnunet.fr/actualite/20041125007

Le tableau de bord du marché national. (2005). Retrieved February 28, 2005, from Observatoire des mobiles, http://www.art-telecom.fr/

Möller, K., Rajala, A., & Svahn, S. (2005). Strategic business nets — their type and management. *Journal of Business Research, 58,* 1274-1284.

Musiwave Press Releases. (n.d.). Retrieved February 15, 2005, from http://www.musiwave.net/MW_press_release.php

Netsize Corporate Brochure. (n.d.). Retrieved March 16, 2005, from http://www.netsize.com/pdf/en/Netsize_Corporate_Brochure.pdf

OECD Key ICT Indicators. (n.d.). Retrieved May 15, 2005, from http://www.oecd.org/document/23/0,2340,en_2649_34449_ 33987543_1_1_1_1,00.html

Orange in Business. (n.d.). Retrieved February 15, 2005, from http://www.orange.com/English/orangeinbusiness/default.asp

Orange Products and services. (n.d.). Retrieved February 15, 2005, from http://www.orange.com/English/productsandservice/default.asp

Profil du groupe Vivendi Universal. (n.d.). Retrieved May 12, 2005, from http://www.vivendi-universal.com/vu/fr/group/default.cfm?idR=15

Sabat, H. K. (2002). The evolving mobile wireless value chain and market structure. *Telecommunications Policy, 26,* 503-535.

Salcedo, L. (2004). *European country focus. Data essentials. France* (Volume 6). New York: Jupiter Research.

Services SMS SNCF. (n.d.). Retrieved February 15, 2005, from http://www.voyages-sncf.com/go/sms/services_cc.htm

SFR Mobile Business services. (n.d.). Retrieved February 15, 2005, from http://www.sfr.fr/sfr_entreprises/

SFR Products and services. (n.d.). Retrieved February 15, 2005, from http://www.sfr.fr/do/Home

SMS+ Info. (n.d.). Retrieved February 15, 2005, from http://www.smsplus.org/

Steinfield, C., Caby, L., & Vialle, P. (1992). Internationalization of the firm and impacts of videotex networks. *Journal of Information Technology, 7*(December), 213-222.

Vialle, P. (1998). *Stratégies des opérateurs de télécoms.* Paris: Hermès.

Vialle, P. (2003, August). *The emergence of m-business: An analysis of the case of the French market.* Paper presented at the 14th European International Telecommunications Society Conference, Helsinki, Finland.

Vialle, P., & Epinette, O. (2001, July). *The attitudes and perceptions of ICT managers of large firms towards m-business Internet adoption: Beyond the magic.* Paper presented at the Conference on Telecommunications and Information Markets (COTIM), Karlsruhe, Germany.

Vialle, P., & Epinette, O. (2002, Sept). *Mobile Internet strategies of the French operators for business customers.* Paper presented at the 13th European International Telecommunications Society Conference, Madrid, Spain.

Vialle, P., & Epinette, O. (2003, Jan). *The impact of demand for integrated solutions on distribution channel strategy and management :The case of France télécom.* Paper presented at the 8th International Conference on Marketing and Development, Bangkok, Thailand.

Vodafone live! (n.d.). Retrieved February 15, 2005, from http://www.sfr.fr/FR/info_nouveautes/vodafone/index2.jsp

ENDNOTES

[1] SMS+ are premium SMS that allow content providers to bill customers for the provision of ringtones and logos, or to participate in TV contests. The average price is 0.59 euros, to compare with 0.10 euros for a plain SMS message.

[2] These figures are based on users' assertions in a survey and not on traffic measurement.

[3] When ISDN was launched in France in 1981, video telephony was envisioned as the ultimate achievement for ISDN based services.

[4] Orange charges the same price for video telephony as for voice as a promotional offer only in 2005, and will charge the equivalent of two minutes of voice call from 2006.

[5] Average number of SMS per month and per active customer. Active customers represent 98.4 percent of the total number of customers.

[6] Dauphin Telecom and Outremer Telecom, operating in overseas departments and territories.

[7] DoCoMo Java: a specific version of Java technology for mobile handsets that has been developed by DoCoMo and Sun Microsystems. Java-enabled handsets have a dynamic memory allowing them to download and store specific programs. In the case of Cityneo Plan, it allows a faster, more intuitive and precise use of this service.

[8] Un SMS pour l'Asie.

[9] More popular under the name of its terminal: Minitel.

This work was previously published in M-Commerce: Global Experiences and Perspectives, edited by N. Dholakia, M. Rask, and R. R. Dholakia, pp. 90-111, copyright 2006 by IGI Publishing, formerly known as Idea Group Publishing (an imprint of IGI Global).

Chapter XII
Wireless Technologies for Mobile Computing and Commerce

David Wright
University of Ottawa, Canada

INTRODUCTION

At the time of writing (1Q06) most countries have a small number (2-6) of major cellular operators offering competing 2.5G and 3G cellular services. In addition, there is a much larger number of operators of WiFi networks. In some cases, a major cellular operator, for example, Deutsche Telekomm and British Telecom, also offers a WiFi service. In other cases, WiFi services are provided by a proliferation of smaller network operators, such as restaurants, laundromats, airports, railways, community associations and municipal governments. Many organizations offer WiFi free of charge as a hospitality service, for example, restaurants. Cellular services offer ubiquitous, low data rate communications for mobile computing and commerce, whereas WiFi offers higher data rates, but less ubiquitous coverage, with limitations on mobility due to business as opposed to technology reasons.

Emerging networks for mobile computing and commerce include WiMAX and WiMobile (Wright, 2006), which offer higher data rates, lower costs and city-wide coverage with handoff of calls among multiple base stations. These new technologies may be deployed by the organizations that currently deploy cellular and WiFi networks, and also may give rise to a new group of competitive wireless network operators.

This article identifies the capabilities needed for mobile computing and commerce and assesses their technology and business implications. It identifies developments in the wireless networks that can be used for mobile computing and commerce, together with the services that can be provided over such networks. It provides a business analysis indicating which network operators can profitably deploy new networks, and which network operators need to establish business and technology links with each other so as to better serve their customers. The resulting range of next generation service, technologies and network operators available for mobile computing and commerce is identified.

WIRELESS NETWORK ARCHITECTURES

Figure 1 illustrates the network architectures for WiFi, Cellular, WiMAX and WiMobile, including the radio access network on the left and the wired core network on the right.

The cellular architecture is the most sophisticated in that the core network includes a circuit network (for legacy circuit switched voice calls), a packet network (for data calls) and an IP Multimedia Subsystem, IMS (for migration of all traffic onto the Internet).

These three networks essentially allow the cellular operator to maintain control over all calls

to and from the mobile device, and hence derive revenue from them. In particular the IMS network contains servers for establishing voice and video calls over IP, authenticating users, maintaining records of the current location of a mobile user, accounting, and security. Cellular operators are migrating traffic from their circuit and packet networks onto the IMS.

By contrast, WiFi (IEEE, 1999a, 1999b, 1999c, 2003), WiMAX (IEEE, 2006; Ghosh et al., 2005), and WiMobile (IEEE, 2006; Lawton, 2005) are simply radio access technologies and do not specify a core network. They therefore allow more direct access from a mobile device to the Internet. In particular, the WiMobile specification, which is under development at the time of writing, emphasizes that its design is being optimized for operation with IP. This more open access to the Internet allows a mobile user to set up, for instance, a VoIP call using a third party

Figure 1. Wireless network architectures

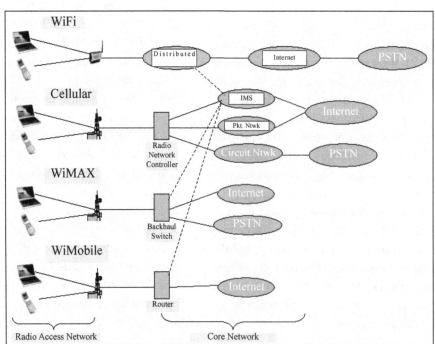

service without the involvement of the wireless network operator. As the user moves from one access point to another, the call can be maintained using Mobile IP, involving servers maintained by the user's ISP, not by the wireless network operator. Mobile IP can operate over diverse wireless access technologies as described by Benzaid et al. (2004).

If the operator of a WiFi, WiMAX or WiMobile network wishes to maintain more control over the traffic passing through their network and hence participate more in the revenue generated by that traffic, they can build an IMS network. Alternatively if they already operate a cellular network, they can provide access to their existing IMS network, as shown by the dashed lines in Figure 1.

REQUIREMENTS FOR MOBILE COMPUTING AND COMMERCE

Any wireless transmitter/receiver has a limited range in order to comply with government regulations regarding maximum power output. A mobile user therefore may move out of the range of its current wireless access point, and it is necessary to handoff the communication to another access point using either the same or a different wireless technology. Handing off the communication means that the current IP session is maintained, for example, the user continues to browse a Web site as a registered user, a VoIP call is not interrupted, and an enterprise user with a laptop-based secure VPN to an enterprise network continues to use the same VPN. There are four requirements in order to achieve handoff suited to mobile computing and commerce:

1. It must be possible to switch the call from one access point to another
2. If the user is receiving quality of service, QoS, for example, a guaranteed low latency,

that QoS is maintained after the handoff, and an acceptable number of packets are lost during handoff.
3. If the access points are operated by different network operators, there must be a business arrangement between them regarding mediation of the billing for the call.
4. The organization deploying the wireless access network must be able to make a profit or to have a business model that focuses on hospitality service.

Requirements 1 and 2 are technology related and are discussed next, followed by the business requirements 3 and 4.

TECHNOLOGY ISSUES

A mobile device that is capable of using multiple wireless access technologies, such as those described above, can continuously scan its radio environment to search for access points that it could potentially use. Some of them may not be available, if, for instance, they are operated by companies with which the user does not have a subscription. In order to choose among the available access points within range the mobile device can apply criteria including: data rate, cost, ability to handoff seamlessly, and QoS; delay (important for voice) and packet loss rate (important for data). For instance, a mobile device with an interactive voice/video call in progress could choose the lowest cost network that provides acceptable delay. A device downloading a large data file could choose the network with the highest data rate given limitations on cost and packet loss rate. Once the network is selected, handoff is initiated.

Handoff among WiFi, WiMAX and WiMobile is handled by IEEE (2006). Handoff between cellular and one of these three technologies is complicated by the need to interwork with the cellular circuit, packet and IMS networks.

- In the case of WiFi, this interworking is provided by a specification from the industry consortium UMA, Unlicensed Mobile Access (2006), which is incorporated as part of the GSM cellular network specifications, release 6.
- In the case of WiMAX, similar issues are involved and are being resolved by the WiMAX Forum (2006).
- WiMobile is at an early stage of development and interworking with cellular is not a priority at this stage. A specification may be developed later, or alternatively, WiMobile may differentiate itself from the other technologies by becoming a "native-IP" access mechanism, similar to DSL and cable modem in which customers have direct access to the Internet.

This discussion addresses requirements 1, 2 above. We now move on to requirements 3, 4.

BUSINESS ISSUES

This section presents business strategies for wireless access network operators that take into account sources of revenue related to mobile computing and commerce, plus the need to compete with other technologies and network operators. Earlier work in this area (du Preez & Pistorius, 2003) dates from a time when 3G and wireless data services were emerging technologies. The present section incorporates developments in technology and services to date.

The sources of revenue are given in Table 1 and are classified in two ways:

1. Whether the service is provided by a content provider or a network operator, which may be the wireless access network operator or another network operator. For instance, a VoIP service could be provided by the wireless operator or by a third party such

Table 1. Wireless access network operators revenue sources

Revenue Source	Service provided by: (N) Network Operator (C) Content Provider	Revenue accrues to: (W) Wireless Network Operator (3) Third Party Service Provider (S) Shared with Content Provider
Voice/video calls	N	W 3
Audio content	C	S
Video content	C	S
Gateway to PSTN	N	W 3
Geographic info (e.g., travel directions, highway safety)	N C	W S
Location enabled advertising	N C	W S
Location enabled buddy lists	N	W
Multimedia Messaging Service	C	W 3 S
Gaming	C	S
QoS	N	W
VPN	N	W 3

Table 2. Strategy for wireless access network operators

	Cellular Operators	Hospitality providers	Competitive Wireless Network Operators
Technologies	2.5G, 3G, WiFi, WiMax, WiMobile	WiFi, unlicensed WiMAX	WiMAX, WiMobile
Revenue sources	Generate revenue from the full range of services	Provide Internet access for the full range of services.	Generate revenue from the full range of services
IMS strategy	Lock customers into IMS-based services.	Establish partnerships and interfaces to the IMS of other operators	Build IMS. Establish partnerships and interfaces to the IMS of other operators
Competitive strategy	Buy up competitors.	Avoid competing with other operators by a competitive bid process.	Differentiate from incumbents by offering low cost services, focusing on IP, developing next generation services, for example, presence, location, QoS.

as Vonage. Either way it is provided by a network operator.

2.   Who receives the revenue for the service: the wireless access network operator, a third party or a sharing arrangement with a content provider.

It can be seen from Table 1 that there is a large number of mobile computing and commerce services that can be provided by a mix of wireless network operators, content providers and third parties. In addition there are non-revenue generating services such as e-mail and Web browsing. A clear business strategy is needed to operate successfully in competition with the other players. Strategies suited to the different types of wireless network operators are given in Table 2.

Table 2 divides wireless access network operators into three groups: incumbent cellular operators, hospitality providers such as restaurants and municipalities, and new competitors, who are starting operations based on the availability of new technology. The incumbent cellular operators have complex core networks as shown in Figure 1 and incur costs of operating legacy technologies. They seek to deploy all possible wireless technologies in order to accommodate the needs

of all customers. By contrast the new competitors seek to reduce their costs by only operating the most recent technologies. Both these groups are operating commercial services and therefore use licensed spectrum so that their customers do not experience interference from other users. The hospitality providers, however, are providing a free service. Their customers accept that the performance may vary according to the demands of other users and therefore the operators reduce their costs by using unlicensed spectrum.

Both the incumbents and the new competitors aim to deliver the full range of services listed in Table 1 to their customers, typically from the IMS, so as to maintain control over the revenue. The hospitality providers, however, are typically providing access only, allowing their customers to get services from any third party they wish, since they do not seek to generate revenue from their networks. For location-based services, the hospitality provider can provide the third party with information about the customer's current location.

The cellular incumbents typically already have an IMS in place and aim to lock customers into service provided by that IMS. The new competitors need to build an IMS and then establish partnerships with other wireless operators so that calls originating on one IMS can be handed off to another operator. These partnerships are also important to the hospitality providers since they typically have no interest in developing their own IMS.

The competitive strategy of incumbent cellular operators towards WiFi operators historically has been to buy them up, and this strategy is also appropriate for WiMAX and WiMobile operators. The strategy of hospitality operators is to avoid competition, and this is particularly important for municipalities, who should not be seen to use tax dollars to compete against private industry. In order to avoid this perception, they can use a competitive bid process allowing any operator the opportunity to bid on the contract to build and operate their network. The strategy of the new competitors is to compete on three fronts. First, they can offer low cost services, since they do not have the cost of operating legacy networks. Second, they can offer a full range of next generation services, such as presence and location-based services, thus positioning themselves as state-of-the-art suppliers. Third, they can sell QoS guarantees to their customers, since new technologies such as WiMAX and WiMobile are particularly suited to providing such guarantees.

CONCLUSION

The enabling technologies for mobile computing and commerce are developing rapidly. New wireless technologies such as WiMAX and WiMobile offer extended coverage and improved QoS compared to WiFi; and higher data rates and lower costs compared to 2.5G and 3G cellular. A wide range of services is available over these technologies including services that generate revenue (a) for the wireless operator, such as location-based services, (b) for a third party, such as VoIP and (c) for a content provider, such as entertainment.

Wireless network operators, including incumbent cellular operators, hospitality providers and new competitive wireless network operators, need to develop strategies that allow handoff of calls among the different technologies and operators. Strategies include locking customers into an IMS, interworking with other operators' IMSs, buying out competitors and developing a broad range of state-of-the-art services such as location and presence services.

The mobile computing and commerce user can therefore expect a proliferation of services (Table 1), a number of different network operators (Table 2), an array of different wireless technologies, WiFi, 3G, WiMAX and WiMobile, and a mobile device that can make the best choice among these alternatives at any point in time and space.

REFERENCES

Benzaid, M., Minet, P., Al Agha, Kh., Adjih, C., & Allard. G. (2004). Integration of mobile-IP for universal mobility. *Wireless Networks, 10*(4), 377-388.

du Preez, G. T., & Pistorius, C. W. I. (2003). Analyzing technological threats and opportunities in wireless data services. *Technological Forecasting and Social Change, 70*(1), 1-20.

Ghosh, A., Wolter, D. R., Andrews, J. G., & Chen, R. (2005, February). Broadband wireless access with WiMax/802.16: Current performance benchmarks and future potential. *IEEE Communications, 43*(2), 129-136.

IEEE. (1999a). *802.11 Wireless LAN: Medium access control (MAC) and physical layer (PHY) specifications.* New York: IEEE Publications.

IEEE. (1999b). *802.11a high-speed physical layer in the 5 GHz band.* New York: IEEE Publications.

IEEE. (1999c). *802.11b higher-speed physical layer (PHY) extension in the 2.4 GHz band*. New York: IEEE Publications.

IEEE. (2003). *802.11g further higher-speed physical layer extension in the 2.4 GHz band*. New York: IEEE Publications.

IEEE. (2006a). *802.16e air interface for fixed and mobile broadband wireless access systems: Amendment for physical and medium access control layers for combined fixed and mobile operation in licensed bands*. New York: IEEE Publications.

IEEE. (2006b). *802.20 mobile broadband wireless access* (In Progress). Retrieved March 2006, from http://grouper.ieee.org/groups/802/20

IEEE. (2006c). *802.21 media independent handover services* (In Progress). Retrieved March 2006, from http://grouper.ieee.org/groups/802/21/

Lawton, G. (2005). What lies ahead for cellular technology? *IEEE Computer, 38*(6), 14-17.

UMA. (2006). *Unlicensed mobile access*. Retrieved from http://www.umatechnology.org/specifications/index.htm

WiMAX Forum. (2006). Retrieved March 2006, from www.wimaxforum.org

Wright, D. (2006). Wireless technologies for mobile computing and commerce. In D. Taniar (Ed.), *Encyclopedia of mobile computing and commerce*. Hershey, PA: Idea Group Reference.

KEY TERMS

IMS, IP Multimedia Subsystem: Part of the wired core network containing servers for establishing voice and video calls over IP, authenticating users, maintaining records of the current location of a mobile user, accounting, and security.

Location-Based Services: Services that take into account the users current geographical location, for example, advertising locally available products and services, providing directions and alerting drivers to traffic congestion and road accidents.

Mobile IP: An Internet standard that allows a mobile user to move from one point of attachment of the network to another while maintaining an existing TCP/IP session. Incoming packets to the user are forwarded to a server in the user's new access IP subnetwork.

Presence: The ability of a user device to specify characteristics, such as whether the user is online, whether the user is willing to receive calls, whether the user is willing to receive calls of a given type (e.g., voice, video, data, MMS) from specified other users and what is the user's current location to a specified degree of accuracy.

Quality of Service (QoS): Features related to a communication, such as delay, variability of delay, bit error rate and packet loss rate. Additional parameters may also be included, for example, peak data rate, average data rate, percentage of time that the service is available, mean time to repair faults and how the customer is compensated if QoS guarantees are not met by a service provider.

WiFi: A commercial implementation of the IEEE 802.11 standard in which the equipment has been certified by the WiFi Alliance, an industry consortium.

WiMAX: A commercial implementation of the IEEE 802.16 standard in which the equipment has been certified by the WiMAX Forum, an industry consortium.

WiMobile: Another name for the IEEE 802.20 standard, which is in course of development at the time of writing (1Q06).

Chapter XIII
A Theoretical Approach to Evaluate Online and Traditional Trading on the NASDAQ Stock Exchange

Haroun Alryalat
Brunel University, UK

Yogesh Kumar Dwivedi
Brunel University, UK

Jasna Kuljis
Brunel University, UK

Ray J. Paul
Brunel University, UK

ABSTRACT

The aim of this chapter is to discuss current online and traditional trading on the NASDAQ stock exchange using theoretical approach. The paper aims to derive future trends for the online stock trading. The following are objectives of this paper: (1) To describe the current state of online trading; (2) To compare the execution of quality trades between market makers and electronic communications networks (ECNs). By achieving set objectives, this paper will provide insight into how ECNs are used and what impact they have on the overall NASDAQ market performance.

INTRODUCTION

The trading of stock involves three primary functions: the gathering of trading orders, the execution of these orders, and the settlement of the trades. The cost structures and the social externalities of these three functions differ. Furthermore, each has different regulatory issues. The ultimate goal of a well-functioning stock market is to bring together all possible buyers and sellers, so that the market price reflects the combined preferences of all participants.

The advent of online stock trading represents a unique opportunity to study the effect of changes in the mix of naïve and sophisticated traders on market behavior. This setting allows us to investigate the descriptive validity of recent models of trade with asymmetrically informed investors. Most of the models of trading behavior group traders into one of two categories: informed traders (who know something about the true price of the security) or liquidity traders (who need to trade for reasons of liquidity) (Barclay, Hendershott, & McCormick, 2001; Barber et al., 2001).

Technology that allows services traditionally provided by people in buildings to be replaced by services provided by the software industry and computers is challenging traditional practices in the brokerage industry and stock exchange.

Traditionally, stockbrokers have been known for their "full service," as the friendly "financial consultant" whom you knew for over 10 years, and who knew your risk appetite. They would provide news about stocks and markets. They would also provide liberal financial advice. But they would also offer advice, service, and preference in initial public offerings (IPOs) and blame it on the broker. For these "services" they charge a commission that would sometimes amount to a percentage of the value that you had traded. The key issue in full-service brokerages is that the brokers are compensated on trading volume, and not on the performance of your portfolio.

Discount brokers—known as such for their "discounting" of the commission—began the practice of flat fees for trading. The Internet helped the onset of online discount brokerages (Web broker). Online brokerages replace people and telephones with computers and code, they offer cost-efficient trades, 24-hour service, fast trade execution, banking facilities, access to IPOs online, access to market information, and no one to blame. Because of online services, the fee percentage declined dramatically.

The start-up fixed costs of setting up an online firm are far lower than setting up a traditional full-service brokerage (Barber et al., 2001). Traders tend to have very different preferences for trading with market makers and trading on an ECN (which automatically matches, buys, and sells orders at specified prices) because of their different trading motives. These developments are commonly attributed to the efficiency of "friction-free" electronic markets that lower transaction and information processing costs by reducing human intermediation (Konana, Menon, & Balasubramanian, 2000).

The Internet serves as an excellent tool for investors, allowing them an easy and inexpensive way to research investment opportunities. On the other hand, the Internet is also an excellent tool for fraudsters. For this reason, investors should always think twice before investing in any opportunity for trading through the Internet. Online trading investors need to understand the risks of online trading or in securities trading in general.

The aim of this chapter is to evaluate current online and traditional trading on the NASDAQ stock exchange using theoretical approach. The chapter aims to derive future trends for the online stock trading. The following are objectives of this chapter: (1) To describe the current state of online trading; (2) To compare the execution of quality trades between market makers and ECNs. By achieving set objectives, this chapter will provide insight into how ECNs are used and what impact they have on the overall NASDAQ market performance.

Section 1 briefly introduces online stock trading and defines aims and objectives of this paper. Section 2 presents a background of the structure of U.S. stock market and online stock trading in the NASDAQ stock exchange. The section includes the different trading mechanisms to match, buy, and sell orders resulting in diverse market outcomes in terms of execution price and speed. Section 3 then goes into more detail about how online investors affect markets. The section provides background of investor's behavior on financial market to understand the investor's performance. Section 4 presents the existing regulation relative online trading with respect to a number of important factors. Finally, section 5 presents the conclusion.

THE STRUCTURE OF U.S. STOCK MARKETS

Equity markets worldwide are in a state of change. Technology and the Internet have and will continue to have a profound impact on the structure of the equity markets (Blume, 2000). A U.S. investor will be able to trade with just a click on any market that provides advantages over the markets in the United States. Investors in the U.S. stock are desperate; there are institutional investors, households with substantial assets, a large number of households with limited assets, day traders, less active traders, foreign investors, after-hour traders, and so on. The different ways of trading will evolve to satisfy their varying needs.

An essential concept of national market system (NMS) was to make information on price, volume, and quotes for securities in all markets available to all investors, so that buyers and sellers of securities, wherever located, can make informed investment decisions and not pay more than the lowest price at which someone is willing to sell, or not sell for less than the highest price a buyer is prepared

to offer (SEC, 2000). The Securities ad Exchange Commission (SEC) believes full disclosure will ultimately produce informed investors and will eventually put increase competitive pressure on brokerage firms (Fan, Stallaert, & Whinston, 2000; Yue, Chaturvedi, & Mehta, 2000).

A trading system is crucial to an exchange market and plays a critical role in determining the overall efficiency of the market. Market efficiency is largely affected by the way trading is organised (Fan et al., 2000). Despite proposed changes in the securities trading process and the introduction of electronic trading systems, other processes determining market efficiency, including order flow, price discovery, and order execution, remain largely unchanged (Figure 1).

Konana et al. (2000) find that for efficiency to move beyond the user interface into the actual trading process, investors need a transparent window to observe the actual flow of orders, the time of execution, and the commission structure of various points in the trading process.

Some researchers have argued that institutional rules, regulations, and monitoring functions would play a significant role in promoting efficiency and transparency along the value chain in electronic markets.

Transparency across market centers help to mitigate the effects of the fragmentation. Last trade and quote reporting provide a great deal of transparency across U.S. market centers, but market centers are not fully transparent. For greater transparency of price and quote information, the SEC in 1997 instituted new order handling rules (Schwartz, 2000).

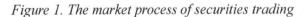

Figure 1. The market process of securities trading

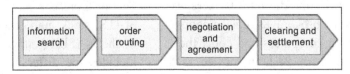

Table 1. Market share of trade and daily share volumes of ECNs (SEC, 2000)

Vendor	Exchange/Broker	Market Share of ECN Trades	Daily Share Volume
Archipelago	Filed as Exchange	1%	25 million
Attain	Filed as Exchange	?	?
B-Trade	Broker	7%	35 million
BRUT	Broker	<1%	7 million
Instinet	Broker	70%	150 million
Island	Filed as Exchange	20%	95 million
NexTrade	Broker	<1%	275,000
REDIBook	Filed as Exchange	<1%	17 million
MarketXT	Broker	<1%	2 million
TOTAL		**100%**	**181.25 million**

Current trends in the market structure for trading stocks will be worldwide. The physical location of the market center where the trade happens will not matter. Technology will make the location of the market center, the currency, and the time of trade a matter of choice. Today, a major hindrance to the development of a global market is settlement and the clearing mechanism (Blume, 2000).

The Current Scene at NASDAQ

Most dramatic in the United States was the National Association of Securities Dealers' (NASD's) acquisition of the American stock exchange in June 1998 (Blume, 2000; Schwartz, 2000). The NASDAQ is not a physical entity. It is an over-the-counter market (OTC) and it relies on market makers to facilitate trading and liquidity in stock (ensure that there are always buyers and sellers for NASDAQ-tested securities, and enable trades to be filled quickly and efficiently).

For each stock, there is at least one market maker; NASDAQ is mainly a dealership market with an average of approximately 12.3 market makers per NASDAQ stock. But the emergence of ECNs has added an auction element in the NASDAQ market (Fan et al., 2000). Rather than being an auction market, NASDAQ is a communication network between thousands of computers, which transmits real-time quote and trade data to more than 1.3 million users in 83 countries (www.nasdaq.com, 2002). Instead of brokers calling out orders, market makers place their name on a list of buyers and sellers, which is then distributed by the NASDAQ in a split second to thousands of other computers. If an investor wishes to buy a stock that trades on the NASDAQ, the broker will either call up a market maker with the information of the trade or enter an order into a NASDAQ-sponsored online execution system.

NASDAQ market makers that trade listed stocks are currently linked to the exchanges through NASDAQ's CAES system's interface with the Intermarket Trading System (ITS) (these market makers are known as ITS/CAES market makers). ITS is an electronic order routing system that facilitates intermarket trading of exchange-listed securities by allowing a broke-dealer in one market center to send an order to another market center trading the same security at a better price.

The NASDAQ is currently working on the technical and programming modifications to its systems needed to support this linkage (SEC, 2000). Currently, there are nine ECNs (Table 6.1) operating in the U.S. equities markets (Instinet, Island, Bloomberg Tradebook, Archipelago, REDIBook, Brut, Attain, NexTrade, and Mar-ketXT) linked to NASDAQ through SelectNet. This link allows each ECN to display its best order for NASDAQ securities in the NASDAQ system, and allows the public to access those orders.

The NASDAQ is developing market structures to trade any stock in any nation in any currency. These new developments are in their infancy, but they point the way to the future. In recent years, the SEC has been extremely active in encouraging competition across market centers. These initiatives have had the most impact on NASDAQ. There are three main initiatives: the manning rules, the order display rules, and alternative trading system (ATS) rules. Each of these can be understood through their interaction with each other and the market.

The manning rules require that a market maker in NASDAQ stocks execute a customer's limit order before executing an order for its own account (Blume, 2000). Under the manning rules a market center had no obligation to display a limit order that improved the NBBO.

The order display rules required that a market maker that receives a bid or offer that betters the NBBO take one of three actions, execute the limit order immediately against its own inventory, display the better price as part of its own quote, or send the limit order to another market maker who would then have the same three choices. The order display rules also required that the quotes of ECNs be integrated into the NBBO. The immediate effect of the order display rules was to narrow spreads on the ECNs.

The alternative trading system rules made it easier to establish a new exchange and to fully integrate them into the national market system (NMS). Alternative trading systems could choose to be a market participant and register as a broker-dealer, or to be a separate market and register as an exchange (SEC, 2000).

ECN and Market Maker Trades

The trading of NASDAQ-listed stocks is spread over many more market centers. There are two principal types of market centers: market makers and ECNs. As of June 2000, there were an average of 12.7 market makers per listed stock, while for the top 1% of issues by dollar volume, there were an average 52.9 market makers. Although this number seems large, there is a high degree of concentration of order flow in any stock in a limited number of market makers. Furthermore, all of these market makers are linked together through electronic trading systems.

A major barrier to a new market center is obtaining a critical mass of order flow to thrive. Order flow is critical to every market center's business. More order flow means more revenue and trading profits (Fan et al., 2000). To displace an existing market requires that the new market offers significantly better services than the established market.

It is useful to pause to consider the difference between an ECN and an exchange. ECNs are broker-dealers regulated by NASD; they match public orders and do not act as principals. Both the ECN form of organisation and an exchange have advantages and disadvantages. A major advantage of an ECN is that NASD performs the regulatory function and frees the ECN from this activity. A major advantage of an exchange is that an exchange receives what is termed "tape revenue." Such tape revenue comes from the sale of quote and last trade data to public vendors. This can represent between 20% to 40% of an exchange's revenue. As an ECN, the revenue goes to the NASD. Another advantage of an exchange is that it may have more latitude in setting its own rules (Blume, 2000).

ECNs are being viewed as a competitive threat to the traditional market both in the United States and abroad. The preponderance of stock exchange around the world now has electronic trading platforms. The electronic systems are fast, inexpensive, eliminate intermediaries, and provide anonymity. Electronic technology has made it possible to combine systems in new ways so as to give users some of the options they want for working their orders.

The ECN phenomenon is attributable to technological and regulatory developments, and to an intensely competitive environment. ECNs' enforced consolidation, transparency, and accessibility of price information are causing the flow of limit order to fragment onto multiple books, and ECNs' cheap, fast, anonymous, and extended hours of trading is forcing NASDAQ to alter its trading systems and organisation structures (Schwartz, 2000).

Technological innovations that enable high-speed, low-cost electronic trading systems are dramatically changing the structure of financial markets. In the United States, ECNs are involved in more than a third of total NASDAQ trading volume.

Today, ECNs account for approximately 30% of total share volume and 40% of the dollar volume traded in NASDAQ securities. ECNs account for approximately 3% of total share and dollar volume in listed securities. In contrast, in 1993 ECNs accounted for only 13% of share volume in NASDAQ securities and only 1.4% of listed share volume (SEC, 2000).

NASDAQ ECN trading volume has grown rapidly over the past several years, transforming NASDAQ's operations. ECNs' operational efficiency (e.g., Island, one of the largest ECNs, has only about 60 employees) promises low costs in addition to improved limit order exposure, anonymity, and increased speed.

Investors' choices of whether to send their orders to market maker or to an ECN will depend on the total expected trading costs, including the implicit, explicit, and opportunity costs (Naik & Yadav, 1999).

For some institutional investors the choice of trading venue is dynamic. Institutional investors can examine the price and depth offered by ECNs and by market makers and chooses the venue that will provide the best execution. For retail investors, however, the choice is generally static.

Several previous papers have examined the effect of ECN quotes on market quality. ECN quotes play an important role in reducing trading costs. Barclay et al. (2001) found that an increased ECN trading improves market quality as measured by effective, realised, and time-weighted quoted spread. These improvements occur in the overall market as well as for market maker trades and quotes. We can explain that because, first, ECNs facilitate customer-to-customer trades that occur at better price than trades with intermediaries; second, ECNs attract a higher fraction of the informed orders than the uniformed order. This reduces the adverse selection costs faced by market makers. Finally, the lower spread available on ECN increase competition and dissipate any quasi-rent on preference market maker trades.

ECNs offer several advantages over market makers such as spread of execution and anonymity. The main factor affecting the quality of execution is price improvement (which is the opportunity, but not the guarantee, for an order to be executed at a better price than what is currently publicly), and market makers give more price improvement to small trades than ECNs. Barclay et al. (2001) suggests that retail customers benefit when their small orders are sent to a market maker instead of to an ECN. Because the ECNs were not integrated into the NASDAQ market, many retail investors traded at prices inferior to those displayed by market makers and other subscribers on ECNs. This created a tow-tiered market—the traditional public market and the new ECN market with better prices and limited access. Market makers could post quotes in private ECNs that were better than the quotes they posted in the public market. This allowed market makers to charge higher prices to retail customers and lower price to more price-sensitive institutional investors.

Best execution does not require market makers to match the rounded or nondisplayed quotes on an ECN. Thus, customers may go directly to the ECN to get those better prices.

ECN subscribers submit limit orders, which are posted on the system for other subscribers to view. The ECN then matches contra-side orders for execution. In most cases, the buyer and seller remain anonymous, as the trade execution reports list only the ECN as the contra-side party. Subscribers may use additional features of the ECN, such as negotiation or reserve size (Barclay et al., 2001).

ECNs are challenging the traditional markets by providing low-cost trading and liquidity through electronic limit order matching systems (Barber & Odean, 2001).

When an order is placed to buy or sell stock, one might think about where and how the order is executed can impact the overall costs of the transaction, including the price paid for the stock. Many investors who trade through online brokerage accounts assume they have a direct connection to the securities market, but they do not. Just as investors have a choice of brokers, brokers also generally have a choice of markets to execute the trade.

The broker may route the order—especially a limit order—to an ECN or market maker. Some brokers now offer active traders the ability to direct orders in NASDAQ stock to the market maker or ECN of their choice.

Online trading is not always instantaneous; investors may find that technological "choke points" can slow down or prevent their order form reaching an online firm. For example, problems can occur where:

- An investor's modem, computer, or Internet service provider is slow or faulty.
- A broker-dealer has inadequate hardware or its Internet service provider is slow or delayed.
- Traffic on the Internet is heavy, slowing down overall usage.

A capacity problem or limitation at any of these choke points can cause delay or failure in an investors' attempt to access an online firm's automated trading system (SEC, 2000).

Who Trades on the Web?

This section provides a profile of those who go online. Barber and Odean (2001) found that young men who are active traders with high incomes and no children are more likely to switch to online trading. Those who switch to online trading seem to experience an unusually strong performance prior to going online and trade more speculatively after going online. Those who switch also have higher levels of self-reported investment experience and a preference for investing in small-growth stocks with high market risk.

Online investors do not generally receive such personal assistance; they do have access to a vast array of financial information, often at no charge, such as market data, historical charts, industry reports, and analyst report. This information can assist them in making trading decisions (GAO, 2000).

To help investors make informed decisions, the SEC and self-regulatory organisations (SROs) require that broker-dealers furnish investors information relating to margin trading. They have proposed rules concerning privacy of information, and recommend that broker-dealers also furnish information about trading risk and best execution of trades. These are key investor protections.

Through greater speed of execution, online trading allows investors to make profitable trades that would not have otherwise been available. Despite the press given to Internet trading, only 11% used the Internet to buy or sell stock in 1998. These individuals tended to be younger, more affluent, and better educated than the typical investor (Blume, 2000).

Some investors may anticipate unusual liquidity needs and switch online in hopes of facilitating liquidity-driven purchases or sales more easily. Investors trade more when they go online simply because of greater ease of access, lower trading costs make more trade potentially profitable. Lower trading costs, liquidity needs, speed of execution, and ease of access do not explain why rational investors would trade more actively, more speculatively and less profitably after going online (Barber & Odean, 1999).

Choi, Laibson, and Metrick (2001) document several other patterns: young, male, and wealthy participants are more likely to try the Web for trading. Participants who try the Web tend to do smaller than phone trades both in dollars and as a fraction of the portfolio being traded. Lastly, "short-term" trades make up a higher proportion of phone trades than Web trades.

There is even a relatively new breed of market participant known as "day traders," that is, retail customers of brokerage firms who attempt to make profits intraday on small changes on the price of stocks who may also affect price for some securities. Some day traders may add to market depth by providing instant liquidity while those who try to profit from short-term momentum cycles probably increase market volatility (Barber & Odean, 2001).

The Investment Style of Online Investors

The investment style of online investors differs from other investors. Online investors tilt their investments towards small-growth stocks with high market risk. Since the tilt towards small-growth stocks with high market risk is apparent

both before and after online trading, Barber and Odean (1999) found that it does not appear that the switch from phone-based to online investing is accompanied by a significant change in the stock investor's own style.

An investor may trade common stocks for many reasons. An investor with a bonus to invest or a large bill to pay may buy or sell for liquidity reasons. If one security in his/her portfolio appreciates considerably, he/she may rebalance to restore diversification to his/her portfolio. He/she may sell to capture a tax loss or may trade to speculate. The proposition that more information leads to better decision making is intuitively appealing. But the truth of the proposition depends on the relevance of the information to the decision and how well equipped the decision maker is to use the information. Similarly, abundant data may encourage investors to try to beat a market that is not fully efficient, but few have the ability to beat through skill (Barber & Odean, 2001).

Competitive markets will become fragmented in response to the diverse demand of investors. Some investors will prefer one type of market, while others will prefer other types. No single market structure will satisfy the needs of all investors. Some fragmentation is a natural result of competition (Blume, 2000).

HOW ONLINE INVESTORS AFFECT MARKETS

Web access could be expected to increase activity. Since the prevalence of such behaviour, especially when motivated by noise, can play a role in stabilising or destabilising markets, it is useful to know whether such activity is indeed increased by this new technology. Choi et al. (2001) found that the Web affected both trading frequency and trade size.

It is very difficult to test whether a stock is mispriced. Furthermore, to some economists it is nearly technological that the market price of a stock is the right price. The experimental economics literature has spelled out the conditions that are most conducive to prolonged mispricing and speculative bubbles: when there is greater uncertainty about the future value of a security. E-commerce and the market have helped to create the conditions (Barber & Odean, 2001).

These very active investors are often making decisions in a situation of high uncertainty. One measure of these heterogeneous beliefs and uncertainty is the volatility of stock returns. The volatility of individual stock has increased dramatically since the 1960s. In the 1990s, the volatility of these high-turnover stocks rose to nearly double its highs from the previous three-decade levels (Choi et al., 2001).

Effects of ECN Trading on Overall Market Quality

The total cost to trade includes not only the commission charge but also differences in stock purchase or sale price that may result from different methods of executing trades.

Determining whether investors were getting the best possible executions of their orders was difficult because the quality depended on a number of factors, such as price, speed, and the likelihood of execution. Some online brokerages had problems ensuring quality execution of trading orders, SEC and NASD require broker-dealers to obtain the best execution available under the circumstances for their customer orders.

Online investors can take steps to help ensure quality trade executions. The SEC found that many online broker-dealers would accommodate a customer's request to route an order to a specific market center, although the customer would likely be charged higher commission fees. Investors may be able to offset the higher fees by getting better prices for their trades. The chairman of the SEC said investors would benefit greatly from more information about execution quality.

Overconfidence and Trading on Financial Markets

There has been much speculation that the development of the Internet and the World Wide Web has had a significant impact on financial market behaviours (Yue et al., 2000). The change in trading behaviour that takes place when investors go online have increased stock market volume and volatility (Choi et al., 2001). This research attempts to provide a description of the theory that overconfidence leads to excessive trading.

The only careful analysis of the behaviour of online investors is Barber and Odeon (1999), who focussed on the trading behaviour and investment performance of investors who switch from the phone to an online channel. Data constraints prevented detailed studies of individual investor's behaviour and performance. Barber and Odeon (2001) discovered many stylized facts: for investors who stay off-line, the more investors trade, the worse they perform (after transaction costs), and men perform worse than women. Barber and Odeon show that many of these results can be reconciled if investors are overconfident of their investment success.

Overconfident investors may trade even with their expected gains although tradings are not enough to offset trading cost (Odean, 1999). Lower costs and more alternatives clearly benefit investors. Many of today's investors are new to the market. Placing trades directly, rather than through a broker, can give such investors an exaggerated sense of control over the outcome of their trades. The vast amount of online investment data available will enable investors to confirm their prior beliefs and may lead them to become overconfident in their ability to pick stock and other securities. Faster feedback may focus the investor's attention on recent performance. Markets in which valuation are uncertain, investors are active and inexperienced, and money to invest is readily available are prone to speculative bubbles, which can hurt all investors (Barber & Odean, 2001).

The Internet has brought changes to investing which may bolster the overconfidence of online investors by providing an illusion of knowledge and an illusion of control, while also changing the decision criteria to which investors attend. These very active investors are often making decisions in a situation of high uncertainty. Online investors have concentrated their trading in e-commerce and other high-tech firms. Many e-commerce firms have novel, untested business plans. Many have little or no earning. Values are based on distant projections, about which there is much disagreement. However, due to the illusions of knowledge and control, and the tendency of people in an information-rich environment to become more set in their beliefs, the volume and variety of information available online have probably led to greater dispersion of beliefs and greater investor overconfidence (Barber & Odean, 2000).

Overconfidence led them to trade active, and active trading caused subpar performance. Overconfidence occurs when factors ordinarily associated with improved performance in skilled situations, such as choice, task familiarity, competition, and active involvement are present in situations at least partly governed by chance.

As an innovative communication medium and information source, the Web has a great capacity to alter trading behaviour along many dimensions (Choi et al., 2001). Online investors have access to vast quantities of investment data. These data can foster an illusion of knowledge, which increases overconfidence. Online investors generally manage their own stock portfolios and execute trades at the click of a mouse. This fosters an illusion of control, which reinforces overconfidence (Barber & Odean, 1999).

The basic idea is that risk averse, overconfident traders trade more aggressively based on valid information than do rational traders (Odean, 1999). As a result, overconfident traders are better able to exploit risky profit opportunities created

by the trades of liquidity—motivated traders or the mistakes of noise traders (Hirshleifer & Luo, 2001; Yue et al., 2000).

REGULATION

Regulation has facilitated the ECNs' inroads into NASDAQ trading. The ECNs new order handling rules (the limit order display rule and the market maker rule) have made it much easier for a new ECN to capture public order flow (Schwartz, 2000).

Alternative Trading System (ATS)

In the United States, alternative trading systems (ATS) have been used since 1969 (instinet) and were able to acquire a significant market share by offering integrated electronic order routing and matching services for securities trading, by providing benefits to retail and institutional investors, such as better price and lower commissions as the traditional exchanges. Thus, they attract not only professional but also retail investors to their systems (Holtmann, Lattemann, Stefan, & Weinhardt, 2001).

The SEC (2000) defines ATS as "automated systems that centralise, display, match, cross or otherwise execute trading interests, but that are not currently registered with the commission as national securities exchanges or operated by registered securities association."

ATS typically have sophisticated IT infrastructures that have been designed from scratch to support the relevant phases in the transaction process—particularly the automated matching and price discovery (SEC, 2000; Holtmann et al., 2001). This enables ATS to

- Underbid the fees exchanges charge to their customers.
- Act more flexibly to varying customer demands or market trends.

- Establish themselves as competitors for the traditional exchanges.

Global Trading

The market of tomorrow will be global. Technology will allow a market center or order gathering function to be located anywhere in the world. A national market system assumes that one market will best serve the needs of all investors. Investors have different needs and different markets will develop to serve these needs.

Monitoring and regulating this movement to global trading will be one of the major regulatory challenges over the next decade. It will require that domestic regulators coordinate their regulations with those of other countries.

NASDAQ has formed an alliance with the Hong Kong Stock Exchange to trade some of the more active NASDAQ stocks in Hong Kong in Hong Kong dollars during Hong Kong business hours. NASDAQ has also formed a joint venture to trade Japanese stock and U.S. stocks in Japan. Once it becomes cheap and easy to trades across borders, there will be increased trading across borders.

Today, a major barrier to the trading of U.S. equities worldwide is the settlement process. The settling of trades is even more centralised for any particular issue, if the issue is registered either directly in the name of the owner or indirectly through an intermediary. In the United States, the Depository Trust and Clearing Corporation (DTCC) is the focal point for this transferring of ownership from one entity to another. The DTCC guarantees the contra-party risk. The problems that must be overcome in establishing global settlement platforms are interrelated (Blume, 2000).

It is imperative that U.S. regulatory bodies change their focus from the regulation of a domestic U.S. equity market to the challenges of regulating in a global market.

CONCLUSION

This chapter presented what extant of the subject area of this research. Online stock trading mechanisms at exchanges are often hybrid of dealer and auction markets. Different aspects of trading execution, which is the most commonly used market centre at present, were discussed. This led to discussion of the way of execute order is organised and what is the impact on effective market performance, trading costs, and investor behaviour.

The chapter's objective led to establishing the case for the research question: To investigate the impact, if any way, of online trading with ECNs, on effective market performance, trading costs, and investors' behaviour as opposed to market makers. In the future, researchers should empirically compare stock trading with ECNs and market makers. This will establish the impact of online trading on market performance. The findings will be helpful for investors to make cost-effective investment strategies.

REFERENCES

Barber, B.M., & Odean, T. (1999). *Online investors: Do the slow die first?* (Working paper). Davis: University of California.

Barber, B.M., & Odean, T. (2000). The Internet and the investor. *Journal of Economic Perspectives, 15*(1), 41–54.

Barber, B.M., & Odean, T. (2000). Trading is hazardous to your wealth: The common stock investment performance of individual investors. *The Journal of Finance, 4*(2), 773–806.

Barber, B.M., & Odean, T. (2001). Boys will be boys: Gender, overconfidence, and common stock investment. *The Quarterly Journal of Economics*, February, 261–292.

Barclay, M.J., Hendershott, T., & McCormick, T. (2001). *Electronic communications networks and market quality.* University of Rochester, NY, May 2001, pp. 1–38.

Blume, M.E. (2000, October 16). The structure of the U.S. equity markets. Paper presented at the *Financial Markets Conference,* Federal Reserve Bank of Atlanta, Sea Island, Georgia, University of Pennsylvania.

Choi, J.J., Laibson, D., & Metrick, A. (2001). How does the Internet affect trading? Evidence from investor behaviour in 401 (K) plans. *The Rodney L. White Center for Fianncial Research,* March, 1–68.

Daniel, K., Hirshleifer, D., & Subrahmanyam, A. (1997). A theory of overconfidence, self-attribution, and security market under- and over-reactions. February 19, pp 1–57.

Fan, M., Stallaert, J., & Whinston A.B. (2000). The Internet and the future of financial markets. *Communications of the Association for Computer Machinery, 43*(11), 83–88.

Hirshleifer, D., & Luo, G.Y. (2001). On the survival of overconfident traders in a competitive securities market. *Journal of Financial Markets,* 1–39.

Holtmann, C., Lattemann, C., Stefan, S., & Weinhardt, C. (2001). Transforming financial markets to retail investors. *Proceedings of the 34th Annual Hawaii International Conference on System Sciences (HICSS), 34*(1), 1–8.

Konana, P., Menon, N.M., & Balasubramanian, S. (2000). The implications of online investing. *Communications of the Association for Computer Machinery, 34*(1), 35–41.

Naik, N., & Yadav, P. (1999). The effects of market reform on trading costs of public investors: Evidence from the London Stock Exchange. June, 1–46.

Odean, T. (1999). Do investors trade too much? *American Economic Review,* December, 1–39.

Schwartz, R.A. (2002). Building a better stock market: New solution to old problems. *Social Science,* January, 1–29.

U.S. General Accounting Office (GAO). (2000). On-line trading: Better investor protection information needed on brokers' Web sites. May, 1–43.

U.S. Securities and Exchange Commission (SEC). (n.d.). Investor tips: Trade execution. Retrieved June 30, 2002, from *www.sec.gov/investor/pubs/tradexec.htm*

U.S. Securities and Exchange Commission (SEC). (n.d.). Investor tips: Trading in fast-moving markets. Retrieved June 30, 2002, from *www.sec.gov/invstor/pubs/onlinetips.htm*

U.S. Securities and Exchange Commission (SEC). (n.d.). Special study: Communication network and after-hour trading. Retrieved June 30, 2002, from *www.sec.gov/news/studies/ecnafter.htm*

Yue, W.T., Chaturvedi, A.R., & Mehta, S. (2000). Is more information better? The effect of traders' irrational behaviour on an artificial stock market. Purdue University, pp. 660–666.

This work was previously published in Internet Strategy: The Road to Web Services Solutions, edited by M. W. Guah and W. Currie, pp. 67-85, copyright 2006 by IRM Press (an imprint of IGI Global).

Chapter XIV
M–Commerce Payment Systems

Valli Kumari Vatsavayi
Andhra University, India

Ravi Mukkamala
Old Dominion University, USA

ABSTRACT

With mobile operators having a large customer base and e-payments getting popular, there is a shift of focus on the huge potential that the mobile commerce (m-commerce) market offers. Mobile payment (m-payment) service is the core for the success of m-commerce. M-payments allow customers to buy digital goods from anywhere and anytime using Internet and mobile environments. Ubiquity, reachability, localization, personalization, and dissemination of information are the characteristics that favor m-payments and encourage the consumers and merchants to use them. This chapter examines various aspects of m-payments like architectures, limitations, security, and trust issues. It also discusses and compares the existing payment procedures of several different companies providing m-payment services. While exploring the advantages of shifting to m-payments, the problems that have to be dealt with when adopting new solutions are discussed. Finally, the chapter concludes by identifying a common set of requirements criteria for successful global m-payments.

INTRODUCTION

M-commerce allows customers to buy goods from anywhere and anytime using the Internet and mobile environments. The content for which the payment is made may be digital goods (e.g., downloading software, e-books, and tickets) or services (e.g., auctions, games, booking tickets, trading, healthcare, and auto parking).

Mobile-phone-based services are becoming an important target for business. M-payment is about using the mobile phone for making payments. This provides a good experience combining convenience with flexibility to the customer while making payments. The customer does shopping online and uses the mobile phone to pay for a product or service or make transactions. There is no need to carry a personal wallet. A customer is required to give a unique code for recognition by the bank when making payments. The payment is made only after validation is done. Shopping is finished, after delivery of the goods depending on the type of goods and mode of delivery. Requirements of mobility by consumers and businesses show a need for rise in the m-payment services. M-payments are an important aspect of M-Commerce that allow and enable secure payments and settling credit and debit claims.

In 2002 and 2003, due to the hype and later crash of new technologies, companies resisted investments in new technologies; since then the number of mobile device users has grown dramatically. According to Lombardi (2006) as of December 2005, there were more than 2 billion mobile connections globally. According to the Mercator Advisory Group (2006), almost 208 million Americans in the year 2005 were cell phone subscribers, as shown in Figure 1.

In China, according to China's Ministry of Information, the number of mobile phone users has passed 400 million in February 2006 and by 2009 it is expected to pass 600 million (Nystedt, 2006). In the European Union (EU) more than 80% of the population has mobile phones (Damsgaard & Marchegiani, 2004). With consumers spending in excess of £700 million during 2005 in the UK, and German consumers spending an average of €4.50 each month on mobile downloads, it is a lucrative market. According to Telecom Regulatory Authority of India (TRAI), there are 90 million cell phone subscribers in India. Mobile

phone penetration has almost saturated a few Asian countries as shown in Figure 2 (Mercator Advisory Group Report 2, 2006).

Thus m-commerce has the potential for explosive growth and that m-payments could be the next "killer application" for business (Aswin, 2003). Though the m-payment market did not live up to the expectations because of multiple service providers and a variety of payment solutions and technologies, it has gained a reasonable level of acceptance. Obviously any customer would adapt to a new payment technology if thorough solutions to his prime concerns of cost, convenience, and security are provided. Mostly the transactional costs that the customer will have to pay should be negligible when compared to the cost of the transaction. Finally, the m-payment vision is to transform the mobile phone into a personal mobile wallet holding credit cards, debit account information, and mobile cash for transactions (Ding & Unnithan, 2004).

A few m-payment applications suggested in the literature are (Gross, Fleisch, Lampe, & Miller, 2004):

- Automated point-of-sales payments (vending machines, parking meters, and ticket machines).

Figure 1. Cellular subscriber growth in USA (Mercator Advisory Group Report 1, 2006)

Year	Approx. Customers (millions)	Approx. annual Revenues in $(billions)
1995	45	20
1999	75	42
2001	125	64
2005	230	100

Figure 2. Mobile phone penetration and subscribers in Asia (Mercator Advisory Group Report 2, 2006)

Country	Mobile subscribers (millions)	Mobile penetration
China	400	31%
Japan	90.7	71%
South Korea	37.5	77%
Taiwan	22.7	99%
Malaysia	19.5	81%
Hongkong	6.8	99%
Singapore	4.3	97%

- Attended point-of-sale payments (shop counters, taxis).
- Mobile-accessed Internet payments (merchant wireless application protocol [WAP] sites).
- Mobile assisted Internet payments (fixed Internet sites using phone instead of credit card).
- Peer-to-peer payments between individuals.

Several m-payment schemes have been successful, but all have been limited in implementation and geography (Bradford, 2003). In order that consumers and merchants accept m-payments globally, an interoperable set of standards and payment systems is needed. Implementing m-payment infrastructure and consumer adoption is fairly complex and is exemplified by the retraction of several m-payment mediators like Paybox (Jones, 2003).

In this chapter, several issues faced by m-payment systems are discussed along with their implementations, successes, and failures. The perspectives and challenges in providing effective m-payment solutions are discussed. Initially, the requirements and the need for m-payments are discussed. Later, categorization of m-payments based on various criteria is given. Then, various existing successful payment system processes and the technical and security issues are discussed. A comparison of these systems is given. Based on these observations a common set of requirements criteria for successful global m-payments is suggested.

E-PAYMENTS TO M-PAYMENTS

Introduction

Any payments made through an electronic terminal to order, instruct, or authorize a financial institution to debit or credit an account is called

Figure 3. Expected popularity of m-commerce/m-payments region wise (Little, 2004)

Year	Europe	Asia & Australia
2004	2%	0%
2006	6%	43%
2008	51%	71%

as an *electronic payment*. Mobile Payment Forum (www.mobilepaymentforum.com), defines *"mobile payment* as the process of two parties exchanging financial value using a mobile device in return for goods or services."

An electronic payment requires a connection to the Internet to fulfill the payment. In m-payment, the mobile device uses a wireless connection to interact with multiple parties involved in the transaction. There are several factors that are driving the merchants to shift to m-payment-based solutions. One of the main reasons is that the device used by the consumer for making payments is usually the personal trusted device. The other possible reason could be to tap the potential mobile services market. The services can be offered round the clock as m-payments are location independent and can be used anytime and anywhere.

Already, the m-payments market started becoming popular around the world. Based on the table shown in Figure 3 the penetration of m-payments services is greater in Asia and Australia when compared to Europe and the USA (Little, 2004). Currently, Japan is the only country in the world that has fully adopted m-payments to exchange e-mail, search for restaurants, train schedules, store photos, and listen to music.

Key Players in M-Payments

The key players in the payment process are (Stallings, 2000):

Figure 4. Simple m-payment process (MeT, 2003)

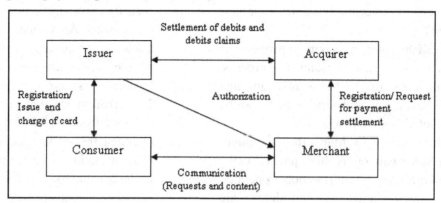

- **Consumers:** A consumer or a customer is an authorized party, allowed to make payments through his/her mobile device. He/she is usually registered with mobile network operators or financial institutions usually called issuers. A consumer holds an account with them from which credits and debits are made.
- **Merchants:** A merchant is an organization or a person that has goods or services to sell to the consumer. A merchant is usually associated with an acquirer.
- **Issuer:** An issuer is usually a financial institution or a mobile network operator, who maintains the accounts of consumers and makes payments on behalf of the consumer.
- **Acquirer:** An acquirer is a financial institution or a mobile network operator who maintains the account on behalf of merchant and performs transfer of funds on his behalf.
- **Certification authority:** It is an authority that issues X.509 v3 certificates to banks, consumers, and merchants. These certificates allow in distribution of public keys of banks, consumers, and merchants.

M-payment process (Figure 4) has the following steps in general:

1. **Registration:** The consumer registers with an issuer for the payment service.
2. **Payment submission:** The merchant communicates to the user about the goods and services. The consumer selects goods and submits payment.
3. **Authentication:** The merchant authenticates the consumer and requests authorization by contacting the issuer.
4. **Authorization:** The issuer sends authorization information. The merchant sends this information to acquirer. Acquirer and issuer settle the claims by performing appropriate debits and credits.
5. **Confirmation:** The consumer gets confirmation message after the transaction is completed.

Now we discuss the general requirements, advantages, and limitations of m-payments systems.

Why M-Payments?

In this section reasons that support a shift from e-payments to m-payments are given:

- **Personalization and convenience:** Consumer uses the mobile device which is easy to carry and is usually a personal device. This ensures traceability and trust for merchants.

- **Established airtime payment process:** E-payment is already an established process. Payment for airtime too is an established one. Hence payment service costs can be computed in an amicable way.
- **Mobile operators know the customers and hence can act as third party:** As the consumer registers with the mobile operator, consumer's whereabouts and identity are known. Thus, the mobile operator can act as a third party for all transactions between merchant and consumer.
- **Allows both voice and text communication:** Mobile devices allow both voice and data to be communicated. This enables multiple services to be offered to consumers.
- **Ubiquity:** Accessibility from any part of the world; transactions can be done instantaneously irrespective of time and place.

- **Security:** SIM card and PIN ensure more security of transactions when compared to e-payments. As mobile network operators know the consumers, the transactions done by the consumers are authenticated and hence more secure.
- **Localization:** Depending on the geographical area from which the device is being operated, the services according to the local customs and preferences may be provided to the consumers.
- **Existing consumer base and Less time to adapt:** Existing customer base of e-commerce is a potential for m-commerce, and the time and effort required to shift to m-commerce is less.
- **Availability in remote towns and villages:** Mobile services can reach remote villages and towns and would give the merchants access to a wide range of consumers.
- **Person-to-person (P2P) transactions:** Interpersonal (P2P) transactions are easy with mobile phones.

In addition, Figure 5 lists a set of benefits ordered by priorities assigned by a group customers when asked about why they prefer m-payments (Little, 2004).

Issues with M-Payments

Most of the limitations of m-payments are due to the mobile device constraints. For instance keyboard, display, memory, processing, and bandwidth are some of the limited resources which prevent implementation of highly secure and efficient m-payment solutions. But as the capabilities of mobile devices are increasing, possibly in future the aforementioned limitations may soon be void, as large screens and broad band access may make them attractive.

Other than the device restrictions, the issues that are restricting m-payments solutions from being adopted are:

Figure 5. Benefits of m-commerce/m-payment for consumers (Little, 2004)

Benefits	Importance (1 to 5 point scale)
Less limitations in time and space	4.4
Avoiding counting and carrying coins	3.5
Customer security	3.4
Life style	3.1
Cost effective payment method	2.7
Avoiding carrying different cards	2.6
Customer anonymity	2.6
Avoiding carrying different currencies	2.1
Access to additional source of credit	2.1

- **Anonymity:** Sharing data with many parties keeps the customers away from online payments, even though it is convenient, they wish to be anonymous.
- **Possibility of theft:** The mobile device gets lost more easily than a credit card. So, consumers may refrain from using the mobile device as a wallet.
- **Signal reception:** Quality of signal reception can be limited (e.g., in buildings). This may prevent transactions from being carried out or completed with less reliability.
- **High costs:** As currently, there are no interoperable global solutions for m-payments settlement of roaming becomes complex. Usually, the mobile operators or banks have a high credit risk. Other than these costs, the service provider investment is high for implementing and upgrading the solutions.
- **Hardware and software flexibility:** Hardware and software used for the m-payment solutions is relatively inflexible.

Requirements for M-Payments

The success of m-payments entirely depends on consumer and merchant willingness to adopt the payment process. The different characteristics based on which consumers and merchants would choose the payment model are broadly classified into three categories: strategic, operational, and participant characteristics (Kreyer, Pousttchi, & Turowski, 2002). The identification of strategic characteristics allows the choice of a payment model based on payment scenario or the size of the payment. Operational characteristics depend on the type, mode, frequency, time, and basis of payment. The participants are the key players mentioned in the previous sections and their characteristics might also lead to choice in the payment system to be adopted. Based on Ondrus and Pigneur (2006) and considering customer and merchant perspectives, the following are the general

characteristics required of effective and successful m-payments.

- **Ease of use/convenience:** The payment process should be simple to learn and convenient to use to enable more consumers to prefer the payment method.
- **Low cost to implement:** For the merchant and the service provider, process should take less investment in terms of infrastructure and technologies upgrading.
- **Reliability:** The process should be reliable and less prone to fraudulent activities.
- **User/market acceptance:** A user obviously gets inclined more to use a widely accepted payment process. Thus maturity of the process is the key factor that counts for an m-payment's success. Existing solutions should be used where applicable. Any payment solution should offer better profits to all parties concerned.
- **Security:** End to end security has to be guaranteed. In this process the essential security services like authentication, confidentiality, integrity, and non-repudiation should be possible. Banks should be able to authenticate their customer while providing banking and payment services. No party should deny having done any transaction, thus enabling non-repudiation. The details about the transactions should not be visible to third parties, thus achieving confidentiality. The messages sent and received during transactions should not be modifiable and should ensure integrity. In addition to these, many users wish to remain anonymous while making payments (Nambiar & Lu, 2005).
- **Flexibility:** The system should be flexible in nature, that is, it should be possible to enhance and include new features, as the requirements of the customers and technologies change day to day. Open and non-proprietary solutions, if used, will make the solutions more flexible.

- **Speed:** In spite of the fact that mobile devices have their own limitations with respect to memory and computing power the payment transactions should be completed at desirable speeds. The ACID properties (atomicity, consistency, independence, durability) should hold good for the transactions.
- **Scalability:** The payment solutions should be scalable in nature.

Generally speaking, it is observed that unless security is high, and the payment solution is convenient and simple, the customer would not be convinced to adopt the m-payment solution. After the customer wishes to use the mobile device for payment he/she would choose a solution only if it is broadly accepted, costs less, and the customer is free to choose the handset, the bank, and the mobile network operator independent of each other. The additional services opted by the customer are usually anonymity, traceability, convertibility, and portability.

On similar lines the merchant requirements include, guaranteed payment for services provided, customer relationship and high diffusion into the customer community. And the cost to adopt the solutions should be less. Based on these requirements factors, an assessment of several successful and unsuccessful payment systems is done in the later sections.

Security in M-Payments

Most of the time the level of security required is based on transactions amount. There are a few cases where no security is required at all, say for picopayments. In such low-valued transactions the cost of implementing security is more than the worth of the transaction and hence no security may be provided. But if the consumer requires that irrespective of the value of the transaction, any transaction should be made only by him/her, then a PIN may be used for encryption. It is known only to the consumer and no one else can perform

the transaction. In cases where the transactions will have to be authenticated, digital certificates (X.509 v3) based keys may be used for both authentication and encryption. A more advanced and reliable technique to make transactions secure are the use of smart cards. By using smart cards high levels of security can be achieved.

Many communication security protocols are used for m-payments. WAP (McKitterrick & Dowling, 2003) provides a mechanism for displaying Internet information on a WAP-enabled mobile device. The basis for WAP 1.x security is Wireless Transport Layer Security (WTLS) standard, which is on the other hand based on TLS. WAP 2.0 provides enhanced security as it encompasses several standards that ensure security at application level, transport level, and management level. Several standards used in WAP are: (1) WAP Identity Module (WIP) which is a tamper resistant smart card chip stored on mobile device and is capable of storing Public Key Infrastructure (PKI) keys; (2) WMLSCrypt, WML Script Crypto API is an application programming interface that uses security functions in WMLS Crypto Library (WMLSCLib) and WIM for providing basic security services; and (3) Wireless PKI (WPKI) is an optimized extension of traditional PKI for wireless environment.

CATEGORIZATIONS OF M-PAYMENT SYSTEMS: A SURVEY

In this section, several categorizations are given to enable a better understanding of the m-payment systems. These categorizations can then be used to develop a requirements framework for global m-payment systems.

Payment Systems Categorization

In this section we give a broad overview of different categorizations proposed in the literature (Buhan, Cheong, & Tan, 2002; Kountz, 2002;

Ondrus, 2003; Schwiderski-Grosche & Knospe, 2002).

Categorization Based on Money Model

- **Token based:** A token is issued for exchange of money. This token represents monitory value. This instead can be used for a goods purchase, and this token is then en-cashed with the issuing financial institution.
- **Notational:** The value equivalent to some cash is stored in an account with a financial institution and is exchanged by authorization.

Categorization by Proximity

- **Remote payments:** Remote mobile transactions span from the purchase of ring tones and logos sent to the mobile phone, for purchasing goods, services, and content during a browsing session with online mobile merchant sites (Ondrus, 2003). In remote transactions there are at least four parties involved: (1) merchant, (2) acquirer, (3) issuer, and (4) customer. A customer registers with the issuer. This enables the merchant to trust the customer. The customer visits the Web site through a mobile network and selects the item to be purchased, the payment method, and confirms the request through a PIN. The customer then receives the acknowledgement receipt. The goods are then delivered to the appropriate place.
- **Local payments:** Local payments are usually done through communication protocols like Radio Frequency Identification (RFID) and Blue tooth, Infrared, WLAN 802.11. Local payments are usually made when using vending machines or through a parking fee or toll gate fee. Europay, MasterCard, & Visa(EMV) is also used for mobile environments.

Categorization Based on Time of Payment

- **Pre-paid systems:** With prepaid accounts the customer pays before obtaining the content.
- **Pay-now systems:** In this system a customer's account is debited at the time of payment.
- **Post-pay systems:** In this system a merchant's account is credited before the customer's account is debited.

Categorization by Seller/Buyer Origin

- **P2P m-payments:** In a P2P payment system there are three parties involved: consumer, merchant, and the P2P payment service provider. The consumer and merchant hold an account with the service provider. The service provider keeps track of funds available to both the consumer and merchant. With P2P, if the consumer has deposited the appropriate funds at the P2P payment service then the transaction is approved and the purchase amount is deducted from the consumer's account and added to the merchant's account. The most popular P2P service is PayPal.
- **Business-to-consumer (B2C) m-payments:** B2C payment services are usually used for services like mobile ticketing and mobile gaming.
- **Business-to-business (B2B) m-payments:** The demand for retail m-commerce may drive the B2B payments and applications. Banks can use the infrastructure used for retail m-payments and brokerage services for corporate customers too. While corporate customers' payment information is stored in bank servers, the retail payment information is stored on a phone chip, card readers attached to the phone, or on a central server accessed via internet (Aswin, 2003).

Categorization Based on Applications Installed

Mobile wallet is a trusted application installed in the mobile phone, which allows cards, tokens, tickets, reminders, and receipts to be stored. Most of the global payments are card based. It is possible that in the future multiple virtual cards issued by different parties will have to be dealt with by the mobile devices. The wallet also helps in making remote and local payments possible. The wallet can be secured using a PIN and other such mechanisms. It is also possible to access other security elements like WIM from wallet applications (MeT, 2003). There are two categories based on whether devices are installed with applications or not (Seah et al., 2001).

- **Device without payment applications:** The wallet is held in a remote site, like in PayBox. The charges are debited from the subscriber's account.
- **Device with payment applications:** Payment applications are installed in the devices in this category.

Categorization by Clearing and Settlement Method

- **Bilateral:** Bilateral payments are limited to just one mobile operator and one bank, which restricts participation to the mutual customers of just these two organizations.
- **Multilateral:** Multilateral payment offsets the debits and credits accumulated by each member against the other members in the process of transactions. The advantage of multilateral clearing or payments is that multiple currencies can be supported.
- **Using intermediaries:** A third party can be used as an intermediary to settle payments.

Categorization by Mode of Registration

- **Registration required:** A few services require the consumers to register with the payment solution provider, by giving some personal information.
- **Registration not required:** A few payment systems do not require any prior customer registration.

Categorization by Type of Transaction

- **Pay per view (PPV):** It is a service where conditional access is given to use a particular program. A popular service is a pay television program for which a consumer pays a separate fee for each program like a movie or a sporting event.
- **Pay per unit (PPU):** The payment made is made whenever a unit of goods is bought like when buying a ring tone. Each time the ring tone is downloaded, a payment has to be made.
- **Subscription:** Instead of viewing a program just once, a service can be subscribed for a given period of time.

Categorization by Scenarios

- The following are the scenarios mentioned by Kreyer et al. (2002). M-commerce (all service), e-commerce (all kinds of B2C transactions like purchasing goods via the Internet using debit/credit cards), stationary merchant (face to face [F2F] conventional purchase like a purchase in super market, auto parking using cash or debit/credit cards), and customer-to-customer (C2C) (transfer of money between individuals through cash or offline transactions).

Categorization Based on Payment Amount (Size of Amount)

- **Pico-payments:** The transaction is done for very small amounts. A survey (Kreyer et al., 2002) reported that consumers prefer payments with mobile devices when the amounts are small to average.
- **Micro-payments:** The transaction is done for average amounts.
- **Macro-payments:** The transaction has large value.

Categorization by Type of Purchase

- Physical goods, digital/electronic goods, rights: The digital products can be general services or entertainment content or services.
  General Services:
  - Messaging services (notification etc.)
  - Directory enquiries (phone numbers, addresses, etc.)
  - Commercial content (news, etc.)
  - Off-line applications (dictionary, road maps)
  Entertainment:
  - Messaging content (voice greetings, etc.)
  - Online games (multiple choice, etc.)
  - Online services(like chatting)
  - Off-line games (Pac man)

Categorization Based on Validation Payments

- **Online validation:** A trusted third party is used to establish a trust relationship between two or more entities unknown to each other. All the transactions are validated by the trusted third party.
- **Off-line:** No third party is involved in transactions between merchant and the consumer.
- **Semi-online:** There is some involvement of the trusted party, but not at each payment.

Categorization by Technology Used

- **SMS based:** All the SMS-based payments are made through text messaging to a given number, amount, and the destination of the payment. A popular SMS based payment is PayPal Mobile.
- **WAP:** The simplest form of WAP-based payment is the basic key-entered transaction. Using a mobile device, the payment application prompts a merchant through a series of screens for key, entering the transaction amount, card number, and expiration date to receive an authorization. This method is the lowest cost of entry for a mobile merchant, but it is less secure.
- **Dual-slot/dual card phone:** A SIM card is inserted like in ItiAchat payment system in the traditional slot of the mobile phone and the payment card is inserted in the second slot.
- **Special payment software:** A few payment solutions require specific applications to be installed.

Categorization Based on Solution Provider

The provider could be a financial service provider like Mobile operators, Banks, Ecash providers, or payment service providers like IBM, Unwire, and so forth.

Categorization by Geography

A few solutions are specific to a region, while a few others are applicable to consumers in several nations. Thus, a few solutions support just single currency, while others allow exchange of currencies. Hence the categories are:

- Domestic/Cross-border
- Single currency/multiple currency

Categorization by Location of Payers' Account Details

A few categorizations focus on the whereabouts of money stored on a smart card (hardware based), electronic money stored on mobile device in a file format (software based) device, and money kept in a background account.

- Network/server based
- Client based (device/card)

Categorization Based on User Preferences

According to Zmijewska, Lawrence, and Steele (2004), m-payments should be categorized based on user preferences, as user-centric categorizations will allow system providers to see how their systems are perceived by the consumer, comparing those of their competitors. The dimensions that were proposed are: change of phone requirement, registration requirement, available phone operating company to which the company has to subscribe, available applications, communication of consumer's number to start transaction, communication of transaction details to user, acceptance of transaction by user, confirmation to customer, payment occurrence, brand visible of consumer, value of payment, registration fee, transaction cost for consumer, and time of transaction.

Kreyer et al. (2002) proposed a morphological box of m-payment characteristics, though exhaustive, it is quite difficult to assess a given payment system. The characteristics given are: payment scenarios, payment heights, involved parties, receiver of customer data, the need for pre-registration, technology required, basis of payment, payment frequency, deduction time, and method for settlement.

M-PAYMENT SYSTEMS

We discuss a few existing mobile systems (Carat, 2002; Meister, 2005; Ondrus & Pigneur, 2006; Zmijewska et al., 2004) in this section.

Vodafone M-Pay Bill

Vodafone m-Pay Bill is a simple, easy to use system that supports virtual point-of-sale (POS) for micro and small payments. Bill is charged via customer's phone bill or from prepaid airtime. There are three entities in this system: customer, merchant, and m-Pay Bill server. The Vodafone customer registers for m-Pay Bill online by entering their mobile phone number, PIN, and other credentials. The amount is then charged along with the phone bill or deducted from prepaid airtime.

The only problem with the system is that the customer data is maintained in a server and is shared with other service providers for interoperability and thus this prevents privacy. Though there is no joining fee, the customer needs to register as a member.

TextPayMe

TextPayMe (https://www.textpayme.com) allows P2P payments to be sent from both the mobile phone and the Web browser. TextPayMe aims to solve the unattended parking market, simple F2F transactions with merchants, and transfer of funds between individuals for tasks as simple as splitting dinner bills. The only requirement is that the phone should be able to send and receive text messages. No installations are necessary. Even if the mobile device is lost, the consumer need not worry as enough steps are taken to prevent fraud. The payment steps are as follows. The customer needs to initially select a credit card or bank account as the source of funds. The customer sends an SMS to TextPayMe with a mobile number specified. Then the mobile phone authorization process can be initiated. A phone call is received after that asking for a PIN to authorize the payment and complete the transaction. Cancellation of the transaction is also possible.

TextPayMe claims providing a convenient and secure solution that works with virtually every mobile phone model across all major carriers in the United States. Currently, TextPayMe users are limited to sending and receiving a maximum of USD $500 a month.

M-Pay

PBS, Orange, and Gemplus support the m-pay system (http://www.m-pay.com). A WAP-enabled phone is required to use this system. It is based on server-based credit/debit cards and a WAP-based mobile phone or PC and the Internet. Initially the customer has to register with the payment server. A PIN is allocated which is installed on a SIM card in the mobile phone. The customer then sends a purchase request via SMS to a merchant. This message is sent to the payment server. The payment server authorizes the payment request by sending a confirmation request to the customer. The customer confirms by entering the PIN. The server then debits the amount from the appropriate account. Confirmation is then sent to the payment gateway, which in turn generates a receipt and sends it to the merchant.

To use the m-pay system, the customers will have to register for free. Customers will then have to buy airtime and the amount is automatically drawn from their credit/debit card account. The advantage of this system is that customer's sensitive information is not put online. The system also claims fraud prevention mechanisms. The user's identity is defined on a SIM card in the mobile phone and is further secured by entering a special PIN either on a phone or payment terminal. The payment terminal and payment center authenti-

cate mutually with a digital signature based on the Elliptic Curve Cryptography (ECC) cryptographic system (public key cryptography using elliptic curves). Data encryption is performed according to a validated digital signature. End-to-end encryption is available for third parties, such as banks.

Paybox

Paybox.net (http://www.paybox.de) AG was founded in July 1999 and launched in 2000 by Deutsche Bank, Debitel AG. It covers Germany, Austria, Spain, Sweden, and the UK. This is used for P2P and also real and virtual POS payment via mobile phone. Registration with Paybox is needed and Paybox provides the user with a PIN. The consumer communicates his/her phone number to the merchant. The merchant communicates this phone number and the price to Paybox via a free phone number. Paybox calls the payer and asks for payment authorization (merchant name and amount are repeated). The payer authorizes by using a PIN. Paybox informs Deutsche Bank as credit institute to settle the payment using a common payment instrument. All the settlements are done via the customer account and hence can be used for various payment frequencies. The procedure is almost the same with Internet payments. Both users and merchants are charged a small fee. Paybox works with any mobile phone independent of financial institution and mobile operator. Paybox is suitable for both micropayments and macropayments. Paybox also promises fraudulent detection techniques. The disadvantage is that Paybox uses interactive voice response (IVR) to make voice calls to the customer. There is no data privacy and no proof of transaction. Transactions are possible with only Global System for Mobile Communications (GSM)-enabled phones. According to Jones (2003), Paybox started too early. Though it was a failure for a brief period of time, the concept resulted in raising interest in the m-commerce market. Technically speaking it was strong, but the other key players were not prepared for the technology. The system ensures secure encryption and the authentication and authorization is done via GSM voice channel using CallerID and mobile subscriber integrated services digital network (MSISDN) for authentication and a Paybox PIN for authorization.

i-Mode

This payment procedure was initiated by NTT DoCoMo, the largest network provider in Japan (http://www.imode.com). This works in m-commerce and e-commerce payment scenarios. The user has to dial a premium number and his/her bills are settled via the phone bill. NTT DoCoMo serves as telco and payment provider and settles the accounts with the merchants. This procedure was also initiated in Europe in 2002 by NTT-DoCoMo and KPN Mobile. NTT-DoCoMo claims 30 million subscribers in just 4 years around the world.

OboPay

OboPay (http://www.obopay.com) was launched in April 2006. This Palo Alto based startup claims to be the first U.S. company to allow cell phone users to make purchases as well as sending and receiving funds on their mobile phones. Their main targets are theatre tickets and restaurant bills. Obopay relies on a java client on the phone instead of SMS or text message payments like Pay-Pal Mobile and TextPayMe. While this provides for a richer and more secure interface, Obopay is of use only to people who have phones that support Java. It is supported by major carriers Cingular and T-Mobile. Five different handset manufacturers are represented in this group (i.e., Nokia, Motorola, Kyocera, Samsung, and Sony Ericsson). They are currently targeting all of the handsets that are used by the consumers and all the major carriers.

The service allows for P2P payments between phones. Users are also to be issued a debit card attached to the account for real-world payments, including ATM withdrawals. After installing the application on the mobile phone, any amount can be sent to a receiving person. A small transaction fee is also charged.

To use OboPay, an account has to be created and an application has to be downloaded. Once the account is created, request for payments from friends and family, checking the balance, and viewing payments is possible. After creating the account a debit card is received through the mail. The debit card can be used at an ATM or to make purchases in retail. Obopay is associated with MasterCard. The amount of money in the phone is the same as in the debit card. So balances can be checked anywhere and anytime. All the transactions done are stored and hence can be tracked.

LUUP

LUUP (http://www.luup.com) is a new m-payments company in the UK. It is also called LUU-PAY in Germany. It allows consumers to use their mobile phone like a wallet to shop with retailers or send and receive money on a P2P basis—with cash, debit/credit card, and bank account functions built-in. The service is independent of mobile phone operators. LUUP is fully integrated with the UK and German banking systems allowing funds to be accessed from credit cards, debit cards, and bank accounts. One of the major benefits of LUUP is its ability to handle payments between individuals. LUUP users who want to transfer money to a friend or split a restaurant bill can send money with one SMS to anyone with a mobile phone. If the recipient is not a LUUP user, they will receive an SMS with the amount sent to them and an invitation to sign up for a LUUP wallet. Once the LUUP wallet has been credited the recipient can save their money in their account, use it for purchases at LUUP merchants, or transfer it to their bank account. The transaction costs for merchants are very small. Additionally, the purchase process is transparent to consumers who can view all LUUP account activity online in real time helping solve consumer concerns about unfair charges.

LUUP uses 128-bit SSL encrypting, IP, and user password-based client authentication to protect personal data. Online purchases and high value P2P payments are confirmed using a PIN code. Personal information, including credit card details, is not made visible to the merchants.

LUUP is an m-payment solution first launched in Norway under the Contopronto name in July 2002. By May 2006, more than 10,000 customers held LUUP accounts each in the UK, Germany, and Norway. As announced by the media in April 2006, five top mobile operators in UK are planning to launch a service called Pay4It which may challenge LUUP.

MobiPay

Mobipay (Carat, 2002) can be used for payment to stationary merchant or mobile merchant; for payment on the Internet or at a vending machine; for P2P payments; and to recharge mobile telephone pre-paid accounts. A customer's registration with Mobipay is associated with the consumer's telephone number. All the operations are carried out by this number and are authorized by the customer. Usually the authentication is done by a PIN. Once the operation is successful, the transaction charges are remitted through issuer cards or through any client associate. A message is sent to confirm the payment. The Mobipay security system is based on personal Mobipay number, PIN, and encrypted communications through the network.

Paiement CB sur mobile

A France Telecom Mobile launched Paiement CB sur mobile in 2000. The system was previously called as Iti Achat. The system is bank centric and hence is an inter-operator system. This system uses dual slot mobile phones and WAP Internet phones. This M-payment solution is offered to France Telecom mobile subscribers (Itineris network) by using dual slot mobile phones, one of the slots being for chip-based Cartes Bancaires (CB) debit/credit cards. This system allows customers to pay for their purchases on their mobile phones without having to type in their debit or credit card numbers. Users can also reload their prepaid phone accounts and pay utility bills using the CB charge cards.

The customer orders goods by entering his/her mobile phone number (typing it on the merchant Web site in the case of using the Internet or saying it over the mobile phone to the catalog sales merchant). Then the customer receives an SMS with purchase details. If the customer wants to proceed with the purchase, he/she inserts a payment card and types in the PIN. When the transaction is authorized by the bank, a confirmation message is then sent by the bank via SMS to the customer's mobile phone. The merchant receives payment confirmation.

Bibit

Bibit has support from several key companies like Microsoft, IBM, Oracle, Intershop, Mercantec, Allaire and KPN Mobile, and so forth. It covers more than 15 countries. Bibit is specialized in international Internet payments, allowing the consumer to pay a foreign Internet retailer using a payment method which is customary in his/her own country. The consumer is thus able to pay in their own currency using a familiar method, while the retailer is paid in his/her own currency. A customer chooses the product in a virtual shop. The customer is then redirected to the Bibit Payment Service. The customer makes a choice of the payment method. After a successful payment, Bibit notifies the merchant that the order can be shipped. The service is free for consumers. Bibit's

Figure 6. Comparison of different payment systems

Payment System	Payment Initiation	Payment Authorization	Payment Base	Possibility of Interoperability	Security	Cost and Convenience
TextPayMe 2005	SMS	PIN	Bank Card	To be provided in future	Fraud management available	Free
PayPal Mobile 2006	SMS IVR Debit Card	PIN	PayPal account Bank card	Based on PayPal account only, hence not applicable	PIN based security	Fee based on transaction amount
Obopay 2006	Application on handset SMS Debit Card	PIN	Bank Card	Possible	Unauthorized access is prevented. SSL and PIN based security	Sender has to pay the fee
Paiement CB sur mobile 2000	SMS Credit/debit card	PIN	Bank account Debit/credit card	Possible	Secure because of dual chip slot	New handset required registration is free Transaction cost is equal to phone call
LUUP 2002	SMS	PIN	Cash credit/debit card Bank account	Interoperable	SSL based	Nominal transaction fee, no registration fee
Vodafone m-Pay Bill 2002	WAP SMS IVR	PIN	Phone bill Pre-paid airtime	Only for Vodafone registered users but interoperable in different countries	No privacy, as personal data is shared with other networks if necessary	No registration fee and transaction fee
mpay 2001	WAP Credit/debit SMS	PIN (SIM card based)	Credit/debit card	Possible	Uses certificates based on SIM cards, so secure.	registration free confirmation costs
i-mode 2002	Phone	PIN	Phone bill	Possible	Levels of Security provided	New handset required Separate fee
Paybox 2000	IVR	PIN	Debit card Bank account	Interoperable with other networks	Personal data on server but is not shared	Annual subscription Transaction fee

back-office informs merchants of all transactions, irrespective of the payment method used. All software is Java-based. All communication to and from Bibit's server is SSL encrypted. Bibit's Mobile Payment Suite can be used to accept payments on a variety of mobile devices. The solution consists of an application that runs on a mobile device, connected to the Internet. The application takes order and credit card details and performs a real-time authorization of the transaction. In most European countries this is possible using standard technology such as GPRS. This means that one single solution can be used in more than one country.

PayPal Mobile

PayPal (http://www.paypal.com) has more than 100 million accounts around the world. PayPal allows sending and receiving payments online securely and easily with a bank account and an e-mail address. It allows payments to be made to the merchants without sharing any financial information with merchants, thus ensuring privacy.

Previously, payments via Paypal were settled via a credit card. This worked for all the payment scenarios. The customer has to register with PayPal and reveal his/her credit card details. If a device like a PDA is used, specific software must be installed. Paypal is now also used for m-payments. The service is called PayPal Mobile. Money can be sent in two ways: (1) by texting to a given number with the amount and recipient's phone number or (2) calling a number and following a set of instructions specified in the scheme. To use PayPal Mobile, customers first activate their telephones by logging into their PayPal accounts. After registering their mobile telephone numbers, users must choose a secure PIN which protects every m-payment. PayPal Mobile users make payments by sending a text message to PayPal. PayPal calls the user back to confirm the m-payment and then sends the money to the recipient. In the case of a text-to-buy purchase,

after the merchant receives the payment, the item is shipped to the address already saved in the user's PayPal account.

Comparison

In Figure 6, a comparison of different payment systems is made based on security, cost, convenience, interoperability, payment initiation/authorization, and base. Any customer would accept the payment model if it has high security, is easy to use, and the technology based on which the system works is an already known one. Customers are already used to SMS, credit, and debit cards. Interoperability is about support for different networks, different mobile operators, and different financial institutions. Security is about ensuring confidentiality, integrity, authentication, and availability.

FUTURE TRENDS

The failure of acceptance of many innovative payment procedures like eCash and the German GeldKarte show that there is a wide set of criteria to be satisfied for the system to be successfully adopted by customers (Kreyer et al., 2002). Based on the surveyed articles, it is found that there are no globally accepted payment systems, but there are some trial projects running. In order for B2B and B2C m-commerce to be widely accepted, standard payment procedures should exist. The consumer acceptance depends on cost, security, privacy, and convenience. The reason stated against m-payments in several surveys found in the literature was that security is a big concern across all ages with respect to contactless payment technologies.

The design of m-payment systems should target the e-commerce scenario as already it has proved to be successful. And also m-commerce may initially focus on micropayments, until customers get adjusted to it. It is not possible to make consumers shift all of a sudden to m-payments leaving traditional payments. Local practices followed for payments may be difficult to shift. Relatively, teenagers adapt to new technologies faster than aged people. Cash is still a predominant payment device, but that percentage reduces significantly with age.

The main problems to be faced by a global payment system are that the wireless network infrastructure varies, and customer needs are usually dependent on the region and culture.

Another challenge for m-payment providers is to provide a secure environment and convince the consumers and the merchants about the security (Lee, Kou, & Hu, 2005). Most of the security challenges posed by m-commerce are the problems due to Internet and problems due to WAP. Most of the security solutions provided today are based on PKI keys. The different security issues that have to be taken care of are privacy of data, confidentiality, integrity, authentication, non-repudiation, accountability, system availability, and customer protection.

The technical difficulties can however be overcome through software and hardware solutions and standardizations. With proper intermediaries and interoperable standards, a global m-payment solution is always possible.

Requirements for a Common M-Payments Model

Any future payment system should support these steps at the minimum: (1) Registration for the payment service, (2) Transact and authorize, (3) Proof of completion of transaction, and (4) Dispute resolution.

While in Ding and Hampe (2003) and Schwiderski-Grosche and Knospe (2002), several critical success factors are discussed for successful m-payment systems, we consider ease of use, security, divisibility, transferability, interoperability, privacy, popularity or brand, cost, and standardization as critical factors for success of m-payments. The system should be flexible and open for wider acceptance. Smart-card-based payments are more secure and trustable. PKI keys combined with smart cards enhance trust in the transactions.

Any future payment type should support multiple types of payment methods like credit cards, charge cards, debit cards, direct debit to bank account, and account-based stored value. Banks should not insist the customers to use a particular network service provider. The system should be independent of mobile network operators, bank, and type of device used. The customers should be given an open choice to choose a combination of network service provider and the bank, only then the m-payments will be most widely adopted.

Evolving Standards and Technologies

There are scores of standards for handheld devices and also a lot of network standards like Bluetooth, 802.11a, 802.11b, HyperLAN2, and 802.11g WLANs. Though currently most of the WANs follow 2G or 2.5G, 3G systems will dominate the wireless cellular services. The standards proposed for 3G are CDMA 2000 proposed by Qualcomm and WCDMA proposed by Ericsson. The WCDMA system is capable of internetworking GSM networks and is strongly supported by EU, which calls it UMTS. CDMA 2000 is widely deployed in United States. Other than these, there are a few m-payment specific standards, organizations, and forums. For almost all the standards bodies, the common issues are: (1) security, (2) interoperability, (3) convenience, and (IV) ease of use.

- **Mobile Payment Forum:** It creates a framework for m-commerce using payment card accounts (www.mobilepaymentforum. com). Mobile Payment Forum is also working on standardization of the phases in the m-payment life cycle, namely device set-up and configuration, payment initiation, authentication, and payment completion.

- **Mobile Electronic Transactions:** MeT focuses on aspects of digital signatures and PKI for mobile devices (http://www. mobiletransaction.org). The main objective is to ensure the interoperability of mobile transaction solutions.
- **Mobey Forum (Mobile Financial Services):** It focuses on how to use the end-user mobile phone as a personal trusted device. This addresses security issues for mobile execution of financial services: payment, remote banking, and brokerage (http://www. mobeyforum.org). Mobey Forum facilitates aims at facilitating business and security requirements; evaluation of potential business models and technical solutions and by making recommendations to standard bodies; handset manufacturers; payment schemes; network operators; regulators; and technology suppliers in order to speed up the implementation of solutions.
- **PayCircle (Payment group):** PayCircle addresses a business-enabling infrastructure for Web services with the focus on micro payment (http://www.paycircle.org).
- **Radicchio:** Radicchio promotes digital signature and PKI for the mobile environment (http://www.radichchio.org).
- **GMCF:** GMCIG enables security and interoperability for mobile macro payments (http://www.gmcf.org). The Global Mobile Commerce Forum (GMCF) promotes the development of m-commerce services. Its membership includes operators, content providers, suppliers, financial institutes, and other organizations involved with m-commerce. The aim of GMCF is construct standards to facilitate the implementation and use of m-commerce applications and devices.
- **Liberty Alliance Project:** (http://www. projectliberty.org/) For secure interoperability, the Liberty Alliance, a consortium

representing organizations from around the world, was created in 2001 to address the technical, business, and policy challenges around identity and identity-based Web services.

- **Oasis PKI Forum:** (http://www.pkiforum. org/) The OASIS PKI Member Section is a group of OASIS members who work together to advance the use of the PKI as a foundation for secure transactions in e-business applications. It was formed in November 2002 with the migration of PKI Forum to OASIS.
- **Open Mobile Alliance:** (http://www. openmobilealliance.org/) The mission of the Open Mobile Alliance is to facilitate global user adoption of mobile data services and ensure service interoperability across devices, geographies, service providers, operators, and networks.

FUTURE RESEARCH

In order to make consumers and merchants naturally get adapted to m-payments, a global and interoperable set of standards for payments needs to be created. It is not just the technical issues that need to be researched, but developing business models that would benefit network operators and banks along with customers and merchants is equally important. A lot of fraudulent activities have been identified in recent literature. The virus, theft of devices, and so forth are a big problem for payments. Hence, fraud management is one issue that can be looked into. Security policies of different countries are a major hindrance to global m-payments. The issues and challenges that arise out of interoperability problems and security problems can be researched further. Anonymity and privacy are important topics in security, which are related to customer personal data, transactions, and content purchased. Mobile operators already have a large customer base. Several operators may collude to share the customer base through the involvement of intermediaries. The trust factor comes into play whenever an intermediary plays an important role in any transaction. Hence, trust in m-commerce is also an important topic when we speak about global m-payments. Trust and security must lie on both the merchant and customer sides.

CONCLUSION

M-payments are quickly catching up in almost all parts of the world. Various m-payment methods have been proposed and implemented in the literature. This chapter has attempted to give an overview of existing m-payment systems, their payment procedures, and limitations. The identified requirements in general, to adopt m-payments are: convenience; cost to implement and use; reliability; user and market acceptance; security; flexibility; speed of transaction; response; and scalability. The issues of concern with most of the existing m-payments are: anonymity, possibility of theft, poor signal reception in certain areas, and inflexible hardware and software solutions. The age of customers, culture, region, type of purchase, size of amount, devices used, and the network operators influence the use of m-payments in a global context. The issues and challenges that arise out of interoperability problems can be solved through proper standards derivation and common security policies. Standards should consider payments in different perspectives. The chapter also includes several payment categorizations based on different issues to enable derivation of better standards.

REFERENCES

Aswin, R. (2003). *From e-commerce to m-commerce: The wireless proposition, HSBC's guide to cash and treasury management in Asia.* Retrieved October 29, 2006 from www.infosys. com/industries/banking/white-papers/11_Wireless_RoongtaHSBC.pdf?page=bcmwphsbc

Bradford, A. (2003). *Consumers need local reasons to pay by mobile.* Retrieved October 29, 2006 from http://www.gartner.com/resources/115600/115603/115603.pdf

Buhan, D., Cheong, Y. C., & Tan, C. (2002). *Mobile payments in m-commerce.* Retrieved October 29, 2006 from http://www.capgemini.com/tme/pdf/MobilePaymentsinMCommrce.pdf

Carat, G. (2002). *E-Payment systems database: Trends and analysis.* Retrieved October 29, 2006 from http://epso.jrc.es/Docs/Background-9.pdf

Damsgaard, J., & Marchegiani, L. (2004). Like Rome, a mobile operator's empire wasn't built in a day! A journey through the rise and fall of mobile network operators. In J. Marjin, et al. (Eds.), *ICEC'04, ACM Sixth International Conference on Electronic Commerce* (pp. 639-648).

Ding, M. S., & Hampe, J. F. (2003, June 9-11). Reconsidering the challenges of mPayments: A roadmap to plotting the potential of the future M-Commerce Market. Paper presented at the *16th Bled eCommerce Conference eTransformation*, Bled, Slovenia.

Ding, M. S., & Unnithan, R. C. (2004). Mobile payments (m-payments)—An exploratory study of emerging issues and future trends. In P. C. Deans (Ed.), *E-commerce and m-commerce technologies.* Hershey, PA: Idea Group.

Gross, S., Fleisch, E., Lampe, M., & Miller, R. (2004). *Requirements and technologies for ubiquitous payment.* Retrieved October 29, 2006 from http://www.vs.inf.ethz.ch/res/papers/MKWI_UPayment.pdf

Jones, N. (2003, January 28). *Pay box retrenches, but its technology remains active.* Retrieved October 29, 2006 from http://gartner11.gartnerweb.com/resources/112800/112827/112827.pdf

Kountz, E. (2002). Mobile commerce: No cell, no sale? *Card Technology, 7*(9), 20-22.

Kreyer, N., Pousttchi, K., & Turowski, K. (2002). *Characteristics of mobile payment procedures.* M-Services 2002. Retrieved October 29, 2006 from ftp.informatik.rwth-aachen.de/ Publications/CEUR-WS/Vol-61/paper1.pdf

Lee, C-W., Kou, W., & Hu, W-C. (2005). Mobile commerce security and payment methods. In W-C. Hu, C-W Lee, & W. Kou (Eds.), *Advances in security and payment methods for mobile commerce.* Hershey, PA: Idea Group.

Lombardi, C. (2006, April 10). *Cell phone subscriptions surge in India.* Retrieved October 29, 2006 from http://news.com. com/Cell+phone+subscriptions+surge+in+India /2110-1037_3-6059482.html

McKitterrick, D., & Dowling, J. (2003). *State of the art review of mobile payment technology.* Retrieved October 29, 2006 from http://www. cs.tcd.ie/publications/tech-reports/reports.03/ TCD-CS-2003-24.pdf

Meister, R. (2005, June 27). *The situation of M-Commerce after Simpay's retreat.* Retrieved October 29, 2006 from http://www.payboxsolutions.com/327_397.htm

Mercator Advisory Group Report 1. (2006). *A research report on mobile payments in the United States: SMS and NFC implementations enter the market.* Retrieved October 29, 2006 from http://www.paymentsnews.com/mercator_advisory_gr/index.html

Mercator Advisory Group Report 2. (2006). *A research report on predicting mobile payment success in Asia.* Retrieved October 29, 2006 from http://www.mercatoradvisorygroup.com/index. php?doc=emerging_technologies&action=view_ item&id=137&catid=5

MeT. (2003). *MeT white paper on mobile transactions.* Retrieved October 29, 2006 from http:// www.mobiletransactions.org/pdf/R200/white_ papers/MeT_White_paper_on_mobile_transactions_v1.pdf

Nambiar, S., & Lu, C. (2005). M-payment solutions and m-commerce fraud management. Mobile Commerce Security and Payment methods. In W-C. Hu, C-W. Lee, & W. Kou (Eds.), *Advances in security and payment methods for mobile commerce.* Hershey, PA: Idea Group.

Nystedt, D. (2006, February 24). *China passes 400 million mobile phone user mark.* Retrieved October 29, 2006 from http://www.infoworld. com/article/06/02/24/75849_HNchinaphoneusers_1.html

Ondrus, J. (2003). *Mobile payments: A tool kit for a better understanding of the market.* Retrieved October 29, 2006 from http://www.hec.unil.ch/ jondrus/files/papers/mpayment.pdf

Ondrus, J., & Pigneur, Y. (2006). A multi-stakeholder multi-criteria assessment framework of mobile payments: An illustration with the Swiss public transportation industry. In *Proceedings of the 39th Hawaii IEEE International Conference on System Sciences* (pp. 1-10).

Schwiderski-Grosche, S., & Knospe, H. (2002). Secure mobile commerce. In C. Mitchell (Ed.), *Special issue of the IEE Electronics and Communication Engineering Journal on Security for Mobility, 14*(5), 228-238. Retrieved October 29, 2006 from http://www.isg.rhul.ac.uk/~scarlet/ documents/Secure%20m-commerce%20ECEJ. pdf

Seah, W., Pilakkat, S., Shankar, P., Tan, S. K., Roy, A. G., & Ng, E. (2001). *The future mobile payments infrastructure: A common platform for secure m-payments.* Retrieved October 29, 2006 from http://www.itu.int/ITU-D/pdf/4597-13.3bis-en.pdf

Stallings, W. (2000). *Network security essentials: Applications and standards.* Pearson Education.

Zmijewska, A., Lawrence, E., & Steele, R. (2004, July 12-13). Classifying m-payments—A user-centric model. In *Proceedings of the International Conference on Mobile Business 04,* New York.

Chapter XV
Barcode Applications
for M–Business

Eusebio Scornavacca
Victoria University of Wellington, New Zealand

Stuart J. Barnes
University of East Anglia, UK

ABSTRACT

One pertinent area of recent m-commerce development is in methods for personal transaction and
information transfer. Several companies around
the world have begun to use barcodes for the
provision of m-commerce services. This chapter
provides background on the enabling technological platform for providing such services. It then
continues with three cases where mobile barcodes
have been used—in Japan, New Zealand, and the
UK. Subsequently, these are used as the basis for a
discussion and analysis of the key business models,
and strategic implications for particular markets.
The chapter concludes with predictions for the
market and directions for future research.

INTRODUCTION

With well over a billion mobile handsets worldwide, wireless technologies are enabling e-businesses to expand beyond the traditional limitations
of the fixed-line personal computer (Bai, Chou,
Yen, & Lin, 2005; Barnes, 2003; Barnes & Huff,
2003; Barnes & Vidgen, 2001; Bergeron, 2001;
Chen, 2000; Clarke, 2001; de Haan, 2000; Emarketer, 2002; Kalakota & Robinson, 2002; Sadeh,
2002; Yuan & Zhang, 2003). According to a study
by Telecom Trends International (2003), global
revenues from m-commerce could grow from $6.8
billion in 2003 to over $554 billion in 2008.

As each mobile device is typically used by
a sole individual, it provides a suitable platform

Figure 1. Technology convergence between OCR and mobile phones

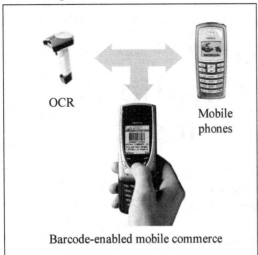

OCR

Mobile phones

Barcode-enabled mobile commerce

for delivering individual-based target information, purchasing goods or services and making payments (Barnes, 2003; Barnes & Scornavacca, 2004; Bayne, 2002; Kannan, Chang, & Whinston, 2001; Newell & Lemon, 2001; Scornavacca & Barnes, 2003). One recent development in m-commerce is the application of barcodes solutions (NTT DoCoMo, 2003). This revolutionary development benefits from the convergence of two widespread technologies: optical character recognition (OCR) and mobile telephony (see Figure 1). Through barcodes, users of mobile phones can, for example, purchase tickets, receive coupons, access information, make payments, and interact with point-of-sale information systems (Airclic, 2003; AsiaTech, 2003; Bango, 2003; Barcode 1, 2003; Ecrio, 2003; NTT DoCoMo, 2003; Wireless Newsfactor, 2002).

This chapter aims to explore the applications of barcodes in mobile commerce. The following section provides a brief explication of barcodes and OCR technologies. This is followed by three case studies of the application of barcodes in m-commerce: in Japan, New Zealand, and the

United Kingdom. Subsequently, we explore the business models being employed, and analyze the strategic implications of these models for different m-commerce markets. The chapter concludes with a discussion about the future of mobile commerce and directions for further research.

TECHNOLOGICAL FOUNDATIONS: OPTICAL CHARACTER RECOGNITION AND BARCODES

OCR technology has been used in business for nearly half a century. OCR devices transform specially designed marks, characters, and codes into a digital format. The codes can contain any kind of information, such as alphanumeric codes, date, time, names, and so on. The most widely used application of optical code is the barcode, and this has become used in a vast range of organizations, including supermarkets and retail stores (point-of-sale [POS] systems), libraries, hospitals, schools, and factories (production and supply chain management) (Uniform Code Council, 2003).

There are several varieties and standards for barcodes. The symbol found on most retail products around the world is based on UPC/EAN standards (Figure 2a). The Universal Product Code (UPC), developed by the Uniform Code Council (UCC), was the first barcode symbol widely adopted in the world. In 1973, the grocery industry formally established UPC as the standard bar code symbology for product marking in the United States. European interest in UPC led to the adoption of the European Article Numbering (EAN) code format in 1976 (EAN, 2003). Today, EAN International is a global not-for-profit organization that creates, develops, and manages jointly with the UCC open, global, multisectoral information standards, and the EAN/UCC standards. All businesses must apply for membership in order to be assigned a unique company identification number for use on all its products (Uniform Code

Figure 2. Examples of barcodes

(a) EAN/UPC barcodes   (b) Data Matrix 2-D barcode

Council, 2003). There are now five versions of UPC and two versions of EAN. The Japanese Article Numbering (JAN) code has a single version identical to one of the EAN versions. UPC and EAN symbols are fixed in length, can only encode numbers, and are continuous symbologies using four element widths (Barcode 1, 2003). The barcode used on books, for example, is generated based on the International Standard Book Number (ISBN).

In terms of business use, barcodes have been promoted largely as a machine-readable "license plate," where each label provides a unique serial number coded in black and white bars linking to a database entry containing detailed information. More recently, end users have sought to code more information; making the barcode a portable database rather than just a database key (Barcode 1, 2003). One good example is the Data Matrix barcode, a two-dimensional (2-D) matrix code (Figure 2b). A Data Matrix symbol typically stores between one and 500 characters. The symbol is also scalable, from a 1-millimeter square to a 14-inch square. Theoretically, a maximum of 500 million characters to the inch is possible, but the practical density will be limited by the resolution of the printing and reading technology used (Barcode 1, 2003).

Barcodes have been widely used and accepted in the business world for decades. Given the existence of a solid infrastructure, it is interesting to note the development of barcode applications for mobile e-commerce (Airclic, 2003; AsiaTech, 2003; Bango 2003; Barcode 1, 2003; Ecrio, 2003; NTT DoCoMo, 2003; Vodafone, 2003; Wireless Newsfactor, 2002). Given a solid platform, there is potential for these applications to become commonplace in the mobile world. The next section provides more details about specific barcode applications in m-commerce, examining the value added by this technology.

CASE STUDIES OF BARCODE USE IN M-COMMERCE

In this section, we examine specific mobile barcode applications offered by companies in Japan, New Zealand, and the United Kingdom. We have focused on exemplars of existing applications that are being offered to and used by consumers in each of the respective markets. Let us consider each of these in turn.

NTT DoCoMo (Japan)

NTT DoCoMo is Japan's leading mobile communications company with more than 50 million customers. The company provides a wide variety of leading-edge mobile multimedia services. These include i-mode, the world's most popular mobile Internet service, providing e-mail and Internet access to over 43 million subscribers; and FOMA (Freedom of Mobile Access), launched in 2001 as the world's first third-generation (3G) mobile network service based on W-CDMA (Wideband-Code Division Multiple Access) (NTT DoCoMo, 2005).

Combien?

Since May 2002, NTT DoCoMo customers have been able to pay monthly mobile phone bills at convenience stores using a 2-D Data Matrix barcode on the screens of their mobile phones. The service is available nationwide in over 2,000 Am/Pm, Lawson, and Mini-stop convenience stores. Since the service eliminates the need for a hard-copy invoice, customers can pay their bills whenever they visit a participating convenience store. There is no fee for the service, although users must pay a transmission charge to download the barcode (via the i-mode portal). To prevent double payment, the barcode is valid only on the day when it is downloaded. A dedicated scanner is used by the merchant to read the 2-D barcode, after which the customer pays the bill. The procedure for downloading the barcode is presented in Figure 3.

This application allows customers to benefit from the large network of convenience stores in Japan. Alongside, they are able to pay their mobile phone bills 24 hours a day, 7 days a week. For the operator, NTT DoCoMo, the main benefit is the capability of collecting payments from customers remotely and safely, reducing collection costs, eliminating invoice handling, and transferring delivery costs to the customer.

Although currently limited to bill payment, this system is planned for use in other areas in the future. Indeed, it is expected that the core of wireless payments (including electronic invoices) will be the integration between financial institutions and wireless services providers (Scornavacca & Barnes, 2003).

505i Series

Another dimension of mobile barcode solutions is the development of hardware capable of reading barcodes. DoCoMo's 505i series has a built in camera and barcode-reader software. Figure 4 presents an example of an application that allows a user to transform printed information into digital format. Figure 4a shows a business card with a 2-D barcode. The barcode contains all the information printed on the card. Figure 4b displays the built-in camera on the 505i device. The user takes a picture of the barcode on the business card (Figure 4c) and the information—typically name, title, company, telephone, mobile, and fax

Figure 3. NTT DoCoMo's Combien? (NTT DoCoMo, 2003)

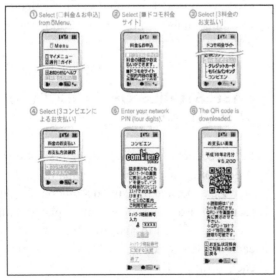

Figure 4. NTT DoCoMo's 505i Series barcode reader (NTT DoCoMo, 2003)

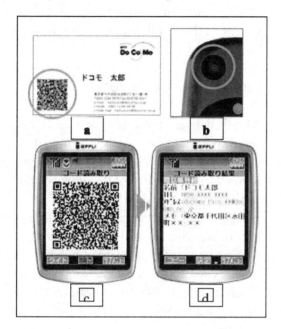

numbers—is automatically added to the user's address book (Figure 4d).

The number of possible applications of this technology is limited only by one's imagination. For example, users could retract information from products simply by scanning their barcode. Barcodes could also be used to access Web site addresses, which can be cumbersome using a mobile phone keypad.

Another possible development that may stem from integration between financial institutions and wireless services providers is using the mobile phone to scan barcodes printed on invoices (as utility bills) and subsequent payment using a mobile phone account. One candidate for this is NTT DoCoMo's DoCommerce payments service. DoCommerce enables both 2G and 3G users to shop using their mobile phone with just a single user ID and password. An account aggregation feature enables DoCommerce users to check—simultaneously and on one single screen—the

balances of their various financial accounts held with banks and credit card companies. Some 15 financial institutions, including VISA and Master-Card, are now part of the service (NTT DoCoMo, 2003). One possible development emerging from the barcode-reader capability and future financial service integration could be bill payment.

Vodafone and mTicket (New Zealand)

The Vodafone Group plc acquired its New Zealand business in November 1998 (previously known as BellSouth New Zealand). At the time of purchase, BellSouth had 138,000 customers. Vodafone New Zealand now has 1.3 million customers and a network coverage of 97%. Vodafone provides its GSM (Global System for Mobile) digital communication service on the 900 and 1,800 megahertz parts of the radio spectrum (Vodafone, 2003).

MTicket was the first commercially available mobile ticket system. The company is based in Europe and the Asia Pacific and provides applications for customers such as Vodafone, O2, and EMAP.

Mobile Ticketing

Developed by mTicket, "mobile ticketing" is a box-office system that allows event organizers to market, sell, distribute, and redeem tickets to events using text messages. The service has been available from Vodafone New Zealand since November 2002. In essence, a ticket is a good that can be easily delivered through electronic media. For mTicket, customers are able to send event keywords to a three-digit short code and receive information about events; accordingly, they may then select tickets and make a purchase using short message service (SMS) text messages (MTicket, 2003). Event information, terms, and conditions are all available using system keywords. To purchase tickets, customers are asked to choose seating areas, ticket types, and the quantity of tickets. Ticket costs are added directly to the mobile phone user's monthly bill, or deducted from prepaid credit. The ticket(s) are sent in the form of an SMS or multimedia message service (MMS) message (which contains a unique mTicket number or booking reference) or as a barcode (which may facilitate data input and access to the event).

Events that have previously sold mTickets include the Football Kingz (soccer), Netball New Zealand, the Heineken Open and ASB Classic tennis tournaments, and many music events ranging from dance to live music. The key benefit for consumers is the ability to purchase goods and services anywhere and at anytime using a mobile phone. For Vodafone and the event promoter the main benefits are the capabilities to collect payments from customers and to deliver tickets electronically via the mobile phone. This cuts the costs of collection, handling, delivery, fraud, and call centers (Vodafone, 2003). Alongside, impulse purchases may play a factor in increasing sales.

Clearly this application is less sophisticated than those found in the Japanese market. The principal reason for this is the current technological limitation of most handheld devices in New Zealand. On the other hand, it is extremely creative and it allows users to experience and become familiar with purchases through a mobile phone.

12snap (UK)

12snap is a major player in mobile marketing across Europe (12Snap, 2003). By exploiting the tremendous possibilities offered by the development of the mobile phone as a new media channel, 12snap offers personalized and targeted wireless marketing. The company specializes in "opt-in" advertising schemes. In essence, "opt-in" involves the user agreeing to receive advertising before anything is sent, with the opportunity to change preferences or stop messages at any time (Scornavacca & Barnes, 2003). 12snap currently

has over 18 million aggregated permission-based users in the UK, Germany, Scandinavia, and Italy, with a further 3 million across the rest of Europe, making it the mobile media market leader in the these territories.

Mobile Barcode Coupons

12snap delivers marketing and customer relationship management (CRM) programmes by combining SMS, voice/sound, the Web, wireless application protocol (WAP), enhanced message service (EMS), and MMS with its own technology. It has built up a reputation for running groundbreaking interactive campaigns and is at the forefront of innovation in the mobile marketing industry. Recently, the company adopted barcodes in its campaigns. Figure 5 illustrates the process of a typical campaign utilizing mobile barcode coupons.

A brand or a retailer contacts the campaign manager in order to deliver coupons directly to targeted customers. An agent can support the development of the campaign strategy. Coupons containing a barcode are delivered via SMS. In order to redeem any relevant offer the customer simply displays the barcode embedded on his/her mobile phone at the POS. The cashier scans the barcode displayed with a barcode reader and the

Figure 5. Business model for mobile barcode coupon campaigns (12Snap, 2003)

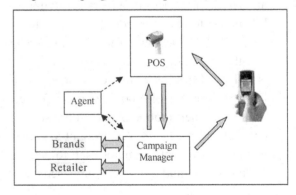

retailer's electronic POS (EPOS) informs the campaign database that a coupon has been redeemed. (Concurrently, the system identifies the client at the point of purchase through its barcode ID and detects other available offers.) Once a coupon is redeemed, it is automatically cancelled. Finally, a "thank-you" message is sent to the customer.

Overall, this business model allows a better measurement and understanding of return on investment (ROI) for mobile marketing (Scornavacca & Barnes, 2003). The solution is considered secure and integrates into EPOS software and hardware providing real-time reporting capabilities, tracking consumer behavior from initial contact through to in-store redemption (12Snap, 2003). A key advantage of the system is that it can be customized to a particular retailer, product, or customer. In addition, because it is based on an electronic format, retailers do not have to manually count, store, and ship coupons via a clearing house. This solution combines the power of couponing with the precision of mobile marketing. However, it is worth bearing in mind that mobile marketing has a more invasive nature than any other media, and a lot of attention must be given to permission issues in order to make the mobile marketing experience pleasant to the users. It must produce a win-win situation between user and advertiser. That said, mobile barcode coupons can certainly help marketers to develop mobile marketing through a better understanding of consumer preferences and behavior.

NEW MODELS OF M-COMMERCE USING BARCODES

The examples of mobile barcode applications and the discussion presented above demonstrate the use of two basic barcode-enabled m-commerce business models: "push" and "pull." Figure 6 presents a conceptual model for barcode-enabled m-commerce business models.

Push business models are based in the concept of interaction between a mobile device and a separate OCR device, usually at a POS or via a "gatekeeper" to service provision. This interaction is possible via a barcode displayed on the mobile device screen. Combien?, 12snap's coupons, and mTicket are examples of this kind of business model. This is the most prevalent business model used for m-commerce.

Figure 6. Barcode-enabled m-commerce business models

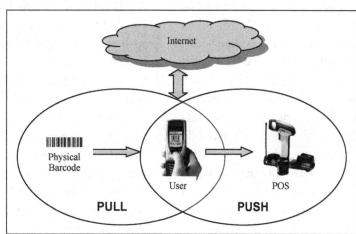

Figure 7. Strategic framework for mobile barcode applications

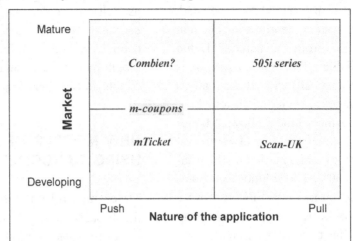

Pull business models are based on the concept of interaction between a mobile device and a physical barcode. This interaction is possible by decoding a printed barcode. This business model is typically dependent on the mobile device being OCR enabled (by camera or barcode reader). The built-in camera and barcode-reader software on DoCoMo's 505i series is a clear example of this application. An interesting example of an OCR-independent pull business model is that of Scan-UK, trialed in 2000. Scan-UK's service enables a user to check if a specific book or CD that they are considering purchasing from a physical store is cheaper online. The user enters the barcode number of the desired product via SMS, sends the message to the service, and the system sends back a list of how much e-tailers are asking for the same product (BBC News, 2000).

A combination of push and pull business models is also possible. A *push-pull* business model would occur in the situation when a mobile device interacts with a physical barcode and later interacts with an OCR device. An example of this would be when a user scans and stores a physical barcode into his/her mobile phone and later uses the scanned barcode at a POS.

Besides the nature of the application (push and/or pull) another important strategic variable for implementing barcode applications in mobile commerce is the market environment. Figure 7 presents a framework that helps understand the relationship between market maturity and business models. When analyzing barcode applications in mobile commerce, we understand market maturity as the dynamic combination of OCR infrastructure, payment systems integration, m-commerce acceptance, mobile phones market penetration, and hardware development.

The Japanese market is considered a mature market. It has a high penetration of Internet-enabled mobile phones, and most are equipped with a camera and a high-definition colour screen (Scornavacca & Barnes, 2003). Japan also has a solid infrastructure of POS systems, equipped with OCR devices. Combien? can be placed in the upper-left quadrant (mature-push). Typically, this type of application is characterized in a mature market where the advanced mobile technology platform available for customers takes profit of the integration between merchants (e.g., convenience stores) and wireless services providers. DoCoMo's 505i series can be placed in the upper-right quadrant (mature-pull). Notice that this application requires that the user's device is equipped with OCR.

In New Zealand, the mobile market still in a developing stage. Most of the handsets have low definition screens and are without camera or barcode reader. Nevertheless, it also has a high penetration of mobile phones and has a solid infrastructure of POS systems equipped with OCR devices. mTicket occupies the lower-left quadrant due to its push nature and market environment.

The UK market is close to that of New Zealand, but driven by a much larger consumer base, more sophisticated hardware, a greater variety of mobile services, and competition among the larger number of operators. It also has a high penetra-

tion of mobile phones and a solid infrastructure of POS systems equipped with OCR devices. The mobile barcode coupons provided by 12snap are positioned in the middle of the left side of the matrix; the UK is supported by a good OCR infrastructure at POS and a reasonable display quality. On the other hand, Scan-UK would be placed in the lower-left quadrant. This application was trialed in 2000. At that point in time, the UK market environment was in a developing stage. Also, this application would be more convenient and accurate if customers could simply scan the product barcode.

The model allows us to understand some strategic implications of barcode-enabled m-commerce business models. Table 1 examines

Table 1. Characteristics of barcode-enabled m-commerce business models

Business model	Characteristics of the model	Benefits	Specific issues
PUSH	A barcode is sent to a mobile device, typically via messaging. Service interaction occurs when the barcode is read from the screen via an external OCR, such as a merchant or another device equipped with OCR capability.	Convenience to the user (time and location) Potential for personalization and CRM Ubiquity of mobile infrastructure (phones) Interaction (passive) Cost reduction to the operator and service provider	Suitable for developing markets where mobile devices are not yet OCR capable. Relies primarily on existing OCR infrastructure of merchants. "Passive" interactivity—the user cannot interact with printed barcodes. Interactivity is driven by the operator or service provider.
PULL	A mobile device is equipped with OCR capability, such as a camera and OCR software. Service interaction occurs when the user pulls information from printed barcodes or other sources, such as screens of mobile devices, computers, or TV.	Convenience to the user (time and location) Customer driven Ubiquity of mobile infrastructure (phones and OCR) Interaction (active) Cost reduction to the operator and service provider	Usually hardware dependent—requires sophisticated mobile devices with OCR capability More suitable for mature markets where advanced devices are in use and commercial activity has begun An "active" model, based on the user's desire for information and interaction

some of the characteristics of barcode-enabled m-commerce business models, as derived from the above discussion.

A key benefit for all the solutions is the *convenience* of the services provided, which can potentially be used by the user on the move at any time and from anywhere. The penetration of mobile telephony means that such services have a high degree of *ubiquity*. The technological platforms enable business models with considerable customer *interaction*, with broad possibilities for the development of services that engage the user. At the same time, by motivating the user to engage in activities enabled by mobile devices, *costs are reduced* significantly via digitization—including such things as collection costs, handling, delivery, fraud, and call centers. Push services, being based on existing OCR infrastructure, are better suited to developing markets. In more mature markets, where devices are more sophisticated, pull services allow the user to interact with printed barcodes, expanding the possibilities for service interaction.

CONCLUSION

The convergence of traditional OCR technology and mobile telephony has provided some exciting possibilities for new mobile e-commerce business models. In this chapter we have explored the background to barcode technology, and how such technology can be employed in the new mobile environment. In particular, we have examined the case studies of a number of companies leading the field in three countries—the UK, New Zealand, and Japan. Each of these involves real exemplars of commercial use of mobile barcodes. By examining these, we have discovered two distinct business models being used—push and pull—each with their own benefits and problems. Moreover, by combining the choice of business model with an examination the maturity of the market environment, we can distinguish a number

of strategic positions for the provision of mobile barcode services.

The development of mobile barcode applications, like m-commerce, is still relatively new and emerging. Technological development may have a strong impact on its future direction. One area of current development that may provide a substitute for barcodes is the use of wireless in personal area networks (PANs) to enable m-commerce. Standards such as Bluetooth and IEEE 802.11 allow a new wave of short-range device interactivity and provide cheap, low-power, high-data-rate connectivity for portable devices in a limited area. Here, for example, the roaming phone user can be provided with information, alerts, or even advertisements based on local interaction with PANs. Customers could also conduct transactions with their mobile phones at the POS—vending machines and ATMs being the best-known examples. In a more complex scenario, the customer looking for a specific product or price could conceivably scan or enter a code into a phone; when the customer walks past a store with the right product or price the phone could send an alert. Stores could even send advertising alerts in an effort to tempt customers inside. Whether short-range wireless will replace barcodes is unclear. Clearly there are also areas of synergy between the technologies, and the use of PANs could enable new types of push and pull application in Figure 7. What is clear, however, is that the infrastructure for barcodes is already in place, and will take some time for POS have short-range-enabled devices of a common standard.

Given the emergent nature of mobile services, this is an area ripe for future research. In particular, we have a number of questions that will provide a future research agenda for mobile barcode research:

• What is the user's acceptance of digital barcode services? Do the user's benefits for these services really outweigh their personal cost? How does this vary among users?

- How can the business use mobile barcodes to build and manage customer relationships?
- How can mobile services become potentially more targeted and measurable? How can businesses measure ROI?
- Which business models and barcode applications are most likely to be successful?
- How will short-range wireless technologies change the nature of interactivity and business models?

Our own research will attempt to examine these questions in more detail utilizing empirical data to provide a firmer base for strategic understanding.

REFERENCES

12Snap. (2003). Mobile barcode coupons – the marketing revolution for marketeers. Retrieved October 23, 2003, from *www.12snap.com/uk/help/couponsshort.pdf*

Airclic. (2003). Airclic devices. Retrieved October 27, 2003, from *www.airclic.com/devices*

AsiaTech. (2003). PaySmart: Cashless payment solution. Retrieved October 27, 2003, from *www.asiatech.com.au/capter ii/chapterii02 a.htm*

Bai, L., Chou, D.C., Yen, D.C., & Lin, B. (2005). Mobile commerce: Its market analyses. *International Journal of Mobile Communications, 3*(1), 66–81.

Bango. (2003). Camera-enabled mobiles and PDAs scan barcodes for instant access to WAP. Retrieved June 4, 2003, from *http://corp.bango.net/corporate/media/releases/_31_iwdemo.asp*

Barcode 1. (2003). Barcode 1. Retrieved October 27, 2003, from *www.adams1.com/pub/russadam/isbn.html*

Barnes, S.J. (2003). The mobile commerce value chain in consumer markets. In S.J. Barnes (Ed.), *mBusiness: The strategic implications of wireless communications* (pp. 13–37). Oxford: Elsevier/Butterworth-Heinemann.

Barnes, S.J., & Huff, S.L. (2003). Rising sun: iMode and the wireless Internet. *Communications of the ACM, 46*(11), 78–84

Barnes, S.J., & Scornavacca, E. (2004). Mobile marketing: The role of permission and acceptance. *International Journal of Mobile Communications, 2*(2), 128–139.

Barnes, S.J., & Vidgen, R. (2001). Assessing the quality of WAP news sites: The WebQual/m method. *VISION: the Journal of Business Perspective, 5*, 81–91.

Bayne, K.M. (2002). *Marketing without wires: Targeting promotions and advertising to mobile device users.* London: John Wiley & Sons.

BBC News. (2000). Mobiles bag barcode bargains. Retrieved October 25, 2003, from *http://news.bbc.co.uk/1/hi/sci/tech/782578.stm*

Bergeron, B.P. (2001). *The wireless Web: How to develop and execute a winning wireless strategy.* New York: McGraw-Hill.

Chen, P. (2000). Broadvision delivers new frontier for e-commerce. *M-Commerce, October, 25.*

Clarke, I. (2001). Emerging value propositions for m-commerce. *Journal of Business Strategies, 18*(2), 133–148.

de Haan, A. (2000). The Internet goes wireless. *EAI Journal, April,* 62–63.

EAN. (2003). EAN International. Retrieved October 27, 2003, from *www.ean-int.org/index800.html*

Ecrio. (2003). Mobile commerce. Retrieved October 20, 2003, from *www.ecrio.com/sol mobilecommerce.shtml*

Emarketer. (2002). *One billion mobile users by end of Q2*. Retrieved May 27, 2003, from *www.nua.ie/surveys/index.cgi?f=VS&art_id=905357779&rel=true*

Kalakota, R., & Robinson, M. (2002). *M-business: The race to mobility*. New York: McGraw-Hill.

Kannan, P., Chang, A., & Whinston, A. (2001, January). Wireless commerce: Marketing issues and possibilities. *Proceedings of the 34th Hawaii International Conference on System Sciences*, Maui, HI.

Lau, A.S.M. (2003). A study on direction of development of business to customer m-commerce. *International Journal of Mobile Communications, 1*(1/2), 167–179.

MTicket. (2003). Tickets for a mobile generation. Retrieved October 27, 2003, from *www.mticket.co.uk*

Newell, F., & Lemon, K.N. (2001). *Wireless rules: New marketing strategies for customer relationship management anytime, anywhere*. New York: McGraw-Hill.

NTT DoCoMo. (2003). DoCoMo Net. Retrieved October 27, 2003, from *www.nttdocomo.co.jp* (in Japanese)

NTT DoCoMo. (2005). DoCoMo Net. Retrieved January 27, 2005, from *www.nttdocomo.co.jp* (in Japanese)

Sadeh, M.N. (2002). *M-commerce: Technologies, services, and business models*. London: John Wiley & Sons.

Scornavacca, E., & Barnes, S.J. (2003). Mobile banking in Japan. *International Journal of Mobile Communications, 2*(1), 51–66.

Telecom Trends International. (2003). M-commerce poised for rapid growth. Retrieved October 27, 2003, from *www.telecomtrends.net/pages/932188/index.htm*

Uniform Code Council. (2003). Uniform Code Council. Retrieved October 27, 2003, from *www.uc-council.org*

Vodafone. (2003). What's hot. Retrieved October 27, 2003, from *www.vodafone.co.nz*

Wireless Newsfactor. (2002). Mobile technology gives pointing new meaning. Retrieved September 12, 2003, from *www.wirelessnewsfactor.com/perl/story/16561.html*

Yuan, Y., & Zhang, J.J. (2003). Towards an appropriate business model for m-commerce. *International Journal of Mobile Communications, 1*(1/2), 35–56.

This work was previously published in Unwired Business: Cases in Mobile Business, edited by S. J. Barnes and E. Scornavacca, pp. 66-81, copyright 2006 by IRM Press (an imprint of IGI Global).

Section IV
Utilization and Application

Chapter XVI
E–Commerce Opportunities in the Nonprofit Sector:
The Case of New York Theatre Group

Ayman Abuhamdieh
Indiana State University, USA

Julie E. Kendall
Rutgers University, USA

Kenneth E. Kendall
Rutgers University, USA

EXECUTIVE SUMMARY

To what extent does having a Web presence reflect on an organization's e-commerce operations? Will a mere brick-and-mortar organizational Web site guarantee online success? This case presents the experience of the New York Theatre Group (NYTG), a nonprofit performing arts organization, in integrating e-commerce in its business practices. The case begins with a very broad overview of the nonprofit sector, the performing arts industry, its delivery channels, and the theatrical production process in general. Then attention turns to NYTG itself in terms of its history, organizational structure, its market segmentation, market trends, and forecasted growth. The strategic planning at NYTG, and the programs put in place to help it achieve its objectives and mission, are detailed. A survey that maps the demographic attributes of NYTG's patrons and subscribers is discussed. The case concludes with the current e-commerce challenges facing NYTG in particular and the nonprofit performing arts organizations in general.

ORGANIZATION BACKGROUND

Sam Jones works at the renowned New York Theatre Group (NYTG), a large nonprofit theatre organization that has been in operation since 1970. He started working there in early 1996 as a marketing associate/Web site manager. At that time, the Internet was burgeoning into an unprecedented scale, and he thought, "This is a great, new way to reach our audience. It's fun, too. How hard can it be to set up a Web site? I already have my own home page." But things didn't materialize the way he had envisioned. "Shouldn't people be rushing to get on the Web site? Why aren't more audience members using it? What should we do to get more of them to the Web site? Provide tickets online? Let them donate to us online?" he asked.

To answers some of these questions, he set out to do a small research project examining the industry he works in, and the Web presence operations he is responsible for at NYTG. He gathered some data about the nonprofit sector and its contribution to the economy, and then he learned about the current state of the theatre industry in the US in terms of the players, owners, and operations. Since he is working in the marketing area, he needed to know more about the theatre production process and the delivery channels used to present the works developed in the theatre. He distributed a survey to a small sample of the theatre subscribers to know more about their demographics, since he is aiming at attracting more of them to the theatre's Web site. He also did a market analysis of the area serviced by the theatre. He will submit a report summarizing his findings to his manager, Don Anderson.

What makes Sam's job interesting is the fact that he works in a nonprofit organization, which is part of a large nonprofit sector that has many players, including relief organizations such as the International Committee of the Red Cross (www. icrc.org/), environmental organizations such as the World Wildlife Fund (www.worldwildlife. org/), and social services organizations like the Robin Hood Foundation (www.robinhood.org/). Sam reviewed some studies that examined the role e-commerce plays in nonprofit organizations and found that competence in organizational e-commerce operations through their Web presence reflects positively on their performance, and helps customers in prepurchase decisions because they can access the information they need

online before they buy (Saeed, Grover, & Hwang, 2005). Despite this established relationship, many nonprofit organizations have lagged behind in adopting e-commerce. Some of this reticence is due to the lack of IT expertise, uncertain and fluctuating funding, lack of clear benefits for the establishment of a Web presence, and the views of some managers who consider organizational Web presence frivolous and unnecessary. There are about 1.4 million nonprofit organizations of all types and sizes in the US, 60,239 of which belong to the arts, culture, and humanity category (NCCS, 2005). The nonprofit theatre industry occupies a small niche of a billion-dollar field of 1,477 theaters (Voss & Voss, 2004).

Sam learned that nonprofit organizations use the Web in many different facets, such as research, fund-raising, volunteerism, e-commerce, and career development (Oehler, 2000). Fundraising is one of the most sought-after Web activities by nonprofit organizations because of the global reach of organizational Web presence, the high customizability of online messages, and the convenience of online transactions (Roufa, 2000; T'eni & Kendall, 2004). It also emphasizes the critical importance of having a Web presence for these organizations, and especially for nonprofit theatres (Kendall, 2006)

The Current State of the Theatre Industry in the United States, With Emphasis on New York City

Sam works in an industry that is divided into two main categories represented by two main bodies: the Theatre Communications Group (TCG) (http://www.tcg.org/) that speaks for the nonprofit sector, and the League of American Theatres and Producers (http://www.livebroadway.com) that represents the commercial theatre sector (O'Quinn, 2000). Seventeen theatre houses on the famous Broadway Street in New York City are rented by Gerald Schoenfeld, the chairman of the Shubert Organization. The country's two publicly subsidized theatre houses are Lincoln Center Theatre and the Roundabout Theatre Company. Both reside in New York City. Other theatre houses are either for profit, such as Disney, or not for profit, such NYTG and the Roundabout.

There are about 1,477 professional nonprofit theatres in the United States, 258 of which are members of the Theatre Communications Group, which was established in 1961. The TCG serves over 18,000 individual members and offers many programs and services such as publishing the American Theatre magazine and the ArtSEARCH employment bulletin. It also conducts a yearly fiscal survey that started in 1997 and maps the latest attendance, performance, and financial indicators of the theatre industry about participating members. The latest survey which was conducted in 2004 included 1,477 theatres, divided into 258 members and 1,219 nonmembers.

Approximately 60% of the theatre income is earned through ticket sales, concessions, and other earned sources, while 40% are contributions from individual and corporate giving, foundation donations, and other sources. More than 104,000 artists, technicians, and administrators are on theatre payroll. These are divided into artistic positions (64%), technical personnel (24%), and administrative staff (12%). Eleven thousand productions translated into 169,000 performances that were presented attracted about 32 million attendees, of which 1.8 million were active subscribers (Voss & Voss, 2004).

The general trend of the industry is characterized by an increasing number of established theatres replacing or adapting aging buildings, while newer and smaller theatres are acquiring new buildings or expanding their facilities (Channick, 2000). Attracting young talents to the theatre movement has been difficult mainly because of low remuneration, especially in the nonprofit sector (Coen, 2000). This difficulty extends beyond artistic talent to IT professionals such as Web masters who can design and deliver any needed changes in house. The hindrance lies

in the cost factor, where a Webmaster would cost in the range of forty to fifty thousand dollars on average. Many theatres do not believe this is an essential expense to incur, and many simply outsource their Web operations.

The number of audiences, artists, performing arts organizations and their budgets has increased across the board. The number of audiences is increasing but is biased toward the recorded and broadcast productions. The number of artists has grown over the years between 1970 and 1990, and their pay and job security has marginally improved. The number of nonprofit performing arts organizations has increased by about 80% between 1982 and 1997 (McCarthy, Brooks, Lowell, & Zakaras, 2001).

The Performing Arts Delivery Channels

The theatre is part of the performing arts that presents art work dramatically in different forms on stage. Figure 1 shows the different categories of art. Art itself is not an easy concept to define, since it is a composite concept that describes many things. The most widely accepted definition of it is "art is an imitation of an imagined or real object or thought" (Huberman, Pope, & Ludwig, 1993). Art has been categorized into two major parts: applied arts that are valued for their specific uses, and fine arts that are valued aesthetically.

Fine arts are classified into two main categories: spatial and temporal. Graphic and plastic arts are material created and manipulated in space. Anything that is created by the manipulation of sound, symbols, moving forms, and any combination thereof over a period of time is considered time art. Poetry and narratives are categorized under the literary arts while dance, music, and drama are categorized under the performing arts.

Art must be presented and delivered to its audience to be appreciated. To that effect, several delivery systems facilitate that function. Figure 1 presents three main channels of performing

Figure 1. The categories of art, adapted from Huberman, Pope, & Ludwig (1993).

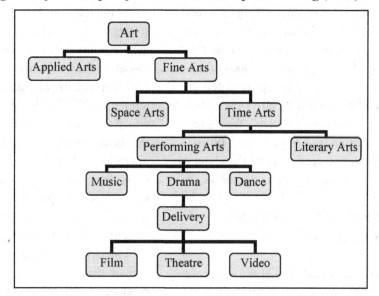

arts delivery: film, theatre, and video. Since the commercial use of the Internet is rather recent, the Web (as one of the Internet applications) has been used as a means of publicizing performances and selling tickets rather than a fourth delivery channel. This has to do in large part to the nature of the theatrical presentation, which is by definition a *live* performance. This is one of the challenges that faced Sam in his quest to integrate the theatre's operations in its Web presence.

THE THEATRICAL PRODUCTION PROCESS

E-commerce or e-business did not have a significant impact on the production of a play or a musical, which remains in large part a humanistic endeavor. A manuscript produced by a playwright is the first step in creating a performance. Many playwrights have agents who represent them vis-à-vis producers and theatre houses. The manuscript runs through several readings and filtrations before it reaches an artistic director, who has the final decision. If the manuscript is produced, the producer gets involved and he/she has the final go/no-go production decision. If the producer's expectations are positive for a good audience response, then the producer works on finding a director for the play. The director's role is to envision the whole production process and assign the duties to the individuals in the production.

Live performances have the special characteristic of individuality, unlike traditional movies, where each movie is an identical copy of the original production. This presents a challenge for the director who works on tying the work together to give it a consistent and coherent form each and every time it is presented. The production finally goes live on stage to a divergent audience that includes critics, reviewers, and patrons, and could have either a favorable or an uncomplementary reception.

Most stages in this process are not dependent on technology, and certainly the Internet played little role in altering any of them. Although e-mail and attachments are in wide use today, this form of communication did not disintermediate agents that are required by many theatre houses as the only venue for play submission. Casting for a role in a performance is done in person, and the Web did not substitute for that. The most visible role the Web has played was to present opinions of critics and reviewers about a production to potential audiences. Whether using a theatre's own Web site, or through other media outlets' Web sites, reviews of performances are presented online, and in many instances, readers have the chance to respond to a particular opinion or review.

A Short History of the New York Theatre Group (NYTG)

The theatre was established in 1970 as a nonprofit organization. The early strategic vision was to produce a large number of off-Broadway plays of high standards to qualify for outstanding awards. This was achieved by producing 23 plays in six weeks in the early days of the theatre's existence. Afterwards, NYTG was awarded several grants from different foundations. In the early years of the Internet commercialization, around 1997, NYTG launched a creative and an ambitious program called TheatreConnection. This program uses the Internet to connect schools and students together in order to produce and discuss plays made by other schools (the program is described in more detail in the theatre programs section.) By 2005, the theatre had produced more than 40 award-winning or award-nominated (Obie, Drama Desk, and Tony awards) productions, created a base of over 20,000 subscribers and 1,000 patrons who provide between $5 and $8 million dollars annually, and expanded its production facilities to the famous Broadway theatre district in New York City.

Organizational Structure and Management Responsibilities

NYTG is organized into a traditional hierarchical structure, headed by the executive producer.

His main responsibilities include developing and implementing NYTG's long range plans and strategies. The executive producer supervises the general manager, who is responsible for the day-to-day operations, and oversees five departments: development, finance, production, education, and marketing. The development department performs one of the most critical functions for NYTG, and that is to provide the needed funds to support its operations when traditional revenue from ticket sales does not cover the expenses (and usually it does not). Despite its importance, NYTG did not use its Web presence to support this function, although it is technically possible.

The artistic component is managed by the artistic director who, along with the executive producer, heads the development and production of the performances presented by the theatre. The director is aided by an associate artistic director who oversees some of the programs supported by the theatre. Before a musical or a play is presented on stage, it goes through several filtration processes, starting from readings by the literary assistant and ending with the artistic director. The artistic director and the executive producer work in tandem to determine which performance will be produced.

Market Segmentation, Trend, and Growth

NYTG's target market could be divided demographically, psychographically, and geographically. Demographically, patrons and subscribers have an average age of 50 years or more, occupy the upper middle to upper class (more than $80,000 annual income on average), are evenly divided between the male and female gender groups, and have at least college education. Psychographically, they are theatre advocates and supporters who give annual monetary and other support to theatre activities. Geographically, they are mainly the dwellers of the tri-state area (New York and specifically New York City, New Jersey, and Connecticut). About eight million live in the greater New York City region. The average per capita income in the tri-state area is $37,390. As the baby boomer generation begins to retire from the work force, stronger demand is forecasted for recreational and leisure activities.

SETTING THE STAGE

Sam works in a theatre bustling with activity. Back stage tours are scheduled almost every week, while casting for roles in new performances is a daily act. Sam's day begins around eight o'clock in the morning, when he checks his calendar for any appointments or meetings. Then he opens his e-mail client (he prefers Microsoft's Outlook) and responds to e-mails and sends out new ones for invitations and special events that were or are posted on the theatre's Web site. He also instructs the Web site hosting company on any changes or new deployments of new ideas or initiatives. The latest one aims to appeal to the younger audience, which included announcing free tickets and subscriptions for winners of a contest that asked the Web site visitors to identify the main characters of different performances presented by the theatre over the past decade.

The traditional venues of phone and fax are used to receive between $5 and $8million in donations, subscriptions, and ticket sales, and Sam wants to change that. Instead of faxing in their ticket and subscription requests and donations, which will take time for someone to receive these faxes, verify their information, and send a fax back to finalize the transaction, Sam sought to automate that through an online transaction system (OLTS). "This should make the transaction round time much faster for the patrons and the theatre, and will free our sales associates' time to focus on other marketing initiatives," comments Sam.

Management acknowledged the importance of technology by facilitating computer use in the

theatre by almost everyone, where all had Internet access, from the receptionist to the theatre director. However, in 1997, when the Web was flourishing into an unprecedented means of communication, transaction, and information delivery, the theatre outsourced selling tickets and subscriptions online to a third party (www.broadway.com). What it kept was enabling users to print out donations or subscription forms, which could be downloaded or viewed online, fill out the forms, and send them back through fax or snail mail. Although the Web site was redesigned several times, ticket and subscription sales were still handled by a third-party company (broadway.com) to handle the transactions.

In addition to musicals and plays presented, the theatre hosts many events that connect it with its audience and the community, such as stage tours, meetings with directors, writers, and other performance members. All these events are announced in print either through the Playbill publication, or via flyers given after performances, or are sent by mail. Mass e-mail is used occasionally to announce some of these events, but Sam does not like to rely on it often because of the sensitivity of some patrons and subscribers to spam. When the Web site was established, it was viewed as an ideal cost-cutting outlet to disseminate all this information without resorting to print, except in limited occasions such as the end of year financial reports.

CASE DESCRIPTION

The main objective of this case is to explore the experience of NYTG, a nonprofit performing arts organization, in using the Web and other online technologies to facilitate its activities and further its strategic vision. This is accomplished through presenting and analyzing its mission statement, describing its programs and the objectives it seeks to achieve through its Web presence, and portraying its business model and target market. It is important to understand the organic and dynamic nature of integrating and translating traditional brick-and-mortar business operations into the online domain. This challenge, while undertaken everyday by established organizations, is still insurmountable by many, and is not a panacea to business models seeking online lifeline and support. Bringing a historically deep-rooted cultural and organizational activity into the twenty-first century is a multidimensional challenge that demands an equivalent response (Andersen, Beck, Bjorn-Andersen, Wigand, & Brousseau, 2004; Winter, Saunders, & Hart, 2003).

NYTG uses information technology to manage its information resources. Computer systems are used to manage the accounting and financing functions, and in interoffice and general communication needs. Its Web site is outsourced to Broadway.com, which manages its design and hosting, and is supervised by Sam Jones, the Web site administrator. The following discussion will focus on how the theatre strategically uses its Web presence, and how it is tied to its marketing and management strategies.

When strategy of an organization is discussed, it is important to examine its mission statement. Part of the NYTG mission is to be "the creative and artistic home for America's most gifted theatrical artists, producing works of the highest quality by both established and emerging American and international playwrights...NYTG nurtures and develops new talent in playwriting, musical composition, writing, directing, acting and design... and it reaches out to young audiences with innovative programs in education and maintains a commitment to cultivate the next generation of theatre professionals with internship and professional training programs... [NYTG is a] leader in developing innovative ways to bring theatre to the widest possible audience. These include extending the life of its productions in house, transferring its productions to larger theatres and coproducing plays with fellow institutions" (NYTG, 2005). To fulfill its mission, NYTG has developed several

programs, which are either executed in house, in cooperation with other institutions, or online. The following section briefly describes these programs.

NYTG's Programs

Several active programs fill the schedules of artists, staff, and management at the NYTG. Except for TheatreConnection, execution of these programs does not rely in large part on information technology or the Web. However, it is one of the challenges that Sam is facing, which is translating or integrating these programs into the theatre's Web presence. Despite the fact that many of these programs are developmental and not transactional in nature, integrating them into the theatre's Web presence and using the Web technology to enhance their productivity will reflect indirectly and positively on the theatre, and ultimately on its patronship and finances.

TheatreConnection is an advanced project for introducing theatre education into schools. It uses the Internet to enable students to study and create theatre together. In 2001, nine schools (divided into three different units) from across the country participated in the project. The Web's multimedia capability is used to transmit original ideas and achievements. Students at each site write an original scene based on an NYTG play they have read and send some of its parts online; the scene is then staged and videotaped by students at a partner school. Through the TheatreConnection Web site, students meet with each other and with NYTG teaching artists throughout the process. The site also provides teachers and students with project syllabi, production terms, guidelines, and bulletin boards.

The play writing program encourages writers to produce manuscripts for the stage specifically, and it provides a laboratory-like evaluation and experimentation setting that guides promising scripts and writers through the development process. Members of the NYTG's artistic staff act as dramaturgical guides for plays in anticipation of their production, and they support playwrights at every stage of their professional development. Playwriting fellowships support early career writers with a living stipend, a commission for a new play, and the opportunity to observe the development and the rehearsal process for an NYTG production. NYTG's readings provide playwrights with the opportunity to hear early drafts of their works performed by talented actors. Workshops aid writers in answering important questions about plot and character development and help directors in resolving early staging issues.

The musicals program was established in 1993. It encourages composers and lyricists to write for the stage, nurture the next generation of musical theatre writers, identify new directors, choreographers, and performers, provide them with the chance to practice their work, and reach out to artists in other fields, such as popular and symphonic music. It provides the needed developmental support that leads a work from conception to production.

The educational program aims to develop new audiences for the theatre and arts in general, deepen the students' understanding of themselves and the world through the medium of the theatre, stimulate students' creativity and critical thinking through the active engagement with challenging new theatre works, and improve the ability of classroom teachers to teach the arts and to incorporate arts education into the curriculum. It began in 1998 and is serving a wide and diverse population with different social, cultural, and economic backgrounds from all over New York City area.

The center program brings students to a matinee of an NYTG production after a series of in-class preparatory workshops. The workshops provide specific insights into the plays under study, and a deep understanding of the theatre in general.

The interactive project gathers students from two culturally, economically, and geographically diverse communities to study and attend a play. Activities in the workshops include acting, writing, discussing, and debating with a group of their peers.

Writers for the future asks students to write and revise original plays inspired by an NYTG production they have studied. A team of professional actors, directors, and classroom teachers supervises the students' revisions, and the project culminates in a performance of the students' work by professional actors.

Teacher development workshops focuses on the collaboration between teachers and NYTG artists through providing teachers and school administrators with instructional tools and techniques for integrating NYTG's educational programming into their school curriculum.

Since other renowned performing arts houses have gone online and were successful in retaining and enhancing patron loyalty (Olson & Boyer, 2005; Vence, 2003), in addition to showing a positive result on their bottom lines, Sam wanted to follow suit and use the theatre's Web presence to inform the public in general and theatre patrons and subscribers in particular about these programs. He also wanted to make sure tickets and subscriptions to current and new patrons are sold online, and enable individuals and institutions to support NYTG online as well. Hence, Sam's vision of the theatre's Web presence is to

- Inform the public of NYTG's productions
- Sell tickets and subscriptions to these productions online
- Promote programs engaging the public in general and theatre enthusiasts in particular in different theatrical activities, such as playwriting, directing, and casting
- Develop and maintain a NYTG patron and subscriber bases
- Provide information about NYTG's educational programs, such as writers for the

future, internships, and fellowships

• Provide information about the space available for rent at NYTG's production houses.

• Preserve a loyal theatre subscriber and patron bases through email and listservs.

NYTG's Objectives Translated Onto Its Web Presence

High service quality perceived by users of a Web site reflect positively on their satisfaction with their Web presence visit experience (Kuo, Lu, Huang, & Wu, 2005). Sam wanted to provide NYTG's Web site visitors with the best experience they can find anywhere online. Information push (Kendall & Kendall, 1999) is used to supply NYTG's site visitors with almost everything they need to know about the theatre, its staff, programs, current and past seasons, and available rent space at its Creative Center. Ten out of nineteen main links on the NYTG's Web site are devoted for this purpose. The other links are used to "pull" information from the site visitors, such as asking for information about them when they want to subscribe, buy tickets, get involved in an internship or an employment opportunity, participate in a gala, or join the mailing or e-mail lists. Although NYTG management embraces technology and supports the use of the Internet and the Web in its operations, it has a policy of not accepting unsolicited manuscripts from individuals either electronically or otherwise. It only accepts them through agents. This is due to the large number of manuscripts that would be submitted by individuals in the absence of such a policy.

Subscribers and patrons are kept informed about the theatre activities through the traditional snail mail and e-mail. Several in-house activities are designed to strengthen ties with them through programs such as the 7x7 (readings of new productions) and backstage tours. Information about schedules of meeting times and places are regularly updated on the Web site. Stage and hall

space available for the theatre is not always used, so it is rented out to other institutions, which provides an additional source of funding. Funding is critical for NYTG's survival, and opportunities for support are found in several places on the site, whether in selling tickets online, or providing support through donations and gifts, gala events, and space rental.

The Technology Used To Build NYTG's Web Site

NYTG's Web site is composed of HTML, JavaScript, and Macromedia's Cold Fusion and Flash pages for interactivity. The Flash plug-in is needed to play the multimedia content on some pages. Although it is an attractive visual component, Web site visitors who have slow Internet connection expressed difficulty in accessing such pages, either because the Flash plug-in is not installed, or the Flash content has a large size and is slow to download. Tables are heavily relied upon to present the site's contents, which have the advantage of allowing it to remain unchanged in the event that viewers decided to change browser window size. High-level strength SSL (Secure Sockets Layer) 128 bits encryption is used to protect the information exchanged between users of the theatre's Web site and the servers hosting it.

NYTG's Business Model

NYTG's business model is based on expanding its subscriber and patron bases, and relies on converting performances, grant applications, and other fund-raising initiatives (galas, space renting, etc.) into income. The value cluster that NYTG offers is not limited to the stage performances, but it also includes the diverse programs that aim to develop and nurture new talents, whether performers on stage or writers behind the scenes. In addition, the theatre has many programs that strengthen its ties with its patron and subscribers, such as meetings that take place every week with interested subscribers to discuss the latest performance with the director, writers, and other performance producers.

Table 1 in the appendix categorizes NYTG's sources of income. About 84% of the theatre's income is from patron, subscriber, and nongovernment foundation contributions and grants. This departs from the traditional income ratio for nonprofit performing arts organizations, where 40% comes from public support and 60% from private sources. These numbers and ratios assist NYTG in determining the marketing and fund-raising sources and strategies. Most of this income is received through the phone and fax. Few subscribers and patrons do their transactions online, despite its availability and ease of use. Subscriber and patron demographic data might give a hint as to why this could be the case. Table 2 summarizes NYTG expenses. The greater proportion of expenses, 69%, is on programs produced by NYTG. The remaining expenses, or 31%, are for management and fundraising activities.

Target Market Survey

To better understand NYTG's market, and in an attempt to learn why patrons and subscribers do not use the theatre's Web presence to buy tickets or subscriptions online, or to simply donate or bestow gifts, Sam distributed a survey to its patrons and subscribers to discover their demographics and theatre attending habits.

Subscribers/Patrons

There are about 20,000 subscribers and 1,000 patrons who support NYTG. A small sample consisting of 77 respondents, divided into 31 patrons and 46 subscribers, agreed to respond to his survey. There is a categorical difference between patrons and subscribers for NYTG. A patron is a contributor at different monetary levels, each having a different label and privileges (for example: supporter, contributor, benefactor, and

so on). Subscribers, on the other hand, are purchasers of specific subscription levels to NYTG's performances. They buy these subscriptions and are entitled to attend a certain number of shows depending on their subscription level (3-play series, 4-play series…).

NYTG's Patrons and Subscribers Demographics and Theatre Attendance Behavior

There are 31 males and 46 females in the sample. About two thirds, or 68%, are over 50 years old. Only one respondent is in the age range of 23-29 years. More than 89% are either college graduates or have a graduate degree. About 73% had a yearly income higher than $80,000. A detailed cross-tabulation of respondents' income with subscriber/patron categories reveals that all patrons have an average annual income over $80,000. More than 35% attend theatre weekly, 45% attend theater monthly, and about 16% attend theatre twice or three times a year. Hence, about 82% attend theatre performances at least every month—that's more than 12 times a year.

CURRENT CHALLENGES/ PROBLEMS FACING THE ORGANIZATION

Theatre attendance used to be mostly for the privileged and royalty in the pre-industrial revolution era. When factories started appearing in major cities and people moved there to become factory workers, theatres sprung up everywhere to entertain the masses. This trend continued until television and moving pictures (movies) were invented around the 1900s, which drew some of the theatre attendees. People could now see identical presentations on a small or a big screen. Theatre attendance continued to decline after the invention and widespread use of the video cassettes in the 1970s, and the compact disc or CD and DVD optical media in the 1980s and early 1990s. People's lives and business operations where forever changed when the private sector was allowed to use the Internet for commercial purposes around 1994. All sorts of audio-visual entertainment experiences became available at the touch of a button or a click of a mouse.

Opening the Internet for commercial activity and the birth of electronic commerce, or e-commerce, leveled the playing field for commercial institutions, where a giant corporation has an equal footing on end user screens with an around-the-corner micro mom-and-pop shop. It also changed how entertainment is consumed. The availability of on-demand streaming audio and video 24/7/365 in one's home is very different from the need to schedule a particular time frame to physically attend a play in a theatre house with tens or hundreds of others. Also, live performances cannot be replayed or repeated with a click of button, and even a play or a musical that is presented every night will be different and unique, which is the hallmark of a live performance. In contrast, identical copies of movies and other audio-visual entertainment on DVD media, for example, could be paused and replayed repeatedly with identical outcome.

In this new age of entertainment delivery, some of the challenges facing theatre houses in general and NYTG in particular include:

1. Finding new, and for the theatre industry, revolutionary distribution channels different from the traditional wooden stage.
2. Attracting and sustaining a viable patron and subscriber base in current and future markets.
3. Enabling the current Web presence to be not only an integral but a primary source of funding for the theatre.
4. Incorporating the e-business and e-commerce technologies within the theatre operations and production processes.
5. Enabling individual internal contributions

to the current Web presence through content management software to decentralize online information dissemination.

The first issue pertains to exploring new delivery channels. Theatrical production is presented live on stage, which is the only prevalent delivery method. Online technologies and e-commerce activity is by far limited to selling tickets and subscriptions, and playing an informational role about the theatre and its activities. Discovering new channels of theatrical production delivery is one of the onerous tasks theatres are facing in the new online-connected world today. How could online technologies be used to transfer live experiences? The seating-limited number of persons attending a live performance on stage could become limited only by the number of online connections logged on to view the performance. This could translate into a revolution in funding streams theatres have not experienced before (Adelaar, 2000). Technologies that stream live performances are available today, but they face many hurdles, such as stage design copyrights (for example, attendees are not allowed to take photographs of the stage before, during, or after a performance), and matching the experience of witnessing a performance through a screen with attending a live one. The connection between finding new delivery channels and expanding the theatre's funding streams could not be more overemphasized.

The second issue relates to attracting and sustaining an online customer base, which is a challenge not limited to not-for-profit organizations. When NYTG introduced its Web site, few of its subscribers and patrons knew about it. Even after the theatre carried out a promotional campaign for its seasons and included a reference to its Web site, a temporary surge in Web site visits occurred. Contributions and ticket sales through the Web site did not change dramatically, as most of those sales, grants, and gifts were made through the traditional phone and fax channels.

This shows that having a Web presence does not translate into immediate or subsequent use. However, the Web presence is not isolated from the theatre constituents, since the age group of the theatre audience is a contributing factor (Van den Poel & Buckinx, 2005).

NYTG is trying to widen its base and focus on the younger audience through different means. Many of the current theatre subscribers and patrons are over 50 years old, so there is a whole market of younger audiences that is yet not well tapped. The programs sponsored by NYTG are in many respects aimed at youth, but to what extent that will effectively translate into more subscribers, supporters, and patrons is yet to be seen. Despite the numerous redesigns that the NYTG's Web presence has undergone, it fell into the general pattern of organizations who were providing more information than by adding e-commerce features (Benbunan-Fich & Altschuller, 2005). The younger generation is more computer-savvy and connected, and new Web features that command younger attention are needed. Many young Web surfers belong to online communities, and use different communication technologies to stay in touch. Thus, the theatre could use virtual communities' technologies, such as online bulletin boards or Web logs (blogs), to enable those groups to express themselves and return to the theatre's Web site for the latest news and information they could be interested in (Abuhamdieh, 2003). When such a young audience is present en masse, it becomes a potential for other sources of income beyond ticket and subscription sales, such as online advertising and promotions for that group.

Funding is the third issue for the theatre. The strategic positioning of the theatre's Web presence within its bundled offerings could have a significant effect on its operations. Web presence redesign, for example, increases the value of service organizations similar to NYTG (Benbunan-Fich & Fich, 2005). Web sites are much easier, cheaper, and faster to update, and information

is distributed to users instantly, compared to the traditional print, audio, visual, and other offline media. Responsibility of the Web site is delegated to Sam, the associate marketing manager, and site design and development is outsourced to Broadway.com. Ticket sales are also delegated to another organization (telecharge.com). Despite the fact that the theatre's income from ticket sales and contributions is over $8 million, its Web presence has not taken a strategic role to secure some of these funds, or add to its incoming fund stream.

For the theatre's Web presence to play a larger role in transforming its funding stream, a different online strategy is needed. For example:

1. Patrons, subscribers, and theatergoers in general need to be aware of the existence and viability of the theatre's Web presence. As described earlier, the theatre's patrons knew about its Web presence and actually visited it only after a short marketing campaign. In today's e-commerce world, online Web presence needs to be part of an organization's identity and an important means of connecting to it, not merely a sign that reads "we are here."

2. Patrons need to be encouraged to use that presence through all sorts of incentives, such as discounts and free tickets or subscription contests. They should also know the benefits of using the Web site for the theatre and themselves, such as reduced costs and speedier transaction time.

3. The Web presence should be built on ease of use and usefulness principles for end user computing (Davis, 1989; Venkatesh, Morris, Davis, & Davis, 2003). Many Web sites use the highest and most sophisticated technology to build, with extensive information and capabilities, but are not used simply because they confuse users rather than aid them in finding what they need.

Incorporating e-business and e-commerce technologies into the theatre's production processes is the fourth issue. Agents are required prerequisites to the submission of the manuscript, and even that is not taking place through the theatre's Web presence. In addition, casting is carried out traditionally, where personal presence is an essential step toward securing a role in a performance. Introducing online technologies into the core business process operations at NYTG goes beyond structural to cultural and strategic changes (Cao & Schniederjans, 2004). Opening up the window for anyone to send their manuscript electronically will result in a flood of material that needs a small army of staff members to carefully screen them and make a sound judgment on what is lean and what is corpulent and promising. Also, casting is customarily done in person. Doing so using online video conferencing, for example, poses significant challenges such as connection speed and reliability, in addition to the technical setup.

The last issue pertains to enabling staff members in the theatre's different department to directly contribute information about their activities on the theatre's Web presence using content management software, which helps in decentralizing information dissemination to the theatre's constituents. Immediate updates are possible without the need to pass through the desk of the Web manager.

Web presence visitors identify with what they view on a site's layout and design. Organizational Web presence is of critical importance because it influences an organization's existence, creativity, and customer appreciation. It is the image of the organization itself, and how its customers and patrons perceive it is directly related to how they perceive the organization itself. Thus, this close identity relationship should be on the mind of any manager responsible for the e-commerce operations of any organization.

REFERENCES

Abuhamdieh, A. (2003). Educational institutions portal system utilization: A student perspective. *Journal of Informatics Education Research, 3*(1), 29-40.

Adelaar, T. (2000). Electronic commerce and the implications for market structure: The example of the art and antiques trade. *Journal of Computer-Mediated Communication, 5*(3).

Andersen, K., Beck, R., Bjorn-Andersen, N., Wigand, R., & Brousseau, E. (2004). European e-commerce policies in the pioneering days, the gold rush and the post-hype era. *Information Infrastructure and Policy: An International Journal on the Development, Adoption, Use and Effects of Information Technology, 9*(3-4), 217-232.

Benbunan-Fich, R., & Altschuller, S. (2005). Web presence transformations in the 1990s: An analysis of press releases. *IEEE Transactions on Professional Communication, 48*(2), 131.

Benbunan-Fich, R., & Fich, E. M. (2005). Measuring the value of refining a Web presence. *Journal of Electronic Commerce in Organizations, 3*(1), 35.

Cao, Q., & Schniederjans, M. (2004). Empirical study of the relationship between operations strategy and information systems strategic orientation in an e-commerce environment. *International Journal of Production Research, 42*(15).

Channick, J. (2000). Promise and progress. *American Theatre, 17*(7), 4.

Coen, S. (2000). The field and its challenges. *American Theatre, 17*(1), 98-107.

Davis, F. D. (1989). Perceived usefulness, perceived ease of use, and user acceptance of information technology. *MIS Quarterly, 13*(3), 319.

Huberman, J. H., Pope, B. L., & Ludwig, J. (1993). *The theatrical imagination*. Fort Worth, TX:

Harcourt Brace College Publishers.

Kendall, J. E. (2006). Theatres, metaphors, and e-collaboration: An examination of Web-based cooperation of regional nonprofit theatres. *International Journal of E-collaboration, 2*(1), 41-60.

Kendall, J. E., & Kendall, K. E. (1999). Web pull and push technologies, The emergence and future of information delivery systems. In K. E. Kendall (Ed.), *Emerging information technologies, improving decisions, cooperations, and infrastructure.* Thousand Oaks, CA: Sage.

Kuo, T., Lu, I.-Y., Huang, C.-H., & Wu, G.-C. (2005). Measuring users' perceived portal service quality: An empirical study. *Total Quality Management & Business Excellence, 16*(3), 309.

McCarthy, K., Brooks, A., Lowell, J., & Zakaras, L. (2001). *The performing arts in a new era.* Santa Monica, CA: Rand McNally.

NCCS. (2005). *Number of nonprofit organizations in the United States 1996-2004.* Retrieved August 22, 2005, from http://nccsdataweb.urban.org/PubApps/profile1.php?state=US

New York Theatre Group. (2005). Mission statement [Electronic Version]. *Annual report.* Retrieved August, 2005.

O'Quinn, J. (2000). Why can't we all just get along? We can. *American Theatre, 17*(7), 82.

Oehler, J. E. (2000). Not-for-profit organizations can profit by investing in the Internet. *The CPA Journal, 70*(12), 65.

Olson, J. R., & Boyer, K. K. (2005). Internet ticketing in a not-for-profit, service organization:

Building customer loyalty. *International Journal of Operations & Production Management, 25*(1), 74.

Roufa, M. (2000). Can nonprofits really raise money on the Interne? *Nonprofit World, 17*(3), 10-12.

Saeed, K. A., Grover, V., & Hwang, Y. (2005). The relationship of e-commerce competence to customer value and firm performance: An empirical investigation. *Journal of Management Information Systems, 22*(1), 223.

T'eni, D., & Kendall, J. E. (2004). Internet commerce and Fundraising. In D. R. Young (Ed.), *Effective economic decision-making by nonprofit organizations* (pp. 167-189). New York: The Foundation Center.

Van den Poel, D., & Buckinx, W. (2005). Predicting online-purchasing behaviour. *European Journal of Operational Research, 166*(2), 557-575.

Vence, D. (2003). Boston orchestra tunes up net campaign. *Marketing News, 37*(13), 5-6.

Venkatesh, V., Morris, M., Davis, G. B., & Davis, F. D. (2003). User acceptance of information technology: Toward a unified view. *MIS Quarterly, 27*(3), 425.

Voss, Z. G., & Voss, G. B. (2004). *Theatre facts 2004*: Theatre Communications Group.

Winter, S. J., Saunders, C., & Hart, P. (2003). Electronic window dressing: Impression management with Web sites. *European Journal of Information Systems, 12*(4), 309.

APPENDIX

Table 1. Categorization of NYTG sources of income for the fiscal year 2002

Expenses	Dollars	Percentages
Program services	9,571,726	69%
Management and general	1,607,731	12%
Fundraising	2,540,729	19%
Total	13,720,186	100%

Table 2. Categorization of NYTG expenses for the fiscal year 2002

NYTG's Income	Dollars	Percentages
Ticket Sales	5,233,775	31%
Royalties, subsidiary rights, and co-production	713,064	4%
Other income	305,281	2%
Government contributions and grants	1,600,384	10%
Nongovernment contributions and grants	8,968,084	53%
Total	16,820,588	100%

This work was previously published in International Journal of Cases on Electronic Commerce, Vol. 3, Issue 1, edited by M. Khosrow-Pour, pp. 28-47, copyright 2007 by IGI Publishing, formerly known as Idea Group Publishing (an imprint of IGI Global).

Chapter XVII
E–Commerce Links for SMEs within the Industry Value Chain

Sylvie Feindt
SFC, Germany

Judith Jeffcoate
University of Buckingham, UK

Caroline Chappell
The Trefoyle Partnership, UK

ABSTRACT

The objective of this chapter is to evaluate the use of e-commerce across the value chains of several companies. In order to fulfil this objective, two different types of supply chain are analysed: the first type consists of buyer groups in the consumer goods sector; the second is dynamic networks in the manufacturing sector. Having identified what value activities are automated, the chapter examines the level of ICT and how value activity interactions between organisations are supported with e-commerce. Building on the analysis of e-commerce technology usage, the development of virtual structures is examined and the roles that SMEs can play in these. The chapter seeks to demonstrate that, with the introduction of e-commerce technologies in value activities across companies, the role of the current players is changing. Finally, the extent to which the traditional supply chain tiers change into more virtual value chain structures is evaluated.

OBJECTIVES AND APPROACH

This chapter is based on research carried out as part of the EU research project KITS, which looked at the use of e-commerce by small and medium enterprises (SMEs) in value chain relationships. The objective of this chapter is to evaluate the use of e-commerce across value chains of several companies. In order to fulfil this objective, two different types of supply chains are analysed. The first type is represented by three buyer groups in the consumer goods sector, the second by two dynamic networks in the manufacturing sector. They represent promising concepts for SMEs in terms of increased competitiveness. The research in this report focuses on firms engaged in the production and distribution of well established product types or services. The aim is to examine changes in existing commercial patterns as a result of the adoption of e-commerce in value chain relationships.

Porter's (1984) nine value activities were used as a starting point. Porter says: "Every company is a collection of activities that are performed to design, produce, market, deliver and support its product. All these activities can be represented using a value chain." Porter's value chain separates company activities into strategically important activities called value activities. These are physically and technologically distinct activities that the company performs.

For this chapter an analysis was carried out of value activities that are inter-linked across different organisations using e-commerce technologies. This approach enables the capture of types of electronic links between SMEs and their business partners which shape the organisation, the value chain itself, and the way in which business processes are carried out. As a result of differentiation and integration of economic activities across company boundaries, a network or value chain can stretch from one or several interwoven sectors. The unit of analysis is thus extended beyond the company to include some inter-organisational elements.

SAMPLE

In order to extend the unit of analysis in this way, it was essential that the companies interviewed were connected together in different types of supply chains. The aim was to interview as many companies linked together as possible, excluding individual SMEs, in order to capture different types and levels of value activity integration through electronic means. The supply chains targeted include large-scale companies but also included network structures, which were particularly favourable for SMEs. An additional requirement was that the interviewed chains and networks should use e-commerce technologies among them. In order to interview inter-linked companies, central points of the network or chain were identified. If the company in the central position refused to be interviewed, the whole chain was dropped.

The sample was composed of 24 companies as shown in Table 1. In addition, two interviews with industry representatives were carried out.

Broadly speaking, the sample is composed of two types of value chains that seem to group many SMEs:

- **Consumer Goods Sectors:** The first type of supply chain is grouped around buyer groups which seek to obtain better conditions with suppliers for their retail or wholesale members. These organisations can take the form of a company or an association. Some

Table 1. Sample structure

Type S	ector	Number of companies	Country
Consumer Goods	Textiles	12 G	ermany, Austria, Switzerland
F	ood	2	UK
W	ood Wholesale 2	G	ermany
Manufacturing	Aerospace	4	UK
M	anufacturing 4	G	ermany

of these buyer groups are very large, servicing more than a thousand retail or wholesale members. They exist in all food and nonfood sectors. The companies in this sample are representative of this rather typical model for SMEs in the retail-wholesale area. The fashion supply chain has as a starting point three buyer groups that cooperate and which not only commonly procure but also organise the production of own labels, and the provision of other services for their retail members. They cooperate with producers, transport companies, and service providers.

- **Dynamic Networks in the Manufacturing Sector:** In these cases, companies have joined forces in a dynamic network to bid for larger projects, subcontract to each other but also to participate in a learning environment. Regional development agencies, universities, research institutes, or consultancies often facilitate these networks.

RESEARCH QUESTIONS

In order to focus on supply chain integration through electronic means, it was important to understand which value activity interactions were being automated using the Internet. Accordingly, the main propositions for KITS relate to industry value chain partnerships and activities, keeping the focus on inter-organisational cooperation:

- Which value activity interactions are being automated with B2B e-commerce and in which types of sectors/value chain/value chain roles? Is there a relationship between these value activity interactions and the ranking of the value activities carried out by the interviewees?
- What levels of automation are being applied to different value activity interactions and in what circumstances? What are the

incentives of moving from value activity interactions with simple levels of support from information and communications technologies (ICT) to more complex levels with advanced technology support?

- What is the impact of the Internet on industry value chains? And which roles can SMEs play in virtual value chains?

In order to discover this, interviewees were asked to:

- Rank their value activities as defined by Porter (1984) on a scale from 1 to 5.
- Describe the automation and integration of highly ranked activities, as internal system integration is a prerequisite for inter-linking efficiently with partners. Respondents were asked to describe their internal electronic links between value activities, as well as how they automate value chain interactions with business partners, customers and suppliers.
- Describe network connections with partners up and down the value chain. Respondents were asked about their upstream and downstream links in the industry value chain to discover how many of these links each company had and why they were significant.
- Explain how they use technologies to support the links with their business partners and to what extent their success in the industry value chain depends on the technologies that they use or adopt over time. Technologies cover network connections, information exchange, the use of applications (e.g., messaging and marketing), and the use of external services (e.g., value-added networks [VANs], application services providers [ASPs] or Web hosting companies).

Drawing on the interconnected cases, the automation of B2B value activity interactions is assessed. Having identified what value activities are automated, the chapter examines the level of ICT and how value activity interactions between organisations are supported with e-commerce. Building on the analysis of e-commerce technology usage, the development of virtual structures was examined and the roles that SMEs can play in these. The chapter seeks to demonstrate that, with the introduction of e-commerce technologies in value activities across companies, the role of the current players is changing. Finally, it evaluates the extent to which a move to more virtual value chain structures changes the traditional supply chain tiers.

AUTOMATING B2B VALUE ACTIVITY INTERACTIONS

The interviews clearly demonstrate that there is a link between the ranking of value activities and the use of ICT and e-commerce technologies to support them internally and across organisational borders. One company in the sample that fails to rank its value activities also has not automated its value activities. This company, a wholesaler of toiletries, cosmetics, and household goods, is at a basic stage of B2B e-commerce adoption and does not appear to be interested in it beyond using the Web as an advertising medium. It tells how one of its customers—the following mentioned home delivery grocery—is reducing the amount of business it is putting through the toiletries wholesaler and diverting it to a much larger, member-owned buyer group.

If a company is not able to grade the importance of its value activities, it risks automating the wrong process or, as in the case of one interviewee, not being able to use ICT and e-commerce technologies to improve its process, thus risking losing business.

Analysis of Value Activity Rankings

The following graph shows the average ranking of a value activity by sector. The emphasis on value activity automation varies from sector to sector. Companies from all sectors have ranked operations top of the scale. Accordingly most companies have internal automation for operations in place. Across sectors, supply chain management systems dominate, which support the value activities inbound and outbound logistics, procurement and sales. Very few companies have enterprise resource planning (ERP) systems, which automate and integrate a high number of value activities, including infrastructure, operations, inbound and outbound logistics and even sales and marketing in some cases. The highest levels of internal automation within the sample were found in manufacturing.

Companies providing business services seem to use shared databases, collaborative work tools, or document management systems rather than supply chain management systems. These tools correspond best to their need to have rapid access to data on the part of past and ongoing projects or clients and they also help to codify know-how. In nearly all value activities, business services ranked the value activities as being less critical. When looking at the ICT usage in value activity interactions, it becomes clear the support levels are very low on average.

Analysis of Automation of Value Activity Interactions

Also, companies have started to link up value activities of suppliers or customers. Different types of service provider have e-commerce solutions at different levels of complexity. Consultancies support value activity interactions with e-mail,

Figure 1. Interviewees were asked to rank their value activities on a scale from 1 to 5

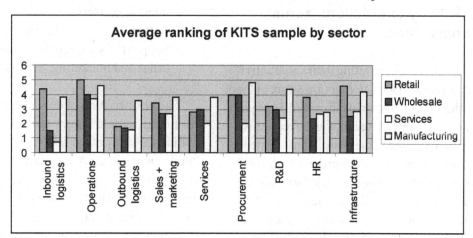

while a software producer has a comprehensive online application supporting service-based interactions.

Manufacturers, retailers and buyer groups have ranked procurement at the top of the scale, indicating their starting point for value activity integration. Also apparent is the correspondingly high ranking of inbound logistics by retailers and outbound logistics of the manufacturers. For example retail companies—ranking inbound logistics and procurement top of the scale—have linked their supply chain management systems via EDI with suppliers or the buyer groups they belong to. Alternatively, they have access to extranets or intranets to their wholesalers or buying organisations, which supports the ability to order online. Buyer groups ranked outbound logistics low as manufacturers are responsible for the delivery of the goods to the retailer members. The overall use of this technology should however not be overestimated. A buyer group reported that it has had an online ordering facility in place since 1997, but only 10% of its retailers make use of it. According to one retailer this, however, is not necessarily due to the technology. If the products or services offered online are not attractive themselves in terms of price or proposed items, even the most user-friendly service will not be used.

A home delivery grocery within the sample, however, is developing its own system that links it up with suppliers. A lot of its daily produce delivered by suppliers is invoiced according to weight delivered. This leads to lots of errors and invoicing problems as weight has to be checked and keyed into the system. It also imposes a daily administrative overhead on the company. The new proprietary system will link the grocery's order processing system (inbound logistics) with electronic scales on the suppliers' premises (outbound logistics). Suppliers will weigh their goods on the scales and this information will be sent immediately to the grocery's system, which will automatically generate an invoice.

The link between the scaling of the value activity and the level of automation is also underpinned by the differentiated scoring of outbound logistics with retailers: If the retailer sells exclusively through his shop, the value activity score zero. If the retailer has an online shop, outbound logistics scores a little higher, and it scores top of scale for an online grocery that carries out the delivery itself to home or office.

Extending the Use of Automated Value Activity Interactions across the Supply Chain

Companies that are integrating their value activities with suppliers and customers are aware of the benefits they gain. Companies advanced in the use of ICT and e-commerce technology, irrespective of their position in the value chain, want to extend these e-commerce supported processes to other supply chain partners. The rationale for this is that cooperating more intensely with fewer suppliers will result in mutual benefits. Others cooperate in intra-industry structures in order to strengthen their competitive position and avoid being driven out of the market. As such partnerships develop, they need collaborative tools and management systems to manage inter-organisational cooperation. Participation in such networked organisations leads to more advanced e-commerce support in all member organisations. The following section discusses which level of automation is required for specific types of cooperation and value activity integration within the sample.

WHICH LEVEL OF AUTOMATION IS REQUIRED?

Looking at the sample, it becomes clear that certain actors in the value chain will automate certain types of activities:

- Retailers focus on procurement and related inbound logistics.
- Buyer groups prioritise downstream links with members (sales and marketing, services) to overcome the groups' information gap regarding the sales data of retail members. However, they also consider putting their members in direct contact with listed suppliers on virtual market places.

- Service providers also focus on downstream integration (services, sales and marketing) so that they can collaborate with partners.
- Suppliers focus on downstream integration (sales and marketing, outbound logistics).

The prioritisation of downstream integration within the sample is very much in line with the findings of study of the U.S. Center for Advances Purchasing Studies. Among large U.S. companies implementing supply chain management systems, the customer side of most companies receives more attention and is more clearly in focus than the supply side. Most companies spend more time on, and dedicate more resources to, building strong customer relations, than to selecting and developing a world-class supply base (Fawcett, 2001).

The analysis of the complexity level of automation in the value chains interviewed draws on the concept of levels of control in inter-organisational systems (IOS). An IOS is a network of computers that enables companies to share information and information processing across organisational boundaries. Applegate, McFarlan, and McKenney (1999) applied the concepts of levels of control and interaction patterns to the American Hospitals Supply Company (AHSC) and American Airlines cases and defined four levels of control:

- **Level 0:** internal operations/management control, forms basis for expansion.
- **Level 1:** data control (EDI). Participant performs no information processing and merely enters or receives data. May be one way or two ways. Protocols defined and controlled by participants.
- **Level 2:** process control. Participant develops and maintains software that controls the underlying business processes. One or more companies invest to gain access to market information.

- **Level 3:** Network control. Participant owns or manages the network and computer processing resources. May be separate from other participants.

At each increasing level of control, responsibility, cost, commitment and organisational/technical complexity also increases.

Within the sample there are still companies, even large ones, that are working their way towards level 0. Other companies that do support their internal processes—in particular in the business services sector—see no need to integrate with partners.

Cases that use e-commerce technologies for their value chain interaction combine data control (level 1) and process control (level 2). The majority of interactions between organisations are still limited to e-mail, but companies are (selectively) upgrading. Members of a networked organisation believed they do not need more complex e-commerce solutions than e-mail and access to an Intranet, thus achieving data control (level 1). The network, however, is implementing an order management system. This would mean that partners cooperating for the limited period of a particular contract would need the support of a more advanced e-commerce solution at level 2, process control. Once the contract is completed, the level of cooperation could fall back to level one, which seems entirely sufficient for the purpose.

Throughout the supply chains, there are different levels of complexity used in e-commerce solutions and upgrading does not happen systematically. A retailer might have a mix of e-commerce solutions and manual interactions in place:

- A shop-in shop using vendor-managed inventories
- NOS with a specific supplier
- Order occasionally online from its buyer group by e-mail
- Procure in a traditional way with a listed supplier of his purchasing organisation.

However, others are moving quickly to a high level of complexity, pulling their value chain partners with them.

Within the sample there is no case applying network control (level 3). At the network control level, one or more inter-organisational system participants own and/or manage the computer managing resources. Level 3 control was developed to explain the service provided by companies such as GEIS, which had their own network infrastructure based on proprietary network standards. Traditionally cost and complexity increase dramatically at this level. However, the use of the Internet has altered the complexity and cost. The Internet is not "owned" by anyone and uses common industry standards. Therefore, it is possible to create application services over the Internet that are only Level 2. The provider does not need to own the network infrastructure and anybody can connect to it with a standard Web browser—there is no need for the provision of specialist application.

Between Data and Network Control (Level 1 and 2)

The levels of control were developed when there was little use of the Internet and really apply to EDI. The interesting thing about the Internet is that both sides of an interaction no longer have to do information processing to make the interaction work. With Web access, all processing can take place on the application developer's (i.e., buyer group's) site, without the retailer or supplier having to have an application that "talks the buyer group's language" on their side. This was not the case with EDI. Companies that want to talk EDI system to system both have to implement an application (level 2 to level 2). The following section presents three cases of automation of value activity interactions from the textile supply chain, which comprise a mix of level 1 and/or level 2 complexity. These are:

- An online information and purchasing system.
- A vendor managed inventory system.
- Customer and ASP services.

For each case, the levels of control achieved is described, together with a discussion as to whether the level is sufficient or whether upgrading is required.

Online Information and Purchasing System

Despite the long-standing cooperation of the three buyer groups, there is no integrated information system between the retailers, the cooperating buyer groups, and suppliers. Interviewing the three independent organisations, it appears that a piecemeal approach to the automation of interactions has been pursued with little coordination in the past. The current online information and purchasing systems are not integrated. The retail members of all buyer groups have access to the online purchasing system via e-mail (level 1).

The most advanced system has been implemented by the Austrian buyer group. Its intranet platform allows administration of meta data (this is processing, therefore level 2) originating from suppliers and partners as well as specific information on product groups, conditions and pricing structures. It has also developed a marketplace function (level 2) where members can offer stocks to improve sales quota and stock turnover. A B2B e-commerce solution could be built on the intranet platform, which would benefit in particular smaller members.

Impacts of Higher Levels of Automation

Retailer members currently make very limited use of the online ordering facility of the German buyer group. An interviewee reported that the offered items do not correspond to what he wants to purchase and the prices are not really interesting. He also judges that the intranet is not really fitting his needs. By not moving to a higher level of value activity integration, the buyer groups continue to suffer from an information gap and the retailers are likely to remain unsatisfied with the provided service. Higher complexity e-commerce solutions would allow moving to process control (level 2). This would help to optimise forecasting, procurement and the service spectrum, thus strengthening the buyer groups, as a higher percentage of the retailers' turnover could be procured from listed suppliers.

The buyer groups have realised the shortcomings and are trying to move to level 2—process control. One buyer group aims to integrate the supply chain management system of the members via EDI, to generate aggregated sales data on, for example, specific colours, sizes, volumes, and price categories ordered. It aims to start with 20 to 25 members but is anticipating a snowball effect. It is aware that it will need to do a lot of convincing of retailer members as currently less than 10% of their members use EDI to order from their manufacturers. However, 60% of their members are using the supply chain management system of the software provider within the sample, which is also in the process of integrating the supply chain management systems of its customers in order to generate anonymised sales and market data. The rest of its members do not want to participate (30%) or have a different system (10%). As the project would need a clearinghouse for the data, the software provider would be a good candidate for such a service. In addition the three buyer groups are discussing the inter-linking of their systems. It is evident that the three buying groups have no common strategy. The consequence is overlapping and competing initiatives, emerging conflicts of interests with partners and a confusing service offering to retail members. This might endanger the position of the buyer groups within the supply chain.

Vendor-Managed Inventory Solutions

Vendor-managed inventories are an example of process control (level 2). Three out of the four interviewed fashion retailers have currently implemented vendor-managed inventory solutions. Whereas one retailer has implemented such a system with a single supplier, a second is integrated with three of its largest suppliers, including the purchasing group it belongs to. A third retailer has integrated its supply chain management system with 10 suppliers. It has the most advanced partnership currently with a large supplier that has the control of a defined sales space and receives sales reports from its integrated system. All three retailers are integrated with one of the suppliers within the sample, and two of the retailers use the supply chain management system of the software provider within the sample.

The integration of systems in retail only makes sense if a product range has been agreed with the manufacturer. This requires not only a management decision but also the willingness to share information, the adaptation of processes and the implementation of technology that will support these processes. An example is the point of sale system that the third retailer has implemented with a large supplier. This concept included sales area management and consequent sales area servicing. The supplier's personnel analyse the present range of products and replaces poor selling items, while items that sell well are enhanced. In addition, some of the suppliers, who generate the largest turnover, also provide support for shop design and marketing.

Figure 2 shows the integration of activities required for vendor managed inventory concepts. The supplier takes over part of the value activities of the retailer, which are in the figure shaded in dark grey. The supplier is responsible for the procurement of items in the shop-in-shop solutions as well as for their delivery (procurement and inbound logistics). Under this system manufacturers do not replenish buyer's warehouses, rather they predict store-level demand per stock keeping unit and replenish each store (Au & Ho 2002). As the supplier is also responsible for the optimisation of the product mix to be sold in its shop-in-shop, it takes over management decisions of the retailer (infrastructure). The more vendor-managed inventory systems the retailer

Figure 2. KITS adaptation of Porter (1984)

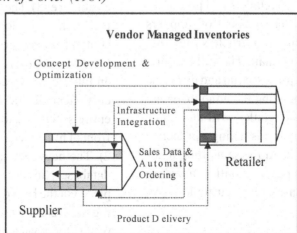

implements with different suppliers, the larger the share of procurement, inbound logistics, and management decisions taken over by suppliers. An extensive use of such systems has the effect that the creative part of the work of a retailer, procurement and item optimisation moves upward in the value chain to suppliers.

This integration impacts, however, on nearly all value activities within the organisation of the supplier, and has an impact on its own suppliers (areas shaded in light grey). Not only inbound and outbound logistics and sales and marketing are affected, but also operations, infrastructure, and product (technical) development. Accordingly, a supplier in the sample makes extensive use of IT to coordinate interaction of system components so that there is a perfect flow of goods to the customer (level 2). The supplier designs, organises the production, and markets 12 collections per year. In addition, it has programmes that correspond to its vendor managed inventory strategy with its retailers. This includes direct delivery of fast moving basics (quick response, NOS); immediate reproduction of items that have sold very fast (repeat system) and fast reaction to unexpected trends (flash programmes). All these processes require very high levels of control, and therefore heavy use of complex e-commerce solutions (for example, the extraction of sales data from the retailer) and for the support of logistics as the sales point receives new products every other day.

As a result, about 400 retailers and producers are connected via EDI. The majority of suppliers are networked using European Article Numbering (EAN) codes and also e-mail. The full automation of the value chain processes up and down the chain (for example, enabling the announcement of delivery times to the retailer) will take time. However, the manufacturer is taking a proactive role in implementing it. At the same time it abstains from selling its products online, avoiding channel conflicts with its retail customers (Au & Ho, 2002).

Impact of Higher Levels of Automation

The fast growing supplier previously described is one of the rare cases where the supply chain management spans from suppliers to customers' customers. A study analysing supply chain management practice of major US companies concluded "nobody is managing the entire supply chain from suppliers' supplier to customers' customer. True integration beyond the first tier in either direction is rare… Most companies do not take a holistic approach to supply chain management" (Fawcett, 2001). However, the availability of such systems, enabling process efficiencies, and higher profitability for retailers and manufacturers, will be a selection criterion for suppliers to wholesalers and retailers.

Customer and ASP Services

The third example is the software provider, which carries out customer service and software maintenance remotely via phone-based help desk or e-mail (level 2—it processes data in order to provide the e-commerce-enabled service to customers). The customers access the service via level 1 e-mail. The provider has direct access to cashier terminals to change the configuration when personnel change (level 2 to level 2, because some processing is done at the customer end). The heart of their customer service is a customer information system (CIS), which contains all activities, requests, and phone calls for all customers. The system is accessible via an Intranet to which all outlets have access. If a customer calls, the responding employee has the entire service history of the calling customer in front of him and can provide adequate help (level 2). The new customer contact is inserted in the database. Ninety-five percent of the service takes place via the help desk; the rest is mainly installing the system with a new customer and training of staff of new customers.

The starting point of the software provider for becoming an ASP is its new product, an information system based on the integrated supply chain management systems. This is a closed user group currently accessed by a growing number of members. The underlying statistics programme is a by-product that has been developed out of the software provider's work on the SCM systems. The system potentially interconnects all the supply chain management systems of its customers. The sales information is sold to customers for a monthly subscription fee. Retailers are very much interested in having access to the sales data generated from the system (level 2). They are, however, hesitant to provide their own data on sales, stock and turnover, a precondition to make the system work. To ease the situation, participating retailers do not need to provide their more sensitive data on profitability or gross proceeds.

Soon the system will include an interactive feature: participating retailers will receive information on surplus stocks of other participating retailers and have the possibility of announcing their own remaining stocks (level 2). They will be able to buy surplus stocks from other retailers if the item happens to sells well at their shops.

Impact of Higher Levels of Automation

The proprietary software, combined with the ASP concept, will create relatively high exit barriers for customers (for example the implementation of standardised codes will tie them in). Also, the more retailers participate in the services, the more valuable it will become and the higher the incentive to buy the underlying supply chain management system. The ASP has the potential of opening new market segments and creating a virtuous circle for the software provider.

Benefits

It has been demonstrated that a mix of level 1 and 2 control governs the automation of the different value activity interactions. More complex e-commerce solutions integrate automated value activity interactions (Just as ERP systems integrate automated value activities). They not only automate value chain processes in a linear fashion, but they automate "bundles" of value activity interactions. Benefits include:

- The opening of new market segments
- New revenue streams through new services
- Improved customer service and loyalty
- Cost reductions
- Improved logistics for a optimised stream of materials and goods
- The creation of virtuous circles mutually re-enforcing benefits of products and services for customers
- Re-enforcement of the competitive position through creating higher profits for the company itself and partners

The absence of advanced e-commerce solutions could, in the long run, endanger the position of a company in the value chain. Partners up and down the value chain might migrate (at least partially) to competitors or new market entrants that have the technological capacity to reap the potential benefits from value activity integration.

The advent of the Internet seems to have made network control (level 3) superfluous as there is no need to control the network infrastructure In effect it is being outsourced to ISPs and others who do control the infrastructure. Also there is no requirement that both involved parties have to implement the same system. If they want to use any sort of private network or extranet, they will, however, have to implement compatible systems. The level of control depends thus on the role that a company wishes to play in its value chain. SMEs do not necessarily need advanced levels of support. The following section looks at potential roles that SMEs can play.

SME ROLES IN VIRTUAL CHAINS

In the first stage of the KITS research[1] four roles for SMEs in the virtual organisation were identified:

- **Value Activity Provider:** In this role, an SME carries out one or more value activities, or parts of a value activity, on behalf of a customer, or group of customers.
- **Value Activity Coordinator:** In this role, an SME coordinates the value activities of all the participants in the virtual organisation.
- **Value Activity Partner:** In this role, an SME works in a joint partnership with another company, combining value activities to better serve their customers.
- **Value Activity Market-Maker:** In this role, an SME brokers value activity interactions between groups of customers and groups of suppliers. Hagel (2002) calls this role "network orchestrator". Using the large Hong Kong-based trading house Li & Fung (Magretta, 1998) as an example, he presents the management of value activities as a strategy for growth through the leverage of the assets of others.[2]

To validate the four identified roles interviewees were asked if they carry out value activities for other companies, either in whole or in part, as well as, if other companies carry out value activities form them. As the virtual structures are just emerging, it is not surprising that most companies in the sample are not identifying the roles that they can potentially play in such structures. Whereas most buyer groups provide value activities (e.g., procurement) for their members, they all fail to recognise that using ICT and e-commerce technologies, they have a strong potential to play the role of a market-maker or a value activity coordinator, depending on their strategy.

None of the retailers realised their potential role as a value chain partner. However, some very advanced companies such as the hub of the cluster and an initiating company of the manufacturing cluster pointed to their potential roles as value chain coordinators. By the same token, a cluster member realised that he could play the role of a value activity provider, and a manufacturer that makes extensive use of vendor managed inventory systems with its retailers identified itself as a value chain partner.

Virtual structures are still at an early stage of the development. As such, most companies in the sample fail to identify a potential role for their own organisation. As brokers and market-makers tend to be the creators and drivers of virtual structures, their inability to identify the role and the related potential will slow down the development of inter-organisational systems or indeed leave room for the entry of new IT-driven competitors.

There is evidence that some new entrants as well as some established players, who are using e-commerce technologies in an integrated and innovative way, are putting pressure on other established players in the value chain. A marketplace, linking suppliers with retailers, puts into question the existence of established wholesalers. Manufacturers implementing vendor managed inventory concepts with retailers also circumvent marketplaces and wholesalers. Such pressure will force companies to precisely define their role and the value that they can add to the supply chain. They will also have to support their strategies with appropriate e-commerce technologies. Also membership in networked organisations to enhance competitiveness and to avoid being pushed out of the market requires companies to define their core competence and take specific roles accordingly.

Within the KITS sample three types of partnerships were identified, corresponding to those defined by Applegate et al. (1999).[3]

- **Intra-Industry Partnerships:** Small- or mid-sized competitors see an opportunity or a need to pool resources, thus creating a new technology infrastructure for an entire industry. Within the KITS sample the manufacturing and the aerospace cluster are such partnerships. The cluster is driven by survival: the companies have realised that they stand and fall together. Unless they all deliver to the required standard and price, contracts will go offshore. On the other hand, the manufacturing cluster has come together in a more favourable setting, also targeting a broader market. Via its selection rules, the network explicitly avoids having direct competitors as members. The present members can veto the membership of a competitor. Because of the inherent difficulty of managing the aerostructure cluster, a central hub staffed with experienced industry managers has taken the lead in creating the cluster.

- **Buyer-Seller Partnerships:** Sellers set up partnerships to service their customers. Examples of buyer-seller partnerships within the sample are: the cooperations between suppliers and retailers to introduce vendor managed inventory systems; the relationship that the home delivery grocery has established with its suppliers; as well as the partnerships between the buyer groups and their retail members. These partnerships work to the mutual benefit of both groups. However, there is an inherent power struggle in this type of partnership. For instance, the buyer group has an interest that its members purchase from listed suppliers or own labels. However, unless contractually fixed, the buyer groups have no means of forcing exclusivity of their own product upon the members.

- **IT Vendor-Driven Partnerships:** Technology vendors provide a platform for uninitiated industry participants to offer novel customer services or an information vendor

may form a research alliance with a major customer to bring products to market. An example of this type of partnership is the software provider for the textile retail sector with its efforts to become an ASP. The service offers highly valuable market data and the possibility of buying or selling surplus stocks. Also the information network that one of the buyer groups has established for its members, including the possibility of buying online or the cooperation of the buyer group with a marketplace, fall into this category of partnerships. Interestingly, there is a strong overlap and competition between the initiatives regarding the proposed services as well as in the target audience. Despite cooperation between all players there is no evidence of integration of all existing projects to the benefit of all.

What types of roles are emerging in the different partnerships? In intra-industry partnerships value activity providers and value activity coordinators can be found. In the case of the aerospace cluster the hub take on the coordination function permanently. In the manufacturing cluster every member is in principle a value activity provider. Members can, however, pass on requests or subcontract into the network, thus playing the role of a broker. The manufacturing cluster also has a formal broker within its network whose task is to market the networked organisation and acquire contracts.

When moving to process control (level 2) in a long-term oriented partnership between two companies, value activity providers become value activity partners. Buyer-seller partnerships are thus populated with value activity partners. Suppliers and retailers, or buyer groups and retailers, work in a cooperative mode in the more virtual structures. Buyer groups have, due to their position in the market, the possibility of realising the role of a value activity market-maker. No buyer group in the sample has realised this potential. The higher level of integration between the companies requires adaptation of internal value processes and impacts value activity interactions with suppliers further down the value chain.

The emerging IT vendor partnerships comprise either marketplaces (market-makers) or ASPs (value activity coordinator) or buyer groups with trading platforms for members, where suppliers (value activity providers) can present and sell their products (via market-makers) as well as the targeted retailers (value activity providers). In the sample these partnerships offer services which lack distinction from one another. In all cases, integration is based on e-commerce solutions that connects retailers and collect their sales data to improve forecasting and enable the optimised purchasing with suppliers or the trading of surplus stocks.

It is clear from the proceeding that value activity coordinators and value activity market makers are the drivers in the creation of inter-organisational systems. As they perform brokerage roles they require in principle higher levels of automation; hub organisations, ASP, and market places should aim for network control level. The value activity provider role is highly promising for SMEs. In fact, it is the role that most SMEs are likely to perform in virtual structures. Depending on the type of cooperation, this role can be performed with control levels 1 or 2. Where high value collaboration is necessary, a marketplace or broker may provide the initial match, but the value chain relationship will be value activity provider to customer.

CONCLUSION

Research conducted in this chapter has shown how the automation of value activity interactions with B2B e-commerce technologies is changing the structure of industry value chains and the roles of the players within them. The following key messages are drawn from the research:

- In the supply chains and networks, there are various levels of complexity in the IT infrastructure and e-commerce solutions. Although ICT and e-commerce technologies are considered valuable by the companies interviewed, the importance of face-to-face meetings is underlined, particularly in locally concentrated networks.

While the majority of interactions between organisations are still limited to e-mail, companies are, albeit selectively, upgrading. Throughout the supply chains, there are different levels of IT infrastructure and e-commerce solution complexity and upgrading does not happen systematically and with all partners at the same time. Different levels of complexity coexist at the same time. A retailer might use vendor managed inventory and NOS systems with a specific supplier, order occasionally online from its buyer group and procure in a traditional way with a listed supplier of its buyer group. However, others are moving quickly to a high level of sophistication, pulling their value chain partners with them. More complex e-commerce solutions integrate automated value activity interactions. They not only automate value chain processes in a linear fashion, but they automate "bundles" of value activity interactions. So-called "Triple A" supply chains with high agility, adaptability and alignment exist, but remain a rare species in value chains of SMEs (Supply Chain Challenges, 2003).

The advent of the Internet seems to have made network control (level 3) superfluous as there is no need to control the network infrastructure. Also, there is no requirement that both involved parties have to implement the same system.

Being a member of the networked organisation will move the individual companies to higher levels of automation as the network as a whole upgrade its tools and moves to more integrated order processing. Members of networked value chains stressed the importance of face-to-face ways of doing business in the cluster's first contracts while establishing trust, cooperation and the sharing of information across company boundaries. Cooperation is not just going to happen because the technology is in place. However, virtual structures will want to have a common platform.

Although interviewees agree that inter-organisational systems are to the mutual benefit of participants, there is a great reluctance to quantify the benefits of e-commerce support of value activity interactions. So far some interesting but anecdotal evidence has been obtained.

- There is a trend towards concentration and combined buying power. This represents both an opportunity and a threat, depending on a company's IT capability.

Increased competition in the consumer goods sector has led to concentration processes at all levels of the supply chain. Generally there is a trend for retailers to join buyer groups to increase their chances of survival. The buyer groups seek to obtain better conditions with suppliers for their retail or wholesale members and provide a whole range of services to their members. However, supply chains around buyer groups are characterised by a concentration process at the level of the individual members but also at the level of the buyer groups.

The absence of an integrated system from suppliers to retailers' sales points prohibits the buyer groups from reaping the benefits of their central position with a wealth of untapped information. Instead some new entrants as well as some established players, that are using e-commerce technologies in an integrated and innovative way, are putting pressure on other established players in the value chain. Marketplaces, linking a critical mass of suppliers with retailers, put the existence of established buyer groups in question. Manufacturers implementing vendor managed inventory concepts with retailers also circumvent marketplaces and buyer groups. As a

result retail members, unsatisfied with the services of their buyer groups, may migrate to alternative modes of supply; in fact to many retailers a mix of different procurement modes seems a promising concept.

A trend in manufacturing is that original equipment manufacturers (OEMs) want to cooperate with fewer suppliers but with those on a worldwide scale. As a result, small and medium sized suppliers will be suppliers to integrators, that is, tier 1 or 2 suppliers. There are very few small suppliers that are established in such specialised niche markets so that they can remain direct suppliers to, for instance, the automobile or aerospace industries. A strategy that small companies pursue is to group themselves in networks with the aim to be perceived as a larger organisation and gain visibility. Companies join forces in a dynamic network to bid for larger projects, subcontract to each other but also to participate in a learning environment and benefit from increase purchasing power. To enhance cooperation the structure will quickly establish electronic support tools such as Intranets, shared databases, collaborative tools, or order management systems.

- Emerging virtual structures lead to a change of roles of supply chain members.

Within the sample three types of inter-organisational systems were identified: buyer-seller partnerships, IT vendor-driven partnerships, and intra-industry partnerships. These different kinds of partnerships entail different virtual roles and require different levels of e-commerce technology support. It is not necessary for every SME to invest in technology supporting high complexity levels. The complexity level required depends on the role that a company wishes to play in its value chain.

Virtual structures are still at an early stage of the development. As such, most companies in the sample fail to identify a potential role for their own organisation. As value activity brokers and value activity market-makers tend to be the creators and drivers of virtual structures, their inability to identify the role, and the related potential will slow down the process of creating inter-organisational systems or indeed leave room for new IT driven competitors.

The use of advanced e-commerce technologies in value processes will not only have an impact on the two partners involved and their internal structures, it is likely to affect other partners in the supply chain. The integration of value activities of a supplier and a distributor is, for instance, likely to impact value activity interactions with suppliers further down the supply chain.

REFERENCES

Applegate, L., McFarlan, F. W., & McKenney, J. (1999). *Corporate information systems management* (5th ed.). Irwin.

Au, K. F., & Ho, D. C. K. (2002). Electronic commerce and supply chain management: Value-adding service for clothing manufacturers. *Integrated Manufacturing Systems 13*(4), 247-254.

Benjamin, R., & Wigand, R. (1995, Winter). Electronic markets and virtual value chains on the information superhighway. *Sloan Management Review*, 62-72.

Burns, P., & Dewhurst, J. (1996). *Small business and entrepreneurship* (2nd ed.). Macmillan.

Fawcett, S. E., & Magan, G. M. (2001). *Achieving world-class supply chain alignment: Benefits, barriers and bridges.* Center for Advances Purchasing Studies. Retrieved from www.capsresearch.org

Franke, U. J. (1999). The virtual Web as a new entrepreneurial approach to network organisation. *Entrepreneurship & Regional Development, 11*, 203-229.

Hagel III, J. (2002, October). Leveraged growth: Expanding sales without sacrificing profits, *Harvard Busiess Review.*

Kincade, D. H., Vass, D., & Cassill, N. L. (2001). Implementation of technology and relationships to supply chain performance: Apparel manufacturers' perspectives. *International Review of Retail, Distribution and Consumer Research, 11*(3), 301-327.

Kurnia, S., & Johnston, R. B. (2000). The need for a processual view of inter-organisational systems adoption. *Journal of Strategic Information Systems, 9*(4), 295-319.

Magretta, J. (1998, September-October). Fast, global and entrepreneurial: Supply chain management, Hong Kong Style. *Harvard Business Review.*

Pihkala, T., Varamäki, E., & Vesalainen, J. (1999). Virtual organisation and the SMEs: A review and model development. *Entrepreneurship & Regional Development, 11*, 335-349.

PLS Ramboll Management (2001). *DG Enterprise SME-commerce Project Output Report*, September. Retrieved from http://www.pls-ramboll. com/homepage/uk/news/index_SME-commerce. html

Porter, M. E. (1984). *Competitive advantage.* New York: Free Press.

Porter, M. E. (2001, March). Strategy and the Internet. *Harvard Business Review*, 63-78.

Robeiro, F. L., & Love, P. E. D. (2003). Value creation through an e-business strategy: Implications for SMEs in construction, *Construction Innovation, 3*, 3-14.

Schuh, G., Millarg, K., & Göransson, A. (1998). *Virtuelle Fabrik: Neue Marktchancen durch dynamische Netzwerke.* München, Wien, Hanser.

Supply Chain Challenges: Building Relationships. A conversation with Scott Beth, David N. Burt, William Copacino, Chis Gopal, Hau L. Lee, Robert Porter Lynch, & Sandra Morris, (2003, July), *Harvard Business Review*, 65-73.

Snow, C. S., Miles, R. E., & Coleman, H. J. (1992). Managing 21st century network organizations. *Organisational Dynamics, 20*, 5-16.

ENDNOTES

[1]   Results can be found under: www.sfconsulting.net

[2]   Hagel (2002) also identifies a fifth role of "resources aggregator", which he derives from the example of the investment company Charles Schwab. This role was not identified in the initial SME sample (first stage research) and seems more suitable as a model for large organisations.

[3]   Applegate et al. (1999) have actually identified four types of partnerships: Intra-industry partnerships, buyer-seller partnerships, IT vendor-driven partnerships and joint marketing partnerships. As however no joint marketing partnership was comprised in the KITS sample this type of partnership was omitted. In a joint marketing partnership competitors coordinate certain activities. They may cooperate to gain access to new customers and new markets.

This work was previously published in Global Electronic Business Research: Opportunities and Directions, edited by N. A. Y. Al Qirim, pp. 133-157, copyright 2006 by IGI Publishing, formerly known as Idea Group Publishing (an imprint of IGI Global).

Chapter XVIII

A Fuzzy Logic–Based Approach for Supporting Decision–Making Process in B2C Electronic Commerce Transaction

Fahim Akhter
Zayed University, UAE

Zakaria Maamar
Zayed University, UAE

Dave Hobbs
University of Bradford, UK

ABSTRACT

The purpose of this article is to present an application of fuzzy logic to human reasoning about electronic commerce (e-commerce) transactions. This article uncovers some of the hidden relationships between critical factors such as security, familiarity, design, and competitiveness. We analyze the effect of these factors on human decision process and how they affect the Business-to-Consumer (B2C) outcome when they are used collectively. This research provides a toolset for B2C vendors to access and evaluate a user's transaction decision process and also an assisted reasoning tool for the online user.

INTRODUCTION

Electronic commerce (e-commerce) is a widely accepted way of doing business, and within a relatively short time, its services have risen to become a core element of the Internet. A leading market analysis firm, Forrester Research, has indicated that online retail sales in the United States exceeded $100 billion in 2003 (Johnson et al., 2004), representing a 38% increase over the previous year. The growth of e-commerce is not only in the U.S., but signs point toward continued growth globally. To this end, we aimed at identifying major elements that back the acceptance of e-commerce among users. This study established the elements that contribute to the growth of users' trust, leading them to complete online transactions.

Fuzzy logic provides a means for coping with the ambiguity and vagueness that are often present in B2C commerce (Cox, 1994; Turban, 1995). Indeed, it was reported (Dahal et al., 2005) that e-commerce is mainly a social activity featured by interaction among consumers, sellers, brokers, and so forth. MATLAB was used because of the built-in support that assisted in understanding the intrinsic relationships between the driving parameters and their effects on the degree of B2C transactions in e-commerce. In conclusion, this study has provided a deeper insight into the factors affecting consumer perception of B2C commerce.

Nowadays, consumers have many online alternatives to explore and to make a sensible and safe purchase decision. They may find the same items offered by different online retailers with different price options in a matter of a couple of clicks. A consumer's buying decision could be influenced by different factors, such as trustworthiness, brand, reputation, familiarity, third-party seal, security and privacy, fulfillment, presentation, and many more. Consumers have to analyze and compare these factors in order to make a final decision of pursuing online transactions. The purpose of this research is to uncover hidden relationships between the critical factors and their effect on human decision process.

RELATED LITERATURE

Trust is an important factor in social interactions and one of the most dominant factors for the success of e-commerce. Since e-commerce operates in a more complex environment than traditional business, a higher degree of trust is required between different stakeholders. In e-commerce, a trading party becomes vulnerable to the other party's behavior (Maamar, 2003). In other words, both vendors and consumers assume risks in a transaction, although they do not meet face to face. A consumer can see a picture of the product but not the product itself. Vendors can make promises of quality and delivery easily, but consumers do not know if these promises will be kept. In order to deal with these issues, consumers and vendors must expose a high degree of online trust.

A consumer's lack of trust often has been cited as a major obstacle to the adoption and widespread use of e-commerce (Karake-Shalhoub, 2002; & Tassabehji, 2003). The stability of a business depends on the right balance of trust and distrust. Furthermore, people face information overload, increased uncertainty, and risk when they are engaged in e-commerce. As members of an e-commerce community, people cope with these obstacles and risk by relying on trust, as it is argued in this article.

RATIONALE FOR USING FUZZY LOGIC

This study adopts a fuzzy-logic approach and utilizes a mathematical research toolset known as Matlab fuzzy logic toolbox® in order to achieve its objectives. The rationale of choosing the fuzzy-logic approach is based on the underlying reasoning process behind B2C transactions, which is based on human decision-making (Mohanty & Bhasker, 2005). Although many factors influence the decision process of B2C transactions, the perception of an influencing feature is more important than the actual level of the feature itself. For example, if the perceived security level is higher than its actual implementation, then it will contribute positively to the level of B2C outcome. There may be cases where the inverse is true, as well, but for such cases, a high level of persuasion will be needed to alter the perception level.

METHODOLOGY

This study was based on the rationale that the actual level of any B2C transaction is based on two factors; namely, what is the level of trust (T) of the given Web site and how competitive (C) is this site for purchasing purposes? Therefore, we propose to investigate into the truthfulness of the following relationships:

$$T = f(S, F, D) \qquad (1)$$

$$L_{B2C} = g(T, C) \qquad (2)$$

Where S is the level of *security*, F is the level of *familiarity*, and D is the level of *design layout* of the B2C site. The premise is that the factors determining the level of *trust* T are a function of these three parameters. Therefore, any degree of B2C transaction will be based on the level of trust (T) and the *competitiveness* (C) of the Web site. Hence, there is a need to develop an Expert System that simulates the human decision process. This expert system should include factors like security, familiarity, and design as the main trust factors. Consequently, this initial exploration warrants the use of fuzzy logic for this study.

Linguistic Variables and Fuzzy Reasoning

The concept of a linguistic variable is paramount to fuzzy logic, where values of a linguistic variable are expressed as words rather than numerical values. For example, the statement "e-commerce is successful" implies that the linguistic variable *e-commerce* takes the linguistic value *successful*. The term *rule* in Fuzzy logic, which is the most commonly used type of knowledge representation, can be defined as an IF-THEN structure that relates given information or facts in the IF part to some action in the THEN part (Zadeh, 1973). A rule provides some description of how to solve a problem. Rules are relatively easy to create and to understand. Any rule consists of two parts: the IF part, called the *antecedent* (premise or condition) and the THEN part, called the consequent (conclusion or action). Furthermore, a rule can have multiple antecedents joined by the keywords AND (conjunction), OR (disjunction), or a combination of both.

Fuzzy reasoning includes two distinct parts: (1) evaluating the rule *antecedent* and (2) implication or applying the result to the *consequent*. In classical expert system, if the rule antecedent is true, then the consequent is also true. In fuzzy systems, where the antecedent is a fuzzy statement, all rules fire to some extent, or, in other words, they fire partially. This also can be understood that if the premise is true to some degree, then the conclusion also will be true to the same degree. It is required to examine the various hedges of this set, which automatically will create some additional subset of the trust indicators. When articulating perceived level of trust, then one can make a distinction of its actual level by the following expressions:

- Very low trust (*VLT*)
- Low trust (*LT*)
- Moderate trust (*MT*)
- High trust (*HT*)
- Very high trust (*VHT*)

Since there is no well-defined boundary between, say, low and moderate trust, which again is the premise of fuzzy-set theory, the following relationship between the fuzzy hedges of the same superset (namely, Trust) can be assumed. To determine a given projected level of B2C transaction, it is necessary to combine the levels of trust (five) with the competitiveness of the Web site. Assuming that the competitiveness can be captured at three levels (low, moderate, and high), then the mapping of rules for Trust and Competitiveness will result in 15 unique input mappings. This further assumes that a given level of B2C can be captured as a category (fairly, moderately, and highly), representing the likelihood of a consumer completing a transaction. Hence, the 15 rules will translate into three output groups for B2C.

Complete Inference Diagram

In order to get a complete picture of the fuzzy expert system, an inference diagram can give a detailed explanation of the processes involved. Figure 1 illustrates the steps and processes involved. The process with the crisp inputs to the fuzzy expert system; for example, this might be the crisp input for security and familiarity or design to get a value for the trust level. Similarly, a crisp level of trust and competitiveness will be required as inputs to the second level inference, as given in equations (1) and (2).

It should be noted that the initial input(s) are a crisp set of numbers. These values are converted from a numerical level to a linguistic level. Fol-

lowing that, the fuzzy rules are applied, and fuzzy inference engine is executed. This will result in a given B2C level as varying degree of membership of fuzzy subsets of the B2C superset. The last step is the defuzzification process, which provides a numeric value for likelihood of the B2C transaction.

1. How is this system useful to the consumer?
2. What benefits can the B2C vendor expect from utilizing such a tool?

For the consumer who is unaware or unable to reach a sound buying decision, this tool will assist him or her in understanding the parameters that could influence or ascertain the strength and weaknesses of the B2C site. Similarly, the B2C vendor can use this tool to discover the critical factors on which a consumer bases a B2C transaction, irrespective of the product/services offered. Consequently, a more realistic picture can be drawn of the factors influencing a consumer's B2C decision.

Figure 1. Complete fuzzy expert system

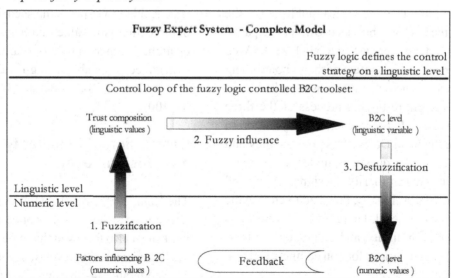

DATA COLLECTION AND ANALYSIS

This study used a Web-based survey (David, 2000) because of its advantages, such as convenience, viable, effective way to access difficult-to-reach respondents. On the other hand, a Web survey has some limitation, such as unequal opportunity (David, 2000). Even though only respondents who have access to the Internet are able to participate in this survey, this condition is exactly what is desired for respondents of this study, which is why a Web-based survey was chosen.

A pilot test was conducted to test the instrument prior to collecting data. The purpose of the pilot test was to access whether the instruments were capturing the phenomena desired. The questionnaires were presented to undergraduate students who were enrolled in different disciplines. The pilot study was used to refine the survey tool used in the study and also to clarify the wording, contents, and the layout of the survey Web site. Participation in this study was voluntarily, and extra credit was given to participants. A total of 150 participants took part in the survey.

Setting Up the Survey Site

An internal Web site was designed to evaluate Amazon.com, Lastminute.com, and Uaemall.com Web sites. Once the Web site was published on the intranet, the URL was provided to the participants. The respondents were asked to analyze the Web sites for purchasing an item of their choice using a credit card. The respondents were asked to go through the entire buying process of the three Web sites but told not to click the buy button to purchase the item. During this process, they had to respond to the questions under five categories: Security, Familiarity, Designs, Trust, and Competitiveness. Finally, they had to choose the appropriate B2C level. There were four questions on security, familiarity, and design, one on trust (but in four categories), four on competitiveness, and one on B2C level.

Choice of the B2C Sites

The three selected Web sites were well-known for their brand recognition globally. Amazon.com is a popular American Web site that sells books, movies, stationery, music, and electronic items on the Internet. Lastminute.com is a British Web site that assists consumers in travel business. Uaemall.com is a popular Web site among Arab consumers who like to purchase electronic equipments, perfumes, branded cloths, and other luxury items.

PROCESSING OF DATA

Calculation of Security Level

This worksheet contains raw data straight from the survey, and no interpretation is provided. In the *security* worksheet, a linguistic input has been assigned a numeric value such as 2, 1, or 0 in order to calculate the accumulated security level. Accumulated security level is the total sum of the four numeric values, and maximum is the percentage of the sum (x/8 multiplied by 100). This security level is then calculated as a percentage of a maximum value (usually 8), and from that, a linguistic security level is drawn. It was decided to express the security level as one of three linguistic values; namely, low, moderate, or high. The percentage of maximum is evenly distributed to establish linguistic security level such as low (0-33), moderate (34-66), and high (67-100).

Calculation of Familiarity and Design Levels

The *Familiarity* worksheet followed the same pattern as used in the *security* worksheet. The *Design* worksheet also followed the same pattern, except the linguistic design level was labeled as poor (0-33), moderate (34-66), and good (67-100).

Calculation of Competitiveness

In the *competitive* worksheet, the linguistic competitiveness is labeled as fairly (0-33), moderately (34 66), and highly (67-100).

Sorting of Trust and Competitiveness to Extract B2C Levels

In the *linguistic data* worksheet, trust, competitiveness, and B2C data have been entered and aligned with security, familiarity, and design levels by expressing them in terms of linguistic parameters, as explained earlier (section or page reference). Some programming also was done using the Visual Basic language. Trust and B2C categories are labeled as very low, low, moderate, high, very high and fairly, moderately, and highly, respectively.

Summary of Trust and B2C Rules

In the *trust rules* worksheet, a maximum of 27 unique rules could be identified from respondents' input by sorting the security, familiarity, and design columns in alphabetical order. In the *B2C_rules* worksheet, a maximum of 15 unique rules could be identified in the same way by sorting the trust and competitiveness columns into alphabetical order.

Table 1. Formation of trust rules

	Linguistic Variables			
Rule #	Security	Familiarity	Design	Trust
1	High	High	Good	Very High Trust
2	High	High	Moderate	Very High Trust
3	High	High	Poor	High Trust
4	High	Low	Good	High Trust
5	High	Low	Moderate	Moderate Trust
6	High	Low	Poor	Moderate Trust
7	High	Moderate	Good	Very High Trust
8	High	Moderate	Moderate	High Trust
9	High	Moderate	Poor	Moderate Trust
10	Low	High	Good	Low Trust
11	Low	High	Moderate	Low Trust
12	Low	High	Poor	Very Low Trust
13	Low	Low	Good	Very Low Trust
14	Low	Low	Moderate	Very Low Trust
15	Low	Low	Poor	Very Low Trust
16	Low	Moderate	Good	Low Trust
17	Low	Moderate	Moderate	Very Low Trust
18	Low	Moderate	Poor	Very Low Trust
19	Moderate	High	Good	Moderate Trust
20	Moderate	High	Moderate	Moderate Trust
21	Moderate	High	Poor	Low Trust
22	Moderate	Low	Good	Low Trust
23	Moderate	Low	Moderate	Low Trust
24	Moderate	Low	Poor	Low Trust
25	Moderate	Moderate	Good	Moderate Trust
26	Moderate	Moderate	Moderate	Low Trust
27	Moderate	Moderate	Poor	Low Trust

CONSTRUCTION OF FUZZY INTERFENCE SYSTEMS

Summary of Rules Providing a Measure for Trust

The rules describing the basis for a given trust level was based on degrees of security, familiarity, and design (Table 1). These degrees were formulated in terms of their linguistic variables, such as low, moderate, and high. The degree for Design level was expressed in terms of poor, moderate, and good. Similarly, the degree for a Trust level ranged from very low to very high in five distinct fuzzy sets.

These rules were derived from the survey data after a thorough organization and analysis and represent the users' views of the Trust level of a given Web site, based on the given factors. A rule from Table 1 can be extracted as:

If (security = high) *and* (familiarity = low) *and* (design = moderate) *then* (trust = moderate trust)

Summary of Rules Indicating B2C Level

Table 2 displays the users' preferences for B2C level, based on their perceived level of trust and competitiveness.

Note here that the Trust is given in terms of five fuzzy sets, while the competitiveness and B2C level is represented in terms of three linguistic labels for fuzzy sets. A given rule from Table 10 can be expressed as:

If (trust = low trust) *and* (competitiveness = highly) *then* (B2C level = moderate)

There were a total of 27 rules for trust deduced from the survey. Similarly, the rules disclosing the B2C level for various inputs were found to be 15. These rules form the basis of the compounded inference system consisting of two separate but interconnected systems to postulate a B2C level for given values for security, familiarity, design, and competition levels of the Web site.

Table 2. Formation of B2C rules

Rule No	Trust Linguistic Value	Competitiveness Linguistic Value	B2C level Linguistic Value
1	High Trust	Fairly	low
2	High Trust	Highly	high
3	High Trust	Moderately	moderate
4	Low Trust	Fairly	low
5	Low Trust	Highly	moderate
6	Low Trust	Moderately	low
7	Moderate Trust	Fairly	low
8	Moderate Trust	Highly	moderate
9	Moderate Trust	Moderately	moderate
10	Very High Trust	Fairly	moderate
11	Very High Trust	Highly	high
12	Very High Trust	Moderately	high
13	Very Low Trust	Fairly	low
14	Very Low Trust	Highly	low
15	Very Low Trust	Moderately	low

ANALYSIS OF FACTORS INFLUENCING TRUST

In this section, we shall analyze all factors influencing trust as set up in this study. It will be attempted to view the factors from various angles in order to disclose any unexplored relations between them.

Trust vs. Security

In order to fully understand the contributions from various factors contributing to the Trust level, it is required that we examine contribution from each factor separately. Figure 2 shows contribution to Trust of a given Web site originating from the Security. Therefore, the contribution from Familiarity and Design has been kept constant at three levels; namely, low, moderate, and high, corresponding to numeric values for Familiarity and Design of (1-4 and 7). Figure 8 shows that Trust level is monotonically increasing for increasing perceived security of a Web site for any given level of Familiarity and Design (F&D). However, when both F&D are High (numeric value of 7), the Trust level is at its maximum for maximum Security. The three curves have one common feature that they exhibit a staircase-shaped curvature.

It is interesting to note that for low and moderate levels of F&D, the developed Trust is almost identical up to a Security level of about 5. Then, there is a sharp change on the Trust level between low and moderate, and the perceived Trust for moderate F&D is approaching that of high. A general observation is that Trust is positively related to Security for any given value of Familiarity and Design. This observation is also plausible to the Human mind. One feature that is disclosed from this figure is that for high levels of Security, the Trust difference is less significant for moderate and high levels of F&D. This result could not be anticipated from the outset.

Figure 2. Trust vs. security for constant familiarity and design

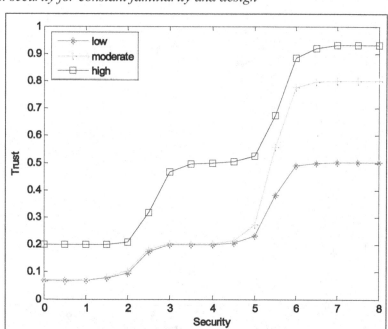

Trust vs. Familiarity

Let us now examine how Trust is contributed from Familiarity (Figure 3) for constant values of Security and Design (S&D). The values for low, moderate, and high have the same interpretations as explained in the previous section. This figure is considerably different from the previous one. One stunning point to note is that trust levels remain low for any value of Familiarity when S&D is low. This means that Familiarity is not an important feature of a Web site, if Security and Design is compromised upon. When S&D is moderate, then the Trust level is only affected when Familiarity levels are higher than 5 and exhibit a sudden sizeable jump, only to flatten out after Familiarity levels of 6 and higher.

When S&D is high, then Trust remains high and is rather constant (at a value of about 0.8) with increasing Familiarity. One peculiar feature is that the curve is somewhat concave for moder-

ate Familiarity and marginally convex for high Familiarity. This tends to suggest that Trust is positively related to Familiarity for high S&D but exhibits a ramp-shaped behavior for Familiarity value of about 3. Also, Trust is high for S&D levels being high with increasing Familiarity. One general point to note about the figure is that the hump is softer as S&D increases and as Familiarity decreases. This means that, although increasing Familiarity has a positive affect on Trust, the relative increase is more visible for moderate values of S&D.

Trust vs. Design

Figure 10 is noticeably identical to the figure in the previous section on Trust as a function of Familiarity. This means that for all intentions and purposes, we can substitute Familiarity with Design and vise versa without compromising perceived Trust level. This relationship is

Figure 3. Trust vs. familiarity for constant security and design

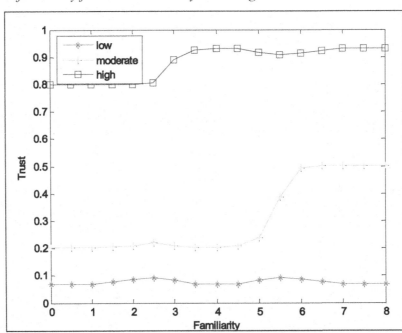

Figure 4. Trust vs. design for constant security and familiarity

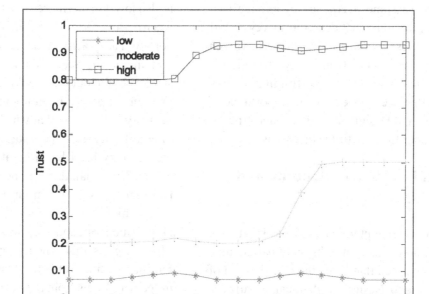

Figure 5. Trust level is positively related to levels of security and familiarity

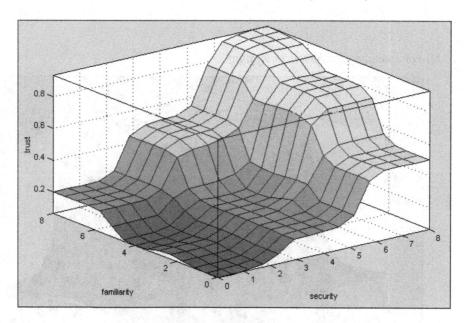

somewhat awkward and difficult to digest. One could almost assume that the surveyors have been complacent in doing justice to the survey. But if one remembers the premise for the level of a given factor (i.e., the level of Familiarity or Design is based on the levels of their constituting factors), it may be that users have kept the importance of Familiarity and Design on par with each other or have been confused with the questions.

Trust as Function of Security and Familiarity

We shall now attempt to visualize the Trust level as a continuous function of its input parameters. It should be noted that since the contribution of Familiarity and Design is identical, it suffices to view Trust as a function of Security and one other factor, say Familiarity. Figure 5 attempts to portray variation of Trust as encapsulated in the rules for Trust.

Figure 5 shows that Trust level is positively related to Levels of Security and Familiarity. That is,

when Familiarity and Security are low, then Trust is also low. Furthermore, Trust is at its maximum when both Security and Familiarity are maximum. For low Familiarity, Trust is increasing in steps with increasing Security, attaining its maximum at a level of about 0.5. Looking at Figure 5 from its topmost point, the gradient perpendicular to Security is less than that which is perpendicular to Familiarity axis. This suggests that lowering the Security level has a greater detrimental effect on Trust than that attained when decreasing Familiarity levels of similar magnitude.

The highest gradient for Trust is when Familiarity is moderate and Security is moderate to high. This suggests that when people are somewhat familiar with a Web site, then a small increase in security levels from between moderate to high security will boost their trust in a significant way. Looking at Figure 5 diagonally from (low, low) to (high, high) levels of Security and Familiarity, one observes three plateaus where the last one is around 0.925 and remains at that level, even when the input factors are increased further. This result

Figure 6. Mirror symmetry of the trust mapping

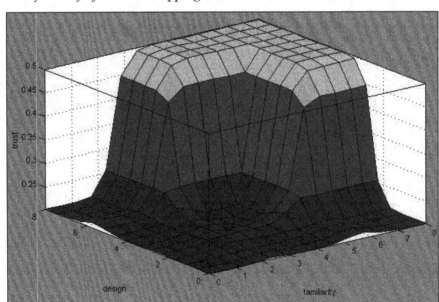

is somehow unexpected and may be due to the fuzzy nature of the expert system where a Trust or Truth level of 100 % is unrealistic.

Trust as Function of Familiarity and Design

The contributions of Familiarity and Design levels on Trust are similar and, in fact, identical. This also can be deduced from Figure 6, showing complete mirror symmetry of the Trust mapping.

One interesting point to note, however, is that for maximum Familiarity and Design, the Trust level is never higher than 0.5. This plateau also is reached fairly rapidly with high gradients from both sides of the input variables.

INFLUENCE OF TRUST AND COMPETITION ON B2C

In order to get a better understanding of how to promote online purchase of goods and services, one must develop a better understanding of the core factors influencing Business to Consumer (B2C) transaction levels. In this study, we have found Trust level and Competitiveness being the two most significant factors affecting a consumer's willingness to conduct online transactions. The second Fuzzy Inference System (FIS) consists of rules containing a user's mind for executing B2C transaction to a given degree for various combinations of the supporting factors; namely, Competitiveness and Trust. A total of 15 rules were derived, based on the survey. Figure 7 displays the B2C level as a function of Trust and Competitiveness. It is evident that as Trust and Competitiveness increases, the B2C level increases. However, for low Trust, the B2C level attains a level of 0.5 for high Competitiveness. This result is plausible, as one would not expect to conduct business on a Web site if the Trust were low, even if it was highly competitive. For Moderate to High Trust, the B2C level remains at a plateau of about 0.5, even for maximum competitiveness. This conspicuous result shows that people are highly Trust-conscious and not

Figure 7. B2C level as a function of trust and competitiveness

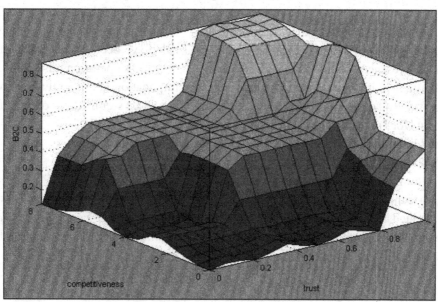

ready to take risks in an effort to catch a good deal. The second plateau occurs when the Trust level is High to very High, and then for increasing competitiveness, the B2C level is increasing rapidly. There is, however, a small unexpected dip for Trust of around 8 and Competitiveness of about 6.25. This dip occurs after the B2C level has reached a maximum. This is a peculiarity of the B2C surface that is not easy to explain, and one must refer back to the B2C rules.

SUMMARY

Consumers can be categorized broadly into two groups; namely, those that are technically critical of a site and capable of measuring its security features and those that are not. This survey can be used to follow step by step the instructions and, based on actual level of a feature, decide its contribution in a category and consequently derive a total value of a factor, say Security. Hence, the survey can make a buying decision more solid, based on actual appearances of various features. An added advantage would be to feed this data to the FIS for Trust and B2C, and the user could compare his or her buying decision with that of others, based on the outcome of the Fuzzy Expert System.

For those who are not necessarily technically inclined, this survey will assist them in trying to gauge the presence of a feature, say security seals, and attach to it a certain contribution (i.e., yes = 2, no = 0, and don't know = 1). After all the requirements for Trust are completed, the FIS for Trust could be used to provide a perceived level that the user could compare with his or her own. Similarly, the B2C level both could be guessed by the non-technical user and computed based on input valued and presented to the user for comparisons. Now, since this category of users is non-technical, the perceived B2C level also

could be compared with previous users who were technically inclined and presented as a possible different B2C level to reflect upon. This procedure would assist even the non-technical user to make an informed online purchase.

The vendor would benefit from the survey data that are aggregated over time and used to amend or refine existing rule-sets. Since the data would be accumulated over time, the responses would be a blend from both technical and non-technical users. Hence, the actual occurrence of a feature would be replaced by its perceived equivalence. The existence of a feature is relevant only to the user if it can be acknowledged, and if it cannot, then the vendor must seriously reconsider inclusion of this aspect on the Web site.

In addition, the vendor can use the survey data to ascertain the Trust level of the site as per the user's perception and rectify, if needed, if this is not obvious or if it is having a negative impact on the Trust level. Furthermore, a measure of the competitiveness is directly deductible from this survey and could be used to retain or to increase market share. Lastly, as the usage of the survey procedure matures (possibly by providing incentives such as discounts on a completed transaction), the Fuzzy Inference Systems could be modified and adjusted where necessary. One limitation of the constructed FIS of this study is that all premises in the antecedent part of a rule have been connected with AND operation where OR operations also could be deployed. The implication and aggregation from the rule then would be significantly different.

REFERENCES

Cox, E (1994). *The fuzzy systems handbook: A practitioner's guide to building, using, and maintaining fuzzy systems.* Cambridge: Academic Press.

Dahal, K., Hussain, Z, & Hossain, M. (2005). Loan risk analyzer based on fuzzy logic. In *Proceedings of the IEEE International Conference on e-Technology, e-Commerce and e-Services*, Hong Kong.

David, J. L. (2000). You've got surveys. *American Demographics, 22*(11), 42-44.

Johnson, C. et al. (2004). *2003 eCommerce: The year in review*. Forrester Research.

Karake-Shalhoub, Z. (2002). *Trust and loyalty in electronic commerce: An agency theory perspective*. Westport, CT: Quorum Books.

Maamar, Z. (2003). Commerce, e-commerce, and m-commerce: What comes next? *Communications of the ACM, 46*(12).

Mohanty, B. K., & Bhasker, B. (2005). Product classification in the Internet business — A fuzzy approach. *Journal of Decision Support Systems, 38*, 611-619.

Tassabehji, R. (2003). *Applying e-commerce in business*. Thousand Oaks, CA: Sage Publications.

Turban, E. (1995). *Decision support and expert system: Management support systems*. Englewood Cliffs, NJ: Prentice Hall International.

Zadeh, L. (1965). Fuzzy sets. *Information and Control, 8*(3), 338-353.

Zadeh, L. (1973). Outline of a new approach to the analysis of complex system and decision processes. *IEEE Transactions on System, Man, and Cybernetics, 3*(1), 28-44.

This work was previously published in International Journal of E-Business Research, Vol. 2, Issue 2, edited by I. Lee, pp. 54-67, copyright 2006 by IGI Publishing, formerly known as Idea Group Publishing (an imprint of IGI Global).

Chapter XIX
Evaluating E-Commerce Trust Using Fuzzy Logic

Farid Meziane
University of Salford, UK

Samia Nefti
University of Salford, UK

ABSTRACT

Trust is widely recognized as an essential factor for the continual development of business to customer electronic commerce (B2C EC). Many trust models have been developed, however, most are subjective and do not take into account the vagueness and ambiguity of EC trust and the customers' intuitions and experience when conducting online transactions. In this article, we develop a fuzzy trust model using fuzzy reasoning to evaluate EC trust. This trust model is based on the information customers expect to find on an EC Website and is shown to increase customers trust towards online merchants. We argue that fuzzy logic is suitable for trust evaluation as it takes into account the uncertainties within e-commerce data and like human relationships; it is often expressed by linguistics terms rather then numerical values. The evaluation of the proposed model will be illustrated using two case studies and a comparison with two evaluation models was conducted to emphasise the importance of using fuzzy logic.

INTRODUCTION

Business to consumer (B2C) electronic commerce (EC) has seen a phenomenal growth since the development of the Internet, and there is a growing interest from many organizations to use it as a way to improve their competitiveness and reach a wider customer base. In B2C EC, the concept of trust is crucial because it affects a number of factors essential to online transactions, including security and privacy. It is widely acknowledged that without trust EC cannot reach its full potential (Cheskin Research Group, 1999). Among the most cited concerns of EC customers are the low level of personal data security, inconvenience systems, disappointing purchases, unwillingness to provide personal details, and mistrust of the technology (Cheskin Research Group, 1999; Lewicki & Bunker, 1996; Matthew & Turban, 2001; Mayer et al., 1995; Shapiro et al., 1992).

Kasiran and Meziane (2002) developed a trust model for B2C EC that is based on the kind of information customers are looking for on a vendor's Website to help them decide whether to engage in a transaction or not. The model identified four major factors that need to be present on a merchant's Website to increase customers' trust when shopping online. These factors are: existence, affiliation, policy, and fulfilment. The information the customer needs to collect to satisfy the existence factor include physical existence, such as the merchant's telephone number, fax number, postal address, mandatory registration, and peoples' existence. These are known as variables. The affiliation factor looks at third-party endorsement, membership and portal and the policy factor looks at information with regards to customer satisfaction policy, privacy statement, and warranty policy. Finally, the fulfilment factor looks at delivery methods, methods of payment and the community comments. Hence, a total of 12 variables have been identified as summarized in Figure 1.

Given the large amount of information the model requires, an information extraction system

has been developed to automate the data collection process (Meziane & Kasiran, 2003, Meziane & Kasiran, 2005). Indeed it has been reported that users are finding it difficult to identify specific information on Websites (Center for the Digital Future, 2004). In addition, we do recognize that users may not be able to make proper use of the collected information. For this purpose, we developed tools to evaluate the trustworthiness of an EC Website based on the collected information. Two models have been developed in (Meziane & Kasiran, 2005) for evaluating the trust factor; the linear model and the parameterized model. More details about these two models will be provided in the comparison section.

However, for both models, we do recognize that this is not the natural way customers use to evaluate their trust towards online merchants or make the decision to buy or not. As with any other business transaction, customers develop in their mind some sort of ambiguity and uncertainties when purchasing online (Mohanty & Bhasker, 2005). The customer may wish to classify the merchants using different preferences or take into accounts other parameters such as the cost or the brand of the product. The decision to buy or not to buy online is often based on user's human intuitions, common sense, and experience rather than on the availability of clear, concise, and ac-

Figure 1. The trust model (Kasiran & Meziane, 2002)

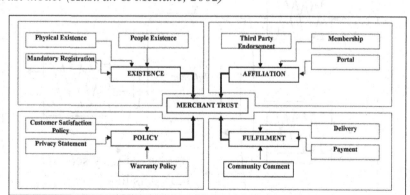

curate data (Akhter, Hobbs, & Maamar, 2005). In this article, we develop a new trust evaluation model using fuzzy reasoning to evaluate the trust factor as it allows the encoding of the information available on the merchant's Website in a form that can be used to reflect the way customers reach the decision to engage in an EC transaction.

The remaining of the article is organized as follows. In the second and third sections, we describe the fuzzy inference and fuzzy logic system and we construct the rules base in the fourth section. We evaluate the newly developed fuzzy model in the fifth section and we compare it with the linear and parameterized models in the sixth section. In the seventh section we report some related work and underline the advantages of our fuzzy system and we conclude in the final section.

THE FUZZY INFERENCE SYSTEM

There are two concepts within fuzzy systems that play a central role in our application domain. The first one is a linguistic variable, that is, a variable whose values are words or sentences in a natural or synthetic language. Fuzzy set theory, which is based on such paradigm, deals with the ambiguity found in semantics (Zadeh, 1965). The second concept is that of a fuzzy IF-THEN rules, in which the antecedent and the consequent parts are propositions containing linguistic variables (Mamdani, 1994). These two concepts are effectively used in the fuzzy logic controller paradigm as shown in Figure 2. The numerical values of the inputs $x_i \in U_i$ with $(i = 1,..., n)$ are fuzzified into linguistic values $F_1, F_2,..., F_n$ where F_j's are defined as fuzzy sets in the input universe of discourse $U = U_1 \times U_2 \times ... \times U_n \subset \mathcal{R}^n$.

A fuzzy inference engine judges and evaluates several linguistic values $G_1, G_2, ..., G_n$ in the output universe of discourse V by using fuzzy IF-THEN rules which are defined in the rule base:

$$R^{(j)}: IF \; x_i \in F_1^j \; and...and \; x_n \in F_n^j$$
$$Then \; y \in G^j \tag{1}$$

where $(j = 1, ..., M)$ and M is the number of rules in the principle base. Each fuzzy IF-THEN rule

Figure 2. The fuzzy logic controller

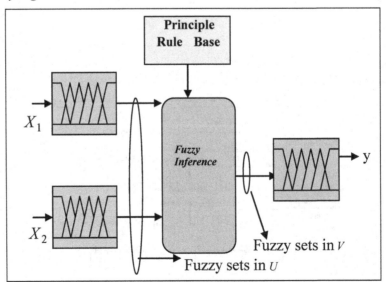

in the form of (1) defines a fuzzy set $F_1^j \times F_2^j \times ... \times F_n^j \to G^j$ n the product space $U \times V$. Let A' be an arbitrary input fuzzy set in U. A fuzzy set B^m in V can be calculated as:

$$\mu_{A' \circ R^m}(y) = \oplus(x_1,...,x_n)^T \in$$
$$U\left[\mu_{A'}(x_1,...,x_n) \otimes \mu_{F_1^m \times ... \times F_n^m \to G_n^m}(x_1,...,x_n,y)\right]$$

(2)

where t-norm $\otimes$ and s-norm $\oplus$ are used for the intersection and the union operations respectively. The final output is a fuzzy set in V, which is a combination of the M fuzzy sets, $A'\circ(R^{(1)}, ..., R^{(M)})$. The membership function of this inferred fuzzy set will be:

$$\mu_{A' \circ (R^{(1)},...,R^{(M)})}(y) = \mu_{A' \circ R^{(1)} \oplus ... \oplus} \mu_{A' \circ R^{(M)}}(y)$$

(3)

The previously shown membership function defines the fuzzy value of the output action $\mu_B(y)$. The crisp value of the output action can be obtained, say, by using the Centre of Gravity (COG) defuzzification method, where the shape of membership function, $\mu_{A' \circ (R^{(1)},...,R^{(M)})}(y)$, is considered to determine the crisp value of the output action $y' = \frac{\sum y\mu_B}{\sum \mu_B}$.

FUZZY LOGIC FOR THE TRUST MODEL

Trust relationships among customers and vendors are hard to assess due to the uncertainties and ambiguities involved in evaluating trust in EC. For example, in the proposed trust model, the community comments variable in the fulfilment factor has a wide range of values as we may have a small or a large number of customers providing positive or negative feedback to the vendor. Hence, the number of comments and their nature will affect the decision made by the associated evaluation module. In addition, in the trust model used,

there are dependencies between some variables. For example the mandatory registration variable in the existence factor is dependent on the membership and third-party endorsements variables in the affiliation factor. Indeed, if an organization is a member of an association or endorsed by a third party, we assume that this organization is fully registered with the required authorities even though the mandatory registration was not extracted by the information extraction system.

Thus, the use of fuzzy reasoning is justified as an adequate approach to deal with evaluating trust in EC as it has the ability to quantify imprecise data and quantify uncertainties in measuring the trust factor of the vendors and to deal with variable dependencies in the system by decoupling them using human expertise in the form of linguistics rules.

The general trust model proposed in this section is composed of five modules. Four modules will be used to quantify the trust measure of the four factors identified in our trust model (existence, affiliation, policy, and fulfilment) and the fifth module will be the final decision maker to quantify the trust factor as illustrated in Figure 3.

The inputs of the existence module are the physical existence, people existence, mandatory registration variable, and the output of the affiliation module. Indeed, as explained earlier in this section, the mandatory registration variable is dependent on the third party endorsement and membership variables of the affiliation module. We also note here that the physical existence variable is composed of three sub-variables, which are the telephone number, the fax number, and the physical address. For the affiliation module, the inputs are the third-party endorsement, membership, and portal variables. For the policy module, the inputs are the customer satisfaction, privacy, and warranty variables. Finally, the fulfilment module has as inputs the delivery, payment methods, and community comments variables. The decision maker has as inputs the outputs of the

Figure 3. The ecommerce fuzzy trust model

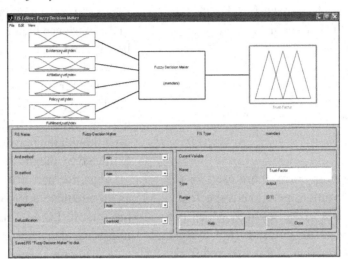

Figure 4. The existence module rules

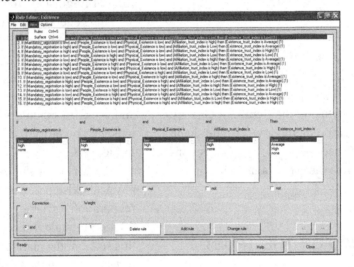

four modules which are Existence_Trust_Index, Fulfilment_Trust_Index, Policy_Trust_Index and the Affiliation_Trust_Index. The output of this module is the trust factor of the merchant's Website. In our model, this trust factor will be determined by the aggregations of the trust indices of all modules. Figure 4 and Figure 5 show a sample of the IF-THEN rules for the existence and fulfilments modules respectively.

In the fuzzification phase, two membership functions described by the labels *"Low"* and *"High"* will be used for each variable related to each module. However, we introduce a third membership function *"Average"* for the outputs. For the decision maker module, we use all three membership functions for the inputs and output corresponding to *Low, Average,* and *High* degree of trustworthiness of the Website. These mem-

Figure 5. The fulfilment module rules

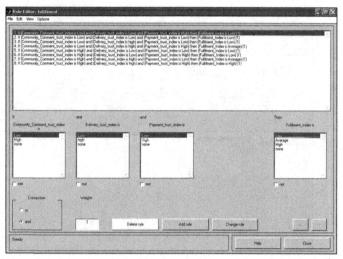

Figure 6. Output of the finale decision maker module

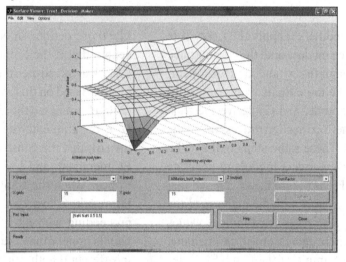

bership functions are represented by Gaussians defined by the centre and the standard deviation parameters. The output values are normalized within the interval (0, 1), with 1 for full trust and 0 for no trust. For example a vendor's Website with 0.75 trust factor is considered high and should be trusted.

The inference rules are subject to the user's choice based on criteria of the risk and the gain as defined by Tao and Thoen (2001). Fuzzy inference is a process to assess the trust index in five steps: (1) register the initial values of each variable as defined by the information extraction system, (2) use the membership functions to generate membership degrees for each variable

Figure 7. The final decision maker module rules

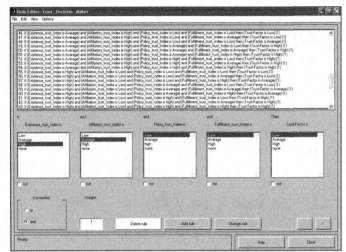

related to each module, (3) apply the fuzzy rule set defined for each module onto the output space (trust index) through fuzzy 'and' and 'or' operations, (4) aggregate the outputs from each rules related to each module, and (5) derive the trust index through a defuzzification process using the centroid method. These same steps will also be used for the decision maker module to generate the trust factor. From Figure 6, we can see that the trust index increases with the increase of the contributing attribute of all trust indices values and decrease when the decrease of all the attribute. Figure 7 shows a sample of the IF-THEN rules for final decision maker module.

THE CONSTRUCTION OF THE RULES BASE

The decision to trust or not to trust EC as a shopping medium is up to consumers' evaluation, which can be based on many factors such as price, convenience, selection of choice, and the information available on the merchant's Website

like those defined in our model. It is widely accepted that if the economic gain is greater than the risk involved then the transaction is reasonably viable. Based on this assumption, Tao and Thoen (2001) formalized the process as: $G_b = P_b L_b$ where G_b is the gain entering the EC transaction, P_b is the risk that the consumer takes for trusting the EC merchants and L_b is the loss the consumer has to bear when the transaction does not produce the result as expected. Consumers are usually proceeding with the transaction if the potential gain is greater than the potential lost and will be indifferent if both values are equal. Thus one has either to maximize the gain G_b or minimize the risk P_b. The risk can be minimized by providing all the information required by the customer on the vendor's Website. Based on this model, we assume that if a large amount of information is available on a vendor's Website and if this information is valid then the vendor can be trusted. However, the importance of these factors can differ from one user to another. To validate our rules we conducted a survey through the use of an online questionnaire.

SYSTEM EVALUATION

To evaluate the fuzzy model developed in this article, we have chosen two random Websites. The first case study is the Denimjunkies[1] site, a vintage clothing shop selling used collectable items such as jeans, jackets, and shirts and the second case study is the Mesh Computers[2] Website, a company selling PCs and peripherals. For each factor, a set of three variables will be considered hence, a total of 13 variables (including the output of the affiliation module which is used as an input to the existence module). Thus combining all variables yield to a total of 12,288 possible combinations for each Website. We use two membership functions for all the inputs, except the output from the affiliation module, which has three membership functions. Given the complexity of the problem, it becomes apparent why we grouped our variables into four factors which are processed by separate modules as defined earlier. This allows us to consider only eight possible combinations per module except the

existence module which has 24 combinations. For the final decision support module, three membership functions are used *Low*, *Average* and *High* and this gives a possible total of 81 combinations. Table 1 summarizes the information extracted from the two case studies.

Table 2 shows the fuzzification of the extracted values related to each variable. In the first case study, the information extraction system found two sub-variables (phone number and address) out of a possible three; hence a value of 0.6 is assigned to the physical existence variable, thus after the fuzzification step the degree of membership function of this value is 0.4 for *Low* and 0.6 for *High*. The remaining two variables (people existence and mandatory registration) in the existence factor were assigned the membership functions 1 (or *High*) In the second case study, all information related to the existence factor was found; thus the degree of membership function of all three existence variables will be 1. After all the selected rules were inferred in parallel, the

Table 1. The extracted information for the case studies

	Variables	http://denimjunkies.com/	http://www.meshcomputers.com
Existence Module	Physical Existence	P/A	P/F/A
	People Existence	yes	yes
	Registration	yes	yes
Affiliation Module	Endorsement	no	yes
	Membership	yes	yes
	Portal	no	yes
Policy Module	Customer Satisfaction	yes	yes
	Privacy Statement	yes	no
	Warranty Policy	no	2 years
Fulfilment Module	Delivery	immediately	delayed
	Payment	Credit C/Debit C/Cheque	Credit C/Debit C/Cheque
	Community Comments	no	no

fuzzy operator 'and' is applied to determine the support degree of the rules. The 'and' results are aggregated and the final trust factor for case study 1 and 2 were is generated by defuzzifying the aggregation using the centroid method as shown in Figure 8 and Figure 9 Respectively.

Example of rules used to process the policy_trust_index for the case study 1 are as follows:

IF customer_satisfaction is Low and privacy_statement is High and warranty_policy is low THEN Policy_trust_index is Low .

IF customer_satisfaction is High and privacy_statement is High and warranty_policy is low THEN Policy_trust_index is Average.

The rules used for the aggregation of the final results for the case studies 1 and 2 and the outputs of the decision maker module are summarised in Table 3.

COMPARISON OF THE FUZZY MODEL WITH OTHER MODELS

Meziane and Kasiran (2005) developed two models to evaluate EC trust using the same model shown in Fig 1, the linear model and the parameterized model. Both models were based on the presence or not of the variables on the EC Website. The linear model is used for new or inexperienced users. The system automatically assigns the value of 1 when a variable is found and 0 otherwise. The total is then divided by the number of variables (12) and a trust factor with a value in the interval (0,1) is calculated using equation (4) were T is the trust factor and v_i represents one of the 12 variables of the trust model.

$$T = \frac{1}{12}\left(\sum_{i=1}^{12} v_i\right) \qquad (4)$$

Table 2. the fuzzification of the extracted information for the case studies

	Variables	http://denimjunkies.com	http://www.meshcomputers.com
Existence Module 1	Physical Existence	{0.4/L; 0.6/H}	H
	People Existence	H	H
	Registration	H	H
	Output 2	L	H
	Output 1	H	H
Affiliation Module 2	Endorsement	L	H
	Membership	H	H
	Portal	L	H
	Output 2	L	H
Policy Module	Customer Satisfaction	{0.2/L;0.8/H}	H
	Privacy Statement	H	L
	Warranty Policy	L	H
	Output 3	H	A
Fulfilment Module	Delivery	L	H
	Payment	H	H
	Community Comments	L	L
	Output 3	L	A

Table 3. The trust factor of the case studies

Outputs	http://denimjunkies.com	http://www.meshcomputers.com
Existence_trust_index	High	High
Affiliation_trust_index	Low	High
Policy_trust_index	High	Average
Fulfilment_trust_index	Low	Average
Trust_factor	Low (0.62)	Average (0.765)

Figure 8. Rules aggregations and output for case study 1

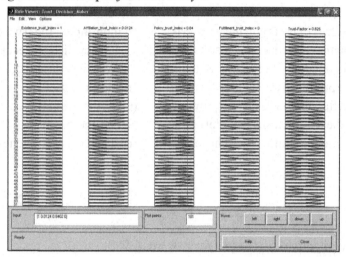

The parameterized model is used with more experienced users who are asked to evaluate the importance (according to their perception) of each variable by assigning the value 1 if the variable is judged important, 0.5 if the variable is fairly important and 0 if it is not important. These values are used as weights to the linear model variables and again a trust factor T in the interval $(0,1)$ is calculated using Equation (5).

$$T = \frac{1}{4}\left(\frac{\sum_{i=1}^{3} E_i w_i}{\sum_{i=1}^{3} w_i} + \frac{\sum_{j=1}^{3} A_j w_i}{\sum_{j=1}^{3} w_i} + \frac{\sum_{k=1}^{3} P_i w_i}{\sum_{k=1}^{3} w_i} + \frac{\sum_{l=1}^{3} F_i w_i}{\sum_{l=1}^{3} w_i} \right)$$

(5)

In both cases, the closer to 1 the trust factor is the higher the trust is towards the merchant's Website. We have compared the results obtained by the Fuzzy model with those obtained by the linear and parameterised model and the results are shown in Table 4. The weights used for the parameterized model used in this experiment, chosen by the authors, are as follows: physical existence (1), people existence (0), mandatory registration (1), third-party endorsement (1), membership (0.5), portal (0.5), customer satisfaction (1), privacy statement (1), warranty (1), delivery (0.5), payment (0), community comments (0.5).

The results obtained by the linear model, which are those provided for a new or inexperienced user, are high compared to those obtained by the other two models. The linear model results are only based on the existence or non existence of the variables on the merchant's Website and this may be misleading as not all variables are of the same importance. The results of the fuzzy and parameterized models are close because in this particular experiment, those who choose the weights for the parameterized model, namely the authors, are themselves experts and have experience in EC transactions. Hence, the results are similar to those produced by the fuzzy systems where experts have produced the IF-THEN rules. By developing the fuzzy model, there is now no need for the use of the parameterized model as the expertise, on a general scale rather then chosen by

individual users, is incorporated in the evaluation process. Users experience is also subjective and the use of the fuzzy model will provide a stronger and a more objective tool to all users regardless of their expertise and experience.

RELATED WORK

Akhter et al. (2005) developed a fuzzy logic based system for assessing the level of trust in B2C EC. In their model the trust (T) is composed of three variables which are security (S), familiarity (F) and the Website's design layout (D) hence $T=f(S, F, D)$. In addition, they have also used competitiveness (C) in the evaluation of the business transaction. Hence the business transaction is a function of trust and competitiveness and formulated as L_{B2C}

Figure 9. Rules aggregations and output for case study 2

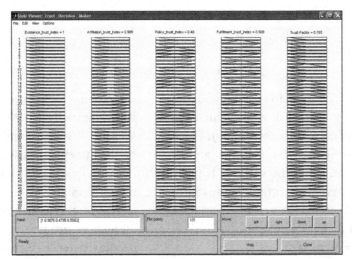

Table 4. Trust models comparison

	Fuzzy Model	Linear Model	Parameterized Model
Case study 1	0.62	0.66	0.60
Case study 2	0.765	0.83	0.79

= $g(T, C)$. However, in their model they are not clear on what factors they use to evaluate each of the three variables S, F and D. They assume that users by just using a Website can decide if the trust is high, average or low with regards to these three variables. Studies on the use of Websites design for example to convey trust are well documented and the characteristics well defined (Basso et al., 2001; Hu et al., 2004; Riegelsberg & Sasse, 2001).

Manchala (2000) proposes a model for the measurement of trust variables and the fuzzy verification of e-commerce transactions. He highlights the fact that trust can be determined by evaluating the factors that influence it, namely risk. He defines cost of transaction, transaction history, customer loyalty, indemnity, and spending patterns as the trust variables. Each variable is measured using semantic labels. His notation is focused on defining when two trust variables are related by an EC trust relationship (ECTR). Using this ECTR, a trust matrix is constructed between the two variables and a trust zone is established. He also describes a method for trust propagation and the construction of a single trust matrix between vendor and customer that governs the transaction. The problem with Manchala's model is that it is (1) unclear, which variables should be used by default for the best results; (2) if it is actually possible for a computer to automatically establish that two variables are related by an ECTR. In his definition, he mentions a semantic relationship between the variables, but neglects to mention how this fact will be specified to the computer so that evaluation can be automated; and (3) if ECTR merging will scale in the face of large trust matrices. These concerns are all related to the viability of implementing his model. These models do not support a theoretic approach to trust and they are not suitable for e-commerce (Tyrone, 2003).

Fuzzy logic was also used for product classification in EC (Mohanty & Bhasker, 2005). When faced with a choice of many products, users need to make a decision on which product to purchase. Taking the case of a car purchase, the authors used five variables which are the cost, re-sale value, mileage, comfort, and maintenance cost. A typical statement would then be to purchase a car with a price around a particular value, a high resale price, with a mileage around certain mileage, comfortable and a low maintenance cost. Such systems would work only on a specific type of products (cars in this case) if one wishes to purchase a personal computer for example, the variables would change as is the fuzzy logic system.

From a technology perspective Jøsang (1998) has shown that it is possible to develop a model for trust and that this model is a model for beliefs. In developing this model, Jøsang has formulated a framework which he calls "subjective logic," which is an extension of standard logic and in part probability theory. It is the assessment mechanism that must be used to evaluate the probability associated to the information and the assessment will then be used to assist in the establishment of the requisite trust. Since the concept of trust is subjective, it creates a number of unique problems that obviates any clear mathematical result.

CONCLUSION AND FUTURE WORK

In this article, we presented a system based on fuzzy logic to support the evaluation and the quantification of trust in EC. Although, the system has addressed many issues that other systems did not such as taking into account the fuzzy nature of trust and using a substantial number of variables, we believe that the system can be improved in many ways. As stated in many trust models, there are other aspects that contribute to the completion of online transactions. This include the price, the rarity of the item and the experience of the customer In order to develop an effective decision support system, future development should include some if not all of these aspects.

The price of the item is certainly an important variable as it is shown in many studies that if the price is reasonably low, customers are ready to take the highest risk to purchase the item. Online transactions also depend on customer's experience and personality. Some customers may value some variables more then others. Hence we believe that future systems should allow customers to rank trust variables according to their own perception and experience.

REFERENCES

Akhter, F., Hobbs, D., & Maamar Z. (2005). A fuzzy logic-based system for assessing the level of business-to-consumer (B2C) trust in electronic commerce. *Expert Systems with Applications, 28*,623–628.

Basso, A., Goldberg, D., Greenspan, S., & Weimer, D. (2001). First impressions: emotional and cognitive factors underlying judgments of trust e-commerce. *In Proceedings of the 3rd ACM conference on Electronic Commerce,* (pp.137-143). Tampa, FL.

Center for the Digital Future (2004), *USC Annenberg School, The digital future report,* http://www.digitalcenter.org/downloads/DigitalFutureReport-Year4-2004.pdf

Cheskin Research group (1999). eCommerce Study Trust, http://www.studioarchetype.com/cheskin/assets/images/etrust.pdf

Han, K.S., & Noh, M.H. (1999). Critical failure factors that discourage the growth of electronic commerce. *International Journal of Electronic Commerce, 4*(2) 25-43.

Hu, J., Shima, K., Oehlmann, R., Zhao, J., Takemura, Y., & Matsumoto, K. (2004). An empirical study of audience impressions of B2C web pages in Japan, China and the UK. *Electronic Commerce Research and Applications,* (3) 176-189.

Jøsang, A. (1998). Modelling Trust in Information Society, PhD Thesis, Department of Telematics, Norwegian University of Science and Technology, Trondheim, Norway.

Kasiran, M.K., & Meziane, F. (2002). An information framework for a merchant trust agent in electronic commerce. In H. Yin, N. Allinson, R. Freeman, J. Keane, & Hubbard S. (Eds), *Intelligent data engineering and automated learning,* 243-248. Springer.

Kasiran, M.K., & Meziane, F. (2004). The usage of third party endorsement in ecommerce websites. *In proceedings of the 7th International Conference on Work with Computing Systems (WWCS2004),* (pp. 794-798). Kuala Lumpur, Malaysia

Lewicki, R.J., & Bunker, B.B. (1996). Developing and maintaining trust in working relationships. In R.M. Kramer & T. Tyler (Eds.), *Trust in organizations,* (pp. 114–139).Thousand Oaks, CA: Sage.

Mamdani, E. (1994). Application of fuzzy algorithms of simple dynamic plants. *In Proceedings of IEEE, 121,* 585-588.

Manchala, D.W. (2000). E-commerce trust metrics and models. *IEEE Internet Computing, March-April,* 36-44

Matthew, K.O., & Turban, E. (2001). A trust model for consumer internet shopping. *International Journal of Electronic Commerce, 6*(1), 75–91.

Mayer, R.C., Davis, J.H., & Schoorman, F.D. (1995). An integrative model of organizational trust. *Academy of Management Review, 20*(3), 709–734.

Meziane, F., & Kasiran, M.K. (2003). Extracting unstructured information from the WWW to support merchant existence in e-commerce. in A. Dusterhoft & B. Thalheim (Eds.), *Lecture Notes in Informatics, Natural Language Processing and Information Systems,* GI-Edition (pp.175-185). Bonn, Germany.

Meziane, F., & Kasiran, M.K. (2005). Strategizing Consumer Logistic Requirements In Ecommerce Transactions: Evaluation of Current Implementations, Proceedings of the 3ʳᵈ European Conference on Intelligent Management Systems in Operations, Salford, Manchester, UK, June 2005, pp.116-125, The Operational Research Society.

Mohanty, B. K., & Bhasker, B. (2005), Product classification in the Internet Business: a fuzzy approach, *Journal of Decision Support Systems, 38*, 611-619.

National Fraud Information Centre, http://www.fraud.org/2002intstats.htm

Riegelsberger, J., & Sasse, M.A. (2001). Trust-builders and trustbusters: The role of trust cues in interfaces to e-commerce applications, Proceedings of the 1ˢᵗ IFIP Conference on e-commerce, e-business, e-government, pp. 17-30, Kluwer.

Shapiro, D., Sheppard, B.H., & Cheraskin, L. (1992, October). Business on a Handshake, *The Negotiation Journal*, 365-378.

Tao-Huan, T., & Theon, W. (2001). Towards a Generic Model of Trust in Electronic Commerce, International Journal of Electronic Commerce, 5(2):61–74.

Tyrone, W. A., Grandison (2003). *Trust Management for Internet Applications,* PhD Thesis, Imperial College of Science, Technology and Medicine University of London, Department of Computing.

Zadeh, L. (1965). Fuzzy Sets, *Information and Control 8*, 338-353.

ENDNOTES

[1] http://denimjunkies.com/
[2] http://www.meshcomputers.com

This work was previously published in International Journal of Intelligent Information Technologies, Vol. 3, Issue 4, edited by V. Sugumaran, pp. 25-39, copyright 2007 by IGI Publishing, formerly known as Idea Group Publishing (an imprint of IGI Global).

Chapter XX
Privacy–Preserving Transactions Protocol Using Mobile Agents with Mutual Authentication

Song Han
Curtin University of Technology, Australia

Vidyasagar Potdar
Curtin University of Technology, Australia

Elizabeth Chang
Curtin University of Technology, Australia

Tharam Dillon
University of Technology, Australia

ABSTRACT

This article introduces a new transaction protocol using mobile agents in electronic commerce. The authors first propose a new model for transactions in electronic commerce, mutual authenticated transactions using mobile agents. They then design a new protocol by this model. Furthermore, the authors analyse the new protocol in terms of authentication, construction, and privacy. The aim of the protocol is to guarantee that the customer is committed to the server, and the server is committed to the customer. At the same time, the privacy of the customer is protected.

INTRODUCTION

Security and Privacy are the paramount concerns in Electronic Commerce (Eklund, 2006). Mobile agent systems are becoming involved in e-commerce (Claessens, Preneel, & Vandewalle, 2003). However, security and privacy within mobile agents must be addressed before mobile agents can be used in a wide range of electronic commerce applications.

The security in the electronic transactions with mobile agents can be classified into two different aspects:

- One is the security of the hosts, to which the mobile agents will travel
- The other is the security of the mobile agents, by which some sensitive information may be transported to the hosts.

The above first security is used to protect the hosts, since the mobile agents may be malicious. For example, the mobile agent may be in the disguise of a legal mobile agent. Therefore, the host will interact with the mobile agent on an electronic transaction. However, the mobile agent tries to obtain some sensitive information (e.g., the secret development plan, the financial report, etc.) about the host. This case will damage the benefit of the host. Therefore, it is very important to maintain the security of the host if some malicious mobile agents travel to the hosts.

The above second security is used to protect the mobile agents, since the hosts may be hostile. For example, when the mobile agents with some sensitive information arrive at the host, those pieces of sensitive information (e.g., the private key, bank account password, home address, etc.) are of paramount importance to the mobile agents' owner. Therefore, the host may try to attain the information through interacting with the mobile agents. As a result, the customer (the owner of the mobile agents) may be blackmailed by the host, since the host holds some sensitive information obtained from the underlying mobile agents. Therefore, it is imperative to design some security mechanism to maintain the security of the mobile agents.

Hosts' security mechanisms include: (1) authentication; (2) verification; (3) authorisation; and (4) payment for services (Claessens et al., 2003). In this article, we will utilise the method of authentication to preserve the security of the host. Authentication is one of the cryptographic techniques. The implication of authentication is to *assure that the entity (customer, host, mobile agents, etc.) requesting access or interaction is the entity that it claims to be.*

Mobile agents' security mechanisms (Kotzanikolaou, Burmester, & Chrissikopoulos, 2000) include: (1) authentication; (2) encryption algorithms; and (3) digital signatures. In this article, we will utilise the digital signature technique. Digital signature is another cryptographic technique. A digital signature scheme is a method of signing a message stored in electronic form. As such, a signed message can be transmitted over a computer network. Also, a signature can be verified using a publicly known verification algorithm. Therefore, anyone who knows the verification algorithm can verify a digital signature. The essence of digital signatures is to convince the recipient that a message (attached to its valid digital signature) is really sent from the signer.

In a virtual community, delegation of signing rights is an important issue since security and privacy are concerned. Consider the following scenario: An international logistics company, AuHouse's President is scheduled to sign a major contract with an Automobile Company in Europe on February 28. However, because of a management emergency, the President is required to attend a meeting held in the General Building of AuHouse in Australia on the same day. This meeting is vital to the future of the AuHouse. However, the contract in Europe is also very important to the organisation. How then can the President be in two places at once and sign the contract, even though he cannot be physically in Europe? Undetachable signature protocol will help the President to solve this issue since the undetachable signature protocol can provide the delegation of signing power while preserving the privacy of the President.

Undetachable signatures are one of the digital signatures which could provide secure delegation of signing rights while preserving privacy. So far only a few undetachable signatures have been created (Coppersmith, Stern, & Vaudenay, 1993; Kotzanikolaou et al., 2000; Sander & Tschudin, 1998). Sander and Tschudin (1998) first proposed the undetachable signatures. The construction is based on the birational functions (Shamir, 1993). However, Stern proved that undetachable signatures based on birational functions are insecure and vulnerable to the attacks (Coppersmith et al., 1993). Another construction on RSA cryptosystem was proposed (Kotzanikolaou et al., 2000). This undetachable signature scheme is secure since its security is based on the security of RSA signatures. However, it is known that RSA signatures usually need to be about 1,024 bit-length or much more in order to maintain an optimal security level (Lauter, 2004). At the same time, mobile agents are working in an environment of mobile communications. Therefore, low bandwidth and efficient communications are much more satisfactory for mobile agents, since the mobile agents often migrate from its owner to a server and from this server to other servers.

Two secure transaction protocols having short signatures have been proposed (Han, Chang, & Dillon, 2005a, 2005b). However, their schemes do not have the mutual authentication mechanism. Therefore, their protocol cannot guarantee that the server is committed to the customer, and the customer is committed to the server.

In this article, we will design a mutual authenticated transaction protocol with mobile agents. We will provide the mutual authentication mechanism to assure that the mobile agent is really the one it claims to be, sent by its owner, the customer. Simultaneously, we will provide a new undetachable signature to protect the privacy of the customer.

The organisation of the rest of this article is as follows: We first provide the model of mutual-authenticated electronic transactions with mobile agents, and the definition of undetachable signatures. Secondly, some mathematical preliminaries are presented that will be used in the new protocol. Thirdly, a new transaction protocol with mutual authentication using mobile agents is proposed. Then, the analysis and proofs are provided, mainly including authentication analysis and construction analysis, as well as privacy analysis—a very important property for a practical virtual community. The conclusions appear in the last section.

MODEL OF MUTUAL AUTHENTICATED TRANSACTIONS WITH MA AND DEFINITION OF UNDETACHABLE SIGNATURES

In this section, we will provide a new model of the transactions using mobile agents (MA) with mutual authentication between the server and the mobile agents (de facto, the customer) and the definition of undetachable signatures. Note that it is the first definition for undetachable signatures, to the best of our knowledge. An undetachable signature scheme consists of four algorithms, namely setup, key, sign, and verify.

Model of Mutual Authenticated Transactions with MA

There are at least four participants involving in the model. The participants are: a customer C (which plays the role of the identifier of the customer), a number of servers (i.e., electronic shops) $S_1 S_2,...,S_n$ (which play the roles of all the servers, respectively), a key certificate authority KCA (which plays the role of the identifier of the key certificate authority), and a number of mobile agents MA_1, MA_2, ..., MA_n (which play the roles of these mobile agents, respectively). Besides these participants, there are six procedures for the proposed model. These procedures deliver the specifications for the mutual authenticated electronic transactions protocol using mobile agents (MAs). The details of this model are as follows:

Setup Algorithm

It generates public key and private key for the customer and also some public parameters for the corresponding servers. In this algorithm, the customer will construct her purchase requirements Req_c according to her purchase plan. The server will construct Bid_S, that defines the bid of the server for a selling activity.

Key Algorithm

In this algorithm, a key certificate authority will also be involved. The customer, a key certificate authority, and some servers will collaborate to assign some public and private parameters. A suitable public key encryption algorithm $E_{pub \otimes prv}$ will be known to the customer and those servers. The private keys and public keys will be certificated by the key certificate authority, respectively. In addition, there is a shared key between the key certificate authority. That will be used for the authentication before the mobile agent migrates to the underlying server.

Mobile Agents Preparing

It involves the interactions between the customer and its mobile agents. The customer will construct some mobile codes for each mobile agent $MA(1 \leq j \leq n)$. These mobile codes include: TBI, Req_c, and a pair of undetachable signature functions; where TBI is the temporary identifier of the customer. The undetachable signature function pair is used to generate the bid tuple on the purchase requirement. Therefore, these mobile agents will travel with the mobile codes to these servers.

Mutual Authentications

This algorithm is used to take authentications between the customer and the servers $S_1 S_2,...,S_n$. Authentication is mutual means that the customer

and the underlying server authenticate in a symmetrical way. It will assure that: *the underlying server is committed to the customer; and the customer is committed to the server.*

Mobile Agent Execution

This algorithm will make the server attend the bidding for the purchase brought with the mobile agent. Each mobile agent will take the mobile codes to the server. Then, the server will design its bid and sign on the bid. In the end, the server arranges the mobile agent to travel back to the customer.

Transactions Verifying

The customer first checks whether the time-stamp is still valid. If it is valid, the customer will verify the signature on the bid. If it is legal, and the bid is an optimal one, the customer will accept this bid.

Definition of Undetachable Signatures

Undetachable signature is, in fact, a kind of encrypted function. Some private parameters will be embedded in the function, and the recipient of this function can execute the computation of the function with some inputs chosen by her self. We utilise the definition proposed by Han and Chang (2006).

Setup is a probabilistic polynomial time algorithm which takes as input a security parameter k and outputs a family of system parameters.

Key is a probabilistic polynomial time algorithm which is executed by a trusted centre and the signers. The input contains system parameters, as well as random parameters which are chosen by the trusted centre and the signers. The output includes a public key $pk \in \underline{K}$ and a corresponding secret key sk.

Sign is a probabilistic polynomial time algorithm, which takes as input a secret key *sk* and a message $m \in \underline{M}$ and outputs a signature $Sig_{sk} \in \underline{S}$. In general, there are many valid signatures for any pair $(m, pk) \in \underline{M} \times \underline{K}$.

Verify is a deterministic polynomial time algorithm. The input includes a message and its allayed signature $Sig_{sk} \in \underline{S}$, as well as system parameters. The output is "Accept" or "Otherwise".

PRELIMINARIES

In this section, we will provide some mathematical knowledge that is used in the design and analysis in the proposed protocol. There are two multiplicative cyclic groups, G_1 and G_2 of prime order q. g_1 is a generator of G_1 and g_2 is a generator of G_2.

A bilinear map is a map $e: G_1 \times G_2 \to G_T$ with these three properties:

Bi-linearity: for any $P \in G_1$, $Q \in G_2$ and x, y $\in$ Z, $e(P^x, q^y) = (P, Q)^{xy}$.

Non-degenerate: if g_1 is a generator of G_1 and g_1 is a generator of G_2, then $e(g_1, g_2) = 1$.

Efficient Computability: There is an efficient algorithm to compute $e(P, Q)$ for any P and Q.

We will use the general case $G_1 \neq G_2$ so that we can take advantage of certain families of elliptic curves to obtain short signatures. Specifically, elements of G_1 have a short representation, whereas elements of G_2 might not.

We say that (G_1, G_2) are bilinear groups if there exists a group G_T, an isomorphism $\psi: G_2 \to G_1$, and a bilinear map $e: G_1 \times G_2 \to G_T$, and e, ψ, and the group action in G_1, G_2, and G_T can be computed efficiently. Generally, the isomorphism ψ is constructed by the trace map over elliptic curves.

Each customer selects two generators $g_1 \in G_1, g_2 \in G_2$, and e(. , .) as above. He will choose $x \in Z_p^*$ and compute $v = g^x_2 \in G_2$. There are four cryptographic hash functions will be used:

$H_1, H_2, H_3,$ and H_4,

where

$$H_1: \{0,1\}^* \times \{0,1\}^* \mapsto Z_p$$
$$H_2: Z_p \mapsto Z_p$$
$$H_3: \{0,1\}^* \times Z_p^* \mapsto Z_p$$
$$H_4: \{0,1\}^* \times \{0,1\}^* \times Z_p \mapsto Z_p.$$

TRANSACTIONS PROTOCOL WITH MUTUAL AUTHENTICATION

A new undetachable signature scheme will be proposed for the protocol of secure transactions. This new undetachable scheme belongs to the domain of short signatures (Boneh & Boyen, 2004; Courtois, 2004; Lauter, 2004). As described in the previous section, short signatures have the characteristics of shorter bit-length of signatures, fast signature generation, as well as fast signature verification. These characteristics are imperative for mobile agents, which take part in the secure transactions between a customer and any server.

Setup Algorithm

Setup algorithm is mainly to set up the compulsory parameters assigned to each participant. We will use the mathematical settings of bilinear mapping groups introduced as above. Each customer will do the following steps:

1. Customer selects $g_1 \in G_1$, $g_2 \in G_2$, two generators;
2. Customer selects bilinear mapping $e(.,.)$ as above;
3. Customer randomly selects $x \in Z_p^*$ and computes $v = g_2^x \in G_2$; and
4. Customer selects two securely cryptographic hash functions H_1 and H_2: $H_1: \{0,1\}^* \times \{0,1\}^* \mapsto Z_p$, $H_2: Z_p \mapsto Z_p$.

In addition, there are another two secure cryptographic hash functions H_3 and H_4, such as SHA-1 (Stinson, 1995, p. 248, pp. 251-253); where $H_3 : \{0,1\}^* \times Z_p^* \mapsto Z_p$ and $H_4 : \{0,1\}^* \times \{0,1\}^* \times Z_p \mapsto Z_p$.

Therefore, the private key of the customer is x; the public key is g_1, g_2, $e(.,.)$, H_1, H_2, H_3, and H_4. All these public parameters are also known to the servers. Note that H_3 and H_4 will be used for the authentication between the underlying server and the mobile agent (de facto, the customer) in subsection 4. D. Another point is that all the public keys are certificated by the key certificate authority, in order to maintain the integration and non-repudiation.

Since we are constructing a transactions protocol, we should specify some corresponding information about the customer and the server. For example, who is the buyer? Who is the bidder (de facto seller). That is, what is the corresponding information of the customer and the server? Here, the server represents the host computer that the mobile agents will visit in the transactions.

For permanent usability, we let C be a permanent identifier for the customer, and let S be a permanent identifier of the server. For a specific purchase (i.e., e-transactions), we define *TSI* as the temporary bidder identifier. In fact, *TSI* is derived from S and the corresponding purchase/selling information (for example, valid period for this bid). We also define *TBI* as the temporary buyer identifier (this may represent the mobile agent). At the same time, t is a time-stamp generated by the underlying server. R is a random element generated by the key certificate authority. R_1 is a random element generated by the customer. These items will be used for the authentication before the mobile agent takes the transactions with the underlying server.

In addition, we denote the constraints of the customer by Req_c, and the bid of the server by Bid_S. The two items are defined as follows:

Req_c defines the requirements of the customer for a specific purchase. It includes: (1) the description of a desired product; (2) an expiration date and time stamp; (3) the maximum price that is acceptable to the customer; and (4) a deadline for the delivery of the product.

Bid_S defines the bid of the server for a selling activity. It includes: (1) the description of the server's product; (2) the minimum price that will be acceptable to the server; (3) a deadline for the delivery of the product; (4) a deadline for paying money into the bank account of the server; and (5) an expiration date and time stamp.

Key Algorithm

The *key algorithm* is a probabilistic polynomial time algorithm. The key certificate authority, the customer, and each server will collaborate to assign some keys. All the keys specified here have two fundamental functions: Some of them are used to maintain the privacy of the underlying participants; the others are used to maintain the authentication between the customer and the underlying server.

1. The key certificate authority determines a practical public key encryption algorithm $E_{pub \otimes prv}$ for the customer and the underlying server. Note that the customer and the underlying server cannot agree on $E_{pub \otimes prv}$ by themselves, since they need mutual authentication in the underlying transactions protocol.

2. The key certificate authority generates a random secret element $k \in Z_p^*$ for the underlying server. Therefore, the key certificate authority and the underlying server will share this element. This key will be used for the authentication before the mobile agent migrates to the server.

3. The key certificate authority sends a pair of public key pub_c and private key prv_C to the customer securely.

4. The key certificate authority sends a pair of public key pub_S and private key prv_S to the underlying server securely.

All these public keys and private keys will be involved when the customer initiates the e-transaction with the server. The public key encryption algorithm can maintain the private communications between the customer and the server.

Mobile Agents Preparing

This algorithm is used to equip the mobile agent with executable codes. The customer constructs the executable codes by using his private key. However, the private key will be presented as a blinded version, since the mobile agent will migrate with the executable does to the underlying server. This will not leak any useful information about the private key. The customer equips the Mobile Agent with executable codes. The executable codes are, in fact, an undetachable signature function pair:

$y() = ()-x_1 \pmod{q}$
and $y_{signed}()=x_2 \times g^{H_2(0-x_1)}$.

where $x_1 = H_1(TBI, \mathrm{Re}q_c)$ is bounded by q;

$x_2 = g_1^{\frac{x_1}{x}} \in G_1$, where the exponentiation is computed modular q. x_2 can be seen as a variant version of the short signature:

$x_1 = H_1(TBI, \mathrm{Re}q_C) \pmod{q}$

$x_2 = g_1^{\frac{x}{x}} \in G_1$

where C is a message, $\mathrm{Re}q_c$ is a random element. Therefore, x_1 and x_2 could be treated as the signature (Han & Chang, 2006): $\sigma=h(m, r)^{\frac{1}{x}}$ on the message m; where $h(m, r)=g_1^{x_1}$. The security is

based on an assumption of q-SDH (Han & Chang, 2006).

Equipped with the executable codes, the mobile agent will migrate from the customer to the server. This agent will carry *TBI* and $\mathrm{Re}q_c$ as part of its data. Also, the mobile agent can sign any purchase (restricted by the purchase requirement) on behalf of the customer. Therefore, this algorithm realises the delegation of signing rights from the customer to the mobile agent.

Before the mobile agent migrates to the underlying server, the customer and the server need to authenticate with each other. Note that this process is actually executed between the mobile agent and the server. Here, the mobile agent, in fact, represents its owner, that is, the customer. However, for the simplicity of the deployment, we arrange the customer and the server to take the process of authentication. The process will assure that: (1) the customer is the purchaser (de facto, the buyer); and (2) the underlying server is truly the bidder (de facto, the seller).

Mutual Authentication

If the mutual authentication is successful, this algorithm can verify that: (a) *the underlying server is committed to the customer for the coming transaction;* and (b) *the customer is committed to the server for the coming transaction.* The customer, the underlying server, and the key certificate authority will attend this algorithm. The following are the details:

1. In order to win the indent (transaction order), the server promulgates her selling information and sends an authentication request to the customer. This request includes *TSI* and *t*.

2. The customer sends *TSI* along with *t* and his permanent identifier *C* to the key certificate authority through a secure channel.

3. After the key certificate authority receives the information, it first checks whether the

permanent identifier C is legal and t is valid. If one of them is not valid, the process stops here; otherwise, the key certificate authority computes $AU_C = H_3 (t,k)$ and $K_t = H_3(R,k)$. Then, the key certificate authority sends the tuple$\{AU_C, R, K_t\}$ to the customer through a secure channel.

4. Once the customer receives the tuple from the key certificate authority, he computes $AU_S = H_4(t, R, K_t)$ and stores it in his database. Then the customer sends the tuple $\{AU_C, R, t\}$ to the underlying server.

5. Once the server gets the tuple, she first checks whether t is valid. If t is valid, the process stops here; otherwise, the server calculates $AU^*_C = H_3(t,k)$ and compares it with the received AU_C. If they are not equal, the transaction is terminated here; otherwise, the customer is authenticated. The server then computes $K^*_t = H_3(R,k)$ and $AU^*_S = H_4(R, t, K^*_t)$, and sends both of them to the customer.

6. After receiving AU^*_S and K^*_t, the customer compares AU^*_S with the one AU_S stored in this database. If the following two equations hold:

$$K^*_t = K_t$$
$$AU^*_S = AU_S.$$

Then, the server is authenticated successfully. After the mutual authentication is completed successfully, the customer will arrange the mobile agent to take the transaction with the underlying server.

Mobile Agent Execution

After the mobile agent arrives at the server, the agent will give all its data and the executable code to the server. The server will execute the executable code provided by the mobile agent, that is, $y($) and $y_{signed}($). The details are as follows:

1. The server computes $y_1 = H_1(TBI, TSI, Bid_S)$ with a bid.

2. The server computes $r = y(x) = y_1 - x_1 \pmod q$. If $r \equiv 0$, the server will stop.

3. The server computes:

$$y_2 = y_{signed}(y_1)$$
$$= x_2 \times g^{H_2(y_1 - x_1)}$$
$$= g_1^{\frac{x_1}{x}} \times (g_1^x)^{H_2(y_1 - x_1)}$$
$$= g_1^{\left(\frac{x_1}{x} + xH_2(y_1 - x_1)\right)(\bmod q)} \in G_1$$

where $g = g_1^x \in G_1$.

4. The server outputs the x-coordinate x_3 of y_2, where x_3 is an element in Z_q.

5. The server hands the mobile agent a tuple $TBI, TSI, Bid_S, y_1, m, x_3$; This tuple will represent part of the transaction.

6. The mobile agent with the tuple migrates to its owner, that is, the customer.

Remark: In the above algorithm, we let TBI and TSI involve the computation of the transaction. This will help to protect the permanent identity of the customer as well as the underlying server. This principle is reasonable, since the temporary identifier is privately linked to the permanent identifier.

Transaction Verifying

This algorithm is used to verify that the fulfilled transaction is an optimal one. If it is, the customer will accept the transaction. The details are as follows: When the mobile agent returns from the server, the customer will check the returned data provided by the mobile agent. The customer will need to follow these steps:

1. The customer will check the undetachable signature (r, x_3) for this transaction by utilising the following formula.

2. The customer will find whether there is a point in G_1: $g_3 = (x_3, y_3)$ (where t is an element in Z_p) such that the following equation holds in G_1:

$$e\left(g_3, v^{H_2(r)}\right) = e\left(g_1, g_2\right)^{(x_1 + x^2 H_2(r)) H_2(r)}$$

If there is no such point, then the customer will not accept this transaction. Otherwise, she will accept this transaction.

That is to say: If the above equality holds, that certifies that the transaction is valid. Then the customer will accept the transaction. Otherwise, the customer will arrange the current mobile agent or another mobile agent to migrate to another server to seek a desirable bid and accomplish the transaction.

ANALYSIS OF THE TRANSACTIONS PROTOCOL

In this section, we will analyse the proposed protocol of transactions with mobile agents and provide authentication analysis, security proof, and privacy analysis. We first provide the authentication analysis - mutual authentication analysis. We will show how the customer is committed to the server, and how the server is committed to the customer. Construction analysis tells how the protocol works, what the principal of the protocol is, and how the mobile agents help the transactions. Security proof shows how to extract the signature scheme from transactions. Subsequently, we will analyse how the privacy is preserved for both the customer and the server.

Authentication Analysis

In this subsection, we will analyse the authentication mechanism. As previously described, we know that the temporary identifier TSI is derived from the permanent identifier S, and the temporary identifier TBI is derived from the permanent identifier C. Therefore, TSI is linked to S, and TBI is linked to C.

1. Mutual authentication fulfils the mutual commitment between the buyer and the seller, that is, the customer and the underlying server. If the seller is committed to the buyer, and the buyer is not committed to the seller, then it will be probable that the buyer would not accept or confirm the transactions. This will result in the buyer presenting no responsibility for the underlying purchase. On the other hand, only the temporary identifiers of the customer and the server are involved in the mobile agent preparing algorithm and the mobile agent execution algorithm. It is known that the temporary identifier has a specific and short-term valid period. Therefore, it is necessary to accomplish the mutual authentication.

2. The mechanism of authentication is as follows: On the one hand, the underlying server is authenticated through: (1) the customer checks whether $K_t^* = K_t$; and (2) the customer checks whether $AU_S^* = AU_S$. In fact, $K_t^* = K_t$ reflects that the underlying server has a shared private element with the key certificate authority. $AU_S^* = AU_S$ implies that the server constructs AU_S^* using the elements from the customer. On the other hand, the customer is authenticated through: (1) the server checks whether the timestamp t is valid; and (2) the server checks whether $AU_C^* = AU_C$. In fact, that t is valid implies that the customer really receives t and replies correctly. $AU_C^* = AU_C$ implies that the customer attains the element AU_C from the key certificate authority, since only the server and the key certificate authority can compute the value of AU_C^* and AU_C.

3. The proposed transaction protocol indicates that the authentication process cannot be forged by the server as well as the customer. Consequently, anyone else (excluding the customer, server, and the key certificate authority) cannot forge the authentication. The security of the mutual authentication is based on the property of cryptographic hash functions (Stinson, 1995).

Construction Analysis

We will deploy the proposed transaction protocol from the construction point of view. This will help us to further understand the transaction protocol.

Note that a key certificate authority is involved in the following three algorithms: setup algorithm, key algorithm, and authentication algorithm. Therefore, the function of the key certificate authority can be deployed according to the three aspects:

a. The key certificate authority certifies the public keys (signing algorithm) for the customer in the setup algorithm.

b. The key certificate authority determines the public key algorithm for the customer and the underlying server in the key algorithm. This assures the private communications between the customer and the server.

c. The key certificate authority helps to accomplish the mutual authentication between the customer and the server. This is realised through: (1) a shared private key between the key certificate authority and the underlying server; (2) computing $AU_C = H_3(t,k)$ and $K_t = H_3(R,k)$; and (3) confirming the legality of the permanent identifier of the customer. All these three are presented in the authentication algorithm.

Next, we deploy the proposed transaction protocol from the delegation-of-signing-right point of view.

In the transaction protocol, the mobile agent is awarded a pair of functions ($y(\ )$ and $y_{signed}(\ )$) and migrates with them to the server. This pair of functions maintains the un-leakage of the signing algorithm (actually the signing private key) of the customer. The input x of the server is linked to the server's bid. At the same time, the mobile agent is also given the certified requirements of the customer (a, b), satisfying

$y(\ ) = (\ )-x^1 \pmod q$,
and $y_{signed}(\ ) = x^2 \times g^{H_2((\ )-x_1)}$ in G_1.

The parameters of function $y(\ )$ are such that the output of this function includes the customer's constraints. The server modifies these by including the bid, Bid_S in the input y_1, in such a way as to satisfy:

• The message m links the constraints of the customer to the bid of the server; and
• It gets an undetachable signature (r, x_3) for the transaction, where $r = (y_1-x_1) \pmod{}$ and x_3 is the x-coordinate of the point *beta*. This serves as a certificate which is authenticated by the customer as follows

$$e\left(g_3, v^{H_2(r)}\right) = e\left(g_1, g_2\right)^{(x_1+x^2 H_2(r))H_2(r)}$$

The certified constraints of the customer Req_c, and the bid of the server, Bid_S restrict the scope of *the context* of *the transaction*, that is, the certificate (r, x_3) to "optimal bid" transactions with the appropriate time-limits (or more generally, to whatever requirements the customer and the server stipulate).

Note that even if a server ignores the customer's constraints Req_C and executes the mobile agent associated with the executable code ($y()$ and $y_{signed}($)) in order to produce an undetachable signature of the customer for a bogus bid, the signature will be invalid. If a server is not willing to bid for a purchase, then the mobile agent will travel to another server to obtain an optimal bid for the transaction.

Privacy Analysis

Privacy is the most concern in respect to financial issues of the participants in the transactions (Eklund, 2006). Therefore, besides the security analysis, it is also necessary to analyse the privacy of the proposed protocol. We will analyse the privacy of the transaction protocol from the following four aspects:

1. Privacy of the signing key of the customer: This privacy is maintained by the mobile agent's executable code, that is, the pair of functions ($y()$ and $y_{signed}()$) since the signing key is implied and embedded in the content of $y_{signed}()$.
2. Privacy of the identity of the customer: This privacy is maintained through the encrypted communication. In fact, when the customer sends the mobile agent to some servers to seek "optimal purchase", she will encrypt the whole or part of the tuple ($y()$, $y_{signed}($), *TBI*, Req_c) (if necessary for the whole content), by utilising her private key prv_C of the underlying public key encryption.
3. Privacy of the context of the transaction initiated between the customer and a server: This privacy is maintained through the mutual encrypted communications between the customer and the server, who will utilise the public key encryption algorithm established in the setup algorithm of the e-transaction protocol.
4. Privacy of the identity of the underlying server: This privacy is maintained through the fact that when the server hands the tuple

TBI, TSI, Bid$_S$, Y_p, r, x_3 to the mobile agent to migrate to the customer, the server will encrypt the part of the tuple in which is related to its identity information, by utilising her private key prv_S of the underlying public key encryption.

CONCLUSION

In this article, we have defined a model of mutual authenticated transactions with mobile agents. Then, a new electronic transaction protocol is presented according to the proposed model. We have provided the corresponding analysis and proofs for the proposed transaction protocol. In detail, there are authentication analysis, construction analysis, and privacy proof. For authentication analysis, we deploy it from the mechanism of mutual authentication, as well as the unforgeable authentication elements. The construction analysis helps to better understand the principles of the proposed protocol. For privacy analysis, it is shown that the privacy is maintained through the involvement of the public key algorithm, an undetachable signature function, and the temporary identifiers.

REFERENCES

Boneh, D. & Boyen, X. (2004). Short signatures without random oracles. In *Proceedings of Eurocrypt 2004, Lecture Notes in Computer Science 3027*, pp. 56-73, Springer Press.

Claessens, J., Preneel, B. & Vandewalle. J. (2003). How can mobile agents do secure electronic transactions on untrusted hosts? *ACM Transactions on Internet Technology 3(1)*, 28-48.

Coppersmith, D., Stern, J. & Vaudenay, S. (1993). Attacks on the birational permutation signature schemes. In *Proceedings of CRYPTO 1993 Lecture Notes in Computer Science 773*, 435-443.

Courtois, N. (2004) *Short signatures, provable security, generic attacks and computational security of multivariate polynomial schemes such as HFE,* Quartz and Sflash. Cryptology Eprint 2004/143.

Digital Signature Algorithm (DSA), RSA (as specified in ANSI X9.31), and Elliptic Curve DSA (ECDSA; as specified in ANSI X9.62), *Federal Information Processing Standard,* 186-2.

Edjlali, G., Acharya, A. & Chaudhary, V. (1998). History-based access control for mobile code. In *Proceedings of ACM Conference in Computer and Communication Security 1998,* 38-48.

Eklund, E. (2006). *Controlling and securing personal privacy and anonymity in the information society.* http://www.niksula.cs.hut.fi/~eklund/Opinnot/netsec.html

Han, S., Chang, E. & Dillon, T., (2005a). Secure e-transactions using mobile agents with agent broker. In *Proceedings of the Second IEEE Conference on Service Systems and Service Management, 2,* 849-855, Jun.13-15, Chongqing University, China.

Han, S., Chang, E. & Dillon, T. (2005b). Secure transactions using mobile agents with TTP. In *Proceedings of the Second IEEE Conference on Service Systems and Service Management, 2,* 856-862, Jun. 13-15, Chongqing University.

Han, S. & Chang, E. (2006). *New efficient undetachable sigantures.* Technical Report, IS-CBS2006, School of Information Systems, Curtin Business School, Curtin University of Technology.

Kolaczek, G. (2003). Specification and verification of constraints in role based access control for enterprise security system. In *Proceedings of the 12th IEEE International Workshops on Enabling Technologies,* Infrastructure for Collaborative Enterprises, 9-11 June 2003, Linz, Austria, IEEE Computer Society 2003: 190-195.

Kotzanikolaou, P., Burmester, M. & Chrissikopoulos, V. (2000). Secure transactions with mobile agents in hostile environments. In *Proceedings of the Fifth Australasian Conference on Information Security and Privacy, 10(12) July 2000,* pp. 289-297, Lecture Notes in Computer Science 1841.

Lauter, K. (2004). The advantages of elliptic curve cryptography for wireless security. *IEEE Wireless Communications Magazine.*

Rivest, R.L., Shamir, A. & Adleman, L.M. (1978). A method for obtaining digital signatures and public-key cryptosystems. *Communications of the ACM 21(2),* 120-126.

Sander, T. & Tschudin, C.F. (1998). Protecting mobile agents against malicious hosts. *Mobile Agents and Security 1998,* Lecture Notes in Computer Science 1419, 44-60.

Shamir, A. (1984). Efficient signature schemes based on birational permutations. *Advances in Cryptology - CRYPTO 93,* Lecture Notes in Computer Science 773, 1-12.

Stinson, D.R. (1995) *Cryptography: practice and theory.* CRC Press, Boca Raton.

Patarin, J., Courtois, N. & Goubin, L. (2001). QUARTZ, 128-bit long digital signatures. In *Proceedings of Topics in Cryptology -* The Cryptographer's Track at RSA Conference 2001, San Francisco, CA, USA, April 8-12, 2001, Lecture Notes in Computer Science 2020, 282-297.

This work was previously published in International Journal of Information Security and Privacy, Vol. 1, Issue 1, edited by H. Nemati, pp. 35-46, copyright 2007 by IGI Publishing, formerly known as Idea Group Publishing (an imprint of IGI Global).

Section V
Critical Issues

Chapter XXI
Factors Affecting Mobile Commerce and Level of Involvement

Frederick Hong Kit Yim
Drexel University, USA

Alan ching Biu Tse
The Chinese University of Hong Kong, Hong Kong

King Yin Wong
The Chinese University of Hong Kong, Hong Kong

INTRODUCTION

Driven by the accelerating advancement in information technology (IT), the penetration of the Internet and other communications services has increased substantially. Hoffman (2000), one of the most renowned scholars in the realm of Internet research, considers the Internet as "the most important innovation since the development of the printing press." Indeed, the omnipresent nature of the Internet and the World Wide Web (WWW) has been a defining characteristic of the "new world" of electronic commerce (Dutta, Kwan, & Segev, 1998). There are a good number of academics and practitioners who predict that the Internet and the WWW will be the central

focus of all commercial activities in the coming decades (e.g., Dholakia, 1998). In particular, Jarvenpaa & Todd (1996) argue that the Internet is alive with the potential to act as a commercial medium and market. Figuratively, discussing the business prospects of the Internet and the WWW is somehow analogous to discussing the Gold Rush of the 19th century (Dholakia, 1995).

Admittedly, the close down of a lot of dot.coms since 2000 has been a concern for many people. However, the statistical figures we have up to now show that the growth pattern continues to be exponential. For example, the latest Forrester Online Retail Index released in January 2002 indicates that consumers spent $5.7 billion online in December, compared to $4.9 billion in November

(Forrester Research, 2002a). There is yet another sign of optimism for online shopping: The Internet Confidence Index (as released in September 2002), jointly developed by Yahoo and ACNielsen, rose 13 points over the inaugural survey released in June 2001, indicating a strengthening in consumers' attitudes and confidence in e-commerce services (Yahoo Media Relations, 2002). Hence, we believe that the setback is only temporary and is part of a normal business adjustment. The future trend is very clear to us. Everybody, be it multinationals or small firms, should be convinced of the need to be on the Web.

While researchers like Sheth and Sisodia (1999) have described the growth of the Internet as astonishing, an even more startling growth is projected in the area of wireless Internet access via mobile devices. The general consensus is that mobile commerce, a variant of Internet commerce (Lucas, 2001) that lets users "surf" their phones (Wolfinbarger & Gilly, 2001), will become part of the next evolutionary stage of e-commerce (e.g., Keen, 2001; Leung & Antypas, 2001; Tausz, 2001). Mobile commerce involves the different processes of content delivery (notification and reporting) and transactions (purchasing and data entry) on mobile devices, and its current landscape resembles the Internet in its first generation in the early 1990s (Leung & Antypas, 2001). According to a study by Strategy Analytics, the rise in demand for mobile commerce services will lead to a market value of $230 billion by 2006 (Patel, 2001). Also a cause for optimism in mobile commerce services is the estimates made by the Yankee Group that the value of goods and services purchased via mobile devices will exceed $50 billion by 2005, up from $100 million in 2000 (Yankee Group, 2001). According to Yankee, the number of wireless consumers using financial services in North America alone will reach more than 35 million in 2005, a leap from the current 500,000.

Research on consumers' online behavior has so far been centered on the World Wide Web. Very few, if any, have specifically focused on mobile access despite the fact that mobile handsets are becoming increasingly popular. This is an important area of study, as the mobile phone is quickly bypassing the PC as the means of Internet access and online shopping. According to the Computer Industry Almanac, there will be an estimated 1.46 billion Internet users by 2007, compared to the 533 million today. Currently, wireless access constitutes a significant, yet limited user share of 16.0%, but by 2007, this number would have increased dramatically to 56.8% (Computer Industry Almanac, 2002). These optimistic projections are further supported by the prediction of Forrester Research that, within 5 years, up to 2.3 million wired phone subscribers in the U.S. would make the switch to wireless access, making an average of 2.2 wireless phones per household by 2007 (Forrester Research, 2002b).

Aided by staggering advances in information technology, mobile devices are now capable of offering a number of Internet-based and Internet-centric services, fueling the growth of mobile commerce. The ascendancy of mobile commerce as a marketing channel warrants researchers' and practitioners' alert even in its current rudimentary stage, not only because of the huge market potential projected, but also because mobile commerce can offer new channels through which enterprises can interact with customers (Leung & Antypas, 2001). In a bid to fill the research void in the realm of mobile commerce, and to afford some insights to firms battling over the electronic commerce arena, this research was conducted with the following two objectives in mind. The first objective is to scrutinize what constitutes the weighty factors as far as transacting through mobile devices is concerned. The second one is to find out how the importance of these factors would vary when consumers are confronted with two different transactions, each with a varying degree of involvement (Celsi & Olson, 1988). The first type of transaction is a low involvement one that involves buying movie tickets with little financial commitment, while the second one is undertaking stock transactions where the stake is high.

In the following, we would briefly summarize what the literature says about important factors that affect online shopping, which forms the basis for us to speculate on factors that may be important for consumers shopping via their mobile phones, the latter being one kind of online shopping, which should resemble to some degree other forms of shopping on the Internet as far as important factors affecting consumer behavior is concerned. Hypotheses are then formulated, which is followed by the methodology. After presenting the results, we discussed the implications and conclusions of this study.

CONCEPTUALIZATION

Regardless of the mode of access, the popularity of online shopping can be partially attributed to the effectiveness and efficiency to acquire information about vendor prices and product offerings (Alba et al., 1997; Bakos, 1997; Cook & Coupey, 1998; Klein, 1998; Peterson, Balasubramanian, & Bronnenberg, 1997; Sheth, Sisodia, & Sharma, 2000; Wolfinbarger & Gilly, 2001), and convenience in overcoming geographical and time barriers (Peterson, Balasubramanian, & Bronnenberg, 1997; Sheth & Sisodia, 1999). In sum, previous literature has found that convenience, site design and financial security are dominant in determining e-satisfaction and likelihood of using the Internet as a shopping channel (Eighmey & McCord, 1998; Szymanski & Hise, 2000; Tse & Yim, 2001).

Given that mobile commerce is also one kind of online shopping, we posit that "convenience," "site design" and "financial security" are the three crucial factors affecting consumers' propensity to transact through mobile phones:

Convenience

One of the widely held perceptions that drives consumers to go online is convenience (e.g., Donthu, 1999; Wind & Mahajan, 2002). The information superhighway has been promoted as a convenient avenue for shopping (Szymanski & Hise, 2000). Driven by the growth of mobile commerce, the convenience of online shopping is further enhanced (Lucas, 2001). Li et al. (1999) find that convenience is a robust predictor of users' online buying status. Similarly, Becker-Olsen (2000) expounds that one of the most important factors that determines whether consumers buy online is the extent to which they perceive the Internet as convenient. The convenience instilled in the electronic marketplace is manifested in time savings, effort economization and accessibility, as perceived by online consumers (Wolfinbarger & Gilly, 2001). Like shopping using a PC, consumers buying movie tickets or completing stock transactions via their mobile phones would be able to save a lot of time and effort that would otherwise be wasted in dealing with agents or ticket offices.

As buying movie tickets is a transaction of low involvement and that undertaking stock transactions is of high involvement, it can be logically reckoned that the convenience factor is different in significance depending upon the situation. Convenience may have a more significant impact on consumers' propensity to transact online in the context of a ticket transaction, as compared to a stock transaction. Consumers should experience greater satisfaction when they can buy movie tickets anytime and anywhere breaking the time- and location-bound facets of traditional "gravitational" commerce (Sheth & Sisodia, 1999). On the other hand, for stock investment, consumers' major concern is security, as the consequence of any mistake can result in a great loss (Rosenbloom, 2000). Hence, we speculate that if an online stock trading system is too convenient, online investors may actually refrain from using it. For example, if, for the sake of convenience, a user is not required to enter a second password to confirm a transaction, the user may end up feeling highly insecure and less satisfied. To test our assertions, we put forward the following hypotheses:

- **H$_{1a}$:** Convenience significantly affects willingness to transact online for both movie ticket and stock transactions.
- **H$_{1b}$:** The importance of convenience in determining whether consumers transact online is greater for a ticket transaction than a stock transaction.
- **H$_{1c}$:** The greater the level of convenience is in an online stock transaction, the lower the intention is in using the system.

Site Design

Site design is considered important in the realm of electronic commerce (e.g., Eighmey & McCord, 1998; Lohse & Spiller, 1999; Wolfinbarger & Gilly, 2001) and mobile commerce (Lucas, 2001). Like any diffusion of innovation, there is a learning curve for most consumers to utilize electronic commerce in a way they feel most comfortable (Li, Kuo, & Russell, 1999). The success akin to the adoption of mobile transactions hinges on, at least in part, the complexity of the utilization of this innovation (Childers et al., 2001; Rogers, 1983). It can thus be understood that meticulously crafted Web sites tend to be more successful in terms of ushering in first-time online shoppers and gaining repeat visits. Empirically, Novak et al. (2000) find that a compelling online experience, which can be engendered by deliberate contrivance of Web sites, is positively associated with expected use in the future and the amount of time consumers spend online. As far as a stock transaction is concerned, we speculate that site design plays a crucial role in facilitating consumers to carry out

the transaction. Users would undoubtedly require an effective design that allows them to orchestrate their portfolio without committing any mistake. Regarding the importance of site design in the use of mobile phones for ticket transactions, we undertook ten in-depth interviews with buyers who had bought tickets with their mobile phone before, and found that since most of the ticket transactions currently completed via mobile devices do not afford consumers the latitude to choose the specific seats they like because of the small screen size, they do not expect the same level of good site design as for stock transactions. Hence, our second hypothesis is formulated as below:

- **H$_{2a}$:** Site design significantly affects willingness to transact online for both movie ticket and stock transactions.
- **H$_{2b}$:** The importance of site design in determining whether consumers transact online is greater for a stock transaction than a ticket transaction.

Financial Security

It has been argued for long that the issue of financial security is pivotal in electronic transactions (e.g., Guglielmo, 1998; Kluger, 2000; Rosenbloom, 2000; Stateman, 1997), specifically in those conducted via wireless devices (Gair, 2001; Goldman, 2001; Hurley, 2001; Laughlin, 2001; Teerikorpi, 2001). As stock transactions entail a significantly larger amount of financial risk than ticket transactions, it can be logically reasoned that financial security plays a more salient role in affecting consumers' propensity to transact online when consumers are confronted with a stock transaction, as compared to a ticket transaction. Our third hypothesis is arrived at as follows:

- **H$_{3a}$:** Financial security significantly affects willingness to transact online for both movie ticket and stock transactions.

- **H$_{3b}$:** The importance of financial security in determining whether consumers transact online is greater for a stock transaction than a ticket transaction.

METHOD

Using a survey design, 192 respondents were selected by convenience sampling and interviewed in three different locations in Hong Kong representing a good cross-section of three different strata of socio-economic groups. The Hong Kong sample is deemed appropriate, by virtue of the fact that Hong Kong is the perfect location for a mobile commerce solutions player and is alive with opportunities fueled by its more than 5.77 million mobile phone subscribers, which represents a mobile penetration rate of 88.88% (Leung, 2002). The research was conducted in shopping malls, where a high customer flow can be found. Respondents were asked to make their evaluations when confronted first with a movie ticket buying scenario, and subsequently with a stock transaction using a mobile phone. For each scenario, before respondents indicate their likelihood of using the channel for the transaction, they were given a detailed description and explanation of the features and functionalities of the phone and the Web site that provide the service. Their likelihood of using the mobile service is captured by a seven-point scale ranging from "–3" to "3," where "–3" means "highly unlikely," "0" means "neither unlikely nor likely," and "3" represents "highly likely."

Each factor described above—convenience, site design, and financial security—is measured by at least four items so that the consistency/reliability of respondents' replies can be assessed. The items for each factor are based on those suggested by Keeney (1999). The factors are presented in bold type below followed by the items used for the factor. For each of the statements below, respondents were asked to indicate the extent to which they agree or disagree with it using again a seven-point scale ranging from "–3" to "3," where "–3" means "strongly disagree," "0" means "neither disagree nor agree," and "3" represents "strongly agree."

Convenience

- The mobile service is convenient.
- The mobile service can maximize transactional speed.
- The mobile service can minimize waiting time.
- The mobile service can minimize personal travel.

Site Design

- The interface is easy to use.
- The interface is designed in such a way that I can contact a service staff easily if needed.
- The interface allows me to get a variety of services easily.
- The design of the interface is of high quality.
- I enjoy using the interface.

Financial Security

- The system is secure.
- Transaction conducted through the system is accurate.
- The system allows me to keep track of my previous transactions without error.
- The system provides me with clear information of my previous transactions.
- The system protects my personal financial information and privacy.

Table 1. Cronbach alphas for all the subscales

Factors	Ticket Transaction	Stock Transaction
Convenience	0.6236	0.8752
Site Design	0.5325	0.7122
Financial Security	0.7552	0.8870

Table 2. Regression coefficients for predictors of transacting online

Panel A: Regression findings for ticket transaction

Predictor Variable	Standardized Coefficient (SE)	t-value (p-level)
Convenience	0.079 (0.046)	0.787 (0.433)
Site Design	-0.122 (0.047)	-1.096 (0.275)
Financial Security	0.097 (0.034)	0.854 (0.395)

Panel B: Regression findings for stock transaction

Predictor Variable	Standardized Coefficient (SE)	t-value (p-level)
Convenience	-0.059 (0.074)	-0.274 (0.785)
Site Design	-0.328 (0.081)	-1.373 (0.175)
Financial Security	0.557 (0.061)	2.216 (0.030)

RESULTS

Table 1 reports the reliabilities of the items for each of the categories for both types of transactions: ticket and stock. All Cronbach's alpha values are greater than 0.7, except those of Convenience and Site Design for Ticket Transactions, which are marginal. However, for exploratory studies like this one, a value of Cronbach's alpha that exceeds 0.5 would be considered acceptable (Nunnally, 1978), and so the summated score of the items under each factor would be used as predictor variables for the statistical analyses described as follows:

Two regression analyses were conducted using the summated scores of the factors as the independent variables and the likelihood of transacting online (buying tickets or consummating stock transactions) as the dependent variable. The results of the regression analyses are depicted in Table 2.

As evinced in Table 2, none of the factors significantly affect the intention to use mobile

Table 3. Difference in effect sizes between ticket and stock transactions

	Convenience			
	Mean[1]	Standard Deviation	Pooled Within Group Standard Deviation	Difference in Effect Sizes[2]
Ticket	6.260	3.965	4.444	-0.058
Stock	6.000	5.206		
	Site Design			
	Mean	Standard deviation	Pooled within group standard deviation	Difference in Effect Sizes
Ticket	1.349	4.255	4.687	0.355
Stock	3.014	5.383		
	Security			
	Mean	Standard deviation	Pooled within group standard deviation	Difference in Effect Sizes
Ticket	1.945	6.065	6.561	0.328
Stock	4.100	7.380		

Note: [1]   Mean level of willingness to undertake respective online transactions.
[2]   positive effect size difference is analogous to a positive treatment effect size using stock as the experimental group and ticket as the control group.

phone for buying movie tickets online. For online stock transactions, financial security exhibits the greatest impact on the likelihood of using the system, with the other two factors playing a non-significant role. Hence, our results do not lend support to H_{1a}, H_{1c} and H_{2a}, and only H_{3a} is supported in so far as high involvement products are concerned.

To test the remaining hypotheses, we need to compute the difference in effect sizes for each factor in the two buying situations. The required differences, computed using the method suggested by Cohen (1977), are shown in Table 3.

The group difference effect sizes shown in Table 3 are free of the original measurement units. They measure the difference in effects of each of the factors under consideration—namely convenience, site design and financial security—on willingness to use a mobile phone to undertake the two different types of transactions. As seen in Table 3, we find that the difference in effect sizes associated with convenience is negative, which is in the expected direction. Tallmadge (1977) provides rough guidelines of difference = 0.25 indicating small effect, and difference = 0.33 for medium effect. Using this guideline, the effect size difference for convenience, is very small, so H_{1b} cannot be said to be supported although the negative direction is consistent with H_{1b}. On the other hand, the differences for site design and financial security are medium in magnitude, thus supporting H_{2b} and H_{3b}.

DISCUSSION AND IMPLICATIONS

The next profound shift in the use of IT will obviously be toward wireless and mobile commerce (Keen, 2001), an emerging discipline (Varshney, 2002). The whole world of mobile commerce is about to explode (Martin, 2002). In many ways, m-commerce is, per se, the continuation of e-commerce with the Palm handheld, wireless laptops and a new generation of Web-enabled

digital phones already on the market. It is even believed that portable devices such as phones, pagers and computers with mobile modems will quickly surpass desktop PCs as the Internet access devices of choice (Lindquist, 2001). The race for dominance in mobile commerce has begun (Nohria & Leestma, 2001). As addressed by Hoffman (2000), scholarly research on the Internet cannot keep abreast with business practice, let alone the scanty, if any, research on the newly emerging mobile commerce. To the very best of our knowledge, the survey we have conducted serves as a pioneer study in the realm of mobile commerce.

Aligning with our initial surmise that the salience of convenience in determining whether consumers transact online is larger for a ticket transaction than a stock transaction, our results, though only marginally supporting the hypothesis, shed light on what is deemed weighty in providing mobile commerce transactions. Enterprises providing electronic ticketing services of recreational activities, which are of low involvement, should pay heightened attention to how the convenience of their services can be enhanced. For example, the waiting time for consummating a ticket transaction as well as the transaction time required should be minimized.

Another noteworthy issue is that the coefficient associated with convenience as a predictor variable of the likelihood of consummating a stock transaction is negative. This may mean that respondents may associate increased level of convenience with increased level of inherent risks, thus hampering their propensity to transact online when the transactions in question are of high involvement. Firms facilitating online stock transactions, or other high involvement transactions, should thus be alert to this issue—they should promulgate their commitment to reduce their clients' risks in line with providing convenience.

Financial security is of paramount concern to online consumers seeking to consummate stock transactions, lending support to our third hypothesis. Indeed, the coefficient associated with financial security for stock transaction is of both practical and statistical significance (0.557; p-level = 0.030), signifying the colossal effects exerting from financial security on the likelihood to transact online. Meanwhile, the effect size difference for security is medium. The implication for our results is pronounced: financial security should be given overwhelming priority to high involvement transactions. Practically, clients should be continually and periodically informed of their online transactions, expressed in unequivocal terms. Building trust with clients is a proper and effective way to alleviate their worry about financial security (Shneiderman, 2000). This can be accomplished by nurturing and fostering a firm's relationship with its clients (Price & Arnould, 1999).

The insignificance of site design serving as a predictor of the likelihood of online transaction is contrary to what is addressed in the extant literature pertaining to traditional electronic commerce. Given the very nature of mobile commerce, we are yet afforded with some novel insights: as screens of mobile phones are miniatures of desktop monitors (Lucas, 2001), the possible designs for a site are constrained—overly fancy site designs cannot be demonstrated in the realm of mobile commerce, rendering site design insignificant in predicting transacting online. Although our study shows that site design does not play a significant role in affecting willingness to transact online, the difference in effect sizes are medium for the two different types of transactions. The latter is an indication that online firms intending to sell high involvement products should spend more on interface design when compared with their counterparts selling low involvement items.

DIRECTIONS FOR FUTURE RESEARCH

As the costs pertaining to the two online transactions delineated previously are somehow kept constant, we have not yet examined the effects of costs on propensity to transact online. The issue should be addressed in future research, since minimizing costs is identified as an objective in online transactions (Keeney, 1999; Leavy, 1999).

The intriguing result of the negative coefficient associated with convenience in the realm of high involvement transactions also warrants further research. Not until forthcoming research renders our intuitive interpretation to empirical scrutiny will a more comprehensive understanding of mobile commerce ensue.

Furthermore, other types of products should be chosen in addition to the ones we have used in this research to improve the generalizability of our findings. Meanwhile, in addition to classifying products based on level of involvement, we may categorize products in other ways. For example, we may classify products as search, experience and credence goods (Klein, 1998), and the relative importance of the three factors studied may be different for these three categories of products.

REFERENCES

Alba, J., Lynch, J., Weitz, B., Janiszewski, C., Lutz, R., Sawyer, A., & Wood, S. (1997, July). Interactive home shopping: Consumer, retailer, and manufacturer incentives to participate in electronic marketplaces. *Journal of Marketing, 61*, 38-53.

Bakos, J. Y. (1997). Reducing buyer search costs: Implications for electronics marketplaces. *Management Science, 43*(12), 1676-1692.

Becker-Olsen, K. L. (2000). *Point, click and shop: An exploratory investigation of consumer perceptions of online shopping.* Paper presented at AMA summer conference.

Celsi, R. L., & Olson, J. C. (1988). The role of involvement in attention and comprehension processes. *Journal of Consumer Research, 15,* 210-224.

Childers, T. L., Carr, C. L., Peck, J., & Carson, S. (2001). Hedonic and utilitarian motivations for online retail shopping behavior. *Journal of Retailing, 77*(4), 511-535.

Cohen, J. (1977). *Statistical power analysis for the behavioral sciences.* New York: Academic Press.

Computer Industry Almanac. (2002). *Internet users will top 1 billion in 2005. Wireless Internet users will reach 48% in 2005.* Retrived December 31, 2005, from http://www.c-i-a.com/pr032102. htm

Cook, D. L., & Coupey, E. (1998). Consumer behavior and unresolved regulatory issues in electronic marketing. *Journal of Business Research, 41,* 231-238.

Dholakia, R. R. (1995). *Connecting to the Net: Marketing actions and market responses.* Paper presented at the International Seminar on Impact of Information Technology hosted by CIET-SENAI, Rio de Janeiro, Brazil, December 6, 1995.

Dholakia, R. R. (1998). Special issue on conducting business in the new electronic environment: Prospects and problems. *Journal of Business Research, 41,* 175-177.

Donthu, N. (1999). The Internet shopper. *Journal of Advertising Research, 39*(3), 52-58.

Dutta, S., Kwan, S., & Segev, A. (1998). Business transformation in electronic commerce: A study of sectoral and regional trends. *European Management Journal, 16*(5), 540-551.

Eighmey, J., & McCord, L. (1998). Adding value in the information age: Uses and gratifications of sites on the World Wide Web. *Journal of Business Research, 41,* 187-194.

Forrester Research. (2002a). *December shopping up from last year in spite of rough economy, according to the Forrester Research Online Retail Index.* Retrieved December 31, 2005, from http://www.forrester. nl/ER/Press/Release/0,1769,678,00.html

Forrester Research. (2002b). Retrieved from http://www.forrester.com

Gair, C. (2001). The next big thing? *Black Enterprise, 31*(10), 62.

Goldman, C. (2001). Banking on Security. *Wireless Review, 18*(7), 22-24.

Guglielmo, C. (1998). Security fears still dog Web sales. *Inter@ctive Week, 5*(273), 44-47.

Hoffman, D. L. (2000). The revolution will not be televised: Introduction to the special issue on marketing science and the Internet. *Marketing Science, 19*(1), 1-3.

Hurley, H. (2001). Pocket-sized security. *Telephony, 240*(18), 42-50.

Jarvenpaa, S. L., & Todd, P. A. (1996). Consumer reactions to electronic shopping on the World Wide Web. *International Journal of Electronic Commerce, 1*(2), 59-88.

Keen, P. G. W. (2001). Go mobile—now! *Computerworld, 35*(24), 36.

Keeney, R. L. (1999). The value of Internet commerce to the customer. *Journal of the Institute for Operations Research and the Management Sciences, 45*(4), 533-542.

Klein, L. R. (1998). Evaluating the potential of interactive media through a new lens: Search versus experience goods. *Journal of Business Research, 41,* 195-203.

Kluger, J. (2000). Extortion on the Internet. *Time, 155*(3), 56-58.

Laughlin, K. (2001). Banking on wireless. *America's Network, 105*(1), 56-60.

Leavy, B. (1999). Organization and competitiveness—Towards a new perspective. *Journal of General Management, 24*(3), 33-52.

Leung, K., & Antypas, J. (2001). Improving returns on m-commerce investments. *Journal of Business Strategy, 22*(5), 12-13.

Leung, T. (2002, May 27). HK trails in mobile data. *Asia Computer Weekly,* 1.

Li, H., Kuo, C., & Russell, M. G. (1999). The impact of perceived channel utilities, shopping orientations, and demographics on the consumer's online buying behavior. *Journal of Computer Mediated Communication, 5*(2).

Lindquist, C. (2001). Mobile Internet access exploding. *CIO, 14*(13), 138.

Lohse, G. L., & Spiller, P. (1999). Internet retail store design: How the user interface influences traffic and sales? *Journal of Computer Mediated Communication, 5*(2).

Lucas, P. (2001). M-commerce gets personal. *Credit Card Management, 14*(1), 24-27.

Martin, N. (2002). Content a la Wmode: Serving up solutions for wireless content. *EContent, 25*(1), 48-49.

Nohria, N., & Leestma, M. (2001). A moving target: The mobile-commerce customer. *MIT Sloan Management Review, 42*(3), 104.

Novak, T. P., Hoffman, D. L., & Yung, Y. (2000). Measuring the customer experience in online environments: A structural modeling approach. *Marketing Science, 19*(1), 22-42.

Nunnally, J. C. (1978). *Psychometric Theory* (2nd ed.). New York: McGraw-Hill.

Patel, N. (2001). *Mobile commerce market update.* Retrieved December 31, 2005, from http://www.strategyanalytics.net/default.aspx?mod=Report AbstractViewer&a0=839

Peterson, R. A., Balasubramanian, S., & Bronnenberg, B. J. (1997). Exploring the implications of the Internet for consumer marketing. *Journal of the Academy of Marketing Science, 25*(4), 329-346.

Price, L. L., & Arnould, E. J. (1999). Commercial friendships: service provider-client relationships in context. *Journal of Marketing, 63,* 38-56.

Rogers, E. M. (1983). *Diffusion of innovations* (3rd ed.). New York: Free Press.

Rosenbloom, A. (2000). Trusting technology. *Communications of the ACM, 43*(12), 31-32.

Sheth, J. N., & Sisodia, R. S. (1999). Revisiting marketing's lawlike generalizations. *Journal of the Academy of Marketing Science, 27*(1), 71-87.

Sheth, J. N., Sisodia, R. S., & Sharma, A. (2000). The antecedents and consequences of customer-centric marketing. *Journal of the Academy of Marketing Science, 28*(1), 55-66.

Shneiderman, B. (2000). Designing trust into online experiences. *Communications of the ACM, 43*(12), 57-59.

Stateman, A. (1997). Security issues impact online buying habits. *Public Relations Tactics, 4*(10), 8-16.

Szymanski, D. M., & Hise, R. T. (2000). E-satisfaction: An initial examination. *Journal of Retailing, 76*(3), 309-322.

Tallmadge, G. K. (1977). *The Joint Dissemination Review Panel ideabook*. Washington, DC: National Institute of Education and U.S. Office of Education.

Tausz, A. (2001). Customizing your world. *CMA Management, 75*(2), 48-51.

Teerikorpi, E. (2001). How secure is the wireless Internet. *Telecommunications, 35*(5), 46-47.

Tse, A. C. B., & Yim, F. (2001). Factors affecting the choice of channels: Online vs. conventional. *Journal of International Consumer Marketing, 14*(2/3), 137-152.

Varshney, U. (2002). Multicast support in mobile commerce applications. *Computer, 35*(2), 115-117.

Wind, Y., & Mahajan, V. (2002). Convergence marketing. *Journal of Interactive Marketing, 16*(2), 64-79.

Wolfinbarger, M., & Gilly, M. C. (2001). Shopping online for freedom, control, and fun. *California Management Review, 43*(2), 34-55.

Yahoo Media Relations. (2001). *Internet confidence index*. Retrieved December 31, 2005, from http://docs.yahoo.com/docs/info/yici/06-02.html

Yankee Group. (2001). Retrieved from http://www.yankeegroup.com

KEY TERMS

Convenience: One of the determining factors for e-satisfaction and likelihood of using the Internet as a shopping channel. It is manifested in time savings, effort economization and accessibility, as perceived by online consumers.

Financial Security: One of the determining factors for e-satisfaction and likelihood of using the Internet as a shopping channel. It refers to the personal financial information protection for the consumers who make online transactions.

Involvement: A consumer's overall subjective feeling of personal relevance.

Mobile Commerce: A variant of Internet commerce that lets users "surf" their mobile devices, for example, mobile phone, PDA.

Online Shopping: Transactions made via Internet rather than at a physical location by consumers.

Site Design: One of the determining factors for e-satisfaction and likelihood of using the Internet as a shopping channel. It refers to the interface quality that a company provides for its consumers to do online transactions.

This work was previously published in Encyclopedia of Mobile Computing and Commerce, edited by D. Taniar, pp. 283-290, copyright 2007 by Information Science Reference, formerly known as Idea Group Reference (an imprint of IGI Global).

Chapter XXII
Privacy and Security in the Age of Electronic Customer Relationship Management

Nicholas C. Romano, Jr.
Oklahoma State University, USA

Jerry Fjermestad
New Jersey Institute of Technology, USA

ABSTRACT

This article presents a value exchange model of privacy and security for electronic customer relationship management within an electronic commerce environment. Enterprises and customers must carefully manage these new virtual relationships in order to ensure that they both derive value from them and minimize unintended consequences that result from the concomitant exchange of personal information that occurs in e-commerce. Based upon a customer's requirements of privacy and an enterprise requirement to establish markets and sell goods and services, there is a value exchange relationship. The model is an integration of the customer sphere of privacy, sphere of security, and privacy/security sphere of implementation.

INTRODUCTION

New technologies have fostered a shift from a transaction-based economy, through an Electronic Data Interchange (EDI) informational-exchange economy, to a relationship-based Electronic Commerce (EC) economy (Keen, 1999). We have moved from *"first order"* transactional value exchanges through *"second-order"* informational value exchanges to *"third-order"* relational value exchanges (Widmeyer, 2004). Three important types of EC relationships have been identified: between enterprises and customers (B2C); between enterprises (B2B); and between customers (C2C) (Kalakota & Whinston, 1996). Additional relationships between Governments (G2G), enterprises (G2B), and customers (G2C) have become more important as EC and e-government have matured, and legislation, regulation, and oversight have increased (Friel, 2004; Reddick, 2004); however, these are not the focus of this article. Relational value exchanges have become central to success and competitive advantage in B2C EC, and it is here that we focus on privacy and security in the age of virtual relationships.

Both enterprises and customers must carefully manage these new virtual relationships to ensure that they derive value from them and to minimize the possible unintended negative consequences that result from the concomitant exchange of personal information that occurs when goods and services are purchased through EC. The need to manage these relationships has resulted in the development of Electronic Customer Relationship Management (e-CRM) systems and processes (Romano & Fjermestad, 2001-2002). E-CRM is used for different reasons by enterprises and customers. It is important to understand how and why both of the players participate in *"relational value exchanges"* that accompany the economic transaction and informational value exchanges of EC.

Enterprises use e-CRM to establish and maintain *intimate virtual relationships* with their *economically valuable* customers to derive additional value beyond that which results from economic value exchanges to improve return-on-investment (ROI) from customer relationships.

Customers obtain goods, services and information (economic value) through EC for purposes such as convenience, increased selection and reduced costs. EC requires customers to reveal personal information to organizations in order for transactions to be completed. The exchange of information between customers and organizations leads to the possibility of privacy violations perpetrated against the customer. It is the responsibility of the organizations to provide privacy policies and security measures that will not endanger customer trust.

In this article, we present a series of models *"sphere of privacy model," "sphere of security model," "privacy/security sphere of implementation model,"* and then integrate them into the *"relational value exchange model"* to explain privacy and security in the context of e-CRM, from the perspective of both customers and enterprises, to provide guidance for future research and practice in this important area. It is important for both customers and firms to understand each others' vested interests in terms of privacy and security, and to establish and maintain policies and measures that ensure that both are satisfactorily implemented to minimize damage in terms of unintended consequences associated with security breaches that violate privacy and lead to relationship breakdowns.

The remainder of this article is structured as follows: First, we explain why privacy and security are critically-important issues for companies and customers that engage in EC, and the consequences that can result from failure to recognize their importance or poor implementation of measures to ensure both for the organization and its customers. Second, we define privacy and security and their interrelationship in the context of CRM. Third, we present our relational value exchange model for privacy and security in e-CRM.

Customer Relationship Management Privacy and Security: Who Cares?

The data contained within a CRM application is often a company's most critical asset, yet because of the pivotal role this information plays in day-to-day business activities, it is also often the most vulnerable to security breaches and disruptions (Seitz, 2006 p. 62).

Before we explain and define privacy and security in detail and present our models and the relational value exchange model, we will describe the costs associated with failure to understand these concepts and failure to effectively ensure that both are protected in terms that firms and customers can understand: dollars and lost customers.

Economic Cost of Customer Security Breaches

The economic cost of security breaches, that is, the release or loss of customers' personal information, has been studied in a number of surveys over the past decade; while some studies show declines in the total and average losses over time, the costs are still staggering for many firms. New threats and vulnerabilities have arisen in the recent past, and these lower costs are most likely offset by increased expenditures to implement security measures and training.

The Computer Security Institute (CSI) and the Federal Bureau of Investigation (FBI) have conducted eleven annual surveys of computer crime and security since 1995. Some of the results of the last seven are presented (Gordon, Loeb, Lucyshyn, & Richardson, 2004, 2005, 2006; Power, 2002; Richardson, 2003). The Ponemon Institute also conducted two surveys on the costs and effects of data security breaches (Ponemon, 2005a, 2005b), and we will also present a portion of their results as well.

The CSI/FBI surveys have tracked the costs (losses) associated with security breaches for thirteen years; we focus on summary data from the last seven years to illustrate trends and changes in the economic costs of security breaches for organizations that responded with loss data. Table 1 reveals some interesting aspects about security breach costs over the past seven years. Several types of costs have been reported across all the years of the survey; these include: theft of proprietary information, sabotage of data or networks, system penetration, insider abuse of network access, financial fraud, denial of service,

viruses, unauthorized insider access, telecom fraud, and laptop theft.

Other types of losses were reported in early years of the period but not in later periods or were reported in only the last three or even only the final survey in 2006, indicating that some threats have been better managed and new ones have arisen or been identified and quantified. Specifically, losses from telecom eavesdropping were reported to be on average from a high of $1.2 million in 2002 to a low on $15,000 in 2003; however, there were no reported losses in 2004, 2005, or 2006. Active wiretapping is another loss that was reported as an average of $5 million in 2000 and $432,500 in 2003, but not reported in any of the other years. Theft of proprietary information was reported as the highest loss for the four years from 2000 to 2003; then viruses took over the top spot in 2004 and remained the highest loss in 2005 and 2006. The results also show that between 2002 and 2003, there is a 62% reduction in the reported losses and, between 2003 and 2004, there is a 90% reduction in the losses. Thus, the enterprises are responding to the need for privacy and security. In 2004, three new loss types were reported: Web site defacement, misuse of a public Web application, and abuse of wireless networks. All three of these losses were also reported in 2005 and 2006. Six new losses were reported in 2006: bots (zombies) within the organization; phishing in which your organization was fraudulently represented as sender; instant messaging misuse; password sniffing; DNS server exploitation; and a general category of other.

The time-series results reveal the dynamic nature of the security environment and the threats and costs over time as companies identify them and take actions to try to minimize or eliminate losses. Figure 1 reveals that losses from security breaches appear to be going down over time, which is a positive finding; however, they do not tell the whole story, because the same surveys from which the data in Table 1 are taken also found

Table 1. Average loss per year per loss type

	2000	2001	2002	2003	2004	2005	2006
Theft of proprietary info.	$3,032,818	$4,447,900	$6,571,000	$2,699,842	$42,602	$48,408	$19,278
Sabotage of data or networks	$969,577	$199,350	$541,000	$214,521	$3,238	$533	$831
Telecom eavesdropping	$66,080	$55,375	$1,205,000	$15,200			
System penetration by outsider	$244,965	$453,967	$226,000	$56,212	$3,351	$1,317	$2,422
Insider abuse of Net access	$307,524	$357,160	$536,000	$135,255	$39,409	10,730	$5,910
Financial fraud	$1,646,941	$4,420,738	$4,632,000	$328,594	$28,515	$4,014	$8,169
Denial of service	$108,717	$122,389	$297,000	$1,427,028	$96,892	$11,441	$9,335
Virus	$180,092	$243,835	$283,000	$199,871	$204,661	$66,961	$50,132
Unauthorized insider access	$1,124,725	$275,636	$300,000	$31,254	$15,904	$48,878	$33,920
Telecom fraud	$212,000	$502,278	$22,000	$50,107	$14,861	$379	$4,033
Active wiretapping	$5,000,000	$-	$-	$352,500			
Laptop theft	$58,794	$61,881	$89,000	$47,107	$25,035	$6,428	$21,223
Web site defacement					$3,562	$180	$519
Misuse of public Web application					$10,212	$3,486	$861
Abuse of wireless network					$37,767	$852	$1,498
Bots (zombies) within the organization							$2,951
Phishing in which your organization was fraudulently represented as sender							$2,069
Instant messaging misuse							$931
Password sniffing							$515
DNS server exploitation							$288
Other							$2,827
Totals	$12,886,153	$10,688,458	$14,702,000	$5,557,491	$438,809	$203,661	$167712

(Data from Gordon et al., 2004, 2005, 2006; Power, 2002; Richardson, 2003)

Figure 1. Total reported losses per year across seven CSI/FBI surveys

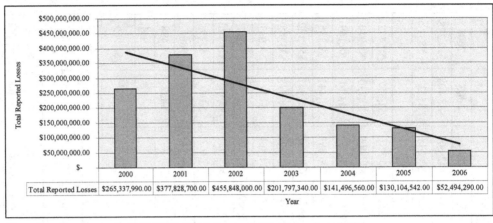

(Data from Gordon et al., 2004, 2005, 2006; Power, 2002; Richardson, 2003)

that budgets in terms of operating expenses and capitol investment for security and training also rose at the same time.

Figure 2 shows the reported average expenditure per employee for operations, capitol investment, and awareness training from 2004 to 2006 for four different-sized companies based on reported revenues. It is important to keep in mind that these are *average* expenditures *per employee,* so for any given company the total outlay would be calculated by multiplying the number of employees in the organization by their actual expenditures, which could be higher or lower than the average.

This time series of expenditures for security reveals interesting trends as well. One is that there appears to be economies of scale for security measures, that is, organizations with higher revenue seem to have smaller expenditures per employee (Gordon et al., 2006), but that may not translate into smaller overall expenditures. A second similar trend is that lower revenue firms seem to have had increases in security expenditures while higher revenue firms have seen decreases. Regardless of these trends, the reduction in losses due to security breaches and attacks have been

accompanied by increased investment in security software, hardware, and training; therefore, it is logical to conclude that either through losses or through increased defense expenditures, security continues to have a large economic impact on firms. Finally, it also reveals that in 2006, firms began to spend funds for security awareness training that were not reported in the previous years of the CSI/FBI surveys.

In November, 2005, the Ponemon Institute (Ponemon, 2005a) surveyed the costs incurred by 14 firms in 11 different industries that experienced security breaches. The size of the breaches in terms of customer records ranged from 900,000 to 1,500 for a total of 1,395,340 records and an average of 99,667 per breach.

Table 2 summarizes total average cost (including direct, indirect, and opportunity costs) for all 14 firms. The average total cost per company was $13,795,000 or $138 per lost customer record. These 14 firms had total losses of $193,103,545.

The economic cost of security breaches is still a staggering amount of money. Many enterprises have been able to reduce the losses by expending large amounts of resources. However, as shown in Table 1, new threats and vulnerabilities are being

Figure 2. Reported average expenditure per employee

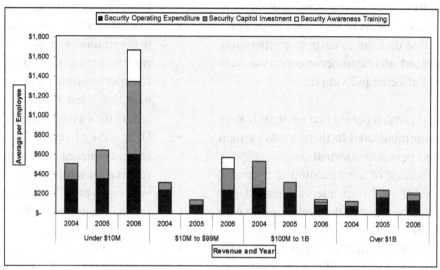

(Data from Gordon et al., 2004, 2005, 2006; Power, 2002; Richardson, 2003)

Table 2. Costs of security breaches for 14 firms in 2005

	Direct Costs	Indirect Costs	Lost Customer Costs	Total Costs
Total Cost for All Companies	$49,840,593	$123,262,952	(factored into indirect costs)	$193,103,545
Average Cost Per Company	$4,990,000	$1,347,000	$7,458,000	$13,795,000
Average Cost Per Lost Record	$50	$14	$75	$138

(Data from Ponemon, 2005a)

unleashed on enterprises every year. The lower costs are most likely offset by increased expenditures to implement new security measures and training. These economic costs are only part of the story, because there are also costs associated with lost customers, and opportunity costs associated with potential customers going elsewhere due to the security breach publicity. The next section discusses losses in these less tangible, but critically-important areas.

Cost of Security Breaches in Terms of Lost Customers

The Ponemon (2005a) survey found that security breaches have potentially severe costs to organizations in terms of lost customers and decreased customer trust in the organizations' ability to secure data and maintain the levels of privacy and confidentiality that customers expect. Ponemon also found that roughly 86% of security breaches involved loss or theft of customer information.

Ponemon (2005b), in "The National Survey on Data Security Breach Notification", polled 9,154 adult-aged respondents in all major U.S. regions, and found that damage to corporate reputation, corporate brand, and customer retention was very high among affected individuals:

- 1,109 (11.6%) reported that an organization had communicated to them a loss or theft of their personal information;
- upon receipt of a notification of a breach, nearly 20% of respondents reported that they had terminated their relationship with the firm;
- 40% of those that received notification reported that they might terminate the relationship due to the breach;
- 58% reported that they believed that the breach had lowered their confidence and trust in the organization that reported it;
- 92% of respondents blamed the company that notified them for the breach;
- only 14% of respondents that were notified of a breach were not concerned; and
- greater than 85% of all respondents reported they were concerned or very concerned about the effect that a data breach would have on them.

Furthermore, the National Survey on Data Security Breach Notification (Ponemon, 2005b) reported that the majority of respondents were not satisfied with the quality of the notification and communication processes. This is where CRM becomes important, and how enterprises communicate security breaches to their customers has an impact. The survey highlighted the following communication experiences:

- Companies that reported breaches to consumers were more than four times (417%) as likely to experience customer churn if

they **failed** to communicate to the victim in a clear, consistent, and timely fashion;
- Companies that sent e-mails or form letters to communicate a breach of consumer data were more than three times (326%) as likely to experience customer churn than companies that used telephone or personalized letters (or a combination of both);
- Over 82% of respondents believed that it is always necessary for an organization to report a breach even if the lost or stolen data was encrypted, or there was no criminal intent. The type of information involved in the breach was also not a factor; and
- About 59% of respondents do not have confidence in U.S. state or federal regulations to protect the public from data security breaches by organizations.

The high cost of security breaches comes from efforts to prevent them and the cost of the aftermath of a breach. Customers appear to be more likely to terminate their relationship with an enterprise after a security breach. In addition, the timeliness and manner in which a breach notification is delivered is important. It appears that telephone calls immediately after (or at least before a public disclosure) followed up with a personal letter, is best to maintain trust and manage the relationship with the customer. Customers are concerned about protecting their privacy and identity, and they expect companies to be vigilant in securing any data they share. In the next two sections, we discuss and define both privacy and security within the context of EC and e-CRM.

PRIVACY DEFINED

The concept of privacy dates back into antiquity: For example, Aristotle (384–327 BCE) made explicit distinctions between a public sphere and political life, 'πολιχ' (*polis,* city) and one's private sphere or family life, 'οικοχ' (*oikos, home) that refers to a separate private domain (DeCew, 2002; Roy, 1999; Rykwert, 2001).*

DeCew (2002) explains that privacy does not have a single shared definition:

The term 'privacy' is used frequently in ordinary language as well as in philosophical, political and legal discussions, yet there is no single definition or analysis or meaning of the term. The concept of privacy has broad historical roots in sociological and anthropological discussions about how extensively it is valued and preserved in various cultures. Moreover, the concept has historical origins in well known philosophical discussions, most notably Aristotle's distinction between the public sphere of political activity and the private sphere associated with family and domestic life. Yet historical use of the term is not uniform, and there remains confusion over the meaning, value and scope of the concept of privacy.

DeCew (2002) further explains that there are several specific types or meanings of privacy that include control of information, human dignity (individual dignity and integrity, personal autonomy, and independence), degrees of intimacy, social relationships, and unwanted access by others. Each of these conceptualizations of privacy is important and meaningful; however, within the scope of this article, information systems (IS) research and practice in general, and EC specifically, we adopt the concept of *"informational privacy"* (DeCew, 2002). Privacy is an important issue for EC because new technologies have enabled personal information to be communicated in ways that were not possible in earlier time periods. Next we discuss the historical background of informational privacy and define privacy within the scope of this article.

Informational Privacy

Warren and Brandeis (*later Supreme Court Justice Brandeis*) (Warren & Brandeis, 1890) in their well-known essay *"The Right to Privacy"* cited *"political, social, and economic changes"* and recognized *"the right to be let alone"* to argue that extent law at the time did afford for protection of individual privacy. In 1890, technologies such as newspapers, photography, and others had led to privacy invasions through dissemination of details of peoples' private lives (Warren & Brandeis, 1890). They argued that the right to privacy is based on the general principle of *"the right to one's personality"* and the more specific principle of *"inviolate personality"* (Warren & Brandeis, 1890).

They asserted that the privacy principle was a part of the common law and the protection of a *"man's house as his castle"*; however, they also argued that new technologies had changed how private information was disseminated and thus required recognition of a separate and explicit protection of individual privacy (Warren & Brandeis, 1890). Their essay laid the foundation for what would become the idea of privacy as a person's control over information about themselves.

Two theories of privacy have stood the test of time and also have figured prominently in major privacy reviews in the 1970's, 1980's, and 1990's (Margulis, 2003): Westin's (1967) four states and four functions of privacy and Altman's five properties of privacy. We focus here on Westin's theory.

Westin (1967) defined four states of privacy; that is how privacy is achieved (Margulis, 2003) and four functions (purposes) of privacy; that is why one seeks privacy (Margulis, 2003):

States of Privacy

1. **Solitude**: an individual separated from the group and freed from the observation of other persons;

2. **Intimacy**: an individual as part of a small unit;
3. **Anonymity**: an individual in public but still seeks and finds freedom from identification and surveillance; and
4. **Reserve:** based on a desire to limit disclosures to others; it requires others to recognize and respect that desire.

Functions of Privacy

1. **Personal Autonomy**: desire to avoid being manipulated, dominated, or exposed by others or control over when information is made public;
2. **Emotional Release**: release from the tensions of social life such as role demands, emotional states, minor deviances, and the management of losses and of bodily functions. Privacy, whether alone or with supportive others, provides the "time out" from social demands, hence opportunities for emotional release;
3. **Self-Evaluation:** integrating experience into meaningful patterns and exerting individuality on events. It includes processing information, supporting the planning process (e.g., the timing of disclosures), integrating experiences, and allowing moral and religious contemplation; and
4. **Limited and protected communication**: limited communication sets interpersonal boundaries; protected communication provides for sharing personal information with trusted others.

Westin's (1967) definition is the one that we adopt for this paper and that we think is the one that should be adopted by IS researchers and practitioners as well as EC customers:

Privacy is the claim of individuals, groups, or institutions to determine for themselves when, *how, and to what extent information about them is communicated to others.* (p. 7)

Westin (1967) also pointed out that privacy is not an absolute but that:

Each individual is continually engaged in a personal adjustment process in which he balances the desire for privacy with the desire for disclosure and communication.... (p. 7)

With this definition in mind, we again turn to recent surveys of consumers and businesses to gain an understanding of how security breaches that violate privacy are perceived and handled. Ackerman, Cranor, and Reagle (1999) surveyed consumers to learn how comfortable they were with providing different types of personal information with businesses, while Ponemon (2005b) gathered data on actual breaches. Table 3 illustrates that data from the Ackerman et al. (1999) survey of consumer concerns and the Ponemon (2005b) survey of actual data breaches reveals that there may be a mismatch in terms of what

Table 3. Comparison of actual data types released and consumer concern

Data Type	Data Released	Consumer Comfort Level
Name	54%	54%
SSN	38%	1%
Credit Card Number	37%	3%
Home Telephone	36%	11%
Mailing address	23%	44%
E-mail Addresses	10%	76%

(Data from Ackerman et al., 1999 and Ponemon, 2005b)

information consumers would prefer not to have revealed and what has actually been lost or stolen. Ponemon (2005b) surprisingly found that some of the more sensitive information that consumers are most reticent to reveal and that could result in the most damage are the ones that are most often released.

Only 1% of consumers surveyed were comfortable always or usually with providing information such as their Social Security numbers (Ackerman et al., 1999), yet 38% of all breaches reported in another survey involved SSNs (Ponemon, 2005b). Similar types of mismatches can be seen for several other data types in Table 3. These results illustrate that companies may not secure the types of personal information that consumers are most concerned about well enough (SSNs, credit card numbers, and home telephone numbers) and may place too much emphasis on the security of information that consumers are more willing to share (i.e., e-mail addresses and mailing addresses). This leads us to question whether firms take into consideration the privacy expectations

of consumers when they decide how to protect different types of data. We think that firms should take consumer expectations and willingness to reveal information into account when establishing security measures to protect different types of information, as this would focus resources in such a way as to engender trust from the consumer and also to minimize potential losses due to breaches.

Figure 3 presents our model of the personal "sphere of privacy" based on Ackerman's findings that illustrates how firms might establish levels of security that are consonant with both consumer willingness (comfort) to reveal information and also with the potential amount of damage that could occur from a breach of specific types of customer information.

We argue that firms should be most vigilant in securing information that consumers would most like to protect and should establish levels or zones of security of different strengths. Later in the paper we will tie this model to security strategies and technology implications.

Figure 3. Model of the customer "sphere of privacy"

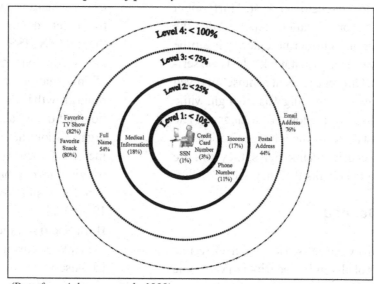

(Data from Ackerman et al., 1999)

Based on Ackerman et al. (1999) and Ponemon's (2005b) data (see Table 3), it is clear that consumers want their SSNs, credit card numbers, and telephone numbers kept private. In other words, consumers place maximum value on these data items in contrast to their mailing address and their e-mail address. Enterprises need to be sure and recognize what information is critical so as to protect it and ensure business continuity (Gordon & Loeb, 2002).

This leads us to the next section on security. Security is the technology and policies that an enterprise and consumer have to keep their valuable information secure.

SECURITY

Security breaches affect most enterprises and government agencies. A recent survey reports that 84% of all enterprises will be affected by a security breach, which is a 17% increase over the last three years (2004-2006) (Ferguson, 2006). Those enterprises and government agencies in the survey reported that when a security breach happened, 54% lost productivity, 20% reported lost revenue, and 25% claimed to have suffered some sort of public backlash with either damage to their reputation or loss of customer trust. Thirty-eight percent of these organizations reported that the breach was internal. Furthermore, according to the survey, many of them did not take the issue seriously enough. Only one percent of those surveyed thought IT security spending was too high, while 38% said it was much too low (Ferguson, 2006). The results suggest that even though organizations are investing in security technologies, they still are not achieving the results that they seek.

Security Defined

The term security can be used in reference to crime and accidents of all kinds. Security is a vast topic including security of countries against terrorist attack, security of computers against hackers, home security against burglars and other intruders, financial security against economic collapse, and many other related situations.

Following are four definitions that provide a narrower focus:

1. **Security**: a very general term covering everything;
2. **Computer Security**: "the discipline that helps free us from worrying about our computers" (Landwehr, 2001, p. 3). Computer security is the effort to create a secure computing platform, designed so that agents (users or programs) can only perform actions that have been allowed. This involves specifying and implementing a security policy. The actions in question can be reduced to operations of access, modification, and deletion. Computer security can be seen as a subfield of security engineering, which looks at broader security issues in addition to computer security;
3. **Information Security**: the protection of information systems against unauthorized access to or modification of information, whether in storage, processing, or transit, and against denial of service to authorized users, including those measures necessary to detect, document, and counter such threats (**NSTISSC**, 1999). IS security has previously concentrated on confidentiality of information stored electronically. The rapid growth in the volume of such information and the uptake of e-commerce within organizations have heightened the need for increased security to protect the privacy of this information and prevent fraudulent activities (Spinellis, Kokolakis, & Gritzalis, 1999); and
4. **Data Security**: the most important part of security - securing the data from unauthorized use.

From the point of view of e-CRM, the above definitions do not help us much. In the section on privacy, information such as SSN and credit card numbers were more critical to consumers than an e-mail address. Thus, we need to look at the security components.

Security Components

A recent meta-analysis of critical themes in electronic commerce research by Wareham, Zheng, and Straub (2005) identified security as an underserved area in IS research. They suggest and support Gordon and Loeb's (2002) assertion that information is an asset of value to an organization and consequently needs to be suitably protected in order to ensure business continuity, minimize business damage, and maximize ROIs and business opportunities (BSI, 1999). The purpose of information security could be characterized as the preservation of confidentiality, integrity, and availability for information assets to keep business value (BSI, 1999; Gordon & Loeb, 2002; Sheth, Sisodia, & Sharma, 2000). Then, in general, IS security is the effective implementation of policies to ensure the confidentiality, availability, and integrity of information and assets to protect from theft, tampering, manipulation, or corruption (Smith & Jamieson, 2006). This also follows from the International Standards Organization (ISO) 17999 Information Security Standard (ISO/IEC, 2005).

The ISO 17799 standard is an internationally-recognized information security management guidance standard (ISO/IEC, 2005). ISO 17799 is high level, broad in scope, and conceptual in nature. This approach allows it to be applied across multiple types of enterprises and applications. It has also made the standard controversial among those who believe standards should be more precise. In spite of this controversy, ISO 17799 is the only "standard" devoted to Information Security Management in a field generally governed by "Guidelines" and "Best Practices" (ISO/IEC, 2005).

ISO 17799 defines information as an asset that may exist in many forms and has value to an organization. Thus, the goal of information security is to suitably protect this asset in order to ensure business continuity, minimize business damage, and maximize return on investments. The objective of the standard is to safeguard:

- **Confidentiality** - ensuring that information is accessible only to those authorized to have access;
- **Integrity** - safeguarding the accuracy and completeness of information and processing methods; and
- **Availability** - ensuring that authorized users have access to information and associated assets when required.

Thus, our basic definition of security in the e-commerce environment is the necessary hardware, software, network controls, data encryption, policies, and procedures in place for an enterprise to ensure that a consumer's information is confidential, has integrity, and is available for e-commerce use.

Enterprise and Consumer Views of Security

Enterprises and consumers will view the security components somewhat differently. Table 4 shows the enterprise and the consumer view. For confidentiality, both the enterprise and consumer expect the security features to prevent unauthorized access to the data. For integrity, the enterprise must use the data supplied by the consumer only for business purposes and must not sell or release the personal data to other enterprises without authorization from the consumer. It is the consumer's obligation to assure that the data is correct. For availability, it is the enterprise's

Table 4. Security components

Security Components	Enterprise/Organization	Consumers
Confidentiality	Prevent unauthorized access Secure all personal information	Prevent unauthorized access How my data is being protected
Integrity	Data used for only business purposes Data not sold without authorization	Data is correct
Availability	Data available for customer Data available for e-commerce	Data available for modification

Table 5. Security threats and vulnerabilities

Internal Threats		External Threats	
Organizations	Consumers	Organizations	Consumers
• Illness of personnel • Temporary staff • Loss of key personnel • Loss of network service • Disgruntled employees • Disgruntled consultants • Labor dispute • Malware • Software bugs	• User misuse • Malware • Software bugs • Poor passwords • Chat room participation	• Severe storms • Utility outage • Natural disasters • Theft of hardware • Software compromise • Hackers • Adversaries	• Severe storms • Utility outage • Natural disasters • Unauthorized access • Unauthorized sale • Theft of computer • Hackers • Denial of service

responsibility to assure that the data is available for the consumer and for e-commerce. From the consumer's point of view, the data needs to be available for modification (*i.e.*, change of address, change of preferences).

IS security has previously concentrated on confidentiality of information stored electronically. The rapid growth in the volume of such information and the uptake of e-commerce within organizations has heightened the need for increased security to protect the privacy of this information and prevent fraudulent activities (Spinellis et al., 1999).

Computer security is the effort to create a secure computing platform, designed so that agents (users or programs) can only perform actions that have been allowed. This involves specifying and implementing a security policy. The actions in question can be reduced to operations of access, modification, and deletion. Computer security can be seen as a subfield of security engineering, which looks at broader security issues in addition to computer security.

Security Threats and Vulnerabilities

Table 5 highlights the major threats and vulnerabilities of enterprise networks and consumer use. Threats are any type of unwanted or unauthorized intrusions, attacks, or exploitations into the system (Volonino & Robinson, 2004). Vulnerabilities are twofold: from the consumer point of view - human error, using poor passwords, or participating in chat rooms; from the enterprise side - the complexity of the software which results in misconfigurations, programming errors, or other flaws. The major Internet security breaches are presented in Table 5 (Volonino & Robinson, 2004).

In a recent trade press article (August 29, 2006), AT&T revealed (Preimesberger, 2006) that an undisclosed number of unauthorized persons had illegally hacked into one of its computer systems and accessed the personal data, including credit card information, of about 19,000 customers who had purchased DSL equipment through the company's online store. The unauthorized electronic access took place over the weekend of August 26-27, 2006, and was discovered within hours, according to a company spokesperson. The electronic store was shut down immediately and remained off-line as we write this article. The cost of this security breach has not been disclosed; however, the company is also working with law enforcement to investigate the incident and pursue the perpetrators. The 19,000 customers are being notified by e-mail, phone calls, and letters. Furthermore, AT&T intends to pay for credit monitoring services for customers whose accounts have been impacted. Clearly breaches are still occurring, even to the largest companies that we would expect would have adequate security in place.

Security: No More than Managing Risk

Gordon and Loeb (2002) suggest that the optimal amount to spend on information security is an increasing function of the level of vulnerability of the information. However, the optimal amount to spend on information security does not always increase with the level of vulnerability of such information. They further suggest that managers should budget for security on information that is in a mid-range of vulnerability to security breaches. Furthermore, managers may want to consider partitioning information sets into low, middle, and high levels of security breach vulnerability.

Some information may be difficult to protect at a high security level and thus is best defended at a more moderate level. Their findings suggest that the optimal amount to spend on information security never exceeds 37% of the expected loss resulting from a security breach.

Smith and Spafford (2004) also suggest that security is managing risk. In addition, they suggest that the major security challenges are:

1. Stop epidemic-style attacks;
2. Build trustworthy large-scale systems;
3. Make quantitative information systems risk management as good as quantitative financial risk management; and
4. Give end users security that they can understand and privacy that they can control.

Kuper (2005) suggests that the sole reason that information technology exists is to leverage the critical asset of data. Thus, security is data and network integrity, the protection of and access to the data. Also, (Kuper, 2005) from 2000 to 2005, enterprises have spent $15 billion on perimeter level security (antivirus, firewalls, and approximately $1.5 billion on encryption software,) one of the more obvious technologies for protecting the data. This supports Gordon and Loeb's (2002) assertion that the amount spent does not always match the required level of vulnerability.

Kuper (2005) suggests several new approaches to data security:

1. Data and network integrity - protecting access to data;
2. Inclusion/exclusion security - trusted, known users are handled differently than unknown users (nodes);
3. Embedded security - more security into all aspects of IT components (hardware, software, or service); and
4. Improved approaches - dynamic XML and Web service architectures.

In this regard, enterprises need to work at the data level (using encryption) to secure the most critical data. The second element is that of trust; trusted consumers should be treated differently than unknown consumers. This is one of the objectives of CRM. Next, embedded security for the enterprise at the hardware/software and server level can help to minimize security breaches. Last, new dynamic approaches can be used.

Table 6 illustrates how privacy and security are interrelated in terms of the levels of data, security strategy, and technologies required to achieve appropriate vigilance. Our model of the sphere of privacy suggests that some information is not as critical to secure (i.e., e-mail address), while other information (consumer's SSN) is critical to secure. Kuper (2005) suggests that initially enterprises focused security at the perimeter, but as they learned from persistent attacks they moved from the edge down deeper, layer by layer, to secure the very data itself through encryption. We rename this as the Enterprise "Sphere of Security" model (see Figure 4). Different technologies are required at the different levels, and the most crucial-level data requires encryption to ensure that it is not released (Volonino & Robinson, 2004).

Table 6. Complementarity of privacy, security, and technology

Sphere of Privacy (Ackerman, 1999)	Sphere of Security (Kuper, 2005)	Technology (Volonino & Robinson, 2004)
Level 4: E-mail	Perimeter	Hardware/Software
Level 3: Full name	Network	Network Security
Level 2: Phone number	Application	Process and Procedures
Level 1: SSN	Data	Encryption

Figure 4. Model of the enterprise "sphere of security"

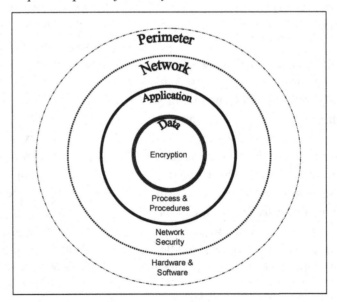

At the perimeter (level 4), firewalls and malware prevention software may offer enough protection for data that is not as sensitive.

Enterprise Privacy/Security Sphere of Implementation

There is an adage that you cannot ensure privacy if you do not first have security. Thus enterprises and consumers need to be prepared for an increasingly hostile public network. Both must provide the right (and updateable) hardware control, data and software controls, and encryption controls to ensure optimal security. Both must also consider the risks, costs, and possible consequences of releasing private information.

A complete solution to either the security or the privacy problem requires the following three steps which become our privacy/security sphere of implementation model:

- **Policy**: The first step is to develop a security or privacy policy. The policy precisely defines the requirements that are to be implemented within the hardware and software of the computing system and those that are external to the computing system, including physical, personnel, and procedural controls. The policy lays down broad goals without specifying how to achieve them.
- **Mechanism**: The security or privacy policy is made more concrete with the mechanism necessary to implement the requirements of the policy. It is important that the mechanism perform the intended functions.
- **Assurance:** The last step deals with the assurance issue. It provides guidelines for ensuring that the mechanism meets the policy requirements with a high degree of assurance. Assurance is directly related to the effort required to subvert the mechanism. Low-assurance mechanisms are easy to implement, but also relatively easy to subvert; on the other hand, high-assurance

mechanisms are notoriously difficult to implement.

CONDITIONAL RELATIONAL "VALUE EXCHANGE" MODEL

Figure 5 illustrates customer data flow and some privacy and security issues related to e-CRM. The Figure shows that each customer has their own personal identity as well as personal and confidential information that they may choose to share, or unknowingly (unwittingly) share with online businesses with which they interact, or with others that obtain the information through some other mechanism than a known direct transfer. The Figure illustrates both intentional and unintentional information transfer from customers to other entities. Three representative customers interact with one or more of three online businesses, as well as other players. Several different scenarios that can affect privacy and security are depicted in the Figure.

Scenarios for Customer John Doe: Mr. Doe interacts with online businesses ABC.COM and PDQ.COM and reveals "some" personally-identifiable information to both, but not necessarily the same information. Once this data is revealed, ABC.COM and PDQ.COM have a responsibility to keep it secure and accurate; however, both may fail in these responsibilities. If they share or sell the information to other companies, there will then be duplicate copies of the information in multiple systems, each of which has different levels of security and protection, and the risk that John Doe's information may be used for purposes other than he intended increases. Additionally, duplicate copies may not be updated if Mr. Doe changes his address, e-mail, or phone number, and thus inaccuracies due to redundant data that is not synchronized can and do multiply. Another possible security and privacy issue is that data from other customers with similar names to John Doe may be inaccurately associated with

Figure 5. Customer dataflow and privacy and security issues

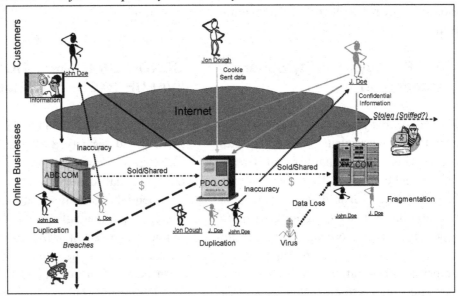

him, or he may be inaccurately associated with their data. This can result in unwanted offers being sent, invalid information being released, or even inaccurate information that changes the customers' status and affects their credit score, ability to purchase, or reputation. The complex data exchange environment and the increase in the number and types of attacks and threats makes it very hard for customers to be confident that their data will be secured and their privacy not violated.

Figures 6 and 7 present our conditional relational "value exchange" model. The basic value exchange model (Figure 6) integrates our customer sphere of privacy with our sphere of security model and the enterprise privacy/security sphere of implementation. If an enterprise is to succeed in the EC environment, it must provide the necessary security to attract and retain customers. Surveys have shown that (Ackerman et al., 1999; Ponemon, 2005a) customers will churn if they feel that their privacy has been or may be violated.

The value exchange model works through the EC system. The customer interested in obtaining information, evaluating a product or service, or even buying a product or service connects with the EC system and then provides the information that is required from their sphere of privacy. Simultaneous with the customer's inquiry or purchase (the customer's value exchange) the e-CRM system is updated. This in turn becomes the enterprise's value exchange. Then, based upon detailed internal and external analysis, the enterprise's privacy/security policies, assurances, and mechanisms should be modified.

Clearly this is a value exchange model. Prabhaker (2000) suggests that businesses can add value to their EC offerings by leveraging Internet technology (the sphere of security) in coordination with proactive measures (privacy/security sphere of implementation) to preserve consumer privacy (the customer sphere of privacy). This is further supported by Schoder and Madeja (2004), who suggest that e-CRM built upon knowledge about their customers and their ability to serve their customers based on that knowledge has proven to be a key success factor in EC. They also suggest that the most effective way to collect customer data

Figure 6. Conditional relational "value exchange" model

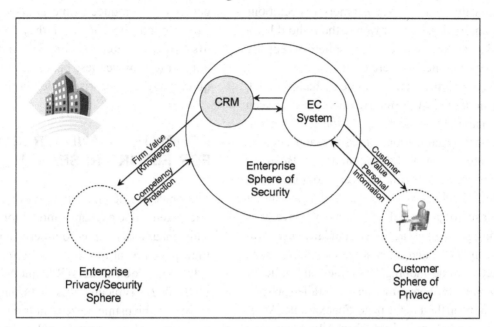

Figure 7. Extended model with watchdogs, government, society, and standards organizations

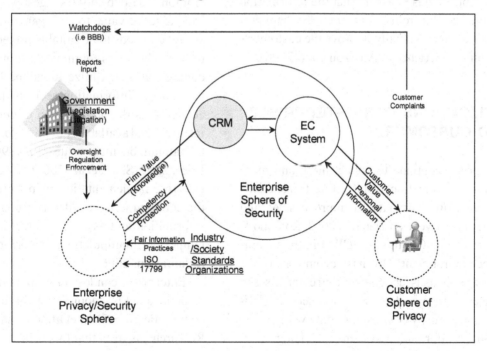

online is through an interactive, feature-rich environment that matches the customers' expectations of an enterprise. In other words, there should be a match between the enterprise's sphere of security and the customer's sphere of privacy.

Figure 7 is the extended value exchange model. This model adds in the interrelationships between the customers, the enterprise, the government, standards organizations, industry and society, and watchdog agencies (i.e., the Better Business Bureau, or BBB). This is a very complex open model. Fletcher (2003) suggests that consumer backlash to perceived invasions of privacy is causing government agencies, standards organizations, industry, and other watchdogs to be more proactive in developing guidelines and policies. Most major EC companies have a detailed privacy statement on their home page. For example, Amazon.com has 11 major items from "What personal information about customers does Amazon.com gather?" to "Examples of information collected". Their objective is to assure that the information that they collect from customers helps them personalize and continually improve the customer's shopping experience at Amazon.com (2006).

IMPLICATIONS FOR ENTERPRISES AND CUSTOMERS

Enterprises continue to collect more and more personal information from online transactions and are using this data to improve sales and service effectiveness (Fletcher, 2003; Romano & Fjermestad, 2003); this is e-CRM in the e-commerce environment. This has become one of the most significant issues confronting enterprises in the electronic age. The issues are securing privacy and security of consumer data while using advanced information systems technology (i.e., e-CRM, business intelligence, data warehousing, and data mining) to sell more goods and services to the consumer.

Consumers, on the other hand, want to get benefits (i.e., reduced time and reduced costs) from e-commerce; however, they are not willing to sacrifice data items such as SSN and credit card number to achieve these benefits. Consumers require that the enterprises safeguard their data.

CONCLUSION AND DIRECTIONS FOR FUTURE RESEARCH

The objective of this article was to develop an integrated value exchange model for enterprises and consumers in an e-commerce environment. Enterprises want to attract and retain economically-valuable customers (Romano & Fjermestad, 2001-2002). Typically this is through e-CRM. However, the prime ingredient is customer data. Thus, an enterprise must employ the right levels of privacy, security, and policy spheres to enable the continued collection and use of consumer data. Gordon and Loeb (2002) suggest that information is an asset of value to an organization and consequently needs to be suitably protected in order to ensure business continuity, minimize business damage, and maximize ROIs and business opportunities. Information security is then characterized as the preservation of confidentiality, integrity, and availability of this information asset to maintain business value (BSI 1999; Gordon & Loeb, 2002; Sheth et al., 2000). IS security is the effective implementation of policies to ensure the confidentiality, availability, and integrity of information and assets to protect it from theft, tampering, manipulation, or corruption (Smith & Jamieson, 2006).

Enterprises can lose customers if they do not respond quickly enough and through the right communication channel after a security breach. Research suggests that this is best handled with personal telephone calls and follow-up personal letters (Ponemon, 2005b). The use of spam e-mail will not be effective and can, in fact, make customers more upset due to feeling disrespected in addition to their personal information being lost.

Our contributions are fourfold. First is our model of the customer sphere of privacy adapted from Ackerman et al.'s (1999) survey findings. This model presents the idea of levels of privacy for a consumer in terms of how willing they are to reveal personal information of different types. The highest level, level 1, corresponds to any personal information that consumers are almost never comfortable revealing, such as their Social Security Number or credit card numbers. Consumers will not reveal such information unless they fully trust the recipient. The lowest level, level 4, corresponds to personal information that many consumers are very comfortable revealing, such as their e-mail address. These levels also correspond with the potential seriousness of consequences from the consumers' information getting into the wrong hands. Release of an SSN or credit card number can result in identity theft or monetary losses, while release of an e-mail address may only result in additional spam e-mail. Both are negative consequences, but clearly the former is much more serious than the latter.

The second contribution is our enterprise sphere of security derived from Kuper's (2005) levels of security. This model represents the level of security required to support customer privacy ranging from the deepest internal data level to the externally-focused perimeter level. Accompanying this model is the technology required to support it. At the perimeter level, hardware and software (i.e., routers and firewalls) provide a modest level of protection, while at the data level more secure technologies such as encryption or perturbation are required to more vigilantly ensure protection of consumer privacy. The third contribution is the enterprise privacy/security sphere of implementation. These are the policies, mechanisms, and assurances to support privacy and security. Many enterprises provide such a policy statement on their Web site.

Our fourth contribution is the integrated value exchange model and the extended model. This model is built upon the interrelationships among the three spheres. The model proposes that both the enterprise and the customer exchange information when they transact via EC. The customer exchanges personal information in order to obtain customer value (reduced time and cost, as well as the goods, services, or information purchased). The enterprise gains customers and, via aggregation and data mining, competitive advantage from the knowledge about their customers. In order to keep their customers, the enterprise must provide competent protection for the customers' information. The extended model shows that there is substantial input from industry, standards organizations, the government, and other watchdog organizations.

In many cases, the major asset of an enterprise is its customers and data about them. There is a delicate balance (as the value exchange model illustrates) that must be maintained. The customers are only a mouse click away from an enterprise's competitors. Customers also have responsibilities to be careful and vigilant in that they must give up personal information in order to receive the benefits of EC. They must provide accurate and reliable information and also verify that a firm is trustworthy and employing adequate levels of security before revealing personal information. They should also think carefully about what information is required for a given transaction and not provide additional information that is not necessary. This can assist customers to make more informed queries and purchases and, at the same time, helps the enterprise market to them and to other customers more effectively through new mechanisms such as recommender systems, cross-selling, and preference discounts.

In the age of e-CRM, Enterprises and Customers have vast new opportunities to exchange value more quickly and effectively than ever before; however, along with these come new vulnerabilities and responsibilities to secure and protect privacy. Enterprises that fail to protect the privacy of their customers may find that many leave for the competition that will do so. E-CRM is about establishing and maintaining intimate relationships with customers to generate additional value and long-term loyalty; enterprises cannot do this if they do not provide the security required to protect their customers' privacy at the level of vigilance they expect. It may be necessary to provide personalized levels of security for the very best customers if they demand it. Just as investors can choose the level of risk they are willing to take for a potential return on investment, consumers will also choose which firms to do business with via EC based on the level of perceived risk they associate with them. Future research and practice in Information Assurance (Security and Privacy) will have to take the consumer's perspective more into account than at present.

REFERENCES

Ackerman, M. S., Cranor, L. F., & Reagle, J. (1999). Beyond concern: Understanding net users' attitudes about online privacy. *AT&T Labs*. Retrieved August 31, 2006, from http://citeseer. ist.psu.edu/cranor99beyond.html

Amazon.com (http:\\www.amazon.com Accessed 8/31/2006)

BSI (1999). *Information security management – Part 1, Code of practice for information security management* (BS 7799-1). London, UK: BSI Group.

DeCew, J. (2002). Privacy: The Stanford encyclopedia of philosophy. E. N. Zalta. Retrieved August 31, 2006, from http://plato.stanford.edu/ archives/sum2002/entries/privacy/

Ferguson, S. (2006, July 7). Study: Security breaches afflict most enterprises, governments. *eWeek*. Retrieved August 31, 2006, from http://www.eweek.com/article2/0,1895,1986066,00.asp

Fletcher, K. (2003). Consumer power and privacy: The changing nature of CRM. *International Journal of Advertising, 22*(2), 249-272.

Friel, A. L. (2004). Privacy patchwork. *Marketing Management, 13*(6), 48-51.

Gordon, A. A., & Loeb, M. P. (2002). The economics of information security investment. *ACM Transactions on Information and System Security, 5*(4), 438-457.

Gordon, L. A., Loeb, M. P, Lucyshyn, W., & Richardson, R. (2004). Ninth annual CSI/FBI computer crime and security survey. *Computer Security Institute*. Retrieved from http://www. theiia.org/iia/download.cfm?file=9732

Gordon, L. A., Loeb, M. P., Lucyshyn, W. & Richardson, R. (2005). Tenth annual CSI/FBI computer crime and security survey. *Computer Security Institute*. Retrieved from http://www.cpppe.umd. edu/Bookstore/Documents/2005CSISurvey.pdf

Gordon, L. A., Loeb, M. P., Lucyshyn, W., & Richardson, R. (2006). Eleventh annual CSI/FBI computer crime and security survey. *Computer Security Institute*. Retrieved from http://i.cmpnet. com/gocsi/db_area/pdfs/fbi/FBI2006.pdf

ISO/IEC (Ed.). (2005). ISO/IEC 17799: 2005 information technology - Security techniques - Code of practice for information security management. *International Organization for Standardization.*

Kalakota, R., & Whinston, A. B. (1996). *Frontiers of electronic commerce, 1st ed.* New York: Addison Wesley Publishing Co.

Keen, P. G. W. (1999). *Competing in chapter 2 of Internet business: Navigating in a new world.* Delft, The Netherlands: Eburon Publishers.

Kuper, P. (2005). The state of security. *IEEE Security and Privacy, 3*(5), 51-53.

Landwehr, C. E. (2001). Computer security. *International Journal of Information Security, 1*(1), 3-13.

Margulis, S. T. (2003). On the status and contribution of Westin's and Altman's theories of privacy. *Journal of Social Issues, 59*(2), 411-429.

NSTISSC (1999). National information systems security (INFOSEC) glossary. *National Security Telecommunications and Information Systems Security Committee (NSTISSC)*, 4.

Ponemon, L. (2005a). Lost customer information: What does a data breach cost companies? *Ponemon Institute* (Tucson, Arizona). Retrieved August 31, 2006, from http://www.securitymanage-ment.com/library/Ponemon_DataStudy0106.pdf)

Ponemon, L. (2005b). The national survey on data security breach notification. *Ponemon Institute* (Tucson, Arizona). Retrieved August 31, 2006, from http://www.whitecase.com/files/Pub-lication/bdf5cd75-ecd2-41f2-a54d-a087ea9c0029/Presentation/PublicationAttachment/2f92d91b-a565-4a07-bf68-aa21118006bb/Security_Breach_Survey%5B1%5D.pdf)

Power, R. (2002). CSI/FBI computer crime and security survey. *Computer Security Issues & Trends, VIH* (1), 1-22.

Prabhaker, P. R. (2000). Who owns the online customer? *Journal of Consumer Marketing, 17(2),* 158-171.

Preimesberger, C. (2006, August 29). Hackers hit AT&T system, get credit card info. *eWeek*. Retrieved August 31, 2006, from http://www.eweek.com/article2/0,1895,2010001,00.asp?kc=EWNAVEMNL083006EOA

Reddick, C. G. (2004). A two-stage model of e-government growth: Theories and empirical evidence for U.S. cities. *Government Information Quarterly, 21*(1), 51-64.

Richardson, R. (2003). Eighth annual CSI/FBI computer crime and security survey. *Computer Security Institute.* Retrieved August 31, 2006, from http://www.reddshell.com/docs/csi_fbi_2003.pdf#search=%22Eighth%20Annual%20CSI%2FFBI%20COMPUTER%20CRIME%20AND%20SECURITY%20SURVEY%22

Romano, N. C. Jr., & Fjermestad, J. (2001-2002). Customer relationship management research: An assessment of research. *International Journal of Electronic Commerce, 6*(3, Winter), 61-114.

Romano, N. C. Jr., & Fjermestad, J. (2003). Electronic commerce customer relationship management: A research agenda. *Information Technology and Management, 4(2/3)*, 233-258.

Roy, J. (1999). Polis and oikos in classical Athens. *Greece & Rome, 46*(1), 1-18.

Rykwert, J. (2001). Privacy in antiquity. *Social Research, 68*(1), 29-40.

Schoder, D., & Madeja, N. (2004). Is customer relationship management a success factor in electronic commerce? *Journal of Electronic Commerce Research, 5*(1), 38-53.

Seitz, K. (2006). Taking steps to ensure CRM data security. *Customer Inter@ction Solutions, 24*(11), 62-64, 66.

Sheth, J. N., Sisodia, R. S., & Sharma, S. (2000). The antecedents and consequences of customer-centric marketing. *Journal of the Academy of Marketing Science, 28*(1, Winter), 55-66.

Smith, S., & Jamieson, R. (2006). Determining key factors in e-government information system security. *Information Systems Management, 23*(2), 23-33.

Smith, S. W., & Spafford, E. H. (2004). Grand challenges in information security: Process and output. *IEEE Security and Privacy, 2*(1), 69-71.

Spinellis, D., Kokolakis, D., & Gritzalis, S. (1999). Security requirements, risks, and recommendations for small enterprise and home-office environments. *Information Management & Computer Security, 7*(3), 121-128.

Volonino, L., & Robinson, S. R. (2004). *Principles and practice of information security.* Upper Saddle River, NJ: Pearson Prentice Hall.

Wareham, J., Zheng, J. G., & Straub, D. (2005). Critical themes in electronic commerce research: A meta-analysis. *Journal of Information Technology, 20*(1), 1-19.

Warren, S., & Brandeis, L. (1890). The right to privacy. *Harvard Law Review, 4*(5, December), 193-220.

Westin, A. (1967). *Privacy and freedom.* New York: Atheneum.

Widmeyer, G. R. (2004). The trichotomy of processes: A philosophical basis for information systems. *The Australian Journal of Information Systems, 11*(1), 3-11.

This work was previously published in International Journal of Information Security and Privacy, Vol. 1, Issue 1, edited by H. Nemati, pp. 65-86, copyright 2007 by IGI Publishing, formerly known as Idea Group Publishing (an imprint of IGI Global).

Chapter XXIII
An Extrinsic and Intrinsic Motivation–Based Model for Measuring Consumer Shopping Oriented Web Site Success

Edward J. Garrity
Canisius College, USA

Joseph B. O'Donnell
Canisius College, USA

Yong Jin Kim
Sogang University, Korea
State University of New York at Binghamton, USA

G. Lawrence Sanders
State University of New York at Buffalo, USA

ABSTRACT

This article develops a new model of Web IS success that takes into account both intrinsic and extrinsic motivating factors. The proposed model begins with the Garrity and Sanders (1998) model of technologic acceptance and develops an extended nomological network of success factors that draws on motivation and flow theory.

INTRODUCTION

The technology acceptance model (TAM) has been the dominant framework for explaining the acceptance and use of IT for nearly 20 years (Keil, Beranek, & Konsynski, 1995). In particular, research has found that *perceived usefulness* and *perceived ease of use* are important predictors of the acceptance of IS technologies (Adams, Nelson,

& Todd, 1992; Davis, 1989; Doll, Hendrickson, & Deng, 1998).

The difficulty comes in applying the TAM model to the Web shopping experience. Unlike traditional organizational IS, Web systems are used for a variety of activities including both work and pleasure. This leads to a disconnect in terms of applying the perceived usefulness and perceived ease of use constructs to the shopping experience because they are typically not the only driving forces behind Web use (Moon & Kim, 2001).

Recent research has extended the TAM model to the Web environment by including intrinsic motivating factors to take into account a wider and more realistic assessment of users' goals (Hackbarth, Grover, & Yi, 2003; Koufaris, 2002; Moon & Kim, 2001; Venkatesh, 2000).

For example, Koufaris (2002) examined the dual role of the consumer in using a Web-based system environment, where an individual can be viewed as both a computer user and a consumer. When viewed as a consumer, Koufaris argues that *perceived shopping enjoyment* (an intrinsic motivator) is important for online shopping since it can have an impact on attitudes and usage intentions. His rationale was based on the findings of Jarvenpaa and Todd (1997a, 1997b). The Koufaris (2002) study found that enjoyment was critically important for online shopping.

However, their model did not adequately explain perceived usefulness and ease of use and their nomological net did not integrate TAM with their intrinsic motivation factor, perceived shopping enjoyment.

This article uses the Garrity and Sanders (1998) model as a vehicle to integrate the individual as a consumer perspective, wherein shopping enjoyment is used as an intrinsic motivator, and the individual is also viewed as a computer user, wherein perceived usefulness is used as an extrinsic motivator and is implemented using *task support satisfaction*. Our approach treats shopping enjoyment as a state variable that emerges from

the interaction between the user and the IS. This perspective is consistent with flow theory (Ghani & Deshpande, 1994; Trevino & Webster, 1992), motivation theory (Deci, 1971; Scott, Farh, & Podaskoff, 1988) as well as environmental psychology (Mehrabian & Russel, 1974).

This article contributes to the literature in three ways. Firstly, the proposed model provides a nomological network of success factors that provides a better understanding of how intrinsic and extrinsic motivation factors impact the use of systems in general and Web sites in particular. Secondly, this paper incorporates two dimensions, *decision support satisfaction* and *interface satisfaction*, as antecedent variables to expand our understanding of perceived usefulness (implemented as task support satisfaction). Thirdly, decision support satisfaction not only provides for enhanced explanatory power in the model, but it can also offer important insights into the decision support provided by consumer shopping-oriented Web IS (Garrity, Glassberg, Kim, Sanders, & Shin, 2005). This is especially important because consumer shopping-oriented Web IS differ from conventional decision support systems (DSS) in a number of ways, including and, most notably, that consumers have an extensive and different decision-making process from managers (O'Keefe & McEachern, 1988).

LITERATURE REVIEW

Garrity and Sanders Model of IS Success and the GSISS Model

Garrity and Sanders (1998) adapted the DeLone and McLean (1992) model and proposed an alternative model in the context of organizational systems and socio-technical systems. They developed a user satisfaction inventory comprised of questions from six well-developed instruments. Garrity and Sanders expand on the DeLone and McLean model by identifying four major factors

Figure 1. Garrity and Sanders (1998) model of IS success

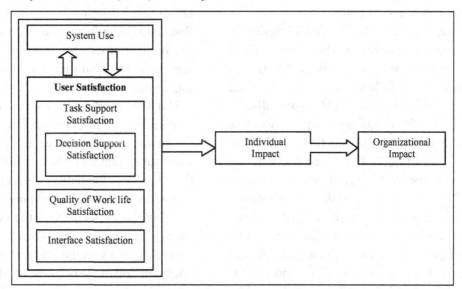

Figure 2. GSISS Model: goal satisfaction-based IS success model

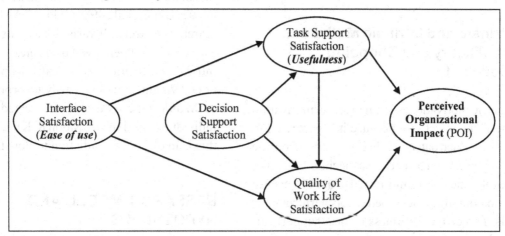

they assert are the basic underlying constructs that make up existing success measures in the IS field (Figure 1). They validate these constructs using a modified Delphi technique whereby IS research experts mapped existing measurement items into one of four factors.

The four factors they identify are *task support satisfaction, decision support satisfaction,* *interface satisfaction,* and *quality of work life satisfaction.*

In order to better understand the underlying dimensions, Kim, Garrity, Sanders, and Sherman (2004) developed and tested a revised model, which arranges the IS success dimensions into a nomological net in order to further understand IS success and to test the construct validity of their dimensions. The revised or detailed model, called goal satisfaction-based IS success model (GSISS model) is presented in Figure 2.

Although the origins of the GSISS model are derived from general systems theory and TAM is derived from the theory of reasoned action (Ajzen & Fishbein, 1980; Fishbein & Ajzen, 1975), the GSISS model is related to TAM. Essentially, interface satisfaction is equivalent to perceived ease of use; and task support satisfaction is equivalent to perceived usefulness. In essence, usefulness is expanded in the GSISS model into two components: (1) usefulness toward task accomplishment or overall job support (task support satisfaction) and (2) usefulness toward decision making (decision support satisfaction). Since most jobs are composed of both decision-making and clerical or processing tasks, the GSISS model provides additional precision and usefulness above and beyond TAM.

Extrinsic and Intrinsic Motivation: Flow Theory and Shopping Enjoyment

Extrinsic motivation is defined as the motivation to perform an activity because it is perceived to produce valued outcomes that are distinct from the activity itself (Webster & Martocchio, 1992). For example, one may be motivated to use IT because it helps one to achieve better job performance. Thus, Perceived usefulness or task support satisfaction would be regarded as extrinsic motivators. In contrast to this, intrinsic motivation is the motivation to perform the activity due to the direct reinforcement of performing the activity per se. An example of this is *enjoyment* towards the system (Davis, Bagozzi, & Warshaw, 1992).

The TAM model was first modified and extended to include intrinsic motivation using the variable enjoyment (Davis et al., 1992). An intrinsic motivating variable or construct that has recently received a great deal of attention in Web-based technology utilization studies is *computer Playfulness* or *playfulness* (Hoffman & Novak,

1996; Moon & Kim, 2001; Novak, Hoffman, & Duhachek, 2003; Novak, Hoffman, & Yung, 2000; Pace, 2004). Playfulness has been operationalized in a number of ways; however, most researchers start with the definition based on the pioneering work on flow theory by Csikszentimihalyi (1975). Csikszentimihalyi's work on flow theory emphasizes the role of a *specific context* rather than *individual differences* in explaining human motivated behaviors. Csikszentimihalyi defines the "flow" as "the holistic sensation that people feel when they act with total involvement."

Flow theory focuses on the *state of playfulness,* which emphasizes the interaction of the individual in a specific context, whereas a strict interpretation of the original TAM model, which is based on the theory of reasoned action (TRA), requires that individual beliefs impact attitudes through perceived usefulness and perceived ease of use (Davis et al., 1989). Thus, TAM forces researchers to treat all variables as antecedents to ease of use and perceived usefulness. Therefore, intrinsic motivation factors such as playfulness or enjoyment cannot be easily incorporated into TAM unless these variables are treated as traits of individuals (as done by Moon & Kim, 2001), but this is in direct contradiction to flow theory.

RESEARCH MODEL AND HYPOTHESES

To operationalize intrinsic motivation into a model of IS success requires decisions on two major issues: (1) the selection of a variable or construct to operationalized intrinsic motivation and (2) the decision to model intrinsic motivation as either a state variable or as a trait variable.

First, we prefer the use of *shopping enjoyment* as a measure of intrinsic motivation since intrinsic motivation is concerned with and defined as the performance of an activity for the inherent reward of doing the activity itself; enjoyment has the advantage of simplicity and also has a great deal of face validity. Finally, shopping enjoyment is a more specific measure that is applicable in the consumer-oriented, Web-based application domain.

Second, we view intrinsic motivation and specifically, shopping enjoyment, as a function of the interaction of the individual within a specific context (with the computer-based artifact or interface). Such an interpretation is consistent with flow theory and the perspective of environmental psychology. According to Mehrabian and Russel (1974), emotional responses to the environment mediate the relationship between the environment and one's behavior. Figure 3 displays the research model and hypotheses, now termed the integrated Web information system success model (IWISSM).

Consumer Trust in the Web Retail Environment

Consumer trust in the Web retail environment is critical for business-to-consumer (B2C) e-commerce, where the possibility exists that a Web retailer can take advantage of online consumers. Trust in the Web retail environment is the "willingness of the consumer to rely on the [Web retailer] when there is vulnerability for the consumer" (Jarvenpaa, Tractinsky, Saarinen, & Vitale, 1999, p. 2). Consumer vulnerability relates to the risk that customers encounter when visiting a problematic site during a purchase. In this context, Web retailers may use personal information to the detriment of the consumer, purchased products may not meet consumer specifications, and or the delivery of purchased products may be late or may not occur at all (O'Donnell, Ferrin, Glassberg, & Sanders, 2004).

Consumers' *trust* in the Web retailer has been empirically shown to influence their *intention to use* the merchant site for e-commerce purposes (Gefen, Karahanna, Straub, 2003; Jarvenpaa et al., 1999; Jarvenpaa, Tractinsky, & Vitale, 2000). Gefen et al. (2003) suggest that trust increases the perceived usefulness of the site by improving the perceived likelihood that consumers will gain expected benefits of product purchases from the site.

Figure 3. An integrated model of Web information system success (IWISSM)

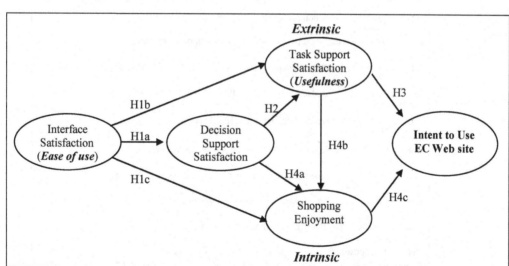

Individual Characteristics

One can expect certain individual characteristics (or traits) to be related to computer shopping enjoyment. Webster and Martocchio (1992) and Hackbarth et al. (2003) found strong associations between computer experience and playfulness (which has a component of shopping enjoyment). Koufaris (2002) also found strong correlations between a consumer/computer user's product involvement and shopping enjoyment. *Product involvement* is defined as the degree to which a consumer is involved with or finds a particular product to be interesting, fascinating, or enjoyable to use. Since a user of a Web-based consumer purchasing Web site is both a consumer and a computer user, one's experience level (or self-efficacy) and one's degree of product involvement should influence one's degree of shopping enjoyment in a particular Web IS context. Table 1 summarizes the study hypotheses.

METHODOLOGY

Data Collection and Experimental Procedure

In order to examine the proposed model in this study, we identified three diverse, commercial Web sites for selecting a digital camera: (1) myCamera.com, (2) Active Buyers Guide, and (3) Amazon.com. myCamera.com is a digital camera comparison guide that lists products and their corresponding critical attributes in a table or list format. Active Buyers Guide is a sophisticated decision guide for the purchase of digital cameras. This Web site provides a number of features and functions to guide a user to "narrow down" the large potential list of products. Amazon.com was selected because it represents a very successful commercial Web site that includes a feature not present in the other two experimental sites—"the average customer rating." The average customer

Table 1. Hypotheses

	Hypothesis
H1a	Interface satisfaction positively influences decision support satisfaction.
H1b	Interface satisfaction positively influences task support satisfaction.
H1c	Interface satisfaction positively influences shopping enjoyment.
H2	Decision support satisfaction is positively associated with task support satisfaction.
H3	Task support satisfaction positively affects intention to use EC Web site.
H4a	Decision support satisfaction positively affects shopping enjoyment.
H4b	Task support satisfaction positively affects shopping enjoyment.
H4c	Shopping enjoyment positively affects intention to use EC Web site.
H5a	Product involvement positively affects shopping enjoyment.
H5b	Web skills positively affects shopping enjoyment.
H5c	Trust positively affects intention to use EC Web site.

rating feature gives users the opportunity to see how other consumers rate the various products.

The data collection was conducted in two steps. First, a pilot test was performed involving 52 subjects and 104 observations. It was used to test the experimental procedure and to refine the items and constructs used in the study. It also enabled the researchers to clarify the wording, content, and general layout of the survey instrument.

Next, the actual experiment was conducted. Students in an introductory computer course at a large research university were given a questionnaire set consisting of two identical sets of survey items for each of the two Web sites assigned. Student subjects were assigned at random to one of six possible Web site combinations. Subjects were given an overview of the task and told that they had a budget of $200 and were asked to select the best camera from the Web site. This budget restriction was used to ensure a moderately involved cognitive task. Specifically, subjects were instructed to visit the Web site listed on their questionnaire packet, select a digital camera from the Web site, and then to fill out the questionnaire. Each questionnaire included a section requiring subjects to list the price, make, and model of the camera selected from the Web site. Subjects were then told to repeat this procedure for the second

Web site listed on their packet. Subjects were given one week to complete the experiment and were given extra credit in the course for their participation. In addition, as extra incentive subjects were informed that completed questionnaires would be placed in a raffle drawing for gift certificates to Circuit City. A total of 300 sets of questionnaires were distributed. One-hundred and ninety questionnaire sets were returned for a response rate of 63% (190/300).

Demographics

Tables 2 and 3 show the demographic and Web access information and the Web use and Web skills for the subjects of this study. Microsoft Internet Explorer was the major Web browser used, and over 90% of the subjects had some prior experience with Internet shopping. Interestingly, the majority (over 60%) of the subjects accessed the Internet through their home office to perform the assignment given for this study.

Operationalization of Research Variables

Measures for product involvement and *Web skills* were adapted from Koufaris (2002). Product

Table 2. Descriptive statistics on demographics and Web access

Demographic Information	N	Minimum	Maximum	Mean	Std. Deviation
Age (in years)	189	18	48	**22.21**	4.308
Gender	188	Male 79 (42%), **Female 109 (58%)**			
Browser used for this survey	187	**Microsoft Internet Explorer 169 (90.4%)** AOL Browser 10 (5.3%) Netscape Navigator 7 (3.7%)			
Location where the Internet was accessed	151	**Home using network 74 (49.0%)** School 48 (31.8%) Home using modem 20 (13.2%) Work place using network 5 (3.3%) Work place using modem 4 (2.6%)			

Table 3. Descriptive statistics on Web use and Web skills

Web Use/Skills Information	N	Minimum	Maximum	Mean	Std. Deviation
G6. I am very skilled at using the Web	188	1	7	**5.74**	1.333
G7. I know how to find what I want on the Web	188	1	7	**5.88**	1.309
G8. I know more about using the Web than most users	188	1	7	**5.26**	1.336
How would you rate your experience with Web technology?	188	1	7	**5.28**	1.089
How many **hours** per week do you use the Internet?	187	0	100	**16.21**	13.584
How many **hours** per week do you spend overall on a computer?	188	0	100	**25.59**	20.039
How long have you been using the Internet?	175	**Between 1 and 1.5 years 170 (97.1%)** More than 3 years 2 (1.1%) Less than 6 months 2 (1.1%) Between 6 months and 1 years 1 (0.6%)			
Number of purchases you have made through the Internet in the last year	189	**1-5 times 91 (48.1%)** 11 or more 53 (28.0%) 6-10 times 32 (16.9%) Never 13 (6.9%)			

involvement was described on the questionnaire as: "We would like to know how interested you are in digital cameras. Please use the series of descriptive words listed below to indicate your level of interest." The instrument then listed two, 7-point semantic differential scales ranging from Un-Exciting to Exciting and from Boring to Interesting. Web skills was implemented using a seven-point Likert scale, anchored by Strongly Disagree to Strongly Agree:

1. I am very skilled at using the Web.
2. I know how to find what I want on the Web.
3. I know more about using the Web than most users (see items G6-G8 in Table 3).

The other major questionnaire items are shown in Appendices A-C. The variables in the study were operationalized based on a variety of sources and existing instruments.

Order Effects and Treatment Effects

The survey questionnaires were designed in six different formats with identical measures. (Each set of the questionnaires includes two Web sites for assessment out of three with the order of Web sites reversed for each of the Web site pairs). Order effects during the experiments were investigated. The results of two-way ANOVA (Table 4) showed that there was no statistically significant difference in behavioral intention to use (the Web site) caused by the order of the presentation of the Web sites on the questionnaire.

The order of site presentation (or evaluation) did not appear to affect respondents' decisions about which site they preferred to buy a digital camera. As shown in Table 5, there was no significant interaction effect between the selected site to buy from and the order of evaluation of e-commerce sites.

Table 4. Tests of between-subjects effects

Source	Sum of Squares	Df	Mean Square	F	Sig.
SITE	12.432	2	6.216	2.945	.054
SITE * SORD	.987	2	.493	.234	.792
Error	785.264	372	2.111		
Total	7206.778	378			
Corrected total	798.912	377			

Note. Dependent variable: Behavioral intention to use an EC Web site
SITE: Target e-commerce sites (Amazon, Decision Guide, and MyCamera.com)
SORD: Site evaluation order by respondents

*Table 5. Selected site to buy from * Site evaluation order cross-tabulation*

	Site Evaluation Order		Total
	1	2	
Buy from Amazon	63	65	128
Buy from Decision Guide	68	60	128
Buy from MyCamera.com	58	64	122
Total	189	189	378

Note. Pearson chi-square value =.826 and p=.662.

ANALYSIS AND RESULTS

We employed the partial least squares (PLS) approach to analyze the data. The emphasis of PLS is on predicting the responses as well as in understanding the underlying relationship between the variables (Tobias, 1999). PLS is a powerful approach for analyzing models and theory building because of the minimal demands on measurement scales, sample size, and residual distributions (Fornell, 1982). In addition, the component-based PLS avoids two serious problems: (1) inadmissible solutions and (2) factor indeterminancy (Fornell & Bookstein, 1982). SEM approaches, such as LISREL and AMOS, are not able to deal with non-standardized distributions (Fornell, 1982), and they can yield non-unique or otherwise improper solutions in some cases (Fornell & Bookstein, 1982). PLS is not as susceptible to these limitations (Wold, 1974, 1985).

Assessment of the Measurement Model

PLS analysis involves two stages: (1) the assessment of the measurement model, including the reliability and discriminant validity of the measures, and (2) the assessment of the structural model. For the assessment of the measurement model, individual item loadings and internal consistency were examined as a test of reliability (See Table 6). Individual item loadings and internal consis-

Table 6. Measures, loadings, and weights

	Decision Support Satisfaction			Task Support Satisfaction			Interface Satisfaction			BI to use EC Web site		
Item	Loadings	Weight	Item	Loadings	Weight	Item	Loadings	Weight	Item	Loadings	Weight
D7	0.8984	0.2818	T7	0.8510	0.3550	I1	0.7904	0.1749	U2	0.8953	0.3563
D8	0.9246	0.2819	T9	0.9020	0.3674	I5	0.8392	0.1784	U5	0.9432	0.3724
D9	0.9096	0.2965	T10	0.9228	0.3973	I8	0.8622	0.2174	U6	0.9254	0.3568
D10	0.8686	0.2534				I92	0.8965	0.2050			
						I13	0.8774	0.1997			
						I16	0.8645	0.1936			

	Shopping Enjoyment			Web Skills			Product Involvement			Trust		
P4	0.8828	0.2778	G6	0.9568	0.3736	PI3	0.8920	0.4707	TR1	0.8709	0.1717
P5	0.9274	0.2800	G7	0.9382	0.3929	PI4	0.9389	0.6179	TR2	0.8584	0.1929
P6	0.9214	0.2637	G8	0.8753	0.3130				TR3	0.9230	0.1859
P7	0.9294	0.2722							TR4	0.8772	0.1526
									TR5	0.9134	0.2104
									TR6	0.9161	0.2054

Note. Items were not included if either: (1) loadings are less than 0.7 and (2) bivariate correlations are higher than .60.

tencies greater than 0.7 are considered adequate (Fornell & Larcker, 1981).

As shown in Table 6, loadings for all measurement items are above 0.8 (except for I1 in interface satisfaction), which indicates there is sound internal reliability. The almost uniformly distributed weights show each item contributes to each construct equivalently. We used PLS-Graph Version 2.91.03.04 to perform the analysis.

Reliability and Validity Tests

In assessing the internal consistency for a given block of indicators, the composite reliability (CR), also referred to as convergent validity (see Werts, Linn, & Joreskog, 1974), was calculated. All the CR values are over 0.9, which suggests that the parameter estimates are sound (Table 7).

The average variance extracted (AVE) was also calculated. AVE measures the amount of variance that a construct captures from its indicators relative to the variance contained in measurement error. This statistic can be interpreted as a measure of reliability for the construct and as a means of evaluating discriminant validity (Fornell et al., 1981). AVE values should be greater than 0.50. All AVEs for the constructs used in this study are greater than 0.70. This indicates that more than 70% of the variance of the indicators can be accounted for by the latent variables.

The AVE can also be used to assess discriminant validity. The AVEs should be greater than the square of the correlations among the constructs. That is, the amount of variance shared between a latent variable and its block of indicators should be greater than shared variance between the latent

Table 7. Composite reliability (CR) and average variance extracted (AVE)

Constructs	CR	AVE	Formula
Decision support satisfaction	0.9449	0.8109	
Task support satisfaction	0.9214	0.7965	
Interface satisfaction	0.9425	0.7322	
Shopping enjoyment	0.9539	0.8377	$CR = (\sum \lambda_i)^2 / [(\sum \lambda_i)^2 + \sum_i var(\epsilon_i)]$
Web skills	0.9460	0.8539	$AVE = \sum \lambda_i^2 / [\sum \lambda_i^2 + \sum_i var(\epsilon_i)]$
Product involvement	0.9121	0.8384	
Trust	0.9596	0.7984	
Behavioral intention to use EC Web site	0.9441	0.8492	

Note. λ_i is the component loading to an indicator and $var(\epsilon_i) = 1 - \lambda_i^2$

Table 8. Correlations of latent variables

	DSS	IFS	TSS	SE	WSKL	PI	TR	BI
Decision support satisfaction	(0.901)							
Interface satisfaction	0.628	(0.856)						
Task support satisfaction	0.699	0.604	(0.892)					
Shopping enjoyment	0.522	0.458	0.613	(0.915)				
Web skills	0.107	0.226	0.057	0.119	(0.924)			
Product involvement	-0.039	-0.075	-0.029	-0.074	-0.123	(0.915)		
Trust	0.421	0.459	0.400	0.429	0.217	-0.129	(0.894)	
Behavioral intention to use	0.532	0.422	0.680	0.668	0.007	-0.031	0.402	(0.922)

Note. The number in parenthesis is the square root of AVE

variables. In this study, the square-roots of each AVE value are greater than the off-diagonal elements (Table 8). This indicates that there exists reasonable discriminant validity among all of the constructs. The correlation between decision support satisfaction and task support satisfaction appears to be a little high although valid in terms of discriminant validity criteria. Such a close but distinctive relationship between decision support satisfaction and task support satisfaction was expected (see Garrity & Sanders, 1998). Hence, decision support satisfaction together with task support satisfaction can be used to provide more insight into the features of the Web site.

Assessment of the Structural Model

The path coefficients in the PLS model represent standardized regression coefficients. The suggested lower limit of substantive significance for regression coefficients is 0.05 (Pedhazur, 1997). In a more conservative position, path coefficients of 0.10 and above are preferable. As shown in Figure 4, all path coefficients except product involvement to shopping enjoyment, Web skills to shopping enjoyment, and trust to behavioral intention are over 0.10 thus satisfying both conservative criteria and the suggested lower limit. They are also statistically significant at p = 0.001. Overall, the

IWISSM model explains a significant amount of variation in the dependent variable, intention to use the EC Web site ($R^2 = 0.57$). Both task support satisfaction as a measure of extrinsic motivation and shopping enjoyment as a measure of intrinsic motivation are significant predictors of intention to use the EC Web site.

The IWISSM model is also a nomological network and can be used to test the construct validity of the success dimensions. Constructs in a nomological network are considered valid if they predict or are predicted by the other constructs consistent with theoretical models and past research (Bagozzi, 1980; Straub, Limayem, & Karahanna-Evaristo, 1995). As shown in Figure 4, a high R^2 for each endogenous variable in the structural model demonstrates that this model can be used to predict each of the success dimensions within the nomological net.

Specifically, over 50% of the variance in task support satisfaction is explained via interface satisfaction and decision support satisfaction, and by the indirect effects of interface satisfaction

through decision support satisfaction. In addition, close to 40% of the variation in decision support satisfaction is explained by interface satisfaction. Over 40% of the variance in shopping enjoyment is explained by interface satisfaction, decision support satisfaction, and task support satisfaction and the indirect effects of interface satisfaction through decision support and task support satisfaction. However, product involvement, Web skills and trust do not provide for significant paths in the model. Table 9 summarizes the results of the hypothesis testing.

DISCUSSION

Interestingly, the major IS success dimensions from the Garrity and Sanders (1998) model all yielded significant path coefficients in the structural model test of the IWISS model (Figure 4). Both the extrinsic motivating factor, task support satisfaction and the intrinsic motivating factor shopping enjoyment, yielded significant paths to

Figure 4. Path coefficients: Integrated model of Web information system Success

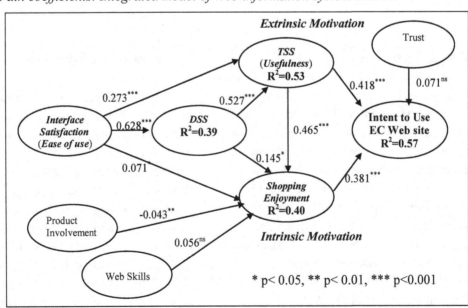

Table 9. Summary of hypothesis testing

	Hypothesis	Support	Significance Level
H1a	Interface satisfaction positively influences decision support satisfaction.	Yes	$p < 0.001$
H1b	Interface satisfaction positively influences task support satisfaction.	Yes	$p < 0.001$
H1c	Interface satisfaction positively influences shopping enjoyment.	Yes	$p < 0.001$
H2	Decision support satisfaction is positively associated with task support satisfaction.	Yes	$p < 0.001$
H3	Task support satisfaction positively affects intention to use EC Web site.	Yes	$p < 0.001$
H4a	Decision support satisfaction positively affects shopping enjoyment.	Yes	$p < 0.001$
H4b	Task support satisfaction positively affects shopping enjoyment.	Yes	$p < 0.001$
H4c	Shopping enjoyment positively affects intention to use EC Web site.	Yes	$p < 0.001$
H5a	Product involvement positively affects shopping enjoyment.	No	
H5b	Web skills positively affects shopping enjoyment.	No	
H5c	Trust positively affects intention to use EC Web site.	No	

the dependent variable, intention to use the EC Web site and helped to explain over 56% of the variance ($R^2 = 0.57$). The model lends support to the IWISS model.

In the Web-based, consumer shopping environment, the primary intrinsic motivating factor is shopping enjoyment. That is, users are motivated by the holistic experience of interacting with computer technology in a manner that promotes enjoyment (and perhaps also captivates their attention and maintains their curiosity).

Interface satisfaction is shown as a significant factor in determining decision support, task support satisfaction and indirectly through those dimensions to shopping enjoyment (intrinsic motivation). This is consistent with the proposed model, since computer tools that are easy to use with well-designed interfaces should be enjoyable and captivating (shopping enjoyment), aid in the support of decision making (decision support satisfaction), and support the entire task process (task support satisfaction).

It is interesting to note that the additional variables from previous Web use studies were not statistically significant. That is, hypotheses H5a, H5b, and H5c are not supported. Although trust has a 0.40 correlation with intent to use the EC Web site, its path is not significant in the model. In other words, the IWISS model accounts for most of the variation in intent to use the EC Web site ($R^2 = 0.57$) but trust does not add significant explanation of intent to use the EC Web site above and beyond what is already explained by the main IS Success factors. The high correlations between trust and the main dimensions of the IWISS model can also be observed in Table 8 and indicate the likelihood of shared variance within the model.

Study results suggest that trust does not directly influence intention to use the Web site *which appears contradictory to prior studies* involving TAM constructs (Gefen et al., 2003; O'Donnell et al., 2004). However, in the development of the IWISS model we were not specifically interested in modeling trust as an additional, endogenous variable or dimension of IS success. In our view, the level of trust of a Web site by a user is best modeled as an independent variable or predictor but not as a component of IS success.

Upon closer examination, *trust is significantly related to the major dimensions of the model, including task support (perceived usefulness) and intention to use, which is consistent with prior studies of trust* (Table 8). The major difference in this study is that the IWISS model already accounts for significant variation in intention to use and trust (modeled only as a direct effect on intention to use) does not explain significant variation above what is already predicted.[3]

A further explanation of trust in this study relates to study participants' perceived level of vulnerability (*risk*) in using the sites. In the absence of risk, trust is not important in choosing one's actions (Lewis & Weigert, 1985; Rousseau, Sitkin, Burt, & Camerer, 1998). It may be inferred that the level of perceived risk could have lessened the importance of trust in our study.

In order to test for moderating influences of perceived risk on trust's direct impact on intention to use, we divided the study sample into a high risk group and a low risk group based on respondents' answers to the following questionnaire item: "I would use my credit card to purchase from this Web site." Subjects that felt their use of the Web site was a high risk undertaking would be reluctant to use their credit card for purchases, whereas subjects in the low risk group are those that are willing to use their credit card.

The correlation between trust and intention to use was 0.13 for the low risk group. This was not statistically significant at the 0.05 level. However, the correlation between trust and intention to use for the high risk group was 0.33, which was significant at the 0.01 level. In addition, the difference in the correlations between the two samples is significant[2] ($p < 0.01$, t-statistic = 3.5). The results lend support to the notion that trust directly impacts behavioral intention to use, but

only when the level of perceived risk is relatively high. Further research should investigate the influence of varying levels of perceived risk on the relative importance of trust on intention to use a Web site.

Finally, the shopping enjoyment factor (*intrinsic motivation*) was modeled as a function of interface, decision support, and task support satisfaction, as well as product involvement and Web skills. Although this model explained over 40% of the variation in shopping enjoyment ($R^2 = 0.40$) both product involvement and Web skills did not have significant path coefficients to shopping enjoyment. This suggests that shopping enjoyment, as implemented in our study, is correctly modeled as a "state variable," meaning that it is a situational characteristic of the interaction between an individual and the situation. Since interface satisfaction, decision support, and task support satisfaction were the primary determinants of shopping enjoyment, this implies that the human computer interaction environment exerts a stronger influence on shopping enjoyment than these individual trait variables.

The nomological network presented in this paper along with the results regarding shopping enjoyment differ from other researchers findings on intrinsic motivation, such as Venkatesh (2000). Venkatesh and Moon and Kim (2001) view intrinsic motivation via playfulness as an individual difference variable (trait) that is system independent. Our results offer an alternative explanation of how intrinsic motivation (viewed as shopping enjoyment) fits within the realm of Web-based IS success and use. Future research will have to explore playfulness or enjoyment as a component of the IS success model, especially in Web-based environments.

CONCLUSION

The IWISS model extends the work of Koufaris (2000) and others by providing and validating a nomological network of factors based on motivation and flow theory and the Garrity and Sanders (1998) model. One of the objectives of this research project was to compare the IWISS model to TAM. In the IWISS model, perceived usefulness is expanded into two closely related but separate dimensions—task support satisfaction and decision support satisfaction. The two dimensions provide additional precision and explanatory power that is helpful to both system designers, who want to design specific support features, and for researchers, who wish to evaluate

the system's impact on task support or decision support satisfaction (Figure 5).

An important goal of our research was to understand why users find Web systems acceptable and useful, and indeed this is important for both researchers and practitioners involved in Web-based systems development. From a practical standpoint, systems that are judged successful become a part of the organizational decision-making framework and or part of the organization's system structure and processes. Additionally, IS success models are used by researchers who wish to build models

Figure 5. Path coefficients: A comparison of TAM only constructs from IWISSM

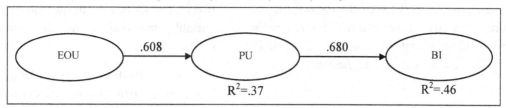

BI = behavioral intention to use the Web site, EOU = ease of use (interface satisfaction),
PU = perceived usefulness (task support satisfaction).

Table 10. Summary of selected studies of Web site usage and explained variance

Literature	Dependent	Independent	Explained Variance (R^2)
This paper, IWISSM model	Intention to use EC Web site	Task support, decision support, interface satisfaction, shopping enjoyment, (trust, product involvement, Web skills)	0.57
Koufaris (2002)	Intention to return	Perceived usefulness, shopping enjoyment, (perceived control, concentration, perceived ease of use)	0.55
Moon and Kim (2001)	Behavioral intent to use Web	Perceived usefulness, ease of use, attitude toward using	0.38
Venkatesh (2000)	Behavioral intention to use	Perceived usefulness, computer self-efficacy, perceptions of external control, computer anxiety, objective usability (playfulness, perceived enjoyment, ease of use)	0.35
Lederer, Maupin, Sena, and Zhuang (2000)	Web site usage	Ease of use, usefulness	0.15

(Variables in parentheses are insignificant within the model tested.)

and enhance our understanding of the factors that generate successful systems. A by-product of this empirical research is the development of normative guidelines that will then be used by practitioners. It is thus imperative for IS success models to be both valid and precise enough to be useful for developing practical guidelines.

The IWISS model provides for additional explanatory power and provides for a greater understanding of the complex factors that may be used to predict Web site use. As Table 10 illustrates, Web site usage models have received significant research attention over the past decade.

From a researcher's perspective, the IWISS model is both a nomological network that can be used to test the construct validity of the variables involved in technology acceptance and IS success measurement as well as a path for conducting future research. Future research should provde further enhancement and understanding of IS success measurement and prediction.

REFERENCES

Adams, D. A., Nelson, R. R., & Todd, P. A. (1992). Perceived usefulness, ease of use, and usage of information technology: A replication. *MIS Quarterly, 16*(2), 227-247.

Agarwal, R., & Prasad, J. (1999). Are individual differences germane to the acceptance of new information technologies? *Decision Sciences, 30*(2), 361-391.

Ajzen, I., & Fishbein, M. (1980). *Understanding attitudes and predicting social behavior.* Englewood Cliffs: Prentice Hall.

Bagozzi, R. P. (1980). *Causal methods in marketing.* New York: John Wiley and Sons.

Csikszentimihalyi, M. (1975). *Beyond boredom and anxiety.* San Francisco: Jossey-Bass.

Davis, F. D. (1989). Perceived usefulness, perceived ease of use, and user acceptance of information technology. *MIS Quarterly, 13*(3), 319-340.

Davis, F. D., Bagozzi, R. P., & Warshaw, P. R. (1989). User acceptance of computer technology: A comparison of two theoretical models. *Management Science, 35*(8), 982-1003.

Davis, F. D., Bagozzi, R. P., & Warshaw, P. R. (1992). Extrinsic and intrinsic motivation to use computers in the workplace. *Journal of Applied Social Psychology, 22*(14), 1111-1132.

Deci, E. L. (1971). Effects of externally mediated rewards on intrinsic motivation. *Journal of Personality and Social Psychology, 18,* 105-115.

DeLone W. H., & McLean, E. R. (1992). Information systems success: The quest for the dependent variable. *Information Systems Research, 3*(1), 61-95.

Doll, W. J., Hendrickson, A., & Deng, X. (1998). Using Davis's perceived usefulness and ease of use instruments for decision making: A confirmatory and multi-group invariance analysis. *Decision Sciences, 29*(4), 839-869.

Doll, W. J., & Torkzadeh, G. (1988). The measurement of end-user computing satisfaction. *MIS Quarterly, 12*(2), 259-274.

Fishbein, M., & Ajzen, I. (1975). *Belief, attitude, intentions and behavior: An introduction to theory and research.* Boston: Addison-Wesley.

Fornell, C. (1982). *A second generation of multivariate analysis.* New York: Praeger.

Fornell, C., & Bookstein, F. L. (1982). Two structural equation models: LISREL and PLS applied to consumer exit-voice theory. *Journal of Marketing Research, 19*(4), 440-452.

Fornell, C., & Larcker, D. (1981). Evaluating structural equation models with unobservable variables and measurement error. *Journal of Marketing Research, 18,* 39-50.

Franz, C. R., & Robey, D. (1986). Organizational context, user involvement and the usefulness of information systems. *Decision Sciences, 17*(3), 329-356.

Garrity, E. J., Glassberg, B., Kim, Y. J., Sanders, G. L., & Shin, S. K. (2005). An experimental investigation of Web-based information systems success in the context of electronic commerce. *Decision Support Systems, 39*(3), 485-503.

Garrity, E. J., & Sanders, G. L. (1998). Dimensions of information systems success measurement. In E. J. Garrity & G. L. Sanders (Eds.), *Information systems success measurement* (pp. 13-45). Hershey: Idea Group Publishing.

Gefen, D., Karahanna, E., & Straub, D. (2003). Trust and TAM in online shopping: An integrated model. *MIS Quarterly, 27*(1), 51-90.

Ghani, J. A., & Deshpande, S. P. (1994). Task characteristics and the experience of optimal flow in human-computer interaction. *The Journal of Psychology, 128*(4), 381-391.

Ghani, J. A., Supnick, R., & Rooney, P. (1991). The experience of flow in computer-mediated and in face-to-face groups. In J. I. DeGross, I. Benbasat, G. DeSanctis, & C. M. Beath (Eds.), *Proceedings of the 12ᵗʰ International Conference on Information Systems* (pp. 229-237).

Goodhue, D. L. (1990). *Developing a theory-based measure of user satisfaction: The task systems fit questionnaire.* Working Paper. Information and Decision Sciences, University of Minnesota.

Hackbarth, G., Grover, V., & Yi, M. Y. (2003). Computer playfulness and anxiety: Positive and negative mediators of the system experience effect on perceived ease of use. *Information and Management, 40,* 221-232.

Hoffman, D. L., & Novak, T. P. (1996). Marketing in hypermedia computer-mediated environments: Conceptual foundations. *Journal of Marketing, 60,* 50-68.

Jarvenpaa, S. L., & Todd, P. A. (1997a). Is there a future for retailing on the Internet? In R. A. Peterson (Ed.), *Electronic marketing and the consumer.* Thousand Oaks, CA: Sage.

Jarvenpaa, S. L., & Todd, P. A. (1997b). Consumer reactions to electronic shopping on the World Wide Web. *International Journal of Electronic Commerce, 1*(2), 59-88.

Jarvenpaa, S. L., Tractinsky, N., Saarinen, L., & Vitale, M. (1999). Consumer trust in an Internet store: A cross-cultural validation. *Journal of Computer Mediated Communications, 5*(2), 1-35.

Jarvenpaa, S. L., Tractinsky, N., & Vitale, M. (2000). Consumer trust in an Internet store. *Information and Technology Management, 1*(1), 45-71.

Keil, M., Beranek, P. M., & Konsynski, B. R. (1995). Usefulness and ease of use: Field study evidence regarding task considerations. *Decision Support Systems, 13*(1), 75-91.

Kim, Y. J., Garrity, E. J., Sanders, G. L., & Sherman, B. A. (2004). *A means-end model of IS success: Toward understanding the cognitive structure of IS users.* Working Paper. State University of New York at Buffalo.

Koufaris, M. (2002). Applying the technology acceptance model and flow theory to online consumer behavior. *Information Systems Research, 13*(2), 205-223.

Lederer, A. L., Maupin, D. J., Sena, M. P., & Zhuang, Y. (2000). The technology acceptance model and the World Wide Web. *Decision Support Systems, 29*(3), 269-282.

Lewis, D., & Weigert, A. (1985). Trust as a social reality. *Social Forces, 63,* 967-985.

Mayer, R. C., & Davis, J. H. (1999). The effect of the performance appraisal system on trust for management: A field quasi-experiment. *Journal of Applied Psychology, 84*(1), 123-136.

Mehrabian, A., & Russel. (1974). *An approach to environmental psychology.* Cambridge, MA: MIT Press.

Moon, J., & Kim, Y. (2001). Extending the TAM for a World Wide Web context. *Information and Management, 38,* 217-230.

Novak, T. P., Hoffman, D. L., & Duhachek, A. (2003). The influence of goal-directed and experiential activities on online flow experiences. *Journal of Consumer Psychology, 13*(1-2), 3-16.

Novak, T. P., Hoffman, D. L., & Yung, Y. F. (2000). Measuring the customer experience in online environments: A structural modeling approach. *Marketing Science, 19*(1), 19-42.

O'Donnell, J. B., Ferrin, D. L., Glassberg, B., & Sanders, G. L. (2004). *The influence of Web site characteristics on consumer trust and the purchase decision.* Working Paper. Canisius College, Buffalo, NY.

O'Keefe, R. M., & McEachern, T. (1998). Web-based customer decision support systems. *Communications of the ACM, 41*(3), 71-78.

Pace, S. (2004). A grounded theory of the flow experiences of Web users. *International Journal of Human-Computer Studies, 60*(3), 327-363.

Pedhazur, E. J. (1997). *Multiple regression in behavioral research: Explanation and prediction.* Fort Worth, TX: Harcourt Brace.

Rousseau, D. M., Sitkin, S. B., Burt, R. S., & Camerer, C. (1998). Not so different after all: A cross-disciplined view of trust. *Academy of Management Review, 23*(3), 393-404.

Sanders, G. L. (1984). MIS/DSS success measure. *Systems, Objectives, Solutions, 4,* 29-34.

Scott, W. E., Farh, J., & Podaskoff, P. M. (1988). The effects of intrinsic and extrinsic reinforcement contingencies on task behavior. *Organizational Behavior and Human Decision Processes, 41,* 405-425.

Straub, D., Limayem, M., & Karahanna-Evaristo, E. (1995). Measuring system usage: Implications for IS theory and testing. *Management Science, 41*(8), 1328-1342.

Tobias, R. D. (1999). *An introduction to partial least squares regression.* Cary, NC: SAS Institute, Inc.

Trevino, L. K., & Webster, J. (1992). Flow in computer-mediated communication: Electronic mail and voice mail evaluation and impacts. *Communication Research, 19*(5), 539-573.

Venkatesh, V. (2000). Determinants of perceived ease of use: Integrating control, intrinsic motivation, and emotion into the technology acceptance model. *Information Systems Research, 11*(4), 342-365.

Webster, J., & Martocchio, J. J. (1992). Microcomputer playfulness: Development of a measure with workplace implications. *MIS Quarterly, 16*(2), 201-226.

Werts, C. E., Linn, R. L., & Joreskog, K. G. (1974). Interclass reliability estimates: Testing structural assumptions. *Educational and Psychological Measurement, 34*(1), 25-33.

Wold, H. (1974). Causal flows with latent variables. *European Economic Review, 5,* 67-86.

Wold, H. (1985). Partial least squares. In S. Kotz & N. L. Johnson (Eds.), *Encyclopedia of statistical sciences* (Vol. 6, pp. 581-591). New York: Wiley.

ENDNOTES

[1]   Some items from frequently used instruments were classified by the expert panel as "out of place," and were later identified as independent variables.

[2]   The correlations were first converted to z-scores and a two-tailed test of significance was performed to determine if the correlations were drawn from the same population.

[3]   Our main concern was to test the validity of the integrated Web information system success model. Alternatively, trust could also be modeled as an antecedent to task support satisfaction.

This work was previously published in Journal of Electronic Commerce in Organizations, Vol. 5, Issue 4, edited by M. Khosrow-Pour, pp. 18-38, copyright 2007 by IGI Publishing, formerly known as Idea Group Publishing (an imprint of IGI Global).

Chapter XXIV
Decision Factors for the Adoption of an Online Payment System by Customers

Fang He
Southern Illinois University at Carbondale, USA

Peter P. Mykytyn
Southern Illinois University at Carbondale, USA

ABSTRACT

Along with the exponential increase in online business transactions, the online payment system has gained in popularity because vendors and creditors realize its growing importance as a foundation to improve their information infrastructure and to achieve "paperless" operating efficiency. However, due to per se different characteristics among customers and Web-systems, both sides' perspectives and technology factors could cause a significant level of variation in customers' acceptance of online payment methods. Our research involving 148 subjects who participated in a field survey examined the impact of a series of possible decision factors including perceived risk, perceived benefits, vendor's system features, and customers' characteristics on the intention to use an online payment system by customers. Some significant associations are observed and their implications are discussed.

INTRODUCTION

It is estimated that by 2006, approximately 68.7% of U.S. residents will be using the Internet. This is complemented by the fact that there has been a growth of 115.5% in Internet use between 2000 and 2005 (Internet World Stats, 2006). Also, eMarketer's (2005) report estimated that U.S. e-commerce retail sales would rise from $56 billion in 2003 to $84.5 billion in 2005, growing at above 20% annually, and that number will further grow to $139 billion by 2008, significantly outpacing traditional retail commerce spending over the next couple of years. This e-commerce growth has provided the impetus and opportunities for traditional business processes (e.g., sales, marketing, payments, collection, financing, and investing) to transfer online. Consequently, the online payment method has become more popular, as it has been increasingly important for financial sectors to improve their information infrastructure (Lee & Cata, 2005). Online payment, also addressed as an electronic payment or an Internet payment, is defined as "an electronic payment made via a Web browser for goods and services using credit or debit cards" (Bitpipe, 2006). Compared with traditional payment methods such as pay-by-check, pay-by-phone, or wire transfer, online payment is considered more time- and cost-efficient, convenient, and flexible for customers and businesses (Sorkin, 2001; Yu, His, & Kuo, 2002). However, customers can differ and Web-based systems can vary in terms of services and features offered, perhaps leading to a significant level of variation in the intention to use online payment systems. What makes e-customers more widely accept online payment methods? What should e-vendors focus on to accelerate such a technology acceptance process? Our study thus focuses on the impact of these decision factors on the adoption of an online payment system by customers, with a framework exploring how the adoption factors drive or impede customers to accept online payment systems.

Recent empirical studies have investigated the impact of key factors on the customer adoption process of various e-commerce activities such as consumer shopping, entertainment, and stock trading (Eastin, 2002; Gefen, Karahanna, & Straub, 2004; Hsu & Lu, 2004; Huang, Hung, & Yen, 2004). These findings jointly suggest that individuals' behaviors could be explained by perceived characteristics of the online transaction methods, vendors' Web site, and product/service characteristics and customer characteristics, not only supporting but also extending the widely-accepted technology acceptance model (TAM) (Davis, 1989), which emphasizes the importance of perceived usefulness (PU) and perceived ease

of use (PEOU) on e-commerce customer decision-making. Lui and Jamieson (2003), for example, incorporate factors such as perceived trust and risk into the TAM; and Ilie, Slyke, Green, and Lou (2005) incorporate perceived relative advantages, perceived compatibility, and gender difference into the TAM framework. Yet, given that online payments are increasingly accepted in the business world, so far few published empirical studies have specifically addressed the underlying factors that could materially affect customers' decisions to adopt online payments. Research progress in this area will help vendors make better plans regarding the replacement of traditional billing and payment tools with integrated online systems that are facilitated with modern technology.

Existing research has analyzed the assessment dimensions for a variety of electronic payment systems. According to the study by Yu et al. (2002), the systems to be assessed include online credit card payment, electronic cash, and electronic checks; and their assessment dimensions cover the technological, economic, social, institution and legal aspects. However, Yu et al. (2002) have not yet empirically estimated or tested the effects of such aspects, nor have they specified the importance of customers' characteristics (Internet experience, age, gender, education, income level, etc.), which could strongly influence a customer's new technology adoption (Akhter 2003; Eastin, 2002). In attempt to fill in this research gap, our study will:

1. Incorporate possible determinants that are previously summarized into an empirical research framework
2. Empirically estimate the influence of those identified determinants

The remainder of this article is organized as follows. Section 2 discusses the advantages of the online payment method and the barriers for switching to online payments. Section 3 presents a research model that illustrates proposed links between determinants and a customer's decision to adopt online payments. Section 4 explains the research method; Section 5 analyzes empirical results; and Section 6 provides a discussion focusing on implications, limitations, and suggestions for future research.

CHARACTERISTICS OF ONLINE PAYMENT METHODS

One of the more prominent points of discussion related to online purchases and payments has been the issue of trust. Odom, Kumar, and Saunders (2002) also investigated consumers' fears and the use of Web assurance seals. Notwithstanding the importance of these trust-related matters, there are other advantages and disadvantages associated with online payment methods. We address several of these as follows.

Major Advantages of the Online Payment Method

- **Efficiency:** Entrepreneurs adopt online payment systems in order to speed up cash inflow, and save money and time by reducing paperwork (Chou, Lee, & Chung, 2004). Within online payment methods, credit cards are particularly favored by consumers because of the efficiencies and protections provided by issuing banks against transaction dispute risks, so they are used for 93% of all online transactions (Caldwell, 2001).
- **Convenience:** Customers can pay their bills at any time and any place where they can access a networked computer because of the versatility of electronic payment methods (Yu et al., 2002). That is, online payers can check and pay their bills at their own time and convenience, without having to wait for their paper bills to be sent to the pre-specified mailing address at a fixed time interval;

this is consistent with our earlier definition of online payment.
- **Flexibility:** Online payments provide customers with the same features as automatic deduction from customers' checking accounts by allowing customers to set and maintain automatic recurring payments (Wright, 2003). Moreover, some online payment systems, including many credit card services (e.g., American Express, 2006) offer customers more flexibility and control over how much they want to pay and when they want the payment to be made.

Major Barriers of Adopting Online Payments

- **Privacy:** The online payment method involves the disclosure of sensitive personal information online and the service providers may potentially misuse such personal information either purposely or accidentally. For example, having long been trusted by cardholders, banks can always access sensitive data of their cardholders. However, negative incidents such as banking scandals, bank closures, mergers due, for example, to poor management, and security problems with Internet banking can all undermine cardholders' trust in banks (Hwang, Yeh, & Li, 2003).
- **Security:** People could feel reluctant to transact and pay online, fearing that their financial account information may fall into the wrong hands. Behrens (2001) reports that 86% of online American adults are very concerned about the security of their bank and brokerage accounts when doing online transactions. A more recent study by Entrust, Inc. (2005) involving 700 online banking consumers in the U.S. found that *18% of all respondents* have decreased or completely stopped their use of online

banking due to fears about the security of their online identity. This research indicates that there is a trend for customers' loss of confidence involving online banking leading to more costly channels such as call centers or brick-and-mortar branches.

- **Reliability:** Online system breakdowns can deeply frustrate buyers and sellers, preventing them from sending/receiving payments, confirming transactions, or accessing funds. Also, online payments may lead to an inadvertent error, intentional misappropriation of funds or fraudulently going out of business (Sorkin, 2001).

DEVELOPMENT OF RESEARCH MODEL

Conceptual Model

In order to address the previous issues, the proposed research framework, as shown in Figure 1, consists of the three categories of possible online-payment-adoption determinants, namely, perceived characteristics of online payment methods, vendors' online system characteristics, and customers' characteristics. These possible decision factors are summarized by prior research regarding various e-business areas (Hsu et al., 2004; Huang et al., 2004), and our study extends this research by examining the impact of these factors specifically on the payers' decision of whether to adopt online payment methods. Furthermore, as was addressed earlier, there are strong linkages between our research model and Davis' (1989) technology acceptance model (TAM). Similar to previous research, our research model, while not specifically testing TAM, does incorporate parallels to it. Recent research by Venkatesh and Remesh (2006) took a similar path by augmenting variables that can complement and strengthen TAM.

Factors That Could Affect the Adoption of Online Payment

Perceived Characteristics of the Online Payment System

(A) Perceived Risk

Pavlou (2003) and Koufaris, Kanbil, and LaBarbera (2002) examine the impact of relative risk on consumer decision-making in using new online transaction tools (Web-based commerce, software agents, etc.), and their findings suggest that when customers consider that the risk of adopting new transaction tools is relatively higher than following the old methods, they will be less willing to adopt. In the current context, the old way to make payments was by regular mail, which may be perceived as more risk-free by individuals. Alternatively, Pavlou (2003) addresses one aspect of perceived risk, environmental uncertainty, which is related to our research. Economic risk and privacy risk are definite concerns due to possible monetary losses as well as loss of private information or illegal disclosure of same; each of these can occur as a result of disclosing credit card information online. If a customer chooses to pay his/her bills online instead, the risk of postal theft/fraud will diminish, but the risk of online theft/fraud (e.g., e-mail interception, network hacking, password stealing, and spyware usage) is present. Therefore, how a customer selects between pay-online and, say, pay-by-mail would then be affected by his or her perception of the relative risk between those two payment methods.

1. **Risk of credit card fraud:** Credit customers have been beset for a long period of time by the risk of fraud/theft related to bill paying activities. In a study by Bhatnagar, Misra, and Rao (2000), significant negative impact of credit card fraud risk was found. In the context of online payment systems, a potential exists for intercepting credit card

Figure 1. Research frameworks for online payment adoption

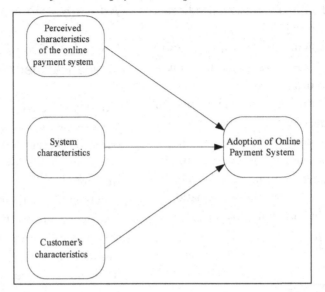

information, such as by transacting business over an unsecure wireless network. Whether transferring the transaction/payment process online will increase the customers' perceived risk of credit card fraud thus emerges as a hypothesis to be empirically tested.

2. **Lack of protection by government policy and legal regulation:** Protection by government policy and legal regulation includes financial and privacy protection. González (2004) reviews the regulatory status of PayPal, the popular consumer-to-consumer (C2C) payment system that is incorporated by auction site eBay. Consumer friendly as it is, such an online payment system causes sensitive legal concerns, including possible liability in cases of fraud, money laundering, the use of the system to pay for illegal or restricted goods/services, or the transactions due to errors or negligence. When feeling the lack of affirmative regulations for online payment systems and legal protections for customer interests, consumers may be less

certain to pay their bills through those online systems.

Biukovic (2002), Strauss and Rogerson (2002), and Baumer, Earp, and Poindexter (2004) compare the Internet privacy law systems between the United States (US) and the European Union (EU). Baumer et al. (2004) summarize the similarities and differences between the 2002 EU Directive on Privacy and Electronic Communications and the projected U.S. Online Privacy Protection Act, and they conclude that with regard to regulations of Web sites and online service providers, the EU provides more strict protections of the right to privacy than the U.S. Biukovic (2002) and Strauss et al. (2002) also argue that self-regulation by the private sector is insufficient to effectively protect clients' online information privacy, so EU-style legislative intervention is needed in the U.S. If consumers feel that there is a lack of governmental and legal policies for online privacy protection, they may be less willing to provide their personal information for online payments.

- **Exposure of personal information:** Customers can hesitate to use online payment systems because of privacy concerns. Invasion of privacy in the area of e-commerce includes the unauthorized collection, disclosure, or other use of personal information such as selling it to another e-vendor (Wang, Lee, & Wang, 1998), and safeguarding privacy would typically cause an added cost to the consumers (Luo, 2002). This too is similar to Pavlou's (2003) environmental uncertainty involving perceived risk associated with exposure of personal information.

- **Concern of system security:** In the network security area, Hwang et al. (2003) indicate that the existing secure electronic transaction protocol needs further revisions to sustain credit cardholders' trust in banks' online card payment networks, particularly in the environment of growing bank mergers and acquisitions. The more customers are concerned about the security of an online payment system, the greater the risk and less trustworthiness they would perceive in using pay-online transactions, and the less their intention would be to adopt the system.

(B) Perceived Advantage

- **Perceived use (PU) and perceived ease of use (PEOU):** The adoption of online payments can be explained in part by the TAM (Davis, 1989). According to TAM, the intention to use a new technology is determined by the PU and PEOU for the specific technology. This model has been widely used and extended by researchers to study technology acceptance behavior and to identify the adoption decision determinants of various e-commerce activities (Gefen et al., 2004; Hsu et al., 2004; Luarn & Lin, 2005). When customers perceive the online payment system as more useful and/or easier

to use, they should be more willing to adopt it.

- **Efficiency:** Daft and Lengel's (1986) media richness theory argues that the selection of communication media depends on the task characteristics and the cost of media usage. The theory suggests that for a rather low-equivocality task of "paying bills at a specific amount by a specific deadline," some leaner media (such as the paperless online media) is better at lowering costs and minimizing excessive message decoding. In addition, Chou et al. (2004) argue that the adoption speed of business innovations (e.g., e-payment system alternatives) is positively affected by technological efficiency and established customer base, but not necessarily affected by technological complexity. By using online payment systems, a buyer can submit a payment "paperlessly" or even "speechlessly," and a seller can receive payments after office hours and ship the goods soon after, instead of answering phone calls (for credit card payments), waiting a few days to receive a mailed payment or taking even longer to clear a check (Sorkin, 2001).

- **Convenience:** Customers favor the mobility and the associated convenience of accessing their bills at any time and any place (Yu et al., 2002). The adoption of an electronic payment method allows online payers to check and pay their bills when and where they want to without having to wait for their paper bills to be sent to a pre-specified mailing address at a fixed time interval. Therefore, when customers can conveniently access the Internet, they should have a greater intention to adopt an online payment system.

- **Financial benefits:** Existing studies investigate various economic factors that might influence the outcome of credit sales, and such factors include customer search cost, membership cost, and interchange fees (e.g.,

Wright, 2003). Adopting an online payment system will significantly reduce the paperwork, cut the postage cost of sending bills, and increase the operating efficiency of vendors such as credit-providing banks. As a result, some credit card issuing banks provide a bonus to customers who switch to a "paperless" online billing system. Chen and Tseng (2003) studied the performance of marketing alliances between Taiwan's credit card issuing banks and the tourism industry, and their findings suggest that credit card clients consider the attached promotional bonus of travel discounts as influential, therefore having positive effects on alliance performance. Nevertheless, Lucas and Bowen (2002) find that in the casino industry, promotional periods fail to significantly influence sales, and the magnitude of prize money generates a positive but insignificant economic impact. As for the e-business, Wilson and Abel (2002) examine the issues that must be considered for developing a successful Internet marketing plan. They emphasize the importance of online and offline promotional activities. So it appears that the influence of using promotional bonuses for marketing new products and/or services could be an industry- and market-specific issue. Whether a promotional bonus can materially enhance customers' willingness to adopt online payment methods is therefore tested.

The hypotheses regarding "perceived characteristics of the online payment system" are summarized as follows:

H1: Perceived risk and benefit of using an online payment system should have a significant impact on a customer's intention to adopt online payment methods.

H1-1: The intention to adopt online payments should be negatively associated with perceived risk factors.

H1-2: The intention to adopt online payments should be positively associated with perceived benefit factors.

Vendor's System Characteristics

(A) Vendors' Service Features

Customers can benefit from adopting online billing and payment systems by minimizing payment efforts ("click-to-pay"), saving postage cost, obtaining payment confirmation, circumventing mail delay, avoiding past-due penalties, and scheduling recurring payments. With regard to automated deductions, however, automated online payments require customers' careful timing and personal financial planning to work consistently, as some of these forgetful and unorganized customers could run into unexpected overdrafts. To solve this problem, some online payment systems provide customers more flexibility and control over how much they want to pay and when they want the payment to be made, and even allow online payers to cancel the pending scheduled payments if they feel need to. Debruyne et al. (2002) and Van Slyke, Lou, and Day (2002) find that the market tends to be more responsive to a new product that can be assessed within an existing product category and less responsive to radical innovations or new products that employ a niche strategy. Their evidence suggests that the public should have relatively less resistance for adopting an online billing and payment system, which is merely an extra new feature added to some well-established existing services (credit sales, automated bank deposits) rather than a "radical innovation."

(B) Vendors' Web site Features

Existing empirical research suggests that both the availability and the quality of design significantly affect customers' interest in and performance of e-business Web sites (Lee et al., 2005; Ranganathan & Ganapathy, 2002). Designing a good Web site is essential for an online payment system, and Liang and Lai (2002) argue that a good design must provide adequate functional support to meet e-commerce customers' needs at each stage of their decision processes.

H2: Vendor's system characteristics should have a significant impact on a customer's intention to adopt online payment methods.

H2-1: The intention to adopt online payments should be positively associated with a customer's overall perception of the features offered on the vendor's Web site.

H2-2: The intention to adopt online payments should be positively associated with a customer's overall perception of the Web site's design.

Customer's Characteristics

(A) Client-Side Technology

The level of anti-virus and/or anti-spyware protection could affect a customer's confidence to pay bills online as the threat of network invasion has been increasing (Hill, 2003). The effectiveness of customers' computer operating systems and the speed of accessing the Internet could also influence their confidence for making online payments.

(B) Demographic Variables

Existing studies indicate that men will be more likely than women to purchase over the Internet because on average men perceive a relatively lower level of risk in online purchasing (Garbarino & Strahilevitz, 2004). Also, when adopting specific information technologies such as instant mes-

saging, men value perceived relative advantage, result demonstrability and critical mass more than women, whereas women value PEOU and visibility more than men (Ilie et al., 2005). Using the 2001 U.S. Census Bureau's population survey data, Banerjee et al. (2005) also found more males use the Internet than females to do financial transactions including security trading and banking. On the other hand, as people age, they tend to exhibit more negative perceptions toward new technologies and feel greater reluctance to adopt new technologies (Gilly & Ziethaml, 1985; Pommer, Pommer, Berkowitz, & Walton, 1980). More recently, Akhter (2003) examined the influence of gender, age, education, and income on the likelihood to purchase over the Internet, and his findings suggest that males in contrast to females, younger people in contrast to elders, more educated in contrast to less educated, and wealthier people in contrast to less wealthy are more likely to use the Internet for purchasing symphony tickets. After reviewing prior literature, our study aims to test those relevant hypotheses in the online payment context.

(C) Internet Experience

Eastin (2002) employs the diffusion model to investigate the adoption of four e-commerce activities: (1) online shopping, (2) online banking, (3) online investing, and (4) electronic payment for an Internet service (such as online auction site or exclusive club membership). The results indicate that when users decide to adopt one of these activities, they tend to also adopt another. Therefore, a customer's e-commerce background could also influence his/her tendency to use online payments. Five factors (computer knowledge, online shopping experience, online trading experience, online auction experience, and online vending experience) are thus selected for testing the influence of customers' Internet experience on the adoption of online payment systems.

H3: Customer's characteristics have significant impact on the adoption of an online payment system.

H3-1: The reliability, effectiveness, and security of client-side technology should be positively associated with the customer's intention to adopt online payment methods.

H3-2: The customer's income level should be positively associated with the customer's intention to adopt online payment methods.

H3-3: Males are more likely to adopt online payment methods than females.

H3-4: The customer's age should be negatively associated with the intention to adopt online payment methods.

H3-5: The customer's level of education should be positively associated with the customer's intention to adopt online payment methods.

H3-6: The level of a customer's Internet experiences should be positively associated with the intention to adopt online payment methods.

The addressed factors that presumably affect one's intention to adopt online payment methods and their corresponding literature are summarized in Appendix I.

RESEARCH METHODOLOGY AND DATA DESCRIPTION

Questionnaire Design, Data Collection, and Descriptive Statistics

To test the series of research hypotheses, a survey-based field study was designed. Prior empirical and conceptual research (see Appendix I) was carefully reviewed to provide the basis for our survey questions, which are listed in Appendix II. The questionnaire includes 22 "subjective" items (Q1-Q22) measured on a Likert-type scale, ranging from 1 ("strongly disagree") to 5 ("strongly agree"). As respondents may hesitate to provide their income information to a non-business-related surveyor, we did not directly inquire about their specific income level, but instead used a "subjective" item (Q22) to indirectly investigate whether a change in the income level might influence their intention to use an online payment system. There are also 8 multiple-choice questions (Q23-Q30) related to the respondents' "objective" characteristics, including their demographic background and Internet experience.

The survey was administered to students and faculty members at a state university located in the Midwestern U.S. The university enrolls approximately 21,000 undergraduate and graduate students with various backgrounds, ranging from full-time students, working people, to retired senior citizens who seek further education; all meet the age requirements to apply for credit cards and/or online banking accounts. After screening the university's Blackboard® user database (listed in alphabetical order with contact information) and selecting at random one out of each 20 users, a total of 200 surveys were randomly distributed through regular campus mail and email beginning early in the semester. A reminder was sent approximately six weeks after the survey was initially distributed. In total, 172 (86%) responded. To test for non-response bias, we used the Mann-Whitney "U" test for comparing the data obtained from those who responded after the first inquiry against the data obtained from those who responded after the second inquiry. Respondents were compared in several key survey areas, including use intention, perceived risk, and perceived benefits. No significant differences were found between the two sets of data. After excluding those who provided incomplete answers, the final sample consisted of 148 (74%) with 98 undergraduates, 43 graduate students, and seven faculty members.

Table 1a. Frequency distributions of respondents' background information (gender, age, education, computer knowledge, online business experience)

Variable	Response (n = 148)				
Q23 (Gender)	Female			Male	
	43.2%			56.8%	
Q24 (Age)	20-29	30-39	40-49	50-59	≥60
	77.7%	12.2%	8.1%	1.4%	0.7%
Q25 (Education)	High School	Associate	Bachelor's	Master's	Doctoral
	10.8%	55.4%	20.9%	8.1%	4.7%
Q26 (Computer Experience)	≤ 1year	2-4 years	5-7 years	8-10 years	>10 years
	1.4%	4.1%	35.1%	20.9%	38.5%
Q27 (Online Shopping)	Never	1-5/mo.	6-10/mo.	11-15/mo.	>15/mo.
	13.5%	42.6%	29.1%	12.2%	2.7%
Q28 (Online Stock trading)	Never	1-5/mo.	6-10/mo.	11-15/mo.	>15/mo.
	45.3%	40.5%	8.8%	2.7%	2.7%
Q29 (Online Auction Bidding)	Never	1-5/mo.	6-10/mo.	11-15/mo.	>15/mo.
	33.1%	39.9%	17.6%	6.8%	2.7%
Q30 (Online Vending)	Never	1-5/mo.	6-10/mo.	11-15/mo.	>15/mo.
	39.9%	38.5%	16.2%	1.4%	4.1%

Table 1a summarizes the frequency distributions of respondents' personal characteristics, including gender, age, education level, computer knowledge background, and their experience with online business. Within our sample of 148 respondents, approximately 43% are females, 90% are between 20 and 39 years old, about 5% possess a Doctoral degree, 75% have an Associate's or Bachelor's degree, and about 95% have at least five years of computer experience. In addition, more than 60% of the respondents have been involved in some sort of online business activity, including shopping, bidding, vending, and/or even security trading.

Table 1b summarizes the frequency distributions of user perceptions (Q1-Q22 item scores) as illustrated in the table.

Out of the 148 respondents, 38.5% "strongly agree" that they would like to use an online payment system to pay their bills (Q1), and another 31.1% also "agree." Put together, approximately 70% of our sample respondents favor online bill paying, while only 21% disfavor it and the remaining 9% feel indifferent. The histograms in appendices also show that the frequency distributions for respondents' opinions to online payment systems are skewed to the left (Appendix III), whereas the respondents' perceived risk for their own online transactions and payments is distributed rather normally (Appendix IV). That is, the respondents as a group consider the risk of online payment frauds to be at the normal level, and paying bills online to be preferable.

Descriptive statistics of the sample data by all 30 items are presented in Table 2.

Table 1b. Frequency distributions of survey question scores regarding use intention, perceived risk, perceived benefits, service features, Web site features, client-side technology and income prospect effects (n = 148)

Score Variable	1	2	3	4	5
Q1	6.8%	14.2%	9.5%	31.1%	38.5%
Q2	5.4%	25.0%	40.5%	21.6%	7.4%
Q3	20.9%	23.0%	21.6%	22.3%	12.2%
Q4	9.5%	39.9%	29.1%	19.6%	2.0%
Q5	12.2%	43.2%	20.9%	21.6%	2.0%
Q6	0.0%	4.1%	8.1%	28.4%	59.5%
Q7	0.0%	3.4%	26.4%	41.9%	28.4%
Q8	0.0%	1.4%	8.1%	50.0%	40.5%
Q9	0.0%	6.1%	8.1%	43.2%	42.6%
Q10	2.7%	16.2%	21.6%	29.7%	29.7%
Q11	1.4%	10.1%	23.6%	33.1%	31.8%
Q12	1.4%	10.1%	27.0%	33.8%	27.7%
Q13	9.5%	21.6	22.3%	27.7%	18.9%
Q14	0.0%	5.4%	11.5%	45.3%	37.8%
Q15	1.4%	9.5%	36.5%	37.8%	14.9%
Q16	0.0%	14.2%	41.9%	33.8%	10.1%
Q17	2.7%	8.1%	18.9%	47.3%	23.0%
Q18	5.4%	17.6%	33.8%	33.8%	9.5%
Q19	0.0%	8.1%	29.7%	33.1%	29.1%
Q20	2.0%	7.4%	22.3%	40.5%	27.7%
Q21	6.8%	8.1%	37.2%	26.4%	21.6%
Q22	8.1%	20.3%	45.3%	18.2%	8.1%

Scale Development and Reliability Analysis

We use the 30 items above to measure the characteristics of an online bill payment system, including customers' use intention (UI), perceived risk (PR), perceived benefits (PB), vendor's service features (VSF), vendor's Web site features (VWF), client-side technology (CST) and customers' characteristics (CC). As shown in Appendix I, a diverse body of research was reviewed to provide the basis for the development of the items incorporated into our instrument The twenty-two subjective items are grouped into seven latent variable scales (Q1 into UI, Q2-Q6 into PR, Q7-Q12 into PB, Q13 and Q14 into VSF, Q15 and Q16 into VWF, Q17-Q21 into CST, and Q22 into IP), with scale scores being calculated, in line with Ilie et al. (2005),

Table 2. Descriptive statistics of online payment survey answers (n = 148)

Item	Min	Max	Mean	t-value	Median	Std. Dev.
Q1	1	5	3.80	7.666**	4.00	1.276
Q2	1	5	2.99	-0.083	3.00	.993
Q3	1	5	2.82	-1.675	3.00	1.325
Q4	1	5	2.65	-4.416**	3.00	.968
Q5	1	5	2.58	-4.979**	2.00	1.024
Q6	2	5	4.43	21.528**	5.00	.809
Q7	2	5	3.95	14.006**	4.00	.828
Q8	2	5	4.30	23.391**	4.00	.675
Q9	2	5	4.22	17.719**	4.00	.840
Q10	1	5	3.68	7.184**	4.00	1.144
Q11	1	5	3.84	9.891**	4.00	1.031
Q12	1	5	3.76	9.173**	4.00	1.013
Q13	1	5	3.25	2.422*	3.00	1.256
Q14	2	5	4.16	16.922**	4.00	.831
Q15	1	5	3.55	7.443**	4.00	.906
Q16	2	5	3.40	5.672**	3.00	.855
Q17	1	5	3.80	9.942**	4.00	.976
Q18	1	5	3.24	2.880**	3.00	1.028
Q19	2	5	3.83	10.719**	4.00	.943
Q20	1	5	3.84	10.475**	4.00	.981
Q21	1	5	3.48	5.203**	3.00	1.122
Q22	1	5	2.98	-0.242	3.00	1.020
Q23	0	1	.57	n.a.	1.00	.497
Q24	1	5	1.35	n.a.	1.00	.746
Q25	1	5	2.39	n.a.	2.00	.954
Q26	1	5	3.91	n.a.	4.00	1.010
Q27	0	4	1.48	n.a.	1.00	.965
Q28	0	4	.77	n.a.	1.00	.919
Q29	0	4	1.06	n.a.	1.00	1.012
Q30	0	4	.91	n.a.	1.00	.989

*Notes: (a) The t-statistics are derived from testing the null hypothesis that the mean value of each variable, Q1-Q22, equals three ("indifference") within a 5-point Likert-type scale. (b) "n.a." denotes "not applicable," as a value of 3 does not refer to "indifference" for variables Q23-Q30. (c) * and ** denotes the rejection of the null hypothesis of "indifference" at the .05 and .01 level of significance, respectively. (d) For Q23 (Gender), we assigned a value of 0 to a female, and 1 to a male. (e) For Q24 (Age), we have no "age below 20" observations in our sample, and we assigned a value of 1 to respondents between 20 and 29, 2 to those between 30 to 39, 3 to those between 40 to 49, 4 to those between 50 to 59, and 5 to those above 60. (f) For Q25 (Education), a value of 1 represented "high school or below," 2 – "associate degree," 3 – "bachelor's degree," 4 – "master's degree," 5 – "doctoral degree." (g) For Q26 (Computer Experience), a value of 1 represented "1 or less years," 2 - "2 to 4 years," 3 - "5 to 7 years," 4 - "8 to10 years," 5 – "more than 10 years." (h) For Q27 – Q30 (frequency of various online business activities per month), a value of 0 represented the response "Never," 1 - "1 to 5 times," 2 - "6 to 10 times," 3 - "11 to 15 times," 4 - ">15 times."*

Table 3. Reliability analysis and descriptive statistics of developed scales

Scale	# Items	Mean	Std. Dev.	Alpha
Use Intention (UI)	1	3.792	1.280	a
Perceived Risk (PR)	5	3.097	0.504	0.795
Perceived Benefits (PB)	6	3.953	0.682	0.813
Vendor's Service Features (VSF)	2	3.701	0.833	0.821
Vendor's Website Features (VWF)	2	3.468	0.775	0.788
Client-side Technology (CST)	5	3.640	0.524	0.764
Income Prospect (IP)	1	2.980	1.017	a

(a) since use intention and income prospect are measured with a single item, no reliability estimate is calculated.

by computing a mean of the items constructing each scale. Descriptive statistics for each scale are reported in Table 3.

To assess the internal consistency of these measurement items, we conducted a reliability analysis by computing Cronbach's Alpha for each scale. All scales are within the commonly accepted range, i.e., $\alpha \geq 0.70$, for this type of research (Kline, 1999).

To assess the convergent validity of the measures, we also conducted a factor analysis by computing rotated component matrix coefficients (i.e., standardized item loadings) corresponding to each factor. In the process, we applied a principal component extraction method with varimax rotation, and specified a seven-factor solution. According to Hair, Tatham, Anderson, and Black (1998, p. 112), a factor loading of greater than 0.45 should be considered statistically significant for a sample size of approximately 150. We found that all measurement items significantly loaded as expected on their corresponding factor, as summarized in Appendix V. Correlation matrices by items and by scales are presented in Appendices VI and VII, respectively. This type of factor analysis has been commonly used in prior research (e.g.,

Gefen et al., 2004; Lee et al., 2005; McKnight & Chervany, 2005). In summary, we consider our item measurement and scale development to have acceptable reliability and validity.

RESULTS

Indifference Analysis

As the aforementioned Table 2 indicates, when commenting on the survey question Q1, the average score is significantly greater than 3 at the .01 level (with t-value of 7.666). On average the respondents accept or even favor online payment methods, instead of feeling indifference or reluctance to pay their bills online. Q2 averages 2.99, not statistically different from 3. Concerning online payment frauds, the respondents perceive themselves to be exposed to the same "normal" level of risk as all the others. Q3, Q4, and Q5 average below 3 significantly, whereas Q6 to Q21 all average above 3 significantly. The income prospect Q22 averages 2.98, not significantly different from 3.

Regression Analysis for Identifying Online Payment Determinants

Using Scales as Explanatory Variables

We next performed a regression analysis with use intention (UI) as the dependent variable, and the other six "subjective" scales in Table 3 (PR, PB, VSF, VWF, CST, and IP) as independent variables. The results, as represented in Equation 1, are outlined in tables 4a and 4b. To account for the possible impact of "objective" characteristics of respondents on use intention, we further incorporated items Q23 (gender), Q24 (age) and Q25 (education) into a regression model. However, in order to ensure that the effects of user perceptions (perceived risk, perceived benefit, etc.) on use intention were not influenced by individual differences in user characteristics, we added gender, age and education factors as covariates, not as independent variables. We also grouped Q26-Q30 (Internet experience) into a new scale, IE, and added it as another covariate. The regression model hence followed without the covariates is:

$$UI_n = \phi_0 + \phi_1 PR_n + \phi_2 PB_n + \phi_3 VSF_n + \phi_4 VWF_n + \phi_5 CST_n + \phi_6 IP_n + u_n,$$

where n = 1, 2, ..., 148. (1)

The regression results are presented in Tables 4a-4b.

A covariate regression analysis was run using UI as the dependent variable, PR, PB, VSF, VWF, CST and IP as between-subjects factors, and gender, age, education and IE as covariates, respectively, in the model. The regression results related to covariates are summarized in the following Table 4c. Among the four covariates, male gender is positively and significantly associated with customer intention of adopting online payments (coefficient = .538, t = 3.624, $p < .001$), while age is negatively and significantly associated

with such a use intention (coefficient = -.527, t = -4.542, $p < .001$). The between-subjects covariate effects of gender and age are also significant on some user perceptions (particularly PB and/or PR). Customer education background and Internet experience, however, are less influential to use intention, as they show no significant associations with UI. However, both education and Internet experience have significant covariate effects on user perceptions (all at the .001 level).

Furthermore, with covariate factors being accounted for, test results of between-subjects effects show that the coefficient estimates (Table 4b) between the use-intention dependent variable and user-perception independent variables are still robust. Regardless of the covariate effects of gender and age, PR, PB, VSF, and VWF remain significantly related to UI, while CST and IP remain non-significant.

Table 4d summarizes the test results of our hypotheses specified previously in Section 3.2. Our findings support some of the hypotheses. Specifically, our respondents have shown a significantly greater tendency to adopt an online payment system if they: (a) perceive a low-level risk to do so (supporting H1-1); (b) perceive benefits of time efficiency or financial savings/bonus to do so (supporting H1-2); (c) find flexible product/service features (supporting H2-1) or attractive Web site features (supporting H2-2) from online vendors. All these regression coefficients are significant at the .01 level. In addition, after PR, PB, VSF, VWF, and IP are controlled for, the use intention of an online payment system is also positively associated with gender, while being negatively associated with age. Ilie et al. (2005) identify a significant gender difference in perceived innovation characteristics of communication technology adoptions, and suggest such a gender difference in perceptions can explain the gender difference in technology use intentions. Our evidence, on the other hand, supports the hypotheses that even among those respondents who perceive the same risk, benefits and vendor's transaction system

Table 4a. OLS model summary & ANOVA analysis related to equation 1

R Square	Adjusted R^2	Std. Error	Durbin-Watson	F	Sig.
.525	.505	.901	2.011	25.806**	.000

Table 4b. Regression coefficients related to equation 1

Dependent Variable	Coefficient	Value	Std. Error	t-value	p-value
Intercept	ϕ_0	-2.553	.721	-3.541**	.001
PR	ϕ_1	.617	.156	3.956**	.000
PB	ϕ_2	.612	.149	4.110**	.000
VSF	ϕ_3	.392	.107	3.667**	.000
VWF	ϕ_4	.381	.112	3.398**	.001
CST	ϕ_5	-.258	.161	-1.603	.119
IP	ϕ_6	.063	.076	.832	.407

Note: ** indicates significance at the .01 level

Table 4c. Covariate effects related to equation 1

Covariate	Regression Coefficient with UI		Covariate Effects		
	Parameter	t-value	Correspondence	F-value	p-value
Gender	.538	3.624**	PB	3.295**	.008
			PR	3.299**	.003
			VSF	.785	.540
			VWF	10.866**	.000
			CST	1.001	.400
			IP	6.739**	.001
Age	-.527	-4.542**	PB	4.383*	.040
			PR	2.587	.082
			VSF	3.382*	.040
			VWF	1.832	.168
			CST	1.007	.371
			IP	1.713	.195
Education	.112	1.475	IP	3.428**	.005
			PB	5.754**	.000
			PR	4.999**	.002
			VSF	4.212**	.003
			VWF	5.275**	.000
			CST	5.992**	.001
IE	.178	1.438	IP	27.086**	.000
			PB	25.382**	.000
			PR	14.506**	.000
			VSF	19.481**	.000
			VWF	34.619**	.000
			CST	10.615**	.000

Note: *, ** indicates significance at the .05 and .01 level, respectively

Table 4d. Hypotheses supported or rejected related to equation 1

Possible Determinant of Use Intention	Hypothesis	Test Result (correlation with UI)
Perceived Risk (PR) at low level	H1-1	Supported (Positive and Significant)
Perceived Benefits (PB)	H1-2	**Supported (Positive and Significant)**
Vendor's Service Features (VSF)	H2-1	Supported (Positive and Significant)
Vendor's Web site Features (VWF)	H2-2	**Supported (Positive and Significant)**
Client-side Technology (CST)	H3-1	Unsupported (negative but insignificant)
Income Prospect (IP)	H3-2	Unsupported (positive but insignificant)
Gender	H3-3	Supported (Positive and Significant)
Age	H3-4	Supported (Negative and Significant)
Education	H3-5	Unsupported (positive but insignificant)
Internet Experience (IE)	H3-6	Unsupported (positive but insignificant)

features, etc., a male is still more likely to adopt an online payment system than a female (supporting H3-3), while one's intention to pay bills online decays with his/her age (supporting H3-4). We attribute this phenomenon to human nature (e.g., variety in risk tolerance) between different genders or ages. For example, even if younger and senior people understand equally well the specific risk for the online payment system itself, younger persons are still more ready to accept the system than seniors, because the former is generally, by nature, more willing to risk trying new technology innovations and abandon the old methods for most of the technology innovations (Gilly et al., 1985).

On the other hand, our findings fail to provide sufficient statistical support for the significance of the other determinants. Comprising multiple measurement items, neither the Client-side technology (CST) scale nor the Internet experience (IE) scale significantly affect customers' intention of adopting online payment methods, therefore not supporting H3-1 or H3-6. Including only a single measurement item, neither the income prospect

(IP) scale nor the education background variable materially influences customers' use intention, therefore not supporting H3-2 or H3-5. Independent of their individual differences in gender and age, customers are by far more concerned about the perceived risk and benefits for using an online payment system, as well as the service option features and Website design provided by vendors in the system.

However, we note that the regression model as Equation 1 is largely based on using scales as explanatory variables, and Table 4b shows that the regression intercept, ϕ_0, is significantly different from zero (coefficient = -2.553, t = -3.541, $p = .001$). The existence of such a significant non-zero intercept suggests that there are other factors missing from our model specifications, and the explanatory power of this regression model can be substantially improved by including additional explanatory variables (e.g., Brav, Lehavy, & Michaely, 2005). Additional analyses to provide extra explanatory powers are not uncommon; see Suh and Lee (2005) and Wasko and Faraj (2005) as examples.

Using All Measurement Items as Explanatory Variables

To further explore the possible underlying factors that may influence a customer's intention to adopt online payment methods, we extended our regression analysis by using respondents' use intention (Q1) as the dependent variable, the other 21 perception items (Q2-Q22) as independent variables, and customer individual difference factors (Q23-Q30)

Table 5a. The OLS model summary & ANOVA analysis related to equation 2

R Square	Adjusted R^2	Std. Error	Durbin-Watson	F	Sig.
.640	.580	.827	2.103	12.290**	.000

Table 5b. The regression coefficients related to equation 2

Coefficient	Value	Std. Error	Test Statistic		Collinearity Statistics	
			t-value	p-value	Tolerance	VIF
β_1	-1.207	.912	-1.323	.188		
β_2	.047	.093	.508	.612	.545	1.835
β_3	.092	.044	2.091*	.047	.511	1.956
β_4	-.098	.104	-.947	.345	.462	2.164
β_5	.422	.112	3.772**	.000	.354	2.821
β_6	.129	.069	1.870	.068	.721	1.388
β_7	.282	.115	2.452*	.022	.514	1.944
β_8	.220	.107	2.056*	.041	.470	2.127
β_9	.138	.071	1.944	.053	.537	1.862
β_{10}	-.115	.129	-.890	.375	.213	4.695
β_{11}	.227	.086	2.651**	.009	.235	4.247
β_{12}	.353	.124	2.840**	.005	.295	3.395
β_{13}	.199	.072	2.758**	.007	.565	1.769
β_{14}	.069	.124	.556	.579	.439	2.276
β_{15}	.233	.103	2.262*	.041	.338	2.959
β_{16}	.010	.119	.085	.933	.450	2.222
β_{17}	.017	.094	.184	.855	.558	1.791
β_{18}	-.189	.096	-1.956	.053	.474	2.108
β_{19}	.043	.084	.508	.613	.741	1.350
β_{20}	.023	.090	.259	.796	.593	1.687
β_{21}	.251	.136	1.838	.089	.504	1.982
β_{22}	-.087	.088	-.984	.327	.572	1.750

*Notes: (a) The t-statistics are derived from testing the null hypothesis that each of the regression coefficients, $\beta_1 - \beta_{30}$, equals zero ("no influence on respondents' preferences"). (b) *, ** indicates significance at the .05 and .01 level, respectively.*

Table 5c. The covariate effects related to equation 2

Covariate	Regression Coefficient with Q1		
	Parameter	t-value	p-value
Q23	.506	2.945**	.004
Q24	-.322	-1.999*	.049
Q25	.252	2.933**	.004
Q26	.149	1.720	.088
Q27	.187	1.462	.146
Q28	.336	3.201**	.002
Q29	-.095	-.812	.418
Q30	.002	.017	.987

Note: *, ** indicates significance at the .05 and .01 level, respectively.

as covariates. The extended model and regression results are presented as follows:

$$Q1_n =$$
$$\beta_1 + \beta_2 Q_{2n} + \beta_3 Q_{3n} + \beta_4 Q_{4n} + \ldots + \beta_{22} Q_{22n} + \varepsilon_n$$
$$= \beta_1 + \sum_{m=2} \beta_m Q_{mn} + \varepsilon_n,$$

where n = 1, 2, ..., 148.   (2)

Table 5a indicates that the R-Square and adjusted R-Square of the model in Equation (2) are respectively .640 and .580, both showing an improvement over Equation (1) with .525 and .505. Cohen and Cohen's (1983) test result (with F-value of 10.651, $p < .01$) also indicates a considerable increase in explanatory power when comparing the item-based Equation (2) with the scale-based Equation (1). The 29 variables (Q2-Q30) which serve as proxies for customers' perceived risk, perceived benefits, online payment service features, vendors' Web site features and customers' characteristics, jointly explain approximately 64% of the variation in customers' intention to adopt online payment methods.

Table 5b estimates the possible impact that each of the explanatory variables may have on customers' payment-method preferences.

- Among the "perceived risk" items, Q3, Q5, and Q6 are significantly and positively associated with the dependent variable Q1, as β_3, β_5 and β_6 are significantly positive at the .05-.10 level. A customer would be more willing to adopt online payments provided that he or she feels safe to provide personal information online, considers legal regulations are sufficient to discipline those engaged in online payment fraud, and considers the vendor/creditor's online transaction network is secure ($p = .068$).

- Among the "perceived benefits" items, Q7, Q8, Q11 and Q12 are significantly and positively associated with Q1, as β_7, β_8, β_{11}, and β_{12} are significantly positive at the .05-.10 level. A customer will be more likely to adopt online payment methods provided that he or she considers meeting payment deadlines and avoiding late penalties as particularly important, considers the online payment system is easy to use and fast, and considers the access to computers and Internet is easy to obtain. However, our respondents do not consider saving postage costs will be particularly important for them to choose "pay-online" as β_{10} is not only insignificant but also negative. The discount/bonus (Q9) provided by creditors/vendors for placing and paying for orders online is marginally influential, as β_9 is marginally positive ($p = .053$).

- Among "vendor service features," Q13 is significantly and positively associated with Q1, as β_{13} is significantly positive at the .01 level. A customer will be more likely to adopt online payment methods provided that the vendor's online payment system offers customers the option feature of recurring automatic deductions. This finding is consistent with the fact that customers highly regard the importance of meeting payment deadlines and avoiding late penalties, since monthly automatic deduction with the minimum amount due is the most time- and cost-effective way to avoid late penalties. Among "vendor Web site features," Q15 is also positively associated with Q1, as β_{15} is positively significant at the .05 level.

- Among the "client-side technology" items (Q17-Q21), all but Q18 are positively associated with Q1, but none of these regression coefficients are significant at the .05 level. From our observations, it appears that a customer's preference to pay bills online does not strongly depend on the hardware or software that he or she is equipped with, including anti-virus/spyware programs, operating system, or even high-speed Internet service such as DSL, therefore reaffirming our earlier result that the scale of client-side technology (CST) does not materially affect use intention (UI). When deciding whether to "pay-online," a customer is concerned more about the vendor's technology level than about his/her own technology level.

- We find no significant results between a customer's intention to pay bills online and his/her family income growth prospect (Q22), as β_{22} is not significantly different from zero.

To further account for customers' characteristics, we once again employed a covariate regression analysis using Q1 (use intention) as the dependent variable, Q20-Q22 (individual items for user perceptions) as between-subjects factors, Q23-Q30 (gender, age, education, and Internet experience items), respectively, as covariates in the model. The covariate effect estimates are shown in Table 5c. The customer's "pay-online" use intention has positive associations with male gender and with education ($p = .004$ in both cases), and a negative association with age ($p = .049$). The between-subjects covariate effects of customer gender, age, education background, and Internet experience are in line with those reported in the scale-variable-based result presented in Table 4c.

The data in Table 5c reaffirms our prior findings that males, younger customers and those with higher education levels are more willing to use an online payment system than their counterparts. In addition, it is interesting to observe that those most willing to pay bills online are those customers who frequently trade securities online (between Q1 and Q28 the coefficient = .336, t = 3.201, $p = .002$), rather than those who frequently shop, bid or sell goods online. One of the possible explanations is that online security trading typically involves larger amounts of electronic funding. Online brokerage accounts require a certain amount of cash deposit to open, and the trader must use bank deposits rather than credit cards to pay for the trades. Compared with online shoppers and bidders who typically use credit cards (with credit card companies allowing customers to dispute unauthorized payments) and pay relatively smaller amounts for their deals, online security traders have experienced considerably greater risk within their online payment/funding process; therefore, they will be more inclined to accept online payment methods and less likely to overestimate the risk related to making online payments.

When comparing results in Tables 5a, 5b, and 5c with those in Tables 4a, 4b, and 4c, we find that instead of using scales, using measurement items as explanatory variables and/or as covariates can improve the statistical performance of regression analysis for online-payment-adoption determinants. (1) The R-square and adjusted R-Square improved, implying a greater explanatory power for the model; (2) The constant coefficient becomes insignificant, considerably reducing the "unexplained" portion for the model; and (3) we find some new significant evidence supporting the positive impact of a customer's education and Internet experience on his or her pay-online use intention.

However, we were concerned that multicollinearity might arise for a regression model like Equation 2 that incorporates all twenty-nine measurement items as explanatory variables. If multicollinearity does exist, it would cause a severe problem of biased and unreliable regression estimates, which by far outweighs the "improvement in statistical performance." Therefore, we performed a collinearity analysis, and the resulting statistics are documented in the last two columns in Table 5b. We find that all individual VIF statistics are below 10, the average VIF value is below 6, and none of the tolerance values is below 0.1. Our regression estimates appear not to be materially affected by the multicollinearity problems. As a further proof, our regression estimates remain stable even after we drop from the model some of the explanatory variables that might seem highly correlated, such as Q4 vs. Q5, Q18 vs. Q21, etc. Thus, we feel reasonably confident with the unbiasedness of coefficient estimates obtained from the regression analysis that uses the 21 "user perception" measurement items (Q2-Q22) as explanatory variables and the eight "user individual difference" items (Q23-Q30) as covariates.

DISCUSSION

This study has empirically examined an individual's intention to engage in online bill payment, and estimated the influence of a number of determinants impacting that intention. Our findings are based upon a survey of a 148 students and faculty members from a state university within the Midwestern US. The results show that:

- A majority of our respondents favor and support the option of making online payments, and they also consider the risk related to making online payments as normal. Their biggest motive to adopt an online payment system is to meet payment deadlines and avoid past-due late penalties.
- A customer's willingness to pay bills online depends significantly on his/her perceived risk and benefits of using the online payment system, on the option features offered in the system, and on the quality of vendors' Web site designs.
- In particular, a customer will be significantly more likely to adopt online payment methods provided that (1) the vendor's transaction network is secure; (2) the online payment methods are easy to learn; and (3) the vendor's online payment system offers customers the option feature of recurring automatic deductions, as it is viewed as the most time- and cost-effective way to avoid past-due late penalties.
- Those customers who are male, younger, with higher education levels, with more computer application experiences, and particularly those who have been frequently trading securities online, are significantly more willing to use an online payment system than the others.

Theoretical Implications

Like much prior research dealing with technology adoption, our research is an extension of the traditional TAM (which concentrates on PU and PEOU) with additional factors that could determine customers' intention to adopt technology innovations. In the specific "pay-online" e-commerce section, such determinants beyond PU and PEOU (which are conceptually similar to perceived benefit) include user perceptions of risk, of vendor-side service and Web site features, of user-side technology feature, and income prospect. According to our findings, even after adjusting for the covariate effects of customer characteristics, most user perceptions of the characteristics of an online payment system significantly affect users' adoption likelihood. For example, customers are exposed to financial risk in the pay-on-line process, and customers with background variations differ in risk tolerance (Gilly et al., 1985). It is interesting to note, however, the impact of customers' perceived risk on their use intention persists across customer groups differing in gender, age, education level, and Internet experience. On the other hand, we do not find evidence that supports the importance of a customer's client-side technology level (e.g., Hill, 2003) or income prospect (e.g., Akhter, 2003) in affecting his/her intention. It appears that when customers decide whether or not to use online payment methods, they are not particularly concerned about their own income prospects or hardware/software technology availability. The necessity to include factors such as client-side technology and customer income prospects might depend on the specific types of technology innovations or e-commerce initiatives.

Practical Implications

To speed up the transformation process and encourage customers to switch to using online payment methods, vendors/creditors should pay particular attention to improving the security and the ease-of-use of their transaction network, and should also add necessary option features such as recurring automatic deductions. Other features that may prove to be relevant include ease with which payments can be made to payees who do not have an account number and minimizing the amount of time between when a customer directs a payment to be made and the date the payment is actually made. Although not specifically addressed in this research, these services are integral to online payment systems today, suggesting that vendors should examine their use.

Limitations and Future Research Agenda

This study empirically investigated the possible underlying factors that could affect a consumer's intention to adopt an online bill payment system. However, at this stage our survey sample merely consisted of students and faulty members from a Midwestern U.S. public university. These surveyed students and faculty covered a variety of courses, and many students are working people who registered in evening classes; yet to obtain results that are more convincing and to better represent the population that pay bills, the sample should be more diversified (in terms of geographical regions, ages, etc.). For example, as Table 2b illustrates, nearly 80% of the respondents are young people with ages between 20 and 29. Future research should not only extend the sample coverage into various social settings, but also investigate whether the findings in this study hold in consumers' adoption process of various e-finance tools other than online bill payment systems.

With regard to measurement items for the questionnaire, a customer's intention to use online payment systems was measured with a single item. Consistent with much of the research today assessing intention to use, a multi-item construct would be more appropriate.

REFERENCES

Akhter, S. H. (2003). Digital divide and purchase intention: Why demographic psychology matters. *Journal of Economic Psychology, 24*(3), 321-327.

American Express. (2006). *Payment flexibility: Extended payment options.* Retrieved from http://www.americanexpress.com/lacidc/en/prcards/paymentflexibility.shtml

Banerjee, S, Kang, H., Bagchi-Sen, S., & Rao, H. R. (2005). Gender division in the use of the Internet applications. *International Journal of E-Business Research, 1*(2), 24-39.

Baumer, D. L., Earp, J. B., & Poindexter, J. C. (2004). Internet privacy law: A comparison between the U.S. and the European Union. *Computers and Security, 23*(1), 400-412.

Behrens, L. (2001). *Privacy and security: The hidden growth strategy.* Retrieved from http://www.gartnerg2.com/site/searchresults.asp

Bhatnagar, A., Misra, S., & Rao, H. R. (2000). On risk, convenience, and Internet shopping behavior—why some consumers are online shoppers while others are not. *Communications of the ACM, 43*(11), 98-105.

Bitpipe. (2006). *IT information: White papers, product literature, Webcasts, and case studies.* Retrieved from http://www.bitpipe.com/tlist/Online-Payments.html

Biukovic, L. (2002). Unification of cyber-jurisdiction rules: Just how close are the EU and the US? *Telematics and Informatics, 19*(2), 139-157.

Brav, A., Lehavy, R., & Michaely, R. (2005). *Using expectations to test asset pricing models.* Working Paper, Fuqua School of Business, Duke University, February.

Caldwell, K. (2001). The public policy report. *CommerceNet Newsletter, 35.* Retrieved from http://www.nii.org.tw/cnt/info/Report/20010504.html

Chen, H. M., & Tseng, C. H. (2003). The performance of marketing alliances between the tourism industry and credit card issuing banks in Taiwan. *Tourism Management, 26*(1), 15-24.

Chou, Y., Lee, C., & Chung, J. (2004). Understanding m-commerce payment systems through the analytic hierarchy process. *Journal of Business Research, 57*(12), 1423-1430.

Cohen, J., & Cohen, P. (1983). *Applied multiple regression/correlation analysis for the behavioral sciences* (2nd ed.). Hillsdale, NJ: Erlbaum.

Daft, R. L., & Lengel, R. H. (1986). Organizational information requirements, media richness, and structural design. *Management Science, 32*(5), 554-571.

Davis, F. D. (1989). Perceived usefulness, perceived ease of use, and user acceptance of information technology. *MIS Quarterly, 13*(3), 318-339.

Debruyne, M., Rudy, M., Griffin, A., Hart, S., Hultink, E. J., & Robben, H. (2002). The impact of new product launch strategies on competitive reaction in industrial markets. *Journal of Product Innovation Management, 19*(2), 159-170.

Eastin, M. S. (2002). Diffusion of e-commerce: An analysis of the adoption of four e-commerce activities. *Telematics and Informatics, 19*(1), 251-267.

eMarketer. (2005). *E-commerce in the U.S.: Retail Trends.* Retrieved April 19, from http://www.emarketer.com/Report.aspx?ecom_us_may05

Entrust. (2005). *Consumers and regulators call for additional security to protect identities and reduce fraud.* Retrieved November 08, from http://www.entrust.com/news/2005/6126_6342.htm

Garbarino, E., & Strahilevitz, M. (2004). Gender differences in the perceived risk of buying online and the effects of receiving a site recommendation. *Journal of Business Research, 57*(7), 768-775.

Gefen, D., Karahanna, E., & Straub, D. W. (2004). Trust and TAM in online shopping: An integrated model. *MIS Quarterly, 27*(1), 51-90.

Gilly, M. C., & Ziethaml, V. A. (1985). The elderly consumer and adoption of technologies. *Journal of Consumer Research, 12*(3), 353-357.

González, A. G. (2004). PayPal: the legal status of C2C payment systems. *Computer Law and Security Report, 20*(1), 293-299.

Hair, J. F., Tatham, R. L., Anderson, R. E., & Black, W. (1998). *Multivariate data analysis* (5th ed.). NJ: Prentice Hall.

Hill III, G. D. (2003). The trend toward non-real-time attacks. *Computer Fraud and Security, 11*(1), 5-11.

Hsu, C. L., & Lu, H. P. (2004). Why do people play online games? An extended TAM with social influences and flow experience. *Information & Management, 41*(3), 853-868.

Huang, S. M., Hung, Y. C., & Yen, D. C. (2004). A study on decision factors in adopting an online stock trading system by brokers in Taiwan. *Decision Support Systems, 40*(2), 315-328.

Hwang, J. J., Yeh, T. C., & Li, J. B. (2003). Securing online credit card payments without disclosing privacy information. *Computer Standards & Interfaces, 25*(2), 119-129.

Ilie, V., Slyke, C. V., Green, G., & Lou, H. (2005). Gender differences in perceptions and use of communication technologies: A diffusion of innovation approach. *Information Resources Management Journal, 18*(3), 13-31.

Internet World Stats. (2006). *Internet usage statistics for the Americas.* Retrieved from http://www.internetworldstats.com/stats2.htm

Kline, P. (1999). *The handbook of psychological testing* (2nd ed.). New York: Routledge.

Koufaris, M., Kanbil, A., & LaBarbera, A. P. (2002). Customer behavior in Web-based commerce: An empirical study. *International Journal of Electronic Commerce, 6*(1), 115-138.

Lee, S. M., & Cata, T. (2005). Critical success factors of Web-based e-service: The case of e-insurance. *International Journal of E-Business Research, 1*(3), 21-40.

Liang, T. P., & Lai, H. J. (2002). Effect of store design on consumer purchases: Van empirical study of online bookstores. *Information and Management, 39*(6), 431-444.

Luarn, P., & Lin, H. H. (2005). Toward an understanding of the behavioral intention to use mobile banking. *Computers in Human Behavior, 21*(6), 873-891.

Lucas, A. F., & Bowen, J. T. (2002). Measuring the effectiveness of casino promotions. *International Journal of Hospitality Management, 21*(2), 189-202.

Lui, H., & Jamieson, R. (2003). Integrating trust and risk perceptions in business-to-consumer electronic commerce with the technology acceptance model. *Proceedings of the 11th European Conference on Information Systems*, Naples, Italy.

Luo, X. (2002). Trust production and privacy concerns on the Internet: A framework based on relationship marketing and social exchange theory. *Industrial Marketing Management, 31*(2), 111-118.

McKnight, D. H., & Chervany, N. L. (2005). What builds system troubleshooter trust the best: Experimental or non-experimental factors? *Information Resources Management Journal, 18*(3), 32-49.

Odom, M. D., Kumar, A., & Saunders, L. (2002). Web assurance seals: How and why they influence consumers' decisions. *Journal of Information Systems, 16*(2), 231-250.

Pavlou, P. A. (2003). Consumer acceptance of electronic commerce: Integrating trust and risk with the Technology Acceptance Model. *International Journal of Electronic Commerce, 7*(3), 69-103.

Pommer, E., Pommer, M. D., Berkowitz, E. N., & Walton, J. R. (1980). UPC scanning: An assessment of shopper response to technological changes. *Journal of Retailing, 56*(2), 25-44.

Ranganathan, C., & Ganapathy, S. (2002). Key dimensions of business-to-consumer. *Web sites, Information, and Management, 39*(6), 457-465.

Slyke, C. V. (2002). Gender differences in perceptions of Web-based shopping. *Communications of the ACM, 45*(8), 82-86.

Sorkin, D. E. (2001). Payment methods for consumer-to-consumer online transactions. *Akron Law Review, 35*(1), 1-30.

Strauss, J., & Rogerson, K. S. (2002). Policies for online privacy in the United States and the European Union. *Telematics and Informatics, 19*(2), 173-192.

Suh, K., & Lee Y. (2005). The effects of virtual reality on consumer learning: An empirical investigation. *MIS Quarterly, 29*(4), 673-697.

Van Slyke, C., Lou, H., & Day, J. (2002). The impact of perceived innovation characteristics on intention to use groupware. *Information Resources Management Journal, 15*(1), 5-12.

Venkatesh, V., & Ramesh, V. (2006). Web and wireless site usability: Understanding differences and modeling use. *MIS Quarterly, 30*(1), 181-206.

Wang, H., Lee, M. K., & Wang, C. (1998). Consumer privacy concerns about Internet marketing. *Communications of the ACM, 41*(**3**), 63-70.

Wasko, M., & Faraj, S. (2005). Why should I share? Examining social capital and knowledge contribution in electronic networks of practice. *MIS Quarterly, 29*(1), 35-47.

Wilson, S. G., & Abel, I. (2002). So you want to get involved in e-commerce. *Industrial Marketing Management, 31*(2), 85-94.

Wright, J. (2003). Optimal card payment systems. *European Economic Review, 47*(3), 587-612.

Yu, H. C., His, K. H., & Kuo, P. J. (2002). Electronic payment systems: An analysis and comparison of types. *Technology in Society, 24*(3), 331-347.

APPENDIX I.

Summary of Online System Adoption Factors Addressed in Related Literature

Category	Dimension	Factors	Literature
Perceived characteristics of online payment methods	Perceived risk	Credit card fraud	Bhatnagar et al. (2000)
		Lack of protection by government policy and legal regulation	Biukovic (2002) González (2004) Strauss et al. (2002)
		Exposure to personal information	Luo (2002) Wang et al. (1998)
		Concern of system security	Hwang et al. (2003) Pavlou (2003)
	Perceived benefits	Perceived usefulness (PU)	Davis (1989)
		Perceived easiness of use (PEOU)	Davis (1989)
		Efficiency	Chou et al. (2004) Daft et al. (1986)
		Convenience	Yu et al. (2002)
		Financial benefits	Chen et al. (2003) Lucas et al. (2002) Wilson et al. (2002)
Vendor's system characteristics	Product or service features	Multiple functions of product or service	Debruyne et al. (2002)
	Web site features	Web site satisfaction	Lee et al. (2005) Liang et al. (2002) Ranganathan et al. (2002)
Customer's characteristics	Client-side technology	Reliability	Hill (2003)
		Effectiveness	
		Security	
	Demographic variables	Gender	Banerjee et al. (2005) Garbarino et al. (2004)
		Age	Gilly et al. (1985) Pommer et al. (1980)
		Education	Akhter (2003)
		Income	
	Internet experience	Computer knowledge	Slyke (2002)
		Online shopping	Eastin (2002)
		Online stock trading	
		Online auctions	
		Online vending	

APPENDIX II.

Questionnaire for Pay-Bills-Online Experience

Please rank the statements below from (1) Strongly Disagree to (5) Strongly Agree					
	Strongly Disagree	**Disagree**	**Indifferent**	**Agree**	**Strongly Agree**
Customers' Use Intention					
Q1: I would like to use an online payment system to pay my bills.	1	2	3	4	5
Perceived Risk					
Q2: The risk of credit card fraud for online transactions and Payments is low for me.	1	2	3	4	5
Q3: I would feel free to submit my personal information online to creditors (vendors) so that they can better serve my online-transaction needs.	1	2	3	4	5
Q4: Existing government policies are sufficient to keep online transactions and payments safe and secure.	1	2	3	4	5
Q5: Existing legal regulations for online transactions and payments can effectively protect my information privacy.	1	2	3	4	5
Q6: I have confidence in the security of the existing online transaction network.	1	2	3	4	5
Perceived Benefits					
Q7: Learning to use the online payment system is easy.	1	2	3	4	5
Q8: The online payment system enables me to pay my bills faster.	1	2	3	4	5
Q9: I would prefer to pay bills online if I can get a discount and/or bonus from creditors and vendors.	1	2	3	4	5
Q10: I would prefer to pay bills online if I have many credit accounts to pay off, because it can save postage costs.	1	2	3	4	5
Q11: I would prefer to pay bills online if I have many credit accounts to pay off, because it can help me better meet the payment deadline and avoid the late penalty.	1	2	3	4	5

APPENDIX II.

continued

Q12: I would prefer to pay bills online as I can easily find access to computers and the Internet.	1	2	3	4	5
Vendors' Service Features					
Q13: I would prefer to pay bills online if my payments can be scheduled for automatic deductions at regular intervals each month.	1	2	3	4	5
Q14: I would prefer to pay bills online if I have control over how much I want to pay and when I want to pay.	1	2	3	4	5
Vendors' Web site features					
Q15: It's easy to interact with the Web site of the online payment system.	1	2	3	4	5
Q16: The Web site design of the online payment system looks attractive to me.	1	2	3	4	5
Client-Side Technology					
Q17: Having famous-brand anti-virus and firewall software installed on my computer(s) would make me more willing to pay bills online.	1	2	3	4	5
Q18: A higher speed (transmission rate) for my Internet access would make me more willing to pay bills online.	1	2	3	4	5
Q19: The newest version of my operating system should be more secure for online payments and less vulnerable to online thefts.	1	2	3	4	5
Q20: Having non-Microsoft-Windows operating system installed on my computer(s) would make me more willing to pay bills online.	1	2	3	4	5
Q21: I would be more likely to pay bills online with DSL-type Internet service being available at my home or office than without.	1	2	3	4	5
Customers' Characteristics					
Q22: I would be more likely to pay bills online after my family income grows.	1	2	3	4	5

APPENDIX II.

continued

Q23: What is your gender?	**Female**			**Male**		
Q24: What is your age?	**<20**	**20-29**	**30-39**	**40-49**	**50-59**	**>60**
Q25: What is your education background?	High school or below	Associate	Bachelor's	Master's	Doctoral	
Customers' Internet Experience						
Q26: How many years of computer experience do you have?	**1 or less**	**2-4**	**5-7**	**8-10**	**>10**	
Q27: How many times per month do you do online shopping?	**Never**	**1-5 times**	**6-10 times**	**11-15 times**	**>15 times**	
Q28: How many times per month do you do online security trading?	**Never**	**1-5 times**	**6-10 times**	**11-15 times**	**>15 times**	
Q29: How many times per month do you participate in online auctions (bidding)?	**Never**	**1-5 times**	**6-10 times**	**11-15 times**	**>15 times**	
Q30: How many times per month do you do e-business (online vending)?	**Never**	**1-5 times**	**6-10 times**	**11-15 times**	**>15 times**	

APPENDIX III.

Frequency Distributions of Respondents' Intention to Pay Bills Online

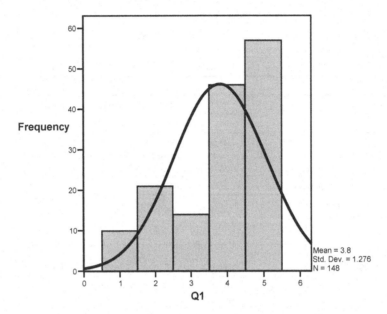

APPENDIX IV.

Frequency Distributions of Respondents' Perceived Risk to Pay Bills Online

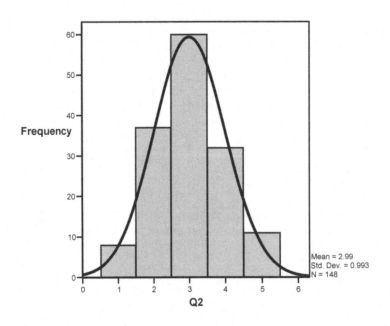

APPENDIX V.

Factor Analysis of Measurement Items: Loadings from Rotated Component Matrix

Scale	Items	Loadings
UI	I would like to use an online payment system to pay my bills.	.572
PR1	The risk of credit card fraud for online transactions and payments is low for me.	.641
PR2	I would feel free to submit my personal information online to creditors (vendors) so that they can better serve my needs for online transactions.	.531
PR3	Existing government policies are already sufficient to keep online transactions and payments safe and secure.	.819
PR4	Existing legal regulations for online transactions and payments can effectively protect my privacy of personal information.	.895
PR5	I have confidence in the security of the existing online transaction network.	.586
PB1	Learning to use the online payment system is easy.	.665
PB2	The online payment system enables me to pay my bills faster.	.733
PB3	I would prefer pay bills online if I can get a discount and/or bonus from creditors and vendors.	.719
PB4	I would prefer to pay bills online if I have many credit accounts to pay off, because it can save postage costs.	.742
PB5	I would prefer to pay bills online if I have many credit accounts to pay off, because it can help me better meet the payment deadline and avoid the late penalty.	.782
PB6	I would prefer to pay bills online if I can easily find access to computers and the Internet.	.556
VSF1	I would prefer to pay bills online if my payments can be scheduled for automatic deductions at regular intervals each month.	.555
VSF2	I would prefer to pay bills online if I have control over how much I want to pay and when I want to pay.	.665
VWF1	It's easy to interact with the Web site of the online payment system.	.773
VWF2	The Web site design attracts me to use the online payment system.	.753
CST1	Having famous-brand anti-virus and firewall software installed on my computer(s) would make me more willing to pay bills online.	.800
CST2	Having non-Microsoft-Windows operating system installed on my computer(s) would make me more willing to pay bills online.	.809
CST3	The newest version of my operating system should be more secure for online payments and less vulnerable to online thefts.	.935
CST4	A higher speed (transmission rate) for my Internet access would make me more willing to pay bills online.	.545
CST5	I would be more likely to pay bills online with DSL-type fast Internet service being available at my home or office than without.	.613
IP	I would be more likely to pay bills online after my family income grows.	.778

APPENDIX VI.

Factor Analysis of Measurement Items: Component Correlation Matrix by Items

Item	1	2	3	4	5	6	7	8	9	10	11	12	13	14	15	16	17	18	19	20	21	22
UI	1																					
PR1	.69	1																				
PR2	.66	.52	1																			
PR3	.81	-.2	.25	1																		
PR4	.71	.32	.36	.65	1																	
PR5	.55	-.1	.10	.12	.07	1																
PB1	.33	.70	.28	.12	.04	-.1	1															
PB2	.33	.74	.23	.12	.10	.24	.37	1														
PB3	.44	.72	.35	.11	.12	.08	.20	.16	1													
PB4	.51	.84	.43	.09	.12	.09	.29	.40	.46	1												
PB5	.47	.81	.34	.14	.19	.09	.23	.51	.45	.39	1											
PB6	.60	.42	.69	.12	.15	.08	.27	.40	.47	.34	.42	1										
VSF1	.39	-.3	.39	.59	.10	.20	-.0	.24	.19	.38	.30	.41	1									
VSF2	.45	-.3	.26	.68	.14	.17	.17	.12	.55	.49	.51	.48	.26	1								
VWF1	.48	-.2	.41	.10	.07	.76	.60	.37	.28	.29	.23	.41	.11	.26	1							
VWF2	.28	-.1	.16	.12	-.2	.69	.28	.18	.25	.22	.14	.41	.08	.17	.53	1						
CST1	-.1	.14	-.0	.05	-.1	.18	-.1	.03	-.1	.66	-.1	-.1	.22	-.1	-.1	-.1	1					
CST2	-.2	.15	-.1	.04	-.1	.12	-.0	-.1	-.2	.79	-.2	.05	.23	-.2	-.2	.19	.55	1				
CST3	.06	-.1	-.1	.01	.05	.04	.10	.12	.01	.06	.06	.18	.56	-.1	.14	.32	-.1	.11	1			
CST4	.15	.09	.02	.20	.04	.20	.23	.18	-.1	.18	.03	.21	.91	.19	.17	.28	.10	.23	.08	1		
CST5	.35	.05	.11	-.1	-.1	.13	.22	.39	.24	.68	.42	.37	.12	.26	.17	.28	-.1	.51	-.1	.29	1	
IP	.05	-.2	-.1	.01	.13	.29	-.1	-.1	.12	-.1	.33	-.1	-.1	.06	-.3	.37	.04	.11	.07	.01	.30	1

APPENDIX VII.

Factor Analysis of Measurement Items: Component Correlation Matrix by Scales

Scale	1	2	3	4	5	6	7
UI	1.000						
PR	.750 (.000)	1.000					
PB	.682 (.000)	.447 (.000)	1.000				
VSF	.596 (.000)	.371 (.003)	.543 (.000)	1.000			
VWF	.510 (.000)	.141 (.087)	.476 (.000)	.203 (.013)	1.000		
CST	-.111 (.177)	.253 (.062)	.249 (.002)	.191 (.019)	.189 (.021)	1.000	
IP	.101 (.545)	.020 (.812)	-.108 (.189)	-.035 (.671)	.194 (.018)	.151 (.066)	1.000

Note: In parentheses are p-values (two-tailed).

This work was previously published in International Journal of E-Business Research, Vol. 3, Issue 4, edited by I. Lee, pp. 1-32, copyright 2007 by IGI Publishing, formerly known as Idea Group Publishing (an imprint of IGI Global).

Chapter XXV
On the Need to Include National Culture as a Central Issue in E–Commerce Trust Beliefs

David Gefen
Drexel University, USA

Tsipi Heart
Ben-Gurion University of the Negev, Israel

ABSTRACT

Trust and trust beliefs (trustworthiness) are key to e-commerce success but depend, to a large extent, on culture. With e-commerce being an international phenomenon, understanding the cross-cultural aspects of trust creation is therefore arguably required although mostly ignored by current research which deals almost exclusively with the U.S. This exploratory study examines whether definitions of trust beliefs as conceptualized and verified in the U.S. apply in Israel which differs markedly in individualism, uncertainty avoidance, and power distance. The data, cross-validating the scale of trust and its antecedents in both cultures, generally support the proposition that trust beliefs apply across cultures, and may be a relatively unvarying aspect of e-commerce. However, as expected, the effects of predictability and familiarity on trust beliefs may differ across national cultures. Implications about the need to include national culture in the research on trust, in general, and in e-commerce in particular, are discussed.

INTRODUCTION

Despite the differences national culture can cause in e-commerce behavior (Kacen & Lee, 2002; Lynch & Beck, 2001) and despite e-commerce becoming global, research on trust and trust beliefs in e-commerce has mostly ignored the possible effects of national culture.[1] With few exceptions (e.g., Jarvenpaa & Tractinsky, 1999), trust in e-commerce research has been conducted almost exclusively in the U.S. Yet the U.S is in some regards a unique national culture because of its patently high degree of individualism and relatively low degree of uncertainty avoidance (Hofstede, 1984), degrees so different from other national cultures that concerns have been raised in other realms of research as to whether research based on the U.S. can be generalized to other countries (Bagozzi, Wong, Abe, & Bergami, 2000; Hofstede, 1980b).

The underlying proposition of this study is that if national culture and trust are closely related, as proposed in theory (Doney, Cannon, & Mullen, 1998; Fukuyama, 1995; Hofstede, 1984) but not yet verified, then research on trust should include national culture as a prime aspect. This proposition is examined in the context of e-commerce because trust and trust beliefs are major players in e-commerce adoption (Gefen, 2000; Gefen, Karahanna, & Straub, 2003a; 2003b; Kim, Xu & Koh, 2004; McKnight & Chervany, 2002; Pavlou, 2003; Pavlou & Gefen, 2004). Trust in the context of e-commerce has generally been treated as even more significant than in other settings because of the lack of personal contact and the lack of social cues in e-commerce (Gefen et al., 2003a).

Accordingly, the objectives of this study are twofold. First, to verify that the psychometric properties and nomological validity of trust beliefs as created in research about the U.S. applies elsewhere. And second, to verify that the way trust is created and the way it affects e-commerce does vary by culture.[2]

The research model is presented in Figure 1. Trust building processes, namely familiarity and predictability, are hypothesized to affect the three trust beliefs, which in turn, are hypothesized to affect behavioral intentions. The trust beliefs are proposed to apply to both cultures, although the trust building processes are hypothesized to differ in their effect. The outcomes of these consumer trust beliefs are (1) a willingness to buy online from the vendor (Jarvenpaa & Tractinsky, 1999; Reichheld & Schefter, 2000) and (2) a willingness to window-shop at the online vendor (Gefen, 2000; Gefen, 2002b). These trust beliefs are composed of three distinct beliefs dealing with integrity, ability, and benevolence (Gefen, 2002b; McKnight et al., 2002). The effect of national culture on trust beliefs is based on Hofstede (1984) and Doney et al. (1998) and examined by comparing the same model with data collected in the U.S. and Israel.

Figure 1. Research model

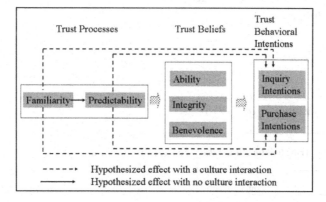

THEORETICAL BACKGROUND CONFLICTING CULTURAL PROCESSES OF TRUST

Trust is the willingness to depend upon another party and be vulnerable to the actions of this other party based on the assumption that the trusted party will deliver without taking advantage of the situation (Mayer, Davis, & Schoorman, 1995). This conceptualization of trust, which is also known as "trusting intentions" (McKnight et al., 2002) and trustworthiness (Jarvenpaa & Tractinsky, 1999), is based on a set of beliefs that others upon whom one depends will behave in a socially acceptable manner by showing appropriate integrity, benevolence, and ability (Doney & Cannon, 1997; Gefen et al., 2003b; Mayer et al., 1995; McKnight et al., 2002). These three beliefs are labeled by most research as "trust beliefs" (Gefen, 2002b; McKnight et al., 2002), although Mayer et al. (1995) label these "trustworthiness." Trust, defined by some research as behavioral intentions, by others as beliefs, and by yet others as a mixture of both, is crucial in many business interactions (Fukuyama, 1995; Ganesan, 1994; Kumar, 1996; Williamson, 1985; Zucker, 1986), including e-commerce (Gefen et al., 2003b; Jarvenpaa, Tractinsky, & Vitale, 2000; McKnight et al., 2002; Pavlou, 2003; Pavlou & Gefen, 2004; Reichheld & Schefter, 2000), e-government (Gefen, Rose, Warkentin & Pavlou, 2004; Warkentin, Gefen, Pavlou, & Rose, 2002), and IT adoption in general (Gefen, 2002a).

Trust is created in many ways. Doney et al. (1998) theorized a model in which trust is built through five processes: calculative, prediction, intentionality, capability, and transference. In the calculative process a party calculates the costs or rewards of another party cheating. The prediction process enables one party to forecast behaviors of another party based on past conduct. The intentionality process deals with the trustor's perceptions about the intentions of the trustee. Trust building through the capability process is based on an assessment of the trustee's capability to meet expected obligations. Transference deals with a trustor transferring trust from a known trusted entity to an unknown one. The intensity and effect of these processes on trust behavior, they hypothesized, depends among other things on culture. Doney et al. proposed 15 propositions, summarized in Table 1, based on Hofstede's (1984) cultural dimensions (see next section for details), namely individualism-collectivism (IDV), power distance (PDI), uncertainty avoidance (UAI), and masculinity-femininity (MAS). The 15 propositions are shown in Table 1, where the plus sign designates the "more likely to use" and the minus sign indicates the opposite. For instance, according to Doney et al.'s propositions, trustors from more individualistic (masculine) cultures are more likely than trustors from more collectivist (feminine) cultures to form trust via a calculative process, but are less likely to form trust via the prediction process.

Table 1. Summary of Doney et al. (1998)

			High
Trust building processes	**IDV (MAS)**	**PDI**	**UAI**
Calculative	+	+	+
Prediction	-	+	+
Intentionality	-	-	+
Capability	+	+	+
Transference	-	-	+

The strength of Doney et al.'s (1998) model is in its incorporation of a vast range of cultural effects on trust-building processes. But incorporating so many propositions also leads to contradictory predictions. What would be the rule for cultures where IDV and MAS do not overlap, such as the U.S. and Japan where the former is the highest on IDV but below average on MAS and the latter is just the opposite, extreme on MAS but below average on IDV? And, what should dominate when a country possesses cultural attributes that conflict in Doney et al.'s model? For example, the U.S. is extreme on IDV but low on UAI. Should the calculative process be affected by individualism, making it stronger, or by the low UAI, making it weaker?

Similar concerns were articulated by Noorderhaven (1999), who also mentioned that some of Doney et al.'s basic assessments were not supported by previous research. For example, while Doney et al. (1998) base their propositions on the assumption that collectivist groups tend to trust one another more than individualistic societies, Yamagishi and Yamagishi (1994) show the opposite. In fact, Hofstede himself states that in the more individualistic societies, people will tend to develop higher initial trust. In other words, in these cultures people will expect others to adhere to the accepted basic rules of conduct ("value standards should apply to all"), based on the assumption that people will want to do so because such conduct is beneficial to the majority (Hofstede, 1984, p. 235).

Conflicting Definitions of Trust

In addition, there is a conceptual lack of clarity in the definitions of trust (Gefen et al., 2003b; McKnight et al., 2002). Most previous research has bundled the three trust beliefs of integrity, benevolence, and ability together with the assessment of trustworthiness, arguing and empirically validating that the constructs are so closely related to each other in many scenarios that they are conceptually and statistically so intertwined as to be inseparable in many cases (Doney & Cannon, 1997; Gefen, 2002a; Pavlou & Gefen, 2004). See Gefen et al. (2003b) and McKnight et al. (2002) for detailed discussions. In the interest of avoiding conflicting terminology, this article adopts Mayer et al.'s (1995), McKnight et al.'s (2002), and Gefen's (2002b) terminology in which the three distinct trust beliefs deal with integrity, benevolence, and ability, which in turn affect behavioral trusting intentions when vulnerability to the trusted party is at stake. It should be emphasized that all these studies on the meaning of trust were conducted in the U.S. The applicability of this three dimensional construct formulation of trust beliefs as composed of integrity, ability, and benevolence, to other cultures remains an open question.

Trust Beliefs and Overall Trust in E-Commerce

Trust is crucial in many social and commerce activities because it reduces social uncertainty (Gefen, 2000). Social uncertainty is the result of other people being free agents whose behavior cannot be controlled and whose behavior may not necessarily be rational. People try to reduce social uncertainty through many social mechanisms, such as laws and institutions, but even then the behavior of other people is fraught with uncertainty. This is where trust comes in. Trust allows people, rightly or not, to subjectively rule out the possibility of undesirable behavior by those they need to rely upon (Luhmann, 1979). Developing this understanding of trust in the Familiarity and Trust model (Gefen, 2000), it has been shown that familiarity with a trustworthy vendor increases people's trust in this vendor, although the effect of familiarity on trust beliefs may be mediated by the nature of the process involved (Gefen et al., 2003b). It should be emphasized, however, that toleration of others as free agents, and hence a more pronounced need for trust in interpersonal activities (Doney et al., 1998), is greater in the

U.S. because of its highly individualistic culture (Hofstede, 1984). Whether the need to trust is as strong also in less individualistic cultures is another open question.

Drawing upon existing models of trust beliefs in e-commerce (Gefen & Straub, 2004; McKnight et al., 2002) and elsewhere online (Jarvenpaa, Knoll, & Leidner, 1998), the research model in Figure 1 assumes, as discussed in detail by previous research (Gefen, 2002b; Gefen & Straub, 2004; McKnight et al., 2002), that the three trust beliefs combined with familiarity will affect consumers' trusting behavioral intentions. Also included in the research model is the prediction process that is hypothesized to increase these trust beliefs, mainly by mediating the effect of familiarity, that is, by increasing the understanding of what to expect (Gefen et al., 2003b). Familiarity with a vendor and predictability also contribute independently to behavioral trusting intentions (Gefen, 2000).

Since culture is hypothesized to affect trust building processes, the study assumes that these processes will differ across cultures. The logic of how they will differ is based mainly on Doney et al. (1998).

Culture and Trust

Trust and culture are interconnected. On the one hand, the meaning, antecedents, and effects of trust are determined by culture (Doney et al., 1998; Fukuyama, 1995; Zucker, 1986). On the other hand, trust is also a central aspect of culture itself, being closely correlated with cultural differences across nations (Hofstede, et al., 1990). Of specific interest is that, in theory, the modes of trust creation depend on national culture (Doney et al., 1998).

This study concentrates on the predictive mode of trust creation (Doney et al., 1998), extrapolating from the originally proposed *interpersonal* relationships of Doney et al. to e-commerce. The calculative process suggested by Doney et

al. (1998) is not included in this study since in the context of shopping at Amazon.com it would be counterproductive for Amazon.com to cheat and risk its reputation, one of its most important assets. Likewise, transference processes are also excluded. Transference typically involves trusting an unknown entity based on its relation to a well known entity. But with Amazon.com being one of the most known online brand names, transference to Amazon seems unlikely.

The hypothesized differences in the trust model in Figure 1 are based mainly on extrapolating relevant propositions of interpersonal trust across cultures as advanced by Doney et al. (1998), based on Hofstede (1984), on McKnight, Cummings, and Chervany (1998), and Gefen (2002b). In the interest of completeness, propositions not readily applicable to e-commerce, and hence not part of the hypotheses, are discussed in endnotes.

Choice of Cultures

The hypothesized effects of national culture on trust beliefs in e-commerce are examined by comparing the same model with data collected in the U.S. and Israel. The choice of these two cultures is especially appropriate considering the research objectives because the two cultures differ in all four cultural dimensions and represent extremes. The U.S. is the most highly ranked on Hofstede's (1984) individualism-collectivism dimension of national culture and midrange on the Power Distance Index (PDI). In contrast, Israel is ranked about midway on IDV and very low in PDI. As such, this comparison contrasts two well-defined national cultures that represent extremes in what are thought to be the major national culture dimensions contributing to trust beliefs (Shaffer & O'Hara, 1995; Shane, 1992) and the processes that create it (Doney et al., 1998; Hofstede, 1984).

Moreover, in both the U.S. and Israel there is a very strong sense of identification with the state combined with a high degree of national pride, which adheres to the recommendations of Straub, Loch, Evaristo, Karahanna, and Srite (2002) about the need to define culture in terms of identification. The choice of the U.S. and Israel is also intended to replicate previous cross cultural research in e-commerce, namely Jarvenpaa and Tractinsky (1999), who focused on Australia and Israel, examining primarily online book purchasing by undergraduate students. Australia has almost identical Hofstede (1984) cultural indexes as the U.S. Jarvenpaa and Tractinsky (1999) found mostly insignificant differences between Australia and Israel with regard to both the measurement and the structural models. However, Jarvenpaa and Tractinsky (1999) examined these beliefs clustered into one construct, which they named trust.[3] This study, in contrast, examines these beliefs as three distinct constructs. Jarvenpaa and Tractinsky concluded that despite their results of insignificant differences, there probably are cross-cultural differences and that more in-depth research is needed to discover them. Examining the U.S. and Israel allows such a reexamination.

Showing that these scales also apply to an equivalent Israeli sample would support, albeit on an exploratory basis, the first objective of this article, that the scales apply also outside the U.S. Showing cultural effects would support, again on an exploratory basis, the second objective because if such cultural differences are shown then there is reason to doubt the automatic generalization of trust studies based on U.S. samples to the rest of the world and vice versa, as suggested by observers (Fukuyama, 1995). It should be noted that as an exploratory study, the latter objective is not to generalize the results but to show their plausibility.

Cultural Differences and Trust

National culture is a set of beliefs and behaviors common to a group of people, or "the collective programming of the mind which distinguishes the members of one human group from another"

(Hofstede, 1984, p. 25). Research has shown that national culture is a major determinant of consumption behavior (see Clark, 1990, for a detailed review). National culture also affects IT management (Tan, Smith, Keil, & Montealegre, 2003), specifically, Hofstede's dimensions affect IT management, development, and use (Ford, Connelly, & Meister, 2003).

Hofstede identified four national culture dimensions: individualism-collectivism, power distance, uncertainty avoidance, and masculinity. Individualism-collectivism deals with whether society is centered on the collective, it being the family and the clan, or on the individual. This dimension deals with the way society prefers to deal with complexity and its related value system of willingness to rely on strangers. When national culture is centered on the collective, it is said to exhibit low individualism or collectivism (Hofstede, 1984). In these cases people generally tend not to rely on strangers or trust them (Fukuyama, 1995). When it is centered on the individual, it exhibits high individualism. In these cases people generally are more willing to rely on strangers and trust them (Fukuyama, 1995). The U.S. has the highest individuality index on this continuum with an index of 91. Americans demonstrate individualistic characteristics such as valuing personal freedom over equality, preferring challenging jobs from which one can achieve a sense of accomplishment, allowing low-context communication, and giving preference to individual interests over collective ones (Hofstede, 1994). Israel, on the other hand, scores about half way on individualism (54 in a 6 to 91 scale), located somewhere between collectivist and individualist societies (Hofstede, 1984).[4]

The picture with PDI in the two nations is the exact opposite. PDI encompasses the attitude toward inequality in society. A higher PDI indicates acceptance of inequality as inherent in society. High PDI shows the tendency of subordinates to depend on "bosses," to respect the more powerful, to accept norms of wide gaps in income, to show preference for a paternalistic and autocratic superior, and to regard benevolence as the primary characteristic of the ideal boss (Hofstede, 1984). The U.S. scores about midrange on Power Distance (40 in a 11 to 104 scale). Israel scores nearly the lowest on PDI (with a score of 13).[5] The low PDI indicates that Israelis generally think that inequality in society should be minimized, that hierarchy in organizations means an inequality of roles, and that hierarchy is established for convenience. They also think of the ideal boss as a resourceful democrat. Generally, Israelis prefer superiors to behave in a consultative and participative manner, where ability and performance are the prominent characteristic of the ideal boss (Hofstede, 1984).

Empirical research on national culture and trust (Shaffer & O'Hara, 1995; Shane, 1992) has shown that customers from high PDI countries hold higher expectations that a service provider will engage in unethical behavior, as compared with customers from low PDI countries. In other words, customers from high PDI countries will express less trust towards a service provider than will customers from low PDI countries (Shaffer & O'Hara, 1995). Furthermore, foreign international investments are negatively correlated with PDI (Shane, 1992).

The third dimension of national culture Hofstede (1984) discusses is UAI, defined as tolerance for uncertainty. The U.S. is low on UAI (46 in an 8 to 112 scale). The combination of individualism and low UAI implies a readiness to adopt innovations when it is believed they will contribute to an individual's performance. Israel scored nearly twice as high as the U.S. in UAI (81), implying that Israelis in general are more intolerant to uncertain situations than Americans. Indeed, e-commerce adoption in Israel was slower than in the U.S., and Israelis in general are less enthusiastic about buying online than Americans (ClickZ, 2004). In Israel e-commerce became significant only in 1999. E-commerce volume in Israel grew from $20 million in 1999 to $60 million in 2000, with

8% of the online population conducting financial transactions in 2002, up from 6% in 2001 (Ebusinessforum, 2002).

The fourth of Hofstede's dimensions is masculinity: the degree to which masculine behaviors, such as competitiveness and assertiveness, are considered desirable and acceptable. Both countries score medium in this index, with the U.S. slightly more masculine at 62 and Israel at 47. Masculinity is not hypothesized to be a reason why trust building processes should differ between these two countries because the two national indexes differ only slightly in this regard.

Modes of Trust Creation and National Culture

Previous research (Gefen, 2002b; Gefen & Straub, 2004; Mayer et al., 1995; McKnight et al., 2002; McKnight et al., 1998) suggested that trust is built through three main beliefs: ability, integrity, and benevolence. In addition, familiarity and predictability have been advocated to influence trust behaviors (Zucker, 1986). Yet, unlike Doney et al.'s interpersonal relationships model, in the context of a well-known online vendor, familiarity and predictability are hypothesized to affect not only trust behaviors, but also the trust beliefs. Familiarity is hypothesized to have a primary effect on predictability, since being familiar with a trustee enhances the ability of the trustor to predict the trustee's behavior (Gefen, 2000).

The hypothesized effect of cultural differences on the way predictability as a trust building process builds trust beliefs and the effect these have on the trust-related behavior of Americans and Israelis is described next.

The predictive mode of trust creation deals with understanding based on experience of what to expect. This is a knowledge-based assessment (Shapiro, Sheppard, & Cheraskin, 1992) and is at the heart of the familiarity concept advanced by Gefen (2000) based on Luhmann (1979) in which familiarity increased trust by letting the trusting party gain a better picture of what to expect. As demonstrated by previous research (Gefen, 2000; Gefen et al., 2003a) familiarity also directly affects behavioral trusting intentions. Although generally individuals prefer to transact with familiar people and organizations rather than to transact with unfamiliar ones, this effect should be more pronounced for Israelis since this tendency is stronger in collectivist societies. The reason for this is that people in collectivist countries make a strong distinction between "us" that is those who make up the perceived ingroup, and "them," that is all the others (Hofstede, 1994). This effect can be quite pronounced with people in highly collectivist cultures shunning interactions with strangers and inherently distrusting them (Fukuyama, 1995). This ingroup vs. outgroup distinction does not necessarily refer only to the group of close family or friends, but can also mean "those who are perceived similar" as opposed to "strangers" (Hofstede, 1994). Even in the highly individualistic U.S. this effect can be quite strong and can be triggered even by belonging to a different organizational department (Gefen & Ridings, 2003; Hogg & Terry, 2000). Typically, individuals and organizations belonging to the ingroup are more trusted, while those belonging to the outgroups are automatically treated with a higher dose of suspicion (Berscheid, 1966; Brown, 1996; Tajfel, 1970, 1978). This avoidance of the outgroup can be so strong in collectivist cultures that it is not an accepted practice to do business with strangers before getting to know them (Hofstede, 1984). Moreover, when group boundaries are salient, as they typically are in collectivist cultures, ingroup members are generally regarded with much higher esteem (Hogg, 1996; Hogg & Terry, 2000; Tajfel, 1970; Turner, 1982). This higher esteem should additionally contribute to making familiarity a stronger predictor of behavioral trusting intentions in collectivist cultures, such as Israel. On the other hand, in high individualism cultures people are generally more inclined to adopt a worldview that everyone should be treated without preference

(Shaffer & O'Hara, 1995), reducing the inherent advantage of familiarity in collectivist cultures. It is thus hypothesized that familiarity will influence behavioral trusting intention more in Israel than in the U.S. Accordingly, this should apply to both types of trusting behavioral intentions

H_{1a}: Familiarity will contribute more to behavioral trusting intention to inquire online in Israel than it will in the U.S.

H_{1b}: Familiarity will contribute more to behavioral trusting intention to purchase online in Israel than it will in the U.S.

Familiarity builds trust because people think they know what to expect, that is because it creates predictability (Gefen, 2000; Luhmann, 1979). But reliance on predictability as a trust creation mode should differ across cultures (Doney et al., 1998).[6] Doney et al. (1998) proposed that low PDI cultures rely less on the predictability process because in these cultures, people expect and accept more personal freedom. Hence, according to Doney et al., adherence to accepted social norms should be a stronger predictor of trust in high PDI cultures than in low PDI cultures. In other words, because Israel is very low on the PDI scale (13 out of 100) and the U.S. is slightly below midrange (40), predictability should be of more consequence in the U.S. in determining the three trusting beliefs.

IDV should also contribute more to trust beliefs formation through predictability in the U.S. Generally, people in high IDV cultures are more willing to trust others outside the extended family in part because of the more prevalent institutional trust mechanisms that society puts in place to regulate activity (Fukuyama, 1995). Accordingly, because it is inherent in the consumer culture in the U.S., people should tend to be more aware of and to more frequently rely on institutional trust mechanisms such as the Better Business Bureau. This increased awareness of the availability of institutional trust mechanisms should result in an increased trust (Gefen, 2004; McKnight et al., 1998; Pavlou & Gefen, 2004; Zucker, 1986). Specifically, predictability should contribute to beliefs in ability because these institutions certify to the quality of the service the vendor provides. Institutional trust mechanisms also vouch for the vendor's adherence to acceptable rules of business, combined with appropriate quality service, that is honesty and caring. Here too, since the reliance on such services is greater in the U.S., so too should their influence. Hence the prediction process is hypothesized to have a stronger effect in the U.S. on all three trust beliefs.

H$_{2a}$: The prediction process will contribute more to trust beliefs in ability in the U.S. than it will in Israel.

H$_{2b}$: The prediction process will contribute more to trust beliefs in integrity in the U.S. than it will in Israel.

H$_{2c}$: The prediction process will contribute more to trust beliefs in benevolence in the U.S. than it will in Israel.

Predictability should also contribute directly to behavioral intentions because predictability reduces the uncertainty in economic activity. This effect should be stronger in the U.S. because in higher IDV cultures people tend to rely more on external regulatory powers and on the government (Fukuyama, 1995). Hence, the predictability created by such external regulatory agencies, such as the IFCC and its Israeli equivalent and the legal system, should have a greater effect in high IDV cultures.

H$_{3a}$: The prediction process will contribute more to behavioral trusting intentions to inquire online in the U.S. than it will in Israel.

H$_{3b}$: The prediction process will contribute more to behavioral trusting intention to purchase online in the U.S. than it will in Israel.

Another way in which trust is created, according to Doney et al. (1998), is capability (referred to henceforth as ability). This mode is akin to what other research typically identify as ability, which is one of the dimensions of trust beliefs (e.g., Gefen & Straub, 2004; Jarvenpaa et al., 1998; Mayer et al., 1995; McKnight et al., 2002, 1998). Ability leads to behavioral trusting intentions because it deals with the ability of the trusted party to meet its obligations (Mayer et al., 1995) and in doing so provides the trusting party with its expected outcome (Gefen, 2002a; Schurr & Ozanne, 1985). Doney et al. proposed that in high UAI cultures, ability should be more critical in building trust because evidence of ability reduces risk (Kale & McIntyre, 1991) and high UAI cultures put more emphasis on avoiding the risks involved with uncertainty.[7] Accordingly, in Israel, as a high UAI country, performance should contribute more to online activity.

H$_{4a}$: Ability will contribute more to behavioral trusting intention to inquire online in Israel than it will in the U.S.

H$_{4b}$: Ability will contribute more to behavioral trusting intention to purchase online in Israel than it will in the U.S.

Perceived size and reputation, originally the antecedents of perceived store trustworthiness in Jarvenpaa and Tractinsky's (1999) study, were not included in this study because only one store, Amazon.com, was examined. The model also includes paths from integrity and benevolence to inquiry intentions and to purchase intentions. These paths are well established and have been extensively discussed in the literature (e.g., Gefen, 2002b, McKnight et al., 2002). These paths are included in the model without explicit hypotheses because integrity and benevolence are expected to affect behavioral intentions regardless of culture.

DATA COLLECTION

Level of Data Analysis

A major consideration in conducting this study was the level of data analysis. The unit of analysis in this study is the national level, as suggested by Ford et al. (2003). This is appropriate because perceptions and behaviors of individuals in a society are affected by cultural dimensions, thus it can be assumed that differences between the two groups of respondents can be attributed to cultural differences (Hofstede, 1984). The variables are tied explicitly to expected outcomes, in this case specific cases of the "Web use" dependent variable as suggested by Saeed, Hwang, and Yi (2003) and corresponding to the applied measures of e-commerce use (e.g., Gefen, 2002b; Pavlou, 2003). This level of data analysis is in accordance with other cross cultural studies (Gefen & Straub, 1997; Hofstede, 1984; Rose & Straub, 1998; Straub, Keil & Brennan, 1997; Warkentin et al., 2002) where national culture is viewed as a collective homogeneity. This choice also allowed for a comparison of the trust belief scales as they were originally developed by Gefen (2000). Moreover, this level of analysis is appropriate here because the study examines the more general theoretical aspects of trust and the implications of the findings to e-commerce vendors when trading in different countries, rather than personalization issues. This choice of level of analysis is also in apparent agreement with Hofstede (1994) who comments that individuals are strongly influenced by national culture, and even young adults are already "imprinted" by the surrounding culture (p. 5).

An alternative level of analysis could have been the individual level as suggested by McCoy, Galletta, and King (2005). McCoy et al. question the cultural homogeneity assumption of previous research based on the apparent changes in the Hofstede scale values between recent studies (McCoy et al., 2005) and the original values. The need to examine cultural differences also on an individual level is raised by Straub et al. (2002) as well. Straub et al. discuss the need to define culture in more than one way because people are influenced by a variety of social circles as proposed by social identification theory (Deaux, 1996; Hogg, 1996; Hogg & Terry, 2000; Tajfel, 1970, 1978). Nonetheless, McCoy et al. (2005) agree there is a need to study cross cultural differences among countries, and social identification theory recognizes national culture as one of the prime sources of an individual's identification (Hogg, 1996).

Details of Data Collection

Recent research on trust belief scales in the specific context of e-commerce has developed statistically distinct scales of these three beliefs. In two unrelated studies by McKnight et al. (2002) and by Gefen (2002b) dealing with Web legal services and with buying books online, respectively, two sets of comparable three dimensional scales of these trust beliefs were developed. Gefen's scale was further validated with minor changes also with regard to online flight booking (Gefen & Straub, 2004). Since this study examines online book buying activity as the context in which trust is compared across cultures, Gefen's (2002b) scales, being developed originally for this specific activity and being cross-validated, were chosen. Gefen's original data from the U.S. were compared with an equivalent Israeli sample. Although there is a time interval between the two samples, it should be noted that Amazon's book selling interface and service process have not changed markedly over this period of time and also that national culture in general is relatively stable and does not change over such intervals. It should also be noted that although Gefen's data (2002b) analyzed here is two years older, these scales were revalidated in other settings (Gefen & Straub, 2004) and shown to have the same pattern of significant paths.

In this study we examine the role of culture on trust beliefs based on comparing the data collected by Gefen (2002b) in the U.S. among mid-Atlantic students with a recent equivalent Israeli sample. The Israeli sample was collected in 2003 with the same data collection procedure and using the same previously validated instrument translated into Hebrew. The original survey was translated into Hebrew and then back again into English, to verify its accuracy. Although both datasets are convenience samples, other research (Gefen & Straub, 2004) has shown the comparable results of these scales and equivalent ones (Serva, Fuller, & Benamati, 2005) with other convenience samples to other scenarios of e-commerce in the U.S.

Replicating Gefen (2002b), the instrument was distributed to undergraduate management students in an Israeli university. (Israeli undergraduate students are on average three to four years older than their American counterparts since they start their studying after a military service of about three years.) Students were approached in an Internet-connected classroom, where each student had a PC. All the PCs had identical configuration, including operating system, Internet browser, installed software and bandwidth, features that could not be changed by users. The students were asked to navigate to Amazon.com, inquire about a course textbook, and go through the procedure of purchasing it but without actually submitting the transaction. Online book purchasing is popular also in Israel. After about 10 minutes of this procedure, the students were asked to complete the experimental instrument. In this questionnaire the students were asked to assess the items in Appendix 1 on a 7-point scale ranging from 1 (strongly agree) to 7 (strongly disagree), with 4 as the midpoint.

The purpose of the study was not revealed to the participants until after the data had been collected. As with the original U.S. data collection procedure, the objective was to elicit responses in natural settings, as is the case with free experiments in general (Fromkin & Streufert, 1976). The objective of this procedure was to refresh the participants' memory. The objective was not to manipulate the participants or create trust. Participation was voluntary. 162 complete instruments from 167 Israeli students were collected and then compared with the 217 original U.S. instruments. In this way, and by sampling university students from the same discipline (management) in both countries, occupation and education were held constant, complying with Hofstede's (1994, p. 29) recommendations.

Among the Israeli respondents, 47% (n = 69) were women, and 53% (n = 78) men, which is about the same percentage as with the American respondents where 52% were women (n = 65) and 48% were men (n = 60); 13 of the original American students did not declare their gender. 52% (n = 76) of the Israeli respondents were in the 21-25 age group and 48% (n = 66) in the 26-30 age group, corresponding to an equivalent percentage among the American students, where 51% were in the 21-25 age group and 43% in the 26-30 age group. The two samples did not differ significantly on age (F = 2.148, p-value = .14), gender (F = 0.398, p-value = 0.53), or whether they had or had not previously bought online (F = 3.145, p-value = 0.08).

DATA ANALYSIS

The data were analyzed with PLS Graph 3.00 Build 1126. First, the convergent and discriminant validity was verified by showing that (1) the square root of the AVE of each construct is much larger than its correlations with other constructs, shown in Appendixes 3 and 4, and (2) that loadings of each measurement item on its assigned factor in a confirmatory factor analysis (CFA) is much higher than on any other factor, shown in Appendixes 5 and 6. The reliability of the constructs is also high, shown in Appendixes 3 and 4. It should be noted that PLS CFA inflate the loadings and that there are no established guidelines about what acceptable CFA loading coefficients should be in PLS. Indeed, comparing PLS and principal components factor analysis (PCA) on the same data show that PLS loadings in the 0.50 and above level correspond to loadings at the 0.30 level in a PCA (Gefen, Straub, & Boudreau, 2000). All item loadings are significant and all the reliability coefficients are above the .80 threshold. The nomological validity of the constructs was established by verifying that in both samples the constructs that should be significantly correlated with each other are significantly correlated. All the trust belief constructs are significantly correlated with trusting behavioral intentions and with familiarity and predictability. Familiarity and predictability are also significantly correlated with trusting behavioral intentions.

Figure 2 shows the results of the two analyses. The percents above the boxes are R^2 values. U.S. values are shown on the left, Israeli ones on the right. Numbers above the arrows are the betas. An asterisk means the beta is significant at the 0.05 level. Two asterisks means significant at the 0.01 level, n.s. means insignificant. The T-values of the path coefficients were estimated with PLS bootstrap.[8]

The U.S. sample shows the same pattern of significant paths as it did with the original analysis

(Gefen, 2002b), albeit the model in this study has predictability added to it. Ability affects inquiry intentions. Integrity affects purchase intentions. Additionally, familiarity affects both inquiry and purchase intentions. As proposed, but not examined by earlier research (Gefen, 2000), familiarity affects all three trust beliefs through its effect on predictability. Predictability also affected inquiry and purchase intentions. In the Israeli sample ability affects both inquiry and purchase intentions, while integrity affects only purchase intentions. Familiarity affects both inquiry and purchase intentions and through its effect on predictability affected ability and integrity but not benevolence. Predictability, however, did not affect inquiry and purchase intentions.

Comparing the two samples, Appendix 2 shows that the differences in trust beliefs were mostly insignificant even though the U.S. sample were more familiar with Amazon.com, which would be expected given that Israelis buy more books in Hebrew than in English, and was therefore more predictable to the U.S. sample who also used it more to both inquire and purchase books. The differences between the samples in their beliefs in integrity and benevolence were insignificant

Figure 2. Research model with path coefficients

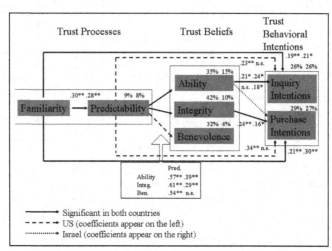

and those in ability were only significant at the 0.05 level, meaning that it was probably not the degree of integrity, benevolence, or ability that caused the differences between the countries in their purchase and inquiry intentions. The hypotheses were examined by comparing the path coefficients based on Wynne Chin as described by Keil et al. (2000). The hypotheses were all confirmed. Table 1 shows these results.

The data analysis also shows significant differences in the paths from integrity to purchase intentions. This may be the result of the U.S. being a highly individualistic culture. In general, highly individualistic cultures have a greater need to install standards and norms in order to prevent

opportunistic behavior, and, accordingly, people in these cultures rely more heavily on adherence to these norms (Hofstede, 1994). Hence, because adherence to behavioral norms is one of the expressions of integrity (Sitkin & Roth, 1993), integrity might have had stronger effects in the American sample as to purchasing intentions.

CONCLUSIONS

Summary of Results

The objectives of this study were twofold: First, to establish the psychometric properties of three

Table 1. Comparison of the path coefficients in both samples

	U.S.		Israel		T value comparing the two countries
	Path Coefficient	Path Standard Error	Path Coefficient	Path Standard Error	
Familiarity will have a stronger effect on trusting behavioral intentions in Israel					
H_{1a}: Familiarity to Inquire	0.1900	0.0746	0.2100	0.0845	2.422*
H_{1b}: Familiarity to Purchase	0.2120	0.0671	0.2970	0.0815	11.041**
The prediction process will contribute more to trust in the U.S. than in Israel					
H_{2a}: Predictability to Ability	0.573	0.0637	0.385	0.0992	-22.208**
H_{2b}: Predictability to Integrity	0.613	0.0467	0.289	0.0852	-46.841**
H_{2c}: Predictability to Benevolence	0.544	0.0493	0.205	0.1156	-38.312**
H_{3a}: Predictability to Inquiry Intentions	0.227	0.0762	0.153	0.1091	-7.705**
H_{3b}: Predictability to Purchase Intentions	0.339	0.0795	0.121	0.0923	-24.468**
Ability will contribute more to trust in Israel than in the U.S.					
H_{4a}: Ability to Inquiry	0.211	0.1017	0.241	0.0953	2.902**
H_{4b}: Ability to Purchase	0.158	0.0941	0.184	0.073	38.254**
Other Significant Differences					
Integrity to Inquiry	0.047	0.0897	0.105	0.0804	16.961** [9]
Integrity to Purchase	0.238	0.09	0.159	0.0792	-8.847**

** means significant at the .01 level * means significant at the .05 level

dimensional scales of trust beliefs and their related familiarity and predictability scales in a culture different from the U.S., where the original scales were developed and verified. Second, having established this, to investigate how the model differs when comparing the U.S. and Israel, a culture which has low PDI, high UAI, and medium IDV. The data show that the psychometric properties and nomological validity of the scales do carry over to Israel, supporting the notion that these trust belief scales apply at least across these two cultures, but, as hypothesized, the data also highlight the need to recognize that trust works differently at least in these two cultures.

This cultural distinction is necessary in studying trust in general because trust is about reducing social uncertainty (Gefen, 2000; Luhmann, 1979) and about the willingness to depend on others (Mayer et al., 1995). These two social aspects are also captured by the IDV, PDI, and UAI dimensions of culture as explained by Hofstede (1984) and hence should affect trust (Doney et al., 1998).

The data also support the theoretical propositions on trust (Mayer et al., 1995; McKnight et al., 1998) that trust beliefs, specifically integrity and ability, affect behavioral trusting intentions involving vulnerability to the trusted party. These trust beliefs are in turn the product of familiarity and prediction processes. Supporting the study's underlying proposition and its hypotheses, there are significant differences in the strength of these processes between the two national cultures. While the data support this proposition, it is reassuring that the three dimensional structure of trust beliefs does carry over across cultures. Benevolence was an insignificant predictor of both types of trusting behavioral intentions. This result in the Israeli sample replicates the results reported by Gefen (2002b) in the U.S. Apparently, while customers in both countries value integrity and ability, in both countries they value less online vendors' benevolence. This is not surprising. Benevolence is a significant predictor of trusting

behavioral intentions among friends (Larzelere & Huston, 1980).

Limitations

The underlying objective of this study was to highlight the need to include national culture in trust research. Showing the generalization of the path coefficients was not. Thus, although the study examined convenience samples of students, which coincidently were also those used by Jarvenpaa and Tractinsky (1999), and hence the generality of the results cannot be assessed, this objective of the study was addressed and supported. Additional research could examine larger and random samples.

Another vein worth studying is other modes of trust creation. This study concentrated on one of the established trust creation modes, namely familiarity. Extending the research to other trust creation modes, such as calculative, intentionality, transference, size, and reputation could add additional aspects of how national culture affects trust beliefs. At this stage, additional research is also needed to examine the research propositions in other cultures. While doing so, examining alternative cultural measures such as Dorfman and Howell (1988) and other levels of identification (Straub et al., 2002) could add insights.

Implications

The central implication of this study is its support of the need to include national culture in e-commerce trust studies. Considering that almost all e-commerce trust is based on studies in the U.S., this should be a wakeup call. If conclusions drawn based on the U.S. cannot be automatically applied to other cultures, researchers should be aware of it.

Another implication is that familiarity and its related predictability process applies differently depending on the culture. While the importance of both familiarity and predictability has been previously demonstrated (Gefen, 2000; Shapiro et al., 1992; Zucker, 1986), showing how this effect changes across cultures is new.

A summary of the differences highlights some of the cultural implications of applying a U.S. model to another culture. The U.S. is a very individualistic and low uncertainty avoidance culture. In such a culture people typically accept others as free agents and hence knowing what to expect of others is a significant antecedent of trusting behavioral intentions. In contrast, Israel is a much more collectivist and uncertainty-avoiding culture. In such a culture, people expect familiar others to behave in accordance with community norms (Singh, 1990), and hence predictability, while still creating trust, is not a significant antecedent of trusting behavioral intentions. Moreover, familiarity is more highly valued in these cultures than in an individualist culture. These observations are supported by the data.

Of the three trust beliefs, integrity was a significant predictor of trusting behavioral intentions in both cultures, while ability was a significant predictor only among Israelis. This difference in the impact of ability may be explained by the difference in PDI between the two cultures. In low PDI cultures, people associate power with ability (Hofstede, 1984). This tendency of Israelis is also reflected by Intel's instructions, based on cultural differences mapped by its research center, to its U.S. employees who are sent to Israel: "When presenting to Israelis be brief, get quickly to the point" (Hermoni, 2004).

The study shows that although trust beliefs as found in the U.S. may be generalized to other cultures, the relative weight of each of these beliefs does differ. This is important because the literature suggests, but has not empirically shown, that trust and trust beliefs should operate differently in different countries (Doney et al., 1998; Fukuyama, 1995; Noorderhaven, 1999). Thus the study clarifies that although these beliefs may operate differently, their nature seems to be the same. This is an important contribution because

previous research that had clustered these three beliefs into one construct (Jarvenpaa & Tractinsky, 1999) did not conclude so, although it did raise the need for additional research to explain these results. Reexamining Jarvenpaa and Tractinsky's conclusion in the same book buying context with the same type of student population, but this time within the currently broader conceptualization of trust as a three dimensional construct of beliefs built through predictability, the study clarifies those counter intuitive conclusions and supports the need to include culture in trust research. This reexamination supports the extension of Doney et al.'s propositions. In doing so, the study opts to contribute to the "deficiencies in developing theoretical structures to better understand the relationship between culture and IS" (Ford et al., 2003, p. 19).

The study also expands existing research on trust formation in e-commerce by including the prediction process as a mediating construct between familiarity and trust beliefs. In doing so the study supports the conclusion that familiarity increases trust indirectly through a better understanding of what is happening (Gefen et al., 2003b), albeit differently between the two cultures.

Afterthought

While additional research is needed before conclusions can be drawn, the data imply that in highly individualist and low uncertainty avoidance cultures vendors might be advised to emphasize predictability, for example through contracts, guarantees and association with trust-elevating institutional institutions. On the other hand, in the more collectivist countries, vendors might be better advised to invest in creating familiarity and a perception of ability. Adding national culture to models of trust in e-commerce, especially trust creation processes, could enhance e-commerce success and allow Web sites to cater to specific national cultural aspects. There is a big wide world out there. It is not all the same.

REFERENCES

Bagozzi, R. P., Wong, N., Abe, S., & Bergami, M. (2000). Cultural and situational contingencies and the theory of reasoned action: Application to fast food restaurant consumption. *Journal of Consumer Psychology, 9*(2), 97-106.

Berscheid, E. (1966). Opinion change and communicator-communicatee similarity and dissimilarity. *Journal of Personality and Social Psychology, 4*(6), 670-680.

Brown, R. (1996). Tajfel's contribution to the reduction of intergroup conflict. In W.P. Robinson (Ed.), *Social groups and identities: Developing the legacy of Henri Tajfel* (pp. 69-190). Oxford, UK: Butterworth-Heinemann.

Clark, T. (1990) International marketing and national character: A review and proposal for an integrative theory. *Journal of Marketing, 54*(4), 66-79.

ClickZ. (2004). Population explosion! Retrieved May 17, 2006, from http://www.clickz.com/stats/big_picture/geographics/article.php/5911_151151

Deaux, K. (1996). Social identification. In E. T. Higgins & A. W. Kruglanski (Eds.), *Social psychology handbook of basic principles* (pp. 777-798). New York, London: The Guilford Press.

Doney, P. M., & Cannon, J. P. (1997). An examination of the nature of trust in buyer-seller relationships. *Journal of Marketing, 61*(1), 35-51.

Doney, P. M., Cannon, J. P., & Mullen, M. R. (1998). Understanding the influence of national culture on the development of trust. *The Academy of Management Review, 23*(3), 601-620.

Dorfman, P. W., & Howell, J. P. (1988). Dimensions of national culture and effective leadership patterns: Hofstede revisited. *Advances in International Comparative Management, 3*, 127-150.

Ebusinessforum. (2002). The Economist Intelligence Unit e-readiness rankings. Retrieved May 17, 2006, from http://www.ebusinessforum.com/index.asp?layout=rich_story&doc_id=5768

EMarketer. (2004). Net users making their mark online. Retrieved May 17, 2006, from http://www.emarketer.com/news/article

Ford, D. P., Connelly, C. E., & Meister, D. B. (2003). Information systems research and Hofstede's culture's consequences: An uneasy and incomplete partnership. *IEEE Transactions On Engineering Management, 50*(1), 8-25.

Fromkin, H. L., & Streufert, S. (1976). Laboratory experimentation. In B. Dunnette (Ed.), *Handbook of industrial and organizational psychology* (pp. 415-465). Chicago: Rand McNally College Publishing Company.

Fukuyama, F. (1995). *Trust: The social virtues and the creation of prosperity.* New York: The Free Press.

Ganesan, S. (1994). Determinants of long-term orientation in buyer-seller relationships. *Journal of Marketing, 58*(1), 1-19.

Gefen, D. (2000). E-commerce: The role of familiarity and trust. *Omega, 28*(5), 725-737.

Gefen, D. (2002a). Nurturing clients' trust to encourage engagement success during the customization of ERP systems. *Omega: The International Journal of Management Science, 30*(4), 287-299.

Gefen, D. (2002b). Reflections on the dimensions of trust and trustworthiness among online consumers. *The DATABASE for Advances in Information Systems, 33*(3), 38-53.

Gefen, D. (2004). What makes ERP implementation relationships worthwhile: Linking trust mechanisms and ERP usefulness. *Journal of Management Information Systems, 21*(1), 275-301.

Gefen, D., Karahanna, E., & Straub, D. W. (2003a). Inexperience and experience with online stores: The importance of TAM and trust. *IEEE Transactions on Engineering Management, 50*(3), 307-321.

Gefen, D., Karahanna, E., & Straub, D. W. (2003b). Trust and TAM in online shopping: An integrated model. *MIS Quarterly, 27*(1), 51-90.

Gefen, D., & Ridings, C. (2003). IT acceptance: Managing user-IT group boundaries. *The DATA BASE for Advances in Information Systems, 34*(3), 25-40.

Gefen, D., Rose, G. M., Warkentin, M., & Pavlou, P. A. (2004). Cultural diversity and trust in IT adoption: A comparison of U.S.A. and South African e-voters. *Journal of Global Information Systems, 13*(1), 54-78.

Gefen, D., & Straub, D. W. (1997). Gender differences in perception and adoption of e-mail: An extension to the technology acceptance model. *MIS Quarterly, 21*(4), 389-400.

Gefen, D., & Straub, D. W. (2004). Consumer trust in B2C e-commerce and the importance of social presence: Experiments in e-products and e-services. *Omega: The International Journal of Management Science, 32*(6), 407-424.

Gefen, D., Straub, D. W., & Boudreau, M.-C. (2000). Structural equation modeling and regression: Guidelines for research practice. *Communications of the Association for Information Systems, 4*(7), 1-70.

Hermoni, O. (2004, July 9). Expect interruptions and hot arguments, don't discuss politics: Intel's tips to its employees visiting Israel. *Haaretz Daily Newspaper.*

Hofstede, G. (1980b). Motivation, leadership, and organization: Do American theories apply abroad? *Organizational Dynamics, 9*(1), 42-63.

Hofstede, G. (1984). *Culture's consequences: International differences in work-related values.* Beverly Hills: Sage Publications.

Hofstede, G. (1994). *Cultures and organizations, intercultural cooperation and its importance for survival, software of the mind.* Glasgow, UK: HarperCollins Publishers.

Hofstede, G., Neuijen, B., Ohayv, D. D., & Sanders, G. (1990). Measuring organizational cultures: A qualitative and quantitative study across twenty cases. *Adminstrative Science Quarterly, 35*(2), 286-316.

Hogg, M. A. (1996). Group structure and social identity. In W. P. Robinson (Ed.), *Social groups and identities: Developing the legacy of Henri Tajfel* (pp. 65-94). UK: Butterworth-Heinemann.

Hogg, M. A., & Terry, D. J. (2000). Social identity and self-categorization processes in organizational contexts. *Academy of Management Review, 25*(1), 121-140.

Jarvenpaa, S. L., Knoll, K., & Leidner, D. E. (1998). Is anybody out there? Antecedents of trust in global virtual teams. *Journal of Management Information Systems, 14*(4), 29-64.

Jarvenpaa, S. L., & Tractinsky, N. (1999). Consumer trust in an Internet store: A cross-cultural validation. *Journal of Computer Mediated Communication, 5*(2), 1-35.

Jarvenpaa, S. L., Tractinsky, N., & Vitale, M. (2000). Consumer trust in an Internet store. *Information Technology and Management, 1*(12), 45-71.

Kacen, J. J., & Lee, J. A. (2002). The influence of culture on consumer impulsive buying behavior. *Journal of Consumer Psychology, 12*(2), 163-176.

Kale, S. H., & McIntyre, R. P. (1991). Distinctive channel relationships in diverse cultures. *International Marketing Review, 8*(3), 31-45.

Keil, M., Tan, B. C. Y., Wei, K. K., & Saarinen, T. (2000). Cross-cultural study on escalation of commitment behavior in software projects. *MIS Quarterly, 24*(2), 299-325.

Kim, H.-W., Xu, Y., & Koh, J. (2004). A comparison of online trust building factors between potential customers and repeat customers. *Journal of the Association for Information Systems, 5*(10), 392-420.

Kollock, P. (1999). The production of trust in online markets. *Advances in Group Processes, 16*(1), 99-123.

Kumar, N. (1996). The power of trust in manufacturer-retailer relationships. *Harvard Business Review, 74*(6), 92-106.

Larzelere, R. E., & Huston, T. L. (1980). The dyadic trust scale: Toward understanding interpersonal trust in close relationships. *Journal of Marriage and the Family, 42*(3), 595-604.

Luhmann, N. (1979). *Trust and power*. London: John Wiley & Sons.

Lynch, P. D., & Beck, J. C. (2001). Profiles of Internet buyers in 20 countries: Evidence of region-specific strategies. *Journal of International Business Studies, 32*(4), 725-748.

Mayer, R. C., Davis, J. H., & Schoorman, F. D. (1995). An integrative model of organizational trust. *Academy of Management Review, 20*(3), 709-734.

McCoy, S., Galletta, D., & King, W. (2005). Integrating national culture into IS research: The need for current individual-level measures. *Communications of the AIS, 15*, 211-224.

McKnight, D. H., & Chervany, N. L. (2002). What trust means in e-commerce customer relationships: An interdisciplinary conceptual typology. *International Journal of Electronic Commerce, 6*(2), 35-53.

McKnight, D. H., Cummings, L. L., & Chervany, N. L. (1998). Initial trust formation in new organizational relationships. *Academy of Management Review, 23*(3), 473-490.

Noorderhaven, N. G. (1999). National culture and development of trust: The need for more data and less theory. *Academy of Management Review, 24*(1), 9-10.

Pavlou, P. A. (2003). Consumer acceptance of electronic commerce: Integrating trust and risk with the technology acceptance model. *International Journal of Electronic Commerce, 7*(3), 69-103.

Pavlou, P. A., & Gefen, D. (2004). Building effective online marketplaces with institution-based trust. *Information Systems Research, 15*(1).

Reichheld, F. F., & Schefter, P. (2000). E-loyalty: Your secret weapon on the Web. *Harvard Business Review, 78*(4), 105-113.

Rose, G., & Straub, D. W. (1998). Predicting general IT use: Applying TAM to the Arabic world. *Journal of Global Information Management, 6*(3), 39-46.

Saeed, K., Hwang, Y., & Yi, M. (2003). Toward an integrative framework for online consumer behavior research: A meta-analysis approach. *Journal of End User Computing, 15*(4), 1-26.

Schurr, P. H., & Ozanne, J. L. (1985, March). Influences on exchange processes: Buyers' preconceptions of a seller's trustworthiness and bargaining toughness. *Journal of Consumer Research, 11*, 939-953.

Serva, M. A., Fuller, M. A., & Benamati, J. (2005). Trustworthiness in B2c e-commerce: empirical test of alternative models. *The DATABASE for Advances in Information Systems, 36*(3), 89-108.

Shaffer, T. R., & O'Hara, B. S. (1995). The effects of country of origin on trust and ethical perceptions of legal services. *The Service Industries Journal, 15*(2), 162-185.

Shane, S. A. (1992). The effect of cultural differences in perceptions of transaction costs on national differences in the preference for licensing. *Management International Review, 32*(4), 295-311.

Shapiro, D., Sheppard, B. H., & Cheraskin, L. (1992). Business on a handshake. *Negotiation Journal, 8,* 365-377.

Singh, J. (1990). Managerial culture and work-related values in India. *Organizational Studies, 11*(1), 75-101.

Sitkin, S. B., & Roth, N. L. (1993). Explaining the limited effectiveness of legalistic "Remedies" for trust/distrust. *Organizational Science, 4*(3), 367-392.

Straub, D. W., Keil, M., & Brennan, W. (1997). Testing the technology acceptance model across cultures: A three country study. *Information & Management, 33,* 1-11.

Straub, D. W., Loch, K. D., Evaristo, R., Karahanna, E., & Srite, M. (2002). Toward a theory-based measurement of culture. *Journal of Global Information Management, 10*(1), 13-23.

Tajfel, H. (1970). Experiments in intergroup discrimination. *Scientific American, 223*(5), 96-102.

Tajfel, H. (1978). Social categorization, social identity and social comparison. In H. Tajfel (Ed.), *Differentiation between social groups* (pp. 61-76). UK: Academic Press.

Tan, B. C. Y., Smith, H. J., Keil, M., & Montealegre, R. (2003). Reporting bad news about software projects: Impact of organizational climate and information asymmetry in an individualistic and a collectivistic culture. *IEEE Transactions on Engineering Management, 50*(1), 64-77.

Turner, J. C. (1982). Toward a cognitive redefinition of the social group. In H. Tajfel (Ed.), *Social identity and intergroup relations* (pp. 1-40). Cambridge, UK: Cambridge University Press.

Warkentin, M., Gefen, D., Pavlou, P. A., & Rose, G. M. (2002). Encouraging citizen adoption of eGovernment by building trust. *Electronic Markets: The International Journal of Electronic Commerce & Business Media, 12*(3), 157-162.

Williamson, O. (1985). *The economic institutions of capitalism.* New York: The Free Press.

Yamagishi, T., & Yamagishi, M. (1994). Trust and commitment in the United States and Japan. *Motivation and Emotion, 18,* 129-166.

Zucker, L. (1986) Production of trust: Institutional sources of economic structure, 1840-1920. *Research in Organization Behavior, 8*(1), 53-111.

ENDNOTES

[1] As of March 2004 there were nearly 186 million online consumers in the U.S. as compared with 945 million users worldwide (EMarketer, 2004).

[2] The latter also take an initial step in addressing the need raised by Noorderhaven's (1999) comment about Doney et al.'s (1998) propositions on how culture affects trust outcomes: "That means we should start with trying to get good and rich data and not more theory" (p. 9).

[3] There is actually quite a mix up in the literature as to what trust is and what trustworthiness is. Some label trust beliefs as trustworthiness (e.g., Mayer et al., 1995) while others named these as trust (e.g., Doney & Cannon, 1997).

[4] Like the U.S., Israel is a country of immigrants. It is composed mostly of Jews from Eastern Europe, where collectivism was especially strong as a means to reduce threats

and maintain self-identity, and from the Arab countries, such as Morocco and Iraq, where society as a whole is collectivistic. Only a relative small percentage of Israeli society can trace its roots to the more individualistic West, but even there the Jewish population was relatively more collectivistic. The kibbutz, a collective form of settlement, formed in Israel at the beginning of the 20th century by Jewish settlers, is an extreme manifestation of collectivism that characterized the early days of Israeli society.

5 The only other country with such an extreme PDI is Austria. As Hofstede explains, the low PDI in Austria is probably the result of the very large proportion of Jews in the *"Inteligentsia"* between the two world wars and their enormous effect on the culture. In fact, it is mostly because of the indexes of these two countries that statistically the PDI and IDV factors are distinct (Hofstede, 1984).

6 Doney et al. (1998) advance conflicting propositions on how predictability should relate to a comparison of national cultures in interpersonal relationships based on PDI, UAI, and IDV. On the one hand, their analysis of PDI, discussed above, suggests that predictability should have a stronger effect on trust beliefs in the U.S. On the other hand, their analysis of IDV suggests that predictability in social settings should be of more consequence in Israel because collectivist cultures put greater value on conformity to social behavior. However, recognizing that buying online is a private activity where conformity plays hardly any role, this proposition was not applied. Along the same lines, Doney et al. also propose that predictability-based trust should be less

influential in social settings in low UAI cultures because predictability cannot logically establish trust in cultures where behavior itself is not predictable and society accepts it as such. But this scenario is also not the case with one of the largest and most reputable online vendors. The behavior of Amazon is very predictable and any variations from what the FTC allows are categorically unaccepted in both countries.

7 The hypothesis is based on Doney et al.'s (1998) proposition concerning UAI. Their contradicting propositions that Ability should carry more weight in building trust in high IDV cultures was not part of the logic here because the reason Ability is less important in low IDV cultures, according to Doney et al. (1998), is that in collectivist cultures the whole group pitches in to help while in individualistic cultures the outcome depends more on the individual. This is not the case with an online vendor. Doney et al. also propose that in high PDI cultures ability should carry more weight in building trust because in these cultures people expect large variance in others people's capabilities based on their social position. Arguably, this too is not the case with online shopping at Amazon.com.

8 An alternative saturated model was also examined. The saturated model contained the same paths as in the research model and also three paths from Familiarity to the three trust beliefs. In the saturated model the same paths as shown in the research model were significant. The three additional paths were not.

9 The paths in both samples are insignificant.

APPENDIX A. QUESTIONNAIRE ITEMS

Familiarity with Amanzon.com	
I am familiar with buying books on the Internet	Fam1
I am familiar with Amazon.com	Fam2
I am familiar with the processes of purchasing books on the Internet	Fam3
I am familiar with inquiring about book ratings at Amazon.com	Fam4
Integrity	
Promises made by Amazon.com are likely to be reliable	In1
I do not doubt the honesty of Amazon.com	In2
I expect that Amazon.com will keep promises they make	In3
Benevolence	
I expect that Amazon.com have good intentions toward me	Ben1
I expect that Amazon.com intentions are benevolent	Ben2
I expect that Amazon.com are well meaning	Ben3
Ability	
Amazon.com understand the market they work in	AB1
Amazon.com know about books	AB2
Amazon.com know how to provide excellent service	AB3
Intention to Buy	
I would use my credit card to purchase from Amazon.com	Use2
I am very likely to buy books from Amazon.com	Use1
Prediction Process	
Amazon.com are predictable	Prd1
I am quite certain what Amazon.com will do	Prd2
I am quite certain what to expect from Amazon.com	Prd3
Intentions to Inquire	
I would use Amazon.com to retrieve information	Inq1
I would use Amazon.com to inquire what readers think of a book	Inq2
I would use Amazon.com to find out about the author of a book	Inq3
I would use Amazon.com to inquire about book ratings	Inq4

APPENDIX B. DESCRIPTIVE STATISTICS

Mean Statistics

	COUNTRY	Mean 1=agree 7=disagree	Std. Deviation	t-value comparing the U.S.A. with Israel (p-value)
Familiarity	U.S.A.	3.3412	1.60231	-8.001 (<.001)
	ISRAEL	4.8912	1.66374	
Integrity	U.S.A.	3.0438	.93918	.352 (.725)
	ISRAEL	3.0023	1.04357	
Benevolence	U.S.A.	3.2251	.92611	.349 (.728)
	ISRAEL	3.1814	1.16142	
Ability	U.S.A.	2.6277	1.01385	-2.095 (.037)
	ISRAEL	2.8957	1.13261	
Prediction Process	U.S.A.	3.2080	.94924	-5.806 (<.001)
	ISRAEL	3.9365	1.14765	
Inquiry Intentions	U.S.A.	2.5501	1.16334	-9.543 (<.001)
	ISRAEL	3.9321	1.63980	
Purchase Intentions	U.S.A.	3.0790	1.51159	-6.929 (<.001)
	ISRAEL	4.4048	1.69238	

APPENDIX C. CORRELATIONS OF LATENT VARIABLES AND SQUARE ROOT OF THE AVE, ISRAELI SAMPLE

	PLS reliability	Pur. Inten.	Ability	Integrity	Ben.	Fam.	Pred.	Inq. Inten.
Purchase Intentions	.93	0.930						
Ability	.84	0.354	0.801					
Integrity	.85	0.337	0.484	0.805				
Benevolence	.91	0.187	0.325	0.459	0.878			
Familiarity	.90	0.378	0.131	0.143	0.034	0.830		
Predictability	.93	0.328	0.392	0.307	0.199	0.276	0.901	
Inquiry Intentions	.94	0.593	0.398	0.325	0.222	0.301	0.349	0.890

APPENDIX D. CORRELATIONS OF LATENT VARIABLES AND SQUARE ROOT OF THE AVE, U.S. SAMPLE

	PLS reliability	Pur. Inten.	Ability	Integrity	Ben.	Fam.	Pred.	Inq. Inten.
Purchase Intentions	.91	0.917						
Ability	.92	0.222	0.900					
Integrity	.92	0.416	0.578	0.895				
Benevolence	.87	0.274	0.679	0.654	0.834			
Familiarity	.91	0.339	0.233	0.274	0.218	0.842		
Predictability	.89	0.455	0.592	0.641	0.561	0.296	0.849	
Inquiry Intentions	.94	0.485	0.424	0.331	0.372	0.313	0.429	0.888

APPENDIX E. CONFIRMATORY FACTOR ANALYSIS, ISRAELI SAMPLE

	Pur. Inten.	Ability	Integrity	Ben.	Fam.	Pred.	Inq. Inten.
USE2	**0.92**	0.30	0.32	0.19	0.33	0.30	0.56
USE1	**0.94**	0.35	0.31	0.16	0.37	0.31	0.55
AB1	0.27	**0.82**	0.48	0.25	0.08	0.27	0.28
AB2	0.14	**0.68**	0.15	0.20	0.00	0.17	0.26
AB3	0.38	**0.88**	0.46	0.31	0.18	0.43	0.39
IN1	0.32	0.42	**0.89**	0.36	0.11	0.26	0.32
IN2	0.27	0.34	**0.78**	0.26	0.21	0.25	0.24
IN3	0.22	0.41	**0.73**	0.53	0.02	0.23	0.22
BEN1	0.12	0.24	0.42	**0.91**	0.02	0.26	0.25
BEN2	0.20	0.30	0.38	**0.90**	0.01	0.10	0.16
BEN3	0.19	0.35	0.40	**0.83**	0.07	0.13	0.14
FAM1	0.31	0.09	0.07	-0.01	**0.84**	0.22	0.22
FAM2	0.22	0.12	0.14	-0.06	**0.74**	0.16	0.20
FAM3	0.36	0.14	0.12	0.02	**0.89**	0.25	0.27

APPENDIX E. CONFIRMATORY FACTOR ANALYSIS, ISRAELI SAMPLE (CONT.)

	Pur. Inten.	Ability	Integrity	Ben.	Fam.	Pred.	Inq. Inten.
FAM4	0.34	0.09	0.15	0.13	**0.84**	0.27	0.29
PRD1	0.28	0.43	0.28	0.27	0.21	**0.89**	0.31
PRD2	0.25	0.26	0.23	0.11	0.20	**0.89**	0.28
PRD3	0.34	0.34	0.31	0.15	0.32	**0.93**	0.34
INQ1	0.56	0.32	0.23	0.12	0.26	0.32	**0.83**
INQ2	0.51	0.34	0.30	0.21	0.32	0.33	**0.93**
INQ3	0.54	0.38	0.36	0.23	0.26	0.27	**0.92**
INQ4	0.53	0.38	0.27	0.23	0.24	0.33	**0.92**

APPENDIX F. CONFIRMATORY FACTOR ANALYSIS, U.S. SAMPLE

	Pur. Inten.	Ability	Integrity	Ben.	Fam.	Pred.	Inq. Inten.
USE2	**0.93**	0.18	0.39	0.25	0.33	0.43	0.42
USE1	**0.91**	0.23	0.37	0.26	0.29	0.41	0.47
AB1	0.20	**0.89**	0.49	0.51	0.24	0.51	0.40
AB2	0.17	**0.90**	0.50	0.62	0.15	0.49	0.37
AB3	0.22	**0.90**	0.56	0.69	0.23	0.59	0.37
IN1	0.35	0.55	**0.90**	0.59	0.29	0.57	0.33
IN2	0.42	0.52	**0.92**	0.60	0.23	0.63	0.30
IN3	0.35	0.48	**0.86**	0.57	0.21	0.51	0.25
BEN1	0.27	0.63	0.60	**0.88**	0.19	0.51	0.38
BEN2	0.20	0.53	0.53	**0.83**	0.16	0.44	0.30
BEN3	0.21	0.53	0.49	**0.79**	0.19	0.46	0.23
FAM1	0.36	0.10	0.18	0.10	**0.84**	0.25	0.21
FAM2	0.23	0.25	0.26	0.20	**0.81**	0.18	0.24
FAM3	0.25	0.21	0.21	0.19	**0.86**	0.26	0.33
FAM4	0.31	0.21	0.27	0.23	**0.85**	0.31	0.27
PRD1	0.40	0.62	0.62	0.57	0.28	**0.86**	0.44
PRD2	0.38	0.37	0.49	0.38	0.21	**0.84**	0.26
PRD3	0.37	0.47	0.50	0.45	0.26	**0.84**	0.37
INQ1	0.44	0.36	0.28	0.28	0.28	0.37	**0.85**
INQ2	0.43	0.35	0.29	0.33	0.29	0.37	**0.91**
INQ3	0.44	0.42	0.32	0.38	0.27	0.43	**0.89**
INQ4	0.42	0.38	0.28	0.32	0.28	0.35	**0.90**

This work was previously published in Journal of Global Information Management, Vol. 14, Issue 4, edited by F. B. Tan, pp. 1-30, copyright 2006 by IGI Publishing, formerly known as Idea Group Publishing (an imprint of IGI Global).

Chapter XXVI
Exploring Decision Rules for Sellers in Business–to–Consumer (B2C) Internet Auctions

Jeff Baker
Texas Tech University, USA

Jaeki Song
Texas Tech University, USA

ABSTRACT

The recent growth of business-to-consumer (B2C) Internet auctions challenges researchers to develop empirically-sound explanations of critical factors that allow merchants to earn price premiums in these auctions. The absence of a comprehensive model of Internet auctions leads us to conduct an exploratory study to elucidate and rank critical factors that lead to price premiums in Internet auctions. We employ Classification and Regression Trees (CART), a decision-tree induction technique, to analyze data collected in a field study of eBay auctions. Our analysis yields decision trees that visually depict noteworthy factors that may lead to price premiums and that indicate the relative importance of these factors. We find shipping cost, reputation, initial bid price, and auction ending time as the factors most predictive of price premiums in B2C Internet auctions.

INTRODUCTION

Over the past decade, Internet auctions have grown from a mere curiosity to a major focus of both researchers and businesses. In their early days, Internet auctions were dominated by individuals selling collectibles such as antiques, celebrity memorabilia, stamps, toys, coins, and trading cards; the vast majority of transactions were consumer-to-consumer (C2C) (Lucking-Reiley, 2000a). More recently, researchers have noted the growth of business-to-business (B2B) and business-to-consumer (B2C) auctions (Bapna, Goes, & Gupta, 2001). In B2C auctions, large merchants such as Dell, Disney, Home Depot, IBM, Motorola, Sears, Sun Microsystems, and Sharper Image have been able to use Internet auctions to sell excess inventory for greater profit than they would receive from using a liquidator (Dholakia, 2005b; Gentry, 2003; Grow, 2002; Vogelstein, Boyle, Lewis, & Kirkpatrick, 2004). As further evidence of the growth of B2C Internet auctions, by the first quarter of 2006, Internet auctioneer eBay alone hosted approximately 383,000 eBay stores worldwide, including 171,000 on Web sites other than their U.S. Web site (eBay, 2006). As firms continue to make extensive use of Internet auctions, the interest in developing sound guidelines for businesses as well as developing theory to advance research will likely continue to grow as well.

While many studies have examined the factors that determine an auction item's final bid price, the number of bids an item receives, whether a sale is completed, or the revenue earned by a seller, the examination of price premiums (above-average final bid prices) is relatively understudied. In economics, price premiums are defined as prices that yield above-average profits (Klein & Leffler, 1981; Shapiro, 1983). Price premiums within the Internet auction context have been defined as *"the monetary amount above the average price received by multiple sellers for a certain matching product"* (Ba & Pavlou, 2002, pp. 247-248). Restated, a number of auctions exist where sellers have earned above-average prices, or price premiums, on the items they have auctioned. In this study, we compare the group of auctions that have achieved above-average prices with those that have not, to observe significant differences. To our knowledge, only two studies have previously examined price premiums (Ba & Pavlou, 2002; Pavlou, 2002). Since it is only by maximizing revenue and profit that a firm can remain viable in the marketplace (Seth & Thomas, 1994), an increased focus on how businesses that rely upon

Internet auctions can earn price premiums may prove beneficial. The focus on price premiums is the first contribution of this study. As we investigate price premiums, we examine many of the independent variables that have been considered in previous studies to determine if they are also predictive of price premiums. The second contribution is the application of CART analysis to Internet auctions as a tool to generate decision rules. CART analysis is a tree-based method of recursive partitioning for explaining or predicting a response to order variables by significance (Brieman, Friedman, Olshen, & Stone, 1984). It generates decision trees and decision rules that may be used as guidelines (by sellers in Internet auctions, in this case). While electronic commerce research has demonstrated that CART analysis can be used to improve one-to-one Internet marketing (Kim, Lee, Shaw, Chang, & Nelson, 2001), CART has not yet been applied to Internet auctions. Thus, our study is, to our knowledge, the first to use a statistically-based decision making technique to demonstrate how sellers can use quantitative data to decide how to sell products in B2C Internet auctions. The third and final contribution of this study is the examination (by CART analysis) of variables that have been found (generally by multiple-regression analysis) to be determinants of auction outcome in previous studies. This confirmation of variables identified as critical factors in other types of analysis is the third contribution of this study.

The article will be organized as follows. We begin by reviewing literature on auctions, including relevant research on both traditional auctions as well as Internet auctions. Next, we present literature on machine-learning techniques that enable the induction of decision trees. Following the literature review, we discuss our methods, including our dataset, variables, and our research design. Specifically, we describe the collection and analysis of field data from Internet auctioneer eBay. We then present the results of our analysis. Following the presentation of our results, we discuss our findings and note the implications of our study. Finally, we conclude by briefly noting the limitations of our study and directions for future research.

LITERATURE REVIEW

Literature pertinent to this study will be selectively drawn from two areas of research. Given that one of the objectives of this study is to investigate factors enabling sellers to earn price premiums in Internet auctions, the first area from which we draw theory is that of auction literature. An additional objective—namely, describing a technique for developing decision rules for sellers in Internet auctions—leads us to the second area of research that is pertinent to the present study: decision-tree induction techniques.

Auctions

Auctions have been described as "*a market institution with an explicit set of rules determining resource allocation and prices on the basis of bids from the market participants*" (McAfee & McMillan, 1987, p. 701). A vast amount of research addresses the topic of auctions. Numerous surveys of auction literature can be found (Engelbrecht-Wiggans, 1980; Klemperer, 1999, 2000; Krishna, 2002; McAfee & McMillan, 1987; Milgrom, 1985, 1986; Rothkopf & Harstad, 1994; Wilson, 1987), including a bibliography of earlier literature (Stark & Rothkopf, 1979) and a review of experimental auction literature (Kagel, 1995).

Auction Mechanisms and Auction Theory

Auction mechanisms are generally categorized as: (1) English or ascending-price auctions; (2) Dutch or descending-price auctions; (3) first-price sealed-bid auctions; or (4) second-price sealed bid or Vickrey auctions (McAfee & McMillan, 1987).

A thorough description of these mechanisms can be found in the recent work of Lucking-Reiley (2000a). Internet auctions on eBay, the point of data collection for this study, have been described by scholars as a hybrid of the English and second-price auctions (Lucking-Reiley, 2000a, 2000b; Ward & Clark, 2002; Wilcox, 2000). Researchers assert that eBay uses a hybrid auction type on the grounds that the presence of a proxy-bidding mechanism ensures that a winning bidder will pay only one increment more than the second-highest bidder's price. Since this study examines only auctions of the hybrid eBay type, a discussion of how various types of auction mechanisms impact auction outcome is beyond the scope of the present study.

Auction theory is often centered around or developed in response to the seminal work of William Vickrey (1961), who described the Independent Private Values Model (IPV). In this model, each bidder formulates a valuation for the item being auctioned without an awareness of competing bidders' valuations. Even if valuations were shared among all bidders, each individual bidder's valuation would be unaffected by the additional information that competing bidders' valuations would provide. In this way, the bidder's value is independent of the influence of competing bidders and is privately determined. In contrast, the Common Values Model (CV) posits that the value of the item being auctioned is common to all bidders, but incomplete information causes each bidder to formulate a valuation for the item that falls either above or below the common value (Rothkopf, 1969; Wilson, 1969). If it is assumed that bidders' valuations are normally distributed about the common value, the winner of the auction is the bidder with the valuation that is farthest above the common value. This person incurs the "winner's curse," because he or she has likely overpaid for the item. An integrative approach, referred to as the Affiliated Values Model (AV), explains that bidder valuations depend upon the bidder's personal preferences, the preferences of others, and the intrinsic qualities of the item being sold (Milgrom & Weber, 1982). Bidders' valuations are described as affiliated because a high valuation by one bidder makes a high valuation by other bidders more likely (Milgrom & Weber, 1982). The AV model is a more general conceptualization of the valuation of items in auctions than the IPV or CV models; both the IPV and CV models can be understood as special cases of the more general AV model (McAfee & McMillan, 1987). Recent studies of Internet auctions rely upon and explicitly mention the merits of the AV model (Dholakia & Soltysinski, 2001; Gilkeson & Reynolds, 2003; Segev, Beam, & Shanthikumar, 2001; Wilcox, 2000). These studies empirically validate the AV model in Internet auctions by demonstrating that bidders may be influenced not only by their own valuation of the item, but also by the behavior of other bidders.

Internet Auctions

Internet auctions have a relatively brief history. Among the earliest electronic auctions were the auctioning of pigs in Singapore (Neo, 1992) and flowers in Holland (van Heck & van Damme, 1997) conducted over a LAN. Auctions on the Internet, conducted via newsgroups and e-mail discussion lists, were the next major development in the Internet auction timeline (Lucking-Reiley, 1999, 2000a). The explosion in popularity of Internet auctions, however, did not begin until the 1995 launches of U.S. Web sites Onsale and eBay (Lucking-Reiley, 2000a). By 1999, there were an estimated 200 auction sites on the Internet (Crockett, 1999). The continued growth of Internet auctions is demonstrated by the performance of international industry leader eBay, a company that operates auction Web sites in 24 countries, includes over 180 million registered users, and generated US$ 4.552 billion in sales in 2005 (eBay, 2006). International competition includes firms such as QXL.com in Europe, Taobao.com in Asia, and MercadoLibre in Latin America. Following

Möllenberg (2004, pp. 360-371), we will define Internet auctions to mean *virtual marketplaces relying on Internet services (such as the World Wide Web) and Internet protocols to conduct auctions.*

In spite of the relatively short history of Internet auctions, they have begun to draw interest not only from economists, but also from researchers in marketing, information systems, and computer science (see Appendix A for a selective listing of recent studies in each of these disciplines). The general questions that many of these studies seek to answer are, "What is the optimal way to auction an item?" or "How is the marketplace changing as a result of Internet auctions?" or "What factors should be considered when buying or selling in an Internet auction?" We will generally limit our discussion of Internet auctions to empirical studies that deal with variables that are under the control of the seller (rather than variables under the control of the other two parties to the auction transaction, the auctioneer and the bidder). Since this study focuses on developing decision rules for sellers in single-item B2C Internet auctions, we will reserve exploration of multi-unit auctions and buyer behavior for other researchers. To organize the list of variables that have been investigated in previous studies, we introduce the categories of: (1) selling information, (2) seller information, (3) product information, and (4) delivery information. We will define and discuss each of these categories in turn.

Selling information includes general information about the auction and the terms of an item's sale. The initial bid price, the availability of a buy-now option, the auction duration, and the auction's ending time are included as selling information variables. Table 1 contains a list of these variables, their definitions, and a list of studies in which they have been investigated. There have been a number of important findings in this area. It has been observed that an item's final bid price can be significantly affected by its initial bid price (Brint, 2003). Bidders have been found to

Table 1. Previous empirical studies measuring selling information variables

Variable	Description	Source
Initial Bid Price	Starting bid price	(Gilkeson & Reynolds, 2003; McDonald & Slawson, 2002; Standifird, 2001; Standifird, Roelofs, & Durham, 2004)
Buy-Now Option	Presence or absence of option for bidder to end auction early by purchasing at a seller-determined fixed price (eBay's Buy-it-Now option)	(Standifird, Roelofs, & Durham, 2004)
Auction Duration	Length of auction in days	(Dholakia & Soltysinski, 2001; Gilkeson & Reynolds, 2003; McDonald & Slawson, 2002; Mehta, 2002; Standifird, 2001; Standifird, Roelofs, & Durham, 2004; Subramaniam, Mittal, & Inman, 2004)
Auction Ending Time	Time of day auction ends	(Dholakia & Soltysinski, 2001; Gilkeson & Reynolds, 2003; McDonald & Slawson, 2002; Mehta, 2002; Standifird, 2001)

Variable	Description	Source
Number of Positive Feedback Ratings	Total number of eBay positive feedback ratings	(Ba & Pavlou, 2002; McDonald & Slawson, 2002; Standifird, 2001)
Number of Negative Feedback Ratings	Total number of eBay negative feedback ratings	(Ba & Pavlou, 2002; McDonald & Slawson, 2002; Standifird, 2001)
Product Information Variables		
Number of Pictures	Number of pictures	(Ottaway, Bruneau, & Evans, 2003)
Number of Bids	Total number of bids submitted for item	(Dholakia, 2005b; Dholakia & Soltysinski, 2001; Gilkeson & Reynolds, 2003; McDonald & Slawson, 2002; Standifird, 2001; Subramaniam, Mittal, & Inman, 2004; Wilcox, 2000)
Delivery Information Variables		
Availability of Expedited Delivery	Availability of express delivery	
Availability of International Delivery	Possibility to Deliver Internationally	
Shipping Cost	Amount of shipping and handling charges	(Gilkeson & Reynolds, 2003; McDonald & Slawson, 2002)

sometimes ignore a buy-now option even when buy-now prices are set below prevailing market prices (Standifird, Roelofs, & Durham, 2004). Setting a buy-now price may, however, enhance revenue for sellers (Budish & Takeyama, 2001) in some situations. The time of day or week that an auction ends, and the duration of an auction are frequently used as either control variables or dependent variables (Bruce, Haruvy, & Rao, 2004; Dholakia & Soltysinski, 2001; Gilkeson & Reynolds, 2003; McDonald & Slawson, 2002; Standifird, 2001; Standifird, Roelofs, & Durham, 2004; Subramaniam, Mittal, & Inman, 2004), but have not, to our knowledge, been conclusively linked to higher closing prices.

Seller information is defined as the various facets of the seller's feedback rating. The ease with which buyers are able to provide feedback has made a seller's feedback rating one of the most significant predictors of auction closing price. Feedback mechanisms can help sellers earn higher prices (Bruce, Haruvy, & Rao, 2004; McDonald & Slawson, 2002; Ottaway, Bruneau, & Evans, 2003) and have been shown in one previous study to play a role in generating price premiums for reputable sellers (Ba & Pavlou, 2002). The number of positive feedback ratings and the number of negative feedback ratings are included as seller information variables in this study (see Table 1). We investigate both positive as well as negative feedback, because it has been found that positive and negative feedback have an asymmetrical effect upon the final bid price. Specifically, positive feedback is mildly influential in determining final bid price, while negative feedback is highly influential (Standifird, 2001). Thus, it has been clearly demonstrated that seller information is also an important subset of variables to examine when researching Internet auctions.

Product information refers to the information provided by the seller or by other bidders about the item being auctioned. Frequently, product information is measured by recording the number of pictures of an item and the number of bids which an item receives (see Table 1). One study has explained that pictures of an item being auctioned on the Internet may affect information processing and ultimately the item's final closing price (Ottaway, Bruneau, & Evans, 2003). Another found that detailed descriptions of the item were significant predictors of a completed sale (Gilkeson & Reynolds, 2003)[1]. Other researchers have included product description as a control variable in their studies (Bruce, Haruvy, & Rao, 2004; Dholakia & Soltysinski, 2001; Gilkeson & Reynolds, 2003; Standifird, Roelofs, & Durham, 2004), giving at least informal credence to the notion that product information, such as pictures of an item, can influence an item's final closing price. Finally, the number of bids and the number of bidders has been shown to be factors leading to higher closing prices (Dholakia & Soltysinski, 2001; Gilkeson & Reynolds, 2003; Wilcox, 2000). Following the lead of these scholars, and in order to reach a more definitive conclusion regarding the possible impact of product description on auction prices, we also include product information in our analysis of Internet auctions.

Finally, *delivery information* simply refers to the cost of shipping and to the available delivery options. The availability of expedited delivery, international delivery, and the item's shipping cost are included here as variables (see Table 1). Relatively few researchers have included this subset of variables within their models. However, one study argues that high seller reputation and delivery efficiency may covary (McDonald & Slawson, 2002), while another includes shipping cost as a control variable (Gilkeson & Reynolds, 2003). We introduce the examination of international delivery because we believe that, with the increasing level of international activity in Internet retailing and Internet auctions, international shipping will become more important to sellers wishing to ensure the largest possible set of potential bidders. To gain a more complete perspective on all factors impacting auction prices, we will include each of the aforementioned delivery attributes in our analysis.

Recent scholarly commentary identifies three approaches that researchers have taken in their studies of Internet auctions: (1) concept discovery, which explores new phenomena; (2) process explanation, which seeks to provide an economic, psychological, or social explanation for behavior; and (3) theory deepening, which uses electronic markets to develop and test theories (Dholakia, 2005a). It has been noted that concept discovery and process explanation have received the majority of researchers' attention, while theory-deepening approaches are relatively few in number (Dholakia, 2005a). In the absence of established theory, continued exploratory work such as this study seems warranted.

While the foregoing findings from Internet auction research are noteworthy in their own right, they have a limited usefulness even when taken in sum. Without being able to ascertain which variables will provide the greatest benefit relative to other variables, businesses are left without guidance for generating price premiums in Internet auctions. In light of this need, we will capitalize upon previous work in a novel way. Rather than simply searching among the myriad attributes of an Internet auction to find those that are predictive of the final closing price, we propose a descriptive model based upon empirical data which ranks the attributes of Internet auctions by their importance. A classification and regression tree will be produced which can be used to guide businesspeople who are making decisions regarding how to auction their products in B2C auctions. At this point, we will turn our attention to decision-tree induction, a technique capable of producing decision rules for sellers.

Decision-Tree Induction Techniques

Decision rules, or rules of classification, can be deduced from data by using various machine-learning techniques (Tsai & Koehler, 1993). Information gained by analyzing data with these inductive learning techniques can be represented in various forms, including mathematical statements, logical expressions, formal grammar, decision trees, graphs, and networks (Kim, Lee, Shaw, Chang, & Nelson, 2001). Decision trees are essentially visual presentations of sets of nested if-then statements. One advantage of using decision trees is that they depict rules that can be readily expressed in words, thus facilitating comprehension by decision-makers (Kim, Lee, Shaw, Chang, & Nelson, 2001).

Several algorithms for building decision trees exist; they include CART (Classification and Regression Trees), QUEST (Quick, Unbiased and Efficient Statistical Tree), SLIQ (Supervised Learning In Quest), CHAID (Chi-squared Automatic Interaction Detector), IC (Interval Classifier), ID3, and C5.0 (Agarwal, Arning, Bollinger, Mehta, Shcafer, & Srikant, 1996; Mehta, Agarwal, & Rissanen, 1996; Quinlan, 1990). While decision-tree induction allows data analysts to deduce decision rules for both continuous and discrete variables, not all algorithms are equally well-suited for use with both types of variables. For instance, CHAID and C5.0 are restricted to the analysis of categorical variables only (Berry & Linoff, 1997; Zanakis & Becerra-Fernandez, 2005). CART, on the other hand, can analyze either categorical or continuous variables. Classification-tree analysis can be used for categorical criterion[2] variables; regression-tree analysis is used for continuous criterion variables (Brieman, Friedman, Olshen, & Stone, 1984). Because of this characteristic of the CART algorithm, and because we intend to make binary splits of our dataset into price premium and non-price premium groups at each node, CART is ideally suited to our study. We now turn to a brief description of the CART decision-tree induction process.

Classification- and Regression-Tree Analysis (CART) is a nonparametric procedure that determines the optimal decision tree for classifying observations on the basis of a large number of predictive variables (Brieman, Friedman, Olshen, & Stone, 1984). CART recursively splits a dataset into non-overlapping subgroups based upon the independent variables until splitting is no longer possible (Kim, Lee, Shaw, Chang, & Nelson, 2001). One of the principal advantages of CART is that it tends to be less-biased than other data analysis methods (Lhose, Biolsi, Walker, & Reuter, 1994; Sorensen, Miller, & Ooi, 2000; Zanakis & Becerra-Fernandez, 2005). For instance, multiple discriminant analysis (MDA) and LOGIT methodologies need to satisfy the assumption of multivariate normality for independent variables; in addition, MDA requires that the groups' covariance structure be equal. Thus, if the variables follow some distribution other than the multivariate normal distribution, MDA and LOGIT will give biased results. The assumptions of multivariate normality and equal covariance can be easily violated in empirical datasets; biased classification can result. In such a situation, CART is preferable because it rests upon more realistic, less-frequently violated assumptions. CART assumes only that the groups are discrete, non-overlapping, and identifiable (Brieman, Friedman, Olshen, & Stone, 1984). Thus, CART is a data analysis technique that may be well-suited to real-world electronic commerce datasets. Now that some of the merits of CART have been described, we turn to an explanation of the process of decision-tree induction with CART.

The decision-tree induction technique begins as a dataset is subdivided into *N* sub-datasets. *N-1* subsets are used as training datasets, and the remaining dataset is used to test the model. The first training dataset is analyzed to find the single most important independent variable for classifying the observations into two groups. CART thus makes its most significant split first, at the root node (Berry & Linoff, 1997; Zanakis & Becerra-Fernandez, 2005). Each subgroup is then examined again with the algorithm to find the next-most important variable for classifying observations. After this partition, the process continues until only inconsequential variables remain (Berry & Linoff, 1997). The possibility of erroneously classifying some observations is computed by summing the predictive error rate at each split (Zanakis & Becerra-Fernandez, 2005). At this point, the tree is "pruned" to remove branches that inflate the error rate without providing substantial improvements in predictive power (Berry & Linoff, 1997). After the decision tree is generated from the first training dataset, the subsequent training datasets are analyzed to refine the tree. This process is known as cross-validation. Analysis of the training datasets thus generates a decision tree—a predictive model for classifying observations. Finally, the test dataset is analyzed to verify that the decision tree generated using the training dataset accurately classifies the remainder of the data as well.

To our knowledge, the use of decision-tree induction techniques to analyze Internet auction data and generate decision rules has not been undertaken. The application of the decision-tree analysis technique to Internet auction data may help to unify and bring coherence to the disparate extant findings in Internet auction research. It may also provide perspective on the relative importance of the numerous factors that have been proven to significantly impact auction outcome.

METHOD

We present the following analysis in order to answer questions about the variables enabling merchants to earn price premiums in Internet auctions and also to describe the decision rules for these variables.

Sample

Data was collected over a one-month period in 2005 from eBay's U.S. Web site. Data from international industry leader eBay has been frequently used as the point of data collection for studies of Internet auctions (Ba & Pavlou, 2002; Brint, 2003; Bruce, Haruvy, & Rao, 2004; Dholakia, 2005b; Dholakia & Soltysinski, 2001; Gilkeson & Reynolds, 2003; Standifird, Roelofs, & Durham, 2004; Ward & Clark, 2002; Wilcox, 2000). Data from eBay is used for three reasons. First, eBay data is often used because the realism of such data is often preferable to data collected in an experimentally-controlled laboratory setting. Field experiments with auctions present an obvious trade-off between experimental control and realism (List & Lucking-Reiley, 2000). Laboratory experiments of auctions have been criticized on the grounds that subjects' behavior in an artificial laboratory environment may not be exactly the same as it would be in real-world conditions (Lucking-Reiley, 1999). It has been argued that experimental subjects have no incentive to develop optimal bidding strategies or apply experience gained from bidding (Ward & Clark, 2002). Collection of data from a field setting reduces questions regarding its generalizability to the marketplace. For these reasons, our goal of developing a guideline for selling in Internet auctions that is both descriptive and prescriptive leads us to follow the precedent of these researchers in using field data rather than experimental data.

The second reason that researchers often use eBay data is simply that eBay continues to be the Internet auctioneer of choice. EBay continues to lead the industry because of the circular effect of high seller volume eliciting high bidder interest, which in turn motivates sellers to continue to utilize eBay (Wingfield, 2001). Thus, eBay provides substantial numbers of auctions to observe and numerous points of measurement.

The third and final reason for the use of eBay data is that eBay is the largest and most international of the Internet auctioneers. Their auction mechanism and terminology are used more widely than any other auctioneer's. Thus, in an endeavor to provide the most generalizable results, we have selected eBay as the point of data collection for this study.

The items examined in this study are a DVD movie (404 auctions) and a popular MP3 player (366 auctions). All DVD auctions were for the same, new, identically-packaged movie title (the popular animated feature "The Incredibles"), and all MP3 player auctions were for the same, new, first-quality, identically-packaged model of the device (the 4 GB Apple iPod). All items were described as "new," "never-used," "new in box," or "brand new." We included these items to sample a reasonably-broad spectrum of items, ranging from inexpensive (DVD) to relatively expensive (MP3 player). We collected data during a three-week window of time to guard against effects due to changes in the market price (due to the release of new versions of the products, or due to a reduction in cost in fixed-price markets). Additionally, these items were examined because their value should not change with the fortunes of a team or individual (as sports collectibles or celebrity memorabilia might). Finally, the high sales volume of these items facilitates data collection.

Variables

The variables for this study are those listed and defined earlier in Table 1. As we noted earlier, variables studied in previous research as predictors of auction outcome can be classified into four categories: selling information, seller information, product information, and delivery information. In addition, the dependent variable of interest is final bid price. We define final bid price as the highest bid submitted for a given item.

Measurement of Variables

Table 2 reports our coding scheme for the variables in the Internet auction. Table 3 reports the descriptive statistics of the data for 404 DVD auctions and 366 MP3 player auctions.

Research Design

This study uses CART to determine the most important variables that sellers should consider to earn price premiums. The reader will recall first, that price premiums have been defined as *"the monetary amount above the average price received by multiple sellers for a certain matching product"* (Ba & Pavlou, 2002, pp. 247-248) and second, that CART is a nonparametric procedure that determines the optimal decision tree for

Table 2. Data coding scheme

Variables	Coding
Criterion (Dependent) Variable:	
Final Bid Price	Continuous: dollars and cents
Independent Variables:	
Selling Information Variables	
(1) Initial Bid Price	Continuous: dollars and cents
(2) Buy-Now Option	Binary: 0—not available, 1—available
(3) Auction Duration	Continuous: duration of auction in days
(4) Auction Ending Time	Categorical: 1: Weekday before 4 PM 2: Weekday after 4 PM 3: Weekend before 4 PM 4: Weekend after 4 PM
Seller Information Variables	
(5) Number of Positive Feedback Ratings	Continuous: number of positive ratings
(6) Number of Negative Feedback Ratings	Continuous: number of negative ratings
Product Information Variables	
(7) Number of Pictures	Continuous: number of pictures
(8) Number of Bids	Continuous: total number of bids submitted
Delivery Service Information Variables	
(9) Availability of Expedited Delivery	Binary: 0—not available, 1—available
(10) Availability of International Delivery	Binary: 0—not available, 1—available
(11) Shipping Cost	Continuous: dollars and cents

classifying observations on the basis of a large number of predictive variables (Brieman, Friedman, Olshen, & Stone, 1984).

We perform two analyses with CART: classification-tree analysis and regression-tree analysis. We first use final bid price as the criterion variable for classification-tree analysis. The classification-tree algorithm identifies the predictors that best separate our data into categories where an auction yields a price premium (denoted in subsequent figures as PP) or fails to yield a price premium (denoted as NPP). Second, we use number of bids as a criterion variable for regression-tree

analysis. We use number of bids as criterion variable because the number of bids is highly and directly correlated with the final bid price. Thus, the results should be substantially similar to those in the classification-tree analysis.

In the tree-building process, CART requires that the user select a computational method for validating the tree. CART provides cross validation in which the dataset is divided into N sub-datasets. $N-1$ subsets are used as training datasets, and the remaining dataset is used for testing the model. To validate our trees, we use 10-fold cross-validation, a procedure in which

Table 3. Descriptive statistics

	DVD Movie (N=404)		MP3 Player (N=366)	
	Mean	Std. Dev.	Mean	Std. Dev.
Criterion (Dependent) Variable:				
Final Bid Price	9.74	2.94	187.58	19.34
Independent Continuous variables:				
(1) Initial Bid Price	4.58	3.89	34.98	69.39
(3) Auction Duration	4.47	2.20	2.93	2.05
(5) Number of Positive Feedback Ratings	849	2616	2374	3176
(6) Number of Negative Feedback Ratings	5.70	9.35	20.04	32.38
(7) Number of Pictures	0.58	0.56	2.58	1.71
(8) Number of Bids	6.14	4.23	23.28	12.60
(11) Shipping Cost	4.20	1.07	16.32	5.50
Independent Categorical Variables				
	Frequencies		Frequencies	
(2) Buy-Now option	No: 384, Yes: 20		No: 357, Yes: 9	
(4) Auction Ending Time				
Weekday Morning	98		164	
Weekday Afternoon	153		48	
Weekend Morning	50		20	
Weekend Afternoon	103		134	
(9) Availability of Expedited Delivery	No: 354, Yes: 50		No: 256, Yes: 110	
(10) Availability of International Delivery	No: 187, Yes: 217		No: 130, Yes: 236	

nine subsets are used as a training sample, and one subset is used as a test sample (Steinberg & Colla, 1997). In the10-fold cross-validation process, the data are divided into approximately 10 equal subsets, where subsets are determined by random sampling on the criterion variable, and the tree-growing process is repeated 10 times.

RESULTS

Figure 1 and Figure 2 demonstrate the decision trees of the two different data sets that have been induced using CART analysis. Table 4 summarizes the decision rules derived from the trees. In the first dataset (the DVD movie), the classification-tree analysis shows that if the initial bid price is greater than $9.63, then the final bid price is above the average final bidding price. In other words, when sellers set the initial bid price at a level greater than $9.63, these sellers earn a price premium (PP). This result (shown both at the top of Figure 1 and also as Rule 1 in Table 4) shows that the initial bid price significantly impacts the final bid price (a finding consistent with earlier regression-based Internet auction studies). The

Figure 1. Decision tree for DVD movie

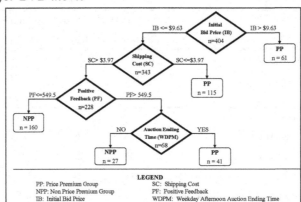

Figure 2. Decision tree for MP3 player

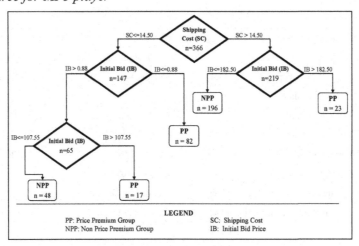

remaining rules pertain to situations in which the sellers' initial bid price is less than $9.63. These rules together show that shipping cost, positive feedback, and the auction ending time are important determinants of price premiums. Rule 2 (see both Figure 1 and Table 4) shows that if the shipping cost is less than or equal to $3.97, a price premium is earned. Rules 3 through 5 indicate that, in the situation of relatively-high shipping cost, positive feedback and an ending time during the PM hours of the weekday are predictors of price premiums. In Rule 3, if the seller has less than

549.5 positive feedback ratings, the seller fails to earn a price premium. Rule 4 and Rule 5 together show that if the seller has more than 549.5 positive feedback ratings, the ending time of the auction plays an important role. If the auction does not end during the PM hours of a weekday, the items fail to earn a price premium.

The fit statistics for the model are as follows. Resubstitution relative cost for the optimal tree is 0.428 and its complexity is 0.006. In addition, error rates for misclassification based on the criterion variable are 0.24 for price premiums and 0.23 for

Table 4. Decision rules based on CART analysis for DVD dataset (N=404)

	Rule for Terminal Node
Classification-Tree Analysis: Dependent Variable = Final Bid Price	
Rule 1	IF Initial Bid Price (IB) > $9.63, THEN Price Premium Group (PP).
Rule 2	IF Initial Bid Price (IB) <= $9.63 AND Shipping Cost (SC) <= $3.97, THEN Price Premium Group (PP).
Rule 3	IF Initial Bid Price (IB) <= $9.63 AND Shipping Cost (SC) > $3.97 AND Positive Feedback (PF) <= 549.5, THEN Non Price Premium Group (NPP).
Rule 4	IF Initial Bid Price (IB) <= $9.63 AND Shipping Cost (SC) > $3.97 AND Positive Feedback (PF) > 549.5 AND Ending Time ≠ Weekday afternoon, THEN Price Premium Group (PP).
Rule 5	IF Initial Bid Price (IB) <= $9.63 AND Shipping Cost (SC) > $3.97 AND Positive Feedback (PF) > 549.5 AND Ending Time = Weekday afternoon, THEN Non Price Premium Group (NPP).
Regression-Tree Analysis: Dependent Variable = Number of Bids	
Rule 1	IF IB <= $ 3.15, THEN Average Number of Bids (AVG-NB) = 9.29
Rule 2	IF IB > $3.15 AND SC > $3.9, THEN Average Number of Bids (AVG-NB) = 2.93.
Rule 3	IF IB > $3.15 AND IB <= $9.25 AND SC <= $3.9, THEN Average Number of Bids (AVG-NB) = 6.28
Rule 4	IF IB > $9.25 AND SC <= $3.9, THEN Average Number of Bids (AVG-NB) = 2.73

non-price premium auctions. In other words, 24% of observations are misclassified to NPP and 23% of observations are misclassified to PP.

In regression-tree analysis, the initial bid price and shipping cost are the most important predictors, just as in classification-tree analysis (see the bottom half of Table 4 for regression-tree analysis). Rule 1 shows that if the initial bid price is less than or equal to $3.15, the average number of bids is 9.29. If the initial bid price is set above $3.15 and the shipping cost is greater than $3.90, then the average number of bids is 2.93 (Rule 2). If, however, the initial bid price is set above $3.15 but the shipping cost is less than $3.90, then the average number of bids is 6.28 (Rule 3). Finally, if the initial bid price is greater than $9.25 and the shipping cost is less than or equal to $3.90, then the average number of bids is 2.73. In regression analysis, CART does not report a misclassification rate.

In the MP3 player dataset, the first rule shows that if the shipping cost (SC) is greater than

$14.50 and the initial bid price (IB) is less than or equal to $182.50, then no price premium (NPP) is earned (see Figure 2 and Table 5, Rule 1). If, however, the shipping cost (SC) is less than or equal to $14.50 and the initial bid price is greater than $182.50, then a price premium (PP) is earned (Rule 2). These results show that the bidders were significantly influenced by shipping cost and the initial bid price. The remaining rules pertain to situations in which the shipping cost is less than or equal to $14.50. Rule 3 shows that if the shipping cost is less than or equal to $14.50, and the seller sets the initial bid less than or equal to $0.88, then a price premium was earned. In Rule 4, if the shipping cost is less than or equal to $14.50 and if the seller set the initial bid between $0.88 and $107.55, then the seller failed to earn a price premium. Rule 5 shows that if the shipping cost is less than or equal to $14.50 and if the seller set the initial bid price higher than $107.55, then a price premium was earned. In this dataset, resubstitution relative cost for the optimal tree is 0.348 and its complexity is 0.008. In addition, error rates for the NPP group and the PP group are 0.06 and 0.27, respectively.

In regression-tree analysis, the initial bid price and positive feedback ratings are the most important predictors, a slightly different result than in the classification-tree analysis. Rule 1 shows that if the initial bid price is greater than $135.40, the average number of bids is 2.27. If the initial bid price is above $85.00 and below $135.40, then the average number of bids is 14.44 (Rule 2). If the initial bid price is between $7.50 and $85.00, then the average number of bids is 21.34 (Rule 3). Finally, if the seller sets the initial bid price lower than $7.50, positive feedback ratings plays an important role. Specifically, if the initial bid price is lower than $7.50 and positive feedback ratings are greater than 2635.5, then the average number of bids is 25.74.

Based on the rules derived from CART analysis, initial bid price, shipping cost, and positive feedback appear as important variables to determine the final bid price for both products.

CONCLUDING REMARKS

Implications for Research

This study contributes to the literature in several ways. This study, with its broad examination of variables from earlier research, is a step towards a comprehensive theoretical understanding of B2C Internet auctions. Exploratory work to this point has identified significant variables, and here all variables have been considered concurrently to find the ones with the greatest relative import. Thus, this study may provide guidance as researchers begin to develop definitive lists of variables that impact the outcome of Internet auctions. The creation of such definitive lists has been identified as a necessary preliminary step to developing theory (Ba & Pavlou, 2002; Pavlou, 2002; Weick, 1995; Whetten, 1989).

More specifically, we have been able to identify three independent variables—shipping cost, initial bid price, and reputation—that may play a larger role in Internet B2C auctions than was

Table 5. Decision rules based on CART analysis for MP3 player dataset (N=366)

	Rule for Terminal Node
Classification-Tree Analysis: Dependent Variable = Final Bid Price	
Rule 1	IF SC > $14.50 AND IB < = $182.50, THEN NPP
Rule 2	IF SC > $14.50 AND IB > $182.50, THEN PP
Rule 3	IF SC <= $14.50 AND IB <= $0.88, THEN PP
Rule 4	IF SC <= $14.50 AND IB > $0.88 AND IB <= $107.55, THEN NPP
Rule 5	IF SC <= $14.50 AND IB > $107.55, THEN PP
Regression-Tree Analysis: Dependent Variable = Number of Bids	
Rule 1	IF IB > $135.40, THEN Average Number of Bids (AVG-NB) = 2.27
Rule 2	IF IB >= $85.00 AND IB < $135.40, THEN Average Number of Bids (AVG-NB) = 14.44
Rule 3	IF IB >= $7.50 AND IB < 85.40, THEN Average Number of Bids (AVG-NB) = 21.34
Rule 4	IF IB < $7.50 AND PF > 2635.5, THEN Average Number of Bids (AVG-NB) = 25.74

previously realized. In particular, the identification of shipping cost as a primary determinant of price premiums has not been previously reported by researchers. Our findings lead us to the conclusion that shipping cost is the single most important factor in earning price premiums in Internet auctions. This is somewhat surprising in light of the fact that so few researchers have considered shipping cost as a part of their models. Positive feedback was also found to be a critical factor in the ability to earn price premiums. This finding is in line with recent studies that place seller reputation in a place of great importance in Internet auctions (Ba & Pavlou, 2002; Bruce, Haruvy, & Rao, 2004; McDonald & Slawson, 2002; Ottaway, Bruneau, & Evans, 2003). Initial bid price was found to be a critical factor in our study, but has not been found to be significant in others (Gilkeson & Reynolds, 2003). We argue that initial bid price is significant because a low initial bid price attracts the greatest number of possible bidders. Sellers desire to have the largest possible number of bidders, because having more bidders helps to ensure that an item does not remain unpurchased. Because of the inconclusive history of this variable, further examination is warranted. Finally, ending time has been proposed as a significant factor in popular literature (Ribeiro, 2004; Witt, 2005) but, to our knowledge, has not been conclusively linked to auction outcome until this study found a weekday afternoon end time to be a significant predictor of the ability to earn a price premium.

We also note that the CART analysis performed here produces results that are similar to the vast majority of existing empirical work on Internet auctions. The majority of previous work has used some form of regression analysis to reach its conclusions; CART corroborates these results using a different methodology. CART has been used in e-commerce research (Kim, Lee, Shaw, Chang, & Nelson, 2001), but has not, to our knowledge, been applied to the specific topic of Internet auctions. One of the strengths of CART is that it is a non-parametric technique, which means that no assumptions are made regarding the distributions of the predictor variables. Normal, non-normal, skewed, categorical, and ordinal variables can be included in CART analyses. These conditions may be present in the datasets collected by Internet auction researchers, thus making CART a potentially useful analytic tool. For these reasons, the application of CART in Internet auction research is a new methodological contribution.

Implications for Practice

Internet Auctions have become a popular sales and marketing channel for businesses seeking to enhance profits. Offering auction services, selling by auction, and adopting the appropriate auction-pricing policy may increase the attractiveness of a Web site, reduce the inventory cost of slow-selling products, reduce transaction costs, and provide valuable insight into customer preferences. In some cases, retailers have realized revenue gains of 50% or more on excess inventory sold through Internet auctions rather than through liquidators (Gentry, 2003).

For the benefit of practitioners, we have demonstrated the use of a relatively new tool, CART Analysis, which can be used to investigate auctions. Businesses can use this tool, available in a number of data mining software packages, to glean insights from their data about how to most effectively list items for auction. Useful outputs of this analysis technique are the decision tree, which gives a fairly intuitive visual representation of the critical variables which are identified, and the table of decision rules, which demonstrates the priority of the critical factors. CART can provide complex, exact models that include decision rules for all variables considered in a given analysis. Here, we have attempted to strike a balance between simplicity and detail by demonstrating a simpler decision tree that indicates only the most important variables. Outputs are simple to interpret (particularly for individuals with little statistical training in regression techniques), provide precise results, and suggest logical, sequential decisions to practitioners. Also, we note that CART analysis is essentially a data-driven method; it is a tool that can be useful even when the analyst has little experience in selling the specific product for which he or she may be developing decision rules. Finally, as noted in the previous section, CART does not require that the data be normally distributed, thus making it a viable option in situations where techniques with more stringent assumptions will not work.

More practically, based upon our findings, merchants desiring to utilize Internet auctions should consider competing with other sellers on the bases of shipping cost, reputation, initial bid price, and auction ending time. We urge caution, however, in applying these findings to products that differ from the ones used in our study. The specific decision rules generated by our analysis may not be widely generalizable to other products (or even to other movie titles or other MP3 players). Investigations of other types of products may generate different decision rules. We encourage sellers to investigate each of the variables listed earlier in Table 1 to find the factors that are most important for the particular product being auctioned. Nevertheless, the growing corpus of literature on Internet auctions indicates that shipping cost, reputation, initial bid price, and auction ending time may be important in the sale of many other types of items as well (e.g., Brint, 2003; Gilkeson & Reynolds, 2003; McDonald & Slawson, 2002; Standifird, 2001).

Limitations

One limitation of this study is the use of a "greedy" classification algorithm. Classification trees use what is known as a "greedy" algorithm to determine splits in the dataset (Harrison, 1997). Some have criticized the use of classification trees because of the use of "greedy" algorithms, instead arguing that splits should be made based upon two or more levels at once (TwoCrows, 1999).

Essentially, the "greedy" algorithm executes its task without considering the impact that any split may have on subsequent splits (TwoCrows, 1999). Other criticisms come from researchers who have expressed a desire for classification systems that make multivariate rather than univariate splits (TwoCrows, 1999). These debates are outside the scope of this study. However, it is worth noting that in spite of these theoretical issues, classification trees continue to be widely used and trusted in data mining applications by researchers and software developers.

Another limitation of our study is that we have analyzed data on only two products. While the fact that we have only examined a DVD movie and an MP3 player does not diminish the fact that CART analysis has been demonstrated as a useful technique in Internet auction research and practice, it is a limitation from the standpoint of identifying significant independent variables. A broader selection of products and different types of analysis might generate more broadly-applicable guidelines for Internet auction retailers. For instance, both DVDs and MP3 players are small, easily transportable, internationally-used products. It is conceivable that different products would generate decision trees with different critical factors. Thus, while our specific decision rules may not be widely applicable, the technique that we have demonstrated is.

Similarly, we have collected data from only one Internet auctioneer. While eBay has a larger international presence than any other Internet auctioneer, we remind readers that caution should be used when applying the findings here to auctions conducted in different contexts.

A different type of data analysis might also present additional useful findings. Other approaches for analyzing Internet auction datasets include, but are not limited to, binary logistic regression (with the auction's final closing price as a binary dependent variable, for instance) and multiple regression (perhaps with number of bids as a dependent variable). Using the same data from which the decision trees were generated, both binary logistic regression and multiple regression identify predictors very similar to those identified in CART analysis (interested readers may consult Appendix B for these results). These analyses identify significant independent variables, but do not generate sequential decision rules. Thus, it is likely that such techniques may be of greater interest to researchers than to practitioners. One final point with regard to alternate data analysis techniques deserves mention. The reader will recall from earlier discussion that regression techniques have more stringent assumptions than CART, and thus regression may not be appropriate for analysis of all datasets.

Future Research

One opportunity for future research is the investigation of auctions of different types of products. DVDs and MP3 players represent only a small fraction of the myriad items that are auctioned on the Internet. It is conceivable that auctions of different types of items may yield different decision rules. An examination of how the type of product impacts auction outcome may be a fruitful area of inquiry for researchers.

Future work will also need to delve into the motivations for bidder, seller, and auctioneer behavior. This is necessary in order to more completely explain the significance of findings in Internet auction studies. Some researchers have examined the roles that bidder experience (Ward & Clark, 2002; Wilcox, 2000), bidder strategy (Bapna, Goes, & Gupta, 2003; Easley & Tenorio, 2004), bidder acceptance of technology (Stafford & Stern, 2002), and bidder motivation (Cameron & Galloway, 2005; Standifird, Roelofs, & Durham, 2004) play in Internet auctions. As this study has assisted in the development of sellers' decision rules and strategies for Internet auctions, we believe future research should continue to examine

bidders' decision rules and strategies as well. Future work could integrate findings from these two streams of Internet auction research, fitting the seller model of behavior to the bidder model. The ultimate goal should be the development of a comprehensive model of buyer and seller characteristics, motivation, and behavior.

REFERENCES

Agarwal, R., Arning, A., Bollinger, T., Mehta, M., Shcafer, J., & Srikant, R. (1996). *The quest data mining system.* Paper presented at the 2nd International Conference on Knowledge Discovery in Databases and Data Mining, Portland, OR.

Ba, S., & Pavlou, P. A. (2002). Evidence of the effect of trust building technology in electronic markets: Price premiums and buyer behavior. *MIS Quarterly, 26*(3), 243-269.

Ba, S., Whinston, A. B., & Zhang, H. (2003). Building trust in online auction markets through an economic incentive mechanism. *Decision Support Systems, 35*(3), 273-286.

Bapna, R., Goes, P., & Gupta, A. (2000). A theoretical and empirical investigation of multi-item on-line auctions. *Information Technology and Management, 1*(1-2), 1-23.

Bapna, R., Goes, P., & Gupta, A. (2001). Insights and analyses of online auctions. *Association for Computing Machinery. Communications of the ACM, 44*(11), 42-50.

Bapna, R., Goes, P., & Gupta, A. (2003). Analysis and design of business-to-consumer online auctions. *Management Science, 49*(1), 85-102.

Bapna, R., Goes, P., Gupta, A., & Karuga, G. (2002). Optimal design of the online auction channel: Analytical, empirical, and computational insights. *Decision Sciences, 33*(4), 557-578.

Berry, M., & Linoff, G. (1997). *Data mining techniques for marketing, sales, and customer support*. New York: John Wiley & Sons.

Breiman, L., Friedman, J., Olshen, R., & Stone, C. (1984). *Classification and regression trees*. Belmont, CA: Wadsworth International Group.

Brint, A. T. (2003). Investigating buyer and seller strategies in online auctions. *The Journal of the Operational Research Society, 54*(11), 1177-1188.

Bruce, N., Haruvy, E., & Rao, R. (2004). Seller rating, price, and default in online auctions. *Journal of Interactive Marketing, 18*(4), 37-51.

Budish, E., & Takeyama, L. N. (2001). Buy prices in online auctions: Irrationality on the Internet? *Economics Letters, 72*(3), 325-334.

Cameron, D., & Galloway, A. (2005). Consumer motivations and concerns in online auctions. *International Journal of Consumer Studies, 29*(3), 181-193.

Chong, B., & Wong, M. (2005). Crafting an effective customer retention strategy: A review of halo effect on customer satisfaction in online auctions. *International Journal of Management and Enterprise Development, 2*(1), 12-26.

Crockett, R. O. (1999). Going, going...richer. *Business Week* (3659), EB16.

Dholakia, U. M. (2005a). Concept discovery, process explanation, and theory deepening in e-marketing research: The case of online auctions. *Marketing Theory, 5*(1), 117-124.

Dholakia, U. M. (2005b). The usefulness of bidders' reputation ratings to sellers in online auctions. *Journal of Interactive Marketing, 19*(1), 31-41.

Dholakia, U. M., & Soltysinski, K. (2001). Coveted or overlooked? The psychology of bidding for comparable listings in digital auctions. *Marketing Letters, 12*(3), 225-237.

Ding, M., Elishaberg, J., Huber, J., & Saini, R. (2005). Emotional bidders - An analytical and experimental examination of consumers' behavior in a Priceline-like reverse auction. *Management Science, 51*(3), 352-365.

Easley, R. F., & Tenorio, R. (2004). Jump bidding strategies in Internet auctions. *Management Science, 50*(10), 1407-1420.

eBay (2006). eBay Inc. announces fourth quarter and full year 2005 financial results. Retrieved April 3, 2006, from www.investor.ebay.com/news/Q105/ebay0420-2932ld.pdf

Engelbrecht-Wiggans, R. (1980). Auctions and bidding models: A survey. *Management Science, 26*(2), 119-143.

Geng, X., Stinchcombe, M., & Whinston, A. B. (2001). Radically new product introduction using on-line auctions. *International Journal of Electronic Commerce, 5*(3), 169-189.

Gentry, C. R. (2003). Recycled returns. *Chain Store Age, 79*(1), 72-73.

Gilkeson, J. H., & Reynolds, K. (2003). Determinants of Internet auction success and closing price: An exploratory study. *Psychology & Marketing, 20*(6), 537-566.

Gregg, D., & Walczak, S. (2003). E-commerce auction agents and online-auction dynamics. *Electronic Markets, 13*(3), 242-251.

Grow, B. (2002). Excess inventory? EBay to the rescue. *Business Week*, 8.

Harrison, J. G. (1997). *Enhancements to the data mining process*. Unpublished Ph.D., Stanford University, CA.

Hu, X., Lin, Z., Whinston, A. B., & Zhang, H. (2004). Hope or hype: On the viability of escrow services as trusted third parties in online auction environments. *Information Systems Research, 15*(3), 236-250.

Kagel, J. H. (1995). A survey of experimental research. In J. H. Kagel & A. E. Roth (Eds.), *The handbook of experimental economics* (pp. 501-586). Princeton, NJ: Princeton University Press.

Kannan, P. K., & Kopalle, P. (2001). Dynamic pricing on the Internet: Importance and implications for consumer behavior. *International Journal of Electronic Commerce, 5*(3), 63-83.

Kim, J. W., Lee, B. H., Shaw, M. J., Chang, H.-L., & Nelson, M. (2001). Application of decision-tree induction techniques to personalized advertisements on Internet storefronts. *International Journal of Electronic Commerce, 5*(3), 45-62.

Klein, B., & Leffler, K. B. (1981). The role of market forces in assuring contractual performance. *The Journal of Political Economy, 89*(4), 615-641.

Klemperer, P. (1999). Auction theory: A guide to the literature. *Journal of Economic Surveys, 13*(3), 227-286.

Klemperer, P. (Ed.). (2000). *The economic theory of auctions.* Cheltenham, UK: Edward Elgar.

Krishna, V. (2002). *Auction theory.* San Diego, CA: Academic Press.

Lhose, G. L., Biolsi, K., Walker, N., & Reuter, H. H. (1994). A classification of visual representations. *Communications of the ACM, 37*(12), 36-49.

List, J. A., & Lucking-Reiley, D. (2000). Demand reduction in multiunit auctions: Evidence from a sportscard field experiment. *The American Economic Review, 90*(4), 961-982.

Lucking-Reiley, D. (1999). Using field experiments to test equivalence between auction formats: Magic on the Internet. *The American Economic Review, 89*(5), 1063-1081.

Lucking-Reiley, D. (2000a). Auctions on the Internet: What's being auctioned, and how? *The Journal of Industrial Economics, 48*(3), 227-253.

Lucking-Reiley, D. (2000b). Vickrey auctions in practice: From nineteenth-century philately to twenty-first-century e-commerce. *The Journal of Economic Perspectives, 14*(3), 183-193.

McAfee, R. P., & McMillan, J. (1987). Auctions and bidding. *Journal of Economic Literature, 25*(2), 699-739.

McDonald, C. G., & Slawson, V. C. (2002). Reputation in an Internet auction market. *Economic Inquiry, 40*(4), 633-650.

Mehta, K. (2002). *Understanding revenue drivers of electronic auctions.* Unpublished Ph.D., University of Illinois at Chicago.

Mehta, M., Agarwal, R., & Rissanen, J. (1996). *SLIQ: A fast, scalable classifier for data mining.* Paper presented at the Fifth International Conference on Extending Database Technology, Avignon, France.

Milgrom, P. (1985). The economics of competitive bidding: A selective survey. In L. Hurwicz, D. Schmeidler, and H. Sonnenschein (Ed.), *Social goals and social organization.* Cambridge: Cambridge University Press.

Milgrom, P. (1986). Auction theory. In T. E. Bewley (Ed.), *Advances in economic theory.* Cambridge: Cambridge University Press.

Milgrom, P. R., & Weber, R. J. (1982). A theory of auctions and competitive bidding. *Econometrica, 50*(5), 1089-1122.

Neo, B. S. (1992). The implementation of an electronic market for pig trading in Singapore. *Journal of Strategic Management Systems, 1*(5), 278-288.

Oh, W. (2002). C2C versus B2C: A comparison of the winner's curse in two types of electronic auctions. *International Journal of Electronic Commerce, 6*(4), 115-138.

Ottaway, T. A., Bruneau, C. L., & Evans, G. E. (2003). The impact of auction item image and buyer/seller feedback rating on electronic auctions. *The Journal of Computer Information Systems, 43*(3), 56-60.

Pavlou, P. A. (2002). Trustworthiness as a source of competitive advantage in online auction markets. *Academy of Management Proceedings*, A1-A7.

Porter, R., & Shoham, Y. (2004). On cheating in sealed bid auctions. *Decision Support Systems,* (39), 41-54.

Quinlan, J. R. (1990). Induction of decision trees. In J. W. Chavlik, W. Jude & T. G. Dietterich (Eds.), *Readings in machine learning* (pp. 57-69). San Mateo, CA: Morgan Kauffman.

Ribeiro, J. (2004, March 2). Researcher compiles auction data for online merchants. Retrieved June 7, 2005, from http://www.computerworld.com/managementtopics/ebusiness/story/0,10801,90668,00.html

Rothkopf, M. H. (1969). A model of rational competitive bidding. *Management Science, 15*(7), 362-374.

Rothkopf, M. H., & Harstad, R. M. (1994). Modeling competitive bidding: A critical essay. *Management Science, 40*(3), 364-384.

Segev, A., Beam, C., & Shanthikumar, J. G. (2001). Optimal design of Internet-based auctions. *Information Technology and Management, 2*(2), 121-163.

Seth, A., & Thomas, H. (1994). Theories of the firm: Implications for strategy research. *Journal of Management Studies, 31*, 165-191.

Shapiro, C. (1983). Premiums for high quality products as returns to reputations. *The Quarterly Journal of Economics, 98*(4), 659-680.

Sinha, A. R., & Greenleaf, E. A. (2000). The impact of discrete bidding and bidder aggressiveness on sellers' strategies in open English auctions: Reserves and covert shilling. *Marketing Science,* (19), 244-266.

Sorensen, E. H., Miller, K. L., & Ooi, C. K. (2000). The decision tree approach to stock selection. *Journal of Portfolio Management, 27*(1), 42-52.

Stafford, M. R., & Stern, B. (2002). Consumer bidding behavior on Internet auction sites. *International Journal of Electronic Commerce, 7*(1), 135-150.

Standifird, S. S. (2001). Reputation and e-commerce: EBay auctions and the asymmetrical impact of positive and negative ratings. *Journal of Management, 27*(3), 279-295.

Standifird, S. S., Roelofs, M. R., & Durham, Y. (2004). The impact of eBay's buy-it-now function on bidder behavior. *International Journal of Electronic Commerce, 9*(2), 167-176.

Stark, R., & Rothkopf, M. H. (1979). Competitive bidding: A comprehensive bibliography. *Operations Research, 27*(2), 364-391.

Steinberg, D., & Colla, P. (1997). *CART: Interface and documentation*. San Diego, CA: Salford Systems.

Subramaniam, R., Mittal, V., & Inman, J. J. (2004). Revenue equivalence in online auctions: The case of Yahoo and eBay. In P. T. L. Popkowski Leszczyc (Ed.), *Advances in consumer research* (Vol. 31, pp. 1-2).

Tsai, L. H., & Koehler, G. J. (1993). The accuracy of concepts learned from induction. *Decision Support Systems, 10*(2), 161-172.

TwoCrows (1999). *Introduction to data mining and knowledge discovery*. Potomac, MD: Two Crows Corporation.

van Heck, E., & van Damme, E. (1997). *New entrants and the role of IT: The tele-flower auctions in the Netherlands*. Paper presented at the 30th HICSS, Hawaii.

Vickrey, W. (1961). Counterspeculation, auctions, and competitive sealed tenders. *Journal of Finance, 16*(1), 8-37.

Vogelstein, F., Boyle, M., Lewis, P., & Kirkpatrick, D. (2004). 10 tech trends to bet on. *Fortune, 149*(4), 75-81.

Ward, S. G., & Clark, J. M. (2002). Bidding behavior in on line auctions: An examination of the eBay Pokemon card market. *International Journal of Electronic Commerce, 6*(4), 139-155.

Weick, K. (1995). What theory is not, theorizing is. *Administrative Science Quarterly, 40*(3), 385-390.

Whetten, D. (1989). What constitutes a theoretical contribution. *Academy of Management Review, 14*(4), 490-495.

Wilcox, R. T. (2000). Experts and amateurs: The role of experience in Internet auctions. *Marketing Letters, 11*(4), 363-374.

Wilson, R. B. (1969). Communications to the editor: Competitive bidding with disparate information. *Management Science, 15*(7), 446-449.

Wilson, R. B. (1987). Auction theory. In J. Eatwell, M. Milgate & P. Newman (Eds.), *The new Palgrave: A dictionary of economic theory*. London: Macmillan.

Wingfield, N. (2001). EBay watch: Corporate sellers put the online auctioneer on even faster track --- Goods from IBM, Disney help dot-com pioneer post a surge in profits --- Why mom and pop are mad. *Wall Street Journal,* A.1.

Witt, L. (2005). Building sales on eBay. Retrieved May 10, 2005, from http://www.fortune.com/fortune/smallbusiness/answercentral/0,15704,601929

Zanakis, S., & Becerra-Fernandez, I. (2005). Competitiveness of nations: A knowledge discovery examination. *European Journal of Operational Research, 166*(2), 185-211.

ENDNOTES

[1] It should be noted, however, that this study examined the sale of sterling silver flatware, including pieces manufactured in the 1890's. This study may only demonstrate the fact that sales of collectible items will likely be disproportionately affected by the quality of the item and the level of detail in its description.

[2] In classification trees, the dependent variable is often referred to as the "criterion variable." We will adopt this usage.

This work was previously published in International Journal of E-Business Research, Vol. 4, Issue 1, edited by I. Lee, pp. 1-21, copyright 2008 by IGI Publishing, formerly known as Idea Group Publishing (an imprint of IGI Global).

Section VI
Emerging Trends

Chapter XXVII
E–Commerce Adoption Barriers in Small Businesses and the Differential Effects of Gender

Robert C. MacGregor
University of Wollongong, Australia

Lejla Vrazalic
University of Wollongong, Australia

EXECUTIVE SUMMARY

Over the last decade, the Internet and Internet technologies such as electronic commerce have experienced phenomenal growth. However, research shows that small businesses have been slow to adopt and to implement e-commerce due to a variety of barriers or impediments. Our understanding of these barriers and their importance has been fragmented and incomplete. This article presents an exploratory study of regional small businesses in Sweden that aims to improve our knowledge about e-commerce adoption barriers and to determine if there are any differences in the level of importance assigned to different barriers by males and females. The results of the study suggest that e-commerce adoption barriers fall into one of two distinct groupings: too difficult to implement or unsuitable to the business. The results also show that while males rate the difficulties of implementing e-commerce as more important, females indicate more concern about the unsuitability of e-commerce. The results of the study have significant implications for government organizations engaged in promoting e-commerce adoption, particularly among small businesses in regional areas.

INTRODUCTION

The last 20 years have seen far-ranging social, political, economic, and technological changes in society. Specifically, there has been a shift from a traditional male-dominated manufacturing economy to a retail and service sector-based economy that has seen females taking far greater levels of participation (Cox, 1999; Teltscher, 2002). The advent of affordable technology has given rise to more flexible working arrangements that have the potential to facilitate global participation and interaction. These changes have led to a greater equality in the makeup of the workforce (Singh, 2001; Teltscher, 2002), in small businesses, in particular. In some areas of the small business sector more than 70% of the workforce is female, with 24% of these small businesses being owned or managed by women (Schmidt & Parker, 2003), while in Asia, women head 35% of small to medium enterprises (Brisco, 2002).

During the same period, the Internet and Internet technologies such as electronic commerce (e-commerce) have experienced a phenomenal growth. Viewed as a potential pot of gold for small business growth and expansion, e-commerce involves the application of Web-based information technologies toward automating business processes, transactions, and workflows, and buying and selling information, products, and services using computer networks (Kalakota & Whinston, 1997). E-commerce technology has the potential to become a major source of competitive advantage to small businesses, because it is a cost-effective way to reach customers globally and to compete on a par with larger counterparts. Governments worldwide have recognized this and have created various funding schemes and initiatives in order to facilitate e-commerce adoption in small businesses. For example, in Sweden, government involvement has included funded studies of e-commerce adoption (Johansson, 2003; Larsson, Hedelin, & Gärling, 2003; Magnusson, 2001; MIEC, 2003) and, more recently, the development of courses in order for small businesses to promote e-commerce adoption.

Yet, despite government support for e-commerce adoption by small businesses, it is mainly larger businesses that have reaped the benefits of this technology (Riquelme, 2002). In contrast, the rate of e-commerce adoption in the small business sector has remained relatively low (Magnusson, 2001; Poon & Swatman, 1998; Van Akkeren & Cavaye, 1999). This sluggish pace of e-commerce diffusion into small businesses has been attrib-

uted to various barriers or impediments that are faced by these organizations. A number of different e-commerce adoption barriers have been documented in research studies (Lawrence, 1997; Purao & Campbell, 1998; Quayle, 2002; Riquelme, 2002; Van Akkeren & Cavaye, 1999). However, the results of these studies paint a fragmented and incomplete picture of factors that inhibit e-commerce adoption. Yet, empirical research to develop and consolidate our understanding of e-commerce adoption barriers has been scarce, and subsequently, the effectiveness of strategies to overcome these barriers has been limited.

Despite the increasing levels of participation by females in the small business sector (Cox, 1999; Gebler, 2000; Singh, 2001; Teltscher, 2002), much of the research concerned with gender differences in e-commerce adoption and use has centered on individual use of Web sites and the Internet (Akhter, 2003; Gilbert, Lee-Kelley, & Barton, 2003; Wolin & Korgaonker, 2003). A number of earlier studies (Mazzarol, Volery, Doss, & Thein, 1999; Perez, Carnicer, & Sanchez, 2002; Venkatesh, Morris, & Ackerman, 2000) have shown that gender, among other factors, was associated with the level of information technology (IT) adoption. However, little has been done to examine whether there are any gender differences in the importance assigned to different barriers in the e-commerce adoption decision-making process.

This article presents some of the findings of a larger, ongoing study of small businesses located in regional areas in developed OECD countries (including Sweden, Australia and the USA) that investigated e-commerce adoption barriers, among other things. The research presented here is part of an extended study of e-commerce adoption in regional small businesses located in Sweden only. The results from other locations are reported elsewhere (MacGregor, Vrazalic, Bunker, Carlsson, & Magnusson, 2004; Vrazalic, MacGregor, Carlsson, Bunker, & Magnusson, 2002). Regional small businesses were chosen due to the disadvantages inherent to their location (Keniry, Blums, Notter, Radford, & Thomson, 2003; Larsson et al., 2003). While it is beyond the scope of this article to describe the entire Swedish study, which examined a number of issues associated with e-commerce, one of the primary aims of the research was to analyze correlations between various e-commerce barriers faced by small businesses in regional areas. A secondary aim was to determine whether any differences exist between male and female small business owners in the level of importance they assign to different e-commerce barriers when making decisions about whether to adopt e-commerce.

The article begins by examining the nature of small businesses and by identifying features that are unique to the sector in order to set the context for the study. Small businesses in regional areas also are discussed specifically. This is followed by a literature review of e-commerce adoption barriers that were used to develop a survey instrument for the Swedish study. The article then provides a review of the previous literature concerned with gender differences in the use of Internet technologies. A description of the study and the results ensues and includes Correlation Matrices and a Factor Analysis. Finally, the results of the study are discussed, along with the conclusion and limitations.

BACKGROUND

This section provides an overview of the relevant background and previous research into small businesses (including small businesses in regional areas), e-commerce adoption barriers, and gender differences in Internet use.

Small Businesses

In Europe, small businesses are defined as organizations that employ less than 50 people (Europa, 2003). Yet, despite their size, small businesses are seen as significant contributors to the prosperity of national economies. The European Commission views small businesses as the backbone of the European economy (Europa, 2003). More than 99% of all businesses in Sweden are classified as small to medium enterprises (SMEs), which means that they employ less than 250 people. Of those, 94% are small businesses with less than 10 employees (MIEC, 2003).

Small businesses are not simply scaled down versions of large businesses (Wynarczyk, Watson, Storey, Short, & Keasey, 1993). Although size is a major distinguishing factor, small businesses have a number of other unique features that set them apart from large businesses. There have been various studies carried out in order to isolate these features (Bunker & MacGregor, 2000; Dennis, 2000; Hill & Stewart, 2000; Miller & Besser, 2000; Reynolds, Savage, & Williams, 1994; Tetteh & Burn, 2001). An extensive review of the available literature was undertaken in order to identify and classify the features and to create a context for the study. An analysis of the features revealed that they could be classified into four general categories: features related to management, decision making and planning processes, features related to resource availability, features related to products/services and markets, and features related to risk taking and dealing with uncertainty. These are shown in Table 1.

Small Businesses in Regional Areas

Small businesses located in regional areas are affected by circumstances inherent to their location. Regional areas are defined as geographical areas located outside metropolitan centers and major cities and include inner and outer regions and remote and very remote areas. The study presented in this article only examined urbanized regional areas, which include inner and outer regions, rather than rural areas, which include remote and very remote areas. Regional areas are of particular interest to governments, because

Table 1. Features unique to small businesses

Features Related to Management, Decision Making, and Planning Processes	Relevant Literature
Centralized management strategy with a short-range planning perspective	Bunker & MacGregor (2000) Welsh & White (1981)
Poor management and business skills	Blili & Raymond (1993)
Strong desire for independence	Dennis (2000) Reynolds et al. (1994)
Decision-making processes rather than based on detailed planning and exhaustive study	Bunker & MacGregor (2000) Reynolds et al. (1994)
Owners and family values have a strong influence on the decision-making process	Bunker & MacGregor (2000) Reynolds et al. (1994) Dennis (2000)
Informal and inadequate planning and record-keeping processes	Tetteh & Burn (2001) Miller & Besser (2000)
Features Related to Resource Availability	
Difficulties obtaining finance and other resources and have fewer resources	Blili & Raymond (1993) Cragg & King (1993)
More reluctant to spend on information technology and have limited use of technology	Walczuch, Van Braven, & Lundgren (2000) Poon & Swatman (1997) MacGregor & Bunker (1996)
Lack of technical knowledge and specialist staff and provide little training for staff	Blili & Raymond (1993) Cragg & King (1993) Welsh & White (1981) Martin & Matlay (2001)
Features Related to Products/Services and Markets	
Narrow product/service range	Bunker & MacGregor (2000) Reynolds et al. (1994)
Limited share of the market (often a niche market) and rely on few customers	Hadjimanolis (1999) Lawrence (1997) Reynolds et al. (1994)
Product-oriented (unlike large businesses, which are more customer-oriented)	Bunker & MacGregor (2000) Reynolds et al. (1994)
Not interested in large shares of the market	Reynolds et al. (1994)
Features Related to Risk Taking and Dealing with Uncertainty	
Less control over external environment and face more uncertainty	Hill & Stewart (2000) Westhead & Storey (1996)
Face more risks and higher failure rates	DeLone (1988) Cochran (1981)
More reluctant to take risks	Walczuch et al. (2000) Dennis (2000)

they are characterized by high unemployment rates (Larsson et al., 2003), a shortage of skilled people, limited access to resources, and a lack of infrastructure (Keniry et al., 2003). Indeed, studies (Keniry et al., 2003) show that those features that are related to resource availability, risk taking, and dealing with uncertainty (see Table 1) are more prevalent in small businesses located in regional areas, compared to metropolitan areas.

Yet, at the same time, businesses located in regional areas have the potential to play a major role in developing those areas. This potential has not gone unnoticed by government organizations. The European Union views small businesses as a catalyst for regional development (Europa, 2003). In 2001, the Swedish Parliament passed legislation that resulted in the creation of Regional Development Councils (Johansson, 2003). The councils have a mandate to promote a positive business climate and sustainable growth in their respective regions. Small businesses have been earmarked as playing an important role in promoting growth, because they are seen as a key source of jobs and employment prospects (Keniry et al., 2003; Larsson et al., 2003).

To encourage growth and development in regional areas, government organizations have been promoting heavily the adoption of information and communication technology (ICT) by small businesses. In Sweden, the Swedish Business Development Agency (NUTEK) runs a national program known as IT.SME, which provides skills training in ICT for small businesses. The program targets regional small businesses, in particular (MIEC, 2003). The agency also runs a similar program that concentrates on increasing the use of ICT in small businesses located in regional areas in order to strengthen their competitiveness in the global market. Specifically, on the e-commerce front, the Swedish Alliance for Electronic Business set an objective of having 80% of small businesses starting to use e-commerce tools by the end of 2004 (MIEC, 2003).

Yet, despite these programs and initiatives, the rate of e-commerce adoption in small businesses has been reported as low. The reasons for this are diverse; however, they generally are categorized as barriers or inhibitors to e-commerce adoption. The following section will examine some of the barriers to e-commerce adoption that are faced by small businesses.

E-Commerce Adoption Barriers

E-commerce has been touted widely as providing small businesses with an opportunity for instant access to global markets and customers (Coviello & McAuley, 1999). However, research shows that it is mostly larger businesses that have benefited from e-commerce adoption (Riquelme, 2002), with small businesses showing a much slower pace of adoption. The reasons for this are diverse and have been examined in various studies as inhibitors or barriers that prevent small businesses from adopting and, subsequently, fully reaping the benefits of e-commerce.

Hadjimanolis (1999), in a study of e-commerce adoption by small businesses in Cyprus, classified these barriers into two types: internal and external. External barriers could be further categorized into supply barriers (difficulties obtaining finance and technical information), demand barriers (e-commerce not fitting with the products/services or not fitting with the way clients did business), and environmental barriers (security concerns). Internal barriers were subdivided further into resource barriers (lack of management and technical expertise) and system barriers (e-commerce not fitting with the current business practices). A summary of different e-commerce adoption barriers in small businesses based on an extensive literature review is presented in Table 2.

A number of previous studies (MacGregor, 2004; Vrazalic et al., 2002) have shown that while the size of the small business (in terms of number of employees) appears to have a bearing on the

Table 2. Summary of e-commerce adoption barriers in small businesses

Barriers to E-Commerce Adoption	Related Literature
High cost of implementation; Internet technologies too expensive to implement	Riquelme (2002) Van Akkeren & Cavaye (1999) Purao & Campbell (1998) Lawrence (1997) Iacovou, Benbasat & Dexter (1995)
E-commerce is too complex to implement F	ielding (1996) Quayle (2002)
Small businesses require short-term ROI and e-commerce is long-term L	awrence (1997) McGowan & Madey (1998)
Resistance to change because of the fear of new technology among employees	Van Akkeren & Cavaye (1999) Lawrence (1997)
Preference for and satisfaction with traditional manual methods (phone, fax, etc.)	Lawrence (1997) Venkatesan & Fink (2002)
Lack of technical skills and IT knowledge among employees; lack of computer-literate/specialized staff	Riquelme (2002) Van Akkeren & Cavaye (1999) Lawrence (1997) Iacovou et al. (1995) Quayle (2002) Damsgaard & Lyytinen (1998)
Lack of time to implement e-commerce	Van Akkeren & Cavaye (1999) Lawrence (1997) Walczuch et al. (2000)
E-commerce not deemed to be suited to the way the organization does business or the way our clients do business	Poon & Swatman (1997) Hadjimanolis (1999) Iacovou et al. (1995)
E-commerce not deemed to be suited to the products/services	Poon & Swatman (1997) Hadjimanolis (1999)
E-commerce perceived as a technology lacking direction L	awrence (1997)
Lack of awareness about business advantages/opportunities that e-commerce can provide	Iacovou et al. (1995) Quayle (2002)
Lack of available information about e-commerce L	awrence (1997)
Concern about security of e-commerce R	iquelme (2002) Van Akkeren & Cavaye (1999) Purao & Campbell (1998) Hadjimanolis (1999) Quayle (2002)
Lack of critical mass among customers, suppliers, and business partners H	adjimanolis (1999)
Heavy reliance on external consultants (often considered by small businesses to be inadequate) to provide necessary expertise	Van Akkeren & Cavaye (1999) Lawrence (1997)
Lack of e-commerce standards	Tuunainen (1998) Robertson & Gatignon (1986)

importance of barriers to e-commerce adoption, e-commerce barriers appear to be uniform across different business types. Other studies (Mac-Gregor & Bunker, 1996; Thong, Yap, & Raman, 1996; Yap, Soh, & Raman, 1992) have shown that, while vendor support as a surrogate for IT skill can reduce the impact of technical barriers, there is no equivalent reduction in organizational barriers.

There are limited studies (MacGregor & Vrazalic, 2005; MacGregor, Vrazalic, Carlsson, Pratt, & Harris, 2005) available about the extent of the e-commerce barriers in regional areas. However, they have shown that many of the barriers listed in Table 2, particularly those related to technical infrastructure, are more pronounced in businesses located in regional areas than those in metropolitan areas.

While research examining the inhibitors to e-commerce adoption in small businesses has identified a large number of barriers that prevent them from implementing e-commerce, there has not been any attempt to correlate the barriers or to examine whether there are any underlying factors to these barriers. Without having a clear awareness of the key issues and underlying factors that affect e-commerce adoption in small businesses, government initiatives such as the ones already described may prove to be ineffective and poorly targeted. Also, there have been no attempts to determine whether differences exist between the levels of importance that male and female small business owners assign to these barriers. The following section will highlight some of the previous research into gender differences in Internet use.

Gender Differences in Internet Use

An examination of the literature shows that very little has been carried out to determine whether any gender differences exist in relation to e-commerce barriers. A similar problem was encountered by Gilbert, et al (2003) in their examination of gender differences in technophobia. Their research combined earlier findings of Bandura (1977, cited in Gilbert et al., 2003) and of Brosnan (1998, cited in Gilbert et al., 2003) with Davis' (1989) original technology acceptance models to justify, as a basis for their own study, the use of literature concerned with gender differences and individual Internet use, since e-commerce literature was unavailable. A similar argument, suggesting that decisions to

adopt and use the Internet are essentially alike, whether they are for private or business use, is put forward here. Therefore, this section will examine previous research into gender differences in Internet use.

A number of studies have explored potential determinants of Internet use and have found gender to be an influential variable in predicting this use (Butler, 2000; Sexton, Johnson, & Hignite, 2002). Others have developed frameworks in order to explain gender differences in Internet use and online behavior (Rodgers & Harris, 2003). For example, prior studies by Singh (2001) and Simon (2001) found that females use the Internet as a tool, while males consider it something to be mastered. Studies also have suggested that males were less anxious than females about using computing technology (Gilroy & Desai, 1986; Meier & Lambert, 1991). Yet, according to Gebler (2000), in the year 2000, female Internet users exceeded male users. The implications of this event are significant, considering the previous research into the use of the Internet by females. Shade (1998) and Sheehan (1999) both found that females were more concerned with privacy and security issues and, subsequently, more cautious about using the Internet for online shopping and trading. Presumably, the same concerns would apply to female business owners considering e-commerce adoption. Kolsaker and Payne (2002) refuted these studies by finding no significant differences between the genders in relation to Internet privacy and security. It should be noted, however, that their study followed the surge of female users after 2000, while the studies by Shade (1998) and Sheehan (1999) preceded the widespread use of the Internet by females.

Although the gap between male and female Internet adoption rates has disappeared, resulting in a more gender-balanced use of the Internet, differences remain in how the Internet actually is used. For example, Akhter (2003) found that men still were more likely to use the Internet for shopping than women were. This would suggest that males may be more open to e-commerce adoption as business owners, because they are more willing to adopt the technology as consumers. However, empirical evidence of such a trend is not available. Although our knowledge of gender differences in relation to Internet adoption as users and consumers is broad, our understanding of gender differences in relation to e-commerce adoption as business owners is scant and inadequate. The exception is a study of e-commerce and teleworking in 112 Spanish small businesses by Perez, et al. (2002). The study, supported by earlier findings (Gilroy & Desai, 1986; Meier & Lambert, 1991) found that small businesses with female managers were significantly more concerned with the difficulty of using the technology than were their male counterparts. The study also cited cost of the technology and changes to work procedures as being of more concern to female managers.

The study described in the following section has two aims: (1) to improve our knowledge about e-commerce adoption barriers faced by small businesses in regional areas and (2) to examine the differences between males and females in the level of importance that they assign to different barriers when making decisions about adopting e-commerce.

METHODOLOGY

A number of research frameworks, including Davis' (1989) technical acceptance model (TAM), Rogers' (1995) Diffusion of Innovation theory, and the use of Grounded Theory (Glaser & Strauss, 1967) were considered and examined. While TAM is concerned with a system's perceived usefulness and ease of use, these factors normally are considered from an individual's viewpoint and in a static business structure. Several studies (Damanpour, 2001; Lee, 2001) have suggested that in order for e-commerce adoption to be valid, organizational restructuring must occur.

Furthermore, this study was concerned with e-commerce barriers from an organizational decision making rather than a personal perspective. As such, TAM was considered to be unsuitable. Rogers' (1995) theory of innovation diffusion also was considered. While it may be argued that e-commerce adoption in regional small businesses is a diffusion of innovation, Rogers' (1995) theory requires the trialability of technology. Since this study is concerned with non-adopters, Rogers' (1995) framework was found to be unsuitable for the research objectives. Furthermore, diffusion of innovation defines how an innovation is spread throughout a social system. Finally, as there were no overriding hypotheses, Grounded Theory also was examined. However, since the study did not employ ethnographic research methods, this framework also was rejected.

A number of previous studies (Daniel, 2003; Shiels, McIvor, & O'Reilly, 2003; Teo & Tan, 1998) that examined the role of business characteristics in the adoption and non-adoption of e-commerce by small businesses were examined. In all cases, the authors expressed the view that no framework adequately suited their approach and that ultimately, they were attempting to develop a model from quantitative analysis. As this study (and others that have been derived from the data presented in this article) ultimately are attempting to develop a model of non-adoption of e-commerce by small businesses, a similar approach is adopted.

The study presented here is part of a larger ongoing study into IT and e-commerce adoption in small to medium enterprises that began in 2002. The larger study was concerned primarily with small businesses located in regional areas, especially since no other research has investigated e-commerce adoption specifically in these areas. As a result, the study was conceived primarily as exploratory in nature. The larger study has been undertaken in Sweden and Australia and, more recently, in the US, with all three countries having similar economies according to the Organisation for Economic Co-operation and Development (OECD) classification, thus allowing for comparisons. The portion of the study presented in this article is concerned with e-commerce adoption barriers in Sweden only. Other issues, such as e-commerce adoption drivers, advantages and disadvantages of e-commerce, and the results from the Australian study, are reported elsewhere.

An examination of the literature concerned with e-commerce adoption in small businesses identified 10 of the most frequently cited e-commerce barriers, all of which were uniquely different and common to the studies examined. In order to both determine the applicability of these barriers and ensure that no other barriers have been excluded, a series of six in-depth, semi-structured interviews were conducted in Australia, where the study of conceived. All interviews were with owners/managers of small businesses (three of those had adopted e-commerce, while the other three had not). All of the identified barriers were found to be applicable, and no additional barriers were forthcoming by the majority of the interviewees. Based on the six in-depth interviews, a survey instrument was developed in order to collect data about e-commerce adoption barriers (among other things). A series of pilot tests of the instrument was conducted in regional small businesses in Australia. Based on the results of the pilot studies, the survey instrument was translated into Swedish (and retranslated back to English for checking purposes). The survey was administered to owners of small businesses as the ultimate decision makers for e-commerce adoption or non-adoption (Reynolds et al., 1994; Welsh & White, 1981). Respondents who had

Figure 1. Question about barriers to e-commerce adoption used in survey

23. This question relates to the reasons your organization is not using e-commerce. Below is a list of statements indicating possible reasons. Please rate each statement on a scale of 1 to 5 to indicate how important each reason was to your decision NOT to use e-commerce, as follows:

1 = the reason was very unimportant to your decision not to use e-commerce
2 = the reason was unimportant to your decision not to use e-commerce
3 = the reason had little importance to your decision not to use e-commerce
4 = the reason was important to your decision not to use e-commerce
5 = the reason was very important to your decision not to use e-commerce

Our organization does not use e-commerce because: R	ating
E-commerce is not suited to our products/services.	1 2 3 4 5
E-commerce is not suited to our way of doing business. 1	2 3 4 5
E-commerce is not suited to the ways our clients (customers and/or suppliers) do business.	1 2 3 4 5
E-commerce does not offer any advantages to our organization.	1 2 3 4 5
We do not have the technical knowledge in the organization to implement e-commerce.	1 2 3 4 5
E-commerce is too complicated to implement.	1 2 3 4 5
E-commerce is not secure.	1 2 3 4 5
The financial investment required to implement e-commerce is too high for us.	1 2 3 4 5
We do not have time to implement e-commerce. 1	2 3 4 5
It is difficult to choose the most suitable e-commerce standard with so many different options available.	1 2 3 4 5

not adopted e-commerce were asked to rate the importance of each barrier to their decision not to adopt e-commerce using a standard five-point Likert scale (as shown in Figure 1). The Likert scale responses were assumed to posses the characteristics of an interval measurement scale for data analysis purposes.

The survey also contained questions used to build a profile of the respondents, including the gender, age, and highest qualifications held by the small business owner, the size of the small business (measured in terms of number of full-time equivalent employees), length of time in business, business sector, market focus, sales turnover, and

Table 3. Profile of survey respondents and non-adopters

E-COMMERCE	Total Number	Percentage
Adopters	152	48.5%
Non-Adopters	123	39.3%
Missing	*38*	*12.2%*
GENDER OF (PRIMARY) OWNER (Non-Adopters Only)		
Male	106	86.2%
Female	17	13.8%
Missing	*0*	*0*
SIZE OF BUSINESS (Non-Adopters Only)		
Single Owner	26	21.1%
1 to 9 employees	67	54.5%
10 to 19 employees	18	14.6%
20 to 49 employees	10	8.2%
Missing	*2*	*1.6%*
NO OF YEARS IN BUSINESS (Non-Adopters Only)		
Less than 1 year	3	2.4%
1 to 2 years	6	4.9%
3 to 5 years	15	12.2%
6 to 10 years	24	19.5%
11 to 20 years	31	25.2%
More than 20 years	43	35%
Missing	*1*	*0.8%*
BUSINESS SECTOR (Non-Adopters Only)		
Industrial	20	16.3%
Service	49	39.8%
Retail	23	18.7%
Finance	0	0
Other	31	25.2%
Missing	*0*	*0*
MARKET FOCUS (Non-Adopters Only)		
Local	74	60.2%
Regional	11	8.9%
National	24	19.5%
International	14	11.4%
Missing	*0*	*0*

computer use in the organization. For the purposes of this article, only the gender of the owner is of primary interest; however, some additional data will be reported in order to provide an insight into the profile of the respondents. It should be noted that where a small business had more than one owner, the gender of the primary owner was used. A primary owner was classified as the individual who either had a controlling interest in the business or, if all the owners had an equal interest, undertook the majority of the day-to-day management of the business.

Sweden was chosen as the location for the study for several reasons. As a developed country, Sweden has a large number of small businesses located in regional areas, and the Swedish government is eager to promote e-commerce adoption by small businesses in these areas (as described previously). Furthermore, ease of access to small businesses in regional areas of Sweden was a major contributing factor. To qualify as a regional area, the following criteria were developed and applied to several areas in Sweden:

- The location must be an urban regional area and not a major/capital city or rural area.
- A viable government-initiated Chamber of Commerce must exist and be well patronized by the small business community.
- The location should have access to a full range of educational facilities (including a university/college).
- The business community must represent a cross-section of business ages, sizes, and market sectors.

As a result of applying these criteria, four municipalities in the Värmland county (regional area) were selected: Karlstad, Filipstad, Säffle, and Arvika. A total of 1,170 surveys was distributed by post to randomly selected small businesses in the county. A return envelope was provided so that respondents could return their completed surveys anonymously. The mode of the data collection was

selected, based on previous research by de Heer (1999), which indicated that Scandinavian countries had historically high mail survey response rates (although he notes that this is declining).

RESULTS AND FINDINGS

Responses were obtained from 313 small businesses, giving an unexpectedly low response rate of 26.8%. It is interesting to note that the low response rate supports de Heer's (1999) findings that survey response rates in Sweden are falling. Of the 313 surveys received, 275 responses were considered to be valid and usable. The total number small business respondents not using e-commerce (i.e., non-adopters) was 123, representing 44.7% of the valid responses. A profile of the survey respondents who had not adopted e-commerce is shown in Table 3.

It is of interest to note that, while the official MIEC (2003) figure for the percentage of small businesses with less than 10 employees is 94%, the current sample shows the number of respondents with less than 10 employees is 75%. This discrepancy is explained by the fact that the MIEC figure is a national figure encompassing rural, regional, and metropolitan small businesses and, as such, would include single-owner agricultural as well as retail businesses.

The responses of the 123 non-adopter respondents were examined in detail, and it was determined that 89 of them responded to every statement in the question regarding barriers to e-commerce adoption. The responses of these 89 small businesses formed the basis for the statistical analysis carried out using SPSS. An inspection of the frequencies indicated that the full range of the scale was utilized by the respondents (i.e., every barrier had at least one instance of each rating from 1 to 5). The aim of the statistical analysis was to establish the correlations between e-commerce adoption barriers in the data set. Prior to this, the scales of measurement for the barriers were tested using a Cronbach Alpha reliability test. Cronbach's Alpha was .9660, indicating a high level of reliability.

Correlation of E-Commerce Adoption Barriers

The correlations between the barriers were examined and the results are shown in the Correlation Matrix (Figure 2). The barriers from Figure 1 have been abbreviated for readability, and correlations that were significant at the .001 level are shown in bold lettering.

The Correlation Matrix shown in Figure 2 indicates an interesting pattern of results. The first four barriers all seem to correlate with each other but show weak or no correlations with the last set of barriers. Similarly, it appears that correlations exist between the last five barriers in the Correlation Matrix. Therefore, two distinct

groupings of results can be identified from the Correlation Matrix. In the first grouping, there is a strong positive correlation between the following barriers: "E-commerce is not suited to our products/services," and "E-commerce is not suited to our way of doing business." These two barriers also show moderately strong positive correlations with the following barriers: "E-commerce is not suited to the ways our clients (customers and/or suppliers) do business," and "E-commerce does not offer any advantages to our organization." In the second group, the barriers relating to the investment, time, number of options, complexity, and lack of expertise about e-commerce adoption generally show moderately strong positive correlations with each other. However, the barriers in the second group appear to be unrelated to the barriers in the first group, with the exception of very weak correlations for the barrier relating to security and time.

Figure 2. Correlation matrix of e-commerce adoption barriers

	No match prod/ services	Not fit our way of work	Not fit client way of work	No advantages	No technical expertise	Complex	Security	Cost too high	No time
Not fit our way of work	**.746**								
Not fit client way of work	**.462**	**.530**							
No advantages	**.482**	**.547**	.280						
No technical expertise	-.030	.054	-.097	.249*					
Complex	-.009	.059	.065	.106	**.544**				
Security	.184*	.303**	.098	.249*	.277*	**.516**			
Cost too high	-.051	-.138	.092	-.104	**.445**	**.481**	.217*		
No time	-.245*	-.261**	-.056	-.195*	**.432**	**.587**	.174	**.448**	
Many choices	-.056	-.005	-.033	.062	**.514**	**.579**	**.334**	**.494**	**.532**

* Correlation is significant at the 0.05 level   *** Correlation is significant at the 0.01 level*

Table 3. Total variance explained

R	otation Sums of Squared Loadings		
Component	Eigenvalue %	of Variance C	umulative %
1	3.252	32.520 3	2.520
2	2.745	27.453 5	9.973

Factor Analysis E-Commerce Adoption Barriers

The findings from the Correlation Matrix (see Figure 2) suggested the use of Factor Analysis to investigate any separate underlying factors and to reduce the redundancy of certain barriers indicated in the Correlation Matrix. The results of Kaiser-Meyer-Olkin MSA (.735) and Bartlett's Test of Sphericity ($\chi^2 = 343$, $p = .000$) indicated that the data set satisfied the assumptions for factorability. Principle Components Analysis was chosen as the method of extraction in order to account for maximum variance in the data using a minimum number of factors. A two-factor solution was extracted with Eigenvalues of 3.252 and 2.745. This was supported by an inspection of the Scree Plots. These two factors accounted

for 59.973% of the total variance. The results are summarized in Table 3.

The two resulting components were rotated using the Varimax procedure, and a simple structure was achieved, as shown in the Rotated Component Matrix in Table 4. Five barriers loaded highly on the first component. These barriers were related to the complexity of implementation techniques, range of e-commerce options, high investments, and the lack of technical knowledge and time. This component has been termed the *Too-Difficult factor*. The barriers highly loaded on the second component are termed the *Unsuitable factor* and are related to the suitability of e-commerce to the respondent's business, including the extent to which e-commerce matched the business' products/services, the organization's way of doing business, its client's way of doing business, and

Table 4. Rotated component matrix

	Component 1: Too Difficult	Component 2: Unsuitable
E-commerce is not suited to our products/services. -	.086 .	844
E-commerce is not suited to our way of doing business.	-.034 .	909
E-commerce is not suited to the ways our clients (customers and/or suppliers) do business.	-.004 .	643
E-commerce does not offer any advantages to our organization. .	076 .	731
We do not have the technical knowledge in the organization to implement e-commerce.	.743 .	074
E-commerce is too complicated to implement. .	852 .	102
E-commerce is not secure.	.525 .	385
The financial investment required to implement e-commerce is too high for us.	.703 -	.092
We do not have time to implement e-commerce.	.742 -	.294
It is difficult to choose the most suitable e-commerce standard with so many different options available.	.800 -	.054

Figure 3. Correlation matrix of e-commerce adoption barriers (male)

	No match prod/ services	Not fit our way of work	Not fit client way of work	No advantages	No technical expertise	Complex	Security	Cost too high	No time
Not fit our way of work	**.629**								
Not fit client way of work	**.600**	**.632**							
No advantages	**.596**	**.647**	**.443**						
No technical expertise	.296*	.320**	.322**	**.471**					
Complex	**.369**	.390**	**.507**	**.419**	**.651**				
Security	**.451**	.390**	**.525**	**.498**	**.550**	**.554**			
Cost too high	.288*	**.506**	**.450**	.281**	**.539**	**.519**	**.357**		
No time	.285	.272*	**.500**	**.361**	**.553**	**.510**	.299**	**.556**	
Many choices	.035	.365**	-.047	.174*	**.539**	**.484**	**.394**	**.407**	**.645**

* Correlation is significant at the 0.05 level   *** Correlation is significant at the 0.01 level*

Figure 4. Correlation matrix of e-commerce adoption barriers (female)

	No match prod/ services	Not fit our way of work	Not fit client way of work	No advantages	No technical expertise	Complex	Security	Cost too high	No time
Not fit our way of work	**.989**								
Not fit client way of work	**.907**	**.920**							
No advantages	**.893**	**.882**	.809**						
No technical expertise	.320	.307	.233	.282					
Complex	.633*	.607*	.522*	.442	.456				
Security	**.739**	.718**	.609**	.540*	.540*	**.896**			
Cost too high	.486*	.450	.529*	.433	.433	.750**	.634*		
No time	.589*	.033	.430	.142	.420	**.907**	.540*	.574*	
Many choices	.035	.075	-.047	.416	.415	.484	.366	.634*	.603

* Correlation is significant at the 0.05 level   *** Correlation is significant at the 0.01 level*

the lack of advantages offered by e-commerce implementation. These two factors are independent and uncorrelated, as an orthogonal rotation procedure was used. It is interesting to note that the barrier relating to security loaded on both factors, although the loading on the too-difficult factor was slightly higher (.525).

Correlation of E-Commerce Adoption Barriers by Gender

The non-adopters then were subdivided by gender into two groups: respondents whose primary owner was male (named *Male*) and respondents whose primary owner was female (named *Female*). The correlations between the barriers then were examined for each gender group individually; the results are shown in the Correlation Matrices in Figures 3 and 4. Once again, the barriers from Figure 1 have been abbreviated for readability; correlations that were significant at the .001 level are shown in bold.

Factor Analysis by Gender

Once again, as Figures 3 and 4 show, there were two distinct groups of barriers in each of the gender groups. Therefore, Factor Analysis was used to investigate the underlying factors. The results of the Kaiser-Meyer-Olkin MSA (.872 for males, .721 for females) and Bartlett's test of Sphericity ($\chi^2 = 578$, $p = .000$ for males, $\chi^2 = 578$, p=.000 for females) indicated that the data sets satisfied the assumptions for factorability.

Table 5. Total variance explained (males and females)

R	otation Sums of Squared Loadings					
Component	Eigenvalue %		of Variance C		umulative %	
	Males	Females	Males	Females	Males	Females
1	4.954	1.435	55.04	15.95	55.04	15.95
2	1.436	5.906	15.96	65.63	71.00	81.58

Table 6. Rotated component matrix (males and females)

	Component 1: Too Difficult		Component 2: Unsuitable	
	Males	Females	Males	Females
E-commerce is not suited to our products/services.	.631	.370	.585	.914
E-commerce is not suited to our way of doing business.	.672	.324	.574	.929
E-commerce is not suited to the ways our clients (customers and/or suppliers) do business.	.739	.281	.292	.904
E-commerce does not offer any advantages to our organization.	.655	.220	.484	.906
We do not have the technical knowledge in the organization to implement e-commerce.	.717	.591	-.255	.008
E-commerce is too complicated to implement.	.850	.909	-.279	.310
E-commerce is not secure.	.838	.779	-.009	.466
The financial investment required to implement e-commerce is too high for us.	.784	.787	-.277	.398
We do not have time to implement e-commerce.	.746	.785	-.404	.272
It is difficult to choose the most suitable e-commerce standard with so many different options available.	.764	.850	-.330	.265

Principle Components Analysis was chosen as the method of extraction in order to account for maximum variance in the data using a minimum number of factors. A two-factor solution was extracted with Eigenvalues of 4.594 and 1.436 for males and 1.435 and 5.906 for females. This was supported by an inspection of the Scree Plots. These two factors accounted for 70.994% of the total variance in males and 81.575% in females. These results are shown in Table 5.

The two resulting components were rotated using the Varimax procedure, and a simple structure was achieved, as shown in the Rotated Component Matrix in Table 6. Once again, the same two components were identified in each gender group: Too Difficult (component 1) and Unsuitable (component 2).

ANALYSIS AND DISCUSSION

The results of the Swedish study already presented show that the e-commerce barriers identified in the literature apply equally to small businesses in regional areas. More importantly, the results are an important first step in improving and consolidating our understanding of barriers that affect e-commerce adoption by small businesses in general, because it appears that correlations between the barriers exist. The correlations indicate that barriers can be grouped according to two distinct factors. These factors have been termed Too Difficult and Unsuitable. The Too-Difficult factor is related to the barriers that make e-commerce complicated to implement, including barriers such as the complexity of e-commerce implementation techniques, the difficulty in deciding which standard to implement because of the large range of e-commerce options, the difficulty of obtaining funds to implement e-commerce, the lack of technical knowledge, and the difficulty of finding time to implement e-commerce. The Unsuitable factor is related to the perceived unsuitability of e-commerce to small businesses. The barriers in

this group include the unsuitability of e-commerce to the organization's products/services, its way of doing business, and its client's way of doing business, as well as the lack of perceived advantages of e-commerce implementation. It can be argued (although further research is required) that the two extracted factors are associated with the unique features of small businesses (presented in Table 1), where the first factor (Too Difficult) is associated with features related to management, decision making, and planning processes, as well as features related to resource availability and features related to risk taking. In contrast, the second factor (Unsuitable) is associated with features related to products/services offered by small businesses and their markets. It would appear that the features unique to small businesses have some bearing on e-commerce adoption barriers; however, the exact nature of this relationship needs to be explored through additional empirical research.

The results of the study also point to a distinct difference in the way that males and females view the importance of different e-commerce adoption barriers. An examination of Table 5 shows that while 55% of male owners felt that e-commerce was too difficult, only 16% of the female respondents rated this as their most important reason not to adopt e-commerce. Instead, 66% of females felt that e-commerce was unsuitable for their business, while 16% of males considered this to be an important e-commerce adoption barrier. Although gender differences have been reported in prior studies, the results of the Swedish study appear to disagree with the results of previous research. Whereas prior studies suggested that males were less anxious about computing technology (Gilroy & Desai, 1986; Meier & Lambert, 1991; Perez et al, 2002), this study implies the opposite, with males reporting difficulties associated with e-commerce as an important adoption barrier. The reason for this may be found in research by Simon (2001) and Singh (2001). Simon (2001) found that females tended to be "less enthralled by technology than males" (p. 30) and used a more comprehensive information-processing scheme when making decisions about technology. In a similar vein, Singh (2001) proposed that females use the Internet as a tool for carrying out activities and not as a technology that must be mastered. Both Simon (2001) and Singh (2001) appear to be suggesting that females are more likely to consider Internet technologies, including e-commerce, in relation to their suitability for a particular activity. In contrast, males view Internet technologies simply as tools that require time, effort, and resources to learn and implement. This may explain the results of the study presented here. The male respondents rated difficulties mastering e-commerce tools as being important barriers, while the female respondents considered e-commerce in relation to the business activities and found the technology unsuitable.

The study presented here is also at odds with previous studies by Shade (1998), Sheehan (1999), and Akhter (2003), who argued that females were more concerned with privacy and security issues and, subsequently, more cautious about using the Internet. Instead, the Swedish study supports the research of Kolsaker and Payne (2002), who found only marginal and statistically insignificant gender differences in relation to privacy and security due to the increased participation by females, which led to a convergence of attitude between the two genders. However, unlike Kolsaker and Payne (2002), this study shows statistically significant gender differences in relation to the difficulties associated with e-commerce and the suitability of e-commerce.

Significance

The results of this study are significant in several ways, because they reduce some of the fragmentation associated with the having a large number of e-commerce adoption barriers, particularly for small businesses located in regional areas. The analysis has shown that 10 of the most common e-commerce adoption barriers can be grouped in relation to two main factors. This gives researchers a powerful explanatory tool, because it reduces the noise in the data. Instead of accounting for a variety of different barriers, the inhibitors to e-commerce adoption can be explained as a result of one of two main factors: e-commerce is either too difficult or thought to be unsuited to the business. The rotated component matrix also enables the prediction of the scores of each individual barrier, based on the score of the two factors and vice-versa for a small business located in a regional area. This has implications for research into e-commerce barriers. Whereas previously, researchers have identified various barriers (e.g., the ones listed in Table 2), this study has shown that these barriers are correlated and can be grouped logically. This makes it not only easier to explain but also to predict barriers to e-commerce adoption.

The results of this study also are significant to government organizations promoting e-commerce adoption in small businesses, particularly in regional areas. The study gives us a more concise understanding of e-commerce adoption barriers faced by small businesses and indicates that, as far as government initiatives are concerned, small businesses in regional areas fall into two categories: potential e-commerce adopters and non-adopters. The non-adopters do not view e-commerce as being suited to their organization at all. This may include small businesses, such as a corner shop selling basic groceries. Government initiatives, therefore, should be targeted more toward potential adopters and should offer them support in two key areas: technical expertise and financial assistance. Both of these areas are significant barriers associated with the Too-Difficult factor, particularly in regional areas that are resource-poor compared to their metropolitan counterparts (Keniry et al., 2003). Only by understanding the correlation and grouping of barriers to e-commerce adoption in regional small businesses can government initiatives provide necessary and appropriate support and result in the development of targeted policies and programs. Furthermore, it would appear that male and female small business owners may require different approaches, since there are differences between the levels of importance they assign to different e-commerce barriers. However, this would require additional support in the form of interviews with male and female small business owners and their attitudes to e-commerce adoption.

E-commerce vendors also will benefit from the results of this study, since small businesses are expressing concerns about the suitability, technical difficulties, and costs associated with e-commerce adoption. To address these concerns, vendors should improve the usability of e-commerce systems and promote the suitability and usefulness of e-commerce to small businesses. Finally, the study has important implications for future research that examines gender differences in Internet adoption and use. While the data confirm the views of Kolsaker and Payne (2002) that attitudes of males and females on privacy and security issues have converged, at the same time, it points to a large divergence in their views about e-commerce.

LIMITATIONS

It should be noted that the study presented here has several limitations. The data for the study were collected from various industry sectors, so it is not possible to make sector-specific conclusions. Also, the choice of variables selected for the study is somewhat problematic because of the complex nature of adoption barriers that change over time. Furthermore, according to Sohal and Ng (1998), the views expressed in the surveys are of a single individual from the responding organization, and only those interested in the study are likely to complete and return the survey. Where mail surveys are used, there is also the risk of not knowing whether the intended person actually completed the survey, despite

clear instructions from the authors requesting that the person should be the primary owner of the small business only. In addition, the cultural background of the respondent may have an effect on the results. Also, only a small number of female primary owners responded to the survey, which implies the necessity to undertake further research with more female owners in order to verify the results presented here. This study was carried out in a Swedish regional area. The results cannot be generalized to regional areas in other countries, unless they possess identical characteristics to Sweden. Finally, this is a quantitative study, and further qualitative research is required to gain an understanding of the key issues.

CONCLUSION

The aim of this article was twofold: (1) to improve our understanding of e-commerce adoption barriers faced by small businesses located in regional areas and (2) to examine the differences between males and females in the importance they assign to different e-commerce adoption barriers. A study of small businesses in a regional area in Sweden was undertaken toward this aim. The total data collected from the study were analyzed, and a Correlation Matrix was produced. The Correlation Matrix indicated two distinct groups of barriers, and a two-factor solution was extracted using Factor Analysis. It was found that e-commerce barriers generally could be grouped, depending on whether e-commerce was deemed to be Too Difficult to implement or Unsuitable for the organization. An additional analysis was performed to determine if any differences existed between the barriers identified by males and females as being important. The results of this analysis showed that females were more concerned about e-commerce being unsuitable for their business, while males expressed more concern about the difficulty of implementing e-commerce.

The implications of the study are significant for government organizations engaged in promoting e-commerce adoption, especially in regional small businesses. While recent studies (Johansson, 2003; Larsson et al., 2003; MacGregor, 2004; MIEC, 2003) suggest that the Swedish government has, in conjunction with universities, concentrated its efforts on e-commerce adoption in regional small businesses, the findings suggest that a number of enhancements are possible. First, the research indicates that the funding should be targeted more explicitly toward potential adopters in the form of technical expertise and financial assistance to acquire the necessary infrastructure (as these concerns are associated with the Too-Difficult factor). Second, government initiatives need to be mindful of the target audience. If these results are indicative of the Swedish regional small business sector as a whole, then the requirements of males differ from those of females. Clearly, further research is required to examine this issue, to establish how potential adopters can be identified, and also to address some of the study limitations described previously.

ACKNOWLEDGMENT

The authors would like to acknowledge the help and support received from Professor Sten Carlsson and Monika Magnusson at Karlstad University in collecting the data in Sweden.

REFERENCES

Akhter, S. H. (2003). Digital divide and purchase intention: Why demographic psychology matters? *Journal of Economic Psychology, 24*, 321-327.

Blili, S., & Raymond, L. (1993). Threats and opportunities for small and medium-sized enterprises. *International Journal of Information Management, 13*(6), 439-448.

Brisco, R. (2002). Turning analog women into a digital workforce: Plugging women into the new Asia economy. *Digital Divide Network*. Retrieved from www.digitaldividenetwork.org.

Bunker, D. J., & MacGregor, R. C. (2000). Successful generation of information technology (IT) requirements for small/medium enterprises (SME's): Cases from regional Australia. *Proceedings of the SMEs in a Global Economy*, Wollongong, Australia (pp. 72-84).

Bunker, D. J., & MacGregor, R. C. (2002, August 9-11) The context of information technology and electronic commerce adoption in small/medium enterprises, *Proceedings of the Americas Conference on Information Systems (AMCIS 2002)*, Dallas, Texas.

Butler, D. (2000). Gender, girls and computer technology: What's the status now? *Clearing House, 73*(4), 225-229.

Cochran, A. B. (1981). Small business mortality rates: A review of the literature. *Journal of Small Business Management, 19*(4), 50-59.

Coviello, N., & McAuley, A. (1999). Internationalisation and the smaller firm: A review of contemporary empirical research. *Management International Review, 39*(3), 223-240.

Cox, B. (1999). Gender gap narrows, changing landscape for e-commerce. *Internetnews*. Retrieved from www. internetnews.com.

Cragg, P. B., & King, M. (1993). Small-firm computing: Motivators and inhibitors. *MIS Quarterly, 17*(1), 47-60.

Damanpour, F. (2001). E-business e-commerce evolution: Perspective and strategy. *Managerial Finance, 27*(7), 16-33.

Damsgaard, J., & Lyytinen, K. (1998). Contours of diffusion of electronic data interchange in Finland: Overcoming technological barriers and collaborating to make it happen. *Journal of Strategic Information Systems, 7*(4), 275-297.

Daniel, E. (2003). An exploration of the inside-out model: E-commerce integration in UK SMEs. *Journal of Small Business Enterprise Development, 10*(3), 233-249.

Davis, F. D. (1989). Perceived usefulness, perceived ease of use, and user acceptance of information technology. *MIS Quarterly, 13*(3), 319-340.

de Heer, W. (1999). International response trends: Results of an international survey. *Journal of Official Statistics, 15*(2), 129-142.

DeLone, W. H. (1988). Determinants for success for computer usage in small business. *MIS Quarterly, 12*(1), 51-61.

Dennis, C. (2000). Networking for marketing advantage. *Management Decision, 38*(4), 287-292.

Europa. (2003). SME definition. *The European Commission.* Retrieved from http://europa.eu.int/comm/enterprise/enterprise_policy/sme_definition/index_en.htm.

Fielding, J. (1996). Getting out in front with EDI. *Inform, 10*(9), 12-18.

Gebler, D. (2000). Rethinking e-commerce gender demographics. *E-Commerce Times.* Retrieved from www.ecommerce times.com.

Gilbert, D., Lee-Kelley, L., & Barton, M. (2003). Technophobia, gender influences and consumer decision-making for technology-related products. *European Journal of Innovation Management, 6*(4), 253-263.

Gilroy, F., & Desai, H. (1986). Computer anxiety: Sex, race and age. *International Journal of Man-Machine Studies, 25*(1), 711-719.

Glaser, B. G., & Strauss, A. L. (1967). *The discovery of grounded theory: Strategies for qualitative research.* Chicago: Aldine.

Hadjimanolis, A. (1999). Barriers to innovation for SMEs in a small less developed country (Cyprus). *Technovation, 19*(9), 561-570.

Hill, R., & Stewart, J. (2000). Human resource development in small organisations. *Journal of European Industrial Training, 24*(2/3/4), 105-117.

Iacovou, C. L., Benbasat, I., & Dexter, A. S. (1995). Electronic data interchange and small organisations: Adoption and impact of technology. *MIS Quarterly, 19*(4), 465-485.

Johansson, U. (2003). Regional development in Sweden: October 2003. *Svenska Kommunförbundet.* Retrieved from www.lf.svekom.se/tru/RSO/Regional_development_ in_Sweden.pdf.

Kalakota, R., & Whinston, A. (1997). *Electronic commerce: A manager's guide.* Reading, MA: Addison-Wesley.

Keniry, J., Blums, A., Notter, E., Radford, E., & Thomson, S. (2003). Regional business—A plan for action. *Department of Transport and Regional Services.* Retrieved from www.rbda.gov.au/ action_plan.

Kolsaker, A., & Payne, C. (2002). Engendering trust in e-commerce: A study of gender-based concerns. *Marketing Intelligence & Planning, 20*(4/5), 206-214.

Larsson, E., Hedelin, L., & Gärling, T. (2003). Influence of expert advice on expansion goals of small businesses in rural Sweden. *Journal of Small Business Management, 41*(2), 205-212.

Lawrence, K.L. (1997). Factors inhibiting the utilisation of electronic commerce facilities in tasmanian small- to medium-sized enterprises. *Proceedings of the 8th Australasian Conference on Information Systems,* Adelaide (pp. 587-597).

Lee, C.S. (2001). An analytical framework for evaluating e-commerce business models and strategies. *Internet Research: Electronic Network Applications and Policy, 11*(4), 349-359.

MacGregor, R., & Vrazalic, L. (2005). The role of small business clusters in prioritising barriers to e-commerce adoption: A study of Swedish regional SMEs. *Beyond Clusters: Current Practices and Future Strategies.* Centre for Regional Innovation & Competitiveness (CIRC), Ballarat.

MacGregor, R., Vrazalic, L., Carlsson, S., Pratt, J., & Harris, M. (2005). How standard are the standard barriers to e-commerce adoption? A comparison of three studies carried out in Australia, Sweden and the US. *Proceedings of the Fourteenth International Conference on Information Systems Development (ISD 2005),* Karlstad, Sweden.

MacGregor, R. C. (2004). Factors associated with formal networking in regional small business: Some findings from a study of Swedish SMEs. *Journal of Small Business Enterprise Development, 11*(1), 60-74.

MacGregor, R. C., & Bunker, D. J. (1996). The effect of priorities introduced during computer acquisition on continuing success with it in small business environments. *Proceedings of the Information Resource Management Association International Conference,* Washington (pp. 271-277).

MacGregor, R. C., Vrazalic, L., Bunker, D., Carlsson, S., & Magnusson, M. (2004). A comparison of factors pertaining to both the adoption and non-adoption of electronic commerce in formally networked and non-networked regional SMEs: A study of Swedish small businesses. In B. Corbitt, & N. AL-Qirim (Eds.), *eBusiness, eGovernment & small and medium-sized enterprises: Opportunities and challenges* (pp. 206-243). Hershey, PA: IGP.

Magnusson, M. (2001). E-commerce in small businesses: Focusing on adoption and implementa-tion. *Proceedings of the 1st Nordic Workshop on Electronic Commerce,* Halmstad, Sweden.

Martin, L. M., & Matlay, H. (2001). "Blanket" approaches to promoting ICT in small firms: Some lessons from the DTI ladder adoption model in the UK. *Internet Research: Electronic Networking Applications and Policy, 11*(5), 399-410.

Mazzarol, T., Volery, T., Doss, N., & Thein, V. (1999). Factors influencing small business start-ups: A comparison with previous research. *International Journal of Entrepreneurial Behaviour and Research, 5*(2), 48-63.

McGowan, M. K., & Madey, G. R. (1998). The influence of organization structure and organizational learning factors on the extent of EDI implementation in U.S. firms. *Information Resources Management Journal, 11*(3), 17-27.

Meier, S. T., & Lambert, M. E. (1991). psychometric properties and correlates of three computer aversion scales. *Behaviour Research Methods, Instruments and Computers, 23*(1), 9-15.

MIEC–Ministry of Industry Employment and Communications. (2003). *The European charter for small enterprises: A review of relevant actions and measures in Sweden.* Retrieved from http://europa.eu.int/comm/enterprise/enterprise_policy/charter/index.htm.

Miller, N. L., & Besser, T. L. (2000). The importance of community values in small business strategy formation: Evidence from rural Iowa. *Journal of Small Business Management, 38*(1), 68-85.

Perez, M. P, Carnicer, M. P. L., & Sanchez, A. M. (2002). differential effects of gender perceptions of teleworking by human resources managers. *Women in Management Review, 17*(6), 262-275.

Poon, S., & Swatman, P. (1997). The Internet for small businesses: An enabling infrastructure. *Proceedings of the INET'95-5th Annual Confer-*

ence of the Internet Society, Honolulu, Hawaii (pp. 221-231).

Poon, S., & Swatman, P. M. C. (1998). Small business Internet commerce experiences: A longitudinal study. *Proceedings of the 11th International Bled Electronic Commerce Conference,* Bled, Slovenia.

Purao, S., & Campbell, B. (1998). Critical concerns for small business electronic commerce: Some reflections based on interviews of small business owners. *Proceedings of the Association for Information Systems Americas Conference,* Baltimore, 325-327.

Quayle, M. (2002). E-commerce: The challenge for UK SMEs in the 21st century. *International Journal of Operations and Production Management, 22*(10), 1148-1161.

Reynolds, W., Savage, W., & Williams, A. (1994). *Your own business: A Practical guide to success.* ITP.

Riquelme, H. (2002). Commercial Internet adoption in China: Comparing the experience of small, medium and large businesses. *Internet Research: Electronic Networking Applications and Policy, 12*(3), 276-286.

Robertson, T., & Gatignon, H. (1986). Competitive effects on technology diffusion. *Journal of Marketing, 50,* 1-12.

Rodgers, S., & Harris, M. A. (2003). Gender and e-commerce: An exploratory study. *Journal of Advertising Research, 43*(3), 322.

Rogers, E. M. (1995). *Diffusion of innovations* (4th ed.). New York: Free Press.

Schmidt, R. A., & Parker, C. (2003). Diversity in independent retailing: Barriers and benefits—The impact of gender. *International Journal of Retail and Distribution Management, 31*(8), 428-439.

Sexton, R. S., Johnson, R. A., & Hignite, M. A. (2002). Predicting Internet/e-commerce use. *Internet Research, 12*(5), 402-410.

Shade, L. R. (1998). A gendered perspective on access to the information infrastructure. *The Information Society, 14*(1), 33-44.

Sheehan, K. (1999). An investigation of gender differences in on-line privacy concerns and resultant behaviour. *Internet Marketing, 13,* 159-173.

Shiels H., McIvor R., & O'Reilly (2003). Understanding the implications of ICT adoption: Insights from SMEs. *Logistics Info. Management, 16*(5), 312-326.

Simon, S. J. (2001). The impact of culture and gender on Web sites: An empirical study. *The DATA BASE for Advances in Information Systems, 32*(1), 18-37.

Singh, S. (2001). Gender and use of the Internet at home. *New Media & Society, 3*(4), 395-416.

Sohal, A. S., & Ng, L. (1998). The role and impact of information technology in Australian business. *Journal of Information Technology, 13*(3), 201-217.

Teltscher, S. (2002). E-commerce and development report 2002. *Proceedings of the United Nations Conference on Trade and Development.*

Teo, T. S. H., & Tan, M. (1998). An empirical study of adopters and non-adopters of the Internet in Singapore. *Information & Management, 34*(6), 339-345.

Tetteh, E., & Burn, J. (2001). Global strategies for SME-business: Applying the SMALL framework. *Logistics Information Management, 14*(1/2), 171-180.

Thong, J. Y. L, Yap, C. S., & Raman, K. S. (1996). Top management support, external expertise and information systems implementation in small business. *Information Systems Research, 7*(2), 248-267.

Tuunainen, V. K. (1998). Opportunities of effective integration of EDI for small businesses in the automotive industry. *Information & Management, 36*(6), 361-375.

Van Akkeren, J., & Cavaye, A. L. M. (1999). Factors affecting entry-level Internet technology adoption by small business in Australia: An empirical study. *Proceedings of the 10th Australasian Conference on Information Systems,* Wellington, New Zealand.

Venkatesan, V. S., & Fink, D. (2002). Adoption of Internet technologies and e-commerce by small and medium enterprises (SMEs) in western Australia. *Proceedings of the Information Resource Management Association International Conference,* Seattle, Washington (pp. 1136-1137).

Venkatesh, V., Morris, M. G., & Ackerman, P. L. (2000). A longitudinal field investigation of gender differences in individual technology adoption decision-making processes. *Organizational Behavior and Human Decision Processes, 83*(1), 33-60.

Vrazalic, L., MacGregor, R. C., Carlsson, S., Bunker, D. J., & Magnusson, M. (2002). Electronic commerce and market focus: Some findings from a study of Swedish small to medium enterprises. *Australasian Journal of Information Systems, 9*(2), 110-119.

Walczuch, R., Van Braven, G., & Lundgren, H. (2000). Internet adoption barriers for small firms in the Netherlands. *European Management Journal, 18*(5), 561-572.

Welsh, J. A., & White, J. F. (1981). A small business is not a little big business. *Harvard Business Review, 59*(4), 46-58.

Westhead, P., & Storey, D. J. (1996). Management training and small firm performance: Why is the link so weak? *International Small Business Journal, 14*(4), 13-24.

Wolin, L. D., & Korgaonkar, P. (2003). Web advertising: Gender differences in beliefs, attitudes and behavior. *Internet Research: Electronic Networking Applications and Policy, 13*(5), 375-385.

Wynarczyk, P., Watson, R., Storey, D. J., Short, H., & Keasey, K. (1993). *The managerial labour market in small and medium sized enterprises.* London: Routledge.

Yap, C. S., Soh, C. P. P., & Raman, K. S. (1992). Information system success factors in small business. *International Journal of Management Science, 20*(5/6), 597-609.

This work was previously published in Journal of Electronic Commerce in Organizatons, Vol. 4, Issue 2, edited by M. Khosrow-Pour, pp. 1-24, copyright 2006 by IGI Publishing, formerly known as Idea Group Publishing (an imprint of IGI Global).

Chapter XXVIII
The Future of M-Commerce:
The Role of Bluetooth and WiMax

David C. Yen
Miami University, USA

Sean Lancaster
Miami University, USA

ABSTRACT

This chapter discusses the growing significance of m-commerce with special focus on Bluetooth and WiMax. There is a detailed investigation of the components involved with, and the marketplace for, m-commerce transactions. The chapter concludes with the future opportunities and obstacles for m-commerce. The authors hope that the reader will gain a better understanding of, not only of m-commerce, but the impact of Bluetooth and WiMax.

INTRODUCTION

As m-commerce continues to grow in overall use and importance for modern business, it is critical to examine future opportunities, trends, questions, and related concerns. By understanding the future implications and outlooks, m-commerce venders, IT/IS developers, and users can continue to pursue this incredible mobile or wireless movement. Additionally, the increasing adoption of short range technologies like Bluetooth, as well as long range technologies like WiMax, are increasingly aiding m-commerce. These technologies have increased the number of applications for mobile users and strengthened the future of m-commerce. It is important to note that m-commerce is not only expected to expand its share of the e-commerce market, but also to expand the overall e-commerce market through rapid evolution of m-commerce services. M-commerce requires careful e-commerce adaptation to include mobile access for enhanced services and business communications that are not only anytime, but also anywhere. This chapter will present the importance of, the components and technologies involved with, the future market forecast, and key future trends and issues for m-commerce.

Figure 1. The relationships, impact, and roles of wireless, Bluetooth, and WiMax

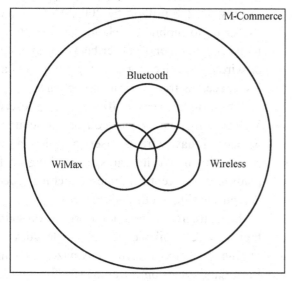

Learning Objectives

- Understand m-commerce and its role in modern business
- Investigate specific m-commerce technologies
- Examine the future trends impacting m-commerce
- Understand the relationship between Bluetooth, WiMax and m-commerce (see Figure 1)

BACKGROUND

A busy executive on a PDA, an anxious driver using a cell phone, and a college student walking to class listening to his or her Mp3 player; all of the aforementioned are common sights in today's world. All are dependent on wireless technology. Wireless has changed many aspects in our lives, including how we conduct business.

M-commerce is the ability to conduct e-commerce transactions over wireless media. Examples of m-commerce include buying and downloading a ring tone to your cell phone, acting on the real-time stock quote on your PDA, or subscribing to have last night's news and highlights sent to your mobile device.

M-commerce requires similar steps as a physical transaction. An m-commerce transaction is more than just checking an e-mail message from a wireless device. A buyer and seller must agree on an item and price, delivery of the product must be made, and payment to the seller must be completed.

That being said, mobility must still be involved during the transaction and a wireless device must be used by the buyer, the seller, or both. Common examples include cell phones; palm pilots or PDAs; or blackberrys. Even more so, the wireless device should be connected to a wireless ISP and not just an extension of a hardwired LAN.

Wireless applications such as pagers, cellular phones, and satellite television have been around for years. Increasingly today, mobile data communication is viewed as an emerging area for many industries, and companies are increasing their investment accordingly. While many recent developments in the wireless industry have been "flops" (including Mobitex messaging, Cellular Digital Packet Data services), the development and acceptance of the Wireless Application Protocol (WAP) has given wireless carriers and mobile service providers sufficient confidence to introduce a new generation of wireless applications like Bluetooth and WiMax.

The PC Industry

Wireless communication has had great impact on the personal computing industry. Most desktop and laptops come readily equipped for wireless devices. WiFi (802.11) and Bluetooth are commonly used in a multitude of applications. Access to hotspots and wireless clouds are routine connections for personal computers.

Another significant impact to the PC industry is that wireless communication becomes a key feature of palmtop computers. 3Com's palm computers now allow users to access their e-mail and to access over 100 different Web sites.

The Communication Service Industry

Most common carriers offer wireless telephone service now. Cell phones are readily used for a variety of reasons ranging from business, to social, to family connections. Recently, Sprint and MCI have been more active on wireless service than their primary competitor, AT&T, which has been more focused on "wired" fiber optic networks.

As more applications over IP networks become possible, there should be even greater impact on the communication service industry. A convergence of television, telephone, radio, and video applications will allow companies who offer wireless bandwidth to compete with large groupings of products and packages.

Other Industries

The microprocessor industry has also responded to the increasing demand for wireless products. In December of 1999, Intel created a new "wireless communications and computing group" that focuses on creating cellular and wireless communication products and technologies. Advanced Micro Devices (AMD), one of the leading providers of wireless communications, has recently formed an alliance with Motorola.

Firms looking to innovate wireless processors that can quickly and efficiently perform the needed tasks while consuming reasonable levels of power. Speed of execution and battery life have become critical components for wireless devices.

Global Society

TIA's 2006 telecommunications Market Review and Forecast (Flanigan, 2006) found that there were more than 194 million wireless subscribers in the United States in 2005. That figure is expected to grow to 270 million by 2009. Most of them subscribe to mobile telephone services, but an increasing number of subscribers take advantage of wireless services for palmtop computers and Web accesses from their mobile phones.

The term the *wireless Web* is used to describe Web sites that can be viewed from these mobile devices. Today, wireless users are viewing the scores of their favorite teams, researching stocks, reading the current headlines, watching videos, and purchasing goods and services.

E-commerce companies work on providing their services available through wireless devices. Online bookstores such as Amazon.com and Barnesandnoble.com are among the first retailers to let handheld users order products. One of the most well known e-commerce companies that take advantage of wireless technology is Peapod Inc., an online grocery store. Peapod believes that services provided through wireless communication are important to their customers, because most people do not have PCs in their kitchens. They currently offer services for the Palm VII platform and plan to expand the service to mobile phones in the future.

M-COMMERCE ISSUES

Businesses should be interested in adapting their e-commerce infrastructures and including m-commerce applications for a variety of reasons. Predominantly, as the wireless title pronounces, m-commerce offers the freedom and flexibility of not needing to be plugged in and tethered to a desk or office. Business can be conducted without the use of the bulky desktop and office environment. An additional benefit of m-commerce is the convenience that goes along with that freedom. This allows business to be extended beyond the traditional norms and truly be conducted from anywhere at anytime.

Along with the aforementioned benefits is the ability to better tap into your data to drive efficient and timely decision making. This allows for businesses to offer higher levels of customer support and to catch and act on potential problems sooner than by relying on hardwired communication. In fact, a true wireless infrastructure, where the business is capable of sending wireless communication and the consumers are enabled to receive, offers enormous one-one marketing capabilities. Wireless environments allow for closer to real-time communications as messages can be received on the fly (Zeng, Yen, & Hwang, 2003).

The increased speed, convenience, and ubiquity of wireless communication should not be underestimated. Consider the move from traditional telephones to cordless phones, and to today's cell phones. Telecom users have shown a preference for the freedom that wireless devices offer.

However, as with any emerging technology, there are a number of critical issues that must be planned for in order to effectively implement a wireless infrastructure. A major downfall for m-commerce, to this stage, is the small size of wireless devices. Whether it is a small display or a tiny keypad, viewing and interacting with wireless content is at a disadvantage versus the high resolution and common keyboards associated with desktop computing. It is easy to recognize the quick clicking of students frantically sending text messages to friends (Bai, Chou, Yen, & Lin, 2005).

Another negative of wireless applications is the potential lack of security. A business must implement and communicate a comprehensive wireless security plan to ensure that its own architecture is not at risk. In addition, these firms must provide a secure wireless environment to their customers and trading partners. The increased freedom and flexibility offered by wireless do come partnered with increased risk of cybercrime.

Finally, as wireless is a relatively new innovation, users will need to have education, training, and continued experience. Wireless operators must struggle with the negative perceptions of the

Table 1. Characteristics of m-commerce

Currentness	Allows for real-time communication from any time or location
Accessibility	Enables users to stay in contact with desired parties
Personalization	Allows for one-one marketing opportunities and personalized data communications
Convenience	Aside from allowing access from any time or location, m-commerce applications are increasingly easy to use
Localization	Allows users to find information on a specific location when used in conjunction with technologies like global positioning systems (GPS)

wireless link. Moreover, the complexity of technical standards, the difficulty and the accompanied expense of roaming outside a given carrier's territory, and the limits to how much information can be displayed attractively on tiny screens are regarded as major obstacles to the operations with relative simple inquiries and responses. Thus, educating the end users about the implications of doing m-commerce on a cell phone or PDA will be a crucial factor for the technology more widely accepted (Yen & Chou, 2000).

A number of key m-commerce characteristics are profiled in Table 1.

M-COMMERCE: COMPONENTS

M-commerce applications use a variety of components. These components are critical in allowing customers to conduct transactions. A diagram

Figure 2. The interpretative relationship of m-commerce components

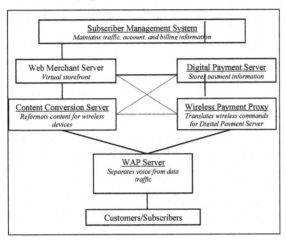

of the relationship between the components is provided in Figure 2. The major components involved are a Web merchant server, a content conversion server, a wireless access protocol server, a digital payment server, a wireless payment proxy, and a subscriber management system (Zeng et al., 2003).

Web Merchant Server. Similar to a brick-and-mortar store for consumers, a Web merchant server is a virtual storefront on the Internet. It maintains and displays the listing of products, descriptions, prices, and availability.

Content Conversion Server. A content conversion server is responsible for taking the existing HTML from a Web page and converting it to a wireless enables format, like WML. This component works as an important gateway to link the Web merchant server and the various wireless devices.

WAP Server. A WAP server connects WAP-enabled hardware, like PDAs and phones with applications hosted on the server. In addition, it routes content based on whether it is voice or data traffic (Leavitt, 2000).

Digital Payment Server. A digital payment server electronically stores consumer's payment information: credit cards, shipping locations, and so forth. This server is essential to the convenience of one-click shopping as it automatically supplies the necessary details to complete the transaction (Karnouskos & Fraunhofer, 2004).

Wireless Payment Proxy. Wireless payment proxy converts wireless commands from mobile devices into commands that can be understood by digital payment servers.

Subscriber Management System. The subscriber management system maintains the traffic, account, and billing information for a firm's wireless operations ensuring a stable and effective m-commerce experience (Zeng et al., 2003).

M-COMMERCE: TECHNOLOGY

Technological innovation has been critical to the adoption of m-commerce. The following sections profile important network and service technologies.

Network Technologies

Network technologies have greatly evolved over the years. TCP/IP enabled the shift from circuit-switched to packet-switched networks. Cellular networks have moved from analog to digital technologies. This evolution over the years has been categorized as first-generation (1G), second-generation (2G), 2.5G and third-generation (3G) wireless. Finally, these technologies encompass short-range communication, including bluetooth and ultra wideband shortwave, as well as local area networks and metropolitan networks, such as WiFi and WiMax (see Figure 3).

GSM

GSM is a 2G standard for mobile communication. The European Telecommunications Standards Institute (ETSI) membership and technical teams

Figure 3. An overview of wireless networking technologies

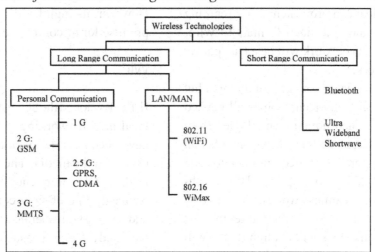

built the GSM standard and The Third Generation Partnership Project (3GPP) now owns GSM along with its own successor standards.

GSM operates in the frequency range of 900/1800 MHz in Europe and 1900 MHz in the US. GSM operates in over 200 countries worldwide providing almost complete coverage in Western Europe, and growing coverage in the Americas, Asia, and elsewhere. For more information visit (http://www.gsmworld.com).

General Packet Radio System (GPRS)

General Packet Radio System (GPRS) is a 2.5G technology that enables higher bandwidth for mobile wireless applications. GPRS allows for multimedia graphics and video to take a larger role in wireless developments. From a historical perspective, GPRS was a crucial step in the move from GSM to Universal Mobile Telephone System (UMTS), from 2G to 3G wireless.

Code Division Multiple Access (CDMA)

A competing standard to GSM, Code Division Multiple Access (CDMA) is the proprietary

wireless standard of Qualcomm and Ericsson. Unlike GSM, CDMA is much more common in the United States than elsewhere in the world. CDMA is considered a "spread spectrum" technology, meaning that it spreads the data from a wireless signal over a much greater bandwidth. A CDMA call may start with a standard rate of 9.6 kbps before spreading to a transmitting rate of approximately 1.23 Mbps.

UMTS

UMTS is a European 3G cellular technology. Under optimal conditions, UMTS can deliver content at a bandwidth of 2 Mbps. However, 384 Kbps is a more realistic expectation in a populated area. Because of the dramatic performance loss, UMTS does have its critics and the adoption of this standard has been slower than originally expected (Holma & Toskala, 2000).

Fourth Generation (4G)

Fourth generation (4G) is considered the future for wireless traffic. The Institute of Electrical and Electronics Engineers (IEEE) considers 4G to be

"3G and beyond." Specifically, 4G is expected to provide significant improvements to streaming high quality audio and video formats to wireless devices. A 4G network will be a true packet switched network.

4G wireless is not one single technology, but a combination of many technologies all packed into one. It will incorporate technologies from WiFi, Bluetooth, and cellular signals to TV and radio broadcasts, and satellite communication. 4G will have the capability to integrate all these technologies into one seamless worldwide network, and all will be able to connect at lightening fast speeds. It will also be small enough that it will allow just about anything from a laptop to a dog collar to have a transceiver in it and be assigned its own IP address. Japan has set out to be the leader in 4G and they expect to have it by 2007 and be able to transfer at speeds up to 100 Mbps (Dursch, Yen, & Huang, 2005).

Bluetooth

Bluetooth is a wireless technology that can be used for short-range communication between different Bluetooth-enabled devices. Common examples of Bluetooth devices include wireless video game controllers, PDAs that can be synched to their docking station, and mobile phone headsets. Bluetooth works in the unlicensed 2.4 GHz industrial, scientific, and medical (ISM) band and uses frequency-hopping spread-spectrum (FHSS) communication, which transmits data over different frequencies at different time intervals. This is accomplished by making "hops" to different frequencies through the ISM band. A device makes about 1,600 hops per second, which is spaced out over 1 MHz (Ersala & Yen, 2002).

Ultra Wideband Shortwave

Ultra wideband is a wireless technology that sends brief, intermittent pulses of high bandwidth communications. Like Bluetooth, it suffers from offering connections at a very short range. However, its high bandwidth capability gives it promise for m-commerce applications.

WiFi

IEEE developed the 802.11x standards for wireless local area networking (LSN). These standards have become quite popular and coined WiFi by users and the media. The 802.11a band operates in the 5 GHz frequency band and is limited to primarily line of sight communication. 802.11b and 802.11g both operate on the 2.4 GHz frequency band and therefore are subject to interference from common household devices such as microwaves and cordless phones. The IEEE has had great success innovating and adding to the original standard improving both available bandwidth and acceptable operating distance. Despite the improvements, WiFi is still viewed as a LAN technology.

WiMax

The IEEE developed the 802.16 with the idea of creating a wireless networking technology suitable for coverage of large metropolitan areas, sometimes referred to as metropolitan area networks (MAN). WiMax, while a wireless standard, joins other high broadband competitors like DSL and cable. It offers great potential as it is the first wireless standard that offers higher bandwidth capabilities than cellular providers.

Service Technologies

Wireless Application Protocol

The purpose of wireless application protocol (WAP) is to provide operators, infrastructure, terminal manufacturers, and content developers a common environment that should enable development of value-added services for mobile phones. Essentially, WAP is the technology that makes it possible to link wireless devices (such as mobile phones) to the Internet by translating Internet information so it can be displayed on the display screen of a mobile telephone or on other portable devices. WAP is an open, global specification developed by WAP forum that has over 500 members. Motorola, Nokia, Ericsson, and the U.S. software company Phone.com (formerly Unwired Planet) were the initial partners that teamed up in mid 1997 to develop and deploy WAP. WAP is an attempt to define the standard for how content from the Internet is filtered for mobile communications. Content is now readily available on the Internet and WAP was designed as the way of making it easily available on mobile terminals.

Unstructured Supplementary Services Data

Unstructured Supplementary Services Data (USSD) is a means of transmitting information via a GSM network. It is to some extent similar to the Short Message Service (SMS), which refers to the ability to send and receive text messages to and from mobile telephones. In contrast to SMS, which is a store and forward service, USSD offers a real-time connection during a session.

The direct radio connection stays open until the user or the application disconnects it. A USSD message can have up to 182 characters. It is relevant for real-time applications, such as mobile stock trading, where a confirmed information transmission is needed. USSD is a WAP bearer service. It is said that USSD will grow with the further market penetration of WAP. We see it used mainly for mobile financial services, shopping, and payment.

M-Commerce: Applications

M-commerce offers many beneficial applications to businesses and consumers. Consumers are able to stay well informed with up-to-the-

minute details of the topics of their choice. Text messaging allows people to stay in contact with each other for both business and pleasure. When higher wireless bandwidth is added into the mix, consumers will be able to demand and expect a richer mobile experience.

Consumers will also have access to a larger number of vendors, as they can now find localized products and firms. An example would be to use your mobile phone to find the nearest restaurant while walking down a city block.

For businesses, m-commerce offers a number of positive applications. For example, inventory can be managed with greater degree of confidence when using mobile devices. The ability to identify and track products from anywhere anytime can help firms better answer supply chain questions. This in turn will allow businesses to better satisfy their customers and build healthy business-business relationships with their trading partners.

Additionally, businesses will be able to collect data about their customers to better understand their needs. As consumers use their mobile devices for business transactions, companies will have an additional avenue to market and support their products.

THE MARKET FOR M-COMMERCE

The following section examines the major stakeholders of m-commerce: customers, technology providers, Web designers and developers, and service providers (see Figure 4).

Customers

Customers, individual and organizational, play a large role in the adoption of m-commerce. As they become the everyday users of wireless devices, their satisfaction and comfort are of the utmost importance. A Nokia study on wireless value-added services found that the primary adopters of wireless technology include:

Figure 4. The market for m-commerce

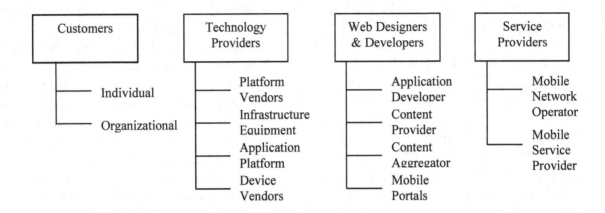

- Teens (18 years and under)
- Students (19-25 years old)
- Young business people (25-36 years old)

It should be noted that the main consumers of m-commerce devices are under the age of 36. These numbers should expand in the future as wireless applications are accepted by larger segments of the population ("Four in ten users," 2002).

Businesses and organizations also use m-commerce products. Similar to the previous section on m-commerce applications, the businesses most likely to posses m-commerce platforms include:

- Businesses that use m-commerce for direct sales to the customer; for example, investment firms selling stocks via wireless devices.
- Firms that have a high demand for real-time, in-house communication. An example of this category of business would include a consulting firm utilizing wireless devices to keep better track of employees.

- Organizations that have a mobile work force; for example, a shipping company using mobile devices to track its deliveries (Bai et al., 2005).

Business customers may use m-commerce applications to check schedules and e-mail, use in-house applications like customer relationship management (CRM) or enterprise resource planning (ERP), or scan products and their associated bar codes or radio frequency identification (RFID) tags.

Technology Providers

Technology providers include the businesses that sell and support the m-commerce platforms, firms that sell the equipment used for the infrastructure of a wireless network, companies that create connecting software and middleware for wireless applications, and the firms that manufacture the actual devices.

Technology Platform Vendors

Mobile devices require similar software and hardware components as other computing devices. Technology platform vendors create the operating systems and specialized applications needed by wireless handhelds, laptops, and cell phones. This industry is largely based around two companies, Microsoft and Symbian, and their respective operating systems, Windows CE and Palm.

Infrastructure Equipment Vendors

Wireless networks require specialized components to create a reliable and efficient communications infrastructure. Companies such as Ericsson, Lucent, Motorola, and Nokia have helped shape the m-commerce environment their products. This is an industry that has seemingly been in a constant state of innovation, with the new and improved products and protocols emerging.

Application Platform Vendors

The wireless application protocols needed to connect different m-commerce applications to help the mobile industry grow and expand. Industry interest groups like the WAP Forum, the Bluetooth Special Interest Group, and the Mobile Data Initiative help to forge agreements and standards to help connect a variety of applications over mobile networks. Additionally, companies like Nokia, Ericsson, and Dr. Materna create and market their own forms of middleware that can ease the connectivity of their products (Bai et al., 2005).

Device Vendors

Handheld computers, cellular phones, and mobile computers are an obvious m-commerce technology provider. There has been a great shift to multi-function devices in this industry, as customers demand products that can mix and match the ability to make phone calls, surf the wireless Web, connect to wireless applications, even listen to music and take pictures. The companies in this industry scramble to offer the right components, but more importantly the right features for consumers. Successful design of these devices is essential to strong consumer loyalty (Cyr, Head, & Ivanov, 2006).

Web Site Designers and Developers

Web designers and programmers play a central role in creating applications suitable for the wireless environment. In the past, these applications have largely been limited by a lack of bandwidth and the limitations of the wireless devices. Both of these characteristics have greatly improved for today's m-commerce designs.

Application Developers

Wireless application developers design and code mobile applications. There is a wide array of tools that can be used in this process. The WAP, The Wireless Markup Language (WML), and the Handheld Devices Markup Language (HDML). In addition, there is a mobile version of Java termed J2ME.

Content Providers

Wireless content providers help to provide Web content to mobile devices. Firms recognizing the attractiveness of using the wireless Web to communicate with consumers have shown a willingness to make available a sometimes limited, or in some case a full featured, version of their Web content. A key challenge for the organizations is to create a suitable version of their content, especially in conjunction with the previously discussed limitations of wireless devices and bandwidth (Saha, Jamtgaard, & Villasenor, 2001).

Content Aggregators

Content aggregators are firms that gather similar content on a topic and make it available to wireless users. For example, a mobile news site may offer subscribers wireless updates of the current headlines. This firm gathers top stories before making them available on mobile devices. Yahoo, AOL, and CNN are all examples of wireless content aggregators.

Mobile Portals

Mobile portals create personalized and localized content to users by providing e-mail, calendar, communication tools, and dynamic information. These portals become the one stop for many wireless users, as they can access a variety of applications from a single location. In addition to being content aggregators, Yahoo and AOL are also mobile portals.

Wireless Service Providers

This section will focus on the firms that supply wireless access. These companies operate and manage mobile networks for subscribers.

Mobile Network Operators

Vodaphone, T-Mobile, Verizon, and NTT Do-CoMo are all examples of mobile network operators. These firms have launched an infrastructure to transport mobile content and data to wireless devices. While some of these firms are traditional cell phone coverage providers, others are moving in and serving more directly as wireless ISPs (Bai et al., 2005).

Mobile Service Providers

Mobile service providers are the firms that provide access to mobile networks. In some cases, the operators and service providers are the same.

For example, Verizon supports and grants access to its mobile network. In other cases, the service providers are simply reselling access over the mobile network, while typically supplying their own content. Vonage has recently announced plans to launch a mobile version of its product (Kharif, 2007).

FUTURE TRENDS

M-commerce is a recent development and it is anticipated that it will exhibit strong growth in the next decade.

Market Forecasts

A 2006 wireless telecommunications industry profile by Datamonitor found the global market value of wireless telecommunications services to be $401.9 billion. This figure is expected to grow to $567.8 billion by 2010 (Global Wireless Telecommunications Services, 2006). These numbers clearly demonstrate scope and potential of wireless networks and mobile applications.

An interesting trend is that Asia and Europe have seen stronger growth of wireless services than the Americas. The United States has been much slower to accept and adopt mobile communications and m-commerce than other areas

Figure 5. Global wireless telecommunications services market segmentation (Source: Global Wireless Telecommunications Services, 2006)

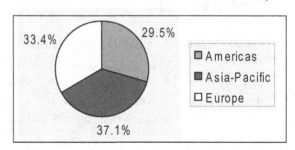

of the world. For this to change, there will need to be continued education of consumers and the emergence of uniform standards with critical applications. A summary of Datamonitor's (Global Wireless Telecommunications Services, 2006) findings is given in Figure 5.

Future Issues

M-commerce is still emerging as a field, industry, and discipline. While there has been some disappointment that it has not evolved faster, there is still great hope for the future. In order for it to reach its promise consumers must continue to accept and even demonstrate a preference for the wireless medium. In addition, firms must continue to deliver products, services, and features that build loyal customer relationships. Finally, two important areas for innovation include security and enterprise applications.

Acceptance of Wireless Technology

In the past, wireless services and devices have been improved upon. We now see products focusing on cross-functional capabilities. This trend will continue but must be echoed by the demands of consumers. The marketplace will drive innovation and lead to more sophisticated products and services.

Customer Loyalty

Wireless firms seek a loyal customer base. Currently, consumers remain loyal through contracts and service agreements that lock them into their current vendors. There is opportunity for the industry to establish service levels that satisfy customers to the extent that they no longer shop for new vendors (Bai et al., 2005).

Enterprise Applications

As the business market grows for mobile applications, firms will seek to implement ERP, CRM, and supply chain management (SCM), and other business intelligence (BI) applications over their wireless infrastructure. This will greatly improve the effectiveness of m-commerce's impact on internal and external decisions like inventory management, customer support, and one-one marketing.

Mobile Security Will Become a Hot Issue

Security has always been a concern for wireless devices. This will continue with increased scrutiny as users accept and adopt mobile solutions. In order for m-commerce to reach its potential, users must trust that the wireless environment is safe and secure to conduct business and to complete financial transactions.

TECHNOLOGY PUSH: BLUETOOTH

Bluetooth is a wireless technology used for short-ranged communication between multiple Bluetooth-enabled devices. An example would include connecting a wireless PDA, camera, or similar device to a desktop computer. The wireless connection would instantly update changes made to either device. Bluetooth works in the unlicensed 2.4 GHz (ISM) band focusing on industrial, scientific, and medical applications. It uses FHSS communication, which transmits data over different frequencies at different time intervals. This is accomplished by making "hops" to different frequencies through the ISM band. A device makes about 1,600 hops per second, which is spaced out over 1 MHz (Ersala & Yen, 2002).

Unlike most devices, Bluetooth-enabled devices communicate with each other automatically. There is no need to specify what type of action is to take place or when it is to happen. When two devices are within range of each other, they will communicate back and forth to determine if there is any information to be passed. During initial communication, it is necessary to create a relationship between unknown devices; this process is referred to as pairing. During the paring process, a secret PIN is created that is only known by the two devices that are communicating. It is better for the user to manually enter a PIN, and make it complex, in order to make the code hard to break (Dursch & Yen, 2004).

Bluetooth has several advantages; one of the most notable is its ease of use. As with every other wireless technology, Bluetooth frees up the user from being bogged down by wires. With an increasing number of peripheral devices, all the wires can become overcrowded and, at times, confusing. If not all the wires and slots are color-coded, it can become very difficult to figure out the location that each wire is plugged into, even for a professional. With Bluetooth, all these wires disappear, saving the user the time that would be spent trying to figure out how to get all the devices connected. When two Bluetooth devices come within range of each other, they automatically make a connection and decide if there is any information that needs to be passed, or if one needs to control the other.

Not only is the fact that Bluetooth devices use wireless communication an advantage, but also that the communication is done automatically. This reduces user interaction time, and tasks can be accomplished more efficiently. Within a wired environment, if the user wanted two devices to be synchronized, data would need either to be reentered by hand or connect the devices by wires. If the user would forget to do the synchronization, the data would eventually become outdated and could lead to data discrepancies. Because of the automatic communication between Bluetooth

devices, the user does not need to worry about forgetting to synchronize, so the data between devices would always match and be up-to-date (Ferro & Potorti, 2005).

Another advantage of Bluetooth is its added security features. The fact that it is a short-range technology (about 3 meters), adds some security in itself, because someone would need to be close to the communicating devices to be able to intercept the signal. As discussed earlier, the authentication process is also much more in-depth and harder to crack than that of other wireless standards.

Even though Bluetooth's short range helps security, there is still the possibility that someone can intercept the signal. The signal that Bluetooth devices send out, is sent in every direction, and can travel through walls. Intercepting the signal could be just as easy as sitting in the next room and listening to someone's conversation. With the increasing speeds of computers and programs, hacking equipment can be made to quickly and easily crack any code. With a wired network, a hacker needs to somehow tap into the company's network. This makes it harder for hackers because they need a physical connecting, whereas with Bluetooth all they need is a receiver that can catch the radio signals being sent out. As this technology continues to grow and mature, there will be better security measures, and someday may be as secure as some of the wired technologies.

The short range poses another disadvantage for Bluetooth. Only being able to transmit to distances up to 30 feet away can be very limiting in an office or production setting. Users cannot go too far away from the device that they are communicating with without losing the signal. If a company were spread out over separate buildings, Bluetooth would not work without help from another networking technology, such as a wired system.

Another disadvantage of Bluetooth is its speed. Today there is a greater need than ever for fast speeds to transfer large quantities of data. Bluetooth is only capable of transferring at speeds of 1 Mbit per second, but the SIG is working on a newer version that would allow speeds to reach 10 Mbits per second. If companies need to continuously exchange large files, Bluetooth would not work for their demands. Bluetooth is only meant for small amounts of data to be transferred at one time.

Bluetooth is already used in a number of real-world applications. Personal area networks use Bluetooth to connect peripherals with desktop and laptop units. Wireless headphone and speaker units to use in conjunction with cell phones are also increasingly more common and use Bluetooth. Most importantly for m-commerce, Bluetooth offers a method of transferring financial data for wireless transactions.

TECHNOLOGY PUSH: WiMax

While Bluetooth was limited in both range and carrying capacity, WiMax is greatly enhanced in both areas. WiMax is a wireless technology that can be used to communicate over much longer distances, up to 30 miles. For this reason the technology is considered a metropolitan area network (MAN), offering the potential to cover large geographic areas. Even though this standard reaches a much larger area than others do, it provides sufficient latency. In addition, WiMax offers bandwidths exceeding 70 Mbits per second.

WiMax is seen as a broadband solution. Whereas the cost of laying cable lines or even extending telecom networks for DSL, are quite high, WiMax offers a cheaper and more scalable solution. For this reason, the standard is seen as a solution to "last mile" problems. Furthermore, its bandwidth potential exceeds cellular networks so it affects other wireless and not just hard-wired solutions (Ghosh, Wolter, Andrews, & Chen, 2005).

A disadvantage of WiMax at the current moment is in its actual adoption. It is seen primarily as an access technology. While it does compete with hard-wired fixed broadband solutions, it cannot match the performance of all, although the hard-wired solutions are not as cost effective.

Additionally, WiMax is sometimes seen as a competitor with the much more established WiFi. In reality, the two technologies would be best used in conjunction with each other. Meshing WiMax and WiFi together, using WiMax as a large area, high-speed backbone and WiFi for LAN needs is a complementary solution (Goth, 2004).

As the world embraces IP-based solutions like television over IP, radio over IP, and voice over IP (VOIP), there is great potential for a high bandwidth, large area wireless networking method. For m-commerce, WiMax offers tremendous potential with both its range and bandwidth. Its ability to mesh with other mobile technologies is vital to providing consumers with a wireless networked solution.

Both Bluetooth and WiMax satisfy and contribute to separate applications of m-commerce. Both have the ability to significantly boost mobile implementations and applications.

Figure 6. The relationships, impact, and roles of wireless, Bluetooth, and WiMax

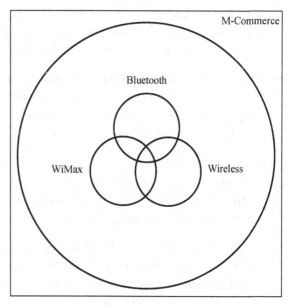

CONCLUSION

There is no question that m-commerce will continue to grow. It is successfully being used. Its reliance on improving standards, both hardware and software, have allowed it to not only develop but to be improved. As more businesses adopt m-commerce solutions, and as additional consumers utilize the flexibility of mobile devices, additional applications will be in demand. M-commerce will also be positively impacted as more Bluetooth and WiMax applications and devices are developed. M-commerce will receive an additional boost as these applications mature and are meshed together on mobile networks. Consumers will have options other than be tied to a desktop plugging into the wall. M-commerce is an area of past growth and future potential for the IT industry.

REFERENCES

Bai, L., Chou, D. C., Yen, D., & Lin, B. (2005). Mobile commerce: Its market analyses. *International Journal of Mobile Communications, 3*(1), 66-81.

Cyr, D., Head, M., & Ivanov, A. (2006). Design aesthetics leading to m-loyalty in mobile commerce. *Information & Management, 43*(8), 950-963.

Dursch, A., & Yen, D. (2004). Bluetooth technology: An exploratory study of the analysis and implementation frameworks. *Computer Standards and Interfaces, 26*(4), 263-277.

Dursch, A., Yen, D., & Huang, S. (2005). Fourth generation wireless communications: An analysis of future potential and implementation. *Computer Standards and Interfaces, 28*(1), 13-25.

Ersala, N., & Yen, D. (2002). Bluetooth technology: A strategic analysis of its role in global 3G wireless communication era. *Computer Standards & Interfaces, 24*(3), 193-206.

Ferro, E., & Potorti, F. (2005). Bluetooth and Wi-Fi wireless protocols: A survey and a comparison. *Wireless Communications, IEEE, 12*(1), 12-26.

Flanigan, M. (2006). *TIA's 2006 telecommunications market review and forecast.* Telecommunications Industry Association. Retrieved from www.tiaonline.org

Four in ten users want to carry out mobile commerce. (2002). *Card Technology Today, 14*(5), 7-8.

Ghosh, A., Wolter, D. R., Andrews, J. G., & Chen, R. (2005). Broadband wireless access with WiMax/802.16: Current performance benchmarks and future potential. *IEEE Communications Magazine, 43,* 129-136.

Global Wireless Telecommunication Services. (2006). London: Datamonitor PLC. Retrieved April 12, 2007, from Business Source Premier database.

Goth, G. (2004).Wireless MAN standard signals next-gen opportunities. *IEEE Distributed Systems Online, 5*(8), 4.

Holma, H., & Toskala, A. (2000) *WCDMA for UMTS: Radio access for third generation mobile communications.* New York: Wiley.

Karnouskos, S., & Fraunhofer, F. (2004). Mobile payment: A journey through existing procedures and standardization initiatives. *IEEE Communications Surveys, 6,* 44-66.

Kharif, O. (2007, February 20). Coming up: Vonage wireless? *BusinessWeek.com.* Retrieved April 20, 2007, from http://businessweek.com/technology/content/feb2007/tc20070220_452876.htm

Leavitt, N. (2000). Will WAP deliver the wireless Internet? *Computer, 33*(5), 16-20.

Saha, S., Jamtgaard, M., & Villasenor, J. (2001). Bringing the wireless Internet to mobile devices. *Computer, 34*(6), 54-58.

Wu, J., & Wang, S. (2005). What drives mobile commerce? An empirical evaluation of the revised technology acceptance model. *Information and. Management, 42*(5), 719-729.

Yen, D., & Chou, D. C. (2000). Wireless communications: Applications and managerial issues. *Industrial Management & Data Systems, 100*(9), 436-443.

Zeng, E. Y., Yen, D., & Hwang, H. (2003). Mobile commerce: The convergence of e-commerce and wireless technology. *International Journal of Services Technology and Management, 4*(3), 302-322.

ADDITIONAL READING

Kane, J., & Yen, D. (2002). Breaking the barriers of connectivity: An analysis of the wireless LAN. *Computer Standards & Interfaces, 24*(1), 5-20.

Varshney, U., & Vetter, R. (2000). Emerging mobile and wireless networks. *Communications of the ACM, 43*(6), 73-81.

Yen, D., & Chou, D. C. (2001). Wireless communication: The next wave of Internet technology. *Technology in Society, 23*(2), 217-226.

This work was previously published in Global Mobile Commerce: Strategies, Implementation and Case Studies, edited by W. W. Huang, Y. Wang, and J. Day, pp. 17-32, copyright 2008 by Information Science Reference, formerly known as Idea Group Reference (an imprint of IGI Global).

Chapter XXIX
Consumer–to–Consumer Electronic Commerce:
A Distinct Research Stream

Kiku Jones
University of Tulsa, USA

Lori N. K. Leonard
University of Tulsa, USA

ABSTRACT

Consumer-to-consumer (C2C) e-commerce is a growing area of e-commerce. However, according to a meta-analysis of critical themes of e-commerce, C2C e-commerce was only represented in the area of online auctions (Wareham, Zheng, & Straub, 2005). C2C e-commerce can encompass much more than just auctions. The question then becomes, "is C2C e-commerce a different research area that deserves its own stream of research?" This study adapts constructs from a business-to-consumer (B2C) e-commerce study of satisfaction (Devaraj, Fan, & Kohli, 2002) to determine what, if any, the differences are in the C2C e-commerce arena. The constructs include elements of the technology acceptance model (TAM), which includes perceived ease of use and usefulness; transaction cost analysis (TCA), which includes uncertainty, asset specificity, and time; and service quality (SERVQUAL), which includes reliability, responsiveness, assurance, and empathy. Participants in the study answered questions regarding these various constructs in relation to their experiences with C2C e-commerce. The findings indicate that TAM, TCA, and SERVQUAL all impact satisfaction in C2C e-commerce. Reliability and responsiveness (areas of service quality) were found to influence C2C e-commerce satisfaction, where as they were not found to be an influence in the B2C study. These findings warrant further research in the C2C e-commerce arena. The study provides implications for future research and practice.

INTRODUCTION

E-commerce is a continuously evolving phenomenon. While media attention of e-commerce has declined in focus, academic research of e-commerce appears to have increased. This can be seen in the amount of e-commerce-specific journals as well as the number of e-commerce-related articles published in the IS main stream journals (Wareham et al., 2005).

In a meta-analysis of the critical themes of e-commerce research, Wareham et al. (2005) performed a meta-analysis of the critical themes of e-commerce research. The analysis included a review of abstracts from "mainstream IS journals," both academic and professional (a full list of the journals used in the analysis can be found in the referenced article), between the years of 1997 and 2003 (65% of which fell between the years 2001 and 2003). At a top level, there are four main areas: (1) business-to-business (B2B), (2) B2C, (3) strategy, and (4) technology adoption. They further refined these broad areas into 17 different themes found in e-commerce research. Of the 17, C2C research was not listed. Some may argue that "Auctions" (one of the 17 themes) covers the full realm of C2C e-commerce. However, C2C e-commerce can encompass much more than just auctions.

C2C e-commerce can also take place in online communities, chat rooms, third-party consumer listing services, and Web-based discussion forums. For example, one consumer recalled a recent C2C e-commerce transaction conducted in a Web-based discussion forum. He indicated to the other participants that he had a car part to sell. Another participant indicated a need for that part. They exchanged address information through the forum. Once the seller received the check from the buyer, he sent the part to him. While the payment and product were sent via postal mail, all interaction regarding the transaction was completed within the Web-based forum. Similar to how third-party consumer listing services

(such as Half.com) or online auctions (such as eBay) facilitate the transaction between sellers and buyers, so did the Web-based forum in this anecdote. The difference comes in the intent of the forum versus the third-party consumer listing service and online auction. However, regardless of the intent of the venue, C2C e-commerce is indeed being conducted in many areas in addition to online auctions. And as such, should be included in the stream of research surrounding C2C e-commerce.

In a quick search for C2C e-commerce, only a few articles could be found which did not solely focus on online auctions and reputation systems. For example, Lin, Li, Janamanchi, & Huang (2006), Livingston (2005), and Melnik and Alm (2002) studied C2C online auctions and reputation systems, and Yamamoto, Ishida, and Ohta (2004) studied C2C reputation management systems, where as Strader and Ramaswami (2002) examined consumer trust in C2C online markets and Armstrong and Hagel (1996) and Orman (2006) described the value of online communities. Even with the online auction and reputation system articles, Wareham et al. (2005) found that only 3% of the articles they reviewed dealt with this area. This lack of research leads one to wonder whether or not C2C e-commerce is a different enough research area to have its own stream of research. Anecdotal evidence suggests that there are enough differences to build a new area of research. This research is an exploratory study to empirically determine if there are indeed differences found in C2C e-commerce and B2C e-commerce research that indicate a need for C2C e-commerce to have its own research stream. To do this, a previous study by Devaraj et al. (2002) that focused on the satisfaction of B2C e-commerce over other commerce methods is modified to reflect C2C e-commerce, utilizing three well-known frameworks: (1) TAM, (2) TCA, and (3) SERVQUAL.

The next section of the paper discusses the research model, followed by the method and sample of the study in the third section. The fourth section provides a discussion of the data analysis and results, and the final section of the paper provides a discussion, limitations, implications for future research, implications for practice, and conclusions based on the study results.

RESEARCH MODEL

New methods for consumers to facilitate their transactions are increasing. C2C e-commerce is one such method. C2C e-commerce is defined in this study as consumers transacting (buying and selling) electronically. The success of this commerce method depends heavily on the consumers' satisfaction. Satisfaction has long been a central measure of IS success. It is "an important means of measuring customers' opinions of an e-commerce system and should cover the entire customer experience cycle from information retrieval through purchase, payment, receipt, and service" (DeLone & McLean, 2004, p. 34). This definition indicates that components of service quality, ease of use, usefulness, reliability, and so forth (DeLone & McLean, 1992, 2003) can have an impact on satisfaction.

Since the C2C area does not have foundation studies at this point, this study builds on the work of Devaraj et al. (2002), who empirically researched consumers' preferences for the B2C e-commerce channel over the traditional brick-and-mortar channel (i.e., physical building where face-to-face commerce is conducted). Their study measured consumer satisfaction utilizing three different frameworks: (1) TAM, (2) TCA, and (3) SERVQUAL. The results of the study indicate that the TAM components have a significant impact on the consumer's satisfaction with the e-commerce channel. In addition, Devaraj et al. (2002) found significant support regarding the TCA components. However, only partial support for the SERVQUAL components was found.

The Devaraj et al. (2002) study focuses on the B2C e-commerce area without making a distinction between B2C and C2C e-commerce. They make reference to B2B e-commerce in the future research section and they encourage researchers to explore their model in this area. However, C2C e-commerce is never mentioned. With the increase in C2C business, it is worth exploring whether or not their model will still hold the same results. That is the focus of our study. Utilizing the same three frameworks, we alter their model to reflect satisfaction of the C2C e-commerce channel. Next is a discussion of the three frameworks to be used in the model.

Technology Acceptance Model (TAM)

TAM is one of the most utilized and referenced models for predicting an individual's use and acceptance of IT (Venkatesh, 1999). In particular, TAM has been used in several empirical studies regarding B2C e-commerce (e.g., Devaraj et al., 2002; Gefen, Karahanna, & Straub, 2003; Gefen & Straub, 2000; Pavlou, 2003) and has been found to be valid in explaining user behaviors in a B2C e-commerce context (Chen, Gillenson, & Sherrell, 2002). TAM indicates that there are two determinants of computer acceptance behaviors: perceived usefulness (PU) and perceived ease of use (PEOU) (Davis, 1989; Davis, Bagozzi, & Warshaw, 1989). PU is described as "the degree to which a person believes that using a particular system would enhance his or her job performance" (Davis, 1989, p. 320). In other words, PU reflects the user's belief that the IT will help him/her achieve specific task-related objectives (Gefen & Straub, 2000). PEOU is described as "the degree to which a person believes that using a particular system would be free of effort" (Davis, 1989, p. 320).

Devaraj et al. (2002) solicited potential respondents from online shoppers, undergraduate and graduate students. Of this mix, 171 agreed to participate in the study. Participants were asked to purchase a product through a traditional brick-and-mortar vendor and then complete an online survey regarding their experience with the channel (not the vendor). They also purchased the same or similar product from an online vendor and answered an online survey regarding their experience with that channel. Only the responses regarding the online channel were analyzed, however the respondents were unaware of this. The study results indicated that both PU and PEOU were significantly related to satisfaction with the e-commerce channel.

Gefen et al. (2003) performed a free-simulation experiment with MBA and senior undergraduate students. The students logged into the Internet and searched for the course's textbook on www.amazon.com. The students went through the process of buying their textbook without the final step of completing the transaction. The students then were given an instrument to fill out regarding their experience. The researchers found that the PU of a given Web site played an important role in determining a repeat customer's intention to purchase on that Web site. Conversely, it was not significant for potential customers. This supports prior research findings that indicate social factors initially affect intention to use.

Davis, Bagozzi, and Warshaw (1992) explain that intrinsic motivation refers to performing an activity for no other reason than the process of performing that activity (e.g., enjoyment of performing the activity). While extrinsic motivation refers to performing an activity in order to reach a goal separate from the activity itself (e.g., PU). Davis et al. (1992) indicate that extrinsic motivation will have a stronger impact on IT adoption than intrinsic motivation. Gefen and Straub (2000) state that PEOU is related to the assessment of intrinsic characteristics of IT (e.g., "ease of use, ease of learning, flexibility, and clarity", p. 1). Their study also utilized a free-simulation experiment method and MBA students. The procedure was the same as the Gefen et al. (2003) study. They

found that PEOU did not affect a consumer's intention to use a website for purchasing; however, PU did have a significant affect on intention. They found for inquiry-based tasks, however, that both PEOU and PU were significant predictors. These studies support the original conclusion that extrinsic motivation is more important than intrinsic motivation.

Pavlou (2003) conducted an exploratory study and then a confirmatory study regarding the TAM components and an individual's intention to transact on a Web site. The exploratory study utilized 103 students in experimental scenarios. Three possible scenarios were used: using Amazon.com (36 students), selecting a Web retailer of their choice (41 students), and discussing Web retailers in general (25 students). Regardless of the scenario, the students were asked to search an item of their choice on the Web retailer's site and discover the process of purchasing that item without actually purchasing the item. The subjects were then asked to complete a questionnaire regarding their experience. This study found that PU was a significant predictor of intention to transact; while PEOU was not found to be a significant predictor. The confirmatory study utilized 155 online consumers. Invitation e-mails were sent to consumers with a URL link to an online survey instrument. The confirmatory study found that both PU and PEOU were significant predictors of a consumer's intention to transact. Pavlou felt the difference in finding was due to the real situation versus the experimental scenario.

Additionally, Chen et al. (2002) used TAM and the innovation diffusion theory (IDT) to examine consumer behavior in a virtual store context. Surveying online consumers, they found PU and PEOU to determine consumer attitudes towards virtual stores. Vijayasarathy (2004) used TAM, among other constructs, to examine consumer intention to use online shopping. Using a mail survey, 281 consumers were assessed. Both PU and PEOU were found to predict attitude towards online shopping. Based on the theory of reasoned action (TRA) and TAM, Shih (2004) developed an extended model to predict consumer acceptance of electronic shopping. Data was collected from 212 participants using questionnaires. The participants were employees of eight small and medium-sized organizations in Taiwan. He found PU and PEOU to affect an individual's electronic shopping attitude. Grandon and Pearson (2004) examined small and medium-sized organizations in the United States to determine factors affecting the adoption of e-commerce. Using an electronic survey, they found PU and PEOU to be determinants of e-commerce adoption. Finally, McCloskey (2006) studied the attitudes and e-commerce participation of older Americans. TAM was used in the study to examine the impact of their attitudes (of PEOU, PU, and trust) on e-commerce usage. She found PU and trust to have a direct effect on usage.

These studies were based on B2C e-commerce. There are no studies utilizing the TAM constructs in a C2C e-commerce setting. It is important to determine if the TAM findings are consistent in this environment.

Transaction Cost Analysis (TCA)

TCA is a framework belonging to the New Institutional Economics paradigm. The framework is based on two main assumptions of human behavior (i.e., bounded rationality and opportunism) and the interplay of the two key dimensions of transactions (i.e., asset specificity and uncertainty) (Rindfleisch & Heide, 1997). Bounded rationality refers to the constraints and limitations of individuals on their cognitive capabilities and rationality. Simon (1977) states that individuals' limited information processing and communication abilities may impede their ability to act rationally. In uncertain environments, these constraints and limitations can become problematic (Rindfleisch & Heide, 1997). Opportunism refers to an individual's quest to serve his/her own self-interests. In uncertain environments, opportunism can increase transac-

tion costs in the form of incomplete or inaccurate information (Devaraj et al., 2002). For example, the seller of a transaction may indicate to the buyer that the product in question is in working condition. However, the seller neglects to tell the consumer that it has been repaired several times. The reason for the seller's incomplete account of the product may be explained by opportunism. Asset specificity refers to any additional investments which have been made to support a relationship. These investments can make it difficult for the buyer and/or seller to switch. However, opportunism may cause the buyer/seller to exploit the relationship in his/her favor (Rindfleisch & Heide, 1997).

Devaraj et al. (2002) (study described in the *TAM section*) found that both uncertainty and asset specificity are significantly related to time. This indicates that the online channels provided good information regarding the product and price. In addition, the wider choice among online channels provided a positive contribution to time savings which, in turn, resulted in a significantly positive relationship between time and satisfaction with the e-commerce channel.

Liang and Huang (1998) did an empirical study utilizing 86 Internet users to determine their purchasing intentions of different products in a B2C e-commerce environment. They found support for their hypothesis that the higher the perceived transaction costs (determined by uncertainty and asset specificity), the less likely a product would be purchased electronically.

Once again, TCA has only been tested in a B2C e-commerce environment. It needs to be tested in a C2C e-commerce environment to determine if the B2C findings hold true.

Service Quality (SERVQUAL)

SERVQUAL was developed to assess general service quality. It measures the difference between the individual's expected level of service and the perceived level of service. This difference is referred to as the gap score. A gap score is calculated on five different dimensions: (1) tangibles (appearance of facilities or Web site; equipment; and personnel), (2) reliability (ability to perform the promised service dependably and accurately), (3) responsiveness (willingness to help customers and provide prompt service), (4) assurance (knowledge and courtesy of employees and their ability to inspire trust and confidence), and (5) empathy (providing caring and individualized attention to customers) (Jiang, Klein, & Carr, 2002).

The use of SERVQUAL in the IS field has been the topic of debate (Jiang et al., 2002; Kettinger & Lee, 1997; Van Dyke, Kappelman, & Prybutok, 1997; Watson, Pitt, & Kavan, 1998). Van Dyke et al. (1997) found there were both conceptual and empirical obscurities. Conceptual obscurities included using the gap score as the operationalized perceived service quality, using the ambiguous expectations construct, and using a single measure of service quality across industries. Empirical obscurities included reduced reliability, poor convergent validity, and unstable dimensionality. Other researchers surveyed various populations

of users to address pieces of these problems such as the reduced reliability (Pitt, Watson, & Kavan, 1997) and dimensionality (Kettinger & Lee, 1997). Jiang et al. (2002) used data from a total of 168 matched sets (IS professionals and IS users) to determine whether or not the problems indicated in the SERVQUAL method were big enough to discredit its use in IS. Their research agreed with previous research that the indicated problems are not substantial enough to lose the capabilities found within the measure.

Kettinger and Lee (2005) tested a new set of scales for SERVQUAL. They posed two levels of IS service quality—desired service and adequate service—and defined the two levels in a zone of tolerance (ZOT). The ZOT represented the satisfactory range of IS service performance. Their research findings indicated validity for a four-dimension IS ZOT SERVQUAL instrument for desired, adequate, and perceived service quality levels. Additionally, Wang and Tang (2003) proposed EC-SERVQUAL (e-commerce service quality) to measure customer perceived service quality of Web sites that market digital products/

Figure 1. Predictors of satisfaction of C2C e-commerce

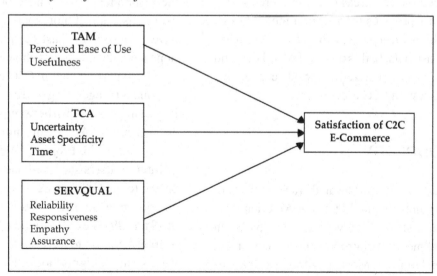

services, and Bauer, Falk, and Hammerschmidt (2006) proposed eTransQual, a transaction, process-based scale for measuring service quality.

Devaraj et al. (2002) (study described in the *TAM section*) found that only the empathy and assurance components of SERVQUAL were significantly related to the satisfaction of the e-commerce channel. Devaraj et al. offer a possible explanation for this finding. It could be that the respondents were not presented with an opportunity to examine the responsiveness and reliability components. These components tend to be established over time and multiple transactions, which was not represented in the study.

Some additional research has been done in the area of service quality and B2C e-commerce (Cao, Zhang, & Seydel, 2005; Gounaris & Dimitriadis, 2003; Lee & Lin, 2005). Varying results indicate that future research is needed to determine additional mediating factors which may be present. It is also easily seen that the issue of how to measure service quality in IS continues to be debated. Since this research is based on the Devaraj et al. (2002) study, the use of a single survey which operationalizes perceived service quality through reliability, responsiveness, empathy, and assurance is used. SERVQUAL has not been tested in the C2C e-commerce environment; therefore, it needs to be tested to determine where, if any, the differences lie between the two areas of e-commerce.

Figure 1 provides the research model of this paper which incorporates the three aforementioned constructs. In this model, TAM, TCA, and SERVQUAL are theorized to impact a consumer's satisfaction with C2C e-commerce.

METHODOLOGY

Undergraduate students located in a Southwestern university in the United States of America were used for this study. They were solicited based on their enrollment in an introduction to management IS course. Drennan, Mort, and Previte (2006) ar-

gue that university students are "representative of a dominant cohort of online users" (p.6). College students represent the most connected (online) segment of the U.S. population, shopping online and spending online. Therefore, they are experienced and frequent users of the Internet.

Participants were given a modified version of the instruments created by Devaraj et al. (2002) used to collect data regarding the TAM, TCA, and SERVQUAL components (see individual statements listed in Tables 1, 2, 3, and 4). Participants were asked to indicate on a 7-point Likert scale the degree to which they agreed with the C2C e-commerce statements. The participants were informed that the survey was completely voluntary and their responses would be kept anonymous and only reported in the aggregate. They were asked to answer the questions regarding their experiences with C2C e-commerce. In addition to these questions, participants were asked to fill out a brief demographics survey. Out of a total of 104 potential respondents, 83 chose to participate (80%).

A majority of the respondents (70%) had participated in C2C e-commerce (such as online auctions, e-mail groups, Web-based discussion forums, and/or chat rooms) as either the buyer or seller. However, 72% had never been the seller of a C2C e-commerce transaction. A majority of the respondents (63%) have purchased an item using this channel more than once; 69% of them have done so in the past 12 months. Online auctions were the method of choice for 76% of those who have participated in C2C e-commerce. The respondents' ages ranged from 19 to 41 with the largest majority (59%) between the ages of 20 and 30. A survey of American adults by Pew Internet & American Life Project (2006) found that 67% of Internet users surveyed had made a purchase online (either B2C or C2C), and that the largest age group of Internet users is between the ages of 18 and 29. They also found a larger percentage of Internet users to have some college education versus only a high school education. Therefore, our sample's demographics are consistent with the demographics of Internet users.

DATA ANALYSIS AND RESULTS

Validity and Reliability of Measures

Self-reported data on two or more variables collected from the same source has the potential to lead to common method variance. Therefore, Harman's (1967) single-factor test was used in this study to test for this bias. This test assumes that if a high level of common method variance is present, then when all of the variables are entered together, all will load on one factor accounting for all of the variance or one factor will account for a majority of the variance. In this study, an exploratory factor analysis (EFA) was performed and seven factors with an eigenvalue greater than

one emerged. The variance explained ranged from 3% to 44% of the total variance. This result provides evidence that common method variance should not be a concern in this study.

The multi-item constructs used in the model were tested for construct validity and reliability. Factors were extracted using principal component analysis (PCA). Each of the TAM constructs' items loaded on one factor. The perceived ease of use construct yielded a Cronbach's alpha score of .77 and the percent of variation explained was 60.66%. The usefulness construct generated a Cronbach's alpha score of .81 with 64.78% of the variation explained. Table 1 shows the results of the factor analysis for the TAM constructs. Variables for each of the TAM constructs (PEOU and PU) were calculated for each subject as the average of those items.

The TCA construct items also loaded on one factor for each construct. The Cronbach's alpha

Table 1. TAM constructs factor analysis

PERCEIVED EASE OF USE (PEOU)	LOADINGS
Overall, I believe that C2C e-commerce is easier than other forms of commerce.	.50
It is easy for me to buy/sell using C2C e-commerce.	.83
My interactions during C2C e-commerce were clear and understandable.	.89
I believe that it is easy to do what I want to do while conducting C2C e-commerce.	.84
Cronbach's alpha	.77
Eigenvalue	2.43
Variance explained	60.66%
PERCEIVED USEFULNESS (PU)	
C2C e-commerce gives me greater control over my buying/selling experience.	.78
C2C e-commerce improves the quality of my decision making.	.92
C2C e-commerce is a more effective way to buy/sell products and services.	.87
Overall, I find C2C e-commerce very useful.	.62
Cronbach's alpha	.81
Eigenvalue	2.60
Variance explained	64.78%

scores for these constructs were calculated as .83, .74, and .75 for uncertainty, asset specificity, and time, respectively. The percent of variation explained was 67.18%, 57.15%, and 69.09%, respectively. Table 2 shows the results of the factor analysis for the TCA constructs. Variables for each of the TCA constructs (UNC, ASSE, and TIME) were calculated for each subject as the average of those items.

The SERVQUAL construct items had similar results to the TAM and TCA constructs. The Cronbach's alpha scores for these constructs were found to be .83, .88, .60, and .84 for reliability, responsiveness, empathy, and assurance, respectively. The percent of variation explained was 66.01%, 81.14%, 56.27%, and 75.95%, respectively. Table 3 shows the results of the factor analysis for the SERVQUAL constructs. Variables for each of

Table 2. TCA constructs factor analysis

UNCERTAINTY (UNC)	LOADINGS
It was easy for me to get/provide relevant quantitative (price, taxes, etc.) information using C2C e-commerce.	.83
I believe that it was possible for me to evaluate the various alternative products using C2C e-commerce.	.72
The C2C e-commerce environment provided adequate information.	.90
The C2C e-commerce environment provided sufficient information about the buyer/seller.	.82
Cronbach's alpha	.83
Eigenvalue	2.69
Variance explained	67.18%
ASSET SPECIFICITY (ASSE)	
There are many Web sites for which the products I have bought/sold are available.	.72
I was satisfied with the number of environments where I could buy/sell products.	.77
C2C e-commerce gives me a wider choice of different sellers/buyers compared to traditional commerce methods.	.79
C2C e-commerce gives me more opportunities compared to traditional commerce methods.	.75
Cronbach's alpha	.74
Eigenvalue	2.29
Variance explained	57.15%
TIME (TIME)	
C2C e-commerce helps me accomplish tasks more quickly.	.69
I did not have to spend too much time to complete the transaction using C2C e-commerce.	.86
I did not have to spend too much effort to complete the transaction using C2C e-commerce.	.93
Cronbach's alpha	.75
Eigenvalue	2.07
Variance explained	69.09%

Table 3. SERVQUAL constructs factor analysis

RELIABILITY (REL)	LOADINGS
I believe that C2C e-commerce is reliable.	.84
I believe that what I ask for is what I get in C2C e-commerce.	.82
I think that the C2C e-commerce seller/buyer with whom I transacted acted in accordance to our agreement.	.74
I trust the C2C e-commerce seller/buyer to complete the transaction on time.	.85
Cronbach's alpha	.83
Eigenvalue	2.64
Variance explained	66.01%
RESPONSIVENESS (RESP)	
I believe that the C2C e-commerce seller/buyer is responsive to my needs.	.90
In the case of any problem, I think the C2C e-commerce seller/buyer will respond promptly.	.90
The C2C e-commerce seller/buyer will address any concerns that I have.	.91
Cronbach's alpha	.88
Eigenvalue	2.43
Variance explained	81.14%
EMPATHY (EMP)	
The C2C e-commerce seller/buyer remembers or recognizes me as a repeat customer/seller (after the first time).	.78
I think C2C e-commerce can address the specific needs of each buyer/seller.	.81
I was satisfied with the payment options (e.g., money order, different credit cards) available with C2C e-commerce.	.65
Cronbach's alpha	.60
Eigenvalue	1.69
Variance explained	56.27%
ASSURANCE (ASSU)	
I felt confident about the C2C e-commerce transaction decision.	.89
I feel safe in my transactions with the C2C e-commerce environment.	.84
The C2C e-commerce seller/buyer had answers to all my questions regarding the transaction.	.88
Cronbach's alpha	.84
Eigenvalue	2.28
Variance explained	75.95%

Table 4. Satisfaction construct factor analysis model testing

SATISFACTION (SAT)	LOADINGS
Overall, I was satisfied with my C2C e-commerce experience.	.87
The C2C e-commerce environment provided information content which met my needs.	.89
It was possible for me to buy the product of my choice easily using C2C e-commerce.	.88
Cronbach's alpha	.85
Eigenvalue	2.33
Variance explained	77.64%

Table 5. Regression on satisfaction: TAM variables

Dependent Variable: SAT					
Independent Variable	Parameter Estimate	Standard Error	t	p	VIF
PEOU	.56	.10	5.60	.000***	2.47
PU	.42	.10	4.03	.000***	2.47
Overall model fit: $p = .000$*** $R^2 = .37$ ***p<.001					

Table 6. Regression on satisfaction: TCA variables

Dependent Variable: SAT					
Independent Variable	Parameter Estimate	Standard Error	t	p	VIF
UNC	.54	.11	4.73	.000***	1.43
ASSE	.26	.13	2.02	.048*	1.33
TIME	.40	.11	3.73	.000***	1.36
Overall model fit: $p = .000$*** $R^2 = .33$ ***p<.001; *p<.05					

the SERVQUAL constructs (REL, RESP, EMP, and ASSU) were calculated for each subject as the average of those items.

The multi-item construct for satisfaction was also tested. A Cronbach's alpha score was found to be .85 with 77.64% of the variation explained. Table 4 shows the results of the factor analysis

for the satisfaction construct. A variable for the satisfaction construct (SAT) was calculated as the average of the items. Each of the constructs in the model exceeded the recommended Cronbach's alpha threshold score of .50 (Nunnally, 1967), but one did not exceed the mostly commonly used threshold in the literature, .70 (Nunnally &

Bernstein, 1994). However, it should be noted that lower (.60) and higher (.80) thresholds are used in the literature (Santos, 1999).

Regression analysis was performed to test the relationships between the construct variables and satisfaction. Residual plots were reviewed for non-random scatter about the zero line. No heteroscedasticity was found in the data. Variance inflation factors (VIF) were examined for each of the independent variables in the model. All values were small (below 10) suggesting there is no problem with multicollinearity in the data.

Table 5 shows the regression results using the TAM variables. Both perceived ease of use and usefulness are positively significant at the .001 level. This indicates respondents are more satisfied with C2C e-commerce when they find the process easy to complete and effective.

Table 6 shows the regression results using the TCA variables. Uncertainty is shown to be positive and significantly associated with satisfaction at the .001 level. Both asset specificity and time are positively significant at the .05 level. This indicates that a respondent is satisfied with C2C e-commerce when information is readily available, there is a variety of choices (both with places to buy/sell and products to buy/sell), and the process can be done quickly.

Table 7 shows the regression results using the SERVQUAL variables. Reliability, responsiveness, and empathy are all positively significant at the .01 level. Assurance was shown to be positively significant at the .001 level. This indicates that respondents are more satisfied with C2C e-commerce when the process is reliable (including receiving the correct products/payment in the agreed upon time frame); the buyer/seller is responsive to the needs, questions, and concerns of the buyer/seller; the buyer/seller recognizes each buyer's/seller's specific needs (including possible payment options); and the buyer/seller provides assurances that the online purchase is correct.

DISCUSSION

The study findings indicate that many individuals are choosing to participate in C2C e-commerce, both as buyers and sellers. With the increase in this type of e-commerce, a look into the factors affecting this area is appropriate. The findings confirm anecdotal evidence that C2C e-commerce is different from B2C e-commerce and deserves its own research theme. Within this new research theme, models specifically dealing with the C2C e-commerce area need to be developed and tested.

Table 7. Regression on satisfaction: SERVQUAL variables

Dependent Variable: SAT					
Independent Variable	Parameter Estimate	Standard Error	t	p	VIF
REL	.45	.13	3.39	.002**	3.73
RESP	.36	.11	3.35	.001**	3.59
EMP	.48	.15	3.21	.002**	1.97
ASSU	.42	.11	3.90	.000***	2.54
Overall model fit: $p = .022*$ $R^2 = .26$ ***p<.001; **p<.01; *p<.05					

The satisfaction model of C2C e-commerce presented and tested here can be a stepping stone for further research.

All model variables from the three constructs, TAM, TCA, and SERVQUAL were found to be significant influencers on satisfaction. More specifically, the ease of use and usefulness of the C2C online environment (TAM); the amount of information provided to eliminate uncertainty, the additional avenues provided for buying and selling (asset specificity), and the time saved when accomplishing buying/selling (TCA); and the buyers/sellers being reliable, responsive, assuring, and empathetic (SERVQUAL) were found to predict satisfaction. It appears that C2C e-commerce relationships can be quite complex, with many factors affecting a consumer's satisfaction with this type of e-commerce.

When comparing these findings to those completed by Devaraj et al. (2002) for B2C e-commerce, there are distinct differences. Devaraj et al. found the same variables to be significant in the B2C online arena except reliability and responsiveness (two components of service quality). With C2C e-commerce, this study found an individual's satisfaction to depend on all four aspects of service quality. The reliability the consumer felt toward another consumer predicted his/her satisfaction. The difference found in C2C e-commerce versus B2C e-commerce may have to do with the feeling of some guarantee of the transaction when a business is involved. This feeling may not be present when dealing directly with other consumers. Therefore, one would expect reliability to influence satisfaction in C2C e-commerce but not in B2C e-commerce. The responsiveness of one consumer to another predicted his/her satisfaction in C2C e-commerce. Again, in a B2C online environment, responsiveness would not be as large of a concern; consumers expect businesses to respond to their needs while they may not hold the same expectation of individual consumers. Therefore, a display of responsiveness

from consumers would increase the satisfaction of C2C e-commerce.

LIMITATIONS AND IMPLICATIONS FOR FUTURE RESEARCH

This research provides evidence that differences do exist in the C2C and B2C online realms. Therefore, further investigation is warranted in the broad area of C2C e-commerce, which has been given little attention up to this point. While there are many articles on online auctions, the other methods for conducting C2C e-commerce have yet to make a dent in the potential research opportunities.

One limitation of this study is that it gathered data regarding all forms of C2C e-commerce, but it did not test for differences between the methods. Differences should be investigated between C2C online auctions and the other forms of C2C e-commerce such as Web forums and chat rooms.

Another limitation of the study is that mediating factors and interactions between model constructs were not investigated. Researchers may want to consider adding mediating factors to the present research model, as well as any interactions between the constructs. For example, a person's age or gender could mediate the factors provided in this model.

This study provided evidence of differences between C2C and B2C based on variables used in a B2C study. There may be additional variables which are worth investigating. For example, trust in C2C e-commerce may be an avenue worth pursuing. The uncertainty found in C2C e-commerce logically seems to be higher than in B2C e-commerce. This may affect how consumers trust one another and their satisfaction level of C2C e-commerce. Another potential future research study could involve product complexity. Product complexity has been proposed as an important factor in the study of buyer/seller behaviors (Zhang & Reichgelt, 2006). Therefore, a modification of the TCA could be pursued in future C2C e-commerce studies. Also, it appears that additional research is needed in the area of service quality in IS research to determine if a universal measure can be obtained.

IMPLICATIONS FOR PRACTICE

Consumers wishing to practice C2C e-commerce may find this study useful in their preparations to conduct e-commerce with other consumers. The findings of this study indicate that there are many aspects of C2C e-commerce which influence their satisfaction. Consumers would be wise to note that simply having a good Web site and/or needed products may not be enough for another consumer to be satisfied with the experience. For example, the study indicates that responsiveness to the needs, questions, and concerns of the buyer/seller impact a consumer's satisfaction. In addition, consumers' satisfaction of C2C e-commerce is impacted by the reliable and complete information provided by the buyer/seller in a transaction. Consumers should keep this in mind when preparing information for potential buyers/sellers.

CONCLUSION

C2C e-commerce is a growing area of e-commerce. As such, the field of research in this area should reflect that growth. This study adapted constructs (TAM, TCA, and SERVQUAL) from a B2C e-commerce study of satisfaction and found different results in the constructs which affect satisfaction in the given area. Namely, reliability and responsiveness (components of the SERVQUAL construct) were found to be predictors of satisfaction in the C2C e-commerce environment but not in the B2C e-commerce environment. This evidence provides support that

C2C e-commerce is deserving of its own research stream. Future research possibilities for this area of e-commerce include overall C2C e-commerce themes (such as trust) and differences between venues (such as between online auctions and online communities). Focusing research in these areas will provide consumers the needed information to conduct C2C e-commerce in the most effective and efficient way.

REFERENCES

Armstrong, A., & Hagel, J. (1996). The real value of on-line communities. *Harvard Business Review, 74*(3), 134-141.

Bauer, H. H., Falk, T., & Hammerschmidt, M. (2006). eTransQual: A transaction process-based approach for capturing service quality in online shopping. *Journal of Business Research, 59,* 866-875.

Cao, M., Zhang, Q., & Seydel, J. (2005). B2C e-commerce Web site quality: An empirical examination. *Industrial Management & Data Systems, 105*(5), 645-661.

Chen, L., Gillenson, M. L., & Sherrell, D. L. (2002). Enticing online consumers: An extended technology acceptance perspective. *Information & Management, 39*(8), 705-719.

Davis, F. D. (1989). Perceived usefulness, perceived ease of use, and user acceptance of information technology. *MIS Quarterly, 13*(3), 319-340.

Davis, F. D., Bagozzi, R. P., & Warshaw, P. R. (1989). User acceptance of computer technology: A comparison of two theoretical models. *Management Science, 35*(8), 982-1003.

Davis, F. D., Bagozzi, R. P., & Warshaw, P. R. (1992). Extrinsic and intrinsic motivation to use computers in the workplace. *Journal of Applied Social Psychology, 22*(14), 1111-1132.

DeLone, W. H., & McLean, E. R. (1992). Information systems success: The quest for the dependent variable. *Information Systems Research, 3*(1), 60-95.

DeLone, W. H., & McLean, E. R. (2003). The DeLone and McLean model of information systems success: A ten-year update. *Journal of Management Information Systems, 19*(4), 9-30.

DeLone, W. H., & McLean, E. R. (2004). Measuring e-commerce success: Applying the DeLone & McLean information systems success model. *International Journal of Electronic Commerce, 9*(1), 31-47.

Devaraj, S., Fan, M., & Kohli, R. (2002). Antecedents of B2C channel satisfaction and preference: Validating e-commerce metrics. *Information Systems Research, 12*(3), 316-333.

Drennan, J., Mort, G. S., & Previte, J. (2006). Privacy, risk perception, and expert online behavior: An exploratory study of household end users. *Journal of Organizational and End User Computing, 18*(1), 1-22.

Gefen, D., Karahanna, E., & Straub, D. (2003). Inexperience and experience with online stores: The importance of TAM and trust. *IEEE Transactions on Engineering Management, 50*(3), 307-321.

Gefen, D., & Straub, D. (2000). The relative importance of perceived ease of use in IS adoption: A study of e-commerce adoption. *Journal of the Association for Information Systems, 1*(Article 8), 1-28.

Gounaris, S., & Dimitriadis, S. (2003). Assessing service quality on the Web: Evidence from business-to-consumer portals. *Journal of Services Marketing, 17*(5), 529-548.

Grandon, E. E., & Pearson, J. M. (2004). Electronic commerce adoption: An empirical study of small and medium US businesses. *Information & Management, 42*(1), 197-216.

Harman, H. H. (1967). *Modern factor analysis.* University of Chicago Press.

Jiang, J. J., Klein, G., & Carr, C. L. (2002). Measuring information systems service quality: SERVQUAL from the other side. *MIS Quarterly, 26*(2), 145-166.

Kettinger, W. J., & Lee, C. C. (1997). Pragmatic perspectives on the measurement of information systems service quality. *MIS Quarterly, 21*(2), 223-240.

Kettinger, W. J., & Lee, C. C. (2005). Zones of tolerance: Alternative scales for measuring information systems service quality. *MIS Quarterly, 29*(4), 607-623.

Lee, G.-G., & Lin, H.-F. (2005). Customer perceptions of e-service quality in online shopping. *International Journal of Retail & Distribution Management, 33*(2), 161-176.

Liang, T.-P., & Huang, J.-S. (1998). An empirical study on consumer acceptance of products in electronic markets: A transaction cost model. *Decision Support Systems, 24,* 29-43.

Lin, Z., Li, D., Janamanchi, B., & Huang, W. (2006). Reputation distribution and consumer-to-consumer online auction market structure: An exploratory study. *Decision Support Systems, 41,* 435-448.

Livingston, J. A. (2005). How valuable is a good reputation? A sample selection model of Internet auction. *The Review of Economics and Statistics, 87*(3), 453-465.

McCloskey, D. W. (2006). The importance of ease of use, usefulness, and trust in online consumers: An examination of the technology acceptance model with older consumers. *Journal of Organizational and End User Computing, 18*(3), 47-65.

Melnik, M. I., & Alm, J. (2002). Does a seller's ecommerce reputation matter? Evidence from

Ebay auctions. *The Journal of Industrial Economics, 50*(3), 337-349.

Nunnally, J. C. (1967). *Psychometric theory.* New York: McGraw-Hill.

Nunnally, J. C., & Bernstein, I. H. (1994). *Psychometric theory* (3rd ed.). New York: McGraw-Hill.

Orman, L. V. (2006). Optimum design of electronic communities as economic entities. *Information Systems Frontiers, 8,* 179-194.

Pavlou, P. A. (2003). Consumer acceptance of electronic commerce: Integrating trust and risk with the technology acceptance model. *International Journal of Electronic Commerce, 7*(3), 101-134.

Pew Internet & American Life Project. (2006). *Demographics of Internet users.* Retrieved January 8, 2007, from http://www.pewinternet. org/trends/User_Demo_4.26.06.htm

Pitt, L. F., Watson, R. T., & Kavan, C. B. (1997). Measuring information systems service quality: Concerns for a complete canvas. *MIS Quarterly, 21*(2), 209-221.

Rindfleisch, A., & Heide, J. B. (1997). Transaction cost analysis: Past, present, and future applications. *Journal of Marketing, 61,* 30-54.

Santos, J. R. A. (1999). Cronbach's alpha: A tool for assessing the reliability of scales. *Journal of Extension, 37*(2), 1-5.

Shih, H.-P. (2004). An empirical study on predicting user acceptance of e-shopping on the Web. *Information & Management, 41*(3), 351-368.

Simon, H. A. (1977). *The new science of management decision.* Englewood Cliffs, NJ: Prentice Hall.

Strader, T. J., & Ramaswami, S. N. (2002). The value of seller trustworthiness in C2C online markets. *Communications of the ACM, 45*(12), 45-49.

Van Dyke, T. P., Kappelman, L. A., & Prybutok, V. R. (1997). Measuring information systems service quality: Concerns on the use of the SERVQUAL questionnaire. *MIS Quarterly, 21*(2), 195-208.

Venkatesh, V. (1999). Creation of favorable user perceptions: Exploring the role of intrinsic motivation. *MIS Quarterly, 23*(2), 239-260.

Vijayasarathy, L. R. (2004). Predicting consumer intentions to use on-line shopping: The case for an augmented technology acceptance model. *Information & Management, 41*(6), 747-762.

Wang, Y.-S., & Tang, T.-I. (2003). Assessing customer perceptions of Website service quality in digital marketing environments. *Journal of End User Computing, 15*(3), 14-31.

Wareham, J., Zheng, J. G., & Straub, D. (2005). Critical themes in electronic commerce research: A meta-analysis. *Journal of Information Technology, 20,* 1-19.

Watson, R. T., Pitt, L. F., & Kavan, C. B. (1998). Measuring information systems service quality: Lessons from two longitudinal case studies. *MIS Quarterly, 22*(1), 61-79.

Yamamoto, H., Ishida, K., & Ohta, T. (2004). Modeling reputation management system on on-line C2C market. *Computational & Mathematical Organization Theory, 10,* 165-178.

Zhang, A., & Reichgelt, H. (2006). Product complexity as a determinant of transaction governance structure: An empirical comparison of Web-only and traditional banks. *Journal of Electronic Commerce in Organizations, 4*(3), 1-17.

This work was previously published in Journal of Electronic Commerce in Organizations, Vol. 5, Issue 4, edited by M. Khosrow-Pour, pp. 39-54, copyright 2007 by IGI Publishing, formerly known as Idea Group Publishing (an imprint of IGI Global).

Chapter XXX
Improving M–Commerce Services Effectiveness with the Use of User–Centric Content Delivery

Panagiotis Germanakos
National & Kapodistrian University of Athens, Greece

Nikos Tsianos
National & Kapodistrian University of Athens, Greece

Zacharias Lekkas
National & Kapodistrian University of Athens, Greece

Constantinos Mourlas
National & Kapodistrian University of Athens, Greece

George Samaras
University of Cyprus, Cyprus

ABSTRACT

Advances in wireless communications and information technology have made the Mobile Web a reality. The Mobile Web is the response to the need for anytime, anywhere access to information and services. Many wireless applications have already been deployed and are available to customers via their mobile phones and wirelessly-connected PDAs. However, as communications and other IT usage becomes an integral part of many people's lives and the available products and services become more varied and capable, users expect to be able to personalize a service to meet their individual needs and preferences. The involved sectors have to meet these challenges by reengineering their front-end and back-end office. This article will examine the interaction requirements regarding a friendlier, personalized and more effective multi-channel services environment. It will present the mobility challenges and constraints implemented into the business sector, investigating the current m-commerce situation and the extended user characteristics presenting a high level user-centric m-commerce architecture.

INTRODUCTION

The Internet revolution has brought about a new wave of conducting business and proved to be an important marketing tool for all sorts of business fields that found this new means as convenient as it is creative. With the emergence of wireless and mobile technologies, new communication platforms and devices, apart from PC-based Internet access, are now emerging, making the delivery of services available through a variety of multi-channel mediums without loosing their integrity or quality of their content (Germanakos et al., 2005a). Inevitably, this increases user requirements, which are now focused upon an *"anytime, anywhere and anyhow"* basis. Moreover, the explosive growth in the size and use of the World Wide Web as well as the complicated nature of most Web structures may lead in orientation difficulties, as users often lose sight of the goal of their inquiry, look for stimulating rather than informative material, or even use the navigational features unwisely. To alleviate such navigational difficulties, researchers have put huge amounts of effort to identify the peculiarities of each user group and design methodologies and systems that could deliver an adapted and personalized Web content. Challenges therefore range not only on adapting to the heterogeneous user needs and user environment issues, such as current location and time (Panayiotou, & Samaras, 2004), but also on

a number of other considerations with respect to multi-channel delivery of the applications concerning multimedia, services, entertainment, commerce, and so forth. That is why, when the next big thing in technological gadgets, the mobile phone flooded the market, offering cheap SMS services using the GSM technology and enabling the extremely successful i-Mode and mobile Internet, various business institutions felt they couldn't stay away from this new rising opportunity.

Relevant channel and distribution strategies are critical for future advancement of m-commerce services to achieve accessible, customer-focused and responsive services. Following the growing user demands and requirements as well as the rapid development of the technological advancements and infrastructure capabilities, the development of m-commerce services should not only focus on making the service available on the Internet, but also examine the different delivery platforms. Indisputably, this is the vision of an interoperable, transparent and secure continent whereby multi-channel service delivery integration is considered fundamental.

This article emphasizes the proliferation of m-commerce services delivery starting with a reference to multi-channel delivery characteristics of user-centric services and the investigation of the m-commerce status and dimensions in various application areas (market fields). The adaptation and personalization considerations with regards to new user requirements and demands is also analyzed emphasizing the significance and peculiarities of user profiling for providing a more personalized m-commerce services result. It further presents a high level architecture for personalizing m-commerce services, introducing a comprehensive user profiling that incorporates intrinsic user characteristics such as user perceptual preferences (visual, cognitive and emotional processing parameters), on top of the "traditional" ones (such as name, age, education, etc.).

SERVICE REQUIREMENTS AND DELIVERY

To struggle against the amplification of the digital divide and therefore to think 'user interaction' whatever the age, income, education, experience, and the social condition of the citizen. (Europe's Information Society, 2004)

The specific theme above reveals exactly the need for user-centric m-government services development and personalized content delivery. In many ways, the new technology provides greater opportunities for access. However, there are important problems in determining precisely what users want and need, and how to provide Web-based services content in a user-friendly and effective way. User needs are always conditioned by what they already get, or imagine they can get. A channel can change the user perception of an m-government application: when users have a free choice between different channels to access an application, they will choose the channel that realizes the highest relative value for them. However, separate development of different channels for a single service (multi-channel delivery) can lead to inconsistencies such as different data formats or interfaces. To overcome the drawbacks of multiple-channel content delivery, the different channels should be integrated and coordinated.

Since successful m-government service delivery depends on a vast range of parameters, there is not a single formula to fit all situations. However, there have been reported particular steps (IDA, 2004) that could guide a provider throughout the channel selection process. Moreover, it should be mentioned that the suitability and usefulness of channels depends on a range of factors, out of which technology is only one element. Additional features that could affect the service channels assessment could be: directness, accessibility and inclusion, speed, security and privacy and availability. To realize their potential value though, channels need also to be properly implemented and operated.

The design and implementation complexity is rising significantly with the many channels and their varying capabilities and limitations. Network issues include low bandwidth, unreliable connectivity, lack of processing power, limited interface of wireless devices and user mobility. On the other hand, mobile devices issues include small size, limited processing power, limited memory and storage space, small screens, high latency, and restricted data entry (Germanakos et al., 2005a).

AN OVERVIEW OF M-COMMERCE/M-MARKETING THEORETICAL FRAMEWORK

It is generally agreed that m-commerce is the use of mobile or handheld devices for communication and commerce transactions without any formal conceptualization of the term currently in existence, due to the continuous technological evolution. Therefore, there is no clear, inclusive and broad definition of all the aspects it might include (Balasubramanian et al., 2002).

What needs to be taken into account is what m-commerce means for an organisation belonging to a specific market field and which definition is more close to the needs of these institutions. Therefore, Easton's (2002) approach could be more descriptive, simple and close to what these organisations need to know about the m-commerce term. Easton claims that: (a) m-commerce is the purchase of a product or a service through wireless devices; (b) there is a number of physical limitations to the above devices indicating to the end-user that it is more convenient to sign up to mobile services by using the traditional interface of the PCs; and (c) the models used by the organisations in the case of m-commerce are more close to "click and mortar" paradigm.

For example, in a theatre context the users will receive information about the performance and the box office contact details through mobile commerce and then they will purchase the ticket at the box office, or payment of the ticket will be done wirelessly with various methods, but still the transaction will be fulfilled when the purchaser attends the performance at the theatre.

Furthermore, what someone should be interested in is not the mobile Internet itself, "the representation of the physical world" in the wireless devices, but rather the mobile marketplace in which different kinds of transactions take place: communication services and wireless purchase. The mobile marketplace covers three dimensions (see *Figure 1*): personalisation according to local position of the holder and the relevance of information to his preferences, localization through the local based services, and immediacy (Lindgren, Jedbratt, & Svebsson, 2002).

As literature indicates, mobile phones are a communication medium that keeps people connected at any place, wherever they go and any time. Therefore, it is accounted as the most effective tool of direct marketing, while wireless marketing involves reaching and servicing customers and developing relationships with them through premium services (Bayne, 2002). Towse & Elgew (2003) describe marketing as "the process whereby the organisation's goals for its products and services are strategically developed and implemented to meet carefully reached price, product, place and promotion preferences of targeted customer groups." In this mentioned marketing mix (5Ps: product, place, promotion, price and, for arts organisations, people) it is clear that the mobile phone sets a new spectrum of marketing applications.

The infrastructures to support great financial transaction through mobile devices are still under development and consequently the mobile phone is used more closely to marketing applications. Therefore, the greater part of analysis in this article mainly concerns the modern m-marketing services era and dedicates a narrower part to the transactional nature of the medium. However, m-marketing is included by definition in the term of "m-commerce," and in the article the terms are used according to each case.

Under the term "m-marketing," two main methods are analyzed: push and pull marketing. Pull marketing method involves the consumers pulling what interests them toward themselves, either the product or information itself. Here the messages are sent instantly after a personal request of the recipient. In the case of push marketing method the marketer sends—or better—pushes the message to the consumers, but in this case the message is sent massively to the subscribers of such service. Another term that is under the umbrella of push marketing is "location-based services" (LBS) or "mobile location services" (MLS). These are "applications that utilize information related to the geographical position of their users in order to provide value-added services to them" (Giaglis et al., 2003).

Mobile Related Technological Aspects

The present technologies used in telecommunication are GSM (générale système mobile/global system for mobile communications), WAP (wireless application protocol), and GPRS (general packet radio service), which, accompanied by

Figure 1. M-marketplace dimensions

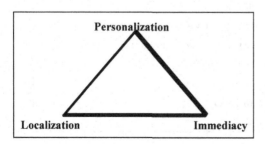

the third generation mobile devices (3G), offer to the end-user a broad variety of capabilities. Mobiles can hardly replace computers due to device limitations such as the screen and the low memory. Even processing capabilities were quite low in the beginning of the 3G development. The first services offered were mostly data services like text alerts for news and entertainment. These alerts are closely related to the wider used form of communication, text messages or else SMS. Text messages are enriched in the later version of the 3G devices with graphics, videos or picture launched as the MMS (multimedia message services) services (Paavilainen, 2002). The services that are slowly launched in the telecommunication markets are the location-based services, which are

Table 1. Challenges of marketing in digital era

Frameworks	Trends
Globalisation	1. global market
	2. global brands, i.e., Tate
	3. Global organizations, i.e., Guggenheim
Society	1. cash rich, time poor → materialistic hedonism
	2. increased leisure time, "the hurried leisure class"
	3. increased technology ownership (mobile, PCs, PDAs)
	4. Individualism
Technology	1. digitalistion of cultural products and data compression, i.e., musical pieces in Mp3 formats, films in DVD
	2. Internet → development of peer-to-peer transactions, e-commerce
	3. rise of Internet → growth of commerce
	4. Information, easy access o data
Virtualisation of digital channels	1. development of new channels, i.e., mobile phones and virtualization of products/services
Virtualisation of payments	1. plastic cards with magnetic stripe/ chip & pin (debit, credit, loyalty cards)
	2. Smart cards
	3. electronic cash/ electronic wallet
	4. Micropayments
Media trends	1. from mass messages to individual
	2. From generic to specific
	3. from print to electronic
	4. from passive to interactive
	5. from plenty of time to fastest way of communication
	6. 24 hours a day/ 7 days a week, global presence
Law	1. Issues of privacy and security
	2. Data Protection Act
	3. Intellectual Property issues
	4. fraud

closely related to the global positioning system (GPS), cell identification and Bluetooth. With these technologies each mobile is detected according to its exact location (Giaglis et al., 2003). With Bluetooth it will be easier to receive text alerts customized to the geographical location, for example, information about the nearest theatre, or receive a promotion alert when the user is near to a theatre house.

The Role of New Media in Modern Society

It would be inadequate to examine the use of mobile commerce and marketing by the various business institutions without presenting the general context of the modern era and what has led to the decision of following this innovative technology. Subsequent to the suggestions that technologies should not be seen without being connected to other processes and factors that set the frameworks, we present an overview to the social and economic tendencies that lead to the spread of m-commerce (Hesmondhalgh, 2002).

The use of mobile is not just a technological trend that needs to be followed. Practice has shown that society accepts technological developments not just for the sake of fashion but when they offer an advanced solution to the needs of each era. The social and economical index change continuously and the market itself decides which technology will spread and survive. The next step is the high penetration of video phones with high resolution screens or i-mode services whose music portals and ringtone downloads have created havoc to the networking marketplace. Therefore, it is the market that allows ideas and technological visions to become part of the everyday consuming life (Knell, 2003). In *Table 1* that follows, we refer to the main issues rising in the modern digital era (Hesmondhalgh, 2002; O'Connor, 2001; Postma, 1999).

Taking into account all these factors, the business institution has to face a number of chal-

lenges in modern life. As consumers live in a multimedia and cross-cultural environment, they demand combinations of forms and new delivery methods, the marketers should keep in mind that they have to satisfy these needs in order to keep their audiences close to their institution.

EVALUATING M-COMMERCE IN RELATION TO VARIOUS MARKET FIELDS

It is quite clear so far that the literature offered on the subject of m-commerce is quite narrow and even sometimes inadequate. In the past five years there were a number of managerial handbooks analyzing the new mobile era either for commerce or marketing. The initial stimuli derived from the book of Turban et al. (2002) where the authors dedicate the last chapter to mobile commerce as a natural evolution of e-commerce through a new portable medium. The m-commerce is perceived as a follower of e-commerce (Easton, 2002) as long as mobile Internet is developed and so the consumers are able to use portable devices to purchase items. Mobile phone is seen by many authors as the physical transformation of the Internet and the leader of the new media (Stafford et al., 2004; Candace, 2005).

Paavilainen (2002) introduces the mobile Internet as the alternative of desktop Internet. Mobile advertising, text alerts and mobile commerce models are described through different case studies from the commercial sector. Mobile entertainment, that is, ringtones, downloads and text alerts, is rich with cases from music and film industries, as sector journals like the New Media Age show. Although someone would think that this marketing trend would hardly expand in other forms of the business institutions, like culture, there is a release by the DigiCULT (2004) scheme that proves the opposite. Mobile devices applying location-based services (LBS) can be integrated in a museum or gallery exhibition giving the option to be another communication channel after the audio guides and the information kiosks. Moreover, scenarios like booking tickets through mobile, receiving text alerts for the latest exhibition or information how to get to an art gallery are becoming more obvious examples in the cultural sectors. The referred applications are included according to Mahatanankoon et al. (2005) in two modes of m-commerce: (i) the content delivery mode and (ii) the transaction mode.

Mobile Marketing

As part of the new strategies, the use of the mobile as a marketing and communication tool plays mainly an important role. With the introduction of text messaging boom marketers were totally influenced and seized the SMS as a new advertising chance. Haig (2002) describes the history of SMS and introduces various applications of mobile devices in marketing like the text alerts. With the introduction of the third generation mobile phones (3G) the capabilities of the devices to support image, sounds and movie clips grow, increasing the number of applications. Marketers find themselves holding a powerful interactive and totally personal marketing tool. However, there are still a great number of barriers which limit the widespread of the medium and its success according to Scharl et al. (2005), and they have to do either with the technological features of the devices, the transmission process or customer behaviour itself.

Customer Behaviour

Kleijnen et al. (2004) used the Technology Acceptance Model (TAM) to examine a number of factors that influence the quicker penetration of mobile technologies in the market in order to explain this trend of text messaging. Factors like cost of the devices and services, the value they offer to the end-user as well as the easiness of use are important in order to make special

mobile services apart from voice mail more acceptable. Moreover, Brumer & Kumar (2005) also introduced the influential factors of utility, convenience and fun, which are the most interesting point, for example, for an arts organisation. An innovative and entertaining way of advertising, promotion or ticket booking could be critical in order to catch the customers' attention and make them act. This last factor mainly influences the mobile advertisements (m-advertisement), toward which the attitude of consumers is more positive than toward traditional advertising, as Tsang et al. (2004) claim. What influences the attitudes of the end-users apart from the entertaining way of presentation is the content of the provided advertising services and its amount of information.

A key concept that should be looked into is the limitation of the irritation caused by interfering and unwanted messages. Therefore, it is important for organisation using the mobile services to ask for permission to deliver them to customer. Permission marketing is the term that should be closely related to any action of direct marketing.

Permission Marketing and Trust

Godin's book "Permission Marketing" (2002) is the most common reference in the literature under the subject of mobile marketing (Kavassalis et al., 2003) and there is no critical point suggested by other authors toward what it claims. The introduction of permission in marketing tactics, especially in direct promotions, comes in contraposition to the traditional way of advertising—interruptive marketing, as explained later.

Additionally, trust, security and privacy are the emerging issues for m-commerce. The fear of manipulation of personal data is the main limit in the consumer's shift to positive attitude. Good sources of information about privacy policies are the independent protecting bodies set to protect the end-users [for example, the Data Protection Act of 1998 is followed by the majority of the cases and the organisations show great respect to its lines, the Wireless Location Industry Association (WLIA) declares an adopted privacy policy by its members and so did the Mobile Marketing Association (MMA) with a relative declaration]. It must also be said though, that in cases of transactions through mobile phones, the risk of hacking is lower than that of the Internet due to the evolving technologies and the use of high standard encryption.

Effectiveness

How could effectiveness be defined in a very unstable context? This is the main question underlying this subject. It is quite difficult to find research on the effectiveness of the new medium due to the very recent introduction of mobile commerce in the market. The given difficulty still rises given the peculiarities of the various market fields. More specifically, for an arts organisation, for example, it is even more difficult to define effectiveness, as this can be meant under totally different aspects depending on what aims each cultural institution has set. Drucker (1995) and Heman & Renz (1999) also briefly referred to the effectiveness in non-profit organisations.

The factors that can make mobile an effective new media for organizations were examined in depth. A good attempt to measure the wireless marketing results by introducing the Mobile Return of Investment (ROI) was also made by Bayne (2002) and that is a useful guide for any organisation which wishes to monitor its investment on this new technology. Moreover, Kavassalis et al. (2003) introduced more indicators of effectiveness in their empirical studies, while Frolick & Chen (2004) assess the mobile commerce applications.

The majority of the research converges to the same conclusion. No matter what the effects of the mobile practices are, which in each case can be totally different, what is important is the benefit that someone can gain by being the first in the market for using this new technology.

PRINCIPLE DRIVERS OF AN M-COMMERCE OPEN SERVICE INFRASTRUCTURE

The deployment of a m-commerce open service platform that could be shared by networked private and public institutions could be a promising approach with further insights on maintaining wireless service provision sustainability in a long-term perspective. Wireless technology is about extending the availability of an e-commerce infrastructure to mobile and wireless channels. It becomes more fully developed and, as bandwidth increases with the availability of "always on" connectivity, next generation applications and entirely new practices will arise different from those delivered over existing static networks (Caldow, 2001).

The large array of new communication technology opportunities and the rapid emergence and change of standards, as well as the variety of mobile channels, offer different technical capabilities for sustainable architectures and technology frameworks in order to meet critical requirements like broadband, interoperability, scalability, transparency, personalization, privacy and security (Germanakos et al., 2005a).

Extended User Requirements and the Personalization Problem

The user population is not homogeneous, nor should be treated as such. To be able to deliver quality services, m-commerce systems should be tailored to the needs of individual users providing them with personalized and adapted information based on their perceptions, reactions, and demands. Therefore, a serious analysis of user requirements has to be undertaken, documented and examined taking into consideration their multi-application to the various delivery channels and devices. Some of the user (customer) requirements and arguments anticipated could

491

be clearly distinguished into (Germanakos et al., 2005c): (a) general user service requirements (flexibility: anyhow, anytime, anywhere; accessibility; quality; and security), and (b) requirements for a friendly and effective user interaction (information acquisition; system controllability; navigation; versatility; errors handling; and personalization).

Although one-to-one Web-based service provision may be a functionality of the distant future, user segmentation is a very valuable step in the right direction. User segmentation means that the user population is subdivided into more or less homogeneous, mutually exclusive subsets of users who share common user profile characteristics. The subdivisions could be based on: demographic characteristics (i.e., age, gender, urban or rural-based, region); socio-economic characteristics (i.e., income, class, sector, channel access); psychographic characteristics (i.e., lifestyle, values, sensitivity to new trends); individual physical and psychological characteristics (i.e., disabilities, attitude, loyalty).

The issue of personalization is a complex one with many aspects and viewpoints that need to be analyzed and resolved. Some of these issues become even more complicated once viewed from a moving user's perspective; in other words, when constraints of mobile channels and devices are involved. Such issues include, but are not limited to: what content to present to the user, how to show the content to the user, how to ensure the user's privacy, how to create a global personalization scheme. As clearly viewed, user characteristics and needs, determining user segmentation and thus provision of the adjustable information delivery, differ according to the circumstances and they change over time (Panayiotou & Samaras, 2004).

User Profiling Characteristics: A More Comprehensive Approach

One of the key technical issues in developing personalization applications is the problem of how to construct accurate and comprehensive profiles of individual users and how these can be used to identify a user and describe the user behaviour, especially if they are moving (Adomavicious & Tuzhilin, 1999). According to the Merriam-Webster Dictionary, the term profile means "a representation of something in outline." User profile can be thought of as being a set of data representing the significant features of the user, like preferences, characteristics, and activities, derived from a set of keywords that are compared against information items.

User profiling can either be *static*, when it contains information that rarely or never changes (e.g., demographic information), or *dynamic*, when the data change frequently. Such information is obtained either *explicitly*, using online registration forms and questionnaires resulting in static user profiles, or *implicitly*, by recording the navigational behaviour and/or the preferences of each user. In the case of implicit acquisition of user data, each user can either be regarded as a member of group and take up an aggregate user profile or be addressed individually and take up an individual user profile. The data used for constructing a user profile could be distinguished into: (a) the data model, which could be classified into the demographic model (which describes who the user is), and the transactional model (which describes what the user does); and (b) the profile model, which could be further classified into the factual profile (containing specific facts about the user derived from transactional data, including the demographic data), and the behavioural profile (modeling the behaviour of the user using conjunctive rules, such as association or classification rules). The use of rules in profiles provides an intuitive, declarative and modular way to describe user behaviour (Adomavicious & Tuzhilin, 1999)). Additionally, in the case of a mobile user, by user needs it is implied both the thematic preferences (i.e., the traditional notion of profile) as well as the characteristics of their personal device called "device profile." Therefore, here, adaptive personalization is concerned with the negotiation of user requirements and device abilities. As Web developers regard personalization as the best way to filter out unnecessary or irrelevant information for their users, some argue on issues like it may restrict the extent and the variety of information users receive, that people often do not have well-defined preferences, they need to answer detailed questions to personalize their Web pages, that the recommendation process is a black box for end-users and so on (Wang & Lin, 2002).

But, could the user profiling be considered complete incorporating only these dimensions? Do the designers and developers of m-commerce applications take into consideration the real users' preferences in order to provide them with really personalized Web-based service content? Many times this is not the case. How can a user profiling be considered complete, and the preferences derived optimized, if it does not contain parameters related to the user perceptual preference characteristics? We could define *user perceptual preference characteristics* as all the critical factors that influence the visual, mental and emotional processes liable of manipulating the new information received and building upon prior knowledge that is different for each user or user group. These characteristics, which have been primarily discussed in Germanakos et al. (2006), determine the visual attention, cognitive and emotional processing taking place throughout the whole process of accepting an object of perception (stimulus) until the comprehensive response to it (Germanakos et al., 2005c). The proposed comprehensive user profiling could be considered as the main raw content filtering module of an m-commerce personalization architecture. To our knowledge, nowadays, there is not research that moves towards the consideration of user profiling incorporating optimized parameters taken from these research areas in combination.

Figure 2. An m-commerce personalization architecture

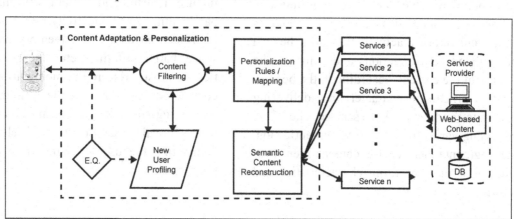

AN OVERVIEW OF M-COMMERCE PERSONALIZATION ARCHITECTURE

Based on the above-mentioned considerations, an m-commerce personalization architecture is overviewed trying to convey the essence and the peculiarities encapsulated. The current system, depicted in *Figure 2*, is composed of a number of interrelated components, as detailed below:

Entry Point

It is the user access interface of the system. It accepts multi-device (enables the attachment of various devices on the infrastructure, such as mobile phones, PDAs, desktop devices, etc.) identifying the characteristics of the device and the preferences as well as the location of the user (personalization/location-based) and multi-channel (due to the variety of multi-channel delivery, for example, over the Web, telephone, interactive kiosks and so on, this module will identify the different characteristics of the channels) requests. It is directly communicating with the "content filtering" component exchanging multi-purpose data.

Content Filtering

This component is considered the main link of the "entry point" with the "'new' user profiling" and the "personalization rules/mapping" components of the architecture. It actually transmits the data accumulated both directions and it makes the filtering of the content, according to the personalization processing characteristics, delivering the adapted and personalized service. The whole processing varies from security, authentication, user segmentation, service content identification, "new" user profiling characteristics and so forth.

"New" User Profiling

This is the main component of the architecture and it is called "'new' user profiling" component. At this component all the requests are processed. It is responsible for the custom tailoring of information to be delivered to the users, taking into consideration their habits and preferences, as well as, for mobile users mostly, their location ("location-based") and time ("time-based") of access (Panayiotou & Samaras, 2006). It also keeps the user logs and retrieves data according to user login to the system. This component accepts requests from the "entry point" component and, after the necessary processing and further communication with the "content filtering" component, either sends information back or communicates with the next component ("personalization rules/mapping") accordingly. This component is comprised of the following two elements:

The "Traditional" User Profile

It contains all the information related to the user necessary for the Web personalization processing. It is composed of two elements: the (a) user characteristics (the so-called "traditional" characteristics of a user: knowledge, goals, background, experience, preferences, activities, etc.), and (b) the device/channel characteristics (contains characteristics referring to the device or channel the user is using and contains information like: bandwidth, size, connectivity, power processing, interface and data entry, memory and storage space, battery lifetime, etc. These characteristics are mostly referred to mobile users and are considered important for the formulation of a more integrated user profile, since it determines the technical aspects of it). Both elements are completing the user profiling from the user's point of view.

User Perceptual Preference Characteristics

This is the new component/dimension of the user profiling. It contains all the visual attention, cognitive and emotional processing parameters that completes the user preferences and fulfils the user profile. User perceptual preference characteristics could be described as a continuous mental processing starting with the perception of an object in the user's attentional visual field and going through a number of cognitive, learning and emotional processes giving the actual response to that stimulus, as depicted in *Figure 3*. These characteristics have been primarily discussed in Germanakos et al. (2006) and Germanakos et al. (2005a).

As can be observed, its primary parameters formulate a three-dimensional approach to the problem.

The first dimension investigates the visual and cognitive processing speed efficiency of the user, the second his/her learning style, while the third captures his/her emotional processing during the interaction process with the information space. All the above dimensions have specific characteristics and implications into the information space based on which the personalization rules in the "personalization rules/mapping" component will be constructed. Suggestively, we present in *Figure 4* the data implications diagram of the learning styles chosen.

For a better understanding of the three dimensions' implications and their relation with the information space a diagram that presents a high level correlation of these implications with selected tags of the information space (a code used in Web languages to define a format change or hypertext link) is depicted in *Figure 5*. These tags (images, text, information quantity, links – learner control, navigation support, additional navigation support, and aesthetics) have gone through an extensive optimization representing group of data affected after the mapping with the implications.

The particular mapping is based on specific rules created, liable for the combination of these tags and the variation of their value in order to

Figure 3. User perceptual preference characteristics—three-dimensional approach

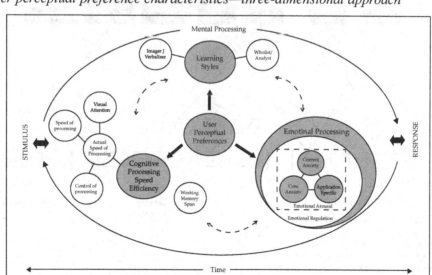

Figure 4. Riding's learning styles characteristics and implications

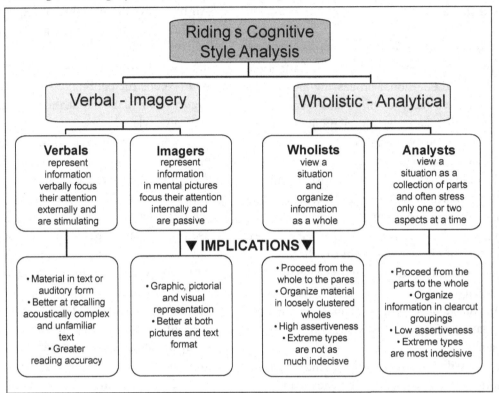

Figure 5. Data: Implications correlation diagram

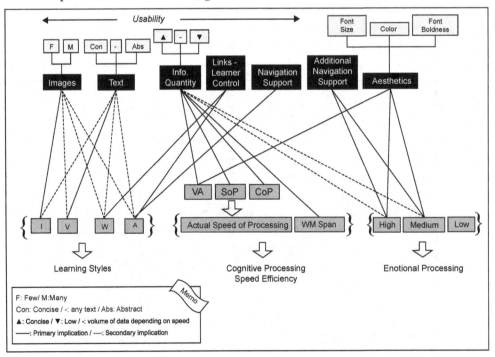

better filter the raw content and deliver the most personalized Web-based result to the user. As it can be observed from the diagram, each dimension has primary (solid line) and secondary (dashed line) implications on the information space altering dynamically the weight of the tags.

Therefore, we include in the learning styles dimension Riding's Cognitive Style Analysis, which applies in a greater number of information distribution circumstances, since it deals rather with cognitive than learning style. Henceforth, for example, the number of images (few or many) to be displayed has a primary implication on imagers, while text (more concise or abstract) has a secondary implication. An analyst may affect primarily the links – learner control and navigation support tag, which in turn is secondary affected by high and medium emotional processing, while might secondary affect the number of images or kind of text to be displayed, consequently. Actual speed of processing parameters (visual attention, speed of processing, and control of processing), as well as working memory span, is primarily affecting information quantity. Eventually, emotional processing is primarily affecting additional navigation support and aesthetics, as visual attention does, while secondary affects information quantity.

A practical example of the Data – Implications Correlation Diagram could be as follows: a user might be identified that is: Verbalizer (V) – Wholist (W) with regards to the learning style, has an actual cognitive processing speed efficiency of 1000 msec, and a fair working memory span (weighting 5/7), with regards to his/her cognitive processing speed efficiency, and (s)he has a high emotional processing. The tags affected, according to the rules created and the Data–Implications Correlation Diagram, for this particular instance are the: images (few images displayed), text (any text could be delivered), information quantity (less info since his/her cognitive speed is moderate), links – learner control (less learner control because (s)he is Wholist), additional navigation support

(significant because (s)he has high emotional processing), and high aesthetics (to give more structured and well defined information, with more colors, larger fonts, more bold text, since (s)he has high emotional processing).

At this point it should be mentioned that in case of internal correlation conflicts primary implications take over secondary ones. Additionally, since emotional processing is the most dynamic parameter compared to the others, any changes occurring at any given time are directly affecting the yielded value of the adaptation and personalization rules and henceforth the format of the content delivered.

Personalization Rules/Mapping

At this component all the calculations such as the user categorization and mapping, content reconstruction and content adaptation takes place. In order for the current component to run properly, Web-based semantic services content is conveyed in the form of metadata from the "semantic content reconstruction" component. Once the provided content is adjusted based on the developed rules to the user characteristics it returns the corresponding adapted and personalized result to the "content filtering" component.

Semantic Content Reconstruction

This component is based on metadata and it is responsible for describing the content (data) available from the "service provider" (service 1, service 2, …service n). In this way a common understanding of the data, that is, semantic interoperability, openness, is achieved. The data manipulated by the system is described using metadata that comprises all needed information to unambiguously describe each piece of data and collections of data. This provides semantic interoperability and a human-friendly description of data. This component is also directly related to the "personalization content reconstruction" component providing the altered Web-based metadata service content. It is consisted of two elements:

- Perceptual provider characteristics: It identifies the provider characteristics assigned to the Web-based services content. They are involving all these perceptual elements that the provider has been based for the design of the content.
- Semantic content properties: This element performs the identification and metadata description of Web-based services content based on predetermined ontologies. It is implemented in a transparent manner removing data duplication and the problem of data consistency.

Service Provider

This is the last component of the architecture and is directly connected to the "semantic content reconstruction" component. It contains transition mechanisms and the databases of Web-based services content as supplied by the provider without being through any further manipulation or alteration.

CONCLUSION

Indisputably, by implementing mobile commerce and mobile marketing a business institution attains a leading image of an organisation close to the technological trends and the needs of modern audiences. It differentiates itself in an era when each institution competes for a share of market and a share of heart not only through its work but also its marketing tactics. The healthy image of an innovative and avant-garde organisation can only work for the benefit of its long-term viability. It is hard to predict what the future will bring. Surely there will be an increasing number of organisations adopting the mobile services. However, the

future is nearer than generally estimated while the circumstances rapidly change. There can be futuristic scenarios which one day might become reality, but what is of more importance is always to know what the end-users finally need. The various institutions need to keep close and open to any kind of evolvement, not only to technological developments but also to how their audiences respond to them.

On these grounds, this article made a reference to the m-commerce content delivery investigating multi-channel delivery characteristics of user-centric m-commerce services and the adaptation and personalization considerations with regards to new user requirements and demands. It analyzed the current situation of m-commerce services, ranging from theoretical considerations to technological parameters, and it underpinned the significance of the user profiling, introducing the comprehensive user profiling that incorporates intrinsic user characteristics such as user perceptual preferences. It has finally presented an overviewed m-commerce personalization architecture that considers cognitive learning styles as its main personalization filter, in an attempt to provide the user with the most personalized m-commerce content result.

REFERENCES

Adomavicious, G., & Tuzhilin, A. (1999). User profiling in personalization applications through rule discovery and validation. In *Proceedings of the ACM Fifth International Conference on Data Mining and Knowledge Discovery (KDD'99)* (pp. 377-381).

Balasubramanian, S., Peterson, R.A., & Jarvnpaa, S.L. (2002). Exploring the implications of m-commerce for markets and marketing. *Journal of the Academy of Marketing Science, 30*(4), 348-361.

Bayne, K.M. (2002). *Marketing without wires*. Wiley.

Caldow, J. (2001). *E-gov goes wireless: From Palm to shining Palm.* Institute of Electronic Government, IBM Corporation.

Candace, D.P. (2005). *E-commerce and m-commerce technologies.* IRM Press.

Drucker, P.F. (1995). *Managing the non-profit organisation: Practices and principles.* Butterworth-Heinemann.

Easton, J. (2002). *Going wireless: Transform your business with mobile technology.* Harper Business.

Europe's Information Society. (2004a). *User interaction.* Retrieved from http://europa.eu.int/information_society

Frolick, M.N., Chen, L.-D. (2004, Spring). Assessing m-commerce opportunities. *Information Systems Management*, pp. 53 -61.

Germanakos, P., Tsianos, N., Lekkas, Z., Mourlas, C., & Samaras, G. (2006). Capturing essential intrinsic user behaviour values for the design of comprehensive Web-based personalized environments. *Computers in Human Behavior Journal*, Special Issue on Integration of Human Factors in Networked Computing. (accepted)

Germanakos, P., Samaras, G., & Christodoulou, E. (2005a). Multi-channel delivery of services—the road from eGovernment to mGovernment: Further technological challenges and implications. In *Proceedings of the First European Conference on Mobile Government* (Euro mGov 2005) (pp. 210-220).

Germanakos, P., Tsianos, N., Mourlas, C., & Samaras, G. (2005b). New fundamental profiling characteristics for designing adaptive Web-based educational systems. In *Proceeding of the IADIS International Conference on Cognition and Exploratory Learning in Digital Age (CELDA2005)* (pp. 10-17).

Germanakos, P., Mourlas, C., & Samaras, G. (2005c). Considering the new user requirements for apt mobile Internet services delivery. In *Proceedings of the IADIS International Conference on WWW/Internet 2005* (pp. 148-152).

Giaglis, G.M., Kourouthanassis, P., & Tsamakos, A. (2003). Towards a classification framework for mobile location services. In B.E. Mennecke & T.J. Strader (Eds.), *Mobile Commerce: Technology, Theory, and Applications.* Hershey, PA: Idea Group Publishing. Retrieved from http://www.eltrun.gr/papers/mBook-classification.pdf..

Haig, M. (2002). *Mobile marketing: The message revolution.* Kogan Page.

Heman, R.D., & Renz, D.O. (1999). Theses on nonprofit organisational effectiveness. *Nonprofit and Voluntary Sector Quarterly, 28*(2), 107-126.

Hesmondhalgh, D. (2002). *The cultural industries.* SAGE.

Interchange of Data Between Administrations. (2004). *Multi-channel delivery of eGovernment services.* Retrieved from http://europa.eu.int/idabc/.

Kleijnen, M., Wetzels, M., & de Ruyter, K (2004). Consumer acceptance of wireless finance. *Journal of Financial Services Marketing, 8*(3), 206-217.

Knell, S. (2003). The shape of things to come: Museums in the technological landscape. *Museum and Society, 1*(3), 132-146.

Mahatanankoon, P., Wen, J.H., & Lim, B. (2005). Consumer-based m-commerce: Exploring consumer perception of mobile applications. *Computer Standards and Interfaces, 27*, 347-357.

O'Connor, J., & Galvin, E. (2001). *Marketing in the digital age.* Prentice Hall.

Panayiotou, C., & Samaras, G. (2006). Mobile user personalization with dynamic profiles: Time and activity. In *Proceedings of On the Move to Meaningful Internet Systems 2006: OTM 2006 Workshops* (PerSys 2006). Part II (pp. 1295-1304).

Panayiotou, C., & Samaras, G. (2004). mPER-SONA: Personalized portals for the wireless user: An agent approach. *Mobile Networks and Applications (MONET), Special Issue on Mobile and Pervasive Commerce, 9*(6).

Paavilainen, J. (2002). *Mobile business strategies: Understanding the technologies and opportunities.* Wireless Press.

Postma, P. (1999). *The new marketing era: Marketing to the imagination in a technology-driven world.* McGraw-Hill.

Stafford, M.R., & Faber, R.J. (2004). *Advertising, promotion and new media.* M.E. Sharpe.

Towse, R. (Ed.). (2003). *A handbook of cultural economics.* Elgew Edward.

Tsang, M.M., Ho, S.-C., & Liang, T.-P, (2004). Consumer attitudes toward mobile advertising: An empirical study. *International Journal of Electronic Commerce, 8*(3), 65-78.

Turban, E., King, D., Lee, J., Warkentin, M., Chung, H.M. (2002). *Electronic commerce 2002: A managerial perspective.* Prentice Hall.

Wang, J., & Lin, J. (2003). Are personalization systems really personal? – Effects of conformity in reducing information overload. In *Proceedings of the 36th Hawaii International Conference on Systems Sciences* (HICSS'03) (p. 222c). IEEE Computer Society.

Index